THE BASQUE SERIES

AMERIKANUAK

BASQUES IN THE NEW WORLD

BOOKS BY WILLIAM A. DOUGLASS

*Death in Murélaga: Funerary Ritual
in a Spanish Basque Village
(University of Washington Press, 1969)*

*Echalar and Murelaga: Opportunity and
Rural Exodus in Two Spanish Basque Villages
(C. Hurst & Co. and St. Martin's Press, 1975)*

*The Changing Faces of Rural Spain
(edited by Joseph B. Aceves and William A. Douglass;
John Wiley & Sons, Inc., 1975)*

BOOKS BY JON BILBAO

*Eusko-Bibliographia
(Editorial Auñamendi, 1970−)*

*Vascos en Cuba: 1492−1511
(Editorial Vasca Ekin, 1958)*

Amerikanuak

BASQUES IN THE
NEW WORLD

William A. Douglass
and
Jon Bilbao

UNIVERSITY OF NEVADA PRESS
RENO, NEVADA
1975

University of Nevada Press, Reno, Nevada 89507
© *William A. Douglass and Jon Bilbao 1975*
Printed in the United States of America
Designed by Dave Comstock

Library of Congress Cataloging in Publication Data
Douglass, William A.
  Amerikanuak.

  (The Basque series)
  Bibliography: p.
  Includes index.
  1. Basques in America—History. I. Bilbao, Jon,
joint author. II. Title.
E29.B35D68   970'.004'9992   75-30830
ISBN 0-87417-043-5

To the memory of
Lynne Fereday
Goian Bego!

*Pour être un Basque authentique, trois choses sont requises:
porter un nom sonnant qui dise l'origine; parler la langue des
fils d'Aïtor, et . . . avoir un oncle en Amérique.*

*(To be an authentic Basque there are three requisites: carry
a sonorous name which states its origin, speak the language
of the sons of Aitor, and . . . have an uncle in America.)*
Pierre Lhande, L'Emigration Basque, *1909*

*L'Amérique est pour les Basques plus qu'une colonie française;
c'est la colonie du pays basque.*

*(America is for the Basques more than a French colony; it is
the colony of the Basque country.)*
Louis Etcheverry, "Les Basques et Leur
Emigration en Amérique," 1886

Contents

Foreword

IT IS TYPICAL of the Basques that their involvement of five centuries in the New World has so successfully avoided historical mention of any general scope. Reticence has always been the deeper mark of the Basque character.

Yet, involved they were to a surprising degree. Seafaring Basques led the way in their pursuit of whales across uncharted oceans, certainly seeing Newfoundland and Canada in the early 1500s and perhaps before. Christopher Columbus's first expedition was dependent upon Basque ships and sailors. From that time on, the Basque presence permeated the conquest and colonization of South America, Mexico, Spanish California, and the American West.

It remained to anthropologist William Douglass and historian Jon Bilbao to undertake the painstaking project of tracing these often obscure threads of Basque activities in the New World.

To do so, they have begun at the beginning. As background to understanding the Basque character and homeland, their first chapter traces the Basques from prehistory to the age of exploration. Suffice to say that it is for me a brilliant sifting of Old World sources in order to produce a capsule view of a people's history.

The six years of research that have gone into *Amerikanuak: Basques in the New World*—in many respects an ongoing project—have taken the authors through ten states of the American West, Mexico, Colombia, Peru, Chile, Argentina, Brazil, and Venezuela. Their work has included the collection of oral histories, personal observation, and questionnaires in western sheepcamps and Basque hotels, examination of myriad official records, and an analysis of newspaper files and published sources, the latter usually of a local and anecdotal nature.

Neither scholar is stranger to the field of Basque studies.

As a beginning anthropologist, William Douglass lived for three years in Basque villages of Vizcaya and Navarra, where he mastered the difficult task of learning to speak and read in the Basque language. Out of this resident fieldwork and subsequent stays in the Basque provinces of Europe was to come his distinguished first book, *Death in Murélaga*, published by the University of Washington Press in 1969, *Echalar and Murélaga: Opportunity and Rural Exodus in Two Spanish Basque Villages*, published by C. Hurst & Co. (London) and St. Martin's Press (New York) in 1975, and a number of articles for scholarly magazines. His work among Basques in the American West began in 1967 under the auspices of the Basque Studies Program in the Desert Research Institute of the University of Nevada.

Jon Bilbao joined the project in 1969. A Vizcayan Basque born in Puerto Rico, he did research work for several years in the Basque provinces and later in Cuba. His first book, *Los Vascos en Cuba*, was published in Argentina. His next project was the preparation of a bibliography of Basque reference works, a task that has consumed the better part of twenty-five years. Four volumes of his projected eight-volume work, *Eusko-Bibliographia*, have been published in Spain.

Of *Amerikanuak*, Dr. Douglass remarks: "The present work is not conceived of as definitive in any respect, but rather as a somewhat general framework within which future scholarship regarding the Basques of the New World might proceed in more productive fashion. In fact, at the very least, we would anticipate that future work—our own and that of others—will require that the argument be overhauled in many of its aspects."

This may or may not be true. As director of the university press, I have found that scholars are often preoccupied with the question of whether their work will stand the test of time and future scholarship.

For a scholar, this is as it should be. But as a reasonably informed layman and an American born of Basque parents, I must conclude that this book—*Amerikanuak: Basques in the New World*—is a milestone of high importance. I suspect that the content of this work will stimulate a considerable refinement of the history of Old World involvement in the North Atlantic, Latin America, and the American West.

ROBERT LAXALT, DIRECTOR
UNIVERSITY OF NEVADA PRESS

Acknowledgments

RESEARCH FOR the present volume was conducted throughout the American West, in several Latin American countries, and in Europe. The project lasted from 1967 to 1974. During this time several hundred persons contributed in some fashion to our efforts and we wish to take this opportunity to thank them. While it is impossible to mention all by name, the contributions of certain persons were so important as to require special acknowledgment. These include Mary Stevenson, Richard Lane, Constancio Castro, Iñaki Zumalde, Rosalie Martínez, Denise Lopategui, Andrés M. Irujo, Francisco Abrisqueta, Linda Gastañaga, Elena Celayeta Talbott, Jess Goicoechea, Ray Goicoa, Sonia Diaz, Robert Laxalt, Yoshiko Hendricks, Eloy Placer, Juanita Hormaechea, Julio Bilbao, Richard Etulain, Joseph Gaiser, Fred Fuldain, Sarah Baker, Louise Dunn, Gene and Mark Etchart, Paul Etchepare, Jean Urruty, Jerome Edwards, and Barbara Wiley Surette.

At the same time we wish to thank the members and officers of the Basque clubs which made information available to us. In the American West these include the Basque organizations of Reno, Ely, Elko, Boise, Chino, San Francisco, and Bakersfield. We also owe a debt of gratitude to the Basque organizations of New York, Mexico City, Bogotá, Caracas, Santiago de Chile, Montevideo, São Paulo, Buenos Aires, and Necoechea (Argentina). The Western Range Association generously permitted us access to their files. The Huntington Library, the California State Library (Sacramento), the McCarran collection of the College of the Holy Names (Oakland), the Bancroft Library, Los Angeles County Museum, the Santa Barbara Mission, the state historical societies of Arizona, California, Colorado, Idaho, Montana, Nevada, Oregon, and Wyoming, and the *Bibliothèque Nationale* (Paris) all provided critical documentation.

The project was financed by the Desert Research Institute of the University of Nevada System, the Gastañaga Basque Studies Endowment of the University of Nevada, Reno, and by National Institute of Mental Health grants 1 RO1 MH18913-01 and 1 KO2 MH24303-01. The opinions expressed are, of course, our own.

WILLIAM A. DOUGLASS
JON BILBAO

January 1975
Reno, Nevada

Introduction

THE NEW WORLD is a mosaic of ethnic groups. No period of its history, no sector of its society, and none of its regions may be understood fully if immigrant traditions and ethnic heritages are ignored. Consequently, the literature (both scientific and literary) dealing with American immigrant and ethnic groups is staggering. But sheer quantity does not guarantee either quality or breadth in coverage. Certain ethnic groups and certain periods in the history of particular groups have received comprehensive treatment while others have remained at the margins of awareness and concern. Such is the case with the Basques, one of the least-studied elements in the pluralistic social fabric of the Americas despite the fact that they were among the first Europeans to emigrate to the New World, as well as one of its most widely distributed immigrant groups. A Basque contingent in Columbus's crew played a significant role in the founding of the first European New World colony, thereby initiating a tradition of Basque overseas emigration which continues to this day. During the intervening centuries, Basques have settled in most countries of Latin America, many islands of the Antilles, and the western region of the United States. Old World Basques refer to these emigrants as *Amerikanuak*, or "the Americans."

Several factors contribute to the relative scholarly neglect of the Basque people of the Americas. With few exceptions, attempts to study the problem have been compartmentalized in intellectual traditions that rarely overlap. In Europe there is considerable Basque scholarship, with an active interest in Basque emigration. The major thrust of this work, reported largely in Spanish and French, is to develop an understanding of the role of the Basques in the colonial ventures of Spain and France. It is not that European scholars are unaware of the existence of extensive Basque communities in the American

West and postcolonial Latin America; rather they are handicapped by lack of first-hand information about them. Their understanding of the role of the Basques in American society is derived largely from first-person accounts of returnees and transatlantic correspondence between friends and relations. Few have utilized published American sources.

In Latin America, there is a second circle of Basque scholars. With few exceptions, however, their efforts and publications deal with either Old World Basque history or Basque accomplishments in the colonial ventures. Comparatively little has been written about Latin American Basques of the nineteenth and twentieth centuries.

The few North American scholars who have speculated about the historical movement of the Basques into the American West have not utilized Spanish and French sources dealing with the periods prior to United States annexation of Texas, New Mexico, Arizona, and California. Their accounts create the impression that the Basques first entered the area in the mid-nineteenth century, probably as a part of the human tide associated with the California gold rush. It is not that they are unaware of the Basque descent of Simón Bolívar, liberator of South America; Juan de Garay, founder of Buenos Aires; or Juan Vizcaíno, explorer of the South American coastline. Instead, they limit their analyses to acknowledgment of these Basque individuals, failing to realize that there were clearly defined Basque ethnic groups of significant size in the Spanish New World.

The inclination of most historians to regard the man from Bilbao just as "Spanish" as one from Madrid and the man from Saint-Jean-de-Luz just as "French" as one from Paris reflects an insensitivity to the historical importance of internal regional differences in Old World Spanish and French society.

For other reasons the Basques of the American West have proven to be an elusive quarry for the interested scholar. Basques entered the United States singly or in relatively small numbers, and most herded sheep. The sheepherding occupation, by its very nature, ruled out the concentration of Basques to the degree that they might become the largest ethnic group in any one area. The isolation inherent in the occupation kept the herders relatively unknown to the wider American population. With the exception of occasional disputes over the use of the range, the Basque herders remained a ghostlike element within the society of the American West, proving elusive for the

journalist and the census taker alike. Furthermore, the investigator who attempts to trace Basque activities through the few
existing newspaper accounts and official documents usually
finds his subjects masked under their French or Spanish nationality rather than identified as Basque. Then, too, with the
exception of the novelist Robert Laxalt, the Basques of the West
have failed to produce their own interpreters.

The fact that Basques are Caucasians protected them from
being made targets of racial discrimination. Because they did
not cause a "social problem," they have not attracted as much
attention in American society as have other immigrant groups.
The value orientations of Basque immigrants did not contrast at
all with highly esteemed values in American culture, such as
dedication to work, thrift, and hygiene. In this respect, Basques
were as "American" as any other immigrant group, possibly
more so than most. Consequently, no major conflict in values
that might have placed the Basques in the public spotlight has
characterized relations between them and the wider society.*

Another factor contributing historically to the low profile
of the Basques in the American West has been their own stance
before the wider society. Basque aloofness and reserve, difficult characteristics for the historian to describe, also contributed to their low profile in the American West. This aloofness
might best be described as a kind of ethnic pride and inscrutabil-
ity, characteristics that have been mistakenly interpreted by
some as sullenness or even hostility.† For the Basque emigrant,
ethnic identity is not particularly a matter for public display; it is
rather the vehicle for one's most private and intimate associations. The most frequent medium of communication employed
in these associations is the Basque language. This enhances the
outsiders' impression of Basque aloofness; so few non-Basques

---

*Although, as we shall see, the Basques' occupational specialization in the
sheep industry did bring them into conflict with other livestock interests.

†Without a certain aloofness *vis-à-vis* others, the Basques, as a viable
society and culture, would have disappeared long ago from the European
scene. The Basque people in Europe have a centuries-long tradition of maintaining a unique identity in the face of intense pressures to assimilate them
into broader national purposes and structures. Too much weight has been given to
the interpretation that Basque culture has survived due to the physical isolation
of the Basque homeland in the Pyrenees, while not enough attention has been
paid to those features of Basque character that allow them to accept outside
influences without surrendering their identity in the process.

have ever heard, let alone learned, the language that it functions
as a secret code for insiders.

By marshaling evidence to explain the paucity of literature
dealing with Basques in the Americas, we have, perhaps,
created an overly negative impression as to the feasibility of
conducting such studies at all. In point of fact, the potential
investigator does enjoy certain advantages. There are still elderly Basques who entered the New World near the turn of the
century. In some cases they were among the first Basque arrivals in their particular area. In other cases they recall anecdotes
about their Basque predecessors. This oral testimony can be
supplemented by a careful reading of newspaper accounts and
public documents. Basque last names are highly distinctive and
unmistakable for the informed.* A further source of information is the thumbnail biographical sketches of Basques that were
published in the vanity† sections of early history books. The
county histories of California are particularly rich in Basque
biographies. Near the turn of the present century, book-length
collections of Basque biographies were published in both the
American West and the Río de la Plata region of South America.
Finally, the Basque-Americans do provide some documentation
concerning their activities. In 1885, a Basque-language newspaper, the *Escualdun Gazeta*, was founded in Los Angeles, and
between 1893 and 1898 another, the *California'ko Eskual Herria*, was published in the same city. The Basque colonies of
Mexico, Argentina, Uruguay, Chile, Colombia, Venezuela,
and Cuba have, at various times, published periodicals. The
Basque social clubs keep records of their meetings and activities
and publish newsletters. Basque hotels maintain records, some
of which have been made available for the present study.
Basques in both Europe and the American West have graciously
consented to provide us with transatlantic correspondence, personal diaries, and photographic materials. Finally, we have

---

*Last names in themselves are not sufficient evidence that the bearers are
culturally Basque. For example, many persons in the American West with
Basque surnames are in fact culturally Mexican and regard themselves as
such. Their last name is likely a result of Basque ancestry which is so remote
that it may have been established by one of the conquistadors of the sixteenth
century.

†It was quite common for the historian of a particular area to finance
publications of his work by selling space to prominent local residents. The
space was filled with a short sketch of the purchaser's life history and possibly
a photograph.

employed the anthropological techniques of surveying and participant observation among the Basques of Europe, Latin America, and the American West.

Murélaga is a small village of slightly more than one thousand inhabitants located in one of the more isolated corners of the Basque Pyrenees (province of Vizcaya). Life in Murélaga is likely to strike the visitor as quaint and idyllic, wholesome and serene. On all sides one hears the Basque language, a rare experience today in many parts of the Basque country. The general impression of rural serenity steeped in folkloric charm is disturbed only slightly in the evening hours when several men return to the village after working the day in the marble quarries or small factories of nearby towns. It is easy for the visitor with a casual knowledge of the village to conceive of Murélaga as one of those forgotten corners of the modern world, largely shielded from outside influences, in which people are pursuing ancestral ways with the mentality of their forefathers. The physical horizons seem to circumscribe the conceptual world of the villagers.

Even the casual visitor is, of course, forced to recognize almost immediately that this characterization is an illusion. The villagers are all bilingual in Basque and Spanish, and one of the irritations for the traveler in search of rural beauty is the increasing ubiquity of television antennas perched on farmhouse rooftops. If one mentions that he is from the city of Bilbao or the industrial town of Eibar, the villager is likely to reply that his brother, son, or cousin is living there.

However, to view Murélaga's contacts with the outside world as limited to the broader Basque area or even to the Spanish nation is equally incorrect. In 1966 one of the present writers conducted a census among the farming population* of Murélaga. An analysis of 165 sets of siblings showed that 100, or 60 percent, had provided at least one emigrant to the Americas or elsewhere, while in 55 cases, or 33 percent, there were two or more emigrants. The 165 sets of siblings included 429 males and 413 females. Of this total of 842 persons, 212 had emigrated at some time. Among the male populace 179, or fully 42 percent, had emigration experience. One hundred and seven, or one out of every four men, had been to the American West or were residing there in 1966. Almost without exception they had worked at least initially as sheepherders. But what of

_____

*Villagers not residing in the village nucleus but, rather, living in hamlets scattered throughout the mountains.

the other male emigrants? Forty-one men had gone out to Australia where, with few exceptions, they had started working as cane-cutters on the sugar plantations. Twelve men had emigrated to Argentina, ten to Venezuela. The remaining nine divided their emigration experiences between Mexico, Peru, Cuba, Chile, and Africa. Most of the emigrants who went to Latin America became well-to-do businessmen, settling mainly in urban areas such as Caracas and Buenos Aires, in marked contrast to those who went to the American West and Australia to work at menial occupations.

Nor should it be assumed that emigration from Murélaga is exclusively a twentieth-century phenomenon. The monumental stone architecture of the dwellings and church gives mute testimony to the wealth of influences, ideas, and material riches that flowed back to the village from the many corners of the Spanish colonial empire.

Thus, the emigration experiences reflected within a tiny, remote village of the Pyrenees encompass at least the last five centuries of world history, with well-developed migratory patterns to three continents—South America, North America, and Australia. Furthermore, Murélaga's emigrants have led a variety of lives in many lands and at different times. One was the archbishop of Lima, Peru, in 1711; others have been businessmen of all sorts; and today's emigrants lead the menial, psychologically trying lives of sheepherders in the American West. This richness and complexity in one local tradition of emigration is easily generalized to large areas of the Basque country, historically one of Europe's prime staging areas for overseas migration.

There is a revealing lesson in Murélaga's emigratory tradition for the would-be author of the historical movement of the Basque people into the Americas. The common format for immigrant histories is to present an initial chapter on Old World conditions that stimulated departures, with the remainder of the work devoted to the history of the emigrants in a particular country of destination. However, such an approach would ignore the fact that there were *several* alternative New World destinations for the Old World Basques, thereby begging such important questions as why, by the latter half of the nineteenth century, a contingent of Basque emigrants braved the uncertainties of life in the desert regions of the American West, in a society where the language presented a formidable barrier, when they likely had established kinsmen in Argentina and could expect to function more easily in a Spanish-speaking country. Nor would such an approach deal with the fact that the first Basque emigrants to California (once that area had been incorporated into the United States) were persons who had formerly immigrated into Argentina and Uruguay, thus making the Río de la Plata region a secondary staging area for Basque emigration to the American West. Such concerns are seldom raised in immigrant histories, although their relevance is by no means limited to the Basque experience.

Finally, our concern with Basque ethnic-group manifestations requires that we employ an unconventional approach to the interpretation of the history of southern Europe, the Spanish Empire in the New World, and the American West. In order to highlight the importance of Old World regional ethnic distinctions, we reject the generally employed technique of writing from a Spanish or French viewpoint in favor of using a Basque perspective. In evaluating New World colonial history, we shall not rely upon the usual procedure of juxtaposing the interests of the Old World-born *peninsulares* and the New World-born *criollos*. Rather, we shall emphasize the importance of Old World regional ethnic distinctions within both circles and as links between them. Finally, in considering the history of the American West, we shall stress those factors that most affected the fortunes of one of its most obscure architects—the Basque sheepman. By employing such heuristic devices it is possible to trace the single thread of Basque ethnic-group life through five centuries of history on three continents.*

---

*In the following text all translations are ours unless otherwise indicated.

CHAPTER ONE

The Basque People

ORIGINS

"What is a Basque?" This is a question that is often heard even in the American West, where for more than a century the Basque people have been identified with the region's sheep industry. The confusion stems from the fact that the Basque homeland in modern times has lacked political sovereignty. Thus, four of the traditional Basque regions—Guipúzcoa, Vizcaya, Alava, and Navarra—are politically integrated into Spain, while the remaining three—Labourd, Basse Navarre, and Soule—are a part of France.

If historical circumstances have frustrated the Basques' claim to a "national" identity, their claim to uniqueness within the broad panorama of European cultures and ethnic groups is secure. There are ample grounds to establish this singularity in the testimony of the Basque language, certain aspects of their physical makeup, the archeological record of the Basque country, and the Basques' own self-concept. Furthermore, the history of the Basque area is a continuous record of a people acting in concert to protect interests that they perceive as differing from those of their neighbors and would-be invaders.

The Basques refer to themselves as *Euskaldunak*. The term means literally "speakers of *Euskera*" or the Basque language. This primal identity invokes the strongest indicator of Basque cultural uniqueness, the language. Despite five centuries of speculation by linguists and philologists concerning possible relationships between Basque and other languages, conclusive affinities have yet to be demonstrated. The enigma of the language, more than any other factor, has led popular writers and scholars alike to depict the Basques as the mystery people of Europe.

Certain features of the physiological makeup of the Basques pose an interesting challenge for physical anthropologists. Basques differ remarkably from surrounding populations in frequency of certain blood types, for example; they manifest the highest rate in any European population of blood type O and the lowest occurrence of blood type B. They also have the highest rate of occurrence of any population in the world of the Rh negative factor; the Basque-speaking Vizcayan population, for example, has a frequency of 27.5 percent.[1]

The body of the evidence concerning these serological peculiarities has been interpreted by some to indicate that they are "racially" distinct from other European populations.* Without entering upon this controversy, it may be stated that at the very least, the serological evidence suggests that the Basque people have remained, over a relatively long period of time, a small and somewhat isolated breeding population. These are the necessary conditions under which genetic drift might be invoked to explain the unusual profile of blood factors reported for the modern Basque population.

The evidence of the archeological record is equally difficult to interpret, admitting a wide range of speculation. It is clear that the present-day Basque homeland in the western Pyrenees has had continuous human occupation since the Middle Paleolithic, or for at least the last seventy thousand years. It is not known, however, whether the direct precursors of the present Basque populace and culture developed *in situ* in the Pyrenees or migrated into the area. Some authorities suggest

---

*The geneticist Boyd has hypothesized that the earliest European race was characterized by a high incidence of the Rh negative factor and no incidence of blood type B. In his view, the Basques are the modern representatives of this hypothetical race.[2] More recent serological work among the Basques suggests that they differ notably from other European populations in terms of their frequency of the $Fy^a(-)$ factor of the Duffy system.[3]

that the Basques are the direct descendants of cave painters who left renowned art treasures at such famous sites as Lascaux, as well as in the caves throughout the present Basque country.[4] Others, skeptical of this claim, date the archeological baseline of the modern Basques in the period of the Pyrenean culture, or from about 5,000 to 3,000 B.C.[5] However, even this most conservative interpretation places Basque precursors in the western Pyrenees well before the invasions of the Indo-European speaking tribes into western Europe during the second millennium B.C. It was these invasions that established the bases for the ethnographic map of Europe as we know it today. Thus, even the most conservative interpretation of Pyrenean prehistory establishes the Basques as one of the most ancient *in situ* peoples in western Europe.

In such areas as material culture, architectural styles, folk art, folk beliefs, and mythology, the Basques are less distinguished for their originality than for their tenacity in retaining pan-western European items, practices, and beliefs. This fact has prompted one investigator to characterize Basque culture as a "living museum" for the student of western European folk traditions.[6]

On the other hand, there is extant among the Basques a self-concept that they are different from any other people. The Basque language contains an extensive vocabulary of terms, many pejorative, to refer to non-Basques. This awareness and claim for Basque uniqueness is not the special province of the Basque scholar; it is expounded upon at length by the factory worker of Bilbao, the peasant of the mountains, and the fisherman of the coastal village.

HUMAN GEOGRAPHY OF THE BASQUE HOMELAND

The Basque country straddles the present French-Spanish frontier at the point where the western range of the Pyrenees meets the Bay of Biscay. Compared with the homelands of other European ethnic groups, the Basque country is quite small both in terms of territory and population. On either a north-south or an east-west tangent the Basque area is barely one hundred miles across. Its total population today is slightly over two and one-half million inhabitants, although scarcely more than

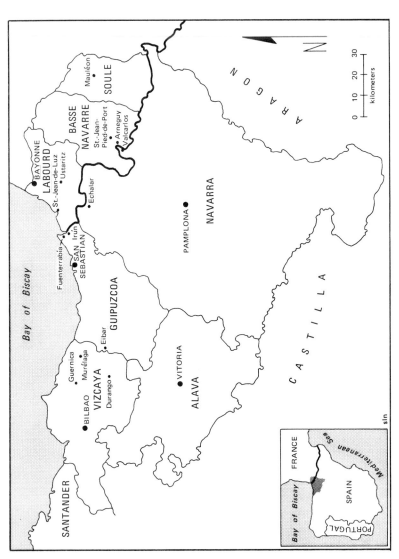

The seven Basque provinces.

700,000 persons can be regarded as culturally Basque (if retention of the language is used as the determining factor).*

The establishment of a Spanish-French border in 1512 created divisiveness in the Basque area that has lasted from the sixteenth century to the present. Basques on both sides of the frontier regard the division as somewhat artificial: few regard as "illegal" the two-directional clandestine smuggling of goods and persons across the border. It is seen in the extensive network of kinship ties that link families on both sides of the frontier. It is reflected in the tendency of many Basques to see their interests as frequently differing from those of Madrid or Paris—an attitude that has led activist elements to clamor for an independent Basque nation (*Euzkadi*) that would include all of the traditional Basque homeland.[12] However, it may not be doubted that the French-Spanish frontier has weakened Basque cultural homogeneity. For several centuries, the four traditional Basque regions of Alava, Vizcaya, Guipúzcoa, and Navarra have been exposed to a large measure of Spanish influence; similarly, the areas of Labourd, Basse Navarre, and Soule have been affected by French culture.

Thus, in everything from loan words in the Basque vocabulary, to the school system, to the nature of administration, the frontier accounts for sufficient internal differentiation of Basque society and culture to provide us with an initial major distinction between Spanish and French Basques. This distinction becomes particularly crucial when attempting to understand differential rates of emigration from regions within the Basque country and at different periods of history. For example, Spain's leadership role in the discovery and exploitation of the

---

*The latest Spanish national census (1970) lists 2,343,503 inhabitants in the four Spanish Basque provinces.[7] French Basque population statistics are more difficult to obtain, since they are reported with those of Béarn under the rubric of the *Département des Basses-Pyrénées* (renamed *Pyrénées-Atlantiques* in 1970). However, by compiling the figures reported in the most recent French national census (1968) of all towns regarded to be French Basque in the Sollube geography,[8] we derive a population total of 218,621 inhabitants for the French Basque area.[9] A recent estimate, based upon the most thorough survey conducted to date, places the number of Basque speakers in Europe at 533,500 persons. Of this total 78,453 are French Basques.[10] In recent years, there has been a tendency toward loss of the language in the more industrialized areas. This represents continuation of a centuries-long process of contraction of the territory in which the Basque language is retained.[11] However, there is currently a movement to establish *ikastolak*, or Basque language schools, even in areas where Basque is no longer the vernacular.

New World provided Spanish Basques with a set of opportunities that were not as directly available to their French brethren. Conversely, the French Revolution and its aftermath affected French Basques more immediately than their Spanish counterparts.

Furthermore, there is considerable geographic and demographic imbalance between the Spanish and French Basque areas. Of the somewhat more than twenty thousand square kilometers constituting the Basque country, over seventeen thousand or six-sevenths of the total land area is located on the Spanish side of the frontier. Some 2.3 million persons, or eleven-twelfths of the total Basque population, reside in the Spanish Basque provinces. They constitute approximately seven percent of the current national population of Spain, whereas the two hundred thousand inhabitants of the French Basque area are but four-tenths of one percent of France's total.

Gross population statistics are eloquent statements of the differing importance of the Spanish and French Basques within their respective nations. The difference is even greater if we look at economics. The Spanish Basque provinces, particularly the industrial zones of Guipúzcoa and Vizcaya, constitute one of the most dynamic sectors of the Spanish nation. The area presently enjoys the highest per capita income of any region of the Iberian peninsula. Historically, it has been a focus of iron mining, steel processing, manufacturing, shipbuilding, and maritime commerce. Conversely, the French Basque area is currently one of the most economically depressed regions of France, receiving more in government subsidy than it pays in taxes. There is little industry, and a scarcely viable form of peasant agriculture is the economic mainstay of the area. French Basque rural poverty is only somewhat alleviated by a summer tourist season.

The distinction between French Basque and Spanish Basque, while somewhat artificial from a Basque viewpoint, is nevertheless a reality. However, there is a more subtle set of regional divisions that plays a greater role in defining the identity of the individual Basque. The seven traditional regions of Vizcaya, Guipúzcoa, Alava, Navarra, Labourd, Basse Navarre, and Soule are differentiated by their political and economic history. Each had its charters (*fueros* and *fors*), which determined the nature of local government and defined the rights of the citizenry. Each has its own history of shifting political alliances that differs from those of neighboring Basque regions, at times making them battlefield adversaries. The Basque regions are further differentiated by the dialects of their spoken and written Basque.

Within the Basque world view there are characterological distinctions between Basques of different regions. Other Basques characterize *Bizkaitarrak*, or Vizcayans, as being extroverted and haughty. *Napartarrak*, or Navarrese, are frequently described as introverted and distrustful. Persons from Alava are seen as aloof and severe, while persons from Soule are described as explosive and unpredictable. A Vizcayan Basque from an interior peasant village refers to persons from the Vizcayan fishing port of Bermeo as loud, pretentious busybodies, while the coastal population views the farmers as sullen, shrewd, and tight-lipped. Persons in northern Navarra call southern Navarrese *ribereños* and see them as violent and hot blooded, whereas in southern Navarra the world view divides the social landscape into at least four *riberas* (drainages of the Ega, Arga, Aragón, and Ebro rivers) and ascribes characterological peculiarities to the inhabitants of each.

Within each region there is a further distinction between Basque-speaking and non-Basque-speaking districts and populaces. In urban centers of the several regions—Bilbao (Vizcaya), San Sebastián (Guipúzcoa), Vitoria (Alava), Pamplona (Navarra), Bayonne (Labourd), and Mauléon (Soule)—the Basque language is no longer the vernacular. The secondary manufacturing centers of Vizcaya and Guipúzcoa are presently transitional as places in which the Basque language is still employed, but with decreasing frequency. Also, there is a sense in which Basques regard the Basque-speaking districts taken as a whole—that is, the French Basque area, extreme northwestern Navarra, and the provinces of Guipúzcoa and Vizcaya as far west as the outskirts of Bilbao—as a kind of *Basque culture area*, a present-day bastion of traditional Basque values. This in contrast to the *Encartaciones* of western Vizcaya, practically all of Alava, and most of central and southern Navarra, where Basque has not been spoken within living memory and where the population has undergone considerable Hispanization. Consequently, within the Basque country as a whole, as well as within each province, there is an important distinction in world view between *euskaldun* zones (Basque-speaking) and *erdeldun* ones (Spanish- or French-speaking).

Finally, Basques make a characterological distinction between urban and rural dwellers. The city dweller regards his rural counterpart as rustic and backward, whereas there is a tendency for the peasantry to view the city with suspicion. The urbanite is depicted in rural circles as shiftless and untrustworthy.

Thus, for the actors themselves the stereotypic view of *the* Basque character is far from monolithic and consensual; it operates at several levels of regional and way-of-life abstractions and interpretative disagreement.

While the Basque country is physically tiny, its geographical situation and topography provide it with a complexity of ecological zones, and hence ways of life. The Atlantic slope of the Pyrenees constitutes a northern ecological zone. The Cantabrian seacoast of Vizcaya, Guipúzcoa, and Labourd, with its rich fisheries and natural inlets, has supported a fishing complex since at least the Middle Ages. It also provides major anchorages at Bilbao, Pasajes, and Bayonne, which permitted development of Basque maritime commerce and shipbuilding activities.

Between the coast and the high ridges of the Pyrenees, there is an area of rolling foothills cut by narrow river valleys. The climate is maritime with cool, fairly moist summers and relatively mild winters. Vegetation is rampant, and agriculture does not require irrigation. The typical settlement of the region is the peasant village. Each river valley is likely to contain one or more small communities of usually less than two thousand inhabitants, whose major economic activity is mixed farming on an individual peasant holding. Each village has a small nucleus that provides services ranging from stores, taverns, and medical care to schools and the village church.[13] The valley floor and the lower hillsides are cultivated by individual families that either own or rent a holding averaging about twenty-five acres in size. The highest elevations of a village's jurisdiction are designated as a commons from which all households can derive forest products (wood and nut crops), mountain pasturage, and bracken (used as animal bedding and subsequently as organic fertilizer).

Until the beginning of the present century, the emphasis in this peasant agricultural system was upon household subsistence. Each household was, ideally, an autonomous social and economic unit.

The elements of the mixed farming economy included grain cropping (predominantly corn or a combination of corn and wheat), an apple orchard (for cider, which was the main beverage), fodder production (to maintain three or four milk cows), pig and poultry raising (the former were pastured for part of the year on forest nut crops), chestnut gathering (used as a staple in both the human and livestock diets), bee keeping (for both a sweetener in the diet and for the wax), and sheep raising (rarely entailing more than one hundred animals, which were allowed to roam freely in the commons under a minimum of controlled herding*). Much of the farming was conducted on relatively small fields with a high degree of slope. Hence, agriculture was labor-intensive, requiring ample investment of human and animal energy (a pair of yoked cows, a mare, or a mule were used commonly for plowing and hauling). The technology was simple, based upon such hand tools as the scythe and hoe. Arable ground was at a premium (seldom constituting more than seven or eight acres of the twenty-five-acre total), and hence the fields were rarely fallowed and crops seldom rotated. Generous use of organic and chemical fertilizers allowed intensive annual fixed cropping of the fields.

Household crafts further enhanced the self-sufficiency of the peasant household. Each man was capable of manufacturing finished timbers from standing trees and furniture from the timbers. Each would burn limestone to fertilize his fields. Footwear was made from animal skins, and eating utensils were carved from wood. Clothing was manufactured from sheep to sock or shirt. These, and many other household handicrafts, reduced dependence upon the market place.

The need for a cash income was minimal, since agricultural produce was bartered directly in the stores, and even medical services and tithes exacted by local religious authorities could be paid in kind. However, cash was required to make some purchases and to pay taxes. Each generation accumulated money to provide dowries for offspring marrying away from the farmstead. Cash was also needed to pay the passages of those anxious to emigrate abroad. These funds were acquired in many ways. In some instances, money was sent back to the household by members who had previously emigrated. The sale of livestock or forest products was another means of making money. Basque peasants frequently engaged in seasonal wage employment locally or migrated periodically to other areas in search of

---

*In some districts household flocks were pooled to form larger bands that were pastured in the high country (central ecological zone) under the care of professional herders.

work. Thus, in the winter months, when the labor demands of agriculture were minimal, the men might work as loggers or charcoal burners in the nearby forests. Others would pursue the same occupation in the Landes area of France or the French Alps. More recently the tourist industry, notably in the French Basque area, has provided girls from peasant villages with summer seasonal employment. Finally, in the frontier areas the ubiquitous contraband traffic provided Basque peasants with *gau lana*, or "night work," at excellent wages.

During the twentieth century much of this household subsistence orientation in the Basque peasant economy has declined due to a rising level of material wants among the rural populace. Many Basque farmsteads have simply been abandoned, their former owners moving to cities in search of factory jobs or opportunity as small-scale shopkeepers. For those remaining behind, the former dedication to subsistence-oriented agriculture, supplemented by seasonal wage employment, is now shifting to an emphasis upon commercial dairying and horticulture for the nearby urban markets. Furthermore, this commercial agriculture frequently involves daily commuting by one or more men of the household to a factory job. Thus, on many farmsteads the active adult males presently limit their involvement in agriculture to the evenings and weekends, causing Basque farming to become increasingly "feminized." Even to this day, however, the Basque farmstead differs from the Iowa farm in more ways than simple scale. Basque agricultural activities still lack significant mechanization, requiring that the labor of every member of the family be invested, at least in part, in agriculture.

This northern ecological zone also contains the iron mining district of Somorrostro and the major urban centers of Bilbao, San Sebastián, and Bayonne. The two former cities have been major industrial zones since the latter half of the nineteenth century. During the twentieth century, industry has penetrated the countryside, converting former agricultural towns into secondary manufacturing centers.

Tourism in the Basque country, of great economic importance since the turn of the present century, is concentrated in the northern ecological zone. The tourist spas are mostly clustered along the seacoast. Biarritz is by far the most widely known tourist center in the Basque area.

There is a high mountain area between the northern and southern regions of the Basque country that might be referred to as the central ecological zone. The higher ranges of the western Pyrenees parallel the coastline on an east-west tangent. The main ridges serve as the approximate dividing line between Vizcaya, Guipúzcoa, Labourd, Basse Navarre, and Soule to the north and Alava and most of Navarra to the south. Only in its extreme northwestern corner does Navarra extend beyond the mountain barrier. Culturally, that portion has more in common with neighboring Guipúzcoa and Labourd than wtih the remainder of the province.

Above approximately six hundred meters the climate is alpine. There are substantial winter snows and few permanent settlements. The area is used during the summer months for high mountain pasturage of sheep, cows, and horses. It is in this region that one encounters the professional herder, charged with several hundred animals, and practicing transhumance which takes the flocks to the lowlands of either the southern or northern ecological zones during the winter months. Such transhumance employs limited numbers of individuals, and few of these professional herders have entered the ranks of the Basque emigrants.

To the south of the main ridges of the Pyrenees, there is a series of plateaus interspersed between secondary mountain chains. Due to their altitude and the barrier effect of the Pyrenees, central Alava and Navarra have a harsh continental climate. Winter wheat and other grains are the main crops. The capital cities of Pamplona and Vitoria are presently undergoing rapid urban growth and industrialization.

Further to the south the landscape tilts gradually to the Ebro River, providing most of southern Alava and Navarra with a plains topography and an arid, Mediterranean-like climate. In the southeastern corner of Navarra, there is a region of rolling foothills covered with scrub vegetation. Known as the Bardenas, the area has for centuries served as winter pasturage for the flocks from the high Pyrenees. There is little industry or tourism in this southern ecological zone. The population resides in rather large farming towns scattered over the landscape at considerable distance from one another. There are several land tenure arrangements varying from the individual peasant holding to the large estate devoted to commercial production. The commonest crops are the Mediterranean trilogy of wheat, grapes, and olives. However, in the irrigated districts such as Tudela, commercial truck farming of both fruits and vegetables is organized on a large scale. There is rigid social stratification of the populace. In some communities aristocratic, frequently absentee, landlords control the lives of the workers through the latter's dependence upon seasonal employment on the estates. Such workers constitute a rural proletariat more than a peasantry. Very few have emigrated to the New World; those who do leave seek the cities of Iberia.

The Basque language is no longer spoken in the southern ecological zone. Culturally, the populace more nearly approximates Castilla and Aragón than Vizcaya or Labourd. Throughout recorded history the area has served as a corridor for the invaders of the Iberian peninsula. Celts, Romans, Goths, and Arabs traversed and settled the region for varying periods of time. Yet today, despite the social, economic, linguistic, and cultural differences between the two populations, there exists some sense of Basque unity between the southerners and northerners.

AN HISTORICAL OVERVIEW: THE ROMAN PERIOD

We have noted that Basque history is seldom written from a Basque perspective. It is only since the sixteenth century that the Basque language has had its own literary and scholarly traditions, both of which remain underdeveloped to this day. Furthermore, throughout much of its history Basque society was essentially rural and marginal to the evolution of the Western world. Until well into the Middle Ages, the Basques were regarded by other Europeans as barbarians, a rustic people who as late as the eleventh century had yet to adopt Christianity.* In consequence, our knowledge of Basque history is derived largely from the accounts of outsiders—Roman, Gothic, Frankish, and Arab chroniclers, for the most part.

History, as determined by written accounts, begins in the Basque area with the commentaries of Roman historians on the imposition of Roman rule in northern Iberia. It is clear that when the Romans arrived there were two major groups of inhabitants in the present-day Basque area. The high mountains and coastal regions of the north were occupied by several tribes that were related ethnically and that probably spoke variations of a common Basque language. The economy of these tribesmen was

---

*It is almost impossible to date with certainty the evangelization of the Basque country.[14] Nor, as we shall see, is it possible to argue that all areas of the Basque country and all sectors of its society adopted Christianity simultaneously.

based upon pastoralism and rudimentary agriculture. Further to
the south, in some of the mountain valleys of central Alava and
Navarra as well as on the broad plains of the Ebro valley, the
inhabitants were sedentary agriculturalists of Celtic origin—the
last of a long line of Indo-European invaders who used the Ebro
as a corridor to reach the Castilian *meseta*. The Basques and the
Celts were at odds.

When the Roman legions first entered Iberia in 218 B.C.,
they encountered their strongest resistance from the Celts, particularly the Cantabrian tribesmen who occupied the mountains
to the west of the Basque country. Upon defeating the Celts in
133 B.C., the Romans established permanent settlements in
much of central and southern Alava and Navarra. They constructed cities, temples, and roads. The rolling plains of the
south and its Mediterranean climate lent themselves to estate
agriculture, and Roman villas proliferated.

The impact of Rome upon the northern areas of the Basque
country is less clear. Roman political control over the mountain
regions, indicated by the presence of either cities or agricultural
villas, was negligible. Roman cities founded at Iruña in Alava,
Calahorra, Pamplona, Jaca, Pau, Saint-Sever, and Dax were all
somewhat marginal to the present-day Basque culture area,
where the language is still spoken. The villas seem to have been
limited to southern Navarra[15] and Alava and the banks of the
Adour and Garonne rivers to the north.

To the extent that the lowlands within and bordering upon
the Basque country were Romanized, Christianity as well may
have been present by the third century.[16] During the period of
Roman rule, however, the Iberian bishopric closest to the
Basque area was based in Calahorra. To the north of the
Pyrenees, the closest Roman dioceses were in Aire, Dax, Lescar, and Oloron.*

The fact that there were no permanent Roman settlements
in the Basque cultural area suggests that Roman political control
remained low key and, at best, indirect. It is not clear why this
was so.

By one interpretation, the Romans were incapable of sub-
jugating a fierce, warlike people accustomed to employing
guerrilla tactics while fighting exclusively on a home terrain
that served them as a kind of mountain fortress. Yet this view is

---

*It was not until the twelfth century that there was clear and adequate
documentation of a church structure in the heartland of the Basque country.[17]

weakened by the fact that the Romans established and maintained a major arterial through the mountains and into southern France. They also constructed secondary roadways into the high country that terminated at Roman-controlled mining operations. Finally, Basque mountain tribesmen were recruited into the Roman legions. In fact, legions that were essentially Basque in makeup served in Rome's Rhine defenses[18] and along the Hadrian wall of Britain.[19] It is likely that the Romans failed to establish a greater visible presence in the northern zone of the Basque country for the simple reason that they had little incentive to do so, particularly as long as the Basque tribes refrained from provocations.

Although the Basques were somewhat insulated from direct Roman control, Rome's influence upon them was nevertheless great. Certainly both items and ideas entered into ancient Basque culture and world view along Roman channels. The high incidence of Old Latin loan words* in the Basque language, many of which label agricultural implements and crops, or deal with commercial and administrative activities, suggests a lively exchange between Basques and Romans.[21] Such borrowing was likely the result both of contacts within the Basque country and the influence of Basques who returned home after serving in the legions.

It is probable that the process of Latinization, or at least of direct Romanization, was interrupted by the incursions of the Germanic tribes into southern Europe during the second half of the third century A.D., in 261, 265, 275, and 284. The last attack destroyed the seat of Roman authority in Cluny, which had jurisdiction over present-day Alava, Vizcaya, and Guipúzcoa, and also demolished the city of Pamplona.[22]

Between 283 and 285 Roman authority in Gaul was challenged by rural unrest. The peasants, or *bagaudae*, were organized into a military force commanded by deserters from the Roman army. While their third-century revolt was suppressed, the *bagaudae* were to reappear as an active force during the fifth century in the southern reaches of the Basque area—the plains of Navarra and Alava.[23]

Rome met these third-century challenges to its authority, and under Diocletian (284–305) the empire was reorganized to

---

*While the Romans exerted control over the Basque area for six centuries, the majority of Latin loan words in Basque (190 B.C. to about A.D. 400), antedate the palatization of the Latin *c*, a phonetic phenomenon that appeared throughout the Roman Empire toward the end of the second century A.D.[20]

provide a greater degree of centralized control. It was divided into twelve dioceses, six in the West and six in the East (which were subsequently to evolve into the two separate empires of Rome and Byzantium). Within each diocese there were several provinces. Gaul to the north of the Pyrenees was divided into two dioceses—Gaul proper in the north and Viennensis in present-day southern France. Within Viennensis there were three provinces—Aquitania, Narbonense, and Novem-populania. This last province was later to acquire the name of *Vasconia* and included the present-day French Basque area. All of Iberia constituted a single diocese, divided into the five provinces of Gallaecia, Lusitania, Carthaginensis, Baetica, and Tarraconensis (which included all of the Basque area south of the Pyrenees).

Despite the reforms of Diocletian, however, the incursions of the barbarians and the insurrection of the *bagaudae* had undermined confidence in the invincibility of the empire. The traditional Roman center of political control, the city, began to show signs of strain. After the third century, no new Roman cities were constructed in or on the periphery of the Basque country. The obligation of collecting taxes, regulating commerce, and recruiting legionnaires increasingly devolved upon rural strong men. Thus, the magistrates of the cities relinquished considerable power to the influential landowners of the countryside, who in turn consolidated their position by further aggrandizing their estates (*latifundii*) while reducing their workers to indentured servitude.[24]

References to Roman administration of the Basque country during the fourth century, though scarce, are sufficient to demonstrate that Roman control had weakened to the point that the mountain tribesmen constituted a military threat. Periodically, the mountain dwellers conducted raids upon Roman establishments in the plains of the Ebro and the Adour. By the middle of the fourth century, the Romans were forced to abandon for a time the city of Iruña (Alava), despite the fact that they had recently fortified it with massive walls that were twelve meters high and five meters wide.[25] Both the fortifications of the city and its abandonment despite them are eloquent testimony of the military pressure to which it was subjected.

By 394, major cities near the Basque area—Calahorra, Bilbilis, and Lérida—were in ruins.[26] Pamplona may have shared their fate.[27] To the north, probably about the middle of the fourth century, the Romans erected fortifications on the site of present-day Bayonne to control the incursions of the mountain dwellers into the Adour region.[28]

By the end of the fourth century the Romans further fortified Iruña and stationed a strong permanent military force there. This was a measure that was taken only in frontier regions deemed to be "dangerous," such as the Rhine and parts of North Africa. At the time, the garrisons surrounding the Basque tribes were the only permanent military outposts within the confines of Roman territory.[29] The magnitude of the Roman defenses suggests that Basque militarism had become organized on a wide scale, probably transcending the population of a single valley or district.

There was to be one last example of Basque-Roman collaboration. In 407 Germanic tribes—the Suevians, Alans, and Vandals—crossed the Rhine, traversed Gaul, and reached the Pyrenees. Here they were delayed for two years by a combined Basque-Roman effort. However, for reasons that are unclear, in 409 the Basques withdrew their support.[30] The Germanic tribes passed through the Basque area without attempting to control it and used the upper valley of the Ebro to enter the Castilian *meseta*. Under continued pressure from the Goths (a Germanic tribe that was threatening the Italian peninsula itself), the Romans relinquished control of Iberia and southern France. The Goths pressed southward, entering Iberia in 415. By 418 they were able to isolate the Suevians in present-day Galicia, to destroy the Alans, and to oblige the Vandals to cross the Strait of Gibraltar into North Africa.

BETWEEN GOTHS AND FRANKS

By the early part of the fifth century the Goths controlled western Europe from the river Loire (the area to the north of which was controlled by the Franks) to the Strait of Gibraltar. They established their capital in Toulouse. Within this larger Gothic region, only the Basques and their immediate neighbors to the west, the Cantabrians, were free of Germanic rule.

The events of the fifth century had far-reaching consequences for the persistence of a separate Basque identity. After six centuries of Roman rule, it is probable that Latin was rapidly becoming the vernacular in the mountain areas. Had Roman hegemony continued unabated for a few centuries longer, the Basque language might have disappeared entirely, just as Latin extinguished several other European tongues and supplanted Basque in parts of the Aquitaine, the central Pyrenees, and the

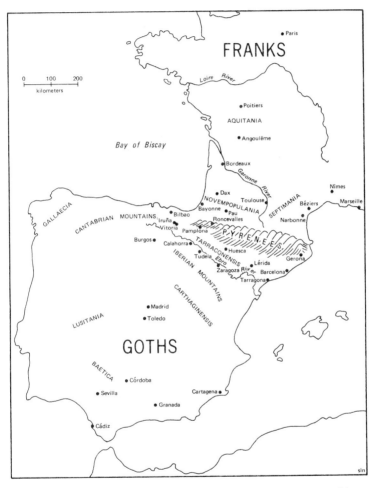

Important place names during the Roman, Frankish, and Gothic
periods of Pyrenean and Iberian history.

drainage of the Ebro. The present Basque language has more loan words of Latin origin than from French, Spanish, or Gascon (the language spoken just to the north of the Basque area). The defeat of the Romans by the Germanic tribes, however, provided the Basques with a respite from outside interference. The Goths were less successful than the Romans in checking Basque militarism. During the first half of the fifth century the Basques remained on the offensive, initiating raids into the lowlands both to the north and south of their mountain fastness.

By the middle of the fifth century the Goths were faced with revolts of the agricultural *bagaudae* in the plains of the Ebro. These revolts were supported by the mountain dwellers, and some authorities believe that the *bagaudae* in question were themselves Basque.[31] The Goths were obliged to deploy their armies to contain the revolts. One of the most important battles was fought at Araceli, which was located along the Roman road between Iruña and Pamplona. The Goths' lack of success is seen in the fact that six years later the *bagaudae* assaulted their city of Tarazona (near the southern frontier of the Basque country). In 454, Theodorus, king of the Goths, sent his brother at the head of a large army to confront the *bagaudae* of the Ebro valley.

These insurrections and the weakness of the Goths to a large extent shielded the Basques from direct military pressure. However, there were certain exceptions. For instance, one chronicle notes that Rekarius, king of the Suevians, traversed the Basque country in 449, laying to waste everything in his path.[32]* In 456 the coastal areas of the Basque country were sacked by maritime invaders.[33] In 472, and again in 481, Pamplona was occupied temporarily by the Goths.[34]

The Franks crossed the Loire and defeated the Goths in the year 507. It is likely that the Basques were involved, because the bishop of Lescar, a town on the northern frontier of the Basque country, raised an army to attack the Goths' rear guard at the same time that a major battle raged near Poitiers. The bishop's forces were not needed; before they could be fielded

---

*He was travelling with an expeditionary force from Galicia to Toulouse where he was to marry the daughter of the Gothic king.

the Goths were routed and driven out of Gaul. They then established their capital in Toledo.

Throughout the first half of the sixth century the Basques enjoyed a period of peace. To the south, the Goths were in disarray, and relations between Basques and Franks were amicable. The Basques even began to extend their influence northward. It was during this period that the area between the Pyrenees and the Loire came to be known as Vasconia. The precise nature of this Basque influence in the Aquitaine is unclear. However, the fact that the Basque language did not become established there suggests that it may have involved little more than the concession of certain privileges to Basque military leaders. It is possible that the privileges dealt with the movements of livestock, since in subsequent periods parts of the region served transhumant Basque flocks and herds as wintering grounds.

There is further evidence—albeit circumstantial—of collaboration between Basques and Franks. The *Chronica Caesaraugustae* states that in 541 five Frankish kings crossed the Pyrenees near Pamplona, laying siege to the city of Zaragoza and looting the surrounding countryside. The chronicles make no mention of hostilities between Basques and Franks.[35] Some authorities believe, however, that the Basques resisted these movements of the Frankish armies. They base their opinion on a poem by Venantius Fortunatus, dedicated in 581 to Chilpericus, king of the Franks. The poet claims that Clotharius, father of Chilpericus, fought during his reign against the Danes, Saxons, Bretons, Goths, and Basques.[36] Yet the poet fails to specify the years in which these battles transpired. The fact that the Frankish armies passed by Pamplona without attempting to occupy it suggests that there existed some sort of treaty between Franks and Basques in 541. There is another piece of indirect evidence that supports this interpretation. According to an account by Saint Isidore,[37] the Goths weathered the attacks and eventually routed the Frankish armies, inflicting upon them great losses. Remnants of the army were trapped on the Iberian side of the Pyrenees. Their condition was so lamentable that the chronicler referred to them as *cetera infelicium turba* or "the remaining crowd of unfortunate men." Most of these soldiers were eventually killed by the Goths, but there is no indication that they were attacked by the Basques.

On the other hand, the poem of Venantius Fortunatus does indicate that relations between Franks and Basques were not always amicable. By the middle of the sixth century the Basques were situated between two powerful forces, the Franks to the north and the Goths to the south, both of which considered themselves heirs to the Roman Empire and hence having political sovereignty over the Basques. That neither was successful in establishing such control is due both to Basque militancy and to the fact that the Franks and Goths continued to fight one another. Throughout this period the Basques employed their military strength in the defense of their independence and remained aloof from the larger political struggle between Franks and Goths. There is no evidence that the Basques aligned themselves with Franks to invade Gothic areas or vice versa. Rather, the Basque forces defended their mountain stronghold and occasionally sallied forth when the moment was opportune against both Frankish- and Gothic-controlled lowland areas adjacent to the Pyrenees.

Toward the end of the sixth century the Basques were subjected to considerable military pressure from their stronger neighbors. In 568 Leovigildus became king of the Goths, and his reign (568−86) was one of almost continual warfare. In 570−72 the Goths waged campaigns against the Byzantines, who had become established in the southeast corner of the Iberian peninsula in 531. In 573 Leovigildus occupied the kingdom of Sabaria, a region along the Duero River (present-day northern Salamanca and southern Zamora). In 574 the Goths occupied and fortified the city of Amaya and thereby exerted control over the Cantabrians.[38] In 575 Leovigildus began a campaign against the Suevians in Galicia which he was forced to abandon due to rebellions in southern Iberia. Again in both 578 and 579 Leovigildus was occupied by new rebellions in the south. However, by 580 he had succeeded in reasserting his control.

It was in 581 that Leovigildus initiated a campaign against Vasconia. The chronicler Juan de Biclara noted that Leovigildus occupied parts of Vasconia in that year and founded the city that he called Victoriaco. The area occupied by the Goths was southern and central Alava, although the exact site of Victoriaco is unclear.* Leovigildus was not able to extend his control into the mountain areas,† but he did inflict a defeat on the Basques and established a fortified city in their territory, with a military garrison that represented a direct and constant challenge to Basque independence.

Meanwhile, the Frankish king Chilpericus, possibly encouraged by the Goths' successes, dispatched the duke of Bladastes against northern Vasconia. This attack, which also took place in 581, had a different outcome. According to one Frankish chronicler, Bladastes was defeated soundly and lost the major part of his army.[41]

This defeat had repercussions in the court of the Franks. The *dux* was the most important post in a Frankish region, and the defeat of Bladastes signaled a new military danger to the south. The anger of the Franks was expressed by the poet Venantius Fortunatus in one of his compositions dedicated to the count of Galactorius, on the occasion of the latter's appointment as ruler of Bordeaux. The poet beseeched Galactorius, "May the Cantabrian fear you, and may the vagabond Basque be terrorized by your arms, and may the Pyrenees relinquish its power to the Alps."[42]

It is interesting to note that the Franks called the Basques "vagabonds," probably because the Basque military forces operated in small mobile units, raiding for booty and protecting Basque interests (primarily their access to winter pasturage for the transhumant herds) in the low-lying regions to the north of the Pyrenees. This view is further supported by subsequent events.

---

*Some authorities believe that present-day Vitoria is the ancient Victoriaco; for others, it was a town near Vitoria, while still others suggest that Victoriaco was built on the site of the Roman city of Iruña.

†The chronicler Juan de Biclara suggested this in his description of Leovigildus's campaigns against the Cantabrians and Basques. With respect to the former he stated, "In these days the king Leovigildus has entered Cantabria, killing the defenders of the province, occupying Amaya, unjustly seizing control of its resources, and subjecting the province to his authority."[39] With respect to the Basque campaign the chronicler noted, "The king Leovigildus occupied a part of Vasconia and founded a city which is called Victoriaco."[40]

This brings us to one of the most frequently cited and misinterpreted* texts regarding the Basques, the account of Saint Gregory of Tours (544–95), written in the year 587:

> The Basques, leaving the mountains and entering the plains, devastated the vineyards and fields, burned the dwellings, and carried away in captivity many inhabitants and their livestock. Austrobaldus [a Merovingian general] sallied forth against them frequently, but with little success.[43]

The text of Saint Gregory does have other points of interest. It relates that the Basques were engaged in a series of punitive raids against the plains of southern France. It declares that they proved to be both formidable and elusive military foes, avoiding population centers while laying waste to the countryside. The reference to vineyards suggests that these incursions probably ranged as far north as Bordeaux and the Armagnac region.

The reasons for the attacks are not clear. Many historians argue that the Basques, besieged in the south by the Goths, were seeking new outlets to the north. However, the fact that Leovigildus, the great warrior king of the Goths, died in 586 gives cause to doubt that the Basques were undergoing severe military pressure from the south one year later. The reverse seems to have been the case, since within a few years Leovigildus's successor, Recaredus, was engaged in defensive actions against Basque attacks.† Thus, although there is no text that states the reason for the Basque incursions against the Franks, it is likely that the trouble stemmed from some sort of violation of a treaty between the two peoples. That the Basques attacked rural areas and concentrated on razing cultivated fields might indicate that they were concerned with protecting winter pastur-

---

*Many Spanish and French historians, in their concern for the historical emergence and development of their respective national states, have interpreted this document as proof of an invasion of southern France from an Iberian Basque stronghold, and hence as the formative period of a "French Basque" area. This interpretation persists in the recent literature on European history. However, there is a crucial question of perspective here, since it is clear that during the time period in question the Basques were an autonomous and independent people, enclaved between the Frankish and Gothic spheres of influence. It seems equally clear that the process of polarization of Basque society between northern and southern spheres of influence was not to begin until several centuries later.

†Saint Isidore, chronicler of the Goths, states that after 590 the Goths were fighting against Basque raiders.[44]

age for the transhumant herds. The need to do so was likely
enhanced by the fact that their traditional grazing area to the
south, the Bardenas of southern Navarra, might have been in the
hands of the Goths.

The expansion of Basque interests into the lowlands north
of the Pyrenees was largely military, although it probably had
economic objectives as well. By this time most of the vestiges of
the Roman economy of southern Europe had disappeared;
money was no longer used as a medium of exchange, and
economic life had reverted to a system of barter.* Livestock
served in some instances as a trade item and measure of
wealth.[46]†

If the mountain-dwelling Basques extended their control to
the plains areas on occasion, there is little evidence that they
were capable of consolidating it for long periods of time. Both
Gothic and Frankish societies were composed of extensive
populations of settled agriculturalists and of some urban centers. The economy and society of the Basques remained
rudimentary and pastoral. Basque warriors were frequently
mounted, and the Basque forces were famed for their mobility.
However, if they were capable of inflicting great damage as
raiders of the unsuspecting plains or as ambushers of would-be
invaders of their mountain stronghold, there is little evidence
that they were able to resist the more determined military
campaigns of their powerful neighbors. It would thus seem that
the very unattractiveness of the Basque territory to a potential
occupier was a major feature of Basque defenses. Most of the
area simply lacked population concentrations that could be
controlled profitably, cities to be subjected to wider political
purposes, or treasure to commandeer.

The attacks of Franks and Goths upon Basque society
appear, then, to be part of a defensive strategy. When Basque
military actions posed a threat to the flanks of the larger empires, the Gothic and Frankish rulers responded in kind. Thus,
in 602 two sons of King Childebertus II decided to restore
Frankish control in the region between the Loire and the

---

*The minting and circulation of money in Christian Europe did not resume
until the tenth century when certain Italian city states initiated commerce with
the Near East.[45]

†In the Basque language the terms used to this day to designate "wealth"
and a "rich man" are *aberastasuna* and *aberatza*, respectively. Both come
from the word *abere* or "livestock."

Pyrenees. They organized a formidable military expedition and succeeded in defeating the Basques, obliging them to accept the authority of an appointed duke *(dux)*. The chronicler Fredegarius relates that the first duke of the dukedom of Vasconia was a man called Genialis and that he ruled the Basques well.[47]

It is of particular interest to note that Genialis was not a Frank, but rather a Gallo-Roman. He belonged to the indigenous population that inhabited most of southern Gaul prior to the invasions of the Franks, a population that had been extensively Romanized through the presence in their territory of the two important cities of Bordeaux and Toulouse. In the final period of Roman control, the area to the west of Toulouse and to the south of Bordeaux—the region later known as Vasconia—was called Novempopulania.* During Roman times the region had enjoyed a certain autonomy with respect to Toulouse and Bordeaux, a fact reflected in an inscription[49] that is conserved in the French Basque town of Hasparren and in the works of Gallo-Roman writers who provide evidence that the inhabitants of Novempopulania were regarded as "foreigners" in the cities.†

However, despite this sense of mutual differences that existed between the wider Gallo-Roman population and the inhabitants of Novempopulania, it is likely that they shared an undercurrent of cooperation. When the Roman Empire collapsed it was the Gallo-Roman population that suffered from the invasion of southern Gaul by the Germanic tribes.

The position of the Gallo-Romans was precarious. The need to deploy their forces in defense of their cities left them vulnerable to attacks in the countryside. There, matters were made even worse by the fact that a large portion of the population consisted of slaves who worked the estates and whose loyalties were dubious. It is likely, therefore, that the Gallo-

---

*There is not complete agreement among scholars on the precise boundaries of Novempopulania. However, it seems to have included the following: Eauze, Dax (Aquenses, Tarbelli), Comminges (Convenae), Auch (Ausci), Bazas (Vasates), Buch (La Teste, Bonates), Couserans (St.-Lizier-en-Ariege), and Bigorre y Ossau (Osquidates).[48] During Caesar's time the region between the Pyrenees, the Garonne River, and the coast was called Aquitania. (To this day the city of Dax is called *Akize* in the Basque language.)

†For instance, in one fourth-century account a Gallo-Roman professor of Bordeaux, in referring to Staphylius, another professor from the area of Ausci, notes, "So far I have kept to the rule of commemorating my fellow-countrymen. . . . Yet it is no sin to couple with my countrymen a single stranger such as you, Staphylius, a son of Novem Populi."[50]

Roman leaders sought and obtained military alliances and support among the surrounding populations such as that of Novempopulania. And of all the inhabitants of the latter region it was the Basques, with their military traditions, their lack of cities to defend or a slave population to control, and their military reserves among the Basque population residing on the Iberian slopes of the Pyrenees, who best qualified for the role of mercenaries in the service of the Gallo-Roman leaders. It may have been such a disposition to engage in mercenary activities that contributed to the spread of the name *vascones* (a denomination of the Romans referring to just one of several Basque-speaking tribes) to all of the Basque-speaking tribes and subsequently to the areas where the Basque warlords were most active *(Vasconia)*.

BASQUE WARLORDS AND THE DUKE OF VASCONIA

It is in light of this line of speculation that the appointment of Genialis, a Gallo-Roman, as duke of Vasconia acquires significance. It may have been that Genialis had prior dealings with the Basque warlords, possibly employing some of them in his service, which might account for the success of his overlordship. This becomes an even likelier explanation in light of subsequent events, when the duke enlisted Basque support in his own personal struggles against the authority of the Frankish monarchy.

The precise dimensions of the dukedom of Vasconia are unknown. In addition to the region between the Garonne and the Pyrenees, it may have included all of the present-day Basque area. The fact that today the three provinces of Vizcaya, Guipúzcoa, and Alava are designated as the *Provincias Vascongadas* (i.e., "of the *vascones*") and not *Provincias Vascas* ("of the *vascos*") may date from this time and may reflect their inclusion in the dukedom of Vasconia.* The fact that by the ninth century a part of the Basque country was referred to as the

---

*The present-day names of the Basque provinces do not appear in the documents until the eighth and ninth centuries, when there begins to emerge a system of feudal countships. For the Romans, the *vascones* were the inhabitants of much of present-day Navarra as well as a portion of the northern slopes of the Pyrenees (Basse Navarre). The Romans discerned several tribes—the Vardulii, the Caristii, and the Autrigones—in the present-day areas of Guipúzcoa, Alava, and Vizcaya.

*Galia commata** suggests the influence in the Basque region of political institutions to the north of the Pyrenees. On the other hand, it is possible that the term *vascones* was simply used to designate all non-Romanized peoples enclaved between the Frankish and Gothic spheres of influence, which would have placed at least parts of the Basque country outside the control of the dukedom of Vasconia. It seems clear that the warlords to the north of the Pyrenees were under the direct authority of the duke of Vasconia. This authority may have extended further into the Basque area, although it likely diminished as one moved south and west.

There is reason to believe that the loyalties of the Basque warlords to the duke were relative. In 636, when Genialis's successor, the Saxon Aighynus, appeared before the king Dagobertus in the company of many Basque warlords, all swore allegiance to the king and his successors, an oath that, as one chronicler complains, the Basques took "in their usual manner," as events were to prove.[53]

The dubious Basque loyalty to Dagobertus reflected the tension between local loyalty to an indigenous political system based upon elected assemblies—the Basque *biltzar*,† in which the popular will rather than personalities dominated—and the necessity to defer in certain instances to the stronger external political forces of feudal Europe. In the former arena issues were debated, compromises reached, and decisions taken collectively—decisions that could be changed by the next *biltzar*. This process was antithetical to the external vassal-suzerain structures dominated by a concern with personal honor and prestige within the framework of an essentially static, divinely prescribed and sanctioned feudal order, in which democratic institutions had no place.

---

*The authorities are not in agreement on the precise dimensions of *Galia commata*. For some it was the ancient territory of the *Vardulii*, that is, northeastern Alava and Guipúzcoa.[51] For others it was northeastern Alava and present-day Navarra.[52]

†In the Basque language any type of assembly is called *biltzar*, but the etymology of the word refers to an "assembly of ancients" *bil-zar*.[54] The precise origins of the system are unknown; however, it clearly antedates codification in the late Middle Ages of its privileges in the many *fueros* and *fors* of the several Basque regions. The antiquity of this essentially democratic institution has prompted some authorities to attribute the Basques with instituting one of the world's oldest democracies.[55] The American president John Quincy Adams was particularly impressed with the ancient Basque form of government.[56]

Consequently, the Basque vassals were of doubtful loyalty. In fact, the beginning of the seventh century ushers in a period of almost constant warfare for the Basques. It was as if the prosecution of wars became their entire reason for existence, and, according to the Christian chroniclers, they were always defeated. The extent of these "defeats" is questionable, however, since the Basques returned to the battlefield time and again, not from generation to generation but almost from year to year.

The Basques were so severely defeated by the Goths in 621 that they were obliged by the victors to erect a fortified city in their own territory (Olite; in Basque, *Iliberri*, or "new city") as a Gothic garrison against future Basque incursions into the valley of the Ebro. Five years later the duke of Vasconia exiled two bishops from the town of Eauze because of their complicity in a rebellion of the Basque warlords. This did not resolve the problem, since in 631 the Franks had to send troops to occupy all of Vasconia.[57] In 635 King Dagobertus dispatched a new military force to the Basque area commanded by no less than ten dukes and several counts. Once again, according to the chronicler Fredegarius, the Basques were soundly defeated, suffering many casualties and losing many prisoners. The victory of the Franks was costly, since Duke Arimbertus and the major part of his troops died in the fighting in Soule.[58]

The following year, the duke of Vasconia again visited the king of the Franks in order to swear his perpetual allegiance. That the Franks did not trust the Basques is evident from an incident that transpired. The duke's Basque companions, fearing for their lives, were forced to seek refuge in the church of Saint Denis, claiming sanctuary and consenting to leave only after receiving personal assurances of their safety from King Dagobertus.*

In 653 there were renewed Basque attacks against the Goths that led to the sacking of the city of Zaragoza and the occupation of Calahorra. The actions were linked to the political machinations of a Gothic leader, Froya, who governed the Jaca region of present-day Aragón. When the king of the Goths, Chindasvintus, died, Froya made an agreement with the Basques to attack nearby cities. The combined forces occupied

---

*The abbey of Saint Denis, near Paris, was the favored church of the Merovingian kings, and especially of the kings Clovis and Dagobertus (the latter was interred there). From the sixth century on, the abbey was known as the protector of "those in danger of their lives."[59]

Calahorra and marched on Zaragoza. According to the bishop of Zaragoza, the Basques committed many atrocities:

> they spilled the innocent blood of many Christians. Some were strangled, others wounded with darts and all kinds of projectiles. They took a great number of prisoners and carried off enormous booty. This unfortunate war entered the temples of God. The sacred altars were destroyed. Many priests were chopped to pieces with swords and many bodies were left without burial as carrion for the dogs and birds. In this fashion and with much reason the words of the seventy-eighth psalm can be applied to this disaster.[60]

The Basques retired to the mountains with their booty, leaving Froya and his forces in the city. Shortly thereafter, a Gothic relief army recaptured both Zaragoza and Calahorra, and Froya was killed in the battle.

By the seventh century there was a clear difference in the Basques' relationships with their respective neighbors to the south and north. The Goths initiated military pressure against the southern reaches of the Basque country in an effort to subject it to their authority. Gothic policy sought to control rather than to incorporate conquered populations. Olite, though constructed by Basques in Basque territory, was to remain subject to the Goths.[61] At no time is there evidence of Basque participation in Gothic ruling circles. For example, the bishop of Pamplona attended Gothic ecclesiastical councils only when the city of Pamplona was in Gothic hands; when the city was under Basque control he was absent.[62] Dealings between Basques and Goths, therefore, were largely restricted to the battlefield.

The relationship between the Basques and the Franks was of a different order. While it might be marred by periodic fighting, it was also profoundly influenced by the existence of the dukedom of Vasconia, through which a number of Basque warlords were drawn into the Frankish political sphere. In this fashion Basque leaders were both influenced by and exerted a certain influence upon developments in the wider world of the Franks.

Toward the middle of the seventh century there began a series of events that were to shape the next several centuries of political history in the Basque area. Felix, duke of Vasconia, resident in Toulouse and ruler of the region between the Loire and the Pyrenees, declared his independence from Frankish authority. The extent to which Basques were involved in this move is suggested by the fact that Felix named his young

Basque protégé, Lupus,* as his successor in 670. Lupus was to establish an hereditary line that controlled the dukedom for more than a century. He was succeeded by his son Eudes (710−36), who was succeeded by his son Hunald (736−44), whose son Waifre was duke from 745−68. In 768 Waifre was succeeded by Lupus II, who was the youngest son of Eudes. So the dukedom became a classical hereditary feudal structure to be passed down a particular family line. In subsequent centuries the kings of the kingdom of Navarra and the counts of Alava were in one fashion or another descended from this original family line initiated in Toulouse by Lupus I.

Lupus I, who assumed power as a young man of twenty-eight, succeeded not only to the dukedom of Vasconia proper, which terminated at the Garonne, but also to the dukedom of Aquitania. Thus, in this personage a Basque leader ruled the entire area from the Pyrenees to the Loire. Lupus I initiated an extraordinary series of political machinations, both within his own sphere of influence and in Frankish and Gothic circles, that seemed designed to create an autonomous Pyrenean kingdom. His efforts either to control or to cajole the church leaders led him to convoke, on his own authority,[64] two ecclesiastical councils held near Bordeaux in 670 and 673.[65]

Lupus took an active role in Frankish politics. He was named in the conspiracy that led to the assassinations of King Childericus II and his wife in 673.[66] Nor was Lupus moderate in his dealings with the Goths; he was implicated in a conspiracy against their king, Wamba. Lupus was involved with both secular and ecclesiastical authorities in the Gothic province of Septimania (located in extreme southeastern France). When the bishop of Nîmes refused to join the plot, Lupus had him imprisoned and sent in exile to Aquitania, replacing him with a Basque abbot. The attempt to subvert Wamba's authority in Septimania appears to have been closely related to Wamba's military successes in the southern reaches of the Basque country. When Wamba learned of the uprisings in the Septimania, he dispatched one of his military leaders, Paulus, and intensified his own campaigns against the Basques.

---

*During the Middle Ages, Basques employed the names of animals as personal names. For example, *Otsoa,* "wolf"; *Garcia* from *artza,* "bear"; *Vela* from *belia,* "raven", for men; or, for women, *Usoa,* "dove"; *Otsanda,* "female wolf"; *Ollanda* from *ollua,* "hen." These names were sometimes Latinized: Basque *Otsoa,* "the wolf," to Latin *Lupus,* "the wolf." The names passed into the Spanish language via Latin in many cases. Consequently *Lope* comes from *Lupus.*[63]

Paulus raised a large army in the province of Tarraconense and crossed the eastern Pyrenees to capture the city of Narbonne, capital of Septimania. But he then declared himself king of the region, forcing Wamba to terminate his campaign against the Basques as rapidly as possible. According to one chronicle, Wamba

> immediately entered Vasconia with all of his army, where for seven days he devastated the fields, destroyed the castles and burned the houses in such a fashion that the same *vascones*, demoralized in spirit, and given to wailing, wished to save their lives and sought a peace concession, not so much by requests as by pleas. From here, having received hostages and tributes, the peace having been secured, Wamba set out directly for the Gauls, passing through Calahorra and Huesca. . . .[67]

Wamba put down the revolts, pursued Paulus to Nîmes, and ended Lupus's efforts to create a Pyrenean kingdom. For the following century, Vasconia continued to enjoy considerable independence in its dealings with the Franks, exerting major political control over the region south of the Loire, but the dukes failed in their continuing ambition to reign as kings.

ARAB OCCUPATION OF PAMPLONA

The relations between the dukedom of Vasconia and the Goths continued to be strained. The military struggles went on year after year, as the fortunes of each side varied, although the Goths were never able to penetrate the mountain areas of the Basque country. At the beginning of the eighth century, however, events altered this stalemate. In the spring of 711 Rodericus, king of the Goths, was locked in a prolonged siege of the city of Pamplona when he learned that Arab forces had crossed the Strait of Gibraltar and invaded the southern areas of his kingdom. The matter was made even more serious by the fact that the invaders had been encouraged by certain Gothic nobles who were unhappy with Rodericus and wanted to replace him with a nobleman named Aquila.[68] Rodericus was forced to abandon his siege immediately. He moved his forces southward and contacted the Arabs in southern Iberia, but as the armies prepared for combat a portion of the Gothic forces deserted. Rodericus was unable to organize effective resistance and was himself slain in a minor battle in 713. His widow married one of the Arab leaders, and the Arabs quickly consolidated their control over most of the Iberian peninsula. Aquila was nominated king of the Goths, but in 714 he traveled with his brothers to Damascus and sold the kingdom to Caliph Walid I (705–15) for lands and money.[69] The remnants of Rodericus's forces, certain nobles and churchmen, took refuge in the mountains of Asturias and Cantabria to organize a resistance.

It was in the year 714 that the Arabs captured the city of Zaragoza, which they were to occupy continuously for the next four centuries, bringing them into contact with the Basques. At first the Arabs occupied Pamplona (in 718) but demonstrated very little interest in the rest of the Basque area. The Arab armies, like previous invaders, preferred to sack cities rather than control forests.*

Meanwhile, an event took place that was to have considerable importance in the future course of Navarrese political history. On the frontier of the Basque area, in the region of Jaca, one of the Christian leaders, the son of a Gothic count, was converted to Islam. It seems likely that he was not the only important convert. While there is little documentation concerning the early relations between Arabs and Basques, it is significant that a century later, when the kingdom of Navarra began to take form, many of its important personages were descendants of this original convert, Fortun ben Qasi. Others of his descendants were to occupy important posts in the Hispano-Arabic world. So during the emergence of the kingdom of Navarra, there were kinship ties linking its leaders and important Arab officials. The proliferation of these ties and the relative absence of conflict between the Arabs and the Basques on the Iberian side of the Pyrenees suggests that Fortun ben Qasi was able to bring over to the Arab side a number of leaders in the Navarra region, or at least to secure their neutrality. Subsequently, Navarra was influenced considerably by Moorish politics.

---

*There are radically different translations of an Arabic text referring to one invasion of the Basque area. The Codera translation states: "having initiated an expedition against the vascones, he [the Arab general Muza] penetrated their territory, until [they] arrived at a town [the inhabitants of which] were like beasts. Later he turned in the direction of the Franks, until he reached Zaragoza."[70] However, the Ribera translation of the same text states: "Muza invaded the country of the Basques and made war against them, until all of them came before him in large bands, as if they were beasts of burden. Then he turned towards the land of the Franks until he reached Zaragoza which he conquered."[71] Other Arab chroniclers underscored the poverty of the Basque area. Al-Himyari, describing Pamplona, stated, "Its inhabitants are poor, they do not eat sufficiently to satisfy their hunger, and they devote themselves to brigandry."[72]

During the first half of the eighth century the Arabs made repeated attempts to cross the eastern Pyrenees in order to lay claim to the Gothic province of Septimania. It was the duke of Vasconia who bore the brunt of these attacks. In 721 Eudes inflicted a major defeat on the Arabs near Toulouse. However, ten years later he was soundly defeated by an Arab army near Bordeaux. With the defeat of Eudes, the renewed Arab threat caused grave concern among the Franks. They mobilized an army under Charles Martel that defeated the Arabs near Poitiers in 732, forcing them back across the Pyrenees.

In certain respects the defeat of Eudes at the hands of the Arabs destroyed the relative autonomy of the dukedom of Vasconia. The name and the dukes persisted, but the dukedom became increasingly dependent upon the Franks. Thus, although Hunald, son of Eudes, who sought to exploit the death of Charles Martel in 742, revolted against the Franks, he was quickly defeated. Subsequent rebellions by the dukes proved to be equally abortive. Under this renewed system of Frankish control a number of Basque warlords dropped their allegiances to the duke of Vasconia, gravitating instead towards the Islamized Qasi leaders to the south.

At about the same time there were new developments in Iberia. The Goths of Asturias and Cantabria, taking advantage of the Arabs' problems in southern France, began to extend their territory. By the middle of the ninth century they controlled all of northern Iberia from Galicia to the Basque country. Thus began a series of attacks and counterattacks in which the Arabs would periodically ascend the valley of the Ebro to engage the Christians. As the Arab armies moved out of southern Navarra, they crossed into Alava, which became the first area to feel the sting of battle. The leaders of Alava and the Christian kings to the west formed alliances, some of which were sealed by marriages.[73]

CHARLEMAGNE: AN ILL-FATED VENTURE

In the year 778 the city of Pamplona was retaken from the Arabs by certain Basque warlords from the mountains who maintained their independence from both the Arabs and the dukedom of Vasconia, which was under the authority of Charlemagne. At the same time the Arab leader in Zaragoza wished to free himself from the control of Córdoba. He asked Charlemagne for assistance. Savoring the opportunity to undermine Arab unity, Charlemagne raised a large army, including troops from as far away as Bavaria and Austria. The duke of Vasconia also participated.

The force crossed the Pyrenees and arrived at Pamplona. There Charlemagne received oaths of loyalty from the Basque warlords, who were theoretically under the authority of the duke of Vasconia but regarded by the Franks as untrustworthy. The army then departed for Zaragoza where it found the gates of the cities closed: the Arab leader had changed his mind. Charlemagne, despite his huge force, and for reasons that are unclear, did not attack. He instead returned to Pamplona where he leveled that city's fortifications before crossing the Pyrenees at Roncesvalles. It was at this point that an army* attacked Charlemagne's rear guard. The Franks' losses were heavy and included a number of noblemen. It was in this battle that Roland was killed, giving rise to the famous ballad, *Chanson de Roland.*

Despite this attack, Charlemagne did not turn back in vengeance. Nor was he to return later. Instead, he changed his political strategies with respect to the inhabitants of the Pyrenees, whom he came to regard as both a buffer and barrier against the further expansions of the Arabs into southern Europe.† Charlemagne underscored the importance of the region by naming his son, Ludovicus, king of Aquitania, placing the dukedom of Vasconia under his authority. The new kingdom was divided into four ecclesiastical dioceses: Bourges, Bordeaux, Auch, and Narbonne. The jurisdiction of the duke of Vasconia was reduced to the district between the Garonne and the Pyrenees. The region from the Garonne to the Adour was called *Vasconia Ulterior* and from the Adour to the high Pyrenees *Vasconia Citerior*.

Ludovicus was at pains to please his Basque subjects. In 785 he appeared at his father's court in the company of young

---

*The precise identity and makeup of this army has eluded historians. In some versions of the famed *Chanson de Roland*, the attackers are identified as Arabs, while in others they are Basques.[74] The very usefulness of the ballad as an historical document has been questioned by those who argue that it is overly mythologized.[75] Employing other sources, some historians have argued that Roland succumbed to a Basque force bent on avenging the destruction at Pamplona.[76] Still others argue that Basques and Arabs combined forces to punish Charlemagne.[77]

†The Arabs were not as resigned about the events. When Córdoba learned of the near alliance between Charlemagne and the ruler of Zaragoza it dispatched a punitive force under the command of Abderraman I which, after capturing Zaragoza, reached the gates of Pamplona (in 781).[78]

Basque warlords of his own age. All were dressed in their traditional garb, which, according to the chronicler, consisted of "Short and round cap, shirt with long sleeves, wide breeches, spurs laced to the footwear and javelin in hand."[79] Ludovicus was successful in attracting to his side many Basque leaders. Consequently, Basque loyalties became split between a Christian Frankish faction and an Islamic faction that maintained close ties with the Arabs of the Ebro region.

The situation in the Basque area at the beginning of the ninth century became confused as events unfolded rapidly. In previous centuries the Basque leaders were referred to generically and anonymously by the outside chroniclers; by the ninth century the documents contain a plethora of names, reflecting the great attention displayed by both the Christian and Arab worlds toward the strategic role of the Pyrenean peoples in the larger struggle for southwestern Europe. Both to the west and the east of the Basque area, the contest transpired on the battlefields. The Arabs maintained constant pressure on the Christians of Iberia, launching five expeditions (through southern Alava) against the kingdom of Asturias between 792 and 816. For their part, the Franks launched attacks against the Arabs in the eastern sector, crossing the Pyrenees to capture the cities of Barcelona and Gerona in 801. Yet Pamplona and its hinterland constituted a crucial arena in which Christian and Arab interests clashed in more than battlefield fashion.

Political intrigue contributed much to the shifting alliances. In 799 the ruler of Pamplona, a Muslim and a member of the Beni Qasi family of Tudela, was assassinated by the Frankish faction in the city.[80] However, if the assassins gained control it was short-lived, since in 803 the ruler of the city was Arista, a Basque kinsman of the beni Qasi. Fortunes were reversed again in 806 when the same Arista family was forced to swear allegiance to Charlemagne. In 812 the entire area from the Garonne to Pamplona rebelled against the Franks. Ludovicus was obliged to attack and was successful in crossing the Pyrenees. He took the city of Pamplona, where he installed a member of the pro-Frank Velasco family as governor. As he returned to France through the Roncesvalles pass, Ludovicus took with him as hostages many prominent Basque families in order to avoid the kind of attack that had been directed at the rear guard of his father's army some years earlier.[81]

In 819 the duke of Vasconia himself rebelled against the Franks, a situation that fermented until 824, when the Franks sent an army against the Pyrenees under the command of counts Eblo and Aznar. They succeeded in capturing Pamplona, but this time the Frankish army was attacked and defeated as it traveled through the pass of Roncesvalles. Both counts were captured. Aznar, who seems to have been related to the Arista family of Pamplona, remained in Basque hands. Eblo was sent to Córdoba as a hostage.

Further evidence of ties between the Basque and Arab worlds is seen in the fact that, by the ninth century, the majority of Arab caliphs and emirs in Iberia were selecting Basque wives.[82] There seems to have been a regular traffic in women between Navarra and Córdoba. At the same time, Navarra became a crucial point in a trading network that developed between Christians and Arabs. One authority believes that Pamplona might have been a major market in which slaves from all over Europe were exchanged for Arab gold and goods.[83] This flowering of Navarrese commerce, as well as the area's strategic position between Gothic Christians to the west, Franks to the north, and Arabs to the south and east, was to culminate in the creation of a new political entity. In 824 a coalition of Basque warlords, including the powerful ben Qasi family of Tudela, recognized one of their members, Eneko Arista, as king of Pamplona. From his kingdom developed the realm of Navarra. Eneko Arista (from the Basque *aritza* or "the oak," i.e., "the strong") was probably from the Salazar valley,[84] or one of the least Christianized areas of Navarra. That this mountain warlord could emerge as king in his own right is somewhat enigmatic. In the western Europe of the period, kingdoms were Germanic in origin and kingships approved by the pope. Although the kingdom of Pamplona was non-Germanic in origin, it was quickly approved by the church and neighboring Christian monarchs. One possible explanation is that the Christian world accepted an autonomous kingdom in Pamplona as an alternative to a possible increase in Islamic influence in the area. At the same time, Eneko Arista seems to have educated his son under Christian tutelage in Leire, since once he succeeded his father in 852, the kingdom of Pamplona broke existing alliances with the Arabs and established closer ties with the Christian kingdom of Asturias.

BASQUE PAGANISM

The emergence of the kingdom of Navarra as an enclave between the Christian and Arab worlds raises the question of the relationship between the Basques and the two great religious traditions. We have noted that during Roman times Christianity may have entered the Romanized lowlands of the Basque country, although there is no evidence that it penetrated the mountainous areas, which presumably remained pagan. The subsequent invasions of the Germanic tribes further delayed the conversion of the Basques to Christianity. Both Goths and Franks were Christians, and it is unlikely that the Basques looked favorably upon the religion of their battlefield adversaries.

Frankish and Gothic chroniclers referred to the Basques as barbarians and pagans.[85] When Saint Amandus entered the Basque area to preach the gospel in about 650, his efforts were thwarted by a heckler who mimicked his every word, destroying the seriousness of the occasion.[86] When Froya sacked Zaragoza in 653, the Basques who fought with him were particularly cruel in their treatment of the city's churches and religious authorities. Similarly, the attack on Charlemagne's rear guard suggests the religious hostility of the attackers. Charlemagne, as emperor of the Holy Roman Empire, was the main secular defender of the Christian faith. Finally, the ease with which Basque warlords switched religious allegiance as they shifted between Christian and Arab political alliances suggests that by the ninth and tenth centuries neither of the great religions was firmly entrenched in the area.

Furthermore, there is reason to believe that pagan beliefs continued to hold sway in the mountainous heartland of the Basque country. As late as the twelfth century two travelers seeking to cross the Basque area reported harassment.[87] One was the French pilgrim Aimeric de Picaud, who was on his way to Santiago de Compostela. He reports that a barbaric people extracted tribute from the pilgrims near St.-Jean-Pied-de-Port. Picaud, in referring to earlier periods, states:

> On this mountain, before Christianity was fully propagated in the lands of Spain, the impious Navarrese and Basques would plunder the pilgrims who were on their way to Santiago. They [the Basques] would mount them as if they were asses, and kill them. . . .[89]*

The second account was written under the direction of the archibshop of Compostela, a contemporary of Picaud. It de-

---

*Mañaricua regards this as sheer calumny on Picaud's part and feels that he lacked hard evidence.[88]

scribes the travels of the bishop of Oporto, who crossed Navarra, Guipúzcoa, and Vizcaya in 1119, while returning home from an ecclesiastical council in Rheims. The chronicler notes that for his safety the bishop did not wear his habit while in the Basque area: "Those remote mountains and places are inhabited by barbaric men, of an unknown language, and given to evil-doing. . . ."[90]

Finally, there is the evidence of Basque legends that refer to *jentillak*, or gentiles, strange mountain inhabitants who were at odds with the Christians. Some authorities believe that even after Christianity penetrated the mountainous regions there continued to be pockets of pagan believers. Lacarra suggests that pagan and Christian communities coexisted in the Basque country for several centuries.[91]

Precisely when paganism was finally abolished among the Basques is unclear. As late as the fifteenth century, a Spanish prelate called into question Basque religiosity.[92] Be this as it may, by the sixteenth century, Basque society was producing titans of the Catholic world. Saint Ignatius of the Guipuzcoan town of Loyola founded the Jesuit order, which was to become the phalanx of the Counter-Reformation. His most famous disciple, Saint Francis, the Asian evangelist, was from the Navarrese town of Javier.[93]

THE DIVISION OF THE KINGDOM OF NAVARRA

For the next two centuries, the kingdom of Navarra occupied a key role in the struggles between the Christians and Arabs. By playing one off against the other and by exploiting the kingdom's strategic position, the kings of Navarra steadily increased their influence and territory. By the tenth century, due to a series of marital and political alliances with the Christian kingdoms to the west, the kings of Navarra were the prime force in Iberian Christian circles.[94] By the beginning of the eleventh century, the kingdom was so powerful that it was exacting tribute from the neighboring Arab rulers.[95]

The apogee of Navarrese power came during the rule of Sancho El Mayor (1000–1035). Under Sancho the kingdom had become one of the most important in western Europe. It controlled the entire present-day Basque country (with the exception of Tudela, which remained in Arab hands until 1119), the ancient dukedom of Vasconia as far north as Bordeaux, all of the Pyrenees including Cataluña (except for a narrow corridor from Urgel to Lérida), and all of Old Castilla. At the death of

Sancho, the kingdom was fragmented among his sons. García de Nájera remained king of Navarra. His reduced kingdom included most of the Basque country. Gonzalo established the kingdom of Sobrarbe and Ribagorza. Ramíro received the eastern area and became the first king of Aragón, while Fernando received the countship of Castilla, which was later to become the core of the kingdom of the same name.[96]

This division had important consequences. The reduced kingdom of Navarra became progressively squeezed between the two expanding kingdoms of Aragón and Castilla as the reconquest of Iberia proceeded steadily southward from these two centers. While certain Navarrese participated in the ventures, and although some Navarrese and other Basque colonies were established to the south in territories newly wrested from Arab control,[97] the kingdom of Navarra remained static while Castilla and Aragón expanded their territories.

In 1076 the Navarrese king Sancho de Penalen was assassinated, and, fearing chaos, certain factions asked the kings of Castilla and Aragón to intervene. The two monarchs divided the kingdom of Navarra into spheres of influence. The present-day region of Navarra passed under the aegis of Aragón (the two areas were to have the same king for the next fifty years) and the remainder was left under the political influence of the king of Castilla.

In 1134 Alfonso I, king of Navarra and Aragón, died and was succeeded by two sons. Ramiro II became king of Aragón proper, while García Ramírez (1134−50) was installed as king of Navarra. The new king found himself in a weakened position with respect to Castilla. The Castilian king Alfonso VII seized the opportunity and occupied the region of the Rioja and some of the lands along the Ebro River.

In the succeeding years Castilla and Navarra continued to dispute sovereignty over these lands. Finally, it was decided to place the matter before Henry II (Plantagenet) of England for arbitration. He decided in favor of Castilla in 1179, and the areas passed permanently under Castilian rule.

Henry Plantagenet was the duke of Normandy prior to his elevation to the English throne in 1154. In 1152 he had married Alionor (Eleanor), the duchess of Aquitania and Vasconia. Consequently, his political sway extended to the Pyrenees. When Henry's daughter Alionor married the Castilian king Alfonso VIII in 1170, her dowry included some rights to the duchy of Vasconia (the area between the Garonne and the

Pyrenees), rights that were also recognized by her brother and Henry's successor Richard the Lion-Hearted. Richard died in 1199.

It was at this time that Alfonso VIII decided to exercise the claims to the duchy of Vasconia acquired through his marriage to Alionor. He marched on Alava and laid siege to Vitoria. After resisting for a year, the city capitulated, and in 1200 Alfonso concluded a pact with Guipúzcoa under which the area severed its ties with the kingdom of Navarra and accepted Castilian protection. Alfonso occupied the area between Arano (near Hernani) and Fuenterrabía, lands that by precedent pertained to the kingdom of Navarra. He crossed the Bidasoa River and captured Bayonne. In 1204 he reached the city of Dax and even managed in 1206 to threaten Bordeaux with a naval attack. Once peace was restored, Alfonso retired his forces from the area but never returned the lands between Arano and Fuenterrabía to the kingdom of Navarra. This was a severe blow for the Navarrese since it landlocked their kingdom. Alfonso stated in his last will and testament, "I promise, if God gives me health, that I shall restore to the king of Navarrra all of that which I possess between the bridge of Araniello [Arano] and Fuenterrabía . . . because I know that . . . it should belong to the kingdom of Navarra and pertain to it."[98] He never did.*

The incorporation of Alava and Guipúzcoa into the Castilian political orbit corresponded to certain economic realities. The seaport facilities of Vizcaya and Guipúzcoa had come increasingly to service the important Castilian wool export trade. Alava straddled the Castilian trade routes to the sea. As economic ties with Castilla increased, towns like Durango (Vizcaya), Vitoria (Alava), and San Sebastián (Guipúzcoa), although chartered originally by the kingdom of Navarra, willingly swore obedience to the king of Castilla. It was a sign of Navarrese weakness that the kingdom could not effectively withstand such challenges to its authority.

The Castilian occupation of Alava and part of Navarra and the alliance between Castilla and Guipúzcoa meant that for the first time in Iberian history a king of the Meseta had direct access to the Pyrenees and the continent beyond. From a Basque viewpoint the arrangement was a wedge that divided the remain-

---

*The Castilian claim to the duchy of Vasconia did, however, revert to the English when king Alfonso X of Castilla conferred it upon Edward I, prince of Wales, when Edward married Alfonso's sister Leonora in 1254.

ing independent Basque polities into Vizcaya to the west and the kingdom of Navarra to the east.

Nor were the Basque areas to the north unaffected by political events during these turbulent years. Sancho El Mayor of Navarra had, in 1023, created the viscounties of Labourd and Soule and several viscounties in Basse Navarre. Richard the Lion-Hearted, upon his marriage to Berenguela in 1191, conceded his rights to the viscounties of Basse Navarre to his brother-in-law, the king of Navarra. Basse Navarre remained tied to Navarra until 1512, when the kingdom was invaded by Aragón and Castilla. However, the viscount of Labourd sold his rights to Richard, placing the area under English hegemony, which lasted until 1451. During this same period the viscounts of Soule were also within the English sphere of influence. With the collapse of English authority on the continent as a result of reversals during the Hundred Years War, Labourd and Soule were incorporated into France.

The political history of Vizcaya during these centuries was somewhat different from that of other Basque areas. The Vizcayans elected their own ruler *(Jauna*)* about the year 870, shortly after defeating an invasion attempt by the king of Asturias. Vizcaya remained independent of outside political embroilment until 1379, when its ruler Juan de Haro by his marriage became king of Castilla. Subsequently, Vizcaya enjoyed considerable political autonomy under its *fueros*, and the king of Spain continued to refer to himself as lord (señor) of Vizcaya among his several titles, but the marriage brought Vizcaya irrevocably into the Castilian political orbit.

Meanwhile, Navarra became embroiled in broader European affairs at the expense of its Iberian involvements. During the twelfth century the Navarrese royal line contributed several queens to European thrones. In 1146 the daughter of King García Ramírez became queen of Sicily. Three daughters of Sancho the Wise (1150−94) married European rulers. Blanca became queen of Champagne, Berenguela married Richard the

---

*Jauna in Basque means *Lord* and seems to have been the term of highest authority within the Basque concept of hierarchy. In Basque the term for God is *Jaungoikoa* ("Lord on High"). There is some question about when and how the first Vizcayan *Jauna* emerged, since historical events are interlaced with legend. According to a Vizcayan tradition recorded in about 1317,[99] the first ruler of Vizcaya was Jaun Zuria ("The White Lord") who was the son of a foreign princess (Scottish) and a serpent. In pre-Christian Basque mythology, the highest divinity was a female and her consort was the serpent.[100]

Lion-Hearted of England, and Margarita became the queen of Denmark.[101] When King Sancho the Strong died without male succession in 1234, the throne passed to his nephew, the count of Champagne, thereby initiating more than a century of Navarrese involvement in French affairs. After a series of internal struggles the throne of Navarra was united with that of France in the person of a single king, drawing Navarra directly into the Hundred Years War. Much of its wealth was dissipated, and its sovereignty over certain territories was contested periodically.

Toward the end of the fourteenth century the Navarrese king, Charles II, lost all of his former French holdings, with the exception of Basse Navarre. Under his son Charles III (1387–1425), the kingdom prospered anew, and the Navarrese court became a major cultural center. The interlude was brief, however, because the death of King Charles triggered a major dispute over succession that destroyed Navarrese unity. With respect to its former glory, Navarra entered the latter half of the fifteenth century as a dismembered, practically defenseless kingdom whose importance rested almost solely on its role as pawn in the machinations of its three more powerful neighbors—Castilla to the south, Aragón to the east, and France to the north.

THE BASQUE ECONOMY: IRON MINES AND SMITHS

To this point we have given little attention to the economic aspects of Basque history. We have noted that Basques were pastoralists who practiced transhumance. The need for access to nearby lowland areas for use as winter pasturage appears to have been a prime factor in the militarism of the mountain dwellers. However, pastoralism was not the sole element in the economy of the Basque area. Basque endeavors in metallurgy, whaling, and maritime trade had a profound impact upon early modern Europe.

The Roman historian Pliny, in the thirty-fourth book of his *Natural History*, remarks, "Iron ore is found in the greatest abundance of all metals. In the coastal part of Biscaya washed by the Atlantic there is a very high mountain which, marvellous to relate, consists entirely of that metal. . . ."[102] The Romans worked these deposits and mined the Basque area for other minerals as well.[103]

It is likely that the Basques' knowledge of iron forging antedated Roman times. By about 1000 B.C. they were in contact with Indo-European tribes that utilized iron implements

and weapons. It has been suggested that certain Basque top-
onyms such as *Aya* and *Ayala* refer to very ancient sites where
iron ore was mined. The Basque area also has a large number of
cromlechs, which are found in association with iron implements.[104]

The earliest documentary evidence of an iron foundry in
the Basque country dates from 871 A.D.[105] From the fifth
century on, however, the chroniclers note that the Basques used
large numbers of throwing weapons on the battlefield, which
suggests that they must have had an abundant supply of iron for
weaponry. The major deposit during the Middle Ages was
located in Guipúzcoa, in the region known as Las Peñas de Aya,
in the geographical heartland of the Basque country.[106] Until
the thirteenth century the foundries were located in the mountains, usually adjacent to the ore deposits. The iron was processed by using large quantities of charcoal produced in the
forests. During the thirteenth century, however, the founding of
iron became organized on an industrial scale. The foundries
were transferred to the river bottoms, where hydraulic power
could be employed, and production greatly increased.

This early industrialization vastly increased both the quantity and the quality of Basque iron production. By the beginning
of the fifteenth century the Basques were famed throughout
Europe for their iron working skills. When the French decided
to establish an ironworks at Quercy, they brought in Basque
technicians.[107] Vizcayan swords were in great demand, and
even Shakespeare referred to the famed *bilbos* in *Hamlet* and
The Merry Wives of Windsor.

In addition to arms, the Basque ironsmiths manufactured
agricultural implements and shipbuilding materials (anchors,
chains, nails, and fittings). By one estimate, about a third of
Basque iron production in the fifteenth century was employed in
naval construction, a third in the manufacture of agricultural
implements and weapons, and a third exported in bulk form
(ingots).[108]

By the end of the century the kingdom of Castilla was
heavily dependent upon Basque iron. In 1480, Queen Isabela
sent an urgent request to the authorities of Vizcaya, Guipúzcoa,
and Alava to drop their other tasks in order to manufacture arms
for the fortresses of Sicily and the fleet that was confronting the
Turks. This request was repeated in 1488 and again in 1489.[109]
At the same time, iron became so fundamental to the Vizcayan
economy that it served as a unit of value. A document of the

period stated that "a farm, a foundry, or a mill in Vizcaya was worth 550 quintals of iron, a mountainside in chestnuts was valued at 30 quintals, while some houses with their lands were worth 130 quintals."[110]*

ERA OF BASQUE WHALERS

Seafaring in Basque coastal waters dates from at least as early as Roman times, when Mediterranean boats used the area's natural harbors.[112]† The fact that the Basque coast was raided by Germanic seafarers during the fifth century A.D. suggests the presence of some level of maritime commerce or other activity. There may have been a small fishing industry, but the lack of a heavily populated hinterland and coastal population centers would have inhibited its growth.

On the other hand, it would seem that the Basques became the earliest whalers in Europe.‡ The presence of whales in the Bay of Biscay was noted as early as the fourth century A.D., when Ausonius of Bordeaux mentioned them in his chronicles. He claimed that the animals were sometimes cast ashore by the winds.[115] It is probable that the Basques learned of the value of the oil, meat, tongue, and bone by experimenting with such accidentally marooned whales and in the bargain became the first Europeans to recognize the commercial possibilities of whaling.

---

*Between the sixteenth and eighteenth centuries annual production averaged about forty thousand tons.[111] During the eighteenth century, the Basque iron industry began to lose its initiative. While the transfer of production from the mountains to the waterways in the thirteenth and fourteenth centuries was innovative and provided a competitive edge, these same facilities were small, inefficient, and uneconomic compared with the foundries installed elsewhere in Europe, and notably in England, during the initial stages of the Industrial Revolution. Attempts during the late eighteenth century to modernize Basque iron production were frustrated by a series of political and economic disruptions. First there was the war with revolutionary France (1794), then the Napoleonic invasion and occupation (1808–13), and finally a series of Spanish civil wars (1822–23, 1833–39, and 1872–76). It was not until the aftermath of this latter civil strife that the Basque iron industry was to undergo renovation, a process that will be considered briefly in chapter 3.

†A preserved Roman vessel was recently discovered near Irún (Guipúzcoa). Irún might have served as a seaport for the Roman mining operations located at nearby Oyarzun.[113] Also, Roman coins have been discovered in the river Nervión.[114]

‡It is impossible to date the beginning of Basque whaling with precision due both to a scarcity of documents and lack of archeological work in Basque coastal areas.

Basque whaling became a highly organized undertaking. Lookouts posted on elevated promontories scanned the waters for signs of prey. A boat, manned by a leader, a harpooner, and four or five crewmen, gave chase. The crew allowed the harpooned whale to tow their craft until the animal died from exhaustion and loss of blood; then they brought it ashore for processing.[116]

It is probable that the creation of the dukedom of Vasconia, which fostered contacts between Basques and Franks, stimulated the development of Basque whaling. Frankish areas had a great demand for the oil, used for lighting, the manufacture of soap, and the preparation of leather and coarse woolen clothes.[117] It should be remembered that southwestern Europe in Roman times depended largely upon olive oil for grease. With the collapse of Rome, however, the major olive-producing regions came to be controlled first by the Goths and then by the Arabs. Whale oil became a substitute. The production of oil from a single whale was enormous, in some cases as much as thirty tons.[118] There are references to Basques selling whale oil in Bordeaux as early as the seventh century A.D.[119]

The Basque coast stretches 130 kilometers from the mouth of the river Adour to that of the Nervión, and the water depths (fifty meters twelve kilometers from shore, to two hundred meters at fifty kilometers) are ideal for marine life. The natural conditions provided a rich fishery and attracted large numbers of whales.[120] Under relentless hunting pressure, however, these animals modified their annual migrations, avoiding Basque waters in favor of an open sea route to the Asturian/Galician coasts. The Basque whalers responded by constructing larger vessels capable of traveling to these new hunting areas. There are records of Basques renting facilities in Asturias and Galicia[121] and possibly on the Brittany coast,[122] where they processed the kill, transporting only the final products back to the Basque country.

It was this demand for larger boats in the whaling trade that created the basis for a Basque shipbuilding industry. It is probable that shipbuilding techniques were adopted in part from the Normans, who occupied the port of Bayonne briefly at the end of the ninth century.[123] The documentation demonstrates clearly that both whaling and shipbuilding were flourishing along the Basque coast during the twelfth century; however, it is probable that both had become significant at least two centuries earlier. That whaling was the single most important coastal activity during the Middle Ages is seen from the fact that the coats-of-arms of almost every port from Bilbao to Bayonne contain harpoons or whaling scenes. The coat-of-arms of Lequeitio, one of the most important whaling centers, bears the inscription *Horrenda cette subjecit*, or "Dominated the horrible cetacean."[124]

The steady expansion of the Basque whaling fleet meant that the whalers were forced to follow their quarry further afield. The numbers of Viscayan whales diminished to the point that some whalers pursued them northward to their polar summering grounds. There the Basque whalers encountered several new species, including the Greenland whale. This latter was the best of prey for many reasons. It was both larger and more timid than the Vizcayan whale. Furthermore, it traveled in schools, unlike the loner Vizcayan species. So as the Basque whalers went northward, their success increased, and they gained incentive to go even further into uncharted climes. This growth of Basque whaling interests peaked in the sixteenth and seventeenth centuries, at which time the Basques were regarded as Europe's best whalers.

There has been considerable speculation as to the extent to which Basque whalers and cod fishermen explored the North Atlantic. There is a literature, dating from the sixteenth and seventeenth centuries, that attributes Basque whalers with the discovery of the New World.[125]* Some believe that it was a Basque sailor who informed Columbus of the existence of land on the other side of the Atlantic.[130]

---

*In his recent work *Northern Mists*, Carl O. Sauer refutes the claims of Basque discoveries. He notes, "How far Biscayan ships went into the northern ocean . . . remains unknown. Their interest was in commerce, in the taking of whales and cod, not in discovery of unknown lands. However far they went they did not discover new land across the sea, nor were they among the first to fish those waters."[126]

Sauer bases this view upon the opinions of the two important Spanish naval historians Fernández de Navarrete and Fernández Duro. The former rejects the claims of pre-Columbian Basque voyages to the New World by citing early sixteenth-century documents that would seem to indicate that Vizcayan and Guipuzcoan mariners were just then inaugurating operations in the North Atlantic. He places particular emphasis on a royal order of 1511, charging a Spanish shipowner to explore the waters of Terranova, in which it is stated, "the persons that you will take with you should be citizens of this kingdom with the exception of two pilots who may be Bretons or from some other nation that has been there."[127] Fernández de Navarrete believes that if Basques had been to Terranova the order would not have given special permission to

While these points remain highly speculative, there is ample evidence of extensive Basque fishing operations along the coasts of Newfoundland and Canada as early as the sixteenth century.* The place names[132] of the two regions reflect this since many either refer to Basques (Isle-aux-Basques) or are in the Basque language (e.g., *Portuchoa*, or "little port"). Tombstones dating from the seventeenth and eighteenth centuries and bearing Basque inscriptions have been found in a

---

include foreign pilots. However, aside from the question of the extent of the Castilian king's familiarity with Vizcayan and Guipuzcoan maritime history (might not fishermen be secretive concerning their fishing grounds?), it should be noted that French Basques were outside Castilian jurisdiction and may have preceded Spanish Basques into the North Atlantic.

Fernández Duro's position is even less supportive. While he musters evidence against possible Basque discoveries in the work cited by Sauer *(Disquisiones Náuticas* 1881), he subsequently published the opinion that Basque mariners indeed landed on the North American coast prior to Columbus's voyage.[128] In 1882, he stated before the Congress of Americanists:

It seems that those heroic mariners [Basque whalers], pursuing a whale or blown by a storm reached the unknown continent, but without claiming the area that they had found. With respect to this there are no documents or overwhelming proofs, but there is one clear indicator, which is the fact that the natives, during the epoch of Columbus's discovery, designated certain places and mountains with Basque names.[129]

*The question of Basque maritime activities in North Atlantic New World waters is currently under investigation by Mlle. Raymonde Litalien (French sources) and Mrs. Selma Barkham (Spanish sources) on behalf of the Public Archives of Canada. This research promises to revise current theories concerning Basque maritime history. Mrs. Barkham (personal communication) is of the opinion that during the sixteenth century one must distinguish carefully between Basque cod fishing and whaling. The former required extensive supplies of salt and the latter a source of metal implements (cauldrons, barrel hoops, harpoons, knives, etc.). French Basques had access to adequate salt supplies and could therefore strike out directly for Terranova, whereas Spanish Basque cod fishermen had first to carry cargo (usually iron) to La Rochelle, Lisbon, Setubal, or Sevilla, pick up salt, and then cross the Atlantic to the fishing grounds. Conversely, Spanish Basques, because of their supply of iron, were favored in the whaling trade. Thus, initially French Basques were largely involved in the cod fisheries while Spanish Basques specialized more in whaling.

Furthermore, the two activities did not coincide in time or space. The cod fishermen left Europe early in the year and returned in some cases by August; the whalers left as late as July and might not return until December. Whalers could still be in the New World in November, and were occasionally iced in

cemetery in Placentia Bay, Newfoundland.[133] The bay itself was probably named after the Basque town of Placencia.†

French explorers in the North Atlantic complained that coastal natives in Canada tried to address them in a kind of pidgin Basque.[134] One chronicle from the seventeenth century claims that Basques had taught the natives to respond to the greeting *nola zaude?* ("how are you?") with *Apaizak obeto!* ("the priests are better off!").[135]

The same natives clearly distinguished between Basques and other Europeans. By one early seventeenth-century account, "they call all the French 'Normans,' except the Malouins, whom they call Samaricois, and the Basques, Bascua."[136] There is evidence that the whalers traded with the natives,[137] particularly for furs.[138] Relations between the Basques and the natives were not always amiable, however. On one occasion, the mariners left a boy with an Indian tribe so that he might learn their language. He was killed and eaten.[139] In another account, unspecified Basque treachery was said to have triggered hostilities between Indians and Europeans and among several Indian tribes.[140] Members of one bellicose tribe underscored its bravery with boasts of being killers of Basques and Malouins.[141] However, the Basques' ability to deal with the natives was legendary. For example, a Jesuit missionary, writing of the Eskimos, noted that they "will never be tamed, except through a miracle, because, ensconced in their naturally hollow and impregnable rocks . . . and ever suspicious, they never allow any person of any nation to approach, not even if he be a Basque. . . ."[142]

---

for the winter. Cod fishing was localized off the Newfoundland coast, whereas whaling centered upon Labrador, and particularly the Strait of Belle Isle.

Finally, cod fishing and whaling differed in terms of economic investment and return. Cod fishing ventures required less capitalization and the catch was sold locally in the Basque market for modest prices. Whaling ventures entailed larger ships and crews, greater risks, and the potential of greater rewards. A whaling ship might have a crew of 120 men and the capability of processing more than 1,000 barrels of oil with a market value of no less than 6,000 ducats when sold in Flanders, France, or England. The purchasing power of this amount may be appreciated by noting that in 1559 for 6,000 ducats one could buy 15,000 *robos* (or about 10,000 U.S. bushels) of wheat, and that in 1564 a Royal Auditor working for the kingdom of Navarra received an annual salary of 90 ducats![131]

†Not to be confused with the inland town of Plasencia in Guipúzcoa. Rather it is the present-day Vizcayan port of Plencia which in medieval times was known as Placencia.

Iceland also felt the Basque presence. In the seventeenth century Icelanders even wrote Basque-Icelandic glossaries.[143]

Thus, throughout the North Atlantic, from Isle-aux-Basques on the Labrador coast to Port-des-Basques in Newfoundland to Bay of Basques in Spitzbergen, Basque whalers were regarded as masters of the trade.* When the English and Dutch began whaling operations at the beginning of the seventeenth century, they used Basque harpooners. Thomas Edge, employed by an English firm in 1611 to outfit a whaling expedition to Greenland, noted the "sixe Biscaines procured for the killing of the whale."[145] Moreover, Edge was enjoined by his employers to treat the Basques "very kindly and friendly during this their first voyage" and to learn from them "that business of striking the whale, as well as they."[146] Edge reported that the Basques distinguished eight different species of whales, for each of which they had a separate name.[147]

In 1612 a flotilla of whalers set sail from Basque ports for Spitzbergen.[148] At about the same time, twelve whaling men from St.-Jean-de-Luz served Holland in the Spitzbergen area.[149] King James I of England wrote the king of Spain in the same year, requesting permission to engage Basque whalers. It must have been granted, since twenty-four Basque harpooners were serving on English vessels in the Spitzbergen area the next year.[150]

Although it is clear from the texts that the English were complete novices in the art of whale hunting, they learned rapidly. In 1619 England, Holland, and Denmark signed a treaty dividing the shores of Spitzbergen among themselves. France was given access only to the extreme northern area known as Cape Biscay. Since at the time it was still necessary to have access to shore facilities for rendering the whales, this posed a serious threat to Basque whaling interests. But the problem was alleviated when a French Basque, François Sopite of St.-Jean-de-Luz, invented a method of processing whales on board ship. This gave the Basques a renewed competitive advantage, since neither the English nor Dutch were able to learn their secret.[151]

---

*The whalers of the North Atlantic used a kind of international argot in their dealings. There was a saying among them, *Christ Maria presenta for mi Balia, for mi, presenta por ju bustana* (if Christ and Mary give me a whale, I will give you the tail).[144] *Bustana* is the Basque word for tail.

In 1636 a French Jesuit missionary report from Newfoundland urged establishment of French whaling activities along the Canadian coast, while acknowledging that at the time whaling in those waters was dominated by the Basques.[152]

Basque whaling and cod fishing declined notably during the eighteenth century. By 1757 international treaty arrangements excluded Spanish Basques (as Spanish nationals) from the fishing grounds of the North American Great Banks.* Nevertheless, French Basques continue to fish the North Atlantic to this day. As recently as the turn of the present century, there was a significant colony of French Basques on the French islands of Saint-Pierre and Miquelon, adjacent to Newfoundland.†

Basque Maritime Commerce

The whaling of the Basques led them naturally into another seafaring activity as well—maritime commerce. Whaling is seasonal, and during the off-season the fleet provided many bottoms that could be employed as merchant vessels. There are reports of export trade from Basque ports by the end of the thirteenth century. Castilian wool was transported to Flanders and Vizcayan iron ingots to England. Basque vessels were also reportedly engaged in the wine traffic.[155] It has been contended that the *Mayflower* was a Basque whaling vessel engaged in commerce on the Bordeaux-to-London run, and that the Pilgrims purchased, refurbished, and rechristened her for their famous voyage.[156]

The symbiosis between Basque whaling and commerce so completely dominated this part of the Atlantic that it came to be known throughout Europe as the Bay of Biscay. Basque port facilities and maritime traffic, benefitted by a long-standing tradition of seamanship and a reserve of whaling vessels, were flourishing fully a century earlier than the other Cantabrian seaports of Castilla, Asturias, and Galicia.[157] As Castilla increased her wool exports, the Basque shippers were able to underbid even their Castilian counterparts of Santander. Basque ports also profited as the major shippers in the trade of the kingdom of Navarra.

---

*In 1758, twelve Guipuzcoan fishing vessels and an undetermined number of Vizcayan ones tested the restriction. All but one vessel were captured by the English.[153]

†The colony even had its own Basque chaplain.[154]

In 1296 most of the seaports along the Cantabrian coast from Santander to Fuenterrabía formed an organization known as the *Hermandad de las Marismas*.[158] The purpose of the alliance was to protect their Flanders run, a sea route that was becoming dangerous due to increasing rivalry between England and France. Over time the *Hermandad* began to engage English shipping, both suffering and inflicting defeats. By the middle of the fourteenth century the *Hermandad* had concluded its own treaty with England; at its expiration, the *Hermandad* sided with France.

Between 1372 and 1380 the vessels of the *Hermandad* defeated an English fleet at La Rochelle, participated in the sacking of the Isle of Wight, raided English channel ports, and ascended the Thames to burn the town of Gravesend. According to Sauer, "The *Hermandad de las Marismas* was in some ways a southern counterpart of the Hanseatic League and acted at times as a sovereign power."[159] Fernández Duro expressed similar sentiments when he noted, "The people of the littoral of northern Spain known by the name of Biscayans, intimately united by community enterprise, constituted a powerful naval force, capable of carrying on war with northern powers independently of the kings of Castile. . . ."[160]

By the fifteenth century commerce had begun to surpass whaling as the major activity of the Basque seafarers. Vessels outfitted strictly for the transport of goods were constructed. Bilbao, the commercial port, eclipsed the fishing and whaling ports of Lequeitio and Bermeo. Basque merchant vessels, taking advantage of the disruption caused in other merchant fleets by the Hundred Years War, began to service Mediterranean trade routes in direct competition with the more established Italian city fleets.[161] By the middle of the fifteenth century most of the commerce of Provence was dependent upon Basque shipping. Similarly, the Basques were engaged in transporting salt from Ibiza to Genoa, Sicilian, Apulian, and Sevillian wheat, Catalan herrings and silk, and Andalusian and Portuguese hides. This traffic proved to be so profitable that Galician, Portuguese, and Andalusian shipping interests followed the Basques into the Mediterranean.[162] Meanwhile, Basque trade in the Atlantic grew to such proportions that by the sixteenth century the Bilbao to Flanders run was regarded as west Europe's single most important trade route.[163]

The Basques were famed for another maritime activity as well—piracy. During the Middle Ages the Bay of Biscay was renowned for its pirates.[164] In the fourteenth century, battles at sea were struggles of "pirate against pirate."[165] By 1400, at least one Basque pirate, Sancho de Butron, was operating in the Mediterranean.[166]

French Basques were particularly prominent in the ranks of Europe's corsairs (men authorized by monarchs to plunder another nation's shipping), first in the service of England and later in that of France. With the discovery of America, Spanish galleons on the Atlantic run became the prime targets for pirates and corsairs alike. However, the galleons were quickly organized into defensible armed convoys when crossing the ocean. For this reason, piratical activity shifted to the Caribbean where single vessels sailing to Veracruz or Havana to join the trans-Atlantic convoys could be preyed upon. One of the most famous of these New World corsairs was Michel Le Basque.[167]

At times the strength of the pirates was such that they assaulted major cities. For example, in June of 1554 French Basques manning two caravels and a patax captured and occupied Santiago de Cuba for one month. Their pillaging was such that according to Bishop Duranga, "the men had not a coat to their backs nor the women a chemise to put on."[168]

In the Basque country, St.-Jean-de-Luz was major home port for pirates and corsairs. The earliest documentation available dates from 1528; however, by that time the town could be characterized as the *nid redoutable de corsaires* ("redoubtable corsair's nest"). The wealth gained from such activities made St.-Jean-de-Luz an architectural showplace.[169]*

By the late fifteenth century, or on the threshold of a period of Iberian dominance of both European and New World history, the Basques were in a unique bargaining position with respect to their more powerful, imperially-minded neighbors. On the one hand the Basques enjoyed a large measure of political independence, while on the other they were masterful seafarers and

---

*The last of the famous French Basque corsairs was Etienne Pellot (1765–1856) from Hendaye. He received his first taste of combat as a cabin-boy on the *Marquise de Lafayette*, a ship of four hundred tons and thirty cannons, which was outfitted in Bayonne by "the ladies of the Court" to fight against England during the American Revolution.[170]

manufacturers of metal products—two indispensable elements in any imperial enterprise. It was by skillfully exploiting these political and economic advantages that the Basques were to secure for themselves a major role in the New World enterprise.

CHAPTER TWO

Mercenaries, Missionaries, Mariners, and Merchants

Shortly after jousting unsuccessfully with the windmill, Don Quixote encountered a coach on the road. The squire who accompanied the coach was a Basque of crude manners and speech. During the argument that ensued this exchange took place:

Don Quixote:

Si fueras caballero, como no lo eres, ya yo hubiera castigado tu sandez y atrevimiento, cautiva criatura.
(If you were a gentleman, as you are not, I should have punished your rash insolence by now, you slavish creature.)

The Basque:

Yo no caballero? Juro a Dios tan mientes como cristiano. Si lanza arrojas y espada sacas, ¡el agua cuán presto verás que al gato llevas! Vizcaíno por tierra, hidalgo por mar, hidalgo por el diablo, y mientes que mira si otra dices cosa.

*(I not gentleman? I swear you liar, as I am a Christian. You throw
down lance and draw sword, and you will see you are carrying
the water to the cat. Basque on land, gentleman at sea. A
gentleman, by the devil, and you lie if you say otherwise!)*[1]

(From Miguel de Cervantes, *El Ingenioso Hidalgo Don Quixote de la
Mancha*, Book I, Chapter 8).

IBERIAN HETEROGENEITY

On the eve of the discovery of America, political jurisdiction on the Iberian peninsula was fragmented among several
independent kingdoms, and a firm dividing line between Iberian
and French spheres of influence had not, as yet, crystallized.
The Basque country was itself divided into several political
entities with loyalties to different sovereigns. The kingdom of
Navarra, comprising the present-day Spanish Basque province
of that name and the French Basque area of Basse Navarre,
retained its independence. However, its ruling dynasty, the
Foix-Albret, established in 1425, was French in origin. The
other two French Basque regions, after three centuries of English rule, had passed under the control of the French monarchy,
Soule in 1449 and Labourd in 1451. However, they retained
their ancient privileges, or *fors*, which guaranteed them a large
measure of autonomy.

In Iberia the kingdom of Castilla exercised considerable
influence over Guipúzcoa, Alava, and Vizcaya. In the year
1200 Guipúzcoa renounced its former loyalty to the king of
Navarra and accepted the monarchy of Castilla. In 1332 Alava
followed suit. Vizcaya remained under a seignorial system of
government. Juan de Haro, through marriage lord of Vizcaya,
became Juan I, king of Castilla in 1379. Thus, throughout the
fifteenth century the monarch of Castilla would be known as
"lord of Vizcaya, king of Guipúzcoa, and king of Castilla."

Castilian royal rule over the Basques remained indirect.
Unlike Cantabria, Asturias, and Galicia, which formed part of
Castilla, and unlike the areas of Extremadura and Andalucia,
newly conquered from the Arabs and incorporated into that

kingdom, the Basques retained sufficient autonomy to give them political leverage in their dealings with the Castilian monarchy. In other words, the Basques were not citizens of a region of Castilla; they were citizens of a land that had accepted the king of Castilla as its sovereign. This is a crucial, if subtle, distinction, since it meant that continued Basque loyalties to Castilla were contingent upon the monarch's respect for local autonomy and tradition as formalized in the *fueros*. These *fueros* were not privileges or concessions conferred at the pleasure of the king; rather, they were based upon centuries-old Basque legal traditions. Under the *fueros*, the popular assemblies, or *biltzarrak*, were vested with legislative authority, and the kings and lords were subject to its laws. Periodically, the sovereign was required to appear before the assemblies to swear to respect their authority; yet the agents of both king and church were excluded from the legislative deliberations. Thus, in the late fifteenth century, there was a strong local political tradition in Basque society that was fully capable of challenging the authority of the broader feudal structures of southwestern Europe.*

The *Fuero Viejo* of Vizcaya, recognized by Castilla in 1456, specified a number of rights of the citizenry that help one to understand Basque involvement in Spain's New World colonial venture. These include:

—Ownership of land in Vizcaya reserved for *vizcainos* (Law 10).

—Exemption from taxes on any maritime activity (Law 12).

—Freedom of every Vizcayan to engage in commerce (Laws 14 and 16).

—Right of due process in all legal proceedings (Law 26).[2]

An important aspect that is not contained in the *Fuero Viejo* of 1452, but which appears in its reaffirmation by Charles

---

*Basque political autonomy as guaranteed under the *fueros* and *fors* remained intact until the late eighteenth and early nineteenth centuries. The French Basque areas were to lose their *fors* (though not without a struggle) during the aftermath of the French Revolution when France was reorganized into new "departments." At the end of the eighteenth century, the Bourbon minister Godoy launched Madrid's campaign to undermine the Basque *fueros*. When the Basques were on the losing side in the two Carlist Wars (1833–39; 1872–76), the more substantive aspects of the *fueros* were voided. To this day, however, both Vizcaya and Navarra are governed by Basque consuetudinary law for certain purposes (e.g., inheritance).

the Fifth in 1526, is the *universal* nobility of the Vizcayans.[3] This point, though it was unimportant in the ordering of the internal life of Vizcaya, was a critical factor in dealings with the kingdom of Castilla. The hierarchical ordering of Castilian society meant that nobles enjoyed privileges and had access to administrative posts, both secular and religious, that were denied to others. Thus, any Vizcayan, regardless of the humbleness of his origins, could aspire to noble privileges and offices,* a fact that was later to condition the relations between Basques and non-Basques in the New World.

A further liberty afforded the Basques under the *fueros* was exemption from obligatory military service outside of Basque territory *(Fuero Nuevo* 1526: Laws 4 and 5).[5] Insofar as the purpose of a military campaign was to guarantee Basque territorial frontiers, each Basque male was obliged to serve without compensation at the call of local officials. But once they left Basque territory, Basque soldiers acted solely as mercenaries, receiving payment in advance. In the event that such payment was not forthcoming, the Basques were likely to abandon the field of battle.†

While Basques could not be conscripted forcibly for military service outside the Basque country, thousands of them left voluntarily to pursue the life of mercenary, largely in the service of Castilla.

BASQUES AND THE EMERGING SPAIN

Part of the reason why Basques were to play a prominent role in the conquest and colonization of the New World is to be found in Old World political developments from 1470 until shortly after the discovery of America in 1492. In 1470 King Enrique IV of Castilla wanted to name one of his nobles (the count of Haro) as lord of Vizcaya. Since they had not been consulted, the Vizcayans viewed this as a breech of the *Fuero*. The count of Haro traveled to the area accompanied by an army but in 1471 was defeated by the Vizcayans at the battle of

---

*To guard against the possibility that migration of commoners into the Basque area could undermine the claim to universal nobility for the populace, any foreigner desirous of settling permanently in either Vizcaya or Guipúzcoa was first required to demonstrate his noble status.[4]

†This happened during the Sicilian campaign of 1500, prompting the commander of the Spanish forces to remark, "I would rather be a lion-tamer than try to rule that nation [the Basques]."[6]

Munguia. In 1472 the Vizcayans declared themselves "de-naturalized" from Enrique's control, swearing allegiance to his sister, Isabela, and proclaiming her lady *(señora)* of Vizcaya.[7]

Two years later Enrique died, and the crown of Castilla was disputed between the supporters of Isabela and those of Enrique's daughter Juana. The kings of Portugal and France both supported Juana's claim (the former was her husband). Isabela was supported by a segment of the nobility of Castilla, her husband Fernando, heir to the throne of Aragón, and the Basques. The kingdom of Navarra was officially neutral; however, its king probably favored Isabela's cause, because he was her father-in-law.

In 1475 Castilla was invaded by the king of Portugal at the command of an army of forty thousand men. Isabela's forces numbered thirty thousand, including ten thousand Basque troops. The Basques also mustered 200 ships placed at Isabela's disposition, which were employed to disrupt maritime communications between the kingdoms of Portugal and France. In the event of victory, the intention of Juana's foreign supporters was to integrate part of Castilla into Portugal and place Vizcaya and Guipúzcoa under French rule. The French king, Louis XI, massed forty thousand troops in Bayonne. However, his invasion of Guipúzcoa was blocked by the forces of Juan de Lazcano, defender of the fortified town of Fuenterrabía.[8]

In 1476 the Portuguese and French forces retreated from Castilian territory and Isabela, until that time solely *señora de Vizcaya*, was proclaimed queen of Castilla. That same year her husband journeyed to the town of Guernica (Vizcaya) to swear beneath the sacred oak, site of the periodic assemblies of the elected representatives of the Vizcayan municipalities, to defend and uphold Basque liberties (the *fueros*).[9]

King Louis XI of France continued his attempts to draw Vizcaya and Guipúzcoa into his sphere of influence, this time by the peaceful means of offering them "all that they should demand."[10] However, the possible attraction for the Basques of union with France was lessened considerably in 1482, when Guipúzcoa negotiated a unilateral commercial treaty with England and opened all English ports to Guipuzcoan commerce.

At the same time, the kingdom of Navarra was converted into a political plum disputed by the more powerful kingdoms of Castilla and France. Until 1483 Louis XI was reasonably certain of influencing Navarrese affairs through his close family ties with King Francisco de Foix. But in that year young King

Francisco died without leaving descendants, and the crown of Navarra passed to his spinster sister Catalina. The Catholic monarchs, Fernando and Isabela, sought to undermine French influence in Navarra by arranging a marriage between Catalina and their son Juan. A number of Castilian ambassadors were dispatched to the court of Navarra to negotiate the union.[11]

The Catholic kings underscored their offer with intimidation as they garrisoned an expeditionary force in Vitoria (Alava). While there with her troops Isabela journeyed to Guernica to take the oath to respect Basque liberties. The French also garrisoned troops in Bayonne as pressure upon Navarra, designed to counteract that of Castilla. But at this critical moment Louis XI died, and his juvenile son Charles VIII assumed the French throne. His regents decided that a new consolidation of French power required some years of peace. They removed French military pressure from Navarra.[12] Meanwhile, the queen mother Magdalena of Navarra decided that Catalina should not marry Juan of Castilla. The ostensible excuse was the difference in ages between the couple, but the political reality was that Magdalena felt that Navarra's interests were more tied to those of France and hence preferred that Catalina marry Jean d'Albret.[13]

At this point, the Catholic monarchs were faced with a clear dilemma. Either they could trigger a war with France designed to annex Navarra or they could devote their energies to the wars of southern Iberia in order to purge the peninsula of the last vestiges of Moorish control. They chose the latter. Pressure upon Navarra was reduced to the level of diplomatic power politics until 1512, when troops of Castilla conquered the Navarrese, thereby bringing the area permanently into the Spanish political orbit.

Basques were to play a major part in the successful campaigns against the Moors in the south, particularly in providing the boats and men that secured for the Catholic monarchs control of the Strait of Gibraltar.[14]

The conquest of Granada (the last Moorish kingdom in Iberia) is the last Castilian conquest and the first "Spanish" one. Although the initiative was Castilian (and Basque), the campaign depended heavily upon Aragonese participation.[15] Aragón was a major Mediterranean power with island holdings (the Balearics, Sardinia, and Sicily). Through the union of Castilla and Aragón, new Mediterranean trade routes were opened to Basque commercial interests. These interests were furthered when Spain occupied Naples in 1504, bringing her into direct competition with Ottoman expansion in the Eastern Mediterranean.

Three major developments which coincided within a very short time span, were to lay the bases for the dominant force in European politics for the next century as well as for the formation of one of the largest colonial empires in human history. In rapid succession, the Spanish nation crystallized out of Iberian political fragmentation; Spain embarked upon an expansionist course into North Africa to the south and the Mediterranean to the east; and the new nation sponsored the " Voyages of Discovery," which were to provide it with the strongest claim and easiest access of any European power to the potential of the New World.

At the beginning of the sixteenth century Spain lacked sufficient population and economic resources to pursue colonialism on all fronts.[16] Hence, a militaristic policy of control, rather than a colonial policy of settlement, was applied to the Mediterranean, whereas Spain's genuine colonizing efforts were reserved for the Indies. But both policies were heavily dependent upon two elements—seapower and a supply of iron products. Without both military and commercial maritime transportation, Spain could not hope either to consolidate her Old World holdings nor to develop her far-flung New World territories. Similarly, efforts to colonize required reliable supplies of iron implements, while military campaigns consumed large amounts of weaponry. Castilla lacked sufficient quantities of both necessities, whereas maritime activities and the mining and manufacture of iron constituted two major underpinnings of the economy of the Basque country.

BASQUE MARINERS OF THE AMERICAN RUN

Commenting upon the economic impact of the discovery of the New World, Vicens notes, "the years that followed the discovery were ones of tremendous disillusionment . . .; absolutely nothing came from America."[17] For the Basque economy, however, the opening of the New World was an immediate stimulant. The metal products of Basque factories were in great demand for the colonial venture. There was a particular need for vessels produced in Basque shipyards. An Armenian bishop who visited the Basque country in 1494 expressed amazement at the quantity of new vessels that were under construction in the little fishing port of Guetaria (Guipúzcoa).[18] In 1498 Queen Isabela offered to subsidize construction of boats larger than 600 tons. In 1502 she offered Basque shipbuilders 50,000 *maravedis*, plus guaranteed cargo for six months, for each vessel larger than 1,500 tons.[19]

Private Basque shipowners themselves responded immediately to the challenge of America. Within three months after Columbus's return to Europe with news of his discoveries, a shipmaster from Bilbao, Juan de Arbolancha, had organized in Vizcaya a fleet of five ships with a total crew of 820 men. However, this fleet did not set sail for America as planned. The Catholic monarchs insisted that it transport refugee Arabs from the defeated kingdom of Granada to North Africa.[20]

Attempts to exploit the American run from the Basque country were frustrated in 1495 when the crown of Castilla named Cádiz (in southern Spain) as the sole port from which ships could depart for the New World. However, this did not effectively exclude Basque participation. Basque maritime interests, through their long-standing involvement in Mediterranean and African trade, had established operations in Cádiz and Sevilla. Cádiz itself was, since at least the beginning of the fifteenth century, the home of a guild of navigators called the College of Vizcayan Pilots (*El Colegio de Pilotos Vizcaínos*).[21] Basque maritime interests were already well ensconced in Sevilla, the result of concessions by Fernando III of Castilla in return for Basque naval assistance in wresting the city from Moorish control (1247).*

In 1503 the monarchs conceded to Sevilla a monopoly on New World trade to be administered by the crown officials of the *Casa de Contratación*. However, Andalusian shipping was so underdeveloped and inadequate to the task that by 1505 the *Casa* named a representative in Bilbao to recruit vessels and

---

*Without a naval squadron to blockade the city and prevent Moorish boats from supplying the besieged from North Africa, the land forces of Fernando had little prospect of success. Fernando dispatched a special emissary to the Basque country to raise a fleet. The concessions offered in return were so attractive that ships from Bayonne (at that time loyal to England) joined the squadron.[22] When the city was captured, Fernando conferred substantial privileges upon the Basques, both with respect to using Sevilla as a home base for maritime activities and the founding of business establishments.[23]

To this day there is a street in Sevilla called Calle de Bayona (which is next to the street that was called Calle de los Vizcaínos). It seems that as early as the fourteenth century merchants from Bayonne lived there, since there is still an inscription on one of the interior arches of the Patio de los Naranjos which says, "San Miguel is . . . mercader de Bayons."[24]

men for the American run.[25] Chaunu notes that at the beginning of the sixteenth century Bilbao surpassed either Sevilla or Cádiz in maritime strength. The city possessed about five hundred vessels.[26] Even the existing Andalusian shipping was dependent upon Basque shipyards. The shells and masts of most Andalusian vessels were constructed in the Basque country.[27]

Thus, "while Sevilla had a monopoly of trade, the north of Spain, especially Biscay, had a monopoly of shipping, for it supplied almost all of the Spanish vessels in the Indies trade."[28]* Basque interests controlled more than shipping; they "supplied capital, equipment, and goods for trade as well as many of its personnel."[30] Several of the previously established Basque commercial interests in Sevilla opened branch operations in the Indies (notably Santo Domingo) under the control of close kinsmen.[31] In fact, it could be stated that "The Sevilla of the early XVIth century was able to meet the challenge of its American mission due to an influx from the North of the Kingdom of Castilla, a Cantabrian-Vizcayan-Basque influx and, ancillarily, old Castilian."[32]

Furthermore, French Basques were also able to participate in the American run, despite strictures against foreign shipping. Vessels from St.-Jean-de-Luz were registered as "Vizcayan" with the authorities.[33] Finally, many of the officials of the *Casa de Contratación* itself were Basques.

Basques in Sevilla constituted one of the city's less assimilated ethnic groups. The historian Ruth Pike notes, "Whereas Castilians generally intermarried with the Sevillian trading families, and in so doing eventually became indistinguishable from them, the Basques in general continued to marry within their own group."[34] The Basques were heavily involved in all aspects of the Atlantic trade, from its financing through banking enterprises, to direct speculation in certain products, to transportation of the merchandise. Pike remarks that, "among the Basques were some of the most active merchant-capitalists in the city, any one of whom could easily have served as the inspiration for one of the characters in Lope de Vega's *Premio del bien hablar*—a Basque trader who became wealthy selling iron in America."[35] Chaunu is even more pointed in his evaluation of Basque commercial involvement and ethnic clannishness in Sevilla. He notes, "in business, and in shipping, [there

---

*Chaunu agrees with the figures but maintains that, rather than Basque shipping alone, they refer to a "Gallegan-Cantabrian-Vizcayan" complex.[29]

was] a heavy Basque involvement, with the circumstances aggravated by signs of pronounced aggressive [ethnic] solidarity."[36]

By 1540 Vizcayans and Guipuzcoans resident in Sevilla formed the *Cofradía de la Nación Vascongada* (Confraternity of the Basque Nation), which was more commonly known as the *Cofradía de los Vizcaínos* (Confraternity of Vizcayans). The Franciscans conceded to the confraternity a site in their church for construction of an elaborate chapel.[37] The chapel served as a crypt in which only Basques, their spouses, and their descendants could be buried. The confraternity was maintained by the voluntary donations of the members and by special payments that they assessed themselves. For example, each Basque-owned boat that arrived in Sevilla paid two ducats to the confraternity; for each box of iron products sold, the Basque merchants gave a half *real*; for each hundred *quintales* of tar that was sold, the confraternity received a half *real*; and for every thousand lances, a whole one.[38]

In sum, the magnitude of Basque involvement in New World maritime traffic was substantial. The historian Lynch notes that 35 boats with a total tonnage of 3,309 plied the seas between Spain and her New World colonies in 1506. By 1550 this figure had grown to 215 boats with a tonnage of 32,355.[39] By Lynch's estimate almost 80 percent of this New World traffic between 1520 and 1580 was Basque-controlled, while between 1580 and 1610 Basque interests represented 50 percent of the total. These figures prompt him to label the Basque area "the nursery of Spanish seamen, which supplied most of the manpower on the American run."[40]

BASQUE EMIGRANTS TO THE NEW WORLD COLONIES

The major thrust of Basque emigration over the past five centuries has been directed at the Americas. Spain's conquest of one and a half continents and France's incursions into the Caribbean, Louisiana, and Canada broadened the horizons of opportunity for the Basques of both nations by providing the new alternative of overseas emigration. What was the magnitude of this Basque emigration? It is impossible to answer this question with any degree of exactitude for the period lasting from the fifteenth through the eighteenth centuries.

Of the two governments of Spain and France, it was the former that sought to impose stringent administrative controls upon emigration to the New World. The Spanish crown required that each emigrant apply for a license and depart through government-established channels. However, violations were flagrant, and the majority of emigrants left Spain illegally and consequently failed to register in the administrators' counts. One Spanish historical demographer, in referring to the magnitude of emigration to the New World colonies between 1509 and 1559, notes with despair, "the quantity of expatriots might have just as well been 150,000 as 23,000.[41]*

If the official statistics are examined in terms of the Iberian regional origins of emigrants, we find that in the period 1509–34, of 7,645 persons 87 percent were from central and southern Spain. Only 239, or 3.1 percent, were from the four Basque provinces.[43]† However, it is extremely unlikely that these figures reflect accurately the initial magnitude of Basque participation in Spain's colonial ventures. The figures fail to take into account the fact that Basque mariners were heavily involved in the sea traffic between Spain and her colonies. With Basques predominating in many crews it is not farfetched to assume that a generous portion of the illegal emigrants were Basques, persons who activated their contacts with fellow Basque seamen in order to secure passage to the New World. Nor is it unlikely that many Basque seamen themselves jumped ship in American ports.

If one looks at the other side of the issue, namely what percentage of the Basque population was availing itself of the opportunity to emigrate, the evidence is equally indirect and incomplete. The practice of counting the population is relatively recent in Spain (the first reliable national census was completed in 1857). By one estimate the population of Spain was 7,414,000 inhabitants in the year 1541. The same work places the population for the year 1717 at 7,500,000, suggesting prac-

---

*The latter figure is derived from a study of official passenger lists. If data on emigration in the first half of the sixteenth century is sparse, it is even more so for the ensuing two hundred years. The official passenger lists for the seventeenth and eighteenth centuries are available but, as yet, remain unanalyzed by historians.[42]

†See Peter Boyd-Bowman (1964) for a partial count of the numbers of Basques present among the European colonizers of Mexico and the Antilles between 1493 and 1519. His estimates run from 5 percent for the island of Cuba to 16.2 percent for Puerto Rico. Between 1520 and 1539 the same author (1968) finds that although Basques constituted only 4.5 percent of the total European population they constituted 17.2 percent of the mariners, 14 percent of the merchants, 8.8 percent of the miners, 8.5 percent of the high-level administrators, and 4.8 percent of the clergymen.

tically no growth at all over two centuries.[44] Emigration to the New World undoubtedly played a major role in undermining the potential population growth of the nation. There were other drains as well, notably the military demands of maintaining the Spanish success. In the sixteenth century the Spanish Empire was not limited to Iberia and the New World; it also included African and Asian holdings, Mediterranean islands, parts of the Italian peninsula, and the Low Countries. Spain in the fifteenth and sixteenth centuries was the major political force in Europe and had all of the military problems implied in the threefold task of defending a gigantic colonial undertaking, controlling subjugated peoples on the European continent, and holding at bay lesser European powers seeking to exploit any sign of weakness. One authority places Spain's losses in the Thirty Years War alone at 288,000 soldiers killed, captured, or missing in action.[45]

It does seem clear that sixteenth and seventeenth century emigration from Spain, and from the Basque area in particular, was essentially masculine. In the year 1511, 4.5 percent of all legal passengers to the Indies were Basques. There was not a single female among them. In 1512, the Basque contingent contained only one woman (from Guipúzcoa).[46]

In 1639 an appeal for donations was published (probably by the government of Vizcaya) to all Vizcayans living in "the Indies, Flanders, Italy, and other provinces. . . ."[47] The document states, "The Seigneury of Vizcaya lacks inhabitants because of the many persons who leave in order to serve His Majesty in his armies and navies. Particularly those [inhabitants] of the ports are absent. . . ."[48] The donations were to be used in part to dower some of the many women who remained single, alleviating the poverty of their husbands and therefore removing the incentive to emigrate. The author of the appeal decried the current situation in which "single women remain unmarried and more exposed to sin, and propagation is lacking. . . ."[49] Another seventeenth century document states, "In 1640 three-fourths of the population of Vizcaya is composed of women due to the number of men who leave never to return."[50]

Thus, the discovery and colonization of the Americas had immediate and substantial demographic consequences for Old World Basque society. By the same token, merchant marine and industrial sectors of the Basque economy benefited greatly from the stimulus of New World enterprises. However, there were equally profound changes in the structuring of rural sectors of the Basque economy.

By the decade of the 1520s two key New World crops, maize and beans, had been introduced into the agriculture of the Basque country—crops that were quickly to become the two basic items in rural Basque cuisine, *talo* (cornbread) and *lapikoko* (a kind of bean soup). The cultivation of maize triggered expansion of rural settlement, since the crop was more dependable and productive than the former staple, millet.[51] In the three centuries from 1530 to 1830 many new farmsteads[52] were established in what were formerly forests, and in many villages (Baigorry, for example) the number of "new houses" surpassed the number of more ancient dwellings.[53] Thus maize and beans, to which were later added another New World crop—the potato—provided the stimulus and base for an agricultural expansion that was in turn to support rapid population growth throughout the northern ecological zone of the Basque country.

ETHNIC GROUP AWARENESS IN THE NEW WORLD CONTEXT

Given the fact that by the fifteenth century the Basques were involved heavily in maritime commerce and mercenary activities, it would be surprising if they were not well represented among the ranks of those who carried out Spain's "Voyages of Discovery and Conquest." A simple listing of every Basque personage in the three centuries of Spain's New World venture, ranging from major figures like the explorer and cartographer Juan Vizcaíno (or Juan de la Cosa), to religious officials like Bishop Zumárraga of Mexico, to lesser-known individuals like mayors and other administrators of Spanish settlements, would literally fill volumes. It is scarcely an exaggeration to state that no major expeditionary force and no ecclesiastical or secular administrative structure was entirely devoid of persons of Basque ethnic origins.*

What we seek to show, however, is not the simple *magnitude* of Basque participation in the New World colonial enterprise but rather the *nature* of Basque involvement. Specifically, we are concerned with demonstrating that Basques in the New

---

*For examples of works documenting the New World exploits of individual Basques see Ispizua (1914–18), Díaz Trechuelo (1965), Otazu Llana (1970) and Lafarga Lozano (1973).

World acted, at least on occasion, as a self-aware ethnic group. This awareness was translated into collective actions, mutual assistance, a common stance toward outsiders, and a perception on the part of outsiders that the Basques were set apart from other Iberian and Creole (New World-born persons of European descent) groups. A number of events in Spain's New World colonial history substantiate this observation.

The first instance could scarcely have come at an earlier time in New World colonial history. In the initial voyage of Columbus, the flagship, the *Santa María*, was Basque-owned and manned, and the crew of the *Niña* was largely Basque. Once again the contractual nature of Basque participation was underscored by the near mutiny against Columbus's authority. The sailors had agreed to sail 750 leagues to the west, the distance that Columbus believed separated the Canary Islands from the Orient. When the boats had sailed for 800 leagues without sighting land, Columbus was still determined to press on. The Basque crew of the *Santa María* threatened to throw him overboard.[54] It was only after the officers of the other vessels intervened that a compromise was reached that allowed the voyage to continue to its successful conclusion.

When the *Santa María* was shipwrecked, Columbus was forced to leave some of his men behind. They founded the first European New World colony at *Fuerte Navidad* on the island of Hispaniola. When Columbus returned on his second voyage, he found that the colony had been destroyed by the Indians. A subsequent investigation revealed that the defeat resulted when the Europeans split into two camps. The division took place along ethnic lines as the Basques seceded. Las Casas states, "Certain Vizcayans joined together against the rest."[55] Herrera remarks "there was a division among the Christians that was caused by the Vizcayans."[56]

In 1509 there was another incident. The royal mandate to explore and conquer the mainland areas was divided between Diego de Nicuesa and Alonso de Ojeda, both from southern Spain. However, the funding for an expedition, the boats, and the manpower came essentially from Basques who were residing on Hispaniola. The Basque Luis de Olano was the highest ranking naval officer in the expedition.

Nicuesa left the island with four boats and a crew of seven hundred men. He explored the coastline from present-day Venezuela to Darién. When the expedition reached Darién, Nicuesa and Olano had a falling out that resulted in the arrest of the latter. Olano, however, sent word to Martín de Zamudio and other Basques who were stationed at a nearby settlement. These men marched on Nicuesa's position, freed Olano, captured Nicuesa, and forcefully put him on a boat for Hispaniola. That this act was carried out along Basque ethnic lines is reflected in the description of the chronicler Oviedo who states, "Lope de Olano was Vizcayan and he knew that one of the officials in Darién, Martín de Zamudio, was a relative of his. Also there were in Darién other Vizcayans, his relatives as well, and other Basques of his language. He wrote to them explaining how the governor had arrested him, and he turned them against Diego de Nicuesa."[57]

From the earliest years of the New World venture, Basques were also involved in collective efforts of colonization. As early as 1501 there was an attempt by Luís de Arriaga, resident of Sevilla, to organize a colony in Santo Domingo. The plan was to settle two hundred Basque families in four townsites. Each family was to receive a *hacienda*, which it was obliged to work for a minimum of five years while paying taxes to the state. In addition, each family would turn over to the government one-half of any gold or mines that were discovered. Arriaga's venture was far from successful, since he was able to recruit only forty Basque families.[58]

The potential benefits of Basque settlement in the New World were recognized by no less a personage than the king himself. In a letter to the governor of Santo Domingo, dated July 25, 1511, the king stated:

> I am displeased by what you tell me, that on the island there is a great need for working people [*gente de servicio*] and Indians. I am advising the Officials of the *Casa de Contratación de las Indias*, who reside in the city of Sevilla, that from now on they shall not harass people who want to leave [for the Indies], as they have done up to now, and that they ignore whatever can be justifiably ignored [*i.e.*, apply emigration regulations loosely]. That they encourage as much as they can the departure of workers, and to attain this end that they publicize in all parts [of Spain] the fact that it is in the interest of this kingdom to discover the many mines found there [the Indies] and the riches therein. . . . And besides this I order them to publicize [this notice] in the mountains of Guipúzcoa where there are many inhabitants and few recourses, so that workers will go out . . . to those parts.[59]

Again, in 1533 there is evidence of royal interest in Basque colonization as sixty Basque farmers, the majority with their wives, arrived in Santo Domingo to found a town. They brought with them "certain capitulations, exemptions and liberties from His Majesty."[60]

During the sixteenth century the Spanish Empire extended its control over most of mainland South and Central America, the Antilles, and present-day Mexico. It was in this latter region, known as *Nueva España*, that Basque ethnic and kinship ties were both to spearhead and to consolidate the expansion of Spanish colonial authority. A sizable number of the troops under Cortez's command were Basque. For the most part, these men were mercenaries who had served in Spain's Italian campaigns and later in the conquest of the Antilles.

However, once a portion of Mexico was conquered a different type of Basque began to enter the territory, the true colonist oriented to developing the land, the educated scribe seeking opportunity in the new administration, and the man of the cloth seeking new converts. One investigator remarks, "If we except the Andalusian-Extremaduran group that formed around Cortez and his relatives, there was not another group more numerous, arriving collectively, and with respect to their place of origin, than the Basques."[61]

Of particular importance was the naming of the Basque Juan de Zumárraga as bishop of *Nueva España* in 1527. Zumárraga surrounded himself with his Basque relatives and compatriots. He even went so far as to recruit colonists from the valleys of his native region of Durango (Vizcaya).[62]

The conquest of Mexico provided the Spanish crown and the conquistadors with a first real taste of the fabulous wealth of the Indies. Mexico City also served as a staging area for further quests. There were two major temptations to fire the imaginations of adventurers. One, to discover a sea route to the Orient, eventually paid handsome dividends, while the other, land explorations to the north in search of the fabled wealth of Quivira, proved to be illusory. Although the Basques played a subordinate role in Cortez's conquest of *Nueva España*, they took the initiative in both of these latter ventures.

With their strong maritime tradition, it is not surprising that Basques would open the sea route between *Nueva España* and the Orient. In 1527 Cortez launched an expedition from the west coast of Mexico in Basque-mannned vessels. The expedition failed to cross the Pacific, but instead discovered the stark peninsula of Baja California. Disillusionment stalled other efforts until two Basque captains, Urdaneta and Legazpi, sailed from *Nueva España* to the Philippines in 1564, thereby bringing part of the Orient within the orbit of Spanish rule.

The thrust northward began under the command of Nuño de Guzmán, a non-Basque. Among Guzmán's forces was the Basque captain Cristóbal de Oñate. Cristóbal de Oñate arrived in Mexico City in 1524. By 1528 he had risen to the rank of *regidor* and had acquired a fortune through ownership of a large *encomienda* located in Michoacán. Cristóbal's brother, Juan, was also in the service of Guzmán. The brothers commanded a force charged with controlling the Indians of present-day Jalisco. Jointly, they founded the city of Guadalajara. They were rewarded with large *encomiendas* in the area, and Cristóbal was named its lieutenant governor, a post that he held until an Indian uprising forced the Europeans to abandon the city. Cristóbal de Oñate later returned with an expeditionary force that included a major contingent of Basques. Most of these Basques stayed on in Jalisco and were to form the backbone of future expeditions.

Among Oñate's men was the Basque Juan de Tolosa, a relative of Bishop Zumárraga. In an expedition of his own, Juan de Tolosa discovered silver at Zacatecas, founded the city of that name, and initiated what was to become one of the most important mining operations in New World history. West notes that, "Beginning with the famous Zacatecas discovery in 1546, Basque miners rapidly overran the foothills northwestward, founding numerous reales, such as San Martín, Fresnillo, Indé, and Santa Bárbara."[63]

Diego de Ibarra, also a relative of Bishop Zumárraga, who joined his Basque compatriots in Jalisco in 1546, is regarded as a cofounder of Zacatecas. He became its first mayor. He later married the sister of Velasco, the *Virrey* (or highest official) of *Nueva España*.

All three men, Cristóbal de Oñate, Juan de Tolosa, and Diego de Ibarra, made fortunes from the mines of Zacatecas. Each attracted to his side relatives from the Basque country and founded his own lineage of descendants, many of whom became personages in the subsequent colonial history of *Nueva España*. Furthermore, these lineages were to become intertwined through marriage. For example, Cristóbal de Oñate brought out to the New World his sister and her husband, Ruiz Días de Zaldívar (from Vitoria). One of their sons, Cristóbal, married a daughter of Juan de Tolosa.[64]

Expansion further northward began when Diego de Ibarra's brother-in-law, the *Virrey* Velasco, conferred upon him the rights to explore and colonize beyond the northernmost frontiers of existing Spanish control. Diego, retired from adventures, gave the task and some financial backing to his nephew Francisco.

Francisco Ibarra had entered *Nueva España* in 1539 as a child. By age sixteen, under the patronage of his uncle Diego, he was placed in command of a company of troops at Zacatecas. From 1554 to 1564 he explored the northern region, founding the new province of *Nueva Vizcaya* and its capital of Durango (which he named after his birthplace in the Basque country). He was made governor and declared that the *Fuero* of Vizcaya would be the law of the newly opened territory. All inhabitants, like those of the Basque provinces in Spain, were to be regarded as nobility and were to be exempted from royal taxation.[65]* Until his death in 1575 he consolidated his gains in *Nueva Vizcaya*, converting it into a new launching area for further incursions to the north.

In 1550 Cristóbal de Oñate fathered a son whom he named Juan. This son married a daughter of Juan de Tolosa. Juan de Oñate employed his family influence to compete for a license to explore and colonize the region that was later to become New Mexico. His chief competitor was another Basque, Francisco de Urdiñola. In 1595 Juan de Oñate received his mandate, and in 1598 he headed an expedition. Unlike previous efforts, which were comprised largely of soldiers and missionaries, the Oñate force included colonists and livestock. In this fashion Oñate introduced the first sheep flocks into what would later become territory of the United States (a fitting early forerunner of massive Basque involvement in the nineteenth- and twentieth-century development of the sheep industry of the American West).† While Oñate included his brothers, some relatives, and

---

*This posture was disallowed by the Spanish crown.

†The distinction must be made between "forerunner" and "founder," since there was no continuity of Basque involvement in the sheep raising of the New Mexico area. Ironically, a Basque, Miguel de Urrutia, was instrumental in introducing sheep into the Argentine *pampas* shortly after 1547, thereby becoming the forerunner of the heavy nineteenth-century involvement of the Basques in the sheep industry of that region.[66]

their wives in his expedition, the large majority of the participants were not Basque.

He met with little Indian resistance as he followed the Río Grande into present-day New Mexico, where he founded a colony and became governor of the area. In 1601 Juan de Oñate explored the region to the north as far as southern Kansas. Failing to find any sign of the golden city of Quivira, he returned to New Mexico, only to discover that the colonists had fled to *Nueva Vizcaya* in the face of Indian uprisings and general pessimism. Oñate returned to *Nueva Vizcaya* and organized a second expedition, founding a colony that was to endure. In 1604 he explored Arizona and the lower Colorado River area, arriving at the Pacific on the coast of Baja California. In 1608 Oñate, disillusioned, resigned his post as governor of New Mexico.[67]

Thus ended two generations of colonial expansion into northern Mexico and the southern United States in which Basque leadership, Basque capital, and Basque manpower carried the brunt of the effort. This expansion left in its wake a social structure whose economy included numerous Basque *hacendados* and mine owners, and whose officialdom was heavy with Basque administrators, soldiers, and clerics. That much of this effort was consciously and collectively Basque is reflected in the many Basque place names found throughout northern Mexico, not to mention the naming of the entire region *Nueva Vizcaya* and its capital Durango, the crowning toponymic monument to Basque efforts in the New World.

But there is further significance in this account. It illustrates the fact that from the earliest years of Spain's New World venture Basques tended to cluster with their fellows in particular areas where they proceeded to convert, or possibly to subvert, objectives of the crown into a favored position for Basque interests. This is a theme that recurs at later points in New World history. Secondly, in the Basque activities of northern Mexico we find evidence of the importance of kinship ties as networks that facilitated Basque immigration into the New World. In the words of one observer, each Basque emigrant "was a window on the world for those who remained behind."[68]

Basque commercial and merchant marine activities were also evident from the earliest years of the colonial venture. Between 1496 and 1514 the Basque shipowner Pedro de Arbolancha was a major provisioner of the budding New World colonies. By the end of the sixteenth century the region of Panama developed into the major focus of trade between Spain and the New World. One fleet would leave Spain and put into the port of Cartagena (present-day Colombia) to await news of the arrival in Panama of the Pacific fleet bringing goods from New World Pacific ports and the Orient. Prices for exchange were set and the goods transferred in Panama. The extent of Basque involvement in this traffic is seen in the fact that, by 1596, two Panama-based Basques of the same last name, Francisco and Miguel de Eraso, owned ninety-nine and eighty-five boats respectively.[69]

New World Basque commercial and maritime interests were not restricted to the Panama area. In 1634 the bishop of Santiago de Chile, Francisco de Salcedo, sent a letter to the king of Spain in which he warned His Majesty that the royal treasury was not receiving its due from the area. The reason given is most revealing. According to Bishop Salcedo:

> The cause of such pernicious effects is that all of the traders, or at least most of them, are *vizcaínos*. The *contador* [harbor authority], although a good man, is also *vizcaíno* as is the *escribano de registro*, whose job it is to examine the cargos. The *alguacil mayor* [chief police authority] of this *Audiencia* . . . is also *vizcaíno*. And since the doctor Jacobo de Adaro y San Martín, *oidor* [chief judicial official] of this *Audiencia* is also *vizcaíno* the Royal Mandates and Orders executed by Your Majesty are not carried out. In all of the warehouses and storage areas the *vizcaínos* guard their goods, which suppose great quantities, and none of them pay to Your Majesty what he owes in taxes. The situation each day is going from bad to worse.[70]

The picture painted by an outsider of a kind of Basque ethnic conspiracy, designed to subvert the official channels of authority and revenue collection, could not be clearer.* By the beginning of the seventeenth century, the magnitude of the Basque presence in Chile was extensive. Thayer Ojeda, who made a detailed analysis of the genealogies of Chilean Basques,

---

*Nor were the fears by the seventeenth century that Basques were capable of subverting crown purposes limited to Chile. In Guatemala, when the Basque Juan Martínez de Landecho was deposed as president of the Audiencia de Guatemala, an observer noted, "It was just to remove Landecho from the presidency, he would have converted the Realm of Guatemala into a *Nueva Vizcaya*."[71]

concludes that Basque immigration into Chile was characterized by "the father bringing over his son, the uncle attracting to his side his nephew, the brother sending for his brother, the cousin inducing his cousin to come, and the friend inducing the friend. . . . This Basque immigration, improperly called Vizcayan, was nothing more than a change of residence of various related families."[72]

Throughout the seventeenth and eighteenth centuries Chile continued to attract large quantities of Basques. Thayer Ojeda estimates that during the two centuries fully 45 percent* of all immigrants in Chile were Basques, and by the nineteenth century half of all illustrious persons in Chilean history and society were of Basque descent.[73] To this day the Basques are one of Chile's most durable and influential ethnic groups.

Bishop Salcedo's denunciations show that there was antipathy between Basques and non-Basques in the New World. The clearest example in New World history of such "bad blood" is found in the annals of the mining district of Potosí (present-day Bolivia) where, at the end of the sixteenth century and well into the seventeenth, there was a veritable race war between Basques and other ethnic groups.

In 1582 Basques and Extremadurans of Potosí engaged in fighting in which a total of eighteen persons lost their lives. The next year a Basque captain was killed in a fight over a game, and the Basques destroyed eight dwellings in the Extremaduran *barrio* of the city.[74] In 1588 additional hostilities took place in which eighty-five persons were killed. In 1593 there was fighting between the Basques on the one hand and both non-Basque Europeans and Creoles on the other, in which sixteen Basques died.[75] In 1608, renewed violence took the lives of fifty-two Basques, twelve Creoles, and seven Portuguese. Again, in 1614, seventy Basques and twenty non-Basques died in fighting. In 1617 the *corregidor*, or ruler of the area, appeared to side with the Basques, provoking a new outbreak of violence that claimed fifty lives.[76] In 1618 the leader of the Creoles declared open season on Basques.[77]

Madariaga cites evidence that some of the tensions and anti-Basque sentiment were due in part to Basque indiscretion in

_____

*Broken down into provinces of origin 16 percent were from Navarra, 15 percent from Vizcaya, 12 percent from Guipúzcoa and 2 percent from Alava.

the display and use of their economic and political power. By one account:

> In the year 1602 the Basques began to stand out in both arms and wealth. Eighty were amalgamators* [silver processors], 160 were traders. There were in the city fortunes of 500, 600, and 800 thousand *pesos* . . . all Vizcayan. Of the twelve silver merchants eight were Basques, of the twelve *veinticuatros* [councilmen] in the town hall six were Basques. In the majority of years the two elected mayors were Basques . . . the mayors of Cerro were also Basques. Of the thirty-eight officials of the mint, twenty-two were Basques, of the ten officials of the Royal Treasury six were Basques, and in like fashion Basques controlled everything else in the Republic, and by their luck, their wealth, and with such offices, they lorded it over everyone in Potosí, and they ignored the other eleven nations [ethnic groups] residing therein. They treated others disdainfully and vituperously. And so the Creoles, who are by their nature aggressive, in consideration of Basque excesses and to terminate Basque vanity, requested that their fathers—Castilians, Andalusians, Extremadurans, and other nationalities—not give their sisters in marriage to Basques under any circumstances. When the Basques saw this they became indignant against all other nationalities. Some Basques resorted to arms and this is civil war.[78]

By 1618 civil war was a constant feature of life in Potosí. The Basques, with their enormous political influence, controlled the support of Spanish officialdom, but the other side, constituted of both Peninsulars and Creoles, waged a strong campaign of intimidation and military force. Known as *vicuñas*, they were led by a man named Xeldres. When Xeldres fled Potosí, after killing a Jesuit priest who had reprimanded him in a sermon, he advised his followers, "let all the nationalities be united with the Creoles. This will quicken the destruction of these *vizcaínos*."[79] From 1622 to 1624 there was constant bloodletting.[80]

In 1624 the Basques used their influence in Lima to request aid. An expeditionary force approached Potosí, and the captain of the local garrison decided to defend the city. However, the situation was defused when a treaty was negotiated. A wedding united a Castilian girl and the son of one of the Basque leaders. While the *vicuñas* continued their harassments for a number of years, their actions degenerated into banditry and general law-

---

*[Of the 132 in Potosi.]

lessness. For all practical purposes the civil war, with its ethnic overtones, was over.[81]

The peace accord in Potosí notwithstanding, Basques and non-Basques in the seventeenth century mining camps of Peru remained mutually antagonistic. Between 1661 and 1666 there were bloody incidents in La Paz.[82] In 1665 in the mining camp of Icazota, there was an abortive plot on the part of the non-Basques to annihilate the Basque population.[83] Under the leadership of a man named Salcedo, the dissidents besieged a company of Basque troops, demanding that some be garroted and others exiled. Many Basques fled the camp, and the local commander was forced to appeal to governors of nearby areas for assistance. The Basque captain Pedro de Garro was sent with an expeditionary force to restore order. Salcedo and his followers fled.[84]

In March 1666 Salcedo returned to Icazota with 800 men, forcing the defenders to barricade themselves in a stockade, at which point the houses and businesses of the Basques were put to the torch.[85] The besieged Basques tried to abandon the town, unarmed and under a sign of truce, but were attacked by Salcedo's men. The carnage raised the total of Basques killed in the trouble at Icazota to 350 persons.[86] The survivors petitioned the local governments in the Basque area to intervene with the king to ensure that Salcedo's deeds would be punished. It was not until several years later, however, that Salcedo was tried and executed for his crimes.[87]

The civil war of Potosí, which festered for several decades, and the events at Icazota are extreme examples of anti-Basque sentiment in New World history. It is clear that envy of Basque economic and political success, as well as their alleged clannishness and highhandedness, were the major causes of the wave of anti-Basque violence.*

Throughout the formative period, and for the first century of Spanish colonial rule in the New World, individual Basques were successful merchants, seamen, conquistadors, missionaries, administrators, miners, and colonists. Furthermore, Basques were sufficiently prone to collective action that they

---

*Many of the anti-Basque statements that appear in the debates over the incidents at Potosí are reminiscent of the characterization of Jews by anti-Semites. The analogy is not far-fetched. In one denunciation an effort was made to demonstrate that the Basques were, in fact, disguised Jews, descendants of a lost tribe of Israel.[88]

constituted a self-aware ethnic group in colonial society—an ethnic group that was perceived as such by outsiders. However, while it is possible to demonstrate Basque ethnic cohesiveness, there is also the danger of overemphasizing it. The outsider's perception of Basque clannishness, tinged as it frequently was with resentment of Basque successes, tends to mask the fact that Basques in many respects were highly individualistic and competitive among themselves. This point may be illustrated by describing one of the blackest episodes in New World history—the ill-fated rebellion of the notorious Lope de Aguirre and his followers, the *marañones*.

In the year 1560 the marqués de Cañete, resident in Peru, organized an expedition to search for the famed mines of *El Dorado*. Command of the groups was given to Pedro de Ursua, a Navarrese Basque who was famous for his successful military campaigns against the Indians in the area of Darién. There were several women in the expedition, including Ursua's mistress and the *mestiza* daughter of the Guipuzcoan Lope de Aguirre. Among the troops there was a large contingent of *vizcaínos* and a non-Basque individual named Fernando de Guzmán, who was to become a pawn in Lope de Aguirre's machinations.

From the outset it was obvious that Aguirre, in company with the *vizcaínos*, was plotting against his commander. When advised of the fact, Ursua's reaction, according to the chronicler Zuñiga, was that "with so many *vizcaínos* in the band there is no need for guards, since at the first word of Basque that he [Ursua] spoke to them they would all come to die at his side."[89] In 1561 Ursua was assassinated by these same *vizcaínos*.

With Ursua's assassination, Aguirre and his companions proclaimed Fernando de Guzmán "King of Peru," Aguirre declaring himself "denaturalized from the kingdoms of Spain." After a period of anarchy in which the band engaged in several murders, Aguirre, Guzmán, and their followers were forced to flee Peru, crossing the Andes and descending the Amazon River.* Many died along the way, some from the hazards of the voyage and others murdered by their companions. Guzmán was himself assassinated, and Aguirre took command. The cruelties perpetrated at the orders of Aguirre are legendary.†

---

*Known as the *Río Marañon*, hence the name of the group.

†In Spanish letters Aguirre is portrayed as the archetypical self-styled anarchical conquistador gone mad, while Ursua is viewed as a kind of paragon of virtue and loyal servant of his superiors. In a recent work, Caro Baroja argues that Aguirre was not really all that evil nor Ursua that innocent.[90]

Aguirre and the *marañones* eventually reached the island of Margarita (Venezuela), where they continued their campaign of rebellion and anarchy. They captured the governor and declared the island free of Spanish authority. Several men from the local garrison joined Aguirre's forces.

The plan was now clear. On the other side of the island there was a good seaworthy boat in which the *marañones* would go to Panama to free black slaves who could then be used in an attack on Peru itself, where the victorious Lope de Aguirre would proclaim the first independent kingdom in the Americas. Aguirre sent his trusted friend and fellow Basque, a man named Munguia, to commandeer the boat. Meanwhile, he destroyed his own small craft to prevent any idea of defection. Munguia failed to carry out his mission. Convinced that the cause was lost, he surrendered voluntarily to crown authorities. Trapped on the island and with little hope of relief, the *marañones* abandoned Lope de Aguirre. As the Spanish forces approached the island, Aguirre stabbed his daughter to death, so that she would not have to suffer the infamy of being "daughter of a traitor."[91]

The case of the *marañones* illustrates that common ethnic ties were not always a guarantee of Basque solidarity. The ill-fated adventures of the *marañones* began with the treacherous murder of Ursua and ended with the defection of Munguia. There is added significance in the actions of Lope de Aguirre, since they constitute what was possibly the most infamous and audacious rebellion against Spanish authority in the annals of New World colonial history. The behavior of Lope de Aguirre and his men could only serve to bolster the fear in many circles that Basques were out to subvert the colonial enterprise.

With the exception of the modest and relatively unsuccessful efforts to form tiny Basque settlements in the Antilles, the examples thus far have dealt with the activities of individual Basques who were largely self-motivated. We have seen that, in different New World areas and at different points in New World history, Basque activities were interpreted by non-Basques as having collective overtones that bordered on an ethnic group conspiracy. Even if individual Basques employed their ethnic ties to gain political favors and commercial success, however, there is no evidence of the existence of *formal* Basque ethnic organizations during the sixteenth and seventeenth centuries.

In the eighteenth century, the Basques did launch a formal

enterprise that deserves special mention: the Royal Guipuzcoan Company of Caracas *(Real Compañía Guipuzcoana de Caracas)*.

Throughout the seventeenth century there was a tendency among European colonial powers to join governmental support with private capital in order to found trading companies to exploit commerce with overseas colonies.* In 1621 the Dutch formed the Dutch West Indies Company; in 1664 the French founded the French East and West Company, while in 1670 the English created the Hudson's Bay Company. Such companies were so obviously successful that there were several efforts throughout the seventeenth century to found Spanish equivalents. However, the Spanish administration defended jealously the monopoly that it exercised over trade with the New World through the *Casa de Contratación* in Seville.[92]

From its inception in 1498 the Venezuela colony remained one of the most remote outposts of Spain's New World empire. During the sixteenth century the area was colonized by Spaniards who were to establish rather large agricultural estates devoted to the production of cacao, tobacco, and hides. The owners of these estates were referred to as *patricios maduanos*. In the seventeenth century there was a new wave of Spanish immigration, primarily from the Canary Islands. These new arrivals constituted the managerial and commercial classes of Venezuela and were to occupy key posts in local government. By the beginning of the eighteenth century the local governors were usually derived from the Canary Islander element in Venezuelan society.[93] Finally, there were Mestizo, Black, and Indian populations that provided most of the workers for the estates.[94]

In terms of its commerce, the region contributed little to the Spanish colonial economy. From 1498 to the 1730s Venezuela was a drain upon the Spanish crown, requiring more funds to administer than it generated for Spain through trade and taxes. This was due not so much to a lack of productivity of the region but to the fact that Venezuelan producers sought to avoid trade with the metropole. The *patricios maduanos* found it

---

*From the viewpoint of the governments such companies had two obvious advantages. First, they could be used to develop resources in marginal areas to which potential colonists did not gravitate by choice. Secondly, they provided a large measure of Old World control over New World commerce, which might otherwise pass into the hands of the colonists or foreigners.

considerably more profitable to traffic directly, if illegally, with Dutch, French, English, and private Spanish ships' captains who put into Venezuelan ports in order both to buy and to sell goods. The Dutch, in particular, were aggressive traders in the Caribbean, establishing warehouses on the islands of Saint Martin, Saint Eustasius, Tortola, Curaçao, and on the mainland in the Guianas. During the seventeenth century the Dutch controlled three-quarters of the trade in the Caribbean, which included the lion's share of Venezuelan commerce.[95]

The major Venezuelan export in this traffic was cacao, a product that was becoming extremely popular in Europe. The Spanish crown attempted to exert control by conceding to Venezuela a monopoly on Spanish colonial cacao production, although laws required that the product had to be exported to Europe via Veracruz and along the cumbersome channels of the Spanish government's absolute monopoly on commerce with the Indies. As a result cacao, worth eight *pesos* per *quintal* in Venezuela, fetched seventy *pesos* per *quintal* in Spain, a price differential that limited demand and excluded the Venezuelan producers from much participation in the profits.[96]

Trafficking with the Dutch and other contrabandists provided Venezuelan cacao growers with considerably higher prices for their product. By the early eighteenth century the situation had deteriorated to the point where in a period of twenty-eight years (1700−28) only five boats left Spain for Venezuela. In the fifteen-year period between 1706 and 1721, not a single officially sanctioned vessel travelled between the two areas.[97] Thus, practically the entire economy of Venezuela was based on contraband. This contraband traffic was so blatant that the Dutch built permanent estates in the Venezuelan region of Tucaras; some twenty Dutch and French vessels openly traded along the Venezuelan coast, and local Venezuelan officials taxed this trade.[98] Thus, Venezuela was in every respect a financial liability and administrative embarrassment for the Spanish crown.

In light of this situation Basque private interests, in conjunction with the government of Guipúzcoa, presented an audacious plan to the king: Guipúzcoa would form a trading company to colonize Venezuela and control its commerce.[99] Unlike other European trading companies that were concessions by a national government to private commercial interests, under Guipúzcoa's plan a regional government solicited a national government for a monopoly on commerce *vis-à-vis* the private sector, other regions of the nation, and the foreign interests.

In 1728, the king approved formation of the *Real Compañía Guipuzcoana de Caracas* and granted a contract for twenty years. Under conditions of the grant the company would send out a minimum of two vessels annually from Guipuzcoan ports. The boats were to be heavily armed and could transport any class of goods to the Venezuelan market. On the return trip, loaded with Venezuelan products (primarily cacao, tobacco, and hides), the vessels would put in at Cádiz where they would pay import duties but would not unload. They would then proceed to their home ports, from which the goods would enter the Castilian market directly without additional payment of the taxes that were applied to other commerce between Castilla and Guipúzcoa. In this initial grant, however, the king refused to concede to the company a monopoly on the Venezuelan trade.[100]

In return the company was obliged to maintain its own coast guard in Venezuela, with the right to capture contraband vessels. Captured vessels could be pressed into service of the company or sold, with two-thirds of the proceeds going to the company coffers and one-third to its ships' crews.[101]

The company was to be capitalized at 1.5 million *pesos* through the sale of 3,000 shares at 500 *pesos* each. The government of Guipúzcoa purchased 100 shares, while the king bought 200 from his private resources. Eight shares were set aside for the souls in purgatory to pay for votive services for persons who were killed in the service of the company.[102] An income of 1,000 *pesos* annually was destined to the Jesuit College of Cádiz, the Andalusian city where the company had one of its offices.[103] Response to the public offering of the remaining shares was disappointing, since a total of only 750,000 *pesos* was subscribed. The Basque backers had to use their personal credit to put the venture on solid financial ground.[104]

In 1730 the first four boats left San Sebastián for the New World. The boats each had between forty and fifty cannons, and their crews totaled 561 men.[105] The reception they were accorded in Venezuela could not have been worse. Not only did the cacao producers refuse to sell to the company, but the arrival of the vessels triggered a rebellion led by a local *caudillo*, who was aided by the Dutch. Several of the Basques and many of the Spanish troops in the local garrison were killed before the governor of Venezuela reestablished his authority.

Despite the adversity, the first two round trips by four of the company's boats produced a net profit of 738,570 *pesos*, or almost a 100 percent return on invested capital. In 1733 the company declared a 20 percent dividend.[106] The efforts to cut off the contraband traffic were successful. In one month of 1733 alone, nine Dutch boats were captured and converted to coast guard use.[107] The king was so impressed that he conceded to the company the desired monopoly. The company established outlets for its cacao in Madrid, Barcelona, Cádiz, Alicante, and San Sebastián.[108]*

Thus began a period that was to last for more than fifty years in which Basque activities converted Venezuela into a productive Spanish colony and a major focus of Basque immigration.[110] The company established more cacao *haciendas*, many under Basque ownership. Cacao exports rose from 60,000 *fanegas* annually in 1730 to 130,000 *fanegas* by 1749. During the same period cattle production tripled. The company also founded new settlements and built new dock facilities at La Guaira and Puerto Cabello, as well as fortifications to protect them.[111] The company covered the costs of government in the area and even produced a surplus which was sent to other areas of the New World to defray administrative expenses.[112]

Between 1739 and 1748 Spain and England were at war, and the company played a major role in Spain's Caribbean defenses. Spanish troops were transported in the eight frigates that the company placed at the king's disposition. From 1742 to 1744 the company maintained between 600 and 1,400 troops in Venezuela at its own expense. It also provided significant financial backing to the crown. In 1741 the king asked for the first in a series of loans that by 1744 totaled more than seven million *pesos*. These were later repaid by charging off duties owed by the company to the crown on the Venezuelan traffic.[113] In return for its war assistance, the company received

---

*In the Basque country, there were publications during the eighteenth century that were obviously designed to stimulate the use of chocolate. In 1754 J. Diaz Bravo published a work in Pamplona with the marvelous title, *Fasting Reformed by the Five Briefs of Our Holiest Father Benedict XIV and in Accord with the Practices of the Primitive Church, An Historical, Canonical-Medical Work of Necessity for Bishops, Priests, Confessors, Doctors, the Healthy and the Infirm. With Particular Attention to the Privileges that Soldiers in Spain Continue to Enjoy even after the Briefs. And an Historical, Medical-Clinical, Physico-Moral Treatise on Chocolate and its Use, Following the New Precepts.*[109]

greater privileges. In 1743 it received the right to charter French boats, which could leave French ports flying the French flag and could traffic directly with Venezuela. In 1746 the king freed the company from the control of crown officials in Cádiz, and by 1747 company boats could leave directly from Cádiz for Venezuela loaded with Andalusian and Castilian goods.[114]

Meanwhile, Basques increased their control in Venezuela itself. By 1737 a Basque, Zuloaga, was the local governor. Under his rule Venezuela acquired full provincial status and was thereby removed from the jurisdiction of Santo Domingo. In 1748 the king prohibited the entry of any additional Canary Islanders into Venezuela.[115]

By 1746 the direct participation of Basques in the benefits of the company's cacao trade was extended even to the ships' crews. Wages were paid in cacao, which the company introduced tariff-free into the Spanish market, thereby providing its employees with an extra bonus. Also, three months' salary of each ship's crewmen was withheld by the company to be invested in cacao, which in turn multiplied their gains.[116]

From the viewpoints of both the king and the Basques, the Company of Caracas was an enormous success and a model of colonial exploitation. However, the Venezuelans were of a different opinion. The Basque monopoly and coast guard activities destroyed the bargaining power of the *patricios maduanos* and forced them to sell their products at more or less fixed prices. By importing its own Basque employees, the company undermined the position of the Canary Islanders in Venezuelan society.[117] The company also assisted other Basques to become established in local commerce and as the owners of *haciendas*. Within a short time these new estate owners had doubled or tripled agricultural production in the area, thereby undermining the prices that all Venezuelan producers could demand from the company. From the viewpoint of the most powerful elements in traditional Venezuelan society, control over the region had passed into the hands of a formidable alien ethnic group that had little in the way of local roots.

Upon termination of Spain's war with England, the Basques controlled most of Venezuela with the exception of the valleys of the river Tuy, where Dutch contrabandists continued to trade with the largely Canary Islander and Creole population. When the company's coast guard vessels captured Dutch ships in the area and put into local ports, the Basque crews were received with threats of physical harm.[118]

The royal charter for the company expired in 1748, but by that time the king's war debts with it were of such magnitude that the charter was renewed with increased monopolistic powers. This could only be interpreted by dissident Venezuelans as threatening to usher in a period of increased Basque control over the colony.

In 1749 the governor of Venezuela substituted a Basque, Martín de Echevarría, for the Canary Islander Juan Francisco León, as "Corporal of War" charged with closing off the illegal trade in the river Tuy region. León refused to accept Echevarría's authority; he raised an army of three thousand Canary Creoles that besieged Caracas under the slogan, "Long live the King, Death to the Vizcayans!"[119] The governor himself was forced to flee and was allowed to return only after promising to forward to the king complaints concerning the behavior and attitudes of the agents of the company. With this guarantee, León withdrew his forces to the river Tuy.

León contended that Venezuela had become nothing more than a province of the company.[120] He accused the Basques of themselves engaging in contraband with the Dutch. He complained that Venezuela was controlled by Basque governors, lieutenants, and commercial interests, and hence the king received no information about the area except that which flowed through Basque channels.[121] León agreed to receive anyone into his area, "Spaniard or Creole . . . but not Vizcayan."[122] Finally, he demanded, "in all of the province [of Venezuela] not one person of this race [Vizcayan] should remain. All of them should leave on the first ship or boat that appears in the bay and lacking this their departure should be hastened by commandeering a boat at the expense of the said Vizcayans."[123]

The rebellion of León caused great consternation in Madrid, provoking a debate on the pros and cons of colonial mercantilism.[124] León demanded abolition of the company, but to do so in the face of open revolt would be to weaken royal authority in the New World and invite challenges to the king from other parts of the Spanish Empire. Conversely, other commercial interests in Spain were desirous of breaking Basque economic hegemony in Venezuela.

After considerable delay it was resolved to send a special emissary to Venezuela with one thousand soldiers in order to reestablish crown control. The emissary was a Basque, Julian de Arriaga.[125] Arriaga was empowered to investigate the leaders of the rebellion to determine their hidden motives. He was to determine what role the Dutch had played in the trouble. He was also to convey to the Venezuelans the fact that the company was not exclusively Basque, since some of the stockholders were from Madrid.[126]*

Arriaga arrived in Caracas in 1749. His efforts at peacemaking were frustrated by the deep resentment against the company that he encountered on all sides. In his own words, "there is scarcely a priest, friar, or nun who does not despise the company."[128] Arriaga also found that León had become a rallying point for *patricios maduanos*, Canary Islanders, and Creoles alike. The rebellious forces were receiving arms shipments from the Dutch. Arriaga's position was also undermined by desertions in the royal forces, since some of his own men sided with León.

The danger of an open and final rebellion was perceived clearly in Madrid. In 1751 Arriaga's successor was ordered to arrest León and send him to Spain to stand trial. León's officers were to be arrested and held in Caracas for garroting in the event that their followers continued the rebellion. Had León decided to organize and fight the outcome would have been in doubt. He decided instead to seek refuge on a Dutch warship. The Spanish forces captured some of his followers, executing four of them.

In light of this obvious crown determination, León's most influential supporters abandoned him. The bishop of Caracas denounced both León and his rebellion from the pulpit. León himself surrendered and was sent to Spain where, in 1752, he died in prison.[129]

The challenge by León, based upon the erroneous belief that the interests of the king could be separated from those of the company, constitutes a watershed in the history of Basque involvement in Venezuela. There is no doubt that the rebellion from 1749 to 1751 was an ethnic conflict that united every other ethnic element in Venezuelan society against the powerful Basques. Old World regional antipathies and racist rhetoric fueled the flames of emotion, even if the real issue was a struggle over control of commerce—a struggle that seemed to be as much between Basques and Dutch as between Basques and Venezuelans.

---

*This was true, because the king was a stockholder and lived in Madrid. But, at least up to January 6, 1749, the only other stockholder who lived outside of Guipúzcoa was one Bartolome Joseph de Urbiba, who lived in Vitoria, the capital of the Basque province of Alava.[127]

The rebellion of León ushered in a period in which the company was to become both more and less "Basque." Basque involvement increased after 1752 simply because both the Old and New World activities of the company increased. The company expanded its interests to include distilleries that it constructed throughout Iberia. It obtained a monopoly on Navarrese forests to be used for shipbuilding. It formed fleets of cod fishing and whaling vessels.[130] It also acquired a monopoly on the slave trade between Puerto Rico (the only authorized Spanish colonial port of disembarkation of Negro slaves) and Venezuela.[131]

In Venezuela itself, the company began new enterprises. It created plantations to grow gall nuts, used to make dyes. It introduced cotton. Two Basque brothers named Arvide, specialists in indigo raising, were brought from Veracruz to start new plantations. By 1774 Venezuela was exporting indigo.[132] Through these and many more expanded New World and Old World activities,* the company provided even greater employment opportunity for Basques who, by virtue of their kinship and ethnic ties, had the inside track to company jobs.

On the other hand, increasing numbers of non-Basques were employed by the company, and Basque control of its ownership and directive board was weakened. In 1751, over the protests of the province of Guipúzcoa, the head office of the company was transferred from San Sebastián to Madrid. The board of directors was to consist of a Spaniard and two Basques. Finally, there was a new stock issue to broaden the base of ownership. Venezuelans were encouraged to purchase shares.[134]

By the end of the 1770s the company was in deep financial trouble. The many schemes that diversified company interests, while diluting its capital and energies, met with uneven success. In 1779 renewed warfare with England disrupted its trade, causing serious financial loss. Also, the Spanish government was employing a liberalized trade policy for political gain in its dealings with the New World colonies. In 1776 Charles III

---

*The activities of the company also stimulated other Basque economic interests. Between the years 1775 and 1777 alone arms factories in Plasencia and Tolosa (both Guipúzcoa), connected with the company through interlocking ownership, received from the king orders totaling, "14,199 firearms of all types, 27,700 swords, lances and bayonets, 3,420 pistols and 12,000 tools for pioneer troops . . . earmarked for America, Peru, Chile and countries about the Caribbean, and all the pioneer tools for Maracaibo."[133]

permitted other trading companies to traffic in Venezuela, and in 1778 New World ports were opened to free commerce.[135]

Thus, by 1780 the company had become a cumbersome, semipublic body, unable to compete in a climate of free commerce with the newer, less diversified, and more aggressive trading companies.

Francisco Cabarrus, a member of the director's commission of the Caracas Company, from Bayonne, proposed in 1784 that the company merge with the Havana Company (another Basque enterprise founded in Cuba in 1740) and the Company of San Fernando. The new enterprise was to be known as the Philippines Company. The consolidation was realized in 1788, and the new company monopolized Spain's Philippines trade for the ensuing twenty-four years.[136]

Mexico City was the setting for a second eighteenth-century example of the founding of a Basque ethnic organization in the New World. We have already noted the intensive activity of Basques in northern Mexico, activity that attracted many additional Basques to the area. Mexico City was one of the major capitals of the Empire, with jurisdiction over all Spanish holdings north of Panama. It was also a key commercial center in Spain's Philippines trade. Goods from the Orient were brought to Acapulco, transported overland to Veracruz, and then shipped out to Europe. The city served as a religious center, attending to the spiritual needs of a large European and indigenous population and spearheading the missionary activity to the north. Thus, throughout the sixteenth, seventeenth, and eighteenth centuries, Mexico City was an important administrative, ecclesiastical, and commercial center. These were three areas of activity in which Basques were prominent throughout colonial history. It is not surprising, therefore, that Mexico City came to have a substantial and influential Basque colony that could trace its origins to the earliest years of Spanish control.

As early as 1584, the merchants of Mexico City, in order to protect their interests, created an association known as the Royal Tribunal of the Consulate *(Real Tribunal del Consulado)*. From its inception, there was an internal struggle for control of the association between two powerful ethnic interests, the Castilians from Santander and Burgos, known as the *montañeses*, and the Basques, referred to generically as *vizcaínos*.[137]

The *montañeses* gained the upper hand, in part due to the support of their larger ethnic religious confraternity the *Cofradía del Santo Cristo de Burgos*. Such confraternities were ostensibly religious but also retained a mutual aid aspect. In return for paying monthly dues, a member received medical care, drugs, burial costs, and financial assistance if he became destitute. He could also borrow money from the church at extremely reasonable rates of interest.[138] The confraternity was housed in a particular church that served as a focus for reunions and fiestas, creating among the members ties of camaraderie that could also serve as business contacts. Thus, membership in a confraternity provided the individual with group support, a measure of personal security, and access to funds and contacts that could be employed to advantage in the world of commerce.

While the Basques of Mexico were prone to collective ethnic action, some of them, after more than a century of involvement in Spain's New World venture, feared that their American successes were undermining their ethnic loyalties. In 1607 Balthasar de Echave published a work entitled *Discursos de la Antigüedad de la Lengua Bascongada* in Mexico City. The work is a fanciful dissertation on the antiquity of the Basque language. It also exhorts the Basques to manifest pride in their ethnic heritage. In the work Echave has the "mother language" address her children, the Basque speakers. At one point she states, "I do not wish nor say that you should not embrace with all possible fervor, the Castilian Foreigner [*"Estrangera Castellana,"* i.e., the Spanish language]. Know her, comprehend her, understand her, as you will thereby know, love; and esteem me better. [But] hold me always foremost and in first place as loyal and obedient sons to their true and legitimate mother."[139]

In 1671 the Basque colony of Mexico City (constituted by that time of both European and Mexican-born Basques) resolved to form a religious brotherhood, which they called the *Hermandad de Nuestra Señora de Aránzazu*, in memory of the miraculous virgin of Aránzazu (Guipúzcoa). The brotherhood was installed in the Franciscan convent of Mexico City. In 1688, the brotherhood inaugurated its own chapel that was also to serve as a cemetery in which Basques, "their wives, children, and descendants" were to be buried.[140] Non-Basques were excluded. The rules of the brotherhood specified that the chaplain be a Basque. A religious festival was to be held every August 15th, the feast of the Assumption. Finally, the offerings

made to the brotherhood, and especially the jewels and adorn-
ments for the statue of the Virgin, were to be independent of the
control of the Franciscans.*

Until 1696 the Basque colony continued to meet in the
sacristy of the chapel without the sanction of Church authorities. In that year, however, the members decided to seek
official recognition of the association as a confraternity *(cofradía)* rather than continue its lesser status of brotherhood
(hermandad). Such recognition could only be obtained by petitioning the archbishop. The recommendation of the legal advisor to the bishop concerning the petition reflects clearly the
extent to which the exclusivism and independence of the
Basques had antagonized the church hierarchy. Not only was
the petition denied but it was suggested to the archbishop that
"the members of the said brotherhood should be severely
punished and denounced for violations of restraints established
under Canon Law, Holy Councils, and Apostolic Bulls, and as
such they should be excommunicated to serve . . . as an example for others."[142]

Before the recommendation was implemented, the
ecclesiastical judge and vicar general of Mexico, Tiburcio de
Anuncibay Anaya, a Basque, intervened, denouncing an excommunication that might "undermine public order" and that
was directed at "some of the leading persons of the Republic,
persons of known nobility, virtue and devotion to the pursuance
of pious works and the cult of the divine."[143] The excommunication was lifted against all but the royal clerk, José Muñoz de
Castro, who had prepared the petition of the brotherhood.
However, within a month this excommunication was also lifted
and four months later the archbishop approved the petition of
the Basques and named José Muñoz de Castro first ecclesiastical notary of the directive of the confraternity.

Elevated to the status of confraternity, the association
further underlined its exclusiveness, and particularly its

---

*An inventory of the chapel made in 1710 gives an idea of the wealth of the
brotherhood. The statue of the Virgin dominated the main altar and was
clothed in a dress that contained 180 emeralds. Her veil included sixty-four
diamonds and her arms were covered with pearl bracelets. There were five
sumptuous minor altars with eleven natural size marble statues robed in silks
from China. The mirrors of the altars were framed in Venetian cut glass. There
were religious paintings by the Mexican-Basque artist Nicolás de Arteaga.
The chapel also contained fifteen silver lamps and eight chalices, two of which
were made of gold.[141]

economic independence, by refusing to ask for alms like the other confraternities and by refusing to accept donations from non-Basques. At the same time, the confraternity refused to allow poor people and mendicant religious to enter the chapel to ask for alms. This provoked an incident in 1728 when a Mercedarian priest, Miguel de Quiroz, entered the chapel during mass to request alms for his order. He was removed from the premises shouting insults at the congregation: "heretical Vizcayan dogs, vile *gachupines* [Spanish settlers in the New World], sobediants, religious backsliders, and excommunicants." He threatened them with trial by the Inquisition, which would "exile all Vizcayans who were living in Mexico."[144] Father Quiroz went to the mayor, who was the son of a *montañés* nobleman, with the request that a list of Basques be compiled to facilitate their deportation from Mexico. The proposal was rejected.

The somewhat stormy history of the confraternity's relations with church authorities prompted the Basques to seek greater protection of their activities. There was in Madrid a powerful Basque religious organization known as the Congregation of St. Ignatius, with which the Confraternity of Our Lady of Aránzazu became affiliated. Through the intervention of the Basques of Madrid, the confraternity was placed directly under the protection of King Philip V in 1729, the year after King Philip had granted the charter to the Basque organizers of the Company of Caracas. When the Basques of Mexico City heard the news, they organized a great celebration in their chapel to which, according to one authority, "were invited, with a certain irony, the archbishop and the fiscal official of the diocese."[145]

With royal protection in hand, the confraternity petitioned the pope, successfully, for the right to prohibit beggars and mendicant religious from begging in the chapel, as well as the right to prohibit the Franciscans from using the chapel and its trappings for their own services.[146]

At this point the Basques of Mexico City proposed to build a major asylum, to be called the College of St. Ignatius, although it came to be known popularly as the College of the Vizcayans (Colegio de las Vizcaínas). The object of the asylum was to provide shelter for "girls and widows, daughters and descendants of Basque families,"[147] who for lack of opportunities were in danger of "not only abandoning the lustrum of dignity but of giving in to a relaxing of propriety and the ruination of their honesty."[148] The college was to provide shelter and protect the virtue and character of both young girls and elderly matrons, while teaching them sewing, housework, reading, and writing. Entry was reserved to persons of legitimate birth. They were to form a living community, disciplined by a rectoress and assistant rectoress, in which the residents would do all of the tasks from cleaning the building and cooking to burying a deceased member.[149]

The central concern of the founders of the college was that it not fall into the hands of ecclesiastical authorities. In the constitution of the college there are articles stating that none of the endowment or income could be administered by religious. Clergymen could not hold administrative posts, nor could the college be converted into a nunnery governed by religious vows. Article 6 stated that any attempt to convert it into such an institution "is declared null, worthless, and without effect, even if, to the contrary, such a change is desired by the College's rector, board of directors, former rectors, treasurer and all the residents." In their constitution the founders petitioned the king to remove his protection from the college if, in fact, its prime purpose of protecting Basque maidens and widows were ever modified.[150]

The Mexican-Basques who went to Europe in the early nineteenth century due to the Mexican Revolution believed that the founding of the college was due to the concern of the Guipuzcoan, Francisco de Echeveste, who was named consul and prior of the royal tribunal of *Nueva España* (a kind of chamber of commerce). Before coming to Mexico, Echeveste had an illustrious career. Twice he was the commander of the fleet of Philippines galleons, and he was also Spanish ambassador to China. According to the oral tradition among the Mexican-Basques, Echeveste was walking through the streets of Mexico City when he was approached by a group of beggar children. He noticed that one was fair-skinned and blonde. He asked her name and was appalled to learn that she was of Basque descent. It was this encounter that reputedly prompted Echeveste to found the college.[151]

Regardless of the authenticity of the legend and whatever the origin of the idea, once launched the project received immediate and substantial support from many Mexico City Basques. In 1731, 181 donors gave a total of 40,033 *pesos*, one and a half *reales*. The largest donation was 6,000 *pesos* from the Basque archbishop of Mexico City, Juan Antonio de Vizarrón y Eguiarreta. The smallest donation was the one and a half *reales* given by a Basque nun, with the permission of her superior. One woman gave a pair of diamond earrings. The donations of the remaining 178 individual donors suggest that there was considerable difference in wealth, generosity, or both among the Basques of Mexico City, as Table 1 shows.

TABLE 1

BASQUE DONATIONS TO THE COLLEGE OF ST. IGNATIUS

Number of Donors	Amount of Donation, *pesos*
8	1,000 – 2,500
79	100 – 600
77	25 – 60
14	5 – 20

Source: Olavarría y Ferrari, *El Real Colegio*, Appendix, pp. 21–31.

In 1732, on the Feast of All Saints, the board of directors of the college held its first meeting. It named a commission to request from the city government the donation of a site for the future building. This was acquired in 1733. Construction began in 1734, and on June 30 of that year the Basque archbishop of *Nueva España*, Vizarrón, and Martín de Elizacoechea, also Basque, and bishop of *Nueva Vizcaya*, laid the cornerstone as part of the religious celebration of the feast day of St. Ignatius, patron saint of the Basques.[152]

The speed with which the work began is in marked contrast to the delays that were experienced before the college was opened. Under the benevolence of Archbishop Vizarrón, there were no special impediments placed in the way of its construction. However, when Vizarrón died in 1747, it was still not completed. Possibly the war with England (1740–49) obstructed progress,* and the magnitude of the undertaking probably delayed its completion. It is possible that construction was delayed awaiting the results of periodic solicitations for funds among the Basque donors. The College of the Vizcayans was to become an architectural landmark of Mexico City, one that still stands.

In 1749 Vizarrón's replacement, Archbishop Manuel Rubio y Salinas, arrived in Mexico City and served immediate

---

*There is an echo of this in the words of the king who, in 1766, upon approving the college's constitution, commented that it seemed impossible for such a work to have been continued throughout a period of calamitous warfare.[153]

notice that he opposed colleges and other institutions independent from ecclesiastical control. He won a suit against the College of Guadalupe and caused that institution to be placed under his immediate jurisdiction. This ecclesiastical victory was a precedent that threatened directly the autonomy of the College of the Vizcayans.[154]

But the Basques were undaunted in their attempts to defend the college's independence. They sent off legal briefs to Madrid and Rome and threatened, if all else failed, to "set fire to that which has cost us our money."[155] The same words were used to communicate to the Basque Congregation of St. Ignatius in Madrid the determination of the Mexico City Basques not to give in to the archbishop.[156]

The ensuing series of legal maneuvers was to last no less than fourteen years. The confraternity commissioned a Basque banker in Cádiz to release the necessary funds to dispute the issue in both the courts of Madrid and the Vatican.[157] In Madrid the Basques' case was argued in part by the king's own chaplain, Don José de Rada Aguirre, and the secretary of state, Don Agustín de Ordeñana, both members of the Congregation of St. Ignatius. In Rome the Basque cause was supported by the Jesuits, since the ecclesiastical advisors of the Confraternity of Aránzazu of Mexico City were all Jesuits.[158] In a letter from the Basques of Mexico to those of Madrid, there is reference to the Jesuit provincial in Madrid and Rome, Father Juan Francisco López, who, it is claimed, "knows our work, esteems it, and loves us."[159]

At this point the struggle dealt with more than an ethnic group's desire for a measure of autonomy. The jurisdictional disputes called into question the relationship between the state and the church, and, within the church, between the regular church hierarchy and the autonomous religious orders. In Madrid and Rome kings died and popes expired; yet the struggle continued in the passageways, palaces, and courts of the two capitals. In 1758 there was a breakthrough in the impasse. The newly elected Pope Clement XIII published a bull that conceded some of the Basques' demands. But the Basques rejected the bull, requiring all or nothing as a condition for opening the college. A major stumbling block was whether or not a church annex, built onto the college, should come under ecclesiastical control. The Basques' answer was that "the church is constructed for the spiritual fruition of the College, the College was not constructed for the church." This stand evoked considerable criticism of the Basques among the clergy of Mexico City.[160]

By 1760 the Confraternity of Aránzazu had spent almost one million *pesos* in construction of the college. Yet it was not until 1763 that there was news favorable to the Basques. The Spanish ambassador in Rome communicated to the prime minister in Madrid that the pope had agreed to modify the bull of 1758 to conform to the requests of the Congregation of St. Ignatius in Madrid.[161] But the Basques of the confraternity rejected the offer anew, since they insisted upon a new bull that would unequivocally guarantee the autonomy of the college. In 1765 the king of Spain lent his prestige to renewed petitioning of the pope, and in 1766, Clement XIII published a bull that was acceptable to the confraternity. Later that same year, King Carlos III took the college under his personal protection.[162]

The jubilant Basques of Mexico City inaugurated the college on September 9, 1767. Thirty-three years had transpired since the dedication of the cornerstone in 1734. The inauguration was splendid. Those in attendance included delegations from other autonomous colleges in Mexico City, a company of honor guards sent by the viceroy, and the new archbishop of Mexico.[163]

The College of the Vizcayans was opened with seventy residents. Today it continues to function. Due to its freedom from church control, it survived the impoundments of church possessions that characterized later periods in Mexican history.

In many contexts of New World colonial history, Basques were viewed as potential subverters of crown interests. In their roles as administrators, ecclesiastics, and colonial mercantilists they also served as the prime handmaidens of crown policy, incurring in the bargain the enmity of other New World groups. Royal support of the Company of Caracas and the Confraternity of Aránzazu suggests that, by the eighteenth century, Basque influence within Spanish administrative circles was not limited to the Americas alone. There is evidence to suggest that Basques had become important figures in both the governmental agencies and commercial circles of the key Iberian cities of Madrid, Cádiz, and Sevilla.

By the beginning of the eighteenth century, both the private and public financial circles of Madrid were dominated by several Navarrese families—Goyeneche, Iturralde, Uztariz, and others.[164] These families originated for the most part in the tiny Basque-speaking northern region of Navarra that included the valley of Baztan and the drainage of the Bidasoa River. Many were from the same small communities. The village of Arizcun provided a number of the most illustrious persons. The complicated business dealings and partnerships that linked the fortunes of these men, superimposed upon a grid of affinal and consanguineal kinship ties, prompted one of the most prominent figures of the circle (Juan de Goyeneche) to remark that the *Baztaneses* constituted "a single house."[165]

A simple listing of some of the activities of the Navarrese magnates gives some notion of the magnitude of their influence. Juan de Goyeneche was personal financial advisor to several monarchs, founder of Spain's first newspaper, founder and protector of a model industrial town (located near Madrid and which he christened *Nuevo Baztan*), and sole provisioner of the Pyrenean timber vitally needed for Spanish shipyards.[166] His intimate friend and frequent business partner, Juan Bautista de Iturralde, compromised an illustrious career as financier and administrator of the crown income from the province of Granada with a rather unsuccessful stint as minister of the patrimony *(Hacienda)*.[167] Pedro de Iturriria, who was involved in several industries, was the administrator of the cacao warehouse of the Company of Caracas.[168] Miguel de Arizcun was the provisioner of foodstuffs to the Spanish fleet, administrator of the wool receipts of Castilla and Aragón, and administrator of the crown income from Galicia.[169] These examples suffice to illustrate the importance of Navarrese interests in Madrid's finances. Furthermore, Navarrese, many of whom had kinsmen in the Madrid colony, were prominent in business and shipping in the two key port cities of Cádiz[170]* and Sevilla.[172]

The qualitative nature of Navarrese involvement in the Spanish economy was more important than its sheer magnitude. The Navarrese businessman of the early eighteenth century was the archetypical capitalist—the true entrepreneur, who was

---

*The extent to which Navarrese ethnic cohesion could be played out in such distant Andalusian points is seen in the case of Ignacio de Enecorena, who left his natal village of the Baztan to join his Baztan-born uncle Miguel de Bergara in Cádiz. The uncle provided him with an education and a post. Ignacio later married Madalena Francisca de Mayora who was born in Cádiz but whose father was likewise a native of the valley of Baztan.[171]

obsessed with both pragmatism and efficiency. The social historian Caro Baroja finds the important contribution of these
Navarrese financiers to be their role as catalysts, introducing
into the Spanish economy the asceticism of Dutch economic
practices and the economic pragmatism of the French minister
Colbert.* It was through the efforts of these Navarrese entrepreneurs that productivity rather than precious metals came to
be viewed in Spain as the basis of the weatlh of nations.

While most Navarrese were nobles by virtue of their collective *hidalguía* (i.e., because they were born in a particular
community or valley that enjoyed collective noble status), the
Navarrese magnates of Madrid used their wealth and power
gained through commerce to acquire individual titles of nobility
(particularly that of *marqués*). This contradicted the
traditionalist notion that the aristocracy ought not to engage in
the mundane and demeaning world of business affairs.[176]

Thus, in the Madrid of the eighteenth century there were
strong manifestations of the same Basque economic pragmatism and success that were so pronounced in Vizcaya in the
fifteenth century or Potosí in the seventeenth. Furthermore, it
should be noted that Caro Baroja restricted his analysis to the
Navarrese role. On several occasions, he suggests that non-
Navarrese Basques were prominent as well. To appreciate this
point, we have only to recall that it was precisely during this
period that the promoters of the Royal Guipuzcoan Company of
Caracas obtained the first private commercial monopoly in the
history of Spanish colonial trade.

Both the Navarrese and the Basques from the other provinces formed religious voluntary associations in Madrid. In
1683 the Navarrese founded the Royal Congregation of San
Fermín of the Navarrese *(Real Congregación de San Fermín de
los Navarros)*. The original membership was 327 persons. In
1685 a special invitation was extended to Navarrese residing
throughout the empire to collect alms for the charitable enter-

---

*Francisco Javier de Goyeneche, son of Juan de Goyeneche, translated into
Spanish a study of the Dutch economy.[173] Jerónimo de Uztariz authored a
treatise in which the Spanish economy was subjected to close scrutiny, while
providing prescriptions for correcting its deficiencies.[174] The economic
pragmatism, asceticism, and entrepreneurial successes of these eighteenth-
century Navarrese financial magnates prompted Caro Baroja to question the
famous thesis of Max Weber concerning the relationship between the "Protes-
tant Ethic" and the origins of capitalism.[175]

prises of the organization,[177] thus underscoring the belief of the Madrid founders that Navarrese everywhere shared a common interest.

In similar fashion the non-Navarrese Basques founded the Congregation of Natives and Those Originated in the Three Provinces of Alava, Guipúzcoa, and Vizcaya *(Congregación de Naturales y Originários de las Provincias de Alava, Guipúzcoa y Vizcaya)* in 1713. The name was later changed to The Royal Congregation of St. Ignatius *(La Real Congregación de San Ignacio)*. The original membership consisted of 124 persons, including 62 Vizcayans, 41 Guipuzcoans, and 21 Alavese. Membership was open to those born in the Basque country, those who owned property there, and those who could simply demonstrate a Basque ancestry.[178] Like the Navarrese Congregation of San Fermín, the organization solicited benefactors in the colonies. Of a list of ninety-five benefactors, thirty-one were residing outside the Iberian peninsula; the largest nucleus was Peru, with fourteen.[179]

While there is ample evidence of Basque collective ethnic activity in the first half of the eighteenth century, it was in the second half that the interlacing of Basque commercial, ecclesiastical, military, and administrative interests throughout the entire Spanish Empire found a common organizational expression. In 1765, the Royal Basque Society of the Friends of the Country *(Real Sociedad de los Amigos del País)* was created. Until this time feedback to the Basque country from the involvement of Basques in the Spanish colonial enterprise was played out along personal and family networks.* With the exception of the Company of Caracas, none of the major Basque-controlled economic enterprises was actually headquartered in the Basque provinces. Basque entrepreneurs who expended their energies in the key centers of the Spanish world (as well as in some of its remote outposts) might use a part of their wealth to embellish the church of their natal village, construct a retirement villa there, or assist other relatives to emigrate. However, they were not overly prone to make direct investments of capital and self in the local economies of the Basque provinces.

By the mid-eighteenth century the very economic successes and the growing cosmopolitanism† of the successful Basque

---

*The results of the appeal[180] made in 1639 to Vizcayans resident abroad to assist the seigneury of Vizcaya are unknown.

†Caro Baroja provides insightful descriptions of the educations provided by the Navarrese magnates to their sons.[181]

entrepreneur prompted several to educate their children abroad. France (and particularly the university cities of Toulouse, Bordeaux, and Paris) was favored. There the sons of Basque financiers were influenced directly by the liberal thought of the Enlightenment. It was a Guipuzcoan, Manuel Ignacio de Altuna, who first introduced into Spain the ideas of the French philosopher, Rousseau. Altuna knew Rousseau well during the years 1743–44, and they continued to correspond after the Basque returned to Guipúzcoa in 1745, where shortly thereafter he became mayor of Azcoitia.

Through the efforts of Altuna and his two friends, Joaquín de Eguía and Francisco Munibe e Idiaquez (conde de Peñaflorida), Azcoitia became a kind of intellectual center. The conde de Peñaflorida proved to be particularly influential. He was a son of one of the founders of the Company of Caracas, and was educated in Toulouse. Shortly after returning to Guipúzcoa in 1746, he organized a series of academic seminars (*juntas académicas*) in Azcoitia for the study of science, history, current events, and music. The loose-knit organization was short-lived, but laid the intellectual bases for the emergence of the Royal Basque Society.[182]

In 1763 Peñaflorida and fifteen other young men presented a plan to the *Juntas Generales*, or legislature, of Guipúzcoa to found an economic society to be called the "Academy of Agriculture, Science, and Useful Arts and Commerce Adapted to the Particular Circumstances and Economy of Guipúzcoa."[183] The idea appeared to be modeled along the lines of several similar French societies. In 1764 the project was approved, and late that winter the society began to function. By this time the concept had been broadened to include the three Basque provinces of Alava, Guipúzcoa, and Vizcaya.[184] The new organization was called the Royal Basque Society of the Friends of the Country.

It is evident that the young idealists who founded the society, in their altruistic concern with the Basque economy, represented a departure from the highly personal economic outlook of the traditional Basque entrepreneur. Furthermore, it is equally clear that they were motivated in large measure by a concern with ethnic group loyalties. The first article of the society's statutes identifies the purpose of the organization as "to cultivate the inclination and the tastes of the Basque Nation [*Nación Bascongada*] towards the Sciences, Letters and Arts . . . and *to further increase the unity of the Three Basque Provinces of Alava, Vizcaya, and Guipúzcoa*."[185] (Emphasis supplied.) There was a careful division of authority among representatives of the three provinces. Each was accorded equal voting rights, and the presidency rotated among them. Every four months during the year, the directorship rotated as well, with each province's delegation assuming it in turn.[186]

One of the most important activities of the society was the creation of a boarding school *(Seminario)* in Vergara. In contrast to the existing pedagogical emphases upon philosophy and theology, the seminary of Vergara concentrated upon physics, commerce, and the natural sciences.* In addition the seminary was concerned with Basque history and current events—thus its full name, the Patriotic Seminary of Vergara *(Seminario Patriótico de Vergara)*. The students were instilled with "love for the king, the nation, and the country [*Patria*],"[188] meaning, of course, the Basque country, which provided the "patriotic" point of reference.†

---

*For example, the French scientists François de Chaveneau and Louis Proust were given chairs of experimental physics. The former discovered how to produce a malleable metal from platinum. The young Swedish scientist Thunborg was given the chair of minerology and metallurgy. Through their experiments in the laboratory at Vergara, the two brothers Fausto and Juan José Elhuyar (of French Basque descent) discovered a new metal, wolfram.[187]

†This is an important distinction since the historian R.J. Shafer, in a study of Spanish Economic Societies of the Eighteenth Century, of which the Royal Basque Society was the first, interprets the references to patriotism from a strictly Spanish viewpoint,[189] whereas an important part of the patriotism of the Basque organizers was of a regional ethnic nature. An as yet unpublished manuscript by the historian Larramendi clearly demonstrates that Basque political nationalism was already a part of the Guipuzcoan scene prior to the founding of the Royal Basque Society. Writing in 1756, Larramendi quotes a member of a hypothetical parliament of Guipúzcoa as saying,

> What reason is there, I repeat, for this privileged nation, and of most noble origin, not to become a separate nation, a nation of its own, a nation wholly independent of the rest? Why should the three provinces of Spain, Guipúzcoa, Alava, and Vizcaya (not to mention the kingdom of Navarra), have to remain dependent upon Castilla, while Labourd, Soule, and Basse Navarre remain dependencies of France?[190]

According to the deputy the new nation would be known as the "United Provinces of the Pyrenees" and would form a "republic totally of Basques."[191]

That such thinking persisted during the period of the society's existence (1765–93) is seen in the fact that when French troops invaded Guipúzcoa in 1794, a part of the Guipuzcoan deputation *(Diputación)* met, declaring the region severed from Spain, while requesting that the French recognize its independence. The effort failed but cost the Spaniards jurisdiction over Santo Domingo, which was conceded to France in return for a French refusal to recognize an independent Guipúzcoa.[192]

The Royal Basque Society maintained four commissions in each province devoted to the scrutiny of such topics as agriculture and rural economics, science and "useful arts," industry and commerce, and humanities *(Bellas Artes)*. Once annually, the society held a meeting at which each of the commissioners made his report. The more interesting projects were published in an annual society organ, the *Extractos*. Through the activities of its several commissions, the Royal Basque Society introduced into the local economy new types of animal fodder, modern agricultural technology, and innovative techniques in the iron industry and the manufacture of paper. In the area of health services, it initiated the practice of vaccination and then defended it against its critics.[193]

Nevertheless, the society was greeted with mixed enthusiasm in the Basque country. Many of the *Extractos* voiced the complaint that the group's activities were viewed with great suspicion.[194] The *Extractos* of 1777 praised the original nineteen founders for enduring "with heroic firmness the criticisms, satires and even calumnies" that were heaped upon them.[195] At the same time it was stated that of the 868 current members of the society,

> The smallest part . . . [is] actually resident in the Basque country itself; in which the town with the largest number [of members] scarcely surpasses those of the remotest parts of Asia [e.g., the Basque colony of the Philippines]. Which justifies stating that it seems that the love of the Basques [for their country] increases in relation to their distance from it.[196]

In the same vein, the 1775 *Extractos* noted the importance of

> The imponderable aids provided to the Basque country by its sons established in the Andalusias and the Americas, benefits which are apparent in everyday life, and which are also enjoyed by the Royal Basque Society.[197]

Close relations were also maintained with the Basque colony of Madrid. In 1775 the Royal Basque Society formally declared its "brotherhood and special unity" with the Royal Congregation of Saint Ignatius.[198] The latter organization, in turn, funded the chair of physics in the seminary of Vergara.[199]

Such contributions of the Basque "diaspora" to the activities of the Royal Basque Society were a frequent topic in the *Extractos*. In 1777 it was noted that

[There is] news from Mexico that Señor Viana . . .
. . . aided by Don Ambrosio de Meabe* and Don Martín de Aguirre Burualde, fervent patriots, had distributed among the countrymen of *Nueva España* a letter of solicitation for the benefit of the Society. [This was done] with the approval of His Excellency Señor Don Antonio María de Bucareli y Ursua, viceroy and captain general of the kingdom of Mexico, who offered to declare himself vice-protector of our royal chapter in those dominions. [The results of the solicitation] were so favorable that . . . one hundred and seventy-one members were inscribed at 7 *pesos* [*pesos fuertes*] per year and in addition eight thousand one hundred and fourteen *pesos* of special donations [were collected].[200]

Another extract mentioned that

a letter was received from His Excellency Señor Don Manuel de Guirior, viceroy of Lima, offering to promote with the greatest zeal the aims of the Basque Society in the kingdom of Peru, initiating the subscription by depositing 500 *pesos*.[201]

Shafer estimates that between 1774 and 1790 almost 1,700,000 *reales vellón* entered the society's coffers from persons in the Indies.[202] So, while the efforts of the Royal Basque Society were aimed at improving conditions in the Basque provinces, its major source of support was clearly the influential and wealthy Basques scattered throughout the empire. For the emigrant, the society provided a means of activating his ethnic loyalties, while the seminary allowed some to even educate their sons in the Basque country. Of the 429 students who attended it between 1775 and 1794, only 117 were born in the Basque country (18 in Alava, 36 in Guipúzcoa, 36 in Vizcaya, and 27 in Navarra). Practically as many, or 111 students, were from the Americas. There were 34 Cuban Basques, followed by Mexico (21), Río de la Plata (9), and Peru (8). But the largest contingent of students, a total of 169, came from the Basque colonies in the other parts of Spain. Fifty-four students came from Andalusia (primarily Cádiz and Sevilla), 19 came from Madrid, and another 19 came from Galicia (particularly from the shipbuilding center of El Ferrol).[203]

The profile of the geographical distribution of the membership of the society reflects a worldwide ethnic organization in which the largest chapters were concentrated precisely in the

---

*Don Ambrosio de Meabe was co-founder of the *Colegio de las Vizcaínas* in Mexico City.

most important and sensitive nerve centers of the Spanish Empire. Thus, of the 1,181 members listed in 1793, the largest contingent, or 496 persons, resided in the New World, and 378 members lived in parts of Spain other than the Basque provinces. In contrast, only 211 members, or slightly more than one-sixth of the total, resided in the Basque country. Forty-four members were listed as with their regiments (post unknown); 28 resided in parts of Europe other than Spain; 23 resided in the Philippines; 1 lived in Africa, and 1 was "travelling."[204] The largest single chapter was Madrid's with 148 members, followed closely by Mexico City, the anchor of Spain's North American holdings, with 132. Lima, the key center of the Empire's South American territories, had 71 members. Havana, the major city of the Antilles, had 44 members, while Manila, the seat of Spanish rule in the Philippines, had 21. On the Iberian peninsula, Cádiz and Sevilla, the most important ports in Spain's trade with the Indies, had chapters of 72 and 54 members respectively. These figures may be contrasted with the 24-member chapter of Vitoria, the 20 members in Bilbao, the 15 members of San Sebastián and the 13 in Pamplona. Thus, the four major cities of the Basque country had smaller chapters than such places as Arequipa (Peru) (32 members) and Puebla de los Angeles (Mexico) (26 members).

But even more impressive than the geographic distribution of the membership was its occupational structure. The 1793 catalogue of membership lists occupations for 470 individuals. One hundred seventy-three had military careers, 182 were administrators, 24 were academicians, and 13 were physicians. The remaining members, one suspects, were largely businessmen without corresponding governmental posts.* Four hundred and seventy occupations in all are specified, but what occupations! They included some of the most prestigious posts within the empire. In Madrid no fewer than eleven members of the Royal Basque Society sat on the Council of Patrimony *(Consejo de la Hacienda)*; six were on the Council of the Indies *(Consejo de Indias)*; five were on the Council of State *(Consejo del Estado)*; three were on the Royal Council *(Consejo Real)*; three on the Council of War *(Consejo de Guerra)*; three served as general directors of the National Income *(Directores Generales de Rentas)*; two were in the Secretariat of State

---

*It should be noted that there was not a hard line between administrator and businessman. Many administrators maintained private business interests, while certain administrative posts were purchased for their business value.

(Secretaría de Estado); and one served on the Accounting Tribunal *(Tribunal de la Contaduría)*. The treasurer of the Inquisition of Sevilla as well as the treasurer of the army of that city were society members. Among the military men there were eight lieutenant generals, one captain general, four brigadiers, three commanders, four squadron chiefs of the Royal Fleet, twenty-four colonels, five lieutenant colonels, and forty-nine captains (the majority were ship's captains). Among the religious there were one archbishop, seven bishops, an abbot, and a large number of canons *(canónigos)*. Several of Spain's ambassadors were members of the Royal Basque Society, including the king's minister to the court of Rome, his personal financial advisor in the Roman court, his ministers in Lucerne, Stockholm, Warsaw, and Copenhagen, his ambassador to Vienna, and the first secretary of his ambassador to London. There were several justices *(oidores)* in the society, including one in Valencia, one in Galicia, one in Manila, one in Caracas, one in Santo Domingo, and two in Lima. In the Indies, society members included such important figures as the regents of the Royal Patrimony *(Regentes de la Real Hacienda)* of Guadalajara, Santiago de Chile, Buenos Aires, and Manila, as well as a minister of the Royal Patrimony *(Ministro de la Real Hacienda)* of Santo Domingo. No less a personage than the viceroy of *Nueva España* was a member as were his subordinates the governor of the Valley of Mexico and Diego de Borica, governor of the Californias (whom we shall discuss further in chapter 4).

The membership of the Royal Basque Society also included such important fiscal officials as the administrators of the State Income *(Administrador de Rentas)* of Majorca, Segovia, Salamanca, Jaen, and Havana. Society members were similarly prominent in the ranks of the superintendents and administrators of customs *(Aduanas)*, including one official in Sevilla, one in Vitoria, one in Lima, one in Havana, one in Manila, two in Arequipa, three in Mexico City, and no less than five in Cádiz.* Given their maritime commercial interests, customs regulations were, as we have seen in discussing the Royal Guipuzcoan Company of Caracas, of prime concern to the Basques. This commercial involvement is also reflected in the list of occupations of the Royal Basque Society member-

---

*Including two inspectors, two accountants, and the superintendent of trade with Mexico.

ship. One was a director of the Royal Company of San Fernando of Sevilla. One was director of the Royal Havana Company. Two were directors of the Royal Philippines Company (successor of the Royal Guipuzcoan Company of Caracas), and the treasurer of the company also belonged to the society.

The organization of Basque involvement in the tobacco monopoly is of particular interest. We have noted that the prominent Navarrese architects of Madrid's eighteenth-century fiscal policy were proponents of a mercantilistic economic philosophy that emphasized production. For the Iberian peninsula this meant industrialization, but colonial mercantilistic economic policy dictated that the emphasis in the colonies should be placed upon production of raw materials, particularly through plantation agriculture. The cacao venture of the Company of Caracas is an obvious example of such thinking. Tobacco, a crop of high value with respect to bulk and with great resistance to spoilage, leant itself well to the transatlantic traffic. While Caro Baroja does not discuss the role of Madrid's Navarrese circle in the tobacco trade, he does indicate that Juan de Goyeneche was proprietor of the building that housed the superintendency and general administration of the tobacco monopoly[205] and Jerónimo de Uztariz was the secretary of the Royal Board of Tobacco *(Junta Real del Tabaco)*.[206] By the end of the century Basque involvement in the tobacco monopoly was pervasive. Members of the Royal Basque Society in 1793 included the minister of the tribunal and accounting and the principal treasurer of the tobacco income in Madrid, the accountant of tobacco income in Segovia, the superintendent of tobacco in Sevilla, two directors of the tobacco monopoly in Mexico City, the accountant director of tobacco in Manila, the director of tobacco in Lima, and the accountant and minister of the tobacco factory in Havana.

In sum, during the second half of the eighteenth century, the twilight years of the Spanish Empire, the long-standing Basque role in Spanish administrative and commercial circles, in combination with the new philosophical influences of the Enlightenment, provide the bases for an ethnic organization that not only embraced the entire Hispanic world but permeated the highest circles of its social, political, and economic life. Although dedicated to improving the standard of living in the Basque country, the Royal Basque Society enjoyed only moderate support there. Conversely, it struck an obvious responsive chord among the Basque emigrés. This in itself is eloquent testimony to the persistence of ethnic loyalties in the Basque diaspora. The question of the extent to which influence, business partnerships, favors, and appointments flowed along Royal Basque Society channels in such centers as Mexico City, as well as between the colonies and the metropole would constitute a study in itself. The profile of the occupations in the society's membership suggests it might have been extensive.*

It is not our intention to present an exhaustive and chronologically arranged treatment of Basque participation in Spanish colonial history. We have instead selected highlights that illustrate some of the salient features of the Basques' involvement. Second, we have been limited, in the main, to

---

*There is the related question of the extent to which Basque ethnic loyalties and the example of the Royal Basque Society contributed to the continued development of interest in commerce and science in the Hispanic world. Between 1765 and 1821 more than eighty economic societies were formed throughout Spain and the colonies. Ruiz Gonzalez and Vicens Vives believe that they were inspired by the example of the Royal Basque Society.[207] R. J. Shafer acknowledges that the Royal Basque Society was the earliest and that the second eldest, the Madrid Society, was founded by Campomanes, a member of the Royal Basque Society.[208] Shafer insists that the remaining societies were probably suggested by, and modeled along, the lines of the Madrid one.[209] While this may have been the case, it should be noted that Shafer himself, without any special concern with the possible influence of Basque ethnic loyalties, provides evidence that members of the Royal Basque Society,[210] officials of such Basque-controlled trading companies as the Caracas Company[211] and the Philippines Company,[212] and both teachers[213] and students[214] of the seminary of Vergara were instrumental in founding some of the other economic societies. Shafer does not discuss the fact that the memberships of many of the other societies contained large numbers of Old World Basques and Creoles of Basque descent. There is also the negative evidence of the inventory of the library holdings of the Guatemalan Economic Society, which contains many works from the Royal Basque Society, but not a single item from the Madrid one.[215] Finally, the Royal Basque Society may have had as many as 2,000 members during its existence, a significant figure indeed when we consider that, by Shafer's own estimate, the eighty societies embraced a total of between 5,000 and 10,000 individuals between 1765 and 1821 (the Madrid Society had 450 members in 1795).[216] Thus, the subsequent history of the Royal Basque Society and the others, as well as the historical importance of the Basque role in Spanish commerce (and particularly during the eighteenth century), make it difficult to accept Shafer's conclusion concerning the founding of the Royal Basque Society, that "It was in part an 'accident' that the first such body was organized in the Basque country."[217]

examples that are high points, somewhat sensational in nature. This is partly a function of the sources. Events such as the race war at Potosí or the rebellion of the *marañones* captured the imaginations of contemporaries and historians alike. The concern of the contemporaries generates the weight of documentation that itself serves as an attraction to later historians. By contrast, an understanding of the everyday lives of ordinary men remains considerably murkier. Thus, the sprinkling of Basque heroes and antiheroes that dots the annals of Latin American history overshadows the lesser accomplishments of thousands, probably even hundreds of thousands, of Basques who entered into the Spanish and French New World colonial ventures.

In one sense, however, the impressionistic weight of the examples should not be discounted out of hand. Both Basques and non-Basques were aware of a kind of black legend of conflict in the history of their mutual dealings. Such awareness of past problems could scarcely help but color their actual relations and their anticipations concerning the likely course of future ones. Most of the New World events that we have considered reinforced this view.

What, then, was the substance of the "black legend"? From a Basque perspective, their incorporation into the Spanish and French nations was something less than voluntary and not entirely desirable. Political dependency upon the Spanish and French crowns, even if not complete, must have occasioned ambivalence in a people who regarded itself as superior to its neighbors. To this day, there is racial antagonism and elitism reflected in the terms that Basques use in referring to the surrounding populations.

With respect to their social and political structuring, there was sharp contrast between the Basques and the respective larger societies. Basque social organization reflected a strong measure of democratic idealism, whereas a feudal heritage characterized Spanish and French societies. Unaffected by the seigneurial proscriptions of physical labor and participation in commerce, hardworking peasants, fishermen and shrewd businessmen wielded considerable political power in the Basque country.

Viewed from the perspective of the wider society, the Basques were latecomers to the national alliance and the least committed to it. In their role as merchants, Basques were seen as opportunists, middlemen who exchanged Mediterranean products and Castilian wool for the goods of northern Europe and who profited at everyone's expense.

The fact that all Basques were entitled to noble status (yet few Basques understood or espoused the values and life style of the nobility) was a potential source of tension. The Basques were resented both by Spaniards denied such status and by those who possessed it but whose lives were dedicated to preserving its values and accoutrements. It is in this light that one may understand the epigraph from *Don Quixote* employed at the beginning of the present chapter. From Don Quixote's Castilian viewpoint, noble status *(hidalguía)* and gentility *(caballería)* were synonymous. For the *vizcaíno*, his personal comportment had nothing to do with his claim to nobility. As in many disputes, the parties to it were simply talking past one another. But Cervantes's stereotype of the precocious, uncouth Basque who, although of obviously* modest origins, laid claim to aristocratic privileges, is significant. Stereotypes generally contain some element of truth, even though they are, by definition, a distortion of it. Cervantes, who wrote toward the beginning of the sixteenth century, presents the *vizcaíno* as the representative of a rustic people with access to noble privilege but without any commitment to its attendant life style and social pretensions. At the same time, he reveals the undercurrent of Spanish resentment of such behavior.

Furthermore, it is certain that common kinship and ties of ethnicity served as channels along which rank, favor, and mutual assistance flowed from Basque to Basque, providing the individual with a measure of ethnic group support in his confrontation with the uncertainties of the New World colonial economy and society.

All of these characteristics served to define a role for Basques in New World colonial history that for others was as galling to live with as it was impossible to live without. The entire colonial venture leaned heavily, though certainly not entirely, upon Basque maritime skills, propensity for hard physical labor, and devotion to task in the face of adversity, as well as their special business acumen. If Basque energies might be turned against crown interests, as was claimed by Bishop Salcedo, they could also serve as the last vital link in maintaining crown authority in the face of the ever present danger of seces-

---

*The language employed by the Basque in addressing Don Quixote is of such an awkward and ungrammatical nature as to defy direct translation.

sion of the colonies, as was the case with the Company of Caracas. If men like Lope de Aguirre could become the archetypical traitor and secessionist in Spain's colonial history, others like Francisco de Ibarra and Juan de Oñate added considerable territory to the Spanish empire.

In sum, the role of the Basques in New World colonial history may only be understood against the backdrop of prior Old World historical events that provided a "group history" to the day-to-day relations between those Basques and non-Basques who participated in the colonial ventures. To this background must be added the characterological differences which distinguished the Basque from his fellow colonists. This combination of antecedence and character obtained for many Basques a measure of success while at the same time making them the objects of charges of elitist, exclusivist, and even subversive behavior. This accusation of ethnic group elitism hounded the Basques throughout their involvement in the colonial period of New World history. It was not until the independence movements of the early nineteenth century that the image of the Basques as held in the wider society of Latin America was modified.

CHAPTER THREE

Sheepmen of
South America

*De los cien millones de ovejas y de los cuarenta millones de bovinos
que pacen en aquella Arcadia infinita [La Argentina], . . .
el mayor número pertenece a los vascos y a los vascos americanos
originarios de la raza eusquérica. No hay exageración al afirmar
que no menos del setenta por ciento de esta enorme riqueza se
halla en las recias manos de los hijos de Aitor.*[1]

*(Of the one hundred million sheep and of the forty million cows that
graze in that immense Arcadia [Argentina], . . . the greater
part belong to the Basques and the Basque Americans descended
from the Basque race. It is not an exaggeration to affirm that no
less than seventy percent of this enormous wealth is found in
the capable hands of the sons of Aitor.)*

THE NEW IMMIGRANTS

In the early years of the nineteenth century, independence
movements swept through Spain's New World colonies. By

1825 all of the continental or mainland former colonies had achieved their autonomy, and Spain's influence in the Americas was reduced to a foothold in the Antilles. The loss of the major portion of her American empire interrupted Spanish emigration to the New World. The previous opportunities for Iberian-born persons in the colonial civil, military, and ecclesiastical structures were gone. Of equal significance for the Basques, who had heavy involvement in merchant marine activities, commerce between Spain and the New World was reduced to a trickle.

Predictably, xenophobia,* and particularly anti-Spanish sentiment, characterized the early years of Latin American independence. Spanish nationals were faced with the choice of either leaving the new Latin American nations or renouncing their Old World citizenship. Moreover, Spain, exhausted by three centuries of colonial and military drain on her population, pursued a policy of restricting emigration for the first half of the nineteenth century in order to replenish the populations of depleted agricultural districts.[3]

Despite restrictive policies on both sides of the Atlantic, Basque emigration to the Río de la Plata area (present-day Argentina and Uruguay) continued throughout the second quarter of the nineteenth century. There are records of French Basques disembarking in Buenos Aires in 1825. In 1829 the Argentine government hired a police force made up largely of foreign mercenaries to secure the city of Buenos Aires. A large contingent of Basques served in this force, some of them settling in the area permanently.[4] However, Latin American xenophobia reached its high point under the Argentine dictatorship of General Rosas (1830–52), which cut off all but clandestine immigration into Argentina.†

By 1830 the main thrust of Basque emigration to the Río de la Plata area was directed at Montevideo. In 1832 agents of an English company, Lafone and Wilson, recruited French Basques for an agricultural colony in Uruguay.[6] According to Defontaines, there was sufficient feedback of successful

---

*Documents from Buenos Aires detail the case of a knifing in 1842 that resulted when three Basques were ordered to stop speaking in their language by two Argentines. One of the Basques was gravely wounded in the attack. It is evident from the accounts that the victims were French Basques, since it was the French chargé d'affaires who filed official protests.[2]

†Such immigration could reach substantial proportions. For example, there were four thousand French nationals residing in Buenos Aires province in 1839 and twelve thousand—three times as many—by 1842.[5]

Basque emigrants from Uruguay to the French Basque area by 1836 to convert the former trickle of emigration into a movement involving thousands of persons.[7]

By 1838 there were local agencies in the French Basque area devoted exclusively to recruiting and transporting emigrants to Río de la Plata. In the event that the potential emigrant was without funds, he could look to the shipping agency for a loan.[8] The Brie brothers of Ispoure employed their two boats (the *Marie-Catherine* and the *Auguste-Victorine*) to service French Basque and Béarnais emigration to South America. By 1840, according to F. Brie, "emigration from France consisted largely of the departures of Basque families."[9]

Defontaines notes that 10,200 French nationals, the majority of whom were Basques and Béarnais, embarked for Montevideo between 1839 and 1842. He estimates the Basque colony in 1842* in Montevideo alone at fourteen thousand individuals.[11] In a siege of the city in April 1845, a Basque regiment formed part of its defense force.[12]

Official statistics given in table 2 reflect the numbers of departures of French Basque emigrants whose destination was the Río de la Plata area.

TABLE 2
FRENCH BASQUES EMIGRATING TO RIO DE LA PLATA AREA

Year	Total Number of Emigrants
1848	672
1849	1,012
1850	1,807
1851–52	not available
1853	1,206
1854	2,838
1855	1,942

Source: Michel, *Le pays Basque*, p. 193.

In 1851, a Béarnais doctor wrote a pamphlet published by the Argentine government for distribution in the Pyrenees: "The Extinction of Agricultural Poverty through Colonization in the

---

*By 1842 the movement of French Basques and Béarnais to the Río de la Plata countries had reached sufficient proportions to attract the attention of writers. In that year Barrère published a work in Pau entitled *Emigration à Montevideo et à Buenos Aires*.[10]

Province of La Plata."[13] This French-language publication received wide distribution in the French Basque country. The Argentine consul in Bayonne (Célestin Roby) also actively recruited potential emigrants for his country. In 1852 alone Roby is said to have sent out 2,800 emigrants from Bayonne to Argentina.[14] By this time, recruiters were combing the interior villages in search of emigrants. In the province of Soule the population remained stable between 1836 and 1841, but between 1841 and 1851 it declined by fifteen hundred persons, and from 1851 to 1856 there was a total loss of 6,633 inhabitants with respect to the 1836 figures.[15] In the province of Labourd between 1846 and 1856 there was a decline of 2,916 inhabitants. While these figures reflect the ravages of a cholera epidemic in 1855, Michel attributes most of the loss to emigration.[16]

Statistics on the emigration of Spanish Basques to the New World during the first half of the nineteenth century are lacking. In 1842, however, twenty-three persons received licenses to emigrate to Montevideo through just one Guipuzcoan notary (Villa de Oñate).[17]* That such emigration was significant enough to cause a local "problem" is seen in the fact that by 1852 the bishop of Pamplona felt compelled to author a pamphlet entitled "Circular In Which the System of Hoodwinking Persons of Both Sexes in Order to Conduct Them to the American Continent under the Seductive Promises of Establishing a Fortune and a Happy Future Is Demonstrated As Being Immoral."[20]

By the 1850s there were profound changes on both sides of the Atlantic in attitudes towards emigration. The revolution of

---

*See Appendix One for a model document describing how one of the Basque personages of the American West, Pedro de Altube, emigrated to Montevideo in 1845, sailing from Bilbao on the *Irurac Bat*.[18] The process of acquiring a license required that someone in Europe guarantee both the fare and the character of the emigrant. The purpose of the latter was to make someone in Europe responsible for possible hidden debts of the departee. The emigrant was to pay the passage money to the shipping company out of his first earnings. The underwriter might be a relative, an agent, or a commercial bank. In Pedro de Altube's case his brother underwrote the departure with a portion of his farmstead. That such arrangements did not always work out satisfactorily is seen in a newspaper ad placed in *L'International* (Buenos Aires) in the May 2 to May 30, 1855, issues by the administrator of the estate of Michel Oyenard of Montevideo. The announcement requests that the persons who came in 1840, 1841, and 1842 on the boats *Ville de Bayonne, Aigrette, Cyrus,* and *Inca* pay the passage money advanced for them more than ten years earlier or suffer the legal consequences.[19]

1852 in Argentina toppled the Rosas dictatorship and brought Urquiza (himself of Basque descent) to power by 1854. Urquiza was from the Entre Ríos district of the nation, one of the major foci of earlier Basque settlement in Argentina. He was influenced by the thought of the famous Argentine-Basque essayist Alberdi, who maintained that "In America, to govern is to populate."* Consequently, Urquiza initiated an open immigration policy, but he was particularly concerned with attracting more Basques. In one of his proimmigration discourses he said, "it is necessary to depopulate the Pyrenees."[22]

Meanwhile, the official Spanish attitude toward emigration underwent change in the mid-nineteenth century. Advances in medical technology, and particularly the techniques of vaccination, were felt almost immediately throughout Europe, and the population of Spain began to rise dramatically. From a national total of 10,541,000 inhabitants in 1797, the population grew to 15,455,000 by 1857, or an increase of almost half.[23] By royal decree, all restrictions on Spanish emigration to South America were lifted in 1853.[24]

If the 1850s witnessed liberalization of Spanish controls over emigration, the converse was true of the attitude of the French government. In 1855 a commission was established to control both emigration and the active recruitment of emigrants in the Basque country. Official reports to the commission state that the French government in 1855 "had no information concerning the Basque emigration that embarks from the ports of Bayonne and Bordeaux."[25] The same commission expressed the fear that, "in certain communes, the major portion of the farmlands would be abandoned for lack of laborers."[26] In 1862 official testimony stated that in the preceding fifteen years there had been twenty thousand passports for Buenos Aires and Montevideo issued in the department of Basses-Pyrénées (the French Basque country and Béarn), and that in many cases a single passport issued to the male head of a family masked the departure of three or four persons leaving as a family unit.[27] French Basque emigration throughout the remainder of the nineteenth century, both to Latin America and the American West, attests to the ineffectiveness of French governmental controls.

---

*In 1810, or on the eve of independence, the European population of present-day Argentina stood at a scant 405,611 persons. In the same discourse Alberdi noted that "[to increase] population is simultaneously the goal and the means."[21]

By the 1850s emigration of both Spanish and French Basques involved thousands of persons annually. The major portion of this emigration was directed toward Latin America, although, as we shall see, by the late 1840s it also included the new destination of California. The notable difference between this movement and the earlier colonial emigration of Basques to the New World was that it was no longer constituted by elitist missionaries, mercenaries, mariners, and merchants. Peasants and the urban lower classes predominated in this search for new opportunity, and they were disposed if need be to enter the lowest rungs of the New World socioeconomic scale.

Whatever its reality in terms of sheer numbers of emigrants, Basque emigration in the first half of the nineteenth century was to pale before the veritable torrent of the second half. Louis Etcheverry notes that official passenger lists for emigration from Bayonne indicate that, between 1832 and 1884, 64,227 persons emigrated from the department of Basses-Pyrénées. He estimates that two-thirds of the total was Basque. Of French Basque emigrants departing prior to 1856, 72 percent went to the Río de la Plata area. After 1856 fully four-fifths of French Basque emigration was to that region. The destinations of the remainder included Chile, Brazil, Peru, Bolivia, Mexico, California, Louisiana,* and Algiers. Etcheverry also remarks that French Basque farmers and sheepherders preferred the Río de la Plata and California, whereas merchants and artisans made up the bulk of French Basque emigration to the other areas.[28]

The impact of emigration upon French Basque rural and urban areas varied at different periods of time. According to Etcheverry, urban artisans made up the bulk of French Basque emigration until the 1850s. Between 1846 and 1856 the urban population in the French Basque area declined by 11 percent, whereas the rural populace diminished by 3 percent. In subsequent periods the trends were reversed. From 1865 to 1874 artisans and other urban dwellers made up only 15 percent of the departees, whereas 53 percent of the emigrants listed their profession as "agriculturalist."[29]

---

*New Orleans was a port of entry for some persons whose final destination was actually California. Prior to establishment of the transcontinental railway, disembarking in New Orleans meant a shorter overland trip to the American West than an east coast disembarcation. Similarly, the overland trip from Louisiana was preferred by many to the several months required to round the South American continent in a boat.

Overall, nineteenth-century emigratory pressure seriously affected the populations of some French Basque agricultural communities. For example, the population of Saint-Jean-le-Vieux (Basse Navarre) went from 1,434 inhabitants in 1792 to 1,135 persons by 1856. By 1896 it had further declined to 884 inhabitants, or a net loss for a century on the order of 38 percent.[30] Etcheverry notes that one French Basque village declined from 1,047 inhabitants in 1841 to 920 inhabitants in 1901. Since births exceeded deaths by 388 during the period, the actual population loss was 515 persons. He attributes nine-tenths of this loss to emigration.[31] Gachiteguy provides even more startling statistics for the villages of Aldudes, Arneguy, and Esterençuby. It is his belief that this small corner of Basse Navarre had the highest rate of out-migration of any area in the Basque country. He finds that of all eighteen-year-old males born between 1862 and 1865 in Aldudes, 87 percent emigrated. Of those eighteen-year-olds born between 1876 and 1879, the majority in all three villages emigrated (Aldudes: 84 percent, Arneguy: 65.3 percent, and Esterençuby: 66.7 percent). Of those who left, less than half returned to establish a family in the Basque country.[32]

The official statistics on French Basque emigration are incomplete on two counts. First, by the 1870s and 1880s many French Basques departed for the New World from the port of Bordeaux rather than from Bayonne.[33] By the late 1880s there were twenty-three travel agencies in Bordeaux servicing Basque emigration to Río de la Plata, working in conjunction with agents of the Uruguayan government and travel bureaus that were actively recruiting potential emigrants throughout the French and Spanish Basque country.[34]

The second factor, illegal departures, is not reflected in official passenger lists. During the nineteenth century both Spanish and French Basques were politically alienated from their respective national governments, as exemplified by the willingness of Basques to evade military service. As early as 1842, the *Conseil Général* of the department of Basses Pyrénées denounced the departures of young men who had been called up for military service.[35]

By the 1850s the French Basques, despite the fact that they constituted a tiny fraction of the national population, accounted for almost one-half of France's evaders. Between 1852 and 1855 there were 1,311 evaders in the French Basque provinces. The French government refused passports to young men who were nineteen years of age, but the measure proved ineffective, since men who were denied passports could slip across the Spanish border and depart from a Spanish port.[36] For the illegal French Basque emigrant the Spanish Basque port of Pasajes proved particularly popular. Boats leaving Bayonne with legal emigrants would put in at Pasajes to take on illegal ones prior to crossing the Atlantic.[37]

Evasion of military service was equally widespread among Spanish Basques. For the years 1913 and 1914 fully 20.76 percent and 22.09 percent, respectively, of all young draftees in Spain failed to report for military service,[38] most of them seeking escape through overseas emigration. The figures in the Spanish Basque provinces, which were close to the French frontier, were considerably higher.* For Spanish Basques the ports of Bayonne and, particularly, Bordeaux provided the means of departure that were denied by the Spanish government. The numerous clandestine departures on both sides of the frontier undermined the accuracy of official emigration statistics.

In light of the above factors Etcheverry estimates total French Basque and Béarnais emigration between 1832 and 1884 at seventy-five thousand to eighty thousand persons, of whom two-thirds, or about fifty thousand, were Basques.[39] Pierre Lhande sees the rate of emigration between 1884 and 1907 as superior to that in the earlier decades. In the year 1905 alone, 3,500 French Basques and Béarnais were entered on the official passenger lists, most of whom declared Argentina as their destination.[40] He places emigration from the French Basque country during the period from 1832 to 1907 at over one hundred thousand persons,[41] an enormous figure from an area whose total population for the period fluctuated around one hundred twenty thousand inhabitants. Spanish Basques were not subjected to national military conscription until 1876, when most of the privileges guaranteed by the *fueros* were abolished as a result of the Basques' defeat in the Second Carlist War.

This picture of a high rate of emigration and relative overall population stability, which characterized nineteenth-century French Basque demographic trends, does not hold true for the Spanish Basque area. In the latter, there was marked population growth throughout the period despite a high rate of emigration.

*He also comments that emigration from the Spanish Basque provinces was at least twice as great.[42]

In 1802 the population of Navarra was 226,467. By 1867 it had increased to 300,328,[43] a figure that remained fairly constant for the remainder of the century: by 1900 the population stood at 307,699.[44] In 1787 the population of Guipúzcoa was 120,176 persons; by 1820 this figure had declined to 112,283 persons (a drop that one author attributes to the effects of the Napoleonic wars).[45] By 1860, despite emigration pressure, the population of the province had grown to 162,547. By 1900 a further increase brought the total to 195,850 inhabitants.[46] The population of Vizcaya, 160,579 in 1857, had grown to 311,361 by 1900.[47] The province of Alava went from a population of 77,475 in 1823 to 96,385 persons in 1900.[48]

While overall population increase characterized all four Spanish Basque provinces during the nineteenth century, not all sectors of the society were so affected. Many rural villages, despite developments favoring population growth (such as a declining mortality rate, increases in the rate of longevity, and a fairly stable fertility rate), experienced population loss. The magnitude of such losses during the second half of the nineteenth century in selected Vizcayan villages may be appreciated by examining table 3. These villages are ones with a known tradition of overseas emigration, particularly to the American West.

TABLE 3
POPULATION LOSS IN SELECTED VIZCAYAN VILLAGES,
1860 – 1920

Name of Village	Population in Actual Residence in 1860	Population in Actual Residence in 1920	Population with Right of Residence in 1920	Net Loss or Gain in Population in Actual Residence since 1860
Villaro	912	792	865	−120
Kortezubi	808	786	879	− 22
Ea	1,289	1,394	1,723* (in 1910)	+105 (in 1910)
Mendata	1,153	1,006	1,119	−147
Navarniz	655	606	647	− 49
Guizaburuaga	338	316	379	− 22
Murélaga	1,419	1,116	1,297	−303

Source: Echegaray, "Provincia de Vizcaya," pp. 740, 797, 800, 828, 847, 874, 894.

*In explaining the wide disparity between the population in residence and that with the right of residence, Echegaray states, "it is due to the large number of sons from this *anteiglesia* who are dedicated to navigation and, above all, to those who emigrate temporarily to California."[49]

Statistics from the Navarrese village of Echalar show a population decline from 1,724 inhabitants in 1842 to 1,397 persons in 1905. That this loss was in part due to overseas emigration is seen clearly in an 1880 document in the village archives, which states that of a total population of 1,381 persons, 142 had emigrated recently* to Argentina, 54 to France, 37 to Cuba, 16 to Uruguay, 6 to California, and 1 to Brazil.[50]

It is clear that in many Spanish Basque villages the rate of departures equalled or outstripped the rate of natural population increase during the nineteenth century. However, is rate of departure to be construed as rate of overseas emigration? For the French Basque provinces, with their overall population stability and relative lack of urban-industrial centers, it would appear that the two are closely related. However, in the Spanish Basque case, there is an alternative possibility that must be considered.

While Navarra and Alava experienced little industrialization and urbanization in the nineteenth century, the same cannot be said for Vizcaya and Guipúzcoa. Table 4 shows the demographic trends of the major urban center in each of the four provinces.

TABLE 4
URBAN POPULATION TRENDS IN SPANISH BASQUE COUNTRY

Name of City	Population in 1857	Population in 1900
Pamplona (Navarra)	22,702	28,885
Vitoria (Alava)	15,569	30,701
Bilbao (Vizcaya)	17,649	83,306*
San Sebastián (Guipúzcoa)	9,484	37,812

Source: Nadal, in Vicens Vives, ed., *Historia*, pp. 53–54.
*A growth due in part to annexation of surrounding towns.[51]

Thus, whereas the population of Pamplona gained slightly and that of Vitoria doubled, San Sebastián and Bilbao both quadrupled in forty-three years.

After the Second Carlist War (1872–76), the iron ore and steel production of Vizcaya began to increase dramatically, in

---

*It should be remembered that 1880 immediately follows termination of the Second Carlist War. Echalar suffered tremendously during the conflict. In fact, the last battle of the war took place in the village.

part because of technological advances and a growing world demand for metals, but also due to the extensive investment of foreign and Basque capital in industry. In the year 1877 alone production doubled to over one million tons of iron ore. In 1899, 9.5 million tons of iron ore were exported.[52] At the same time, Basque-owned steel-processing plants were established. At first these were family-controlled enterprises, but they quickly became broader-based corporations. The powerful steel manufacturing concern of *Altos Hornos* was formed in Bilbao in 1882.

The economy of Vizcaya in the nineteenth century was bolstered further by the maintenance of the tradition of shipbuilding. From 1848 on, Basque shipbuilding yards led the nation in production. From 1841 to 1859 Basque shipyards turned out an average of twelve ships annually, whereas between 1855 and 1879, the annual production average for the rest of Spain was just 4.44 units per year.[53] This shipbuilding activity in turn laid the basis for a formidable Basque-owned merchant fleet. In 1886, 101 boats with a total tonnage of 151,000 operated out of Bilbao, a figure that was second in Spain only to that of the port of Barcelona.[54] By the end of the century Bilbao possessed no less than 39 percent of Spain's total tonnage.[55] By 1885 the Basque-owned shipping company *La Vasco-Andaluza* controlled most of Spain's coastal shipping trade in the Mediterranean.[56]

Basque commerce was further stimulated in the second half of the nineteenth century when Basque financiers founded banking concerns that were to control economic interests throughout the Spanish nation.[57] In 1890 a stock exchange was established in Bilbao.[58]

The upswing in heavy industry, ancillary light industry, and commerce in Vizcaya (and to a somewhat lesser degree in Guipúzcoa) reestablished the area as one of the major industrial zones of the Iberian peninsula. This fact poses a major anomaly for the present study. Why did Spanish Basques emigrate to the Argentine *pampas* and deserts of the American West, areas with underdeveloped economies, when there was apparently burgeoning economic opportunity on their own doorstep? In point of fact, it would appear that an appreciable number of rural Basques did enter the mines, factories, and boats of the booming Vizcayan economy. A large segment of Navarrese emigration, in particular, was directed at the sister provinces of Vizcaya and Guipúzcoa.[59] At the same time, it is evident that in the nineteenth century the industrial zones of the Basque provinces became one of the most favored targets for migrants from other regions of Spain. Between 1797 and 1900 the three Basque provinces of Vizcaya, Guipúzcoa, and Alava grew from 2.6 percent of the national population to 3.2 percent.[60] This growth was realized despite a highly developed nineteenth-century pattern of emigration in the native-born Basque population. So the question remains: why, by the second half of the nineteenth century, were the Basque provinces converted into an area of both in-migration *and* out-migration?

In attempting to account for the fact that Basques preferred overseas emigration to work in the few local factories in the French Basque area (where, as in Vizcaya, the labor force was largely "foreign"), Pierre Lhande states simply that the Basque is a farmer by choice and as such he is reluctant to settle in cities.[61] It is apparent that there was a shift in this attitude during the first three decades of the twentieth century, since Lefebvre, writing in 1933, notes that French Basques were availing themselves of job opportunities in the industries of Bayonne and Mauléon.[62]* Around the turn of the present century, however, there was an entirely different attitude toward city life extant in Basque rural society. To be an *echekojaun*, or "lord of the household," was possibly the most prestigious role available to a man. Conversely, city dwellers were referred to as *kalekuak* ("those of the street") or *errikuak* ("those of the town"), terms that carried a pejorative connotation of desperation, proneness to dishonesty, and a life of misery. Rural life was eulogized in folk songs and sayings as an existence that guaranteed personal dignity and independence.[63] Life in the city, on the other hand, meant toil under the control of others. Hard work was not the demeaning factor, since a willingness to engage in hard physical labor has always been highly esteemed in rural Basque society. Rather, it was the loss of personal autonomy, as implied by working in the despised factory system. It might be added that working conditions, as well as living conditions, in the nineteenth-century industrial districts of the Basque country were far from ideal, facts that were well known among rural Basques.

---

*The same may be said of attitudes in the Spanish Basque provinces. By the 1950s, it was a common practice for rural male Spanish Basques to sign labor contracts to herd sheep in the American West in order to acquire savings that would permit them to purchase housing in the factory zones of the Basque country as the first step in seeking industrial employment.

This explanation in itself may not fully account for local reticence to work in local industry, for it would be difficult to argue that working and living conditions were any easier in the sheep camps of Nevada or the Argentine *pampas*. However, there was one salient difference. In the Basque country there was little possibility of expanding the economic base of agriculture, due to an almost total lack of available uninhabited land,* and the major portion of the economic benefits of industrialization remained in the hands of an extremely small entrepreneurial class of businessmen and financiers. The New World, on the other hand, held the promise that after years of menial work one might eventually become a member of the entrepreneurial class in an expanding frontier economy. It was not that the short-term picture in the Americas was more promising than that at home; rather, it was the greater possibility of economic mobility over the long run that proved irresistible to so many Basque emigrants.

So, despite well-developed local opportunities for wage-earning in industry, a condition that attracted workers from throughout Iberia to the Basque country, Spanish Basques continued to emigrate to the New World. In the official lists of overseas emigration from Spanish ports between 1911 and 1915, some 2,217 emigrants list their natal province as Alava; 1,871 were from Guipúzcoa; 6,750 from Navarra; and 7,709 from Vizcaya, or a total of 18,547 persons in a five-year period.[65] It is also clear that illegal departures of military evaders from French ports was a major problem at the time. Furthermore, the emigration report concludes that many legal departees were leaving from Bordeaux and Liverpool† since there were better shipping combinations and accommodations from those ports to North America. By one estimate, fully 50 percent of all Spanish nationals shipping out of French ports were Basque.[66] If these considerations are taken into account, the reality of Spanish Basque emigration between 1911 and 1915 was considerably greater than the official statistics imply.

---

*It might be argued that improvements in cropping techniques and technology expanded agricultural production on the same land base. However, this increased productivity was narrowly limited and partially offset by a spiraling level of material aspirations in the rural society that was the direct result of modernization in the nearby industrial areas.[64]

†It was common by that time for some emigrants to travel from Vizcaya to Liverpool to await transatlantic accommodations. There was at least one Basque hotel in Liverpool which serviced this traffic.

Although the economic opportunities of the New World provided a powerful stimulus for Basque emigrants, there were also several local stimulants other than an abhorrence of factory work that encouraged emigration from Old World Basque society.

Political considerations caused many Basques to depart. During the French Revolution the French Basque provinces were largely in opposition to the centralist philosophy of the victorious revolutionaries. As a consequence, the area was distrusted, subjected to military control, and stripped of its ancient privileges guaranteed under the *fors*. Many persons were deprived of their land and livestock and interred in concentration camps by the revolutionary officials; some even faced the guillotine.[67]

Immediate disruptions in the Basque country attributable to the French Revolution and its aftermath were restricted largely to the French side of the frontier. Napoleon's rise to power, however, had a much wider impact. The Basque country constituted the major corridor for Napoleon's drive into the Iberian peninsula, as well as the major route of retreat in the face of pressure applied by the forces under the command of Wellington. Several engagements of the Napoleonic wars were fought in the Basque country, and the Basque populace was subjected to recruitment and requisitioning by both sides.

In 1833 a civil war, known as the First Carlist War, erupted in Spain. In response to the policies of the liberal government in Madrid, which was both centralist and anticlerical in its philosophy, the deeply Catholic and regionalist Basque provinces supported the claim of a pretender to the throne. The struggle broke with all the virulence that characterizes civil conflicts. To finance the war, most of the rural areas of the Basque country were subjected to heavy taxation and military conscription by the Carlist forces. Many of the battles were fought in the Basque provinces. The defeat of the Carlists in 1839 saddled the Basques with the payment of heavy war retributions. Under the Treaty of Vergara, the Basque *fueros* were to be respected, but only insofar as they did not conflict with Spanish national interest.

Meanwhile, the French Revolution of 1848 once again found the French Basques alienated from the revolutionary goals and conjured up memories of the excesses committed in the Basque provinces during the earlier revolution. While these fears were not realized, they nevertheless stimulated departures from the area.

By 1872 the Carlist forces in Spain were once again sufficiently powerful to trigger a civil conflict. The Second Carlist War was a repeat of the first. Initial successes of the Carlist forces, financed and realized through heavy taxation and military conscription in rural Basque areas, were reversed. The victorious governmental forces stationed an army of occupation in the Basque country and exacted heavy retributions.[68] This time the *fueros* were all but abolished by the central government.

Thus, nineteenth-century events provided ample reason for Basque political alienation. For the politically sophisticated Basque, these reversals caused deep personal anguish and frustration. For the apolitical populace, sheer fear of warfare and resentment of the abuses of both sides to the various conflicts were sufficient reasons to seek escape.[69]

To the litany of nineteenth-century Basque political disasters might be added the natural disaster of famine that swept the Basque country in 1846−47, when the corn crop all but failed, causing hardship for the urban and rural populace alike.[70]

A number of factors leading to disruption in traditional economic activities were also stimulators of emigration. The Industrial Revolution of the nineteenth century might have spurred overall growth of urban areas but, at the same time, it displaced both rural and urban artisans, who found that their handcrafted products were unable to compete successfully with cheaper manufactured items. Similarly, in southern and central Navarra and Alava, where the economy was dominated by large agricultural estates, employing hundreds of workers on a seasonal basis, advances in agricultural technology undermined the demand for labor.

By the middle of the nineteenth century another traditional Basque economic activity, contraband traffic across the French-Spanish frontier, suffered a setback. New tariff agreements between Spain and France removed much of the former profit, as did the installation of a rail line between the two countries, which lowered transportation costs considerably.[71]

Undoubtedly the single most important factor stimulating emigration was the interplay between land-tenure arrangements and inheritance practices in rural Basque society. Throughout the French Basque area, Vizcaya, Guipúzcoa, and parts of northern Alava and Navarra, peasant farmsteads were the rule.*

---

*This is the area we have defined as the northern ecological zone in chapter 1.

Each farmstead usually supported a single family in agriculture. In many cases the peasants owned the land outright, but rental arrangements were also common. Renter families were, to a degree, less committed to their circumstances and hence were potential candidates for emigration. However, Basque common-law practices that made eviction of renters difficult and that allowed the selected heir of a renter family to continue upon the farmstead, tended to keep some of the landless in their natal villages.

In rural Basque society there has been striking continuity of landholdings. The mountainous nature of the terrain severely limits the amount of available tillable land, and since at least the eighteenth century there has been little expansion in the number of farmsteads in most Basque villages. At the same time there has been strong emphasis in Basque common law that each farmstead should support a single family in agriculture. It has been felt that farmsteads should not be fragmented, either through divisive sales or inheritance practices. Consequently, most Basque farmsteads, as identifiable and unmodified units on the landscape, have a history lasting several centuries.[72] The key to this continuity has been a system of inheritance whereby, in each generation, a single heir to the farmstead was selected from among the former owner's (or renter's) offspring. This practice was guaranteed under the *fueros*, which also stipulated that the siblings of the selected heir could be disinherited, although in practice they were provided with dowries.

The manner in which the heir has been selected varies from place to place within rural Basque society. Caro Baroja reports the custom in some Navarrese villages of selecting a female as heiress while encouraging her to marry an "indiano" (i.e., a male who is returning from the Indies).[73] In certain communities of Vizcaya the heir is determined according to the principle of male primogeniture; in parts of Navarra the heir or heiress is selected on the basis of individual merit and without reference to the candidate's sex or sibling age order.[74] Until quite recently little attention was paid within their natal households to the preparation of departing siblings for their careers elsewhere, with the exception that they were provided with a dowry. If it were determined that a young man was to leave to join his uncle's business in the New World, he might be sent to the parish priest or to a local school teacher for private lessons in Spanish, accounting, and penmanship, but usually for only a few months before his departure. Similarly, young men who aspired to enter administrative posts commonly studied for a few years at places like the University of Salamanca. With the exception of those studying for the religious life, however, young Basques received very little formal education in their home communities.

The disinherited pursued several alternatives in life. If they remained celibate and were willing to live under the authority of the heir, they had the right to remain in their natal household throughout their lifetime. There was always the preferred possibility of marrying the heir in another farming household. A frequent choice was to profess religious vows. But for many the only alternative was migration, either to a nearby urban area or overseas.

It is this structural feature of rural Basque society that provided the bulk of the persons who participated in the Basque activities of New World colonial history. Its traditional organization made rural Basque society a natural seedbed of candidates for emigration. The nineteenth-century demographic pressures that favored population growth throughout Europe certainly enlarged this Basque emigratory pool. However, in the late eighteenth century and throughout the nineteenth century, there were developments that disrupted the traditional system and thereby enhanced the "natural" out-migration of individuals and families.*

The French Revolution, which abolished the *fors*, also introduced the Napoleonic Code of inheritance into the French Basque area. Under the new system the Basque farmstead was to be divided equally in each generation among the legitimate offspring of the former owner. In many instances families used the subterfuge of simulated land sales among siblings to continue the traditional practice of indivisible transfer of farm ownership.[76] By as early as the 1850s the French Basques viewed emigration as a means of salvaging intact the family patrimony. One member of the family would go out to the New World to earn sufficient funds to "purchase" the shares in the farm owned by his siblings.[77] He might then return to it himself or stay on in Latin America, turning over complete ownership of the farm to one of his siblings. In many instances the emigrant remained celibate, retired at an advanced age, and, after decades in the New World, returned to the farm that his efforts had saved from division and ruination.

---

*The rate of out-migration could differ considerably from one community to another, being conditioned by local factors.[75]

But this example required a degree of altruism impossible to achieve in every instance. In practice, many French Basque farmsteads were fragmented to the point that they would no longer support a family in agriculture. In other cases, one sibling would mortgage the property to pay off the claims of the others, running the risk of failure and forfeiture of the lands. Such forfeitures displaced entire families, some of which emigrated to the New World.

A second measure of the French government further exacerbated the situation. Traditionally, Basque peasants augmented their private resources by pasturing livestock on the village commons and otherwise exploiting their communally-held property. However, the state declared village commons to be the property of the national government, closing them to villagers or requiring the payment of fees for their use. This practice had the overall effect of impoverishing the French Basque rural economy.

The traditional inheritance practices of the Spanish Basque provinces of Alava and Guipúzcoa were similarly affected by abolishment of their *fueros* in the nineteenth century (only Vizcaya and Navarra continue to the present day to enjoy legal guarantees for their system of impartible inheritance of rural landholdings). Meanwhile, the traditional economic importance of access to the village commons was undermined in many Spanish Basque villages. In the aftermath of the Basque defeats in both Carlist wars, local villages were required to pay enormous war retributions to Madrid. In most cases these sums could be collected only through sale of the best tracts of the commons. In this fashion much communally-held property was sold to private parties, frequently to urban dwellers, thereby closing them to local peasant households.

Many authors have invoked atavism as an explanation of nineteenth- and early twentieth-century Basque emigration.[78] They argue that the Basque is by his very nature an adventurer; in the inner workings of the Basque psyche there lurks a kind of uneasiness and desire to see the world. Thus, the modern-day Basque is imbued with the same spirit that prompted Juan de Elcano to circumnavigate the globe, Saint Francis Xavier to evangelize the Orient, or Simón Bolívar to challenge an empire. The problem with atavism is that it is almost impossible either to prove or to disprove. Atavism implies a rupture in the flow of awareness, a tradition that resurfaces after being submerged for a period of time. Thus, the response is largely unconscious, difficult to account for, and hence hard to study.

There is an alternative interpretation that might account for a part of nineteenth-century Basque emigration: there was no discontinuity in the awareness of a former emigratory tradition. By the beginning of the nineteenth century practically every Basque village provided at least some evidence of a tradition of emigration to the New World. Money from the Indies had, over three centuries, embellished village churches and reconstructed village dwellings. Particularly in the seventeenth and eighteenth centuries, Basque villages underwent an extensive face lifting. Today's casual visitor is likely to be impressed by the monumental stone architecture of the dwellings. If he looks closely he might find emblazoned on a stone over a doorway, "This house rebuilt in 1721." The source of the funds is best stated in such an inscription still visible on a house in the village of Ainhoa that reads, "This house was redeemed by Maria de Gorritti, late mother of Jean Dolhagarry, from monies sent by him from the Indies; it may not be sold nor mortgaged; done in the year 1662."[79]

Few Basque villages lacked at least one fabulous success story of a native son in the New World as a part of their oral traditions. More importantly, few families in the Basque country lacked at least one relative residing in the Americas, and there was considerable feedback of former emigrants from the New World.* It is, therefore, scarcely an exaggeration to state that, in the nineteenth century, the New World (or more accurately two or three corners of the New World) constituted an integral part of the local frame of reference in each Basque village. Overseas emigration was as much a "traditional" alternative for those displaced in agriculture as was professing religious vows.

Thus, at least to a degree, nineteenth-century Basque emigration was due to simple momentum. The new emigratory movement fed in part upon a long-standing tradition irrespective of the particular economic and political realities of the moment. By the second half of the nineteenth century the embers of this tradition were being fanned by recruiters, some employed by shipping lines and others representing Latin American governments interested in immigrants. A potential Basque emigrant who lacked funds could even expect financial aid from these sources. At the same time, the practice of

---

*In a description of one French Basque village at the end of the nineteenth century, in 25 of the 156 inhabited households the male head was an *American*, "that is to say one of the former emigrants . . . who returned with savings and due to his savings married into one of the best families in the village."[80]

mortgaging the family farm to provide siblings of the selected heir with passage money was instituted on a widespread basis.

If we view nineteenth-century Basque emigration from the perspective of the New World host countries, it is even more difficult to determine with certainty the magnitude of the movement. An examination of Argentine statistics is of some help, although entering Basques were masked under their French or Spanish national identity. Between 1857 and 1915 Argentina alone received 4,445,760 immigrants, of whom 1,497,741 were Spanish nationals. Only 3,370 persons entered between 1857 and 1860, whereas 1,136,666 arrived after 1900.[81] The peak period of Spanish immigration in Argentina was 1901−10, when 652,658 Spaniards entered the country.

The Argentine statistics show that, between 1857 and 1924, 226,894 French nationals entered the country. This movement grew from a relatively modest figure of 9,476 immigrants between 1857 and 1870 to a peak of 93,843 for the decade 1881−90.[82]

The movement of Spanish and French nationals with respect to Argentina was not one-directional. During the period 1857 to 1924, 756,262 Spanish nationals and 120,258 French nationals left the country.[83] In part this reflects the fact that near the turn of the present century there was considerable Basque participation in seasonal labor migration between Europe and the New World.*

If departures are subtracted from arrivals, official Argentine statistics reflect a net gain throughout the sixty-seven-year

---

*Before the mechanization of agriculture in the *pampas*, there was a seasonal demand for labor that could not be met adequately by the local reserve of manpower. This labor-intensive development of agriculture in the Argentine *pampas* coincided with emergence of economical and speedy transatlantic shipping services. The added fact that the agricultural cycle of Argentina, with its southern hemispheric reversal of the seasons, was the mirror opposite of agricultural activities in Europe meant that European peasants and agricultural laborers could complete their own harvests and, in late fall, ship out to Argentina for several months of wage employment. They would return to Europe in the spring in time to seed their new crop. This annual movement involved thousands of workers (referred to in Spanish as *golondrinas* or "swallows"). Thus we find that in June 1910, 15,037 immigrants entered Argentina, whereas in the month of November the figure swelled to 63,675 persons.[84] Departures in November of 1910 numbered only 5,094, whereas in April 1911, 17,022 persons left the country.[85] In this fashion, the immigration statistics for Argentina during a period lasting from the 1880s through the first decade of the twentieth century are inflated considerably.

period in question of 1,024,033 Spanish nationals and 106,636 French nationals. While it is impossible to determine how many of these immigrants were Basques, it is evident that large numbers of them had entered Argentina by the middle of the nineteenth century. Between 1857 and 1869, a proimmigration committee in Argentina published folders for distribution in Europe, describing the opportunities in Argentina. The importance that Basque immigration had acquired is reflected in the claim in one such folder that of every 100 immigrants who were depositors in the Bank of Buenos Aires, 13 were Basques (both French and Spanish). Similarly, of every 100 million pesos placed on deposit by immigrants, 9 million were owned by Basques.[86]

By this time it should be apparent that it is impossible to make an entirely accurate assessment of the magnitude of nineteenth and early twentieth century Basque emigration to the New World. Many Basque emigrants were simply never counted, and those that were usually fell under the broader rubric of the movement of French and Spanish nationals. However, even the most conservative estimates would have to place the number of Basques who arrived in the New World during the period at a minimum of 200,000 individuals. The actual figure might have been considerably higher.*

LIFE IN THE NEW WORLD

It is clear from the pattern of emigration we have examined that the movement of Basques to the New World from the 1820s through the First World War was, in terms of sheer numbers, impressive. It is equally evident that the Río de la Plata countries of Uruguay and Argentina attracted the majority of Basque emigrants. Let us turn now to the opportunities and living conditions that they encountered.

In the 1830s Argentina and Uruguay were countries in which the bulk of the population was concentrated along the coast, while both contained enormous interior frontierlands that lacked such basic installations as roads. Governmental control of the interior was extremely tenuous, and Indian resistance proved a major barrier to permanent settlement by Europeans. The development of the *pampas* was further delayed by the

---

*One estimate made at the turn of the present century places the number of persons with Basque last names in Argentina alone at 250,000,[87] the result of four centuries of Basque immigration into the area, but notably of the mass movement of the nineteenth century.

series of internal revolutions and international warfare over borderlands that characterized the first few decades of independence for the South American republics.

During the 1820s and 1830s the governments of Argentina and Uruguay were committed to policies of Indian control and economic development of the *pampas*. It was during these years that the great Argentine *estancias*, or ranches, employing the romantic *gaucho* (the South American equivalent of the cowboy), proliferated. These huge frontier-adapted cattle operations employed few men and extensive acreage to produce cattle for hides and for salted meat, which was processed in plants called *saladeros* located in Buenos Aires and along the coasts and rivers.[88] The semi-wild cattle were rounded up annually rather than actually herded. With the exception of a brief period in 1826−27, when President Rivadavia of Argentina encouraged creation of small farms to be operated by European peasant immigrants, the *estancia-saladero* interests reigned supreme in the economic and political life of the nation and discouraged immigration. The culmination of control of Argentina by the cattle interests came under the iron-fisted dictatorship of Rosas, who assumed power in 1830. Under Rosas, vast private holdings, some consisting of as much as five hundred thousand acres, were created.* With Rosas's defeat in 1852, there was a dramatic reversal in the official Argentine policy toward immigration, the development of small holdings, and the creation of new industries.

Despite the fact that during the first half of the nineteenth century cattle interests were largely unchallenged as the dominant force in the Argentine economy, the period also witnessed establishment of an Argentine sheep industry. The native grasses of the *pampas* were largely unsuitable as sheep feed, but once areas were grazed extensively by cattle, the tough native perennials were replaced by such annual plants as clovers, thistles, Indian barley, foxtail, and mustard.[90] This permitted sheep raising, while undermining the value of the land as cattle range. As the areas adjacent to the settled coast underwent this transition, cattle raising shifted further into the interior. By the

---

*During the Rosas period, in the words of one historian, "As the state weakened under the impact of revolution and the incapacity of the elite to create an effective substitute for the authority of the Spanish Crown, the *estancia* grew stronger so that the great *estancieros* did not just control the state; they became the state."[89]

1830s sheep raising, mainly in the province of Buenos Aires, accounted for 7 percent of Argentina's total exports. This budding sheep industry was controlled by immigrants. Under President Rivadavia, some thirty thousand Irish immigrants had fanned out over the interior of the province of Buenos Aires, most of whom engaged in sheep raising.[91] They were quickly followed by the Basques, who became the second most numerous ethnic group involved in the industry.[92] Irish herders dominated the northern area of Buenos Aires; by 1840, Basque interests controlled the southern sectors of the province.[93]

In contrast to the cattle operations, sheep raising was both labor- and land-intensive. A herder might raise a flock of as many as fifteen-hundred animals on a permanent pasture of only six hundred acres. These early sheep operations tended to be small in size, and they were further handicapped by the poor quality of Argentine sheep. The marginal nature of the sheepman's livelihood is seen in the fact that as late as the 1840s the value of a sheep in Argentina was at times scarcely equivalent to that of an egg.[94] By another account, sheep were so worthless that they were purchased, killed, and their carcasses used as fuel in furnaces.[95]

The early sheepmen were despised by many *estancieros* who encouraged their *gauchos* to harass the flocks. The Basque ethnic group straddled this *estancieros*-versus-sheepmen competition. Basque families, established in Argentina when the area was a Spanish colony, were among the great cattle-estate owners. Other Basques were employed in the cattle industry as foremen and even as *gauchos*. A few of the nineteenth-century Basque immigrants found employment with budding *estancias* far out in the *pampas*, in areas that were still being wrested from the control of the Indian tribes. However, the major portion of the newly arrived Basques settled either in Buenos Aires, where they pursued urban occupations, or in the more settled areas of the *pampas*, which they converted into sheep range.

During the 1850s the sheep industry began to prosper. The Industrial Revolution in Europe created a seemingly inexhaustible demand for sheep's tallow and wool. By 1862−63 the total worth of sheep exports equalled that of cattle.[96] The more intensive use of the land by sheep made it more profitable for owners of *estancias* to let out their lands on a share system to Irish, Basque, and Scottish herders.

By the 1860s the area within a fifty- or sixty-league radius of Buenos Aires was favored as a sheep run and supported such quantities of animals that there was the definite danger of overgrazing.[97] Latham, writing in 1866, notes that, in the province of Buenos Aires, *"Estancia* after *estancia*, district after district, has passed into the hands of the sheep farmer, or the *estancias* have been dedicated to this by the owners."[98] He further notes that in the previous twenty years the value of sheep had increased tenfold as had the value of grazing land.[99] Thus, many herders realized a 25- to 35-percent annual return on the value of their flocks, and, according to Latham,

> considerable fortunes were made from very small beginnings, and with little or no trouble or outlay in the management. In lieu of payment in cash to shepherds, the owners of the land and sheep freely gave flocks on halves, say half the increase and half the wool, and these men . . . participating in the benefits of this rapid augmentation in value of the stock, throve with their employers; and on the expiration of their contracts, and the division of the increase, moved with their flocks on to lands rented at a mere nominal figure, and finally became purchasers of land, half a league or one or two square leagues in extent, and owners of many thousands of sheep.[100]

However, as the lucrativeness became apparent to the landlords, they reduced the percentage of the profits offered to herder-employees. Finally, by the mid-1860s most landowners in the Buenos Aires area put their herders on a straight wage basis. The more enterprising immigrants were going further out onto the *pampas*, where sheep were cheaper, the land less valuable, and the long-range prospects brighter for a sheep outfit of humble beginnings.

Despite the inflation in the values of land and sheep, Latham—an experienced sheepman himself—estimated that under good management, one league of land and 5,000 ewes purchased at an investment of about seven thousand pounds sterling in 1865 would have produced, by 1870, a wool crop worth between two thousand and twenty-five hundred pounds annually and a flock of animals worth fourteen thousand pounds. The land itself would have a market value equal to the original seven-thousand-pound investment.[101] It is obvious that sheep raising offered ample opportunity for the potential entrepreneur. Rural Argentina was still attractive for the person lacking capital, since jobs were plentiful and wages good.[102]*

---

*There is a contrary view that maintains that the leaseholder or employee on the *pampas* was exploited by both the *estancieros* and the monopolistic local storekeeper and hence was likely to lose most of his profits.[103]

Since few cattle-oriented native Argentinians were attracted by sheep raising, the immigrants were able to acquire control of the industry and, by paying premium prices, to gain ownership of large tracts of the *pampas*. In this fashion the several thousand Irish sheepherders in the province of Buenos Aires at the fall of Rosas swelled to thirty-five thousand by the 1870s and were producing more than half of Argentina's wool exports. Basques remained the second most numerous group in the industry.[104]

From the 1850s through the 1880s the economic competition from sheep forced cattle interests further southward and westward into the *pampas*, where they repeated the transformation of native grasses into suitable sheep range. Hence, expansion of the sheep industry followed closely upon the *gaucho's* heels.[105] Firing the *pampas* was another way to remove the coarse grasses and to convert a particular area into suitable sheep range.[106] In drought years sheepmen would trail their animals many leagues in search of better conditions.[107] This practice was undoubtedly an added stimulus to the rapid spread of sheep outfits throughout the *pampas*.

Much of the development of the Argentine *pampas* was caused by this spread of sheep interests. Sheep raising supported greater populations and in more settled circumstances, than did cattle raising.[108] Servicing centers and transportation facilities such as the railroad network developed. The sheep industry also created changes in the coastal urban centers. In the 1880s British meat packing interests built freezing plants in Buenos Aires and found it easier and more profitable to process mutton rather than beef. The export of frozen mutton to Europe increased the profits of sheep raising. Consequently, by 1889 there were 51 million sheep in the province of Buenos Aires alone,[109] and wool constituted between 50 and 60 percent of Argentina's total exports.[110]

The life of the shepherd was a solitary if sedentary one. Each herder lived in a small hut, frequently with his wife and children, but in many cases as a bachelor.[111] Each day the man would guide his animals to nearby grazing areas, taking care not to mix his band with those of other herders. At night the animals were returned to corrals near the herder's hut. These huts were at great distances from one another, and the only opportunity to socialize came on infrequent trips to a distant *pulpería* (a kind of rural tavern) and during the fiestas held annually, when many of the men and women of a particular district traveled about in shearing crews.[112]

In 1870 President Roca initiated military action against the Indian tribes of the western and southern *pampas*. Roca's successful campaigns opened vast areas to European settlers and ushered in an era of Argentine political stability and rampant economic growth.[113]* The latter depended in large measure upon the continued arrival of large numbers of European immigrants.† The Argentine government sent recruiting agents to Europe, publicized the economic opportunities of the country in both Europe and North America, subsidized transatlantic passages, and created a number of facilities throughout the republic that provided free room and board, transportation, and employment bureau services for the new arrivals.[115]

The arrival of large numbers of peasants, most of whom were Italian in the case of Argentina, transformed the *pampas*. With new refrigeration techniques, large quantities of Argentine meat products could be marketed in Europe. However, European preferences for fresh rather than salted beef caused rejection of the sinewy product of the *pampas*. Argentine beef growers could and did improve the quality of their animals through selective breeding.‡ One further step was required to conform to European desires. Range cattle had to be either fed high-quality fodder in feed lots or pastured on refined alfalfa for several weeks prior to shipment. Such feed lots and fodder-producing agricultural districts appeared first near Buenos Aires and then in the interior.

The labor for transforming grazing land to cultivation was provided by immigrant sharecroppers and tenant farmers. Such an individual received up to five hundred acres of land for a

---

*The extension of governmental control to Indian territory provided a stimulus to expansion of the sheep industry. It also produced the political stability necessary to attract the mass immigration that would eventually bring an army of small-scale agriculturalists to the *pampas* to compete with both the sheepmen and cattlemen for use of the land.

†It seems that Basque livestockmen continued to press southward to the frontier limits of effective governmental control. There is an autobiographical account of an Italian immigrant who, after learning through rumors that there were still good ranch sites to be had for the asking near the headwaters of the Río Negro, set out for the area on horseback. After an eight days' ride through virtually uninhabited country, the author notes, "we reached a Spanish settlement. They were Basques and all were from the same town."[114]

‡Basques made a major contribution to the selective breeding and improvement of Argentine cattle. Denis states, "The Basque dairies established in the district near Buenos Aires sold pedigree-calves to the ranches, and these were used for breeding purposes."[116]

period of three to six years. He might receive implements, seeds, and other assistance as well. In return he would turn over half of his crop to the landlord and at the end of the period would move on to a new plot, leaving behind refined alfalfa pasture or workable ground that could be converted to wheat production. In this fashion, the *pampas* were populated rapidly. Argentina's total population rose from 1.8 million in 1869 to 4 million in 1895, and much of this growth was concentrated in rural districts.[117]

Accompanying this general agricultural development were numerous attempts to form agricultural colonies. In some cases a rich landowner (some were of Basque descent) subdivided an existing estate, offering small plots for sale, usually of less than one hundred hectares in size. In other cases the colonies were founded by agents who sought to recruit persons in Europe and to settle them on private or government-owned lands. Some of the schemes involved establishing a single ethnic group in a kind of closed community, such as those created by the Jewish Colonization Association in the province of Entre Ríos.[118]

We have noted that as early as 1850 both private agents and agents of the Argentine government were recruiting European immigrants for Argentina.[119] The propaganda efforts in the Pyrenees by Dr. A. Brougnes attracted many Basques to an agricultural colony that he founded in Corrientes province in 1855, but the venture proved to be a disaster.[120] A few Basque families participated in the more successful agricultural colonies of Alejandra and Bernstad (both in the province of Buenos Aires).[121] In later years Basques were to found dozens of agricultural colonies in the provinces of Santa Fe,[122] Córdoba,[123] and Entre Ríos.[124]

Basques were considered to be particularly desirable immigrants. Article 17 of the new immigration law authorized advancing passage expenses to certain newcomers. Under the program, "the immigration of Basque families and workers was fomented. . . . the Señores Muñagorri and Iturríos were paid 10 *pesos* for each adult and half as much for each child."[125]

As a result of the general agricultural transformation and population explosion, land values in the *pampas* increased. The magnitude of inflation in land prices during the Argentine land boom of the latter part of the nineteenth century defies the imagination. Some parcels increased in value tenfold within a year. In extreme cases land which sold for as little as 35 pounds per league in the 1870s was worth 35,000 pounds per league by the first decade of the twentieth century.[126]

The Argentine land boom of the latter part of the nineteenth century did not affect all Basque sheepmen in the same fashion. Many had entered the industry at an earlier date with the desire to earn sufficient capital to be able to return to the Basque country as relatively wealthy men. Since they intended all along to leave Argentina, they were not prone to purchase land. By leasing sheep range from the government, or from *estancieros*, their only real capital investment was in the flocks themselves, and these could be sold with relative ease. The inflation of land values, however, made it increasingly difficult for such sheepmen to lease adequate range at a reasonable rental fee. It may be surmised that by the end of the nineteenth century many landless Basque sheepmen were caught in a cost-price squeeze that either forced them out of business or required that they move their operations to less suitable areas. In point of fact, between 1895 and 1908 the total sheep population in Argentina declined by over 7 million animals, whereas the decline in the province of Buenos Aires, the former bastion of the Argentine sheep industry, was on the order of 18 million.[127] Between 1908 and 1915 the sheep population of the province was nearly halved, down from an earlier total of 34 million animals.[128]

Those Basques who had acquired lands as a part of their sheep operation profited enormously by the meteoric rise in land values.* Many thrifty and entrepreneurial herders had acquired large holdings at relatively modest prices on the very eve of the great land boom. Men who had struggled for years in the lonely obscurity of small-scale sheep raising lived to see the value of their holdings increase a hundredfold or more.[130] These developments laid the foundations for a number of modern Argentina's largest fortunes and secured for some Basques a prominent position in Argentina's social aristocracy.

These changes in land value meant that potential immigrants could no longer count upon entrepreneurial opportunities in what had become a traditional field of Basque activity, the sheep industry. The inflated purchase and lease costs of sheep range meant that it required substantial capital to establish one's own sheep outfit. The *estancias* and Basque-owned sheep

---

*Other Basques found success in professions ancillary to actual livestock production, notably as livestock buyers.[129]

ranches paid herders in wages rather than in terms of the former shares system. Thus, a potential Basque immigrant could probably count upon adequate wage employment as a herder, but had little prospect of socioeconomic mobility within the Argentine sheep industry.

ALTERNATIVES TO THE SHEEP INDUSTRY

There are other threads of Basque occupational history in the Río de la Plata area, since not all who immigrated devoted their energies to cattle and sheep raising. Basque immigrants quickly acquired a reputation in Buenos Aires and Montevideo as excellent longshoremen and construction laborers. By 1864 French Basques were the dominant ethnic element in the work force of the tanneries of Buenos Aires.[131]

As the large landowners of Argentina became convinced of the advantages of intensive stock raising practices, literally thousands of miles of barbed-wire fencing were strung across the *pampas*. Basque fencing crews became so commonplace that the word *vasco* became synonymous with *alambrador* (fence stringer).[132]

In the early years of expansion into the *pampas*, the two-directional flow of goods between Buenos Aires and the interior was transported by teams of oxcart drivers known as *troperos*. The occupation was lucrative but the dangers from the elements and the Indians were great. Some of these teams of *troperos* were made up exclusively of Basques.[133] With the coming of the railroads in the latter half of the nineteenth century, the *troperos* disappeared from the rural Argentine scene.

The occupations of *hornero*, *leñador*, and *carbonero* (brickmaker, logger, and charcoal maker) were largely Basque-controlled. Basque brickmaking teams dominated every phase of that industry, from buying suitable deposits of soil to delivering the final product to construction sites.[134] Other Basques formed logging crews and prepared charcoal for the Buenos Aires market. In these pursuits they were able to convert one of their Old World experiences into a New World gain.[135]

Above all, there were two occupations in the greater Buenos Aires region that were known as "Basque activities." By at least as early as 1850 Basques were acquiring leases or ownership of ground within about three leagues of the city that they converted into *tambos*, or dairies.[136]* Some small-scale dairymen traveled daily to Buenos Aires to peddle their wares. Others jobbed their milk to fellow Basques who marketed it from house to house. The figure of the Basque *lechero* or milk vendor was a ubiquitous sight in Buenos Aires during the latter half of the last century.[138]

The second Basque-dominated activity in the Buenos Aires area was that of *saladerista*, or worker in the *saladeros* (meat-salting plants). The work entailed extremely long hours and hard physical labor. Newly-arrived immigrants could count upon employment, thanks to the Basque reputation for physical strength and perseverance. Wages in this industry were quite good.

In the *saladeros* the immigrant was in a thoroughly Basque environment. The Basque language was used as the vernacular. His companions, overseers, and in some cases even the owner, were Basques. Old World Basque dress, including the beret, red sash, and sandals, was the order of the day. Most *saladeros* provided a Basque handball court where the workers played in their leisure hours.[139]

The *saladeros* did not limit the horizons of their employees by rooting them permanently in one spot and within a controlled ethnic environment. Work in them was seasonal, lasting for only six or seven months out of the year. The *saladerista* was forced to seek other opportunities. Many would leave Buenos Aires for the sheep raising districts of the *pampas*, seeking employment or buying and transporting wool.[140] Thus, the *saladeros* provided the young Basque with partial security while forcing him to become better acquainted with Argentina and its opportunities. The young immigrant could try his hand at another occupation for part of the year secure in the knowledge that he could always return the next season to the *saladero*.†

Not all Basque activities were limited to hard physical occupations or entrepreneurial activities related to agriculture.

---

*By the end of the century Basque interests had a stranglehold on the market for dairy products in the area. The major entity exercising this control was a creamery called *La Unión Argentina*, owned by a consortium of ten Basques controlling a total of fifty-two farms.[137]

†One authority dates the period of major Basque involvement in the *saladeros* as beginning about 1845 and lasting until 1871.[141] President Urquiza was himself the owner of a major *saladero* in Entre Ríos province. The Basque workers of the operation organized their own union which frequently threatened management with strikes.[142]

Basque soccer team competing in the Venezuelan national soccer championship in 1945.

Eighteenth-century headquarters in La Guaira, Venezuela, of the Royal Guipuzcoan Company of Caracas reflects Old World Basque architectural style. In modern times the edifice houses La Guaira customs officials.

Jose Antonio Aguirre, *lendakari*, or president, of the Basque government-in-exile, attends mass at the Caracas *Centro Vasco* in the early 1940s.

Children of the *Gure Echea* organization of Buenos Aires in Old World Basque costume. Photo taken in 1935.

"Fiesta criolla" in the *Gure Echea* club of Buenos Aires in which members wear traditional Argentine dress. Photo taken in 1931.

Monument in downtown Buenos Aires to the memory of Juan de Garay, founder of the city. The small oak tree to the right of the statue was grown from a sprout of the original tree of Guernica. The iron railing around its base displays the coat-of-arms of the four Spanish Basque provinces.

Pantheon of the *Laurac Bat* organization of Havana, Cuba, where burial was reserved for Basques.

Entrance to *Euskal Echea* of Buenos Aires. The facility housed a school, orphanage, retirement home, and agricultural station.

A building within the *Euskal Echea* complex of Buenos Aires, bearing the names of its donors.

The *Euzko Etxea (Centro Basko Argentino)* social club of Necochea, Argentina. The complex houses a bar, restaurant, salons, and a *pelota* court.

Quarters of the Basque social club *(Euzko Etxea)* of Bogotá, Colombia.

Modern private dwelling in Lima, Peru, incorporates Old World Basque achitectural features.

...amily portrait taken in 1924 of a farmstead in Elizondo, Navarra Legend details ...e subsequent residence of each person. Individuals 1–3 represent three genera- ...ons of family continuity on the same farmstead, whereas the emigration experi- ...ice of the remainder encompasses France, Uruguay, Argentina, Mexico, Canada, ...d the United States.

1. The retired *echekojaun* of the household who never left the area.
2. Active *echekojaun* who inherited the farmstead and remained in Elizondo.
3. Active *echekoandria* from a farmstead in the nearby village of Arizcun.
4. Brother of active *echekojaun* on a return visit to his natal household after thirty years absence in Puebla, Mexico.
5. Mexican wife of No. 4.
6. Eldest daughter of active couple, now living in Vitoria, Alava.
7. Second eldest daughter, now residing on a ranch near Glasgow, Montana.
8. Third eldest daughter, now residing in Ciboure, France.
9. Only son who presently resides in Elizondo as the actual *echekojaun*.
10. Fourth eldest daughter, now residing in Toronto, Canada.
11. Fifth eldest daughter, now residing on a farm near Azopardo, Argentina.
12. Youngest daughter, emigrated to Uruguay.

The *ikastola,* or Basque language school, of the Basque center in Caracas, Venezuela. During early school years, all classes are taught in the Basque language.

Basques owned many of the stores in Buenos Aires and Montevideo.[143] Similarly, the Basque-owned hotels, restaurants, and bars in the two cities enjoyed considerable success by catering to the Basque trade. But there are also Basque success stories at the level of industrial entrepreneurship. One example is that of a French Basque who established a grain-sack factory that eventually attained an annual production of thirty million sacks and employed one thousand persons.[144] Another example is that of the *Compañia Sansiñena de Carnes Congeladas* which, by the turn of the present century, was Argentina's largest exporter of frozen meat.[145] An example of the importance of Basque kinship solidarity in such entrepreneurial activities is reflected in Hammerton's description of one family: "They are French Basques, and some fifteen or sixteen brothers and cousins are united in a great business, which has important warehouses in every large town along the Atlantic and Pacific coasts of South America, as well as in many of the business centers of the interior."[146]

The striking successes of Basque landowners and entrepreneurs heightened their influence in Argentine financial circles. Some Basques founded banking firms,[147] and Basques were prominent both on the board and as stockholders of one of Argentina's most prestigious commercial institutions, the *Bolsa de Comercio*.[148] During its first half century of existence, eleven of its presidents were Basque.[149]

As in the sheep industry, the opportunity for wage-earning and entrepreneurial activities in a number of these other "Basque occupations" was reduced considerably by the end of the nineteenth century. In light of new technological developments the frozen meat industry eclipsed the *saladeros*, which had been the main processors of Argentine meat products. In 1883 the freezing plants handled only 7,571 sheep; by 1903 they processed 3,427,783 sheep and 254,971 steers. Between 1902 and 1903 the production of the *saladeros* declined from 454,900 to 269,100 steers.[150] The employment opportunity for Basque *saladeristas* was eroding rapidly.*

The same may be said for opportunity in the *tambos* near Buenos Aires. By the turn of the century the marketing of milk products was in the hands of large cooperatives. The Basque

---

*In 1907, by one account, the ethnic makeup of the labor force in the remaining *saladeros* was no longer exclusively Basque, and the *saladeros'* handball courts were in disrepair and seldom in use.[151]

lechero was no longer a common sight on the streets of the city. Moreover, the dairy-farming industry had matured to the point that, while the *tambos* were still largely Basque-owned, there was little opportunity for the newly-arrived Basque immigrant to acquire his own *tambo*. The Basque *tamberos* willingly employed newly-arrived Basques as milkers, but the milker had little prospect of rapid socioeconomic mobility.

Thus, although the Argentine economy continued to expand and attracted a flood of European emigrants from 1900 to the First World War, the country became less attractive for the Basques. By the turn of the present century Argentina had matured to the point where its real offer of opportunity was directed at the potential wage laborer, not at the aspiring entrepreneur. This was particularly true of those activities in which many Basques had previously enjoyed substantial success.

The Basque Entrepreneur

We can better appreciate the experience of the nineteenth-century Basque immigrant in the Río de la Plata region by examining a success story and an account of economic failure.

Pedro Luro's fabulous success story was one of many that quickened imaginations in Europe and fueled further Basque emigration to the New World. Here is Hammerton's translation of an account by the French writer Huret of Luro's life:

> I wish to relate in some detail the story of one of these French Basques (perhaps the most celebrated of them all), as I heard it from one of his sons. . . .
>
> Pedro Luro was born in 1820 in the little town of Gamarthe,* and in 1837 he arrived in Buenos Ayres with a few francs in his pocket. Entering as a labourer in a *saladero*, . . . he contrived to save enough to contemplate matrimony, but suffered the loss of his little savings by robbery. He applied himself with new energy to work; purchasing a horse and a tilt cart, he converted the latter into an omnibus and with himself as driver plied between the Plaza Montserrat and the suburb of Barracas.
>
> He then married a countrywoman, Señorita Pradere, a relative of his own, and with one of her brothers founded an *almacén* (general store) at Dolores, some three hundred kilometres to the south. But soon this store did not suffice for his activity, and leaving his wife and her brother in charge of it, he scoured the Pampa for cattle, wool and hides. Later on, he made

---

*Francisco Grandmontagne maintains that Luro was from the village of Sare.[152]

a proposal to a neighbouring *estanciero* whom he saw planting trees on his ground, and effected a contract with him, the conditions of which are famous still in the Argentine. Luro was to plant as many trees as he liked on two hundred hectares of land, which the *estanciero* was to place at his disposal, and was to be paid for the work at the rate of four centimes for each common tree and twenty-five for each fruit tree. . . .

Calling to his aid a number of his fellow Basques, at the end of five years, Pedro Luro had planted so many trees on these two hundred hectares that the proprietor owed him a sum not only superior to the value of the ground planted, but of the whole five thousand hectares comprising his *estancia* (land was sold at that time in this district at 5,000 francs per league). The *estanciero* did not care to pay Luro, with the result that the astute Basque started an action at law and converted himself into the proprietor of the 5,000 hectares.

About the year 1840, the southern part of the province of Buenos Ayres was still almost desert, the land of small value. These were the times of the Rosas tyranny, and incessant revolutions. All around the abandoned *estancias* dogs had returned to a state of savagery, and cattle wandered free in innumerable herds across these immense spaces. It happened that Luro was assisting at a *batida* (round up) of these animals, rendered mad by being entangled in the lassos and pricked with knives in the hocks. Pondering over the value of all that flesh and fat wasted, for it was then the custom merely to secure the skin of the animal and leave its body to decay, the idea occurred to buy from the land-owner all the animals of the class that were thus to be hunted and killed, at the rate of ten pesos of the old Argentine money. . . . The proprietor was highly amused at the suggestion. "I quite believe I will accept," he exclaimed, laughing, "but do you really think it would be a good business?"

It was with the only system of capture known to the *gauchos*, that is to say the lasso and the *bolas* (three balls attached by long leather thongs, which, thrown with great dexterity at the legs of an animal, entangle these and bring it to the ground), necessitating months and an enormous number of men, that he would be able to bring some thousands of cattle—and in what sad state—to the salting factory.

All the same, Luro insisted with perfect coolness, and the contract was signed.

Now the tactics conceived by the intelligent Basque were as follows: He began by prohibiting the gauchos from scouring the country in cavalcades. During three months, only two men on horseback, going slowly, were allowed to wander about the pasture ground of these wild cattle. Little by little the animals became accustomed to the sight of them and did not fly away when they approached. When some hundreds of cattle had thus been domesticated, they were taken farther away, where others were still in a wild state, and these in turn were easily reduced to the tameness of the first.

In batches of five hundred to a thousand, Luro was soon able to herd the cattle direct to the salting factories, where he sold them at 15, 20, 25, even 30 francs each. At the end of a year, he had thus secured no fewer than 35,000 head of cattle. He had made himself rich, and the proprietor of the *estancia* had received from him at one stroke 70,000 francs, which he had never expected, remaining enchanted with his transaction.

In 1862, Pedro Luro went still further afield, beyond Baha Blanca, whose fort at that time constituted the frontier against the Indians. He was delayed for some time on the banks of the River Colorado, owing to the Indians having robbed him of his horses. Meanwhile, exploring the valley of the river, he quickly grasped the potentialities of the district. Returning to Buenos Ayres, he secured an interview with General Mitre, to whom he proposed to buy from the State 100 square leagues of land (250,000 hectares) at the rate of 1,000 francs per league, with a view to founding a colony of three hundred Basques in that region.

His scheme apparently approved by the President, he then set sail for Navarra Baja in Spain,* where he recruited some fifty families, with whom he returned to the Argentine. But the Government, while agreeing to the sale of land, would not, for some unknown reason, permit the founding of the colony, so the Basques were spread over the land of their compatriot. Many of them, or their descendants, are to-day millionaires, while the land bought at the 1,000 francs the league is valued now at 200 francs the hectare, or say 500,000 francs per league.

Meanwhile, Pedro Luro continued his active commerce in skins and wool. Ere long he had constructed the largest curing factory in all the basin of the River Plate, expending millions of francs on it. Then he set himself to the exploitation of the bathing station of Mar del Plata which had been founded by Señor Peralta Ramos, one of the most fortunate of speculations, from which his heirs, continuing his work there, have benefited immensely. At his death he left to his fourteen children 375,000 hectares of land, 300,000 sheep, and 150,000 cattle, then valued at 40,000,000 francs.

Pedro Luro . . . took to the Argentine more than 2,000 of his fellow Basques, whom he employed in his many agricultural and industrial establishments, providing them with cattle, letting land to them cheaply, lending them money. Almost all of

---

sic, probably Basse Navarre in France.

these have made their fortunes. With Luro disappeared one of those types that are almost legendary, and without doubt the most famous colonist of the epic period of Argentine immigration.[153]

From another source we learn that Luro became a veritable legend of the *pampas*, and not only as an entrepreneur. Zubiaure,* the stereotypic Argentine *gaucho*, once declared, "In this country there are only two *Gauchos*, myself and the Basque Luro."[154]†

Luro's offspring were to enjoy prestigious, if sedentary, lives. The eldest son became the president of the Chamber of Deputies of the province of Buenos Aires. The second son became the governor of the region of the *pampas* that his father first brought under control. The third son was a deputy and the president of the Commission of Finances in Argentina.[156]

Luro's successes stand in stark contrast to the experiences in Río de la Plata of the famous Basque poet and songwriter José María Iparraguirre.[157] In 1858 Iparraguirre and his wife embarked for Buenos Aires from the port of Bayonne.‡ His fame as a performer had preceded him, and he was met on the dock by a large crowd of Basques. They took him to a local Basque hotel operated by Francisco Mendia and his wife (refugees of the First Carlist War). Iparraguirre had a school teacher uncle in Buenos Aires and a cousin in Nueva Palmira (Uruguay). The latter had promised to set him up as a sheepherder. He went to Nueva Palmira where the cousin, whose name was Ordeñana, failed to comply with his word. So Iparraguirre went to Dolores and Mercedes (Uruguay) in search of work with sheep. In Mercedes an Argentine-born Basque doctor, a pharmacist from Navarra, and a man from Guipúzcoa offered to purchase one thousand sheep, which the Iparraguirres would tend and repurchase slowly as the flock produced. When Ordeñana learned of this he was apparently mortified for not having helped earlier. Ordeñana had a bar on a large *estancia* and also rented land from the *estanciero*, where, with the use of employees, he ran flocks of sheep. He offered the Iparraguirres two hundred animals to tend. Their wages were to be one-fourth of the profits.

---

*Zubiaure is also a Basque name, although the individual in question was obviously a *criollo*.

†The general adaptability of Basques to life on the *pampas* was commented upon by several writers.[155]

‡An instance of a Spanish Basque departing for the New World from a French port.

Iparraguirre thus accepted what his wife was later to call "a misery." Her own comments about the arrangement were as follows: "Imagine, sir, the others offered him one thousand sheep to be paid off whenever we could and he preferred the two hundred sheep, and we had to give Ordeñana three-fourths of the profit. Poor Joshe Mari, when it came to business he was a dope!"[158] According to his wife, Iparraguirre accepted Ordeñana's proposition so that "no one could say that we didn't want to be with our relatives."[159]

The Iparraguirres spent three years in a mud hut that they built themselves, three leagues distant from the closest neighbor. As might be expected, the poet was a poor herder. He lost sheep, allowed them to be stolen, and suffered the frustration and extra work of sorting his animals after they mixed with the bands of other herders. He would spend his time singing and composing verses. To this day the place where Iparraguirre herded is known in Uruguay as the "Post of the Troubador."

After three years Iparraguirre had an argument with his cousin and demanded whatever he had coming to him. Ordeñana insisted that they were even. As a result, the Iparraguirres were penniless as they traveled to Montevideo. He earned their daily sustenance by singing and playing his guitar.

In Montevideo a Navarrese agreed to back Iparraguirre in the cafe business. The venture was an instant success due to Iparraguirre's fame. Each night he would entertain the patrons. But there was one problem: he refused to charge the clientele. The backer lost his money, and Iparraguirre lost his cafe.

By this time the Iparraguirres had two children, and they wandered about the *pampas* while Joshe Mari earned something as a performer. A Guipuzcoan took pity on them and placed in their care one thousand sheep *"a medias"* (i.e., half of the profits going to the owner). But Iparraguirre's lack of concern for the animals destroyed this venture as well. After a group of revolutionaries requisitioned most of his sheep, he was left with a mere seven head. He was also quite ill, and friends took him to a local Basque hotel where a Basque-Argentine doctor cured him. He then worked as a herder for five years on the same doctor's *estancia* before changing employers to work for a French Basque. Once again he lost his entire flock to revolutionaries and drought.

At this time Iparraguirre learned that at the end of the Second Carlist War the Spanish government had stripped the Basque provinces of their *fueros*. He believed that there would be another war immediately to recover Basque privileges, and he resolved to return to Europe to join the fight. A Basque organization (the *Laurak Bat*) of Montevideo collected funds to repatriate him, and also sponsored a concert in which Iparraguirre performed his works and other Basque music. Many rich Basques and their sons, who were educated, professional men, attended the performance. When Iparraguirre sang his own *Gernika'ko Arbola*, which had become a kind of Basque national anthem, the older generation wept openly, while the young "dotores," who could no longer understand the Basque language, laughed at the display of emotion. Iparraguirre's wife pleaded with him to use the 2,000 *pesos* he had earned to buy sheep and remain, but he declined, saying that he must defend Basque liberties. He left his wife and eight children in Uruguay. They never saw him again.[160]

The cases of Pedro Luro and José María Iparraguirre might be viewed as brackets around the Basque experience in the Río de la Plata region. Neither is typical. The life of the dedicated, probably ruthless, and certainly gifted entrepreneur Luro is the crowning Basque economic success story in Argentine—or possibly New World—history. The life of the bumbling, hopeless dreamer Iparraguirre is probably the epitome of Basque failure in the Río de la Plata. For most Basque immigrants, the realities of life in the area fell somewhere in between.

Details of the stories underscore other significant points. The reception for Iparraguirre on the docks, the presence of the Basque hotel in Buenos Aires, Iparraguirre's own cafe in Montevideo, the presence of the *Laurak Bat* organization in that city, and the success of his concert all signal the presence of a self-aware ethnic group in the Río de la Plata region. Iparraguirre's benefactors highlight the Basque ethnic channels that transcended kinship ties operative in both Argentina and Uruguay by the 1850s. This point is also underscored by Luro's tendency to hire Basques and his grand scheme to create a Basque colony. The fact that Iparraguirre sought out a kinsman for his first New World job and stayed with this relative in the face of better economic offers reflects what became a common pattern both in Latin America and in the American West. Similarly, Iparraguirre's falling out with his cousin, as well as the cousin's willingness to exploit his newly arrived relative, are practices that occurred with a great degree of frequency.

The kind of rapid socioeconomic mobility attainable by some within a single generation is seen in the occupations of

Luro's offspring and the "doctors" who attended Iparraguirre's concert with their parents. The generational erosion of such cultural traits as the Basque language is seen in Señora Iparraguirre's denunciation of the younger men who failed to understand her husband's music. Finally, the extent of Basque involvement in the sheep business is illustrated by the fact that many Basque storekeepers and professional persons, who were not themselves involved directly in the care of sheep, nevertheless invested in Basque sheep operations.*

This last point helps us to understand why, by the middle of the nineteenth century, the stereotype of the Basque that predominated in Río de la Plata society was that of *sheepman* *(ovejero)* despite the fact that Basques were clearly established in other activities as well. We have seen that many Basques remained in urban centers and occupations, that many of those who went to the *pampas* never rose beyond the ranks of the wage-earning sheepherders, and that many of the successful Basque sheepmen preferred a seminomadic landless existence to a long-term investment of capital and self in the Río de la Plata area. It is equally true, however, that the livestock business remained the major path to rapid socioeconomic mobility for the more entrepreneurial Basques.

Grandmontagne argues that there was a pattern in the emergence of the successful Basque sheepman.[162] He would get his start either herding for a wage or working for a share in the flock's increase. Alternatively, he might begin as a fence stringer, or *alambrador*. In either event he acquired an intimate knowledge of the local terrain and range conditions. For many a future prominent Basque landowner or *estanciero*, the next step was a stint as innkeeper, or *fondista*. The Basque inn, which doubled as a general store, was frequently the first business establishment in a developing rural area. The *fonda* was the center for the social and economic life of a fairly extensive region, and hence a clearinghouse for local news. The proprietor was in a particularly favored position to take advantage of any opportunity that might present itself. He could afford to

---

*There are examples of the reverse. The book *De Vasconia a Buenos Aires* has a case history of a young Guipuzcoan immigrant who worked as a clerk in a Basque-owned store in Buenos Aires. When the business failed, the trusting young man lost his entire savings. Impoverished, he traveled to the provinces where he found employment in another firm. He was befriended by a French Basque sheepman who, impressed with the man's business knowledge, provided the capital that allowed him to start up his own store.[161]

speculate in lands and flocks, since his livelihood did not depend entirely upon his successes with them. His background as herder or fence stringer made him a knowledgeable investor in the local livestock industry. As innkeeper, he had up-to-date information of the availability of range, as well as a clear idea of conditions in the local labor force. He might even wield considerable influence over the latter by extending credit through his store.* It was frequent for Basque *fondistas* to hold controlling interests in several ranches and sheep operations, becoming in time wealthy *estancieros*.[163]

So, although Basques were successful in many sectors of Argentine life, it was in livestock raising and particularly in the sheep industry that a Basque ethnic organization seemed to pervade all levels of activity from herding to ownership, including such tasks as fence stringing, livestock buying, and wool transport. These activities formed the sheepman stereotype of the Basque.

The grim contrast between the life histories of Pedro Luro and José María Iparraguirre highlight the extremes of the Basque experience in nineteenth-century Argentina and Uruguay. Some, like Luro, used livestock raising to amass vast fortunes and considerable power. By the turn of the present century the descendants of both a Basque rural aristocracy and successful Basque urban capitalists were prominent in the professions, the arts, the military establishment, the economy, and the political life of several Latin American countries.

In rural Argentina Basques were most prominent among the ranks of the large landholders. The holdings of some are family patrimonies dating from the eighteenth century (or earlier), while others are of more recent vintage.[164] A list of the fifty largest landowner families in Argentina, published in 1958, contains at least twelve names that are unequivocally Basque.[165] The top three landowners in Argentina and the only ones with over two hundred thousand hectares were all Basques: Alzaga Unzue (411,938 hectares), Anchorena (322,670 hectares), and Luro (232,336 hectares).[166] Furthermore, the descendants of this provincial landed class, including many of Basque descent, have provided Argentina with a major portion of her intellectuals.[167] In a recent study of the Argentine social elite, Imaz notes that Basques and their descendants have pro-

---

*Iparraguirre's cousin Ordeñana was a classic example of the Basque *fondista* with a hand in sheep operations as well.

vided many army officers.[168] Of the forty-nine bishops of the
province of Buenos Aires, seven were Basques, making them
the second most numerous group after the bishops of Italian
descent.[169] In the 1947 edition of *Quién es Quién* in Buenos
Aires, 12.10 percent of those listed had Basque names. Of the
memberships of the two most exclusive social clubs of the city,
29 percent and 19 percent, respectively, had Basque names;
14.26 percent of the members of the bar association were of
Basque descent.[170] By a 1962 estimate, 15.9 percent of the
families constituting the social elite of Buenos Aires were
Basques.[171]

At one point in the late nineteenth century, Errazuris was
president of Chile, Uriburu presided over Argentina, and
Idiarte-Borda was chief executive of the Republic of Uruguay.
All were of Basque descent.[172] Between 1853 and 1943, ten of
the twenty-two presidents in Argentina were of Basque descent.

However, the life of José María Iparraguirre shows clearly
that nineteenth-century Basque history in the Río de la Plata
area was not an unqualified success story. The illustrious accomplishments of a few mask the misery of many. Laboring
conditions in the *saladeros* were among the least desirable in
Buenos Aires and Montevideo. Until the 1850s conditions in the
sheep industry were such that the herder was hard put to survive.
His troubles were further compounded by the animosity of the
gauchos and the Indians.[173]

In 1883 the *Diputación*, or provincial government, of
Alava published in book form the articles of the newspaper
reporter José Cola y Goiti. The articles were written to warn
potential emigrants of the false claims of the recruiting agents
and were directed particularly at the propaganda of the
Uruguayan government concerning opportunities and conditions in that country. Cola described the immigrant traffic as
bordering on slave trade. He wrote of the deplorable conditions
on the transatlantic steamers. He characterized the Uruguayan
wage scale as low and undermined by inflation. Life in the
interior was described as fraught with dangers from the elements and from lack of public security. Cola noted that many
new arrivals were pressed into military service due to Uruguay's
incessant wars and revolutions (twenty over a fifty-two-year
period). He warned young women that entering domestic service in Uruguay is a ready pathway to becoming a mistress or a
prostitute. To underscore his case, he devoted considerable
attention to the Basque organization *Laurak Bat* of Montevideo

whose main purpose was to lend assistance to indigent Basques, and provide those who desired it with passage money to Europe.[174]*

Therefore, it is somewhat misleading to judge the realities of Basque emigration to Latin America on the basis of the social registers of Buenos Aires and Santiago de Chile, or to judge them in terms of the palatial homes of rich "American" returnees that are found throughout the Basque country.† If the annals of nineteenth-century South American history are replete with hundreds of Basque success stories, it must not be forgotten that nineteenth-century Basque emigration to the Americas involved tens or even hundreds of thousands of emigrants.

THE BASQUES AND THEIR INTERPRETERS

It is clear that the Latin American Basques in the second half of the nineteenth century formed a conscious ethnic group capable of collective action. It is also apparent that Basque ethnics had established a group reputation in Latin America. Basque activities were being evaluated in print by non-Basques and Basques alike. In one Uruguayan newspaper article published in 1880, the Basques were characterized as hard-working and even-tempered. But above all, they were praised for their ability to adapt to livestock-raising conditions in the semidesert regions of the Uruguayan interior. Moreover, the report states,

---

*Cola's work received wide distribution in the Spanish Basque country, sponsored officially by the four provincial governments.[175] The Cola book is important to our understanding of the movement of the Basques to the American West. It probably created a climate of suspicion in the minds of potential emigrants concerning life in Latin America. This came at a time when Basque emigration to the American West was increasing dramatically. In 1909 *L'émigration Basque* by Pierre Lhande was published. Lhande was less actively concerned with deterring Basque emigration than was Cola. He states that the conditions of emigration to Latin America had improved considerably since Cola's time.[176] In fact, he reserves his few critical barbs for Basque circumstances in North America.

†An interesting question that is somewhat beyond the scope of the present work is the extent to which the nineteenth-century resurgence of the Basque economy (see pp. 126–28) was due to the contraction in overseas opportunities resulting from the New World independence movements, thereby forcing Basque entrepreneurism to seek local outlets for its energies. As a corollary, it is clear that the feedback of wealth to Europe from the nineteenth-century emigrants was a considerable factor in the economic development of the Basque country. Grandmontagne maintains that no less than 70 percent of San Sebastián's urban growth was financed from the Americas, notably Argentina and Mexico.[177]

[The Basque group] is little represented in criminal statistics; here it sinks down roots which increase the wealth of the nation and from here it sends out family letters which have the immediate effect of attracting to our piers a spontaneous immigration of moral, hard-working persons disposed to begin their activities where they are most needed by the country, that is, outside the cities.[178]

An article that appeared about the same time in the Uruguayan journal *Asociación Rural del Uruguay* characterized Basque immigrants as most desirable, due to Basque moral rectitude, dedication to hard work, and love of liberty. Singled out for particular praise are the Basques' strong family loyalties and propensity to settle the land in family units. The article ended with an appeal to foment future Basque settlement in Uruguay as the "model for colonization."[179]

This view of Basque settlement was seconded in the filiopietistic writings of Latin American Basques. The flavor of the genre is well represented in the efforts of Tomás Otaegui:

The Basques continued to immigrate into the Río de la Plata Republic, forming strong sentimental attachments to the new lands, constructing their homes, and seeding their great biological characteristics. Always individualists and lovers of freedom, they fled the population centers and penetrated the then abandoned deserts. There they fought to colonize as if they were heralds who went about proclaiming the greatness of hard work and bearing the benefits of civilization.

In the melancholy pampa, at the foot of a mountain ridge, by a stream which murmured its song of solitude, there where the cry of the Indian breaks the silence giving voice to his savagery, there amidst heroic distances, the Basques built their ranches and steeled themselves against the environment. In the knowledge that they could rely solely upon their own resources, they intensified their individualism and multiplied their desire. They became more Indian than the Indian if need be, they became versed in creole horsemanship and accustomed to creole wanderings in which they crossed vast horizons, frequently with songs from their native Basque land on their lips. They herded the flocks which scattered over the green pastures.

The Basques became numerous and the flocks and rodeos multiplied and the ranches were converted into nests of love. The sacred smoke of many hearths, climbed through rustic chimneys into the blue sky, announcing the creation of family homes, the fundamental basis of any country.[180]

But not all authors concurred in viewing the Basques as a stable colonizing element. Daireaux notes:

> Many [Basque sheepmen] continue . . . augmenting the number of their sheep, finally forming provisional holdings of twenty or thirty thousand animals, rejecting the possibility of selling some to buy land and establish themselves permanently. For they believe, although they won't admit it, that the day they buy land they will have said an eternal goodbye to their native mountains. In the recesses of their hearts there remains a profound love, unconscious perhaps, for the Pyrenees, and this chronic nostalgia, this insatiable desire to return to their homeland, serves them as a north wind in all of their actions in life to the point of stopping them from buying land, and it is land which has the only real value in this country.[181]*

Recognition of the Basques' energies was not restricted to their roles as stockmen. Carlos Pellegrini, a president of Argentina, noted, "The vigor, activity and energy that the Basques bring to any task makes it almost impossible to compete with them. For this reason, within a short time they monopolize any secondary industry to which they dedicate themselves."[182] Nor has the Basque contribution to Argentine society escaped the awareness of foreign observers. Hammerton states, "When we talk of Argentine emigration, we refer chiefly to the Italian and the Spanish, though the Basque provinces of France and Spain have probably supplied the very finest element of foreign blood in the Argentine nation today."[183]

Basque honesty was legendary and was reflected in the belief that the word of a Basque was as trustworthy as a written contract.[184]† José María Garciarena, commenting upon the esteem in which the Basques are held in modern Argentine society, notes, "In the country, to have a Basque name is to carry credentials; it is the best possible recommendation to gain entry to any circle or to participate in any activity."[186]

ETHNIC IDENTITY MAINTENANCE

We have demonstrated that the magnitude of the nineteenth-century movement of Basques to Latin America was

---

*This view was echoed by the detractors of the Basque itinerant sheepmen of the American West; cf. chapter 6.

†Indeed, Basques were favored as store clerks and stevedores.[185] In both occupations the employer had to place considerable faith in the employee's honesty.

impressive. That Basque immigrants tended to cluster in certain occupations, and that they came to dominate some of them, suggests that Basques cooperated with one another in the economic arena. It remains for us to examine the extent to which Basques maintained an ethnic group awareness and a collective stance with respect to other New World peoples.

Cola states that in nineteenth-century Uruguay there was no question as to the identity of Basques as such: the term *gallegos* (Gallegans) was applied to every Spanish group (Andalusians, Asturians, Gallegans, Valencians, Catalans, and Castilians) except the Basques, who were always referred to as *vascos*.[187]

As early as 1842 there was a residential district in Buenos Aires *(Barrio de la Constitución)* that was primarily Basque. This area was filled with the Basque-owned bars, hotels, and boarding houses that served as employment bureaus and way stations for new immigrants, housing for single men working in the *saladeros*, and places of amusement and relaxation for Basque diarymen and herders in from the *pampas*. To enter these establishments was to enter a world where Basque was the vernacular and Basque songs, the *jota* (a dance), and the card game *mus* were the chief forms of entertainment.[188] As we have seen, the *saladeros* constructed Basque handball courts, and there were also such courts or *frontones* in the Basque *barrio*.[189]* The Basque community of the Río de la Plata preferred and maintained the Old World forms of recreation.

During the first half of the nineteenth century Basque emigration to the New World was made up in large measure by young single males. For example, between 1832 and 1840 only 16 percent of French Basque emigrants were females.[191] By 1855, however, 30 percent of all emigrants in the official† lists were females, a percentage that lasted during the period 1875−77 as well.[192] If we examine the figures for departures to Río de la Plata from the port of Bilbao in 1915, we find that 395 persons, constituting 127 family units, and 139 single males between fifteen and twenty years of age, shipped out to Argen-

---

*By the end of the century Basque *pelota* (the form known as *jai alai* in this country) was a very popular sport in Argentina, and top-flight professional talent was imported regularly from the Basque country.[190]

†It should be noted that practically all female emigrants departed legally, since there was no question of avoidance of military conscription. If the illegal departures are factored in, the percentage represented by females in the overall statistics of Basque emigration would have to be reduced somewhat.

tina.[193] A popular account, published in 1909, confirms the fact that most emigrants left the port of Bilbao in family units.[194]

These statistics tend to support the impression derived from other sources that what was essentially a movement of young single males had become, by the 1850s, a broader movement including young single girls and entire family units. There was a ready demand for single Basque girls as domestics and as serving girls in the Basque hotels of the Río de la Plata region. The Basque hotel, which served as a place of recreation, was a prime context for matchmaking. If the situation of the Basque hotels in the American West is at all comparable, then the turnover of Basque serving girls in the hotels of the Río de la Plata area was brisk.

The movement of entire family units to the New World, coupled with the flow of single girls who tended to marry within the Basque ethnic group, created the basis, by the mid-nineteenth century, for continuity of Basque ethnic awareness in the Latin American context even without the continued immigration of Old World Basques. Such terms as "Argentine-Basque" or "Chilean-Basque" were given substance by the maintenance of Basque ethnicity through the family unit.

By 1854 a Basque religious order, the Congregation of Betharramites, became concerned about the lack of religious guidance available to the scattered Basque population of the *pampas*. Its offer to provide missionary priests to Argentina was accepted by President Urquiza in 1856. The first contingent consisted of eight priests. In less than five years the Betharramites had established thirty missions throughout the interior of Argentina and Uruguay.[195] In 1858 the Basques of Montevideo constructed their own church.[196] The Betharramite priests were referred to locally as the "Basque Fathers." The works of these missionaries included founding the College of San José in Buenos Aires, as well as other colleges in Montevideo, Rosario, Santa Fe, and Asunción (Paraguay).[197]* A special missionary order was founded in Mauléon (Soule) to service the Americas. In addition, French Basque Benedictines established rural missions in both Argentina and Uruguay.[198]

During the second half of the nineteenth century, the continued immigration of Basques into the Río de la Plata republics and the emergence of a New World-born Basque

---

*Parenthetically, these colleges laid the bases of higher education in the Río de la Plata region, providing the schooling for many of its future leaders.

population underscored the need for and feasibility of founding formal ethnic organizations. In 1876 two dozen Basques in Montevideo formed the association *Laurak Bat* (which means "Four in One" in Basque and refers to the unity of purpose of the four Spanish Basque provinces). The organization provided care for indigent Basques (including return passages to Europe if desired). It also extended legal aid to Basques who ran afoul of the many pitfalls in Uruguayan civil life. *Laurak Bat* established a school and library for children of Basque descent.[199]

The formal ethnic organization provided the structure for the kind of collective action required to hold elaborate festivities. In 1880 the Basques of Montevideo celebrated the fourth anniversary of the founding of *Laurak Bat* by sponsoring a fiesta that lasted for two days. The events began with a parade throughout the streets of the city with the band playing typical Basque music. Next a choir sang the Basque national anthem *Gernika'ko Arbola* before an effigy of the tree of Guernica. Basque athletic events followed, including *tiro a la barra* (in which the object is to throw an iron rod the greatest distance), foot races, and a sailing regatta. There was a performance of Basque folk dances, followed by a public dance. The festivities closed with a handball championship and concert performance of a Basque choir.[200]

According to one newspaper account, this fiesta was attended by 30,000 persons. The importance of the Basque colony and the esteem in which it was held is reflected in the fact that among the participants were several ministers of the Uruguayan government, the ambassadors of the United States, Spain, and Chile, and various other notable personages in Montevideo's social life.[201]

In 1876, as a direct reaction against the law of July 21 which abolished the *fueros*, the Spanish Basques of Buenos Aires formed an association which was also christened *Laurac Bat*.[202]* The stated purposes of the organization were to organize an annual protest over the abolition of the *fueros*,[203] to assist needy Basques in Argentina, to help the indigent or ill to return to Europe, and to sponsor Basque cultural events.[204] By 1878 the membership stood at 225, including 105 Guipuzcoans, 61 Vizcayans, 46 Navarrese, and 13 Alavese.[205] One hundred

---

*The orthography of Laura*c* was later changed by the organization to Laura*k*.

and twenty-four members resided in the interior of the country.[206]

In 1878 the organization began publication of a newspaper with the same name. The early issues provide some insight into the circumstances of the Basque colony of Argentina. There were many want ads like one which states, "Needed, a store clerk for Dolores who knows Basque,"[207] suggesting the presence of a substantial Basque clientele. Other announcements reflect considerable human pathos such as the long lists of unclaimed letters and the pleas from Europe for information concerning relatives who had simply disappeared.[208] There was a standing appeal in the newspaper for donations to help the organization repatriate the needy. And when a storm swept the Cantabrian Sea in 1878, killing more than two hundred seamen, a considerable relief fund was collected and sent to Europe.[209] In the following year a Basque festival was organized to raise funds for flood relief in Europe.[210] The festivities included such events as a performance by a recently organized Basque orchestra, the *Euskarina*, a ball match, *tiro a la barra*, foot races, a competition between Basque *bertsolaris*, or versifiers, and dancing of the Basque *zortzico*.[211]

By the year 1880 the *Laurac Bat* organization was promoting construction of a handball court, and in 1881 there was another Basque festival to inaugurate this new *Plaza Euskara*.[212] The celebration included planting a cutting from the tree of Guernica.[213] Shortly thereafter, the *Coro Euskaro*, or Basque choir, was formed, as was a group called *Tradiciones Vascas* ("Basque Traditions") whose purpose was to stage Basque festivities in the streets of Buenos Aires on appropriate days.[214]

At one level the existence of these organizations confirms a collective Basque ethnic stance. However, there is evidence that the Basque community of Río de la Plata was not, in terms of internal organization, monolithic and undifferentiated. Old World Basque regional loyalties and animosities tended to be reproduced in the New World context. As early as the 1850s the considerable French Basque colony of Buenos Aires conducted group activities independently of the Spanish Basques. A French hospital in the city, which employed two French Basque doctors, served the colony as a site for an annual fiesta. One particular hotel, owned by a man from St. Palais, was the favorite hangout for the French Basques.[215] In 1895 twenty-nine members of the French Basque colony organized the *Centro Vasco Francés* in Buenos Aires which had its own building, dance salons, and handball court.[216]* The same year, the Navarrese Basques of Buenos Aires formed their own association, the *Centro Navarro*, which was independent of *Laurac Bat*.[217]

At the end of the nineteenth century there were at least three distinct Basque organizations in Buenos Aires alone.† Furthermore, Basque clubs were proliferating in the various Argentine provinces. Handball championships, pitting region against region, became annual events.[220]

In 1904 a Souletin Basque banker in Buenos Aires launched the ambitious undertaking of *Euskal Echea* (Basque House). *Euskal Echea* incorporated the several Basque clubs of Buenos Aires (overarching regional differences) into a single charitable and educational foundation. Construction was begun in 1908, and within eight years the complex contained twenty-four buildings.[221] Its purposes were varied and included care of destitute Basques, care of orphans, establishment of an old peoples' home, provision of hospital care, repatriation to Europe of needy Basques, schooling for Basque children, and religious guidance. Within a short time 400 orphans and 100 old people were living in *Euskal Echea* facilities under the care of an order of Basque nuns from Anglet (Labourd), who also ran the girls' school. A boys' school operated under the guidance of Basque Capuchin priests.[222] Other activities included sponsorship of choral performances, handball matches, Basque language instruction, a service to find living quarters for young Basque girls new to Argentina, and an agricultural station. A women's auxiliary group, counting as members ladies from some of Buenos Aires's finest families, met weekly to sew garments for the needy. *Euskal Echea* maintained its own cemetery and sponsored monthly masses for its deceased members.

---

*The constitution of the *Laurac Bat* organization excluded French Basques.

†The *Laurak Bat* organization underwent difficulties during this period. Through the *Plaza Euskara* it sponsored *jai alai* matches, importing the best players from Europe. Ultimately *jai alai* became the prime reason for the club's existence and produced a considerable profit. However the money was subsequently lost through speculations in the gold market.[218] *Laurak Bat* was forced to sell the *Plaza Euskara* to cover its debts.[219] With the remaining funds it erected a building in downtown Buenos Aires which still houses the organization.

Euskal Echea received its support from subscribers who made regular monthly contributions. From 141 donors in 1905, the list of subscribers grew to 560 by 1907. They were drawn from all walks of life, including both wealthy entrepreneurs and *saladeristas*. The Luros, one of the most successful pioneer families of the *pampas*, constructed a headquarters building in Buenos Aires for the organization.[223]

Further evidence of Basque collective action is a tendency to found publications. We have seen that in Buenos Aires the *Laurac Bat* organization started a newspaper by the same name in 1878. The *Laurak Bat* association of Montevideo followed suit in 1881. From 1893 to 1913, several periodicals appeared in Buenos Aires incuding *La Basconia* (1893),* *Euskal Herria* (1898), *Vasconia* (1898), *Haritza* (1899), *Irrintzi* (1904), *La Euskaria* (1906), and *Euskotarra* (1913). In 1914 *Esnea* ("Milk"), a publication for dairymen, made its appearance and in 1922 a publication, *Zazpirak Bat*, was founded in Rosario de Santa Fe, Argentina. As of 1912 there was a Basque newspaper called *Euskal Erria* in Montevideo.

BASQUE IMMIGRANTS IN OTHER LATIN AMERICAN NATIONS

While the Río de la Plata area was certainly the most important New World destination of nineteenth-century Basque emigration, other countries of Latin America continued to receive an influx of Basques.

Lefebvre notes that beginning about 1840 there was a fresh movement of Basques to Chile, including a generous contingent from the French Basque country.† Initially, the emigrants to Chile outnumbered those to the Río de la Plata area.[226] However, this was quickly reversed as the majority of Basque emigrants selected Argentina. A comparison of statistics concerning foreigners present in each country near the turn of the twentieth century (Argentina, 1914; Chile, 1907) shows that while there were 829,701 Spanish nationals in Argentina, there were only 18,755 of them in Chile. Similarly, Argentina hosted 74,491 French nationals while the number of French nationals

---

La Basconia was a scholarly publication in Basque studies that was read in Europe as well.

†He further localizes the Old World origins of the movement in the Nive Valley where towns like Ustaritz and Hasparren are, to this day, famed for their wealthy "Chilean" returnees.[224] Espil states, "Chile is the country of America to which the Basques of Labourd have preferred to go."[225]

in Chile was only 9,800.[227] Without maintaining that the ratio of Basques masked under the rubric of the French and Spanish nationalities was necessarily the same for Argentina and Chile, it is still clear that considerably more Basque immigrants entered the former.

Thayer estimates that from 1820 through 1885 only 3,575 male Spanish nationals emigrated to Chile (figures for females are lacking).* From 1886 to 1907, he calculates, a minimum of 16,150 Spanish immigrants of both sexes. From 1907 through 1916, he estimates there were 12,461 Spanish immigrants (of both sexes).[230] Sampling the Old World regional origins of 4,001 Spaniards who entered Chile between 1894 and 1916, Thayer finds that 546, or 13.6 percent, were from the four Basque provinces,[231] a ratio, he argues, that holds true for all Spanish immigration throughout the period.[232]

In small measure this movement was stimulated by the mid-nineteenth-century conquest of the Araucanian Indian tribes of southern Chile. With newly available lands, the Chilean government became highly interested in encouraging the immigration of European agriculturalists. Orders were sent to a Chilean agent in Europe to encourage Basque emigrants to select Chile as their destination.[233]† However, with the exception of a few Basques who became wheat farmers in the south, it appears that most who entered Chile preferred commerce.[236] Thus, there is not much mention of Basque participation in stock raising and other physical occupations in nineteenth-century Chile. Rather, Chilean Basques are characterized by

---

*This is difficult to square with the claim by Ridal that by 1883 Chile had attracted two thousand families from "Biscaye" to its shores.[228] It may be that Ridal is using Biscaye in the broadest sense to cover French Basque immigration as well. Such an interpretation is likely (if the figures are at all accurate), since Thayer notes that Spanish Basques had fallen to fourth place (behind Catalans, Old Castilians, and Andalusians) in their contribution to nineteenth-century Spanish emigration to Chile.[229]

†Parenthetically, the *Laurac Bat* newspaper of Buenos Aires roundly denounced these efforts by the Chilean government as fraudulent. They warned that Basque emigrants to Chile could expect to be slaughtered by the Araucanians and that the government would remain indifferent.[234] When advance word of Cola's book (see pp. 156−57) denouncing emigration to the Río de la Plata reached Buenos Aires, *Laurac Bat* simply assumed that it was emigration to Chile that was being denounced. The editors endorsed Cola's work sight unseen.[235] One can only surmise that they were subsequently chagrined to learn that their area was the prime target of Cola's criticisms.

their involvement as entrepreneurs in the creation of "tanneries, shoe factories, corn mills, canneries, hotels, general stores, fruit and vegetable outlets."[237] The pattern was for a young man to enter the employ of an established relative, learn the business, and then head a branch operation or take over the entire enterprise, allowing his former employer to retire to the Basque country.[238]

Five centuries of Basque emigration to Chile, combined with the Basque tendency to become successful entrepreneurs, have made the Basques a pronounced segment of the social elite of modern Chile. According to Thayer, at the turn of the present century, 10.21 percent of Chile's intellectuals were Basques.[239] Of the 554 most valuable agricultural holdings of Chile, 127, or 22.58 percent, were Basque-owned.[240] Of the 2,498 richest families of Santiago 529, or 21.56 percent, were Basques.[241] In each of these categories, Basques led all other Iberian ethnic groups and other European nationalities.

Colombia and Peru were also early foci of Basque immigration. In the case of the former, it has been suggested that the present-day high incidence of business entrepreneurship in the region of Antioquia is directly attributable to the Basque immigration and hence Basque character traits.[242]* Today few Colombians and Peruvians of remote Basque descent are aware of their ethnic heritage. However, in both Bogotá and Lima there is a small colony of thirty or forty families who emigrated either as a consequence of the Spanish Civil War or because of opportunities for technicians and businessmen. The Bogotá colony has its own social club.

Basque immigration into Mexico may also be divided into an older colonial movement and a newer modern one. We have noted many activities of the Basques in colonial Mexican society. However, the independence movement ruptured the ties of chain migration along which Old World Basques entered the area. Toward 1840 a new Basque emigration to Mexico began, which lasted until the early twentieth century. However, the nineteenth century proved to be a particularly unsettled period in Mexican history, a fact that served to limit the magnitude of Basque emigration to that country.[243]

In 1907 the Mexico City Basque colony founded the organization *Centro Vasco*. The emigrants were, in the main,

---

*For a discussion of the Basque emigrant as entrepreneur, see Kasdan 1965; Douglass 1971, 1973a, 1973b; Brandes 1973; Kasdan and Brandes 1973.

from the three Spanish Basque provinces of Navarra, Guipúz-coa and Vizcaya, but also included some French Basques.

The island of Cuba, which remained under Spanish control until the Spanish-American War of 1898, provided another opportunity for Basque emigrants. Cuba, of all the possible New World destinations, provided the greatest continuity with Spanish colonial traditions and opportunities. Basques could continue to enter Cuba as administrators, merchants, and sol-diers. In 1869, when revolution swept the island, Basque troops were sent from San Sebastián to put down the insurrection. According to one report, they were met in Havana by several Basque delegations and by Basque musical groups. Cuban high society provided the officers of the Basque contingent with a sumptuous welcome.[244]

In 1878 the Basque community of Havana organized the *Asociación Vasco-Navarra de Beneficencia* (The Basque-Navarrese Beneficent Association), whose major purpose was to aid the indigent and sponsor repatriations. One of the first actions of the group was to found a burial society with a cemetery reserved exclusively for deceased members.

By 1887 the association had 365 members in Havana and 228 members in the Cuban provinces, in addition to a number of corresponding members residing in the Basque country. Ap-proximately half of the total were persons of Vizcayan descent with the remainder coming from the other three Spanish Basque provinces. No French Basques were accepted.[245]

By 1884 the association sponsored religious ceremonies in honor of the Virgin of Begoña (Vizcaya), their patroness. The services included a mass in which the singing was in Basque, a sermon that praised Basque achievements, a religious proces-sion, a parade with Basque banners, musicians, folk costumes and folk dancing, and refreshments in a local Basque restaurant. Havana newspapers proclaimed the Basque fiestas as the best that had ever taken place in the city.[246]

In Rio de Janeiro (Brazil) there were enough Basques by 1885 to form a society called *Eskualdunak Orok Bat* ("All Basques in One") which maintained close relations with the Basque societies of Montevideo.[247]

On the other hand, areas that formerly had received sig-nificant Basque emigration received little, if any, during the nineteenth century. A case in point is Venezuela. Aristides Rojas lamented the loss of Basque immigration in *El Elemento Vasco en la Historia de Venezuela* ("The Basque Element in the

History of Venezuela"), written in 1874. After noting that the Company of Caracas was the most important American activity of the Spanish crown during the reign of Philip V,[248] Rojas stated:

> among the various branches of the Spanish nationality from which the population of Venezuela originated, none has greater claim upon our national gratitude than the Basques. Study the Andalusians, Castilians, Catalans, or Canary Islanders and one finds that the only element that has managed to conserve itself and leave behind imperishable accomplishments, despite the effects of passing time, is the Basque element.[249]

Yet from 1830 on, according to Rojas, "only the republics of the Plata enjoy the enviable privilege of witnessing a steady current of immigration originating in the Basque provinces."[250] He complained:

> Why this decisive love for the shores of la Plata? Is it that the *pampas* of Buenos Aires appear to them more attractive than the vast and rich extensions of our plains? Is it that in our Alpine mountains and our hot forests, on the shores of our lakes and on the extensive belt of our coastline they do not see the image of Pyrenean peaks and the Cantabrian sea? Why not come to the soil that was cultivated by their ancestors, where the variety of climates, and landforms, where the richness of the vegetation . . . and the large number of Basque descendants tell them that there in times past was their American center?[251]

By the First World War, there were well-established Basque colonies in several countries of Latin America, most notably the Río de la Plata nations of Argentina and Uruguay.*

---

*Recently an Argentine writer estimated the number of Old World-born Basques and their postcolonial New World-born descendants in Argentina in 1970 at 1.5 million persons. This calculation is derived by applying a natural growth rate of 2.3 percent (the national average) annually to a presumed population of forty thousand Basques present in Argentina in 1869, adding in the additional immigration of Basques through the remainder of the nineteenth century, thereby achieving an estimated Basque population of about six hundred thousand persons by 1910, to which a natural growth rate of 1.8 percent to 1.9 percent (the national rate of growth) is applied to the present.[252]

A problem with this approach is that it fails to consider the probable high rate of departures as Basques left Argentina to return to their homeland or went to another part of the New World. Furthermore, nineteenth-century Basque immigration into Argentina included a large proportion of single males. Taking a cue from the high frequency of celibacy among Basques in Europe and the American West, we may surmise that many of these men never married. Etcheverry notes that in 1866 in the French Basque population there

No region of Argentina was without its Basque population.[256] Buenos Aires province, with slightly over two million inhabitants, was the most populous in the nation. By one estimate, fully 31.5 percent of the province's population were of Basque descent.[258]

In each country the Basques maintained their ethnic group self-awareness, which they converted into formal organizations as they made concerted efforts to maintain Basque cultural traditions. One important expression of this concern was the tendency of Latin American Basques to retain an orientation to the Old World Basque country. The majority of nineteenth-century Basque emigrants left the Basque country with the intention of returning. Few Basque immigrants of long-term residence in Argentina took out Argentine citizenship.[258] This was equally as true for the man who left an impoverished rural society to gain the means to redeem his family farm as for the political refugee who sought a temporary New World haven during and after the Carlist Wars. That many established themselves permanently in Latin America was only natural. However, even they were likely to realize a desire to revisit their natal land. The maintenance of ties with the Basque country is reflected clearly in some of the activities of the Basque organizations in Latin America. For example, in 1913 the *Centro Vasco Francés* of Buenos Aires sent flood relief funds to the mayor of Bayonne, and again in 1920 funds were sent to the three French Basque provinces for war relief. In 1925 100,000 *pesos* were collected to help establish a college in Ustaritz (Labourd).[259]

But possibly the clearest indicator of a continued Old World orientation was seen in the responsive chord that Basque nationalism struck in the thinking of many Latin American Basques.* During the last two decades of the nineteenth cen-

---

were 121 celibate males for every one thousand inhabitants.[253] Gachiteguy states that in the 1950s, 17 percent of the adult Basques resident in California[254] and 15.5 percent of those in Nevada were celibate.[255] These figures include American-born Basques and those immigrants with long standing residence in the American West. If the sample is restricted to Basques of Old World birth, fully 33 percent of those residing in California and 55 percent of those in Nevada were celibate! Also, Basques have a tendency toward late marriage; many males delay it until in their thirties. Hence, it is likely that the natural growth rate in the Basque sector of the Argentine population was somewhat below the national average.

*The issue of Basque nationalism constitutes the most divisive factor in the group life of Latin American Basque colonies. In all of the major colonies,

tury, the Basques of Spain initiated a political and cultural movement that clamored for greater Basque political autonomy and freedom of cultural expression. The works of the precursor of the movement, Arturo Campión, were read widely in Argentina, as were the works of its founder, Sabino Arana y Goiri.[260] It is probably more than coincidental that the Basques of Montevideo founded the *Laurak Bat* organization in 1876, the year the Basques were defeated in the Second Carlist War. The founding of *Laurac Bat* in Buenos Aires the same year was clearly related to the ethnic pride that was outraged by this defeat.[261] A Basque nationalist political organization, *Acción Nacionalista Baska*, was founded near the turn of the century in Buenos Aires.[262] The *Euskal Echea* of Buenos Aires served as a forum for many Basque nationalist political discourses. The American-born Basque Tomás Otaegui became a leading apologist for the Basque Nationalist Movement.[263] In 1919 a bronze plaque, honoring those Basque parliamentarians who were arguing the Basque case in the Spanish parliament, was placed in the building of the *Laurak Bat* society in Buenos Aires. Shortly thereafter, the society planted a cutting of the tree of Guernica at the foot of the statue of Juan de Garay, the Basque founder of the city.[264]

THE BASQUES IN TWENTIETH-CENTURY LATIN AMERICA

The First World War marks the termination of massive Basque emigration to Latin America. Several factors were responsible. By the second decade of the twentieth century the expansion of agriculture in the *pampas* was largely over. The great land boom had driven prices well beyond the means of immigrants and lower-class laborers. Thus, there was considerably less likelihood that an impoverished immigrant could gain rapid social and economic mobility through sheer dedication and hard work. Furthermore, the demand for unskilled workers in both agriculture and urban occupations was waning. Particu-

---

there are groups that refrain from political involvement. In some cases, this difference of opinion caused outright schism in the ethnic organizations. To cite but two examples, in 1929 the apolitical members of the *Laurak Bat* organization of Buenos Aires seceded and formed a new club, *Gure Echea* ("Our House"), which emphasized athletics. Similarly, in the mid-1930s, most of the Navarrese withdrew from the *Centro Vasco* in Mexico City and formed the *Círculo Vasco Español*, which favored good relations with the clubs of other Spanish nationals residing in the area.

larly on the *pampas*, the mechanization of agriculture diminished wage employment opportunities for the unskilled.
With the exception of the war years themselves, Argentine food
products and wool production caught and surpassed the European demand. The sheep industry was dealt a serious blow
about 1900, when a major depression in French and Belgian
wool prices coincided with devastating floods in the *pampas*.[265]

Paralleling the decline of economic opportunity in several
South American countries was a resurgence of natiõnalism
tinged with xenophobia.[266] By the First World War both Chile
and Argentina had vocal proponents of restrictive immigration
policies, although this nationalism did not culminate in anti-
immigration legislation until the Great Depression of the
1930s.[267] The xenophobic sentiment was surely conveyed to
potential emigrants in Europe and undoubtedly weighed in their
decision to emigrate and their choice of destination.

The First World War itself disrupted sea traffic with the
New World and engaged the interests of most Europeans.
French Basques served willingly and with distinction in the
French forces. In fact, the German invasion of France triggered
what might be regarded as the first wave of genuine French
patriotism in the Basque provinces. Spain remained neutral in
the war and as such enjoyed the economic benefits of a nation on
the edge of a major conflict, freed from its adverse consequences, while selling goods to the combatants. The war stimulated Spanish Basque industry, inflated the value of agricultural
products, and provided frontier populations with great
economic opportunity in the booming contraband traffic.

For these reasons, Basque emigration to Latin America
was disrupted considerably during the First World War. Furthermore, this disruption was not of a temporary nature. After
the war economic conditions in Europe improved rapidly. In the
Basque provinces a veritable consumers' revolution of wants set
in and caused a major shift in value orientations, particularly
among the rural populace. The peasants' existence had been
independent and self-sufficient; the peasant household was capable of meeting most of its members' wants through farming
and household crafts. Postwar Basques saw peasant life as
brutish, backward, and anachronistic. Urban living became
idealized as the "good life." Many peasants abandoned their
natal farmsteads and migrated to the cities, where they gained a
foothold in small-scale commerce or in factory jobs. Those who

remained in the countryside sought to emulate their urban counterparts, at least in their reliance upon manufactured goods.

In the Spanish Basque provinces the growth of industry did
not remain centralized in the traditional urban industrial centers
like Bilbao and San Sebastián. Small towns like Guernica,
Durango, Eibar, Villafranca, Vergara, and Irún became industrial zones. Each of these centers affected its immediate hinterland in two fashions. The factory-working population provided
a ready demand for agricultural produce; hence, the peasants
living within easy distance could convert their traditional agricultural system, with its emphasis upon household subsistence, to intensive dairying, poultry raising, and horticulture for
the nearby urban marketplaces. More recently, with improved
transportation facilities individual peasants were in a position to
commute—by bicycle, motor scooter or bus—to a factory job.
The economies of numerous former peasant households became
characterized by a blend of factory work and commercial agriculture.

A further factor reducing post—World War I Basque emigration to Latin America was the new attraction of the American
West. Although the *pampas* were settled and in private ownership, vast areas of the American West remained open to exploitation by the immigrant. A man might hope to enter the American West, seek employment as a sheepherder with a kinsman or
other contact, take his wages in ewes, and within a few years
wander over the open range with his own flocks. Since the early
twentieth century was generally a period of expansion in the
American economy, there were many success stories among the
Basque sheepmen. Also, by 1900 there were numerous wealthy
sheepmen from the American West who had returned to the
Basque country as living proof of American opportunity.

Since the First World War, Basque emigration to Latin
America has been limited, with one notable exception, to a few
hundred individuals annually who usually go to join their established relatives. The exception is the period immediately following the Spanish Civil War, when thousands of Basques were
forced to flee Spain. The Basque government-in-exile exhorted
Basques of the New World to help the refugees. Venezuela,
Argentina, Chile, Uruguay, and Mexico received large numbers of Basque exiles. Between 1939 and 1945, fifteen hundred
Basques entered Venezuela as political refugees.[268] In 1940 a
group called the *Comité Pro-Inmigración Vasca* was estab-

lished in Argentina to provide for any Basque refugee who failed to fend for himself. President Ortiz declared Argentina open to any person of Basque descent. In the following years, fourteen hundred Basques entered Argentina under the plan, none of whom ended up as a ward of the committee or the state.[269]

Although Basque emigration to Latin America was reduced to a trickle when compared with the previous period, the twentieth century witnessed the continued expansion and proliferation of Basque collective activity. In Argentina, for example, membership in the *Laurak Bat* organization had grown to one thousand by 1930. The *Centro Vasco Francés* grew from twenty-nine members in 1895 to five hundred in 1930. By the same year *Euskal Echea* had grown to over two thousand members and the *Centro Navarro* had three hundred. In 1929 a recreational group called *Gure Echea* was formed in Buenos Aires with a membership of five hundred. Furthermore, in the 1920s, several Basque organizations were established outside the capital, including *Euskal Echea* in Quilmes, *Denak Bat* in Arrecifes, *Zazpirak Bat* in Rosario, *Laurak Bat* in Bahía Blanca, and *Euskal Echea* in Comodoro Rivadavia.[270] At present there are at least forty-four Basque clubs in Argentina. In 1955 the *Federación de Entidades Vasco Argentinas* (Federation of Basque-Argentine Entities), which includes twenty-five of Argentina's Basque clubs, was formed. The federation is highly political and has a Basque nationalist orientation. It publishes its own journal and organizes an annual national Basque week sponsored on a rotating basis by one of its member clubs.

During the twentieth century Basque clubs have been organized in other Latin American countries as well. To cite but a few, there are the *Centro Vasco* (1907) of Mexico City; the *Centro Euskaro Español* (1911) and *Euskal Erria* (1912), both of Montevideo; the *Centro Vasco* (1931) in Santiago de Chile; the *Centro Vasco* (1942) of Caracas; the *Eusko Alkartasuna* (1954) of São Paulo, Brazil;* and the *Centro Vasco* (1960s) of Bogotá.

With the collapse of Basque resistance in the Spanish Civil War, many leading Basque intellectuals sought refuge in Latin

---

*Basque technicians have found considerable employment opportunity since the 1950s in the automobile industry of São Paulo. There are presently several hundred Basques in the city, all of whom are relatively recent immigrants.

America. Their presence soon led to the establishment of publications, generally pro-Basque nationalist, in several countries of Latin America. In Argentina these include *Eusko Deya* (1937), *Galeuzka* (1945−46), *Euskalzaleak* (1954), and *Tierra Vasca* (1956); in Montevideo, *Euskal Ordua* (1939); in Santiago de Chile, *Boletín de Euzko-Gaztedija* (1941), *Batasuna* (1941−42), *Euzkadi* (1943), and *Eusko-Etxea* (1959); in Mexico, *Aberri Aldez* (1936), *Alkartu* (1942), *Euzko Deya* (1943), *Aberri* (1946), *Ekin* (1950), *Euzkadi Azkatuta* (1956); and, in Venezuela during the 1960s, *Gudari* and *Zutik*. *Tierra Vasca* of Buenos Aires and *Gudari* and *Zutik* in Caracas are major propaganda organs in the ongoing Basque nationalist movement. Each has wide clandestine distribution in the Basque country.[271]

In 1942 the publishing house *Editorial Ekin* was founded in Buenos Aires with the purpose of publishing works dealing with Basque culture. In 1943 the American Institute of Basque Studies was founded in Buenos Aires; in 1950 it began to publish an important journal of Basque studies, the *Boletín del Instituto Americano de Estudios Vascos*. In 1945 Longfellow's poem *Evangeline* was translated into Basque and published in Guatemala City.[272] The journal *Cancha* (biweekly magazine of Basque *jai alai*) appeared in Mexico City in the same year. In 1950 a Basque cultural magazine, *Euzko Gogoa*, was founded in the capital of Guatemala.

It ought to be pointed out that the seeming effervescence of group activities among the Basques of Latin America masks a growing crisis. Presently, there is little continued immigration of Old World Basques into Latin America, and there is rapid assimilation of Basques into the mainstream of Latin American society. Many of the Basque immigrants are technicians or professional persons with skills that provide them with immediate economic and social advantages. Furthermore, the Old World Basque emigrant is fluent in Spanish, including many French Basques, and is generally conversant with the Hispanic traditions that are a part of Latin America's cultural heritage as well. With few exceptions (the *Centro Vasco* of Caracas, for example), the Basque organizations of Latin America are losing members. In 1930, the *Laurak Bat* and *Centro Vasco Francés* associations of Buenos Aires had one thousand and five hundred members respectively; by 1970, the membership of the former had declined almost a fourth to 776,[273] while that of the latter stood at 368.[274]

There are many lessons in Latin American history for the student of the Basques of the American West. Since Columbus's first voyage to the Indies in 1492, Latin America has served as a focus for Basque emigration and activities. In the sixteenth and seventeenth centuries there was notable clustering of Basques in northern Mexico, the mining districts of the central Andes, and the key commercial and port centers such as Havana, Veracruz, Panama, and Santiago de Chile. At the same time Basques were sprinkled liberally throughout the ranks of the conquistadors, missionaries, and mariners; Basques, either as individuals or in small groups, were ubiquitous throughout the Spanish colonial world.

In the eighteenth century, there was a notable shift of Basque emigration to Venezuela and Chile. In the nineteenth century the Río de la Plata republics were by far the most popular New World destinations of Basque emigrants.

We can only understand the complexities of a Basque emigration that eventually touched every corner of the New World, albeit in differing degrees, by first considering the historical backdrop of shifting political, social, and economic conditions that influenced the Old and New World over the course of several centuries. To understand the nature of Basque emigration to any one area of the world at a particular time, it is necessary to understand the nature of the alternatives and the emigrant's perception of them. To do otherwise is to seek the explanation for the attraction of Chile for Basque immigrants in terms of "the climate . . . , the pearly sky, the infinite verdure of the plains, which never ceased reminding them of the sweet atmosphere of the Basque country with its blue sky tenderly flecked with clouds. . . . Yes, many things there spoke to them of their mother land."[275] This explanation ignores the fact that Basques emigrated to practically every habitable climatic zone of the New World. Of particular interest in this respect is the second major nineteenth-century destination of Basque emigrants—the American West. But in order to begin at the beginning, we must revert once again to the Spanish colonial period of New World history and look particularly at the region that is presently the state of California.

CHAPTER FOUR

Basques in
Spanish California

JESUIT MISSIONARIES IN BAJA CALIFORNIA

During the late sixteenth and seventeenth centuries the Jesuit order was quite influential in Mexican society, particularly among its Basque colony. After all, the very founders of the order, Saint Ignatius (a Guipuzcoan from Loyola) and Saint Francis (a Navarrese from Javier), were both Basques.

While Saint Ignatius was still alive, a fellow Basque, Juan de Arteaga, who became bishop of Chiapas (present-day Mexico) in 1539, wrote to him requesting that the order send priests to his diocese. The project would have been the first entry of Jesuits into the Americas, but it was abandoned when the bishop died suddenly.[1] When Ignatius was beatified in 1610, there were processions in Mexico City led by 150 horsemen in sumptuous dress. According to Alegre's account, "They were all Vizcayans, of the ranks of the most distinguished and wealthy people in the city."[2]

When Ignatius and Francis were canonized together in 1622, the celebration in Mexico City defied the imagination. The jewels and gold used to adorn the statues of the two saints weighed fourteen *arrobas* (an *arroba* is equivalent to about twenty-five pounds).[3] The festival lasted for several days and included parades that had floats representing Navarra, Guipúz-coa, and Vizcaya.[4]

Unlike the Franciscan fathers, who remained essentially a missionary order recruiting their members in Spain, the Jesuits recruited internationally and played a prominent role in colonial society, founding colleges for the instruction of the children of the wealthy. We have already noted that all of the ecclesiastical advisors to the Basque Confraternity of Aránzazu in Mexico City were Jesuits. Jesuit influence in Mexico was further enhanced by the fact that sons of some wealthy colonial families themselves entered the order. However, if the Jesuits were not as publicly self-demeaning, poverty-stricken, and humble as the members of some other religious orders, they were nevertheless imbued with the same missionary zeal—a quality that made them the initial spearhead of the Spanish colonization of California.

In 1590 the Jesuit order began to found missions along the west coast of northern Mexico on the borders of the old province of *Nueva Vizcaya*, the present-day regions of Sonora and Sinaloa. Sinaloa served as a point of departure for several expeditions whose purpose it was to explore the California coast. Jesuit priests participated in many of these voyages, and in 1640 the order petitioned Rome for permission to create missions in Baja California.

In 1678 the Jesuits reached an agreement with the governor of Sinaloa, Isidro Atondo y Antillón (a Basque), to explore the peninsula and to study the possibilities of establishing missions there,[5] but it was not until the arrival in Mexico of the Italian Jesuit Eusebio Francisco Kino in 1681 that the project was begun. Kino and the Basque Matías Goñi together launched the first Jesuit-sponsored expedition. The expeditionaries left the Mexican coast on January 17, 1683, and on April 1 of the same year they landed in La Paz Bay, taking possession of the area in the names of Governor Atondo, the king of Spain, and the bishop of Guadalajara.[6] Two years later the expedition returned to Mexico.

Father Kino and Governor Atondo began a concerted campaign to convince the Spanish administration of the advisability of colonizing California. They received the support of the royal treasurer in Mexico, Pedro de Labastida, a Basque from Alava, who recommended to the crown that it support colonization of California to the tune of "an annual appropriation from the government of 30,000 *pesos* for the support of four missionaries and 25 soldiers with 8 Yaqui families of laborers."[7]

The Jesuit order named another Italian, Father Juan María Salvatierra (half-Spanish; his father's family came from Andújar in Andalucía),[8] as the organizer of the California missions. Salvatierra appointed the Basque priest Juan de Ugarte, professor of philosophy in the Jesuit college of Mexico City, as fundraiser and guardian of the purse strings of the California missions. Ugarte remained in Mexico City while Salvatierra left in 1697 to found missions in California with a formal permission granted by the Spanish crown.

Under the terms of their contract the Jesuits were responsible for financing their expeditions and missions. Soldiers would be provided, but the Jesuits were to pay their salaries. The Jesuits retained authority over the selection and command of their troops. Consequently, Salvatierra was not only the spiritual leader of the missions, but he was also commander in chief of Baja California.[9]

Between 1697, when their first California mission was built at Loreto, until 1767, when the last was erected at Santa María, the Jesuits established a chain of seventeen missions in Baja California.

The international quality of Jesuit recruitment was reflected in the nationalities of the sixty-two friars who serviced the California missions. Seventeen were born in Latin America, fifteen were Germans or Austrians, fourteen were Spaniards, nine were Italians; there was one Croat, one Scotsman, and five were of national origins undetermined by historians. Analyzed in terms of ethnic origins, ten of the sixty-two were of Basque descent. This included two European-born Basques, José de Echeverría and Juan de Muguzabal. Six were Basque-American, including four born in Mexico: Juan Manuel de Basaldua, Sebastián de Sistiaga, Juan Luyando, and Agustín Luyando. The other two Basque-Americans were the brothers Juan and Pedro de Ugarte, born in Tegucigalpa. Finally, two of the Basque descendants, Matiás Goñi and Juan Salazar, were of unknown origin.

The history of the mission of Santa Rosalía de Mulege shows clearly the interweaving of clerical and lay interests along Basque ethnic lines. The mission was founded by Father Juan Manuel Basaldua, born in Michoacán of Basque parents. It was financed by another Basque, Nicolás de Arteaga, a resident of Mexico City (and the artist who decorated the chapel of the

Confraternity of Aránzazu). When Basaldua left for health reasons, he appointed Juan Bautista Muguzabal, also a Basque and a corporal of the mission's military guard, as temporary leader until Basaldua's replacement, the Sicilian-born Father Picolo, arrived to take charge. Muguzabal had arrived in California as a soldier in 1704. However, after his short experience as head of the mission garrison, he resolved to enter the order. He served his noviceship in California under the auspices of the Basque priest Juan de Ugarte and became a Jesuit, thereby being "the first man to pronounce officially his initial religious vows of poverty, chastity, and obedience in California."[10]

After Father Picolo's tenure, two Basques headed the mission of Santa Rosalía: Father Sebastián Sistiaga (1718−26) and Father Juan Bautista Luyando (1727−31). In 1728 these two Jesuits jointly founded the mission of San Ignacio, which they financed out of Luyando's family inheritance (10,000 *pesos*).

Father Sistiaga continued to be a major figure in the Jesuit California missions. The historian Dunne regards him as "a pillar of the California foundations,"[11] and in subsequent periods many Indians received the name Sistiaga in memory of the great missionary.[12]

In their relations with the other colonists the Jesuits of California made many enemies. They prohibited lay persons from colonizing Baja California and also prohibited the development of pearl fisheries along the coast. Near the end of their tenancy, they even forbade their own soldiers and Indian charges to pearl dive. This attitude was little appreciated in the colonies, where California was often viewed as an "el dorado and the padres were dragons guarding its wealth."[13]

In 1767 Spain, following the example of France (1764), expelled the Jesuits from all of the territories of its empire, including California. Captain Gaspar de Portolá was dispatched to Baja California accompanied by troops and by fourteen Franciscans, who were to replace the Jesuits. According to one of the expelled Jesuits, Father Baegert, the soldiers who arrived "imagined that California was paved with silver and that heaps of pearls could be swept together with brooms."[14] However, the only form of wealth that had been nurtured and developed by the Jesuits was livestock. With the exception of missions like San Luis and Dolores, which had problems with Indian raids, the missions were well stocked with cattle and sheep. Dunne cites the list of the last Jesuit inspector (*visitador*) to visit the

California missions, the Basque priest Ignacio de Lizasoain. Lizasoain's estimates of the herds and flocks appear in table 5.

TABLE 5
HERDS AND FLOCKS KEPT BY BAJA CALIFORNIA MISSIONS, LATE EIGHTEENTH CENTURY

Name of Mission	Cattle	Sheep
Loreto	3,000	—
San Gabriel	1,000	1,000
Comundu	2,500	2,000
Santa Rosalía	1,000	2,000
San Ignacio	1,500	4,000
Purisima	700	—
San José	—	16,000
Todos Santos	*	*

Source: Dunne, *Black Robes*, p. 396.
    *Well stocked.

In 1772 the Dominicans replaced the Franciscans in the missions of Baja California. The latter were thereby released to missionize Upper (or Alta) California, at which point we enter into the history of the colonization of the present-day state of California.

VOYAGES OF DISCOVERY IN CALIFORNIA WATERS

At about the time of the expulsion of the Jesuits, the crown initiated a dynamic program of expansion of missions and military bases along the Pacific coast to counter the growing threat posed by Russian and English claims and incursions in the region. In 1765 a special emissary *(visitador)*, José de Gálvez, was sent to Mexico to oversee the Spanish effort. It was immediately clear that Spain required a naval base on the Pacific coast to serve as the home port, both for the launching of new voyages of discovery as well as for the provisioning of new colonies. The base was established in 1767 at San Blas de Nayarit.

Immense physical distances separated San Blas on the Pacific from Spain and the Spanish New World ports on the Atlantic and in the Caribbean. San Blas therefore required a full array of maritime facilities. The port was even outfitted with shipyards for both the construction and repair of vessels. During the thirty-year period between 1767 and 1797, when San Blas was the most important sea base in the north Pacific, Basques were the most prominent and numerous ethnic element among its many maritime officials, naval engineers, and shipbuilders.

The first administrator of the region was the Basque Juan de Urrengoechea y Arrinda. Between 1767 and 1777 the head shipbuilder in San Blas was the Basque Pedro de Yzaguirre, who directed the construction of the schooner *Sonora* and the frigates *Santiago* and *San José*.[15] When Yzaguirre retired to Spain in 1777, he was replaced by the Basque Francisco Segurola, whose previous post was in the shipyards of El Ferrol (Spain). Segurola completed the construction of the frigate *Princesa* before dying in 1787.

Upon Segurola's death, Spanish officialdom encountered considerable difficulty in finding a suitable replacement. After searching vainly in Havana and Spain the crown commissioned the Vizcayan Diego de Gardoqui, the Spanish consul in Boston, to find a skilled American shipbuilder for the vacant post. Gardoqui hired a technician, John Ficus Morgan of Boston, and started him on his journey to San Blas. However, while Morgan was still in Havana the viceroy of Mexico wrote to the Minister of the Indies in Spain refusing to receive the shipbuilder. His letter defines the importance of San Blas and reveals a growing suspicion in Mexico of the emerging nation to the north. To wit, the viceroy states,

> I take it as a matter of course that this foreigner is very good and well qualified; but it does not seem to me convenient to employ him in these dominions, and much less in the construction of ships for a port like that of San Blas, which sustains our recent establishments in California, which facilitates the explorations to the north of that coast, which provides the means of impeding the intentions of Russia, and which, finally, serves as a port for the ships of Callao de Lima and the Philippines. All of these reasons compel me to suspend the carrying out of the royal order . . . [until] there shall come from Spain a good shipbuilder with the requisite qualifications, since none is to be had in Havana.[16]

In light of the viceroy's rejection of Morgan, the crown once again contracted San Blas's master shipbuilder in the shipyards of El Ferrol. The post was given to the Basque Manuel de Bastarrechea who, between 1790 and 1792, constructed four vessels, the *Valdés*, the *Activo*, the *Sutíl*, and the *Mexicana*. These were the last ships to be constructed in San Blas, although other vessels navigating in California waters used San Blas as home port.

Basques played an important role in the many exploratory voyages launched from San Blas. In 1774 an expedition under the command of Juan Pérez, with the Basque missionaries Mugartegui and Murguía on board, sailed as far north as Nootka. However, Pérez did not take formal possession of the area, nor did he establish a colony.

By this time there was growing alarm in Madrid over Russian activities in the North Pacific. In 1774 Julián de Arriaga, minister of the Indies, sent six new officials to San Blas to reorganize the port. According to Thurman, "These new officers who took command of the supply vessels have become legendary in the early history of Alta California: Bruno de Hezeta, Juan Francisco de la Bodega y Quadra, Fernando Quiros, Juan Manuel de Ayala, Francisco Mourelle, Ignacio de Arteaga, and Manuel Manrique."[17] Of the six, the senior officer (Hezeta of Bilbao) and his junior officer (Bodega, born in Peru) were of Basque descent,[18] as was the port official Ignacio de Arteaga, who was appointed by Viceroy Bucareli* specifically as a "partial guarantee against poor administration."[19]

Once installed, the new officials organized expeditions with the specific purpose of taking formal possession of the northern reaches. In 1775 Bruno de Hezeta, with Bodega as his second, sailed from San Blas in command of the three vessels, the *San Carlos*, the *Santiago*, and the *Sonora*. At least twelve of the crewmen were Basques.[20] The expedition reached Alaskan waters, thereby establishing the northernmost claim of sovereignty for the Spanish crown.[21]

In 1776 the minister of the Indies, Julián de Arriaga, died and was replaced by José de Gálvez, the founder of the port of San Blas. One of Gálvez's first official acts was to promote both Hezeta and Bodega and to order that a new expedition be prepared. Since the available shipping in San Blas was already sorely taxed to maintain the supply lines to the California missions and presidios, Bodega went to Callao (Peru) in search of a vessel. Meanwhile, Ignacio de Arteaga ordered the construction in San Blas of the vessel the *Princesa* under the direction of the shipbuilder Francisco de Segurola. In 1778 the vessel was ready, and Bodega returned from Callao with another, the *Favorita*.

In February of 1779 the *Princesa*, under Arteaga's command, and the *Favorita*, under the command of Bodega, left

---

*Himself Basque on his mother's side.

San Blas. One of their pilots was the Basque Juan Bautista de Aguirre who, according to Bancroft, was to be a frequent visitor to California ports between 1775 and 1790.[22] The Arteaga-Bodega expedition reached the Kanai peninsula, which Bodega claimed in the name of the Spanish crown. On their return, the expeditionaries rested for six weeks in San Francisco Bay before arriving in San Blas on the very eve of the declaration of war between Spain and England.

With the new war (1779−85) the priorities for the port of San Blas had to be modified. Its prime mission became to service the vessels defending the Spanish shipping lanes to Manila. During the war years, only two supply boats were dispatched annually to California, and in 1781, none could be sent.[23] In 1782, the California supply boats were the *Princesa*, under the command of the Basque Agustín de Echevarría, and the *Favorita*, commanded by Juan Bautista de Aguirre.

The war with England also prompted a reshuffling in the administration of the port. Hezeta and Arteaga remained in San Blas but Bodega was sent to Cádiz. In 1789 he returned to San Blas as its senior commander.

Between the end of the war in 1785 and Bodega's return in 1789, two expeditions were launched from San Blas, in 1788 and 1789, both of which reached Canadian and Alaskan waters. The force under Gonzalo López de Haro contacted a Russian settlement on Kodiak Island while the second expedition, under the command of Esteban José Martínez, captured two English vessels near Nootka, returning to San Blas with English prisoners.

The presence of Russians and English to the north of California increased consternation among the Spanish authorities. In 1789 Bodega returned to San Blas accompanied by seven officials, among whom were the Basques Francisco de Eliza and Juan Bautista de Matute. Eliza was given command of a new expedition. His orders were to establish a permanent presidio in Nootka for the defense of Spanish interests. He was also to map the Alaskan coast and initiate fur trading with the natives.[24] The *Aránzazu*, under the command of Matute,[25]* was the vessel selected to service the lifeline between Nootka and San Blas.

---

*Once again we find that in important matters Basques sought out fellow ethnics. It is not by chance that in a matter as important as the securing of Nootka, Bodega settled upon Eliza as his right-hand man and Matute as the link between them. The appointments echo the same confidence placed in Bodega some years earlier by his fellow Basque commander Hezeta.

Eliza's expedition left San Blas on February 3, 1790. On the first of April, he dropped anchor in Nootka Sound. During the summer, he established a fortress and dispatched boats to reconnoiter the coast. Meanwhile, Matute and the *Aránzazu* supplied the new base. On November 13 all vessels except the *Concepción*, which remained in Nootka with Eliza, had returned to San Blas.[26] Spain and England concluded an agreement shortly thereafter that ultimately limited Spanish sovereignty in the North Pacific to the two Californias.[27]

The maritime activity on the west coast of Mexico quickly created its own administrative structure and economic activities. By the late eighteenth century crown income from the colonies had shifted from the earlier dependence upon mineral wealth to trade based upon the products of plantation agriculture. Tobacco plantations were established in the region of San Blas, and the first supervisor of the area's tobacco monopoly was the Basque Francisco de Urbieta, appointed by the *visitador* Gálvez.

Gálvez was particularly impressed with the potential of tobacco as a source of crown income.[28] A year prior to his arrival in Mexico in 1764, he had conceded the Mexican monopoly to Juan José de Echeveste, a Guipuzcoan residing in Mexico City. Echeveste was required to deposit 12,000 *pesos* and to pay all costs of the operation.[29] In March 1765 the general director of the tobacco monopoly, Jacinto Espinosa, demanded that Echeveste increase his deposit. When he refused, Espinosa himself assumed control and by August was bankrupt, having spent 35,533 *pesos* against receipts of only 29,754 *pesos*.[30]

When Gálvez arrived in Mexico one of his first official acts was to return the tobacco monopoly to Echeveste.[31] Echeveste's success was phenomenal. The crown's share of the earnings between September 1765 and December 1766 was 239,097 *pesos*. In 1767 it climbed to 417,732 *pesos*. By 1798 the Mexican monopoly had realized 117,482,551 *pesos* for the Spanish crown,[32] or an annual average of over three million. Echeveste established factories in Mexico City, Puebla, Orizaba, and Oaxaca, whose combined work force reached 12,000 employees.[33]*

---

*We have noted in chapter 2 (p. 111) that by 1793 members of the Royal Basque Society occupied key posts throughout the entire administrative structure of Spain's tobacco monopoly.

The tobacco magnate Echeveste was a nephew and heir of General Francisco de Echeveste, whom we have already encountered as a cofounder of the College of the Vizcayans in Mexico City. Juan de Echeveste was likewise active in the college, and he was one of the signatories of a letter sent to the king in 1755 during the long dispute over the college's inauguration. Once the college was functioning, Juan de Echeveste and Ambrosio de Meabe gave 120,000 *pesos* to support forty students.[34] During the biennium 1774–5 Echeveste served as the rector of the Confraternity of Aránzazu and the College of the Vizcayans.[35]

In light of his administrative achievements with the tobacco monopoly, Juan de Echeveste was appointed treasurer of the baker's guild and the crown's purchasing agent for the two Californias in 1770.[36] The same year he traveled to Monterey, after which he was the key administrative figure in the control of California commerce. As author of the "New Code for San Blas and Alta California," written in 1773, Echeveste was instrumental in shaping the future Spanish colonization of California.[37]

Basque Missionaries of Alta California

The Echeveste document was written just four years after the first Spanish attempts to establish permanent settlements in the Alta California region. The first such project was initiated under the personal supervision of the *visitador* Gálvez who sent out two sea expeditions and two land expeditions in 1769 with orders to join forces near present-day San Diego, to found a base camp there, and then to push on to Monterey. If Basques were the most prominent Iberian ethnic group in the voyages of discovery in California waters, the outstanding ethnic group in these early efforts at colonization were the Catalans and Mallorcans.* The Catalan Gaspar de Portolá, at that time governor of Baja California, was the commander of the key expedition. His lieutenant was the Catalan Pedro Fages who headed an elite group of twenty-five Catalan volunteers. There was also a large contingent of Mexican soldiers, under the command of Captain Rivera Moncada. The religious leader of the expedition was a Franciscan friar, the Mallorcan Junípero Serra.

The expedition was plagued with problems from the outset. Of the twenty-five Catalan soldiers, eighteen or nineteen

---

*In terms of Old World regional ethnic divisions, Catalans and Mallorcans are closely related, almost to the point of sharing common ethnicity.

died aboard ship or in San Diego of scurvy.[38] Of a total expeditionary force of ninety men, two-thirds died.[39] It was only the resolve of Father Serra that prevented Portolá from calling off the effort. As it was, Portolá returned to Baja California in the summer of 1770, relinquishing his command to Captain Rivera.

This first attempt at colonization was strictly a military and missionary effort. There were no families, only soldiers, a half-dozen specialists (an engineer, a mechanic, a doctor, a carpenter, and two muleteers), and some servants. A published list of the names[40] of these early colonists contains only three persons with Basque last names (Esparza, Badiola, and Orozco), and it is likely that these men were born in Mexico. Among the six Franciscan friars who arrived in the first year, only one was Basque—Father Juan Viscaino.

Almost immediately there was friction in the new colony between the soldiers and friars. The friars were anxious to convert the Indians to Christianity and to transform them into docile agriculturalists and craftsmen. The friars regarded the soldiers as temporary protectors of the missions against the possible attacks of unconverted Indians and as instruments of justice when corporal punishment had to be meted out to Indian backsliders. At the same time, they regarded the soldiers as the potential exploiters of the Indians and as pernicious influence upon them.

The mission establishment itself was the friars' main instrument of control. The mission constituted a largely self-contained society with living quarters, workshops, fields, and a church. Indians were attracted, cajoled, or coerced, if need be, into becoming permanent residents of the mission. Under the guidance of the friars, they were to be "domesticated" and imbued with the Christian values of hard work and obedience. For the missionary, the Indian was an infant who required careful and constant protection against both the savage customs of the unenlightened Indian tribes and the moral weaknesses* of the European soldiers.

During Portolá's year of command (1770) he founded the presidio of Monterey and the mission San Carlos de Monterey.[42] In the following year the pulse of Spanish colonization

---

*In Serra's view, the fact that the soldiers were without women was a particularly dangerous state of affairs. He made the accusation that the soldiers "lassoed [Indian] women for their lust and killed such males as dared to interfere."[41]

of Alta California quickened. In May ten new friars arrived, the majority Catalans and Mallorcans, and in the autumn twenty-one additional Catalan soldiers reached the presidio. Meanwhile, the relationship between Father Serra and Lieutenant Fages deteriorated to the point that Serra felt obliged to travel to Mexico City to seek a clear mandate to further the projected settlement and pacification of Alta California. In his absence he appointed the Catalan friar Palou as the religious leader of the missions. In 1772 the Dominican and Franciscan orders reached an agreement that the former would have jurisdiction over the missions of Baja California, while the latter would spearhead the creation of missions in Alta California. This released the services of all Franciscan friars currently working in the Baja California missions. Palou selected eight of these friars for the Franciscan effort to the north. Four of the eight were Basques (Gregorio Amurrio, Fermín Francisco de Lasuén, Juan Antonio Murguía, and Juan Prestamero). Amurrio headed the mission of San Diego, Lasuén the mission of San Gabriel, and Prestamero the mission of San Luis Obispo, while Murguía assisted Palou.[43] San Carlos de Monterey was the central mission and remained under the direction of Father Palou.

Among the Basque missionaries of California the most exceptional was Fermín Francisco de Lasuén, whom the historian Bancroft praised as the "first among the California prelates . . . a friar who rose above his environment and lived many years in advance of his time."[44] Lasuén was born in Alava and lived in Alta California for thirty years, from 1773 to 1803. During this time he was president* of the California missions for eighteen years, succeeding Father Junípero Serra in 1784.

Lasuén manifested a clear preference to work with fellow Basque friars. At one point he informed the order that he was unwilling to remain at the San Diego mission if it transferred his "compatriot" Amurrio, a posture that his superiors regarded as improper for a man of religious vows.[49] For his part, Amurrio

---

*While president, Lasuén displayed a strong independent spirit. He placed the welfare of his missions and Indian wards above all else. In 1793, for example, when the king prohibited teaching catechism in the language of the Indians,[45] Lasuén defended his teachers in the strongest terms.[46] To convert the Indians, Lasuén said, "The first principle is patience, and the second is patience, and the third is patience, and so are all the others."[47] Here is how the historian Guest paraphrased Lasuén's attitude toward Indian defectors from mission life: "The Indians returned to their former mode of life in the forest, said Lasuén, for two reasons, first it was free; secondly, it was lazy. And he added, Who can blame them?"[48]

(who had requested the transfer) agreed to stay with Lasuén.[50] Together they founded the mission of San Juan Capistrano, which was inaugurated officially in 1776 by Lasuén, Amurrio, and another Basque friar, Mugartegui.[51]

In 1779 Amurrio left for Mexico due to serious illness, but close ties continued between Lasuén and Mugartegui. When Lasuén assumed the presidency of the missions in 1784, Mugartegui was made vice-president.[52] Two years later Lasuén received a new contingent of six friars, of whom four (Sola, Arenaza, Arroita, and Norberto Santiago) were Basques.[53]

Lasuén's chief aid, Father Mugartegui, was transferred to Mexico City in 1789, where he became *guardián* of missions at the College of San Fernando, the administrative seat of all Franciscan missions in Mexico.[54] The College of San Fernando, founded in 1731, was an outgrowth of the Franciscan convent, which was closely aligned with the powerful Basque colony of Mexico City.

A large portion of the Franciscans of Mexico came from the order's institutions in the Basque country. These included Franciscan colleges in Vitoria (Alava) and Zarauz (Guipúzcoa) and the monastery of Aránzazu (Guipúzcoa). Aránzazu in particular was an important cultural center that maintained close ties with the Basques of Mexico.*

Normally the Franciscan missionaries served for ten years in the California missions, although some remained longer. Between Serra's first voyage in 1769 and the secularization of the missions in 1834, a total of 128 friars worked in California, of whom 26 were Basques.†

During Lasuén's stay in Alta California the number of Basque friars in California at any one time fluctuated between five and nine. From 1803 to 1820 the number increased to between nine and fourteen.[56] Before Lasuén's presidency the total number of mission Indians was 4,655, a figure that rose to 18,186 under his administration.[57] Of the twenty-one missions established in Alta California, nine were founded before Lasuén's presidency, nine during it, and three after he left office.[58]

---

*One of the earliest histories of the miraculous Virgin of Aránzazu was written and published in Mexico City in 1686 by the Basque Franciscan friar Juan de Luzuriaga.[55]

†Amestoy, Amurrio, Arenaza, Arroita, Barona, Calzada, Carranza, Estenaga, Ibarra, Iturrate, Landaeta, Lasuén, Marquinez, Martiarena, Mugartegui, Murguía, Quintana, Saizar de Vitoria, Santiago, Sarria, Sola, Ulibarri, Urresti, Uria, Urria, and Zalvidea.

BASQUE ADMINISTRATORS OF ALTA CALIFORNIA

During the first twenty-four years of the colonization of Alta California, the area was administered as a part of the command of the Internal Provinces. The command had jurisdiction over what is today northern Mexico, the American southwest, and the two Californias. The office of commander of the Internal Provinces was "a position second only to that of viceroy among Spanish officials in America."[59] In 1784 the Basque José Joaquín de Arrillaga was named captain and commander of Loreto, a post that also made him the lieutenant governor of the Californias. In 1785 the Basque Jacobo Ugarte y Loyola was named commander of the Internal Provinces, a post that he held until 1790. According to Bancroft, "Ugarte commanded in person in Sonora and California; had a subordinate in *Nueva Vizcaya* and New Mexico, and another in Coahuila and Texas."[60] All three subordinates were fellow Basques: Diego de Borica in *Nueva Vizcaya* (and future governor of California), Juan Bautista de Anza in New Mexico, and Juan de Ugalde in Texas and Coahuila.[61]

The fact that European Basques and Mexicans of Basque descent occupied important posts in the military administration of what is today northern Mexico and the southwestern United States is simply an extension of the sixteenth- and early seventeenth-century involvement of Basques in the creation of *Nueva Vizcaya* (see chapter 2).* Given the number of Basques who earlier settled the area, it is not surprising to find a large contingent of native soldiers with Basque last names. For the common soldier, it is an open question as to whether there was still an awareness of a common ethnic tie.† At the level of officialdom, however, Basque descent was of both social and

---

*But it is also clear that, even as late as the second half of the eighteenth century, there was continued emigration of Old World-born Basques to the northern reaches of *Nueva España*. There is the case of Joaquín de Amézqueta, who settled in Chihuahua.[62] Also, the Royal Basque Society reported twenty-three corresponding members in Chihuahua in the year 1793.[63]

†It is also likely that many persons with Basque last names were *mestizos*, descendants of Indians who had assumed the last name of a Basque patron. For example, in his list of "inhabitants of California, 1769–1800,"[64] Bancroft identifies many persons, mainly soldiers, as "half breeds." Included in the list are the following Basque last names: Alviso, Amézquita, Orozco, Archuleta, Antuña, Butron, Cariaga, Lisalde, Otondo, Pollorena, Arana, Arriola, Basadre, Galindo, Guevara, Oribe, Salazar, Arruz, Duarte, Garaicoechea, Garibay, Ibarra, Ladron de Guevara, Mojica, Vizcarra, Horchaga, Esparza, Mendoza [Bancroft's spellings].

legal importance. Many military officers were drawn from the ranks of the upper classes, composed in large measure of successful Basque families. The claim to Basque descent became a claim to *hidalguía*, or noble status, a requisite for occupying high posts in the Spanish military system.

At one moment in California history—1790—Basques occupied key posts in both the religious and secular administrations. Mugartegui was the director *(guardián)* and chief of the missions in Mexico. In Mexico City the Basque Mendivil was the postmaster, administering all correspondence with the missions. The commander of the Internal Provinces was Jacobo Ugarte y Loyola, while the lieutenant governor of the Californias was José Joaquín Arrillaga. The commander of the key port city of San Blas, through which California was supplied, was Bodega, and the official of Tepic, who served the Franciscans as the purchasing agent for the California missions, was Esteban Lazcano.[65]

This "Basque network" functioned on all levels, including the clandestine, as an incident illustrates. Mugartegui proposed on one occasion that Lasuén make illegal purchases of otter skins, which could be sold in Mexico for more than the officially determined prices. Father Lasuén assented to this questionable venture and replied that he would send the skins to the College of San Fernando disguised as other merchandise, and he suggested using Lazcano as the intermediary. The project was not carried out.[66]

It is clear that when Basques occupied the key administrative posts in both systems, the tensions between the mission and civil administrations abated. Father Junípero Serra fought bitter battles with Pedro Fages, in great contrast to the harmonious relations that obtained between Father Lasuén and his fellow Basques, Arrillaga and Diego de Borica, both of whom served as governors of Alta California. Serra traveled to Mexico City to denounce Fages publicly. When Governor Borica felt that there were solid grounds to criticize the treatment of Indians at the San Francisco mission, a contention that Lasuén denied, Borica chose a more private avenue to resolve the problem. He wrote a letter to the Franciscan leader in which he appealed to their common ethnic background. Borica asked,

> Won't it be scandalous if two compatriots have a lawsuit . . . ? Yet it is necessary that such be the case, since the obligations of my office prohibit me from glossing over such a serious matter.[67]

In his reply, Lasuén stated,

> No, my Lord and compatriot, there will be no lawsuit. First, because there is no one who would dislike it more than I, and when one is unwilling two cannot argue. Secondly, because an agreement is more worthwhile than a lawsuit. . . . Thirdly, because for your eminence to initiate a lawsuit is a sign that you have evidence, and I choose not to dispute it.[68]

A similar recognition of ethnic ties between fellow Basques in the ecclesiastical and the secular branches of power is reflected in a letter to Father Martín de Landaeta of the San Francisco mission, sent by Governor Arrillaga. The letter ends with this phrase:

> . . . Agur frailea aguindu, que le complacerá gustoso su paisano.*

Upon the death of Governor Romeu of the Californias in 1793, the lieutenant governor, José Joaquín de Arrillaga, became acting governor and took up residence in Monterey. Arrillaga was the first Basque administrator who actually resided in Alta California.† Consequently, during the interim rule of Arrillaga, the Californias became separate administrative divisions directly responsible to the viceroy in Mexico City.[70]

José Joaquín de Arrillaga was born in Aya, Guipúzcoa, in 1750. He served as acting governor until 1794 when his fellow Basque Diego de Borica received the permanent appointment. In 1800, when Borica left, Arrillaga again became acting governor of Alta California until 1804. He was then named to the post permanently, serving until his death in 1814. According to Bancroft, "Arrillaga was an efficient and honest officer of most excellent private character, and a model governor as far as the performance of routine duties was concerned."[71] He was an extremely popular man. He was asked so frequently to serve as a baptismal godfather that he was known as "Papá Arrillaga."[72]‡

---

*Agur frailea aguindu is Basque for "Goodbye friar, I am at your orders," and que le complacerá gustoso su paisano is Spanish for "it will give your compatriot great pleasure."[69]

†A possible exception is Felipe Antonio de Goycoechea, the military commander at Santa Barbara in 1784 and governor of Baja California (1805). While clearly of Basque descent, he was born in either Sonora or Sinaloa in Mexico, and there is insufficient evidence to contend that he conceived of himself as a Basque, although the use of the preposition de in his name might indicate he was conscious of it. De has overtones of claim to hidalgo status.

‡For many years after his death, each November 2, hundreds of Indians placed floral wreaths on his monument at the Soledad Mission.[73]

Diego de Borica y Retegui was Alavese, probably born in Vitoria. In any event, his sister Bernarda lived in that city and maintained relations with the Lasuén family.[74] He served as governor of California from 1794 to 1800 when, due to illness, he left for Mexico, where he died in Durango later the same year.[75] Before coming to California, he served as lieutenant in the presidio of Santa Fe, New Mexico, and in 1780 he married a Mexican-Basque, María Magdalena de Urquidi, a direct descendant of one of the founders of Durango.[76] Bancroft characterized Borica as:

> one of the ablest and best rulers the country ever had, always striving for progress in different directions, avoiding controversy, and personally interesting himself in the welfare of all classes; a jovial bon-vivant, knight of Santiago, and man of wealth.[77]

Borica was a member of the Royal Basque Society of the Friends of the Country and was highly influenced by its liberal ideas and preoccupation with economic development. As governor he was particularly interested in creating a colony of settlers in California. The community was to be named Branciforte (present-day Santa Clara), in honor of the viceroy of that name in Mexico City. Borica believed that Catalans in particular would make good settlers. He publicized the project in the regions of Guadalajara, Zacatecas, Guanajuato, and Valladolid in Mexico. The search was for families of little means but honorable and pure Spanish ancestry. The plan failed. From Guadalajara came nine men convicted of public crimes and from Guanajuato sixteen convicts. There were only three volunteers.[78] Borica's efforts to seek help from Spain for his attempts to develop California's economy were ignored, since Spain was once more at war with England (1796–1802).

In 1804, after Arrillaga had again assumed the governorship, Alta and Baja California were divided into two separate administrative units. Arrillaga was governor of Alta California, while Felipe de Goycoechea governed Baja. Both were directly dependent upon the viceroy in Mexico City, who at that time (1803–08) was José de Iturrigaray, a Basque from Cádiz.

At this time European settlement in Alta California was restricted to a narrow coastal strip running from San Diego in the south to San Francisco Bay. At no point were permanent settlements any further inland than thirty miles. The interior had scarcely been explored, let alone colonized.

In 1806 Arrillaga ordered José Joaquín Maitorena, a Mexican-born Basque, to organize the exploration of the interior.[79] None of Maitorena's efforts resulted in attempts at colonization. The major problem in California was the small population. Alta California remained one of the most remote outposts of the Spanish Empire. In 1790 its European population was a scant 990 inhabitants. By 1800 the number had grown to 1,800 and to 2,130 by 1810.[80]

Developments in Europe during this same period hamstrung the efforts of Borica and Arrillaga to develop California's economy.[81] The Napoleonic invasions of the Iberian peninsula paralyzed Spain's colonial administration, forcing marginal areas to fall back upon their own resources. The authorities in Mexico City became so disinterested in California that the soldiers and friars ceased to receive their salaries.[82] For two years (1811–12), not a single boat reached California from San Blas.[83] It was during this period that contraband commerce with American and Russian sea captains became commonplace in Alta California.

On July 24, 1814, Arrillaga died, and later the same year another Guipuzcoan* Basque, Pablo Vicente Sola, born in Mondragón, was named governor. Sola was the last Spanish governor of California as well as the first of the Mexican period of California history. He governed during the period when the Spanish Empire was shaken by independence movements, for which there was little sympathy in California.[85]†

Sola was a governor in the tradition of Borica. He not only imported schoolteachers from Mexico, but he also supported two of them with his personal funds.[87]

During Sola's term of office the president of the California missions was a fellow Basque, Vicente de Sarria. However, the relations between Sola and Sarria were not as close as those that obtained earlier between Borica and Lasuén. This may have been due to their differences of opinion on the political issues of the day.‡

---

*Although his family was of Navarrese origin, coming from the town of Obanos.[84]

†The disruption of sea traffic did affect California, and in 1818 an Argentine ship's crew tried to convince the inhabitants of Monterey to revolt against Spanish rule. When they were unsuccessful, they sacked the town.[86]

‡Sola may have been a liberal supporter of the constitutionalist forces in Spain, whereas Sarria may well have sympathized with the anticonstitutionalist defenders of the ancient regime, who were supported by most of the clergy. From 1820 to 1823, the constitutionalists, who were also

The transfer of Spanish California to Mexican rule was accomplished with little disruption in 1812. Sola, himself, presided over the ceremony. He later was elected as California's representative to the newly established Congress in Mexico City. While he remained interested in California affairs for years, he never returned to it.

In 1825 a Mexican of Basque descent, José María de Echeandia, was named governor of California, a post that he filled until 1830. During his administration, California was Mexicanized in many respects. The missions were attacked strongly by the authorities, as they contained both the best ranch lands and the potential work force. Both were deemed crucial to the development of California's economy. At the same time, the Mexican authorities regarded California as an ideal place to send convicted criminals.[89] Since there were no prisons in the area, California society was inundated with undesirable persons who immediately became a disruptive element in local life.[90] In Mexico City a "Board for the Development of the Californias" was formed.* It proposed that colonists be sent to California with their voyage subsidized. They were to be given livestock, tools, and a subsidy for three years. All was to be paid by the missions.[92] The proposal was never implemented.

Faced with such sentiment, the missionaries ceased to be a dynamic force in California society and went on the defensive. Father Sarria refused to swear allegiance to the Mexican constitution of 1824 (an oath that demanded loyalty to Mexico in the event that Spain tried to regain control over the former colony). Sarria was condemned to exile, although the sentence was never carried out. Between 1826 and 1829 there was constant bickering between Sarria and the Mexican authorities.[93] For their part, the authorities suggested that the friars had concealed great fortunes in their missions.[94]

In 1834 the missions were secularized, which is to say that they were converted to the legal status of *pueblos* (towns), and the friars became parish priests. The mission lands were distributed among the mission families and to single persons over twenty years of age.[95]

---

anticlerical, ruled Spain. They were removed from power when the anti-constitutionalists, who were strongly supported by the Basque clergy,[88] rebelled. France intervened with an army of one hundred thousand men, placing Fernando VII on the throne as an absolute monarch.

*Of the twenty members, eight were Basques: ex-governor Sola, José Ignacio Ormaechea, Manuel Ibarra, Francisco Cortina, Francisco Fagoaga, Isidro Icaza, Juan Francisco Azcarate, and Tomás Zuria.[91]

Anticipating the secularization, the friars began to slaughter their herds for hides and tallow, which was their only means of converting part of their holdings into money. On some missions, like San Gabriel, all of the stock was slaughtered. The only thing that prevented the friars from destroying the vineyards was the refusal of the Indians.[96] Many of the Indians who left the missions at this time rejoined the tribes of the interior. They and "New Mexican vagabond traders and foreign hunters kept the country in a state of chronic disquietude in these and later years, being the most serious obstacle to progress and prosperity."[97]

In that same year a large contingent of Mexican colonists, composed more of artisans than agriculturalists, arrived in California under the direction of José María Hijar and José María Padrés. In their number was the Basque scribe Antonio Apalategui.* Apalategui became disenchanted with the direction of events in California and, in league with a Mexican doctor, Francisco Torres, tried to initiate a rebellion against Governor José Figueroa.[99] When the attempt failed, both were imprisoned and sent to Mexico for trial.

The years of periodic neglect and bald exploitation of California by the Mexican government created animosity and a growing anti-Mexican sentiment among the residents. In 1842 Manuel Micheltorena was appointed governor of California. Micheltorena was from a prominent Mexican family of Basque descent. During his military career he had distinguished himself in campaigns in Texas.[100] Micheltorena arrived in California with the desire to govern well and in the best interests of the area.[101] However, among the five hundred men who accompanied him as colonists, three hundred had been selected by the Ministry of Justice from among the criminals in Mexican prisons. If they comported themselves well during the journey, they were to receive the "land and implements to become colonists."[102] The excesses of this *cholo* population, as it was called pejoratively by the Californians, was such that in 1845 the local populace rebelled, forcing Micheltorena to resign and leave for Mexico. Micheltorena was to be the last governor sent from Mexico to California. He was succeeded by the native Californian Pío Pico, who was in office in 1848 when the area was annexed by the United States.

---

*Bancroft calls him a "Spanish *escribiente*."[98]

BASQUE MERCHANTS OF ALTA CALIFORNIA

There is yet another thread of Basque involvement in the history of Alta California: Many Basques were among the ranks of the ship captains, their agents, and merchants who provided the region with its provisions.

In many respects the European society of Alta California was of a special nature. Neither the friars nor the soldiers were settlers in the strictest sense of the word; missions and presidios were not economic enterprises. Rather, both were outposts of Spanish civilization that required provisioning rather than generating trade.

The Spanish authorities regarded Alta California as a sensitive military garrison and actually discouraged the settlement of potential colonists. For example, Californians were prohibited from engaging in trade even with the Manila galleons that occasionally put into local ports.[103] All California lands belonged to the king.[104] Occasional land grants were made, usually to retiring soldiers, but those who received them were prohibited from maintaining more than fifty head of any one species of livestock.[105] Whatever the few ranches produced had to be sold exclusively to the presidios and at prices fixed by the military authorities.[106] Similarly, the ranchers were required to buy their goods, which had come from San Blas, at highly inflated prices, from the presidios.[107] Consequently, it is not surprising that in the first thirty years (1769−1800) the European population of California remained at less than one thousand persons.

In the early years the only free commerce was a contraband traffic in sea otter skins with foreign ship captains.* In 1786 there was an attempt on the part of the Philippines Company (successor of the Basque-controlled Caracas Company) to organize the sea otter skin trade of Alta California, but the authorities proposed conditions that were too stringent, and the project was dropped.[109] Other attempts to trade in otter skins were equally unsuccessful.[110]

While there was a certain amount of contraband trade with foreign ships, it was not until 1816 that the official restrictions

---

*We have seen that Father Lasuén and Father Mugartegui tried to organize an illegal flow of sea otter skins along Franciscan missionary channels. Father Landaeta frequently sent skins to his friends in Mexico City.[108]

on trade in California were removed.* By 1818 there was a burgeoning trade in tallow in California ports. The product was purchased largely by Mexican and Peruvian interests. At about the same time, American traders began to purchase California hides.[111]

In the years immediately following Mexican independence, and particularly after the constitution of 1824, the friars had refused to sell their hides and tallows for cash, since they feared that the Mexican government would tax the income. As the friars were little interested in luxury goods, the traders were initially unsuccessful in dealing with them.[112]

In 1834, however, when the friars began to slaughter their vast herds and flocks, there was a sharp increase in the hide and tallow trade, attracting many foreign purchasers into the market. The profits in the hide and tallow trade in California were enormous,[113] but the competition was keen. As the new provisioners of California needs and desires, each ship captain sought to outdo the others in attracting and holding California clients by providing them with the widest possible range of luxury goods. For their part, the Californians responded eagerly, quickly establishing a halcyon life style whose luxury and ease became legendary.

The middlemen in this traffic were the agents of the ship captains known as supercargos. The supercargo was charged with both buying the hides and tallow and selling the luxury items. In this capacity he traveled from ranch to ranch, establishing personal ties and extending liberal credit. In fact, credit was so completely overextended that by 1842 one inspector from a Mexican-based shipping firm observed, "even if all the livestock were killed, not enough hides and tallow would be produced to pay the debt of the Californians."[114]

A key run in the hide and tallow trade was California-Callao (Peru). At that time Callao was a major link in Spain's trade with the Orient, as well as the home port of an impressive fleet of Peruvian merchant vessels. Of the twelve major shipping firms in Lima in 1834, four were Basque-owned.†

The key shipping firm in Mexico participating in the California trade prior to 1834 was the German-owned Virmond

---

*The relaxation was due as much to the fact that Spain could no longer control California waters nor provision the area as to a liberalized trade policy.

†Juan Francisco Izcue, Aramburu Brothers, Urien and Company, and Dalidou Larrabure and Company. The remainder were either English or German firms.[115]

Company of Mexico City. Virmond handled all of the commerce for the Franciscan missions, which had a credit of $400 annually for each mission friar. However, in 1833 a shipping firm was established at Guaymas on the western Mexican coast by the Basque José Antonio Aguirre. In 1834 Aguirre began to challenge Virmond's near monopoly of the California-Mexico trade. Aguirre hired fellow Basques as supercargos, whereas Virmond's key California supercargos were *santanderinos* or *montañeses* (Eugenio de Celis and Arnaz, for example).

José Antonio Aguirre, or "Aguirrón" as he was called in California, due to his enormous size and stature, was born in San Sebastián (Guipúzcoa) about 1793.[116] He was a ship captain on the Manila-Canton-Mexico run, thereby familiarizing himself with commerce in the luxury products of the Orient.[117] Consequently, he became established in Mexico City in a shipping firm specializing in trade with the Orient.[118] In 1830, since he refused to accept Mexican citizenship, he was forced to leave Mexico. He settled in New Orleans, where he took out American citizenship,[119] and in 1833 was able to return to Mexico where he established a shipping firm in the port city of Guaymas. He purchased an American warship, the *Dolphin*, and renamed it the *Leonidas*.[120] By the end of 1833, the *Leonidas* was trafficking with San Francisco.

While Aguirre remained in Guaymas, his chief supercargo in California was Charles Baric,[121] a fellow Basque. Baric remained with the Aguirre firm until his death in 1847.[122]

Aguirre traveled to California frequently, and in 1838 he settled permanently in Santa Barbara, although he continued to maintain close ties with his fellow Basques in Mexico.[123] Between 1836 and 1839, he served as a director on the board of protectors for the *Colegio de las Vizcaínas* of Mexico City.[124]

In 1840 Aguirre paid $13,000 for a two-hundred-ton English vessel, the *Roger Williams*. He renamed it the *Joven Guipuzcoana*.[125]* Aguirre became one of the most prominent citizens of California. He maintained a large house staff, including a tutor who instructed young men recommended by him.[127] Some considered him "the wealthiest merchant of the coast."[128] He married into one of the most prominent Old California families, the Estudillos.

---

*In April of the same year the Mexican government requisitioned the ship to transport to San Blas the Americans who were implicated in the abortive conspiracy of Isaac Graham. In September, the vessel was returned to Aguirre and reentered the service of his company.[126]

The magnitude of Aguirre's economic successes was such that by 1849 he had on deposit with William Heath Davis, the husband of his niece, "between $100,000 and $200,000 in doubloons and gold dust."[129] At the same time he owned extensive lands in both Los Angeles and San Diego. His brother-in-law Miguel de Pedrorena, Davis, two other Americans, and Aguirre were "the projectors and original proprietors of what is now known as the city of San Diego."[130]

Miguel de Pedrorena, Aguirre's brother-in-law by virtue of the fact that he too married an Estudillo sister, was from an important Basque family resident in Madrid. His brother became a minister in the Spanish government,[131] and he himself engaged in commercial activities in Lima, where he formed a company with two Spaniards.[132] His first commercial contact with California was in 1837, when he arrived as the consignatory of a Mexican ship, the *Juan José*.[133] He later bought the vessel and registered it under the Colombian flag. Between 1837 and 1839 he was both the owner and supercargo in California of an Ecuadorian vessel, the *Delmira*.[134] In 1840, he purchased the American vessel, the *Corsair*.[135] At that time he hired a Basque, Pedro Gandara, as his California assistant.[136]*

Pedrorena traveled constantly between California and Peru. When in California, he was a member of the best social circles. He and José Antonio Aguirre frequently cosponsored sumptuous fiestas, particularly in San Diego.[138] By virtue of his marriage, he became the grantee of the El Cajón (1845) and San Jacinto Nuevo (1846) ranchos.[139] After 1846, he openly supported the incorporation of California into the United States.[140] Consequently, he was appointed to the constitutional convention of 1849 and was named customs collector of San Diego.[141]

Another successful Basque merchant in California was Cesareo Lataillade, born in the French Basque town of St.-Jean-de-Luz in 1819. He emigrated to Mexico with two brothers and in 1841 made his first voyage to California as supercargo and part owner of the Mexican vessel *Chato*.[142] He settled in Santa Barbara, where in 1845 he married María Antonia de la Guerra, daughter of one of California's most prominent families.[143] The next year he was named vice-consul of Spain in Monterey,[144] and became the French consul in 1849.[145] In 1848, after the first discoveries of gold in California, he formed a company with the *montañés* Gaspar Oreña to provide supplies

---

*Gandara left the following year for the Río de la Plata.[137]

to the miners of Placer County, realizing "extraordinary profits."[146]

Another Basque ship captain to settle in California was
José Domingo Indart (Yndart). He was owner of the vessel
Keoneana, which operated between California, Acapulco, and
Callao.[147] He married a Mexican woman and settled his family
in California in 1849. He was joined by a nephew, Ulpiano
Indart, who was born in Fuenterrabía Guipúzcoa, in 1828.
Ulpiano established a store in Los Angeles and he moved to
Santa Barbara in 1855, where he purchased the Rancho Najoqui
and entered into cattle ranching.[148] In 1856 he married his
cousin Feliciana, daughter of José Domingo. Later, as a
widower, he married María Antonia de la Guerra,[149] niece of
the María Antonia de la Guerra who was the widow of Cesareo
Lataillade. Ulpiano Indart was highly respected in local affairs
and for many years was the treasurer of Santa Barbara County.
He died at Santa Barbara in 1902.[150]

If there was extensive involvement of Basques in the
missions, administration, and commerce of Old California, the
carryover into the American period was negligible. The success
of the Mexican independence movement foreclosed the possibility that the Old World Basques could obtain administrative
posts in the area. The secularization of the missions terminated
the activities of the Franciscan friars. As for the successful
Basque merchants, few survived much beyond the American
annexation of the area. Cesareo Lataillade died an accidental
death in 1849. Miguel Pedrorena died in 1850. José Antonio
Aguirre died ten years later. Only Ulpiano Indart continued as a
force in the life of the Basque community of the New California.
Thus the basis for a substantial "chain migration" into California was lacking; nevertheless, a new wave of Basque immigration into the area began shortly after California was annexed by
the United States.

CHAPTER FIVE

Basque Beginnings in the New California

*In choosing sheepherders, the best will be found among the Mexicans,
Basques, or Portuguese. These latter two do not, as a rule, take
service except with their own people; their aim is ultimately to possess
a share in the herds, and to rise to the position of owners.
(Major W. Shepherd, Prairie Experiences in the Handling of Cattle
and Sheep, 1885)*[1]

THE EARLY FORTUNE SEEKERS

Among the Basque "old-timers" of Boise it is said that
the first Basque in the American West arrived in 1849. He was a
mariner from Ea (Vizcaya), captain of a Chilean merchant
vessel and married to a Chilean woman. According to the
account, he was accompanied by two other Basques, a man
named Senda and one called "Natxitxu," from the town of

Nachitua (which is located close to Ea).[2] By another Boise account the first two Basques, Pedro Altube and Segundo Ugariza (known as "Sendo"), arrived at San Francisco in 1850. They were sailors on a whaling boat.[3]

There is, of course, no mystery concerning the attraction of California in 1849. On February 2, 1848, under the Treaty of Guadalupe Hidalgo, Mexico ceded Alta California to the United States. In April of the same year there was public disclosure of the first discoveries of gold in the Sierra foothills and in the narrow mountain valleys forming the headwaters of the Stanislaus and Tuolumne rivers. It was in the following year that new discoveries triggered the world-wide rush of the fortune-hunting "argonauts" to the California diggings. The 1848 discoveries were in themselves sufficient to upset the normal routine of California life. In the month of August alone, seventy-four American soldiers deserted their posts at Sonoma, San Francisco, and Monterey to go to the mines.[4]

Due to its sea access to California, Latin America was the departure point for the earliest foreign expeditions to the gold fields. News of the discoveries reached Valparaíso, Chile, on August 19, 1848 and by September 12, the first boatload of Chilean fortune seekers sailed for California.[5] However, the voyage of 6,700 nautical miles required nearly three months.[6] Consequently, well before the arrival of the first Chileans, in October of 1848, caravans of Sonoran Mexican miners were beginning to arrive in California. Between October 1848 and April 1849, five thousand to six thousand persons left Sonora for the gold fields.[7]

By May of 1849 there were at least ninety vessels in San Francisco harbor that had been abandoned even by their captains who, like the crews, had succumbed to the gold fever.[8] A month later, there were 150 vessels in the port, the majority of which had been abandoned.[9] Most of these ships were apparently from Chile.*

By July 1849 more than four thousand persons had arrived by sea in California from Latin America (including 1,452 from Mexican ports, 1,350 from Chile, 1,251 from Panama, 227 from Peru, and 26 from Central America).[11]

During the autumn of 1848 and spring of 1849 there were

---

*Chile at this time had the largest fleet in the Pacific. López Urrutia stated that "the attraction of California gold produced the ruination of the Chilean merchant marine."[10] It is likely that one of the abandoned vessels was under the command of the sea captain in our Boise account.

many new discoveries. The value of the nuggets and gold dust recovered during this period approximated twenty million dollars, of which fifteen million went to "foreign" miners, primarily Chileans* and Mexicans. Only five million of the additional twenty million extracted during the remainder of 1849 was recovered by the foreign miners, reflecting the impact of the newly arrived "forty-niners," United States citizens who reached California by sea or by trekking overland.[12]

In 1849 the mining camps were scenes of frequent violence between the Anglo miners and their foreign competitors. The Anglos regarded themselves as racially superior to the Latins and as the proprietors of California wealth by virtue of the Mexican-American War, the Bear Flag Revolt, and the Treaty of Guadalupe Hidalgo. Foreigners were denounced as opportunists bent upon filling their pockets with American gold that they would then carry off to other lands.

The Anglos had many ideas designed to prohibit foreigners from working the diggings.[13] Such proposals were prevented from becoming law only through the intervention of the Anglo merchants, who did not choose their clientele according to nationality. Nevertheless, the general climate of competition and racism, exacerbated by the naked greed of the gold seekers, was sufficient to force division of the mining district into the Anglo camps of the north and the foreigner-dominated camps of the south. In the words of one observer:

> In the north, one saw occasionally some straggling Frenchmen and other European foreigners, here and there a party of Chinamen, and a few Mexicans engaged in driving mules, but the total number of foreigners was very small: the population was almost entirely composed of Americans, and of these the Missourians and other western men formed a large proportion.
>
> The southern mines, however, were full of all sorts of people. There were many villages peopled nearly altogether by Mexicans, others by Frenchmen; in some places there were parties of two or three hundred Chilians [*sic*] forming a community of their own. The Chinese camps were very numerous; and besides all such distinct colonies of foreigners, every town of the southern mines contained a very large foreign population.[14]

By August 1849, Sonora Camp (named for its large number of residents from the Mexican region of Sonora) had a population

---

*"Chilean" was frequently employed as a generic term for South Americans by their detractors.

of eight thousand persons considered to be either Mexican or South American.[15]

During the succeeding years the largest group of foreigners in the southern camps after the Latin Americans was the French. News of the gold discovery in California reached Paris on November 13, 1848,[16] about one month before Louis Napoleon Bonaparte was elected president of the French Republic, ending the Revolution of 1848. France was in the doldrums, suffering from economic aftereffects of the revolution. California provided hope not only for the individual Frenchman seeking to better his lot, but to the French nation's shattered economy. "Let us . . . not lose this chance to increase our riches and to efface from our memory the suffering of the past year," trumpeted La Californie, a Parisian biweekly periodical devoted to extolling the fabulous riches of the California mines. "We cannot urge the French too strongly to profit in these marvellous discoveries so that they shall not pass into the hands of other people."[17]

The French nourished the illusion of dominating California. "Let France, by force of immigration, make this possession hers," stated one of the dispatches sent from the American West to La Californie, while another writer asked "why . . . doesn't France send a fleet with mining engineers on board, a general officer, some companies of engineers, and 1,500 soldiers? . . . Here is the armed intervention that would benefit France."[18]

The French organized mining companies and emigrant expeditions with such rapidity that a French reporter who visited California at the end of 1849 could write, "the French, after the Americans, are the most numerous element of the present population in California. Nearly 10,000 of them are found either at San Francisco or at the mines."[19]

The established French colonies in Latin America were also influenced by California. The French-language newspaper of Uruguay, the Messager de Montevideo, reported on June 2, 1850, that "on every side expeditions are being formed to exploit the mines of California." In the same year an almanac was published in Paris to orient the prospective emigrant. Its title, Almanach Californien pour 1851, Guide de l'émigrant, Manuel de Commerçant et de l'Actionnaire, Documents complets pour tout le monde sur la Californie, indicates the scope of the work. According to the almanac, by 1850 there were already many French nationals with restaurants and other businesses in towns like San Jose, Stockton, Sacramento, and Sutterville.[20]

By the same token, it claimed that many Frenchmen* had already made their fortunes, returning home to France with suitcases filled with gold.[22]

Within the California gold rush, therefore, we have identified three immigratory currents of particular interest to this study: Sonoran Mexicans, South Americans, and French nationals. Each current constituted a readily discernible and important segment of the total population of argonauts. Each supposes its own peculiar problems for the investigator intent upon discerning Basque immigration into mid-nineteenth-century California.

With respect to Sonora, we have noted previously the extensive sixteenth-century involvement of the Basques in the development of northern Mexico. The upshot is that, as a result of the Basque involvement in the creation of *Nueva Vizcaya*, there was by the nineteenth century a large population in northern Mexico who, despite their Basque last names, culturally were totally divorced from any awareness of their Basque cultural heritage. Consequently, if last names† alone were employed as the criterion for evaluating Basque participation in the gold rush, emigration from Sonora would likely inflate the statistics all out of proportion.

A similar problem arises when we consider the individuals who shipped out of Chilean‡ and other South American ports for the California gold fields. Many immigrants into California

---

*Even the French royal family was entranced with California. Prince Louis Lucien Bonaparte served as president of "La Compagnie Minière du Nouveau Monde," which leased the Mariposa mine to General Frémont.[21] Parenthetically, Prince Bonaparte was one of the great linguists and Bascophiles of the nineteenth century and founded the study of Basque dialectology.

†In evaluating early California census records for Basque last names (as a preliminary, if not definitive, indication of Basque ethnics), the investigator is further frustrated by the fact that some censuses are in poor physical condition (e.g., that of 1852 for Tuolumne County); also, the Anglo census takers frequently misspelled the names of foreigners or glossed them over with entries like "26 Chileans" or "45 Frenchmen."[23]

‡It seems that Valparaíso was frequently the port of embarcation for Argentine and Uruguayan residents who preferred to cross the Andes on horseback instead of braving the difficult and lengthy trip around Cape Horn. Many travelers from Europe also opted to disembark in Montevideo or Buenos Aires, to cross the continent, and then to ship out of Valparaíso, at times in the same boat.[24] This practice is probably the source of a legend extant among some Basques of the American West to the effect that the first group of Basques to arrive in California came from Argentina on horseback,[25] a journey that remains impossible to this day.

from South America had Basque last names, yet their "Basqueness" remains questionable. However, we have noted that by the mid-nineteenth century there was a considerable colony of recent immigrant Old World Basques established in Uruguay, Argentina, and Chile. These persons remained culturally Basque, and there is definite evidence that a number of them were included among the ranks of South American emigrants to California.

South American sources, particularly passport applications, reveal the names of eighty persons with Basque last names who left Buenos Aires for California between 1849 and 1851.* This list is far from complete. We know, for instance, that Bernardo Altube was called to California by his brother Pedro, who had preceded him there after both brothers had worked in Argentina.[26]

The newspaper *El Comercio de la Plata* (Montevideo) lists 155 persons with Basque last names who requested passports listing their destinations as "foreign ports" in late 1848 and 1849. It is likely that most were intent upon reaching California.† Appendix Three lists many persons with Basque names who shipped out for California from the Chilean port of Valparaíso.

There is also early evidence of French Basques coming to California directly from Europe. On August 11, 1851, the San Francisco newspaper *Daily Alta California* announced the arrival of a group of persons from Bayonne.

On January 1, 1850, a French journalist visiting the Murphys Camp diggings reported his encounter with "two Basques who within a space of six square feet got ten to twelve ounces of gold per day and his [*sic*] neighbors found nothing."[27]

There is further evidence that French Basques formed a sizeable contingent in the total population of Murphys, as well as one that was capable of collective action. The German traveler Friedrich Gerstäcker visited the camp in May 1850 and reported on "the French Revolution." Gerstäcker reports:

> An immense number of French, a large part of them Basques, had likewise arrived in Murphys, and a great many French stores sprang up along with those of the Americans. . . .

---

*See Appendix Two for this list.

†It is impossible to crosscheck the Montevideo newspaper announcements with official emigration records, which burned in a fire that destroyed the prefecture of police near the end of the nineteenth century.

There were also Germans, Spaniards and Englishmen in Murphys, but the French outnumbered them by far, and in any case made up three-fourths of the entire population of this little mining town.[28]

The French Basques became incensed when

a law was passed by the California legislature that a tax of twenty dollars per month would be levied on all foreign gold miners in the mines of California, and in case they did not want to pay that, or were not in a position to pay it, they should leave the mines at once. If, in spite of this, they were thereafter to be found at another mine also engaged in gold mining, this would then be considered a crime against the state and punished as such.

. . . Especially the French complained and argued profusely; declared the law infamous, and decided not to pay a penny. Among the Germans were some Alsatians who especially agreed with them, and the Basques brought forth rifles and shotguns, declaring that it would be best to place themselves in armed readiness from the very beginning, so as to win the respect of the Americans.

[The tents] surged with Frenchmen, and especially Basques . . . and [there were] mixed outbursts of anger, such as: Wicked!, Help!, Down with the Americans! . . .[29]

When the French of Murphys heard that two Frenchmen and a German had supposedly been imprisoned at Sonora over the tax, they formed an armed column and marched on the camp, only to find that they had been duped by rumors. They disbanded after almost hanging the rumormonger, and California's "French Revolution" came to a close.[30]

These accounts lead us to surmise that the number of Basques entering California between 1849 and 1851 runs to several hundred individuals.

By 1852 there is evidence of Basque collective action in another of the mining camps. The Canadian traveler William Perkins noted in his diary on January 25, 1852:

Yesterday a Basque was brought in dead from "Los Cayotes" camp. He was shot by the officers of Justice in an attempt to rescue a prisoner. He was buried last night by his countrymen by torchlight, and, according to one of their singular customs, several vollies of musquetry were fired over the grave.*

---

*Perkins's description of the "Basque funeral" is interesting since, despite his contention, it was not usual practice in Basque society to fire graveside volleys. The likely explanation is that the men in question were veterans of the

These Basques are a strange people, *and we have large numbers of them amongst us.* Generally speaking they are peaceable, hard working men, but when their passions are aroused they are very dangerous. They are probably the oldest people of Europe who have retained their customs and original language, if we except perhaps the Welsh. They are very powerful athletic men; their amusements after a hard days work being pitching quoits, and the iron bar, or heaving heavy stones.

These fellows would make the finest soldiers in the world but they are too proud to inlist in any service. Their language is a mixture of barbarous old french and older spanish, and not to be understood by the natives of either side of the Pyrenees. The Mexicans view them with a species of stupid wonder. They can't understand the use of the vast physical exertions of the Basques exhibited for mere amusement. Their astonishment equals that of the Turkish Pasha, who was sadly puzzled at witnessing for the first a ball in England to see the continued and violent exertions of the ladies and gentlemen on the floor.

"Great Allah! why do not these people hire dancers to dance for them instead of killing themselves with fatigue!"[31] (Emphasis supplied).

The earliest immigrants in the California gold rush sent word to kinsmen to join them. Among the group of Basques leaving Buenos Aires in February 1850 was Bernardo Altube, beckoned by his brother Pedro, and Catalina Haegui and her brother Juan, called to California by her husband Jean-Baptiste Batz. Similarly, many of those making the journey together formed friendships that were to last a lifetime, serving as the basis for later business partnerships and marriages. In the early California accounts the names of the shipmates Amestoy, Larronde, Gless, Oxarart, Erreca, and Indart appear in combination frequently, and it was this group of "Argentine" Basques* that was subsequently to stand out in early California society.

First Carlist War (1833-39), forced émigrés of the Carlist defeat, who provided military honors for a fallen comrade-in-arms.

*To the Argentine contingent belongs the credit for establishing in the American West "bascos" as the term of reference for the Basque ethnic group. The transformation of the identity from *vizcaínos* to *bascos* began in the 1830s and 1840s in the Río de la Plata nations. Prior to the secondary movement of Basques with Argentine experience to California, the term for Basques in Mexico continued to be the older *vizcaíno*. As late as 1878, California hispanos used the term *vizcaíno* when referring to Pedrorena (of Navarrese origin) as easily as when referring to the Guipuzcoan José Antonio Aguirre.[32]

California sources* provide biographies of fourteen Basques who entered the region between 1845 and 1860. Appendix Five provides synopses of the backgrounds of these men. In only five cases did the men come to California directly from Europe: eight arrived from the Río de la Plata region, and one came from Mexico.

Nine of the fourteen men first sought employment in the mines. The biographies of the businessmen Ulpiano Indart, Pedro Zabala, and Juan Miguel Aguirre indicate that not all of the argonaut Basques entered the mining camps, and the experiences of José María Andonaegui (tailor in San Francisco) and Jean Etchemendy (baker in Los Angeles) suggest that some Basques were quick to leave the mines for urban occupations. With the exception of Bernard Iribarne, the Basque miners in the sample spent but a short time in the mining districts before settling elsewhere with different occupations. Nevertheless, there is sketchy evidence to suggest that a Basque contingent remained in the southern mining camps throughout the 1850s. Thus the public records of Tuolumne County show that Louise Garat† sold a Sonora lot in 1854 to Juan Dupont, who had himself purchased other real estate from the Irizar brothers.[33] In 1853 another Basque woman, María Azalegui (one of those to arrive in the February 1851 Basque contingent from Buenos Aires), sold a lot in Sonora to Constant Bourguin. The following year it was resold to Pierre Larrei (Larregui?).[34] There is also the case of Bernardo Etcheverry, who entered California

---

*We now enter the uneven terrain of the biographical source materials provided in the "vanity" sections of early county and state history books (see Appendix Four). A word of caution is necessary concerning the reliability and comparability of such sources. The accounts frequently reflect the personal biases, interests, and, one suspects, the deliberate omissions and embellishments of their authors. Thus, they vary considerably in terms of their completeness. The tabulations based upon the composite picture of all the accounts is highly qualified by these drawbacks. For example, when we say that of our sample of 112 Old World Basque California emigrants, 14 made return visits to the Basque country, this cannot be converted automatically into a percentage; we cannot assume that the other 98 did not return to the Basque country, since the authors of the sketches may not have posed the question in every case.

†Louise Garat was thirty-eight years old at the time. She died in 1863 and was buried in a country cemetery near present-day Los Banos, California. Her tombstone is conserved in the Ralph Le Roy Milliken museum of that community.

relatively late (1856) in the company of seven other Basques. He went to Columbia Camp, where he worked for three years as a miner.[35] In 1860 three Basques—José Echenique, Miguel Lassegue, and José María Garamendia—purchased a tavern at Robinson's Ferry on the Stanislaus River.[36] The site was well situated astride the major line of communication for a number of the mining camps. Basques usually established tavern or hotel businesses to service a Basque clientele.

Although some Basques remained in the mines, most did not. Of the nine miners in our sample, six appeared to have enjoyed some success. Because it was the successful man who was likely to make the biographical section of a county history book, we can only surmise that, for every Basque success story in mining, there were numerous failures. What is of particular interest to the present study is the fact that there was a pattern to the later careers of the successful *and* the unsuccessful Basque miners. Of the fourteen men in the sample, twelve subsequently entered the livestock industry. Two became cattlemen, and ten were sheepmen in southern and central California. Basques who became established as livestock men in their own right showed a preference for hiring other Basques, either directly or for a share in the profits (thereby assisting fellow ethnics to enter stock raising). To appreciate this Basque occupational pattern it is necessary to consider the historical background of the California livestock industry during the decade of the 1850s.

California Cattlemen, 1848–1860

Annexation of California by the United States, and the subsequent gold rush, altered drastically the tranquil and provincial nature of Old California society. The burgeoning mining camps and servicing centers such as San Francisco created an instant demand for foodstuffs of all kinds that traditional California agriculture, which emphasized hide and tallow production, was simply unable to meet. In 1848, the population of California was 15,000 (Indians excluded); by 1852 it stood at 92,597, and there were 379,994 inhabitants in 1860.[37]

In 1848 there were less than three hundred thousand head of cattle in the entire state,[38] and the value of a full-grown steer seldom rose above four dollars a head.[39] With the population explosion of 1849 the same steer brought seventy-five dollars in the San Francisco market, and a small calf was worth twenty to twenty-five dollars.[40]

United States annexation opened California to many new American settlers in search of farmland, and their ranks were swollen by disillusioned Anglo miners. The original mining boom centered upon the north-central portion of the state and converted San Francisco Bay into the main port of entry. The potential agricultural worth of northern California in terms of soil and climate was evident, and the traditional land-grantee, large-scale California landowners were quickly regarded as impediments to progress. Despite legal promises by the United States government (as formalized under the Treaty of Guadalupe Hidalgo) to respect Spanish and Mexican land-grant titles, the power and wealth of the native-born "Californios" of northern California were destroyed almost immediately. Anglos employed every tactic, from squatting to law suits, outright intimidation, and bloodshed, while stripping native Californios of their claims. Within a decade after American annexation the majority of land grants in the northern part of the state had been destroyed or considerably reduced.[41]

The situation in southern California differed because it was more isolated from the excitement of the mining districts and therefore failed to undergo rapid population increase. An arid climate made it considerably less attractive to potential settlers interested in plow agriculture. Consequently, the land-grant rancheros of the south were considerably more successful in retaining their holdings and social prominence during the decade after the discovery of gold. The demand in northern California for meat provided the southern stock raisers with their first "local" market (i.e., a market within relatively close trailing distance). Value of stock rose to eight to ten times that of the hide and tallow days, and tens of thousands of cows were driven from southern ranges to northern California markets during the 1850s.[42]

Established southern California livestock interests were in a particularly favored position to fill the expanding demand for meat in northern California, although they were not initially organized to do so, because major drives of cattle and sheep came from points east of the California gold fields during the decade.

In 1852 alone 90,000 cattle passed Fort Kearny en route to California.[43] Beginning in 1855 Texas alone accounted for eight to ten thousand steers driven to California annually.[44] During the 1850s, over five hundred thousand sheep crossed

Nevada on their way to California markets.[45] By the 1860s the trend had been reversed. From 1865 to the 1890s millions of California sheep were trailed from California to the northern mining camps of Idaho and Montana and to railheads in Colorado, Kansas, and Nebraska.[46]

While southern California stockmen enjoyed the great boon to their business, they failed to recognize certain danger signs. Their product was decidedly inferior to imported herds. The careless open-range stock raising practices of Old California had not been conducive to selective breeding and herd improvement. The imported animals fetched considerably higher prices.[47] Furthermore, previously uninhabited areas of the great San Joaquin Valley in central California were being stocked by newcomers employing superior breeds, portending future competition for the southerners.[48]

Although there were 1,234,000 head of cattle in California by 1860, or almost a million more than in 1850,[49] prices had declined to about ten dollars a head.[50] In the following year a report from Santa Barbara stated that, "everybody is broke, not a dollar to be seen, and . . . cattle can be bought at any price. Real estate is not worth anything."[51] The natural disasters between 1862 and 1864 caused further deterioration in the economics of stock raising. The catastrophe reached such proportions that the 200,000 head of cattle in Santa Barbara County in 1962 declined to 5,000 in 1865.[52] In 1864 cattle sold in Santa Barbara for thirty-seven cents a head.[53]

Paralleling the wholesale losses of cattle and the decline in the value of the remaining animals, there was a massive drop in real estate values. In 1853 cattle range in southern California commanded fifty cents an acre. By 1857 bankruptcies of old California families depressed land values to about nineteen cents an acre, and by 1862 the price had dipped further to the astounding figure of eleven cents an acre.[54]

By far the greatest peril to the southerners was to their accustomed life-style. The new wealth of the 1850s was employed to embellish further the already luxurious life-style of the California dons.[55] When cattle prices began to fall sharply in the face of a glutted market after 1856 (a year in which southern California steers brought only sixteen to eighteen dollars a head),[56] the stock raisers of southern California were prone to mortgage their holdings at incredibly inflated interest rates rather than sacrifice their comforts. Such debts, coupled with the newly instituted Anglo custom of land taxation and the exorbitant legal costs incurred in fighting would-be usurpers of the ranchos anxious to prove the falsity of land claims, brought ruination to many of the wealthiest southerners.[57]

The final straw for the beleaguered livestock raisers of the south came in the form of flood and drought. Between 1861 and 1864 the area was whiplashed by one of the greatest periods in California history of winter flooding (1861-62), in which literally thousands of head of livestock were drowned, and the searing drought conditions of 1862-64 from which there was no relief. Between 1860 and 1870 the number of cattle in Los Angeles County declined by 71 percent[58]

It is clear that at least some of the Basques, and particularly those with Argentine experience, promptly recognized opportunity in the California livestock business. The case of Juan Indart is typical. He arrived in California sometime before 1851 and worked in the mines for a few years. He and a partner began to make periodic trips to southern California to buy cattle, which he trailed back to the mining camps.[59] By 1856 Juan Indart was purchasing land in Calaveras County,[60] including the 160-acre Tula Ranch.[61] Nor was he the only Basque cattle buyer in California. In November 1857, at the mouth of the Río Nacimiento, two Basque cattle buyers were murdered by the bandit Jack Powers, who relieved them of more than thirty-five hundred dollars.[62]

By the year 1860 Basques entered into cattle-ranching partnerships with one another. Bernardo Altube formed such a company with Jean-Baptiste Arambide and bought a ranch in Calaveras County.[63] The men had been shipmates from Buenos Aires in February 1851. In the same year Bernardo's brother Pedro formed a cattle company in Santa Barbara County with Antonio Harispuru and Bernardo Ypar (both of whom had come to California from Argentina). They pooled $27,383 for the enterprise, of which Altube put up half. The deal included funds loaned by the Basque Juan Barreneche, of whom we have no further information.[64]

The Altube brothers first entered California by boat from South America. In the late 1840s, according to one account, they amassed considerable funds as livestock buyers in the Río de la Plata region.[65]* In their early California years Pedro and Bernardo Altube were partners as dairymen near San Mateo.[67]

---

*Gachiteguy mistakenly believes that Pedro Altube entered the United States via New York City.[66]

When the city annexed their property, Bernardo purchased
ranch interests near Fresno, while Pedro continued as a dairy-
man near Palo Alto.[68]*

The most famous (or infamous) of these early Basque
cattlemen (also a sheepman) was Miguel Leonis, a French
Basque from Cambo. Sometimes referred to as "the king of the
Calabasas," Leonis controlled "the whole country south of the
Ex-Mission San Fernando grant, west of El Encino and north of
El Malibu."[70] The area in question was "larger than some of the
German principalities and greater than at least one state of the
United States."[71]

Russell provides information showing how Leonis acquired this holding:

> One method of trying to acquire land titles was to buy rights
> from heirs of old grants even though the title had been lost to the
> United States. In one case an old grant had been partly divided
> among some of the heirs before California became a state. Some
> of these titles were validated and some were not. Later part of
> this grant was thrown open to public entry and the settlers came
> in. There was friction with the former owners, but it did not
> become serious until a man known as The Basco appeared upon
> the scene. He was a man of means and offered money to the
> original owners of the grant for the land as well as for whatever
> rights they still fancied they owned. They accepted the offer.
> The Basco was a unique character. Strong as a bull physically,
> he was filled with a determination to clear out the squatters. The
> methods were of no consequence as long as they brought results.
> There were reports of people who disappeared and never reap-
> peared. Of those who disappeared, some did show up again—
> and with no desire for any more land near the area.[72]

According to Pitt, "In the San Fernando Valley, a fero-
cious Basque squatter, Miguel Leonis, armed a hundred countrymen and Mexicans at Calabasas, and clung to land by brute
force, staving off both Yankees and Californians with better
claims than his."[73] According to this statement, other Basques
were in the employ of Leonis.

The lawyer Horace Bell knew him well (having served

---

*Some sources maintain that due to Pedro's extraordinary stature (6'8"), he
was known as "Palo Alto" (Tall Pole) and that the town was named for him.
However, it is more likely that he received the nickname among the Basques
because of his residence near the town, which was itself named for a large
redwood tree.[69]

both as his attorney and as attorney of the plaintiff in suits against Leonis) and wrote a remarkable character sketch:

> He was a giant in statue [sic] and strength, a perfect savage in nature, besotted in ignorance, so illiterate that he could not read a word in any language.
>
> Still, the Big Basque was in a way a great man. He was of indomitable will, industry and perseverance, was a great business manager and became rich. When he was killed in 1889 [while driving his wagon homeward through the Cahuenga Pass, Leonis fell out and his head was crushed under one of the wheels] he left a half million dollars, the most of which was inherited by the lawyers.[74]

Another account claimed that Leonis was impeccably dressed in black and always preferred to ride a large black stallion,[75] habits that made him "the prototype of the villain for a thousand cowboy movies."[76] Leonis was married* to a woman named Espiritu, daughter of an Indian chieftain, a marriage that, claims one author, "alienated him from the rest of the Basque people."[81] Whether for this or other reasons, it is clear that Leonis did not have the unswerving loyalty of all of his fellow ethnics. Leonis lost a major court case that proved to be

---

*Russell reports:

> My father incurred the enmity of The Basco and was involved in several lawsuits with him in later years. In one of these suits The Basco testified that the Indian was his legal wife, so that she could not be brought as a witness against him. This statement was to have important bearing on the disposition of his estate after his death, for his will bequeathed the estate almost in its entirety to his relatives in a foreign country, leaving a relatively small amount to the Indian woman, saying he had never married her.
>
> One of California's bright young lawyers . . . brought suit in her behalf to break the will and allow her a widow's share. My father was subpoenaed and testified that he had heard the Basco say under oath that the Indian was his legal wife. The will was broken and the widow received her share. . . .[77]

The lawsuit in question was both long and bitter. The May 9, 1893, issue of the newspaper *California'ko Eskual Herria* reported the change of residence of Madame Mariana Bonnet, sister of Miguel Leonis, who at the time had been in California for five years contesting her brother's will.[78] Meanwhile, Doña Espiritu had her problems as well. It was announced in the October 26, 1895, issue that she had filed charges of embezzlement against Laurent Etchepare, her personal financial advisor.[79] Finally, the January 11, 1896, issue reported that the entire Leonis fortune had been consumed in the legal costs of years of litigation in which no fewer than forty lawyers had intervened.[80]

the turning point in his control of the Calabasas precisely because Jean Goyheneche and Jean Etchemendy testified against him in court.[82]

The fame of Leonis as a litigation-prone individual was particularly widespread among his Basque compatriots. In the inaugural issue of California's first Basque-language newspaper (the *Escualdun Gazeta*), the editor, Martin Biscailuz, himself a lawyer by trade, wrote a tongue-in-cheek article concerning a lawsuit between Leonis and an Italian vine-cutter. The editorial ends with the statement, "Emasu hor Miguel! Cer behar guinuke guk avocatek eguin su gabe? Hil."[83] (Bravo Miguel! What would we lawyers do without you? Die.)

In the decade of the 1850s and the early 1860s, a handful of Basques became well established as cattlemen in southern California. Their successes coincided with the demise of Old California society, an economic collapse that greatly enhanced the purchasing power of those few Basques who possessed considerable capital. But the entry of Basques into the California livestock industry was not limited to men of means. For several reasons, sheep raising offered a viable alternative to the man with little backing, and the majority of Basque immigrants were in this category.

SOUTHERN CALIFORNIA SHEEPMEN

During the Spanish period of California history there had been some interest in sheep raising. The missionaries favored wool growing as one of the means of securing a maximum degree of economic autonomy for the missions. The Basque governor Diego de Borica championed sheep raising in early California.[84] Borica was a member of the Royal Basque Society of the Friends of the Country at a time when its publications extolled the virtues of wool growing and the related textile industry. He intervened personally, buying and distributing sheep among some of the early California ranchers.[85] During six years of his term of office (1794–1800), the numbers of sheep in California increased from twenty-five thousand head to more than one hundred thousand.[86] By 1822, in the first year of the Mexican period of California history, there were 200,646 head of sheep in California.[87] However, in the subsequent years of disorder, exacerbated by the droughts of 1828–30 and 1840–41,[88] California flocks diminished. The secularization of the missions was particularly instrumental in causing the abandonment or slaughter of sheep. A livestock census for the state of California in the year 1850 placed the sheep population at 17,574 head, roughly the same number as in 1790.[89]*

As with beef, demand in the booming mining and servicing centers of central California forced up mutton prices. In 1851 the first attempt was made to trail sheep from points east to California. This initial experiment did not turn out well, because of 10,000 sheep that began the trek only 3,000 completed it.[91] In the spring and early summer months of 1852, however, thousands of sheep from New Mexico reached California in good condition over the trail.[92] In September 1852 alone, 47,000 head of sheep crossed Colorado on their way to California.[93] These early flocks brought fabulous profits to the successful drovers. In 1853 the partners Kit Carson and Lucien Maxwell purchased over thirteen thousand head of sheep in New Mexico, at no more than $2.50 per head (and probably for less), trailed them to California without incident, and sold them for $5.50 a head.[94] By one estimate, between 1852 and 1860, 551,000 sheep were trailed to California from New Mexico alone.[95]

During the 1850s the indigenous sheep industry of California expanded rapidly. The United States census for 1850 placed the total sheep numbers for the state at less than 18,000 head, and by 1860, the official figure stood at 1,088,002 head.[96]

In the early years of the decade it was believed that the California climate was inappropriate for sheep raising. The hot summers and mild winters did not favor wool production, and the degenerate quality of California sheep strains (the result of years of neglect during and after the secularization of the missions) supported the notion that California was not sheep country. On the other hand, California sheep were famed for their fecundity; twins were common and triplets frequent in the California lambing.[97] Some of the Californios of the south continued to raise sheep, while in the north (to the east of Monterey) Anglos became the established sheepmen, including some of the former drovers like the Flints, Bixby, and Colonel W. W. Hollister.[98] In the second half of the decade sheep flocks were improved through importation of Australian stock and of merino rams from Europe and the eastern United States. Once the breeds began to improve, it became obvious that in normal years sheep thrived in the California climate. Mild winters allowed year-round growth, making California sheep as

---

*Wentworth believes that this figure is too low.[90]

large at two years of age as three-year-old Atlantic states animals. Sheep in California continued to be more prone to multiple births; the lambs had a lower mortality rate, and the common sheep diseases seemed to be less virulent in California climes.[99]

Sheep values remained high throughout the 1850s, but it was only late in the decade—the season of 1859, in the opinion of Wentworth[100]—that sheep flocks really began to proliferate on the California range.

There were other factors that stimulated the development of the California sheep industry. Millions of acres of California rangeland were under federal rather than private ownership. Control of this range remained on a first-come basis. Even as late as 1872, of the 120,947,840 acres of California, only 5,000,000 acres were within fences.[101] Thus, with the simple investment in a flock and a grubstake, the early sheepmen were in business. Similarly, in southern California, the cattlemen utilized their ranges in extensive fashion, employing vast acreage to raise relatively small numbers of livestock. Budding sheep outfits could, for a small rental, acquire access to prime rangeland to supplement their grazing on the generally less-desirable public lands. After the combination of ruinous mortgages and the crushing droughts of the early 1860s had bankrupted many California cattlemen, even more leasable rangeland became available. Leases on such lands near Los Angeles could be acquired at as low as one cent per animal per month.[102]

The flocking nature of his charges provided the sheepman with a further advantage over his cattleman counterpart. By employing dogs, a single herder could control a thousand or more charges and move them about the range quickly and efficiently. A sheep operation could therefore exploit stretches of pasturage located at considerable distance from one another. The manipulation of open-range cattle herds was more unwieldy and labor intensive. During the flooding of 1861 thousands of cattle simply drowned before they could be moved out of harm's way.

Sheep also proved to be more resistant to the periodic drought conditions of southern California. Sheep are browsers whereas cattle are grazers. In time of drought the deep-rooted brushy natural feed of sheep is less affected than the shallow-rooted grasses of the cattle. During the drought years that affected the south, both cattle and sheep suffered and died, but sheep losses were smaller.* The drought of 1862 marks a major transition from cattle to sheep raising on the southern California range.[104]

Finally, the economics of sheep raising proved to be considerably more stable during the 1850s than those of the cattle industry. If Kit Carson sold his charges in 1853 for $5.50 a head, by 1859 sheep were still worth $4.00 each in Los Angeles.[105] While mutton prices held firm, sheepmen, beginning in the following year, enjoyed sharp increases in the worth of their other product—wool. The American Civil War disrupted the cotton market and made wool the prime textile in the northern states.† The advantages afforded the sheepmen by rising sheep prices were further enhanced by sharp declines in cattle prices, the ruination of California cattlemen, and the great droughts of the early 1860s (resisted better by sheep than cattle). By one estimate, cattle numbers of California approximated 1.8 million animals in 1863, but by the following year the *San Francisco Bulletin* reported, "It can safely be estimated that from 1,800,000 head of cattle . . . there have died from starvation and the slaughter . . . not less than one-half the number."[107] One producer alone, Abel Stearns, lost between forty thousand and fifty thousand head.[108] That the cattle industry was not quick to recover is seen in the official statistics, which placed cattle numbers in California at 669,280 head in 1870.[109] During the same decade, sheep numbers more than tripled from 1,080,002 in 1860 to 3,636,000 in 1870. The steady improvement in sheep breeds is reflected in the increase of the wool clip

---

*The ability of sheep to survive without a direct supply of water is reflected in a description of sheep raising on the arid California coastal island of Santa Cruz where "The sheep that lived in the central portion of this waterless stretch, unbelievable as it may seem, never tasted water from birth to old age except what they received from dew or rain or eating a form of ice plant called Siempre Viva."[103]

†In 1864, wool prices were twenty cents a pound minimum; by 1867 they had declined to fourteen cents, a price at which the California woolgrowers could no longer compete with the traditional wool producing areas of Australia, Latin America, and South Africa. California woolgrowers were, in fact, as distant from United States textile markets as foreign producers, since the California product had to be sent to eastern United States ports via Panama or Cape Horn. In the same year (1867), United States wool production was protected when Congress placed a ten-cents-per-pound tariff on importations of foreign wool. In 1869, inauguration of the transcontinental railway facilitated shipment of the California wool clip to eastern markets.[106]

from 3,260,000 pounds in 1860 (an average of a little over three pounds per animal) to 19,472,666 pounds in 1870 (or an average of more than six pounds per animal).[110]

By the 1860s the former land-grant ranchos, in many cases broken into smaller units through forfeitures and sales, were being converted into sheep operations.[111] Those that remained large ranch holdings also became sheep ranches. It is estimated that the sheep population of the Irvines' Rancho San Joaquin reached fifty thousand head.[112] After John Bixby and his partners acquired the Ranchos Los Cerritos and Los Alamitos, they were each stocked with thirty thousand head of improved merino stock.[113] The lands of others like the Rancho La Habra, under the ownership of Abel Stearns, became available to small-scale sheepmen on lease arrangements.[114]

During the first two decades after the discovery of gold, the sheep industry of California expanded at an impressive rate. But who were the financial architects of this expansion, and who provided the labor that made it possible? The native Californio was not, as a rule, personally attracted to sheep raising; as a cattleman, he tended to have a low opinion of sheepherding. Insofar as he engaged in sheep raising prior to American annexation of California, he did so minimally, possibly supporting a small flock under little care on his rancho. The bonanza in beef prices in the early 1850s served to reinforce his commitment to cattle raising. Few of the Californios made the adaptation to sheep raising when cattle prices began to plummet.

The early sheepherders of California represented many different backgrounds. The California diggings attracted a cross section of nationalities and professions, and there was little security in the artificial economy of the mining camps. Conversely, the demand for sheepherders was growing, and the profession held out a guarantee of twenty-five to fifty dollars monthly on a regular basis. All manner of persons sought at least temporary relief in sheepherding. Thus, the nephew of the English Lord Clanmorris worked as a herder,[115] and a sheepman from Nacimiento could claim to have hired as herders an impressive array of college graduates including a bishop's son, a banker, an editor, a civil engineer, and an accountant.[116]

Nor were the opportunities in the sheep industry limited to wage employment. With a relatively modest investment, the enterprising man could turn a rapid profit in sheep. Thus, the March 23, 1860, issue of the newspaper *San Andreas Independent* (Calaveras County) stated:

There is no safer or more remunerative investment for a small amount of capital—say $3,000 to $4,000—than in breeding of sheep. . . . To attend a flock of, say 800 sheep, worth $4,000, but one man and two trained shepherd dogs are required, except in the lambing season, when a couple of extra hands may be required for a single month. A shepherd can be readily hired at $40.00 to $50.00 per month and found. . . . [Thus]:

For stock of sheep	$4,000
wages of shepherd	500
extra help in lambing season	100
price of mule or horse	70
to which add, for salt	30
Total	$4,700

The increase of 800 ewes, in this climate, will be at least 800 lambs, which at the age of ten to twelve months will readily bring $5.00 per head. If they have been well herded and kept on fresh pasture they will average 50 pounds . . . wool will average $1.00

[Thus]

800 yearlings at $5.00 per head	$4,000
1600 fleeces at 50c each	800
Total	$4,800

The profits of this business are more than 100 per cent per annum.[117]

To the many Basques arriving in the state from the Río de la Plata nations, the growth of the sheep industry in California must have seemed like a replay of Argentine history. By the late 1840s the competition in Argentina and Uruguay for adequate sheep rangeland was increasing, and we can only surmise that those Basques who reemigrated to the California diggings were those whose achievements in South America had been modest at best. It is unlikely that the truly successful Basque livestockman of the pampas would risk his "bird-in-the-hand" for the uncertainties of fortune seeking.

The newly arrived "Argentine Basques" brought with them not only an awareness of the economic potential of large-scale sheep raising, but also a knowledge of open-range herding practices under frontierlike conditions not unlike those of southern California. This is a crucial point, because throughout the American West it is still assumed, erroneously, that the success of the Basques in the region's sheep industry is due to their Old World background in the care of sheep. In point of fact, sheep raising in the Basque country has been far from ubiquitous and, where practiced, differed markedly in scale from the New World herding practices. Old World sheep raising involved household flocks, rarely surpassing one hundred animals, which were maintained on a nearby hillside and within walking distance of the dwelling. Since there were no large predators the sheep did not require a herder's constant care. Such flocks were only one item in a mixed farming household economy. This is in sharp contrast to herding practices in the American West, where the sheep band rarely numbers less than one thousand animals, predators make close herding a necessity, climate requires long-distance seasonal transhumance, and herding is a full time occupation.* Basques did import into nineteenth-century California special knowledge of sheep raising that was highly adaptable to local conditions, but it was wisdom acquired as much on the South American *pampas* as on Pyrenean peaks.

Basques newly arrived from Argentina became involved in sheep raising in southern California well before the budding opportunities were clear to everyone. Pierre Larronde, a French Basque from St. Palais, left Buenos Aires for California in February 1851 and found employment as a herder on the Rancho Dominguez near Los Angeles. A short time later he was a

---

*Gomez-Ibañez, in his study of sheep transhumance on the western range, argues that Basque herders probably applied an Old World experience derived in the Pyrenees to the range conditions of the American West. He credits the Basques with establishing sheep transhumance in the United States.[118] This is certainly a possibility, although we are unable to cite clear evidence that Basques were the first to trail sheep out of southern California into the High Sierra. Even if Basques were the earliest, it does not necessarily mean that they were applying an Old World experience.

There are two varieties of sheep transhumance in Europe, the Mediterranean pattern (involving large-scale, long-distance movement of men and animals) and the Alpine pattern (the local movement of flocks from valley floor to nearby mountaintop). The Basques practice the latter, whereas patterns of sheep transhumance in the American West most nearly approximate the former. Gomez-Ibañez makes the somewhat tenuous suggestion that, because Old World Basques shared common Pyrenean pastures with Mediterranean-type sheep drovers from central and southern Spain, they were at least aware of the Mediterranean pattern, even though they were not practitioners of it. Furthermore, none of the biographical information of the early Basque settlers in California reflects a strong Old World background in sheep transhumance. A view of Basque emigration to the American West from 1850 to the present is equally suggestive. While the majority of emigrants did come from rural circumstances, and therefore possessed working familiarity with animals in general, only a few French Basques from the higher villages of Soule and Basse Navarre seemed to have had prior sheepherding experience under conditions of transhumance.

sheepman in his own right.[119] Jean-Baptiste Batz, a French Basque who entered the mines in 1850, had by 1852 purchased the "Wild Rose Ranch" (today a part of Los Angeles), where he engaged in sheep raising.[120] By 1854 other Basques from Argentina like Simon Gless, Gaston Oxarart, and Domingo Amestoy were working as herders in the Los Angeles area.[121]

Prior to the entry of the Basques, herders in California were simply salaried employees. However, as early as 1854 we have evidence of contractual arrangements between a rancher and a Basque sheepman that are strongly reminiscent of those that frequently obtained in Argentina (see pp. 140—154). Essentially, such agreements called for the rancher to provide land and part or all of the flock while the sheepman provided care, operating expenses, and possibly part of the flock. At the end of a one- or two-year period, the sheepman retained a percentage of the animals as his payment. There were advantages on both sides. The rancher was guaranteed excellent care of his animals by a man who had a financial interest in their well-being. Sheep raising was more intensive than cattle raising and promised a greater return per acre if done properly. Finally, the rancher was exempted from a drain on his cash reserves, because he paid no wages for the sheep operation. For his part, the sheepman benefitted in that he was spared working for wages for years in order to accumulate the initial capital to start a sheep operation. The arrangement further allowed him to operate at peak efficiency from the beginning. It was practically as easy, and considerably more profitable, to run a thousand sheep as five hundred.

Thus, on June 26, 1854, Domingo Amestoy (another of the French Basques who arrived in the group that left Buenos Aires in February 1851) signed a sheep raising contract, or "conbenio," with Don Abel Stearns of Los Angeles (see Appendix Six). The document was written in Spanish and witnessed by the Basque Ulpiano Indart. Under the agreement, Stearns entrusted 1,829 animals (including 800 ewes, 395 wethers, 118 rams, 412 lambs, and 114 goats) to Amestoy, as well as rangeland for their maintenance on the Rancho de los Alamitos. For his part, Amestoy was "obliged to care for and raise this flock" for a period of two and a half years beginning May 15, 1854. Amestoy was to pay, at his own expense, "the required servants and all work necessary to the task of caring for the flock." He was to shear the animals and "give all of the wool" to Stearns. He was to "castrate the lambs at the appropriate time . . . and mark them with the brand of Stearns." Amestoy was also to "pay immediately in cash the quantity of one dollar and fifty cents for each of the lambs in order to have rights or ownership of one-half of this year's lambing." Amestoy agreed to reimburse Stearns for "any loss in the flock resulting from his neglect or poor handling." At any time during the agreement, Stearns could demand his wethers, his share of the offspring, his goats, and his rams, although he agreed not to remove those rams necessary for the breeding of the ewes. No ewes or lambs were to be sold until conclusion of the contract period, at which time Amestoy was to return to Stearns "800 ewes and one-half of the increase of the flock." Amestoy retained the other half "as recompense for his labor and expenses."

At the conclusion of the contract period, Stearns and Amestoy entered into a new agreement. A document signed by both men at Las Paredes and dated November 15, 1856, states:

> Today the period of the contract that we have had since the year 1854 terminated. With respect to the flock that Abel Stearns placed in the care of Domingo Amestoy today the animals were counted and they number two thousand seven hundred and ninety nine (2,799) between small and large ones. We have entered into a new contract with the same terms of the other with the exception that Domingo Amestoy will not have to replace the old ewes that die and furthermore that the said Amestoy will retain one-half of the wool at the time of shearing.
> . . .

This new document is interesting for many reasons. First, it suggests that within a space of two and one-half years Amestoy was able to form his own band of approximately one thousand animals (one-half of 2,799 less 800 ewes). This fact gave him greater leverage in his new dealings with Stearns. On the one hand, Amestoy was unwilling to guarantee the continued good health of the aging ewes (note that no ewes were to be sold under the original agreement) and, second, Amestoy was no longer willing to be excluded from the wool profits. Under the new arrangement Amestoy acquired rights in his own wool, while at the same time he was to receive half of the wool profits from the 800 ewes returned to Stearns as per the original agreement.* The alternative for Stearns, of course, was that he

---

*Domingo Amestoy signed a receipt on June 2, 1857, in which he states, "I received from Don Abel Stearns Two Hundred and Thirty Two Dollars for one half of the wool sold from this year's clip."[122]

would simply lose Amestoy's services, an eventuality that he obviously sought to avoid by liberalizing the terms of their agreement.

From Amestoy's viewpoint the original contract was far from generous. He was responsible for replacing lost animals, he had to care for wethers, rams, and goats without sharing in any of their profits, and he had to pay all costs of the operation. Nevertheless, Amestoy was able to parley this modest beginning into a personal fortune. During the 1860s his was one of the biggest sheep operations in southern California. In 1871, Amestoy purchased shares worth half a million dollars in the newly-formed Farmers and Merchants Bank of Los Angeles.[123]

There is another aspect of the Stearns-Amestoy agreement that requires comment. Abel Stearns was one of the more successful Old Californians. Prior to the American annexation of the state, he was well acquainted with Basques such as Miguel Pedrorena, José Antonio Aguirre, and Cesareo Lataillade. The Basque Ulpiano Indart, who appears as a witness on the first contract, entered California in 1849 and established himself as a merchant (Stearns's main activity as well). We might speculate that Indart's involvement reflects a relationship between an established* "California" Basque and a newcomer fellow ethnic of more modest background. It is equally plausible, however, that it reflects a class affiliation and that Indart witnessed the document as a fellow Californio businessman at the request of Abel Stearns.

From more secondary sources, it is evident that Domingo Amestoy was not the only Basque sheepman operating in southern California by the mid-1850s. From the biographical sketches, we know that Jean-Baptiste Batz, Jean Etchemendy, and Pierre Larronde were early sheepmen. Beaudreau[124] identifies Simon Gless, Pierre Larronde, and Gaston Oxarart as sheepmen operating about this time in the Cahuenga Valley (present-day Hollywood). It may be that these men also got their start with lease arrangements (since most of the area was under private ownership); however, this remains speculative in the absence of documentation comparable to the Stearns-Amestoy *"conbenio."*

It is clear that by the decade of the 1860s Basques were becoming established in increasing numbers in the exploding

---

*Although Ulpiano personally entered California at a relatively late date, the Indart family's California credentials were more long-standing (see p. 201).

sheep industry of southern California. By this time most of the new Basque sheepmen came to California directly from Europe, rather than as former sojourners in the Río de la Plata. Some of the newcomers, men like Domingo Bastanchury and José Sansiñena, were to become wealthy landowners after many years of personal sacrifice as sheepherders and small-scale sheep operators.

To take Abel Stearns as an example again, by the late 1860s he preferred simply to lease range on several of his ranches (particularly the Cajón de Santa Ana, Las Bolsas, and the Paredes) to sheepmen rather than entering directly into partnership with them. In the Stearns accounts there are seventeen sheepmen listed as lessees at some time between 1868 and 1870. Of the seventeen, eight are almost certainly Basque—Pedro Etchevery [sic], Miguel Ydegollen [sic], Pedro Archimo, Martin Etchepare, Juan Uristey [sic], Domingo Bastanchury, Jean Larre, and Bautista Yndart. Of the remainder, one has a Basque last name, Cayetano Ybarra, though the first name suggests Mexican origin. One is simply identified as the D. & D. firm and might be Basque. The largest single operator was Pedro Etchevery who, on May 28, 1869, paid a fee for seven thousand sheep.[125] Domingo Bastanchury subsequently became one of the larger sheepmen in the area, running between ten thousand and twenty thousand head on up to twenty thousand acres of Stearns's leases.[126]

It is clear that many *individual* Basque operators were a part of the establishment of the sheep industry of southern California during the decades of the 1850s and 1860s. However, there remains a question as to the importance of the role of the Basque *collectivity* in this development.

Harris Newmark, in his celebrated work *Sixty Years in Southern California* states: "Frenchmen from the Basque country, among whom were Miguel Leonis, Gaston Oxarart, Domingo Amestoy, and Domingo Bastanchury, had commenced to appear here in 1858 and to raise sheep; so that in 1859 large flocks were brought into Southern California."[127]*

---

*The extent to which the interests of these early southern sheepmen were interrelated is described by an article in the December 18, 1897, issue of *California'ko Eskual Herria*. The article reported the bankruptcy of Simon Gless, who listed his assets at $4,800 and his debts (owed mainly to fellow Basques) as $8,627.15. Mr. Gless was identified as the nephew of Simon Oxarart and the husband of Domingo Amestoy's daughter. The article noted that his economic problems were due in large measure to the fact that his share of the sizeable inheritance left by Oxarart had somehow gone to the Amestoy family.[128]

Basque involvement in the sheep industry of southern California was so great by 1858 that a non-Basque observer saw the Basques as founders. The statement is doubly significant because Newmark became a wool and hide buyer in 1862 and therefore had an intimate knowledge of the sheep industry.

Nor was the Basque role in the sheep business limited to that of owner. Sarah Bixby, in *Adobe Days*, a book that deals with the life of an American girl on the Los Cerritos and Los Alamitos ranches (present day Long Beach and Signal Hill) in the late 1870s, states:

> Most of the sheep . . . lived out on the ranges in bands of about two thousand, under the care of a sheepherder and several dogs. These men lived lonely lives, usually seeing no one between the weekly visits of the wagon with supplies from the ranch. Many of the men were Basques.[129]

In *Los Angeles City of Dreams*, Harry Carr writes:

> Sheep were in the hands of the Basques when I came to California [in 1887]. Possibly no race with less fighting qualities could have held their own against the cattlemen. Even as late as my reporter days, the Basque herders and the Mexican cattlemen shot on sight in the hills of Calabasas where many movie stars now have country places on the edges of the city. The Basques are a mysterious people—an ethnological riddle—perhaps the backwash of an early Gothic invasion of southern Europe that became marooned and isolated in the high mountains of the Pyrenees. There were many old families in California speaking this strange Mongoloid tongue, keeping to themselves, scornful of the Spanish fandangos, and saving their money. Their herds were Ishmaelites, grazing the slopes of the foothills, wandering from pasture to pasture. The herders did not go insane as pulp magazine authors insist. They lived in unbelievably crude conditions and thrived on loneliness. I can remember seeing their camps. They slept in boxes raised on high stilts—like an upper Pullman berth out on a lonely plain; this to avoid the danger of rattlesnakes.[130]

A governmental report written in 1880 saw the Basques as small-scale sheepmen:

> The tenure of [California] land has been changing from free ranging to ownership or lease, especially since 1870. . . . In . . . [Los Angeles County], and farther east, the Basques lease land at an annual average of 30 cents per acre.[131]

It is likely that such leases frequently included lands owned by the railroad.[132]

The contention by non-Basques that Basque involvement in the sheep industry of California was extensive is supported by biographical sources. In 110 published biographies of Basque males (see Appendix Four)* who entered California between 1845 and 1920, we find that 93 were involved at some time in the sheep business; 74 started as herders and, of this total, 52 later owned their own sheep outfit. Nineteen managed to acquire their own sheep without mention being made of previous herder experience (although one suspects that in most cases this is due to an omission in the biographical account).†

The Basque involvement in the sheep business of southern California was characterized by itinerancy. A few of the early Basque sheep owners, such as Domingo Bastanchury, José Sansiñena, and Domingo Amestoy, ultimately acquired large landholdings but generally did not do so until later in life, just prior to withdrawal from sheep raising. These large-scale operators preferred to acquire leases from others or run their animals on the public domain exclusively. Thus, despite the early and substantial involvement of Basques in the livestock industry of southern California, we have no evidence of Basques among the ranks of such land barons as Abel Stearns, General Beale, or Flint and Bixby. When the old land grants were coming on the market, and at ridiculously low prices, Basques were little prone to invest in land.

---

*Of the 130 biographies listed in the sample, 2 Old World-born persons were women, while 18 were born in the New World.

†It should be remembered that "successful" men are more likely: (1) to be interviewed by the authors of county histories and (2) to be willing to pay for a biographical sketch in the vanity sections of such books. The Basque who remained a wage-earning sheepherder all of his life is absent from the sample; yet there were many such in nineteenth-century California. A second point concerns the high incidence of sheepmen in the sample and the correspondingly low number of persons who were successful (in order to be included at all), but in enterprises other than sheep. We suspect that there is special significance in the Basque sheepman figures because sheepmen in general remain more obscure in the history of the American West than the more romanticized figures of miners and cattlemen. It is not unusual in some local histories to find sheepmen ignored altogether or passed over in a few (possibly deprecative) lines. Hence we suspect that Basques who were successful in any other enterprise and residing in towns or cities were more likely to make the county histories than their rural sheepman counterparts. (In point of fact, many of the sheepmen in the sketches also owned urban property and had town residences in addition to their rural operations.) Yet in our sample there remains an overwhelming identification of Basques with the sheep business.

We suspect that this reflects the same attitudes ascribed to the Basques in mid-nineteenth-century Argentina, namely their continued orientation to their Old World homeland. Most Basques viewed their New World experience as a sojourn rather than a permanent rupture of Old World ties. An investment in land meant a commitment of self to a New World future that few were willing to make, at least initially.* As long as the population of southern California remained sparse, cheap leases were available and free grazing on public domain was to be had for the taking, so there was little reason to tie up capital in land. Furthermore, land purchases supposed involvement with the little-known world of Anglo business and legal relations, mortgages, assessments, and taxation. Finally, most Basque immigrants entered the American West with little or no money, and sheepherding was not the most lucrative of professions. To accumulate sufficient capital to acquire even a single band of sheep required at best several years (unless one were fortunate enough to find a backer). Had it been necessary initially to acquire cash for sufficient land to support the band all year, the several hundred Basque sheepmen who were operating in the American West by the end of the nineteenth century would undoubtedly have been reduced to a handful.

There were two tendencies present simultaneously in the development of the sheep industry of southern California. One approach was based upon utilizing private lands as the heart of an operation and supplementing them with grazing on the public domain. These were generally large, stable ranch operations with a headquarters, limited mobility, and, ideally, a permanent labor force. In short, they were operations with both a past and a future. In contrast, there were small-scale, landless, mobile outfits operating off the back of the burro that carried the sheepman's tent and supplies. More often than not the Basque sheepman was of this latter variety—labelled pejoratively "tramp sheepman" by the more settled, competing livestock interests. At the same time, the majority of early itinerant sheepmen in southern California were Basques.

As early as the 1870s most Basque sheepmen in southern California were small-scale, landless operators who were more

---

*The California-born Basque Martin Biscailuz, in the first issue of *Escual-dun Gazeta* (1886), complained that of the two thousand Basques in the area only twenty were naturalized American citizens and hence eligible to vote. As a backer of the losing party, Biscailuz was chagrined at recent election results and urged his fellow ethnics to take out citizenship before the next election.[133]

concerned with the short-term vicissitudes of the wool market than with the long-term prospects of the American sheep industry. Their boredom in the solitude of the range was alleviated by dreams of an ultimate return to the Basque homeland. Writing of the southern California sheep industry of this period, Gordon states, "With but one or two exceptions these sheep-husbandmen are prospering, especially the Basques, several of whom have made money enough to retire on, and this has been done within six years."[134]

In the meantime the Basque sheepman contented himself with employing fellow countrymen as herders who, even though they might be exploited in some ways, were also to be helped in their own attempts to become the sheep operators of tomorrow. In many instances the herders were "imported" directly from the Old World, as sheepmen sought to attract their own relatives or fellow villagers to their sides. In such cases the relationship between employer and employee was frequently colored by other than economic considerations. Because he himself intended to return to the Old World, it was easy for the Basque operator to allow kinship and ethnic loyalties to override any fears that he might have of creating, through his protegés, too much pressure upon the available range.

Thus, it became common practice for the herders to take their wages (at least in part) in ewes. The herder was then allowed to run his animals along with those of his employer until his own flock was of sufficient size to support him. At this time he might "hive off," as it were, taking his animals and contracting for his own leases or searching out his own area on the public domain. In some cases, and particularly if he was a kinsman, a herder might enter directly into partnership with his former employer.

One result of these practices was to create considerable turnover of Basque herders, since each was a potential small-scale entrepreneur who might hope to complete the hiving cycle in as little as three or four years. As each of these new sheep owners in turn sent back to the Old Country for assistance, a regular pattern of Old World emigration of sheep-industry-oriented young Basque males was quickly established.

It is improbable that the supply of new arrivals was tailor-fitted to the demand for their services among established Basque sheepmen. While the established sheep operators were prone to seek herders along personal networks of kinsmen or fellow villagers, many young Basques without an "American uncle" assumed the greater risks of emigrating to the West on their own account. By the 1870s they could depend upon assistance from an emerging network of Basque hotels. The hotels provided them with initial lodging, orientation, and job information in a familiar ethnic setting. But most of all, they could count upon the budding Basque reputation (among non-Basques) as the best sheepherders.

It might be argued that the Basque herder had greater incentive to provide special care for his charges, because in many cases some of the ewes were his property. It is also likely that he paid particular attention to learning his trade well since he was not merely an employee but an aspiring independent operator. Thus, as this margin of special care was converted into a Basque reputation for excelling at sheepherding, Basques were hired preferentially by the non-Basque outfits as substitutes for their former Indian, Mexican, Scotch, and Portuguese herders.

This involvement of Basques in the sheep industry of southern California peaked by 1880 and then declined sharply during the next decade. The southern California climate was unpredictable and the ecological balance of the range tenuous. It might be that Basque hiving practices caused too rapid proliferation of itinerant sheep bands on the available range. However, even more significant were the general developments in the economy of the greater Los Angeles region. The establishment of a railhead in Los Angeles in 1876 triggered a population explosion and land boom, fed by speculators who advertised the area as a semitropical paradise. Indeed, as irrigation projects calmed the perennial fears of drought, southern California proved capable of producing a phenomenal range of crops. The sheepmen were caught in a price squeeze as sheep range became too expensive. Los Angeles County had 330,350 sheep in 1880;[135] by 1890 the number was reduced to 87,632 head.[136] At the same time, the small-scale, itinerant Basque sheepmen became increasingly rare in southern California. By the 1880s, however, southern California was no longer the sole California base of operation for the Basque sheepmen.

Northern and Central California Sheepmen

Monterey County comprised a second early and substantial focus of sheepraising in California. In the year 1860 Los Angeles County (with 94,639 head) was actually the second leading producer to Monterey (with 190,656 head).[137] The

Monterey flocks included those of Pereira (30,000 head), Flint and Bixby* (17,000 head), and Colonel Hollister (14,000 head).[138]

Our earliest evidence of Basque sheepmen in northern California comes from San Benito County. During the 1850s Julián Ursua (a Basque name) operated a hotel in San Juan Bautista, which he sold, sometime prior to 1863, to an Italian, Angelo Zanetta, and his Basque wife, María Laborda. Under their ownership the hotel was a major center for sheep and cattle transactions. The guest registers for the years 1863–66 include such Basque names as Julián Ursua, Juan Echeveri, Juan Indart, C. Echeveria, José Aurrecoechea, Mendizabel, Esteban Luyua (Lugea?), Franco Echeveria, Benito Echeveria, and Ramón Chevarria.† In the late 1860s and the 1870s, Basques were acquiring leases to run sheep in San Benito County.[140] By the 1880s a number of Basque sheepmen had purchased ranch properties in the area.[141]

In the Salinas Valley, meanwhile, an Italian sheepman named Alberto Trescony reputedly employed many Basque herders (although precise dates are unclear).[142] Two points are of interest in Trescony's dealings with the Basques. First, he depended upon the Aguirre hotel, a Basque-owned establishment in San Francisco, as a kind of employment agency in acquiring his men. Alberto's son Julius thereby met and married Kate Aguirre, daughter of the hotel's proprietor.[143] Second, the first Basques that Trescony reputedly encountered were itinerant operators who had trailed their sheep into the Salinas Valley from the San Joaquin Valley during a particularly dry year. According to Fisher, "Salinas vaqueros hustled many a Basque herder and his sheep back over the mountain passes at the point of a rifle."[144]

It is likely that the San Joaquin Valley sheepmen in question came from what was known as the "west side" district of areas like Merced County. By as early as 1862, there was a largely Basque-controlled ranching corporation known as the Sentinela Ranch in western Merced County. The three Basque partners Juan Indart, Juan Etchevery, and Salvador Isagar pooled their resources with Sequi Murietta, "a Spaniard," to

---

*These are the same persons who in 1878 acquired the Los Cerritos and Los Alamitos ranches in southern California and converted them to sheep production.

†Spellings are from the registers.[139]

buy the property. They raised horses, cattle, and sheep.[145] Of considerable interest is the fact that the ranch was purchased from another Basque, Faustino Larrondo, suggesting an even earlier Basque involvement in the area. Similarly, the purchase involved other pieces of land as well, including three urban parcels in the Sierra mining town of Murphys.[146] Here is a clear case of simultaneous involvement of a Basque in both the mining activities of the Sierra foothills and the ranching activities of the San Joaquin.

It was during the latter half of the 1870s that the San Joaquin Valley emerged as the key sheep-raising district in California. The 1880 sheep census listed Los Angeles County as still a major producer (330,350 head); Monterey's total had declined (126,644); and several San Joaquin Valley counties were recording substantial totals: Kern (152,041), Merced (167,749), San Joaquin (182,597), Sonoma (156,554), Tulare (126,176), Stanislaus (113,939); Fresno County (383,243) was the state's leading sheep producer.[147]

In his history of Kern County, Morgan claims that its earliest sheepman was Solomon Jewett; the next sheepman was Harry Quinn, who settled the area in 1874. Later, many French itinerant sheepmen, such as J. B. Berges, A. P. Eyraud, Andre Vieux, Pierre Giraud, and the Faure brothers, entered the county.[148] According to Wentworth, the largest operator out of Bakersfield was the firm of Olcese and Ardizzi. Olcese was a Frenchman who, "through financing many Basques, French, and Scotch herders, came to control hundreds of thousands of sheep. . . . Through direct or indirect connections with him, numerous families prominent in the modern sheep industry got their start—The Soldumbehrys [sic], Ansolabeheres, Bastanchurys, Etcheverres [sic], Etchegarays, Etcharts, Espondas and Oronos [all Basques]."[149] In fact, Wentworth noted, "Three European races were strongly successful in the Bakersfield region—Spanish Basques, French Basques, and Béarnais French."[150] The firm of Miller and Lux, which had gigantic holdings throughout the San Joaquin Valley, was also a major employer of Basques. At one time, a Basque (Oyharçabal) was the sheep foreman for the entire operation.[151]

By the 1870s many Basque itinerant sheepmen were firmly established in Kern County, and others were making their appearance in Fresno and Merced counties. By the 1880s Basque herders were established throughout the San Joaquin and Sacramento valleys as far north as Red Bluff.

Sheepmen and cattlemen were not the only agriculturalists to make an early entry into the San Joaquin and Sacramento valleys. The establishment of steamboat traffic along the Sacramento and San Joaquin rivers by the early 1860s facilitated the transport of bulky crops to distant markets. By 1860, wheat farming was an established feature of the valleys' economy.[152]

During the ensuing decade cattlemen and sheepmen competed with each other for the available range and jointly opposed the farmers. Until the early 1870s the burden of protecting his crops fell squarely and solely upon the farmer. If his fields were invaded by livestock, he had no recourse. In the early 1870s, however, the so-called No-Fence laws were legislated, requiring that stockmen supervise their animals and pay all damages to crops. This was disastrous for the cattlemen but considerably less so for sheepmen who utilized constant herding practices anyway. Consequently, the cattlemen of the San Joaquin were forced to curtail their activities, while the sheep industry boomed through the 1870s and 1880s.[153] Furthermore, sheepmen found it to be both possible and profitable to lease stubble after the wheat harvest.

In the San Joaquin and Sacramento valleys there quickly developed certain sheep raising practices that differed from those employed in the formative years of the southern California sheep industry. In the southern reaches of the San Joaquin Valley, notably Kern County, there developed a pattern wherein the flocks were trailed annually into the High Sierra for summering. This southern corridor of sheep transhumance, established as early as 1865, stretched from Kern County across the northern fringes of the Mojave Desert, up the eastern slopes of the Sierra to Mono County, then across the Sierra to the foothills of the western slopes, thence south to Kern County to the wintering grounds.[154] Further to the south, San Diego County sheepmen frequently trailed their animals into the mountains of northern Baja California.[155]

To the north many sheep outfits, more or less from Fresno County to Sacramento County, developed patterns of short-distance transhumance in which the animals were wintered on the valley floor and summered in the high country to the east.

In 1865 Flint wrote that a drought in the summer of 1864 prompted many sheepmen to seek refuge in the High Sierra where they learned that annual migrations would benefit the stock.[156] The California naturalist John Muir was a sheep drover out of the San Joaquin into the headwaters of the Merced and Tuolumne rivers in the summer of 1869.[157] The following summer, in the Tuolumne Meadows alone, Le Conte observed "twelve to fifteen thousand sheep . . . divided into flocks of about twenty-five hundred to three thousand."[158]

Further to the north there was a corridor of sheep trails that ran from Tehama and Butte counties to Lassen and Plumas counties on the eastern slopes of the Sierra. As early as 1883 two hundred thousand Sacramento Valley sheep were summered annually in Lassen County alone.[159] Shortly thereafter both Lassen and Modoc counties had their own populations of itinerant Basque sheepmen.

There were certain advantages (notably improved wool quality and more successful insemination of ewes) to be derived from summering in the High Sierra, but it is more likely that this initial pattern of sheep transhumance was mainly a reflection of growing pressure upon the California range (both private and public) as profits soared and the itinerant bands proliferated.

These patterns of sheep transhumance made it possible for a concentration of sheep outfits to operate out of the central valleys, which, lacking the supplementary summer mountain pasturage, would have overtaxed the carrying capacities of the low country ranges. It was only in the 1890s and early 1900s, when the central valleys entered upon a diversified cropping agricultural boom, that many Basque sheepmen followed the example of others and homesteaded* or otherwise acquired holdings that they converted to plowland. The general "settling" of the valleys curtailed the movements of sheepmen and limited the availability of suitable sheep range. Once again, it was a question of inflated land values pricing out the sheepmen.

By 1900 the economic situation had seriously hampered the activities of many sheep operators; their problems were further aggravated by their first taste of government intervention. In the last decade of the nineteenth century and the first

---

*Between 1886 and 1901, in Merced County alone, homesteads were filed by these Basques: Pedro Aguirre (1891), Salvador Aizegar (1892), Francisco Aldansa (1892), Juana Aniotzbehere (1901), Lauriano Arana (1892), Prudencio Arburua (1892), Arnaud Ardans (1892), Francisco Ardansa (1892), José M. Ariztia (1888), Urbano Ariztia (1889), Martin Arribellaga (1886), Prudencio Arrieta (1891), Juan Behere (1892), Mary Ann Echeverre (1897), Juan Ellisagone (1892), Bernard Etchepare (1891), Pedro Gastambiobe (1890), Martin Obieta (1893), Pedro Idiart (1897), Gracian Indart (1901), John Indart (1901), Peter Indart (1901), Pedro Urdeburu (1892), José Yrigoyen (1892), J. M. Yrigoyen (1893), and Fermin Zalba (1897).[160] (Spellings by Merced County recorders.)

decade of the twentieth, several national parks and national forests were created in the High Sierra.

In many cases, sheepmen, particularly itinerant sheepmen, were denied access by United States Forest Service officials to what had traditionally served them as summer range. Morgan, a historian of Kern County, states,

> The setting apart of a very great area of mountain land as a federal forest reserve and the exclusion of the sheep men from the free ranges which they had formerly enjoyed therein, was the cause of curtailing to a considerable extent the sheep industry in the county, particularly affecting the wandering shepherds, the Frenchmen and Basques who own little or no land and depend on leasing cheap ranges and driving their flocks from section to section to meet the changes of the varying season.[161]

However, the displacement was never complete, and to this day there exists a symbiosis in the San Joaquin Valley between sheep raising and cropping. Contemporary sheepmen (most of whom are Basques) own or lease extensive range in the foothill areas unsuited to plow agriculture, and they lease agricultural lands (grain, cotton, and alfalfa lands primarily) after they are harvested.* Furthermore, some San Joaquin Valley (and particularly Kern County) sheepmen continue to trail or truck at least a part of their sheep into the High Sierra during the summer months.[162]

Although the numbers of California sheepmen were thinned toward the end of the century, many, including a fair number of Basques, continued in the business. During this period, in fact, the ratio of Basques in the ranks of the California sheep growers began to increase markedly, because many new Basque immigrants, by acquiring leases on grainfields and in the nearby foothills, actually became independent operators after 1900.†

The Decline of the California Sheep Industry

California experienced severe drought conditions in 1877, prompting many of the established sheepmen to trail bands of

---

*By restricting sheep to the nearby foothill and high mountain areas during the growing season, and introducing them into the fields after the harvest, sheep feed was multiplied, the farmers received a fee for the otherwise worthless stubble, and the sheep fertilized the fields in the bargain.

†See many of the biographical sketches in Morgan, Vandor, and Tinkham.[163]

several thousand head to northern California, the Sierra, or the states of Nevada and Wyoming.* By one account,

> The losses of 1877 were estimated in southern California at 2,500,000 head of sheep, for the pastures were overstocked before the drought. Sheep were sold at sheriff's sale for from 25 to 30 cents. Stock fled in every direction, to Arizona, to New Mexico, and to the Sierra Nevada.[164]

Some authorities attribute the decline in the sheep business to this drought.[165]† What was more important were developments in California society that created population growth, resulting in the homesteading of parts of the public domain as well as rapid inflation in the value of private land, which soon became too valuable to be utilized as sheep range.

After the Civil War California became more famed for her climate and agricultural potential than for her gold. Land speculators advertised the state as an agricultural utopia in both Europe and the eastern United States.[167] Of particular interest to southern California was the completion, in 1876, of the first rail link into the area. The rapid and cheap transportation of cash crops to outside markets became a reality, and southern California entered upon an era of irrigation projects and plow agriculture. Sheepmen, including those few Basques like Domingo Bastanchury and José Sansiñena, who had acquired land, made fortunes by selling off extensive sheep range to potential farmers or converting it to crops themselves. There also developed a system of leasing land for the purpose of plow agriculture. This California arrangement was quite similar in nature to leasing practices on the Argentine *pampas.*‡

---

*The fact that some chose to go east into the Great Basin is eloquent testimony that large numbers of tramp sheep bands were competing for the High Sierra by this time.

†Many stockmen, Basques included, undoubtedly suffered enormous losses in the 1877 drought. A biographical account written by a longtime San Diego resident relates:

> In May 1877 when I returned with my sheep to the mountains I called at the Santa Maria and saw Mr. Etchevery [*sic*] and found him in a very poor way. He had lost lots of lambs and old sheep during the winter and said, "If I could find anyone who would give me $5000 and pay my debts, I would turn over the ranch to him, and the sheep which were left." I persuaded him not to do it, and he held on and came out all right in the end.[166]

‡Discussing the situation on the Irvine Rancho San Joaquin near the turn of the century, Armor states, "There are about one hundred and ten tenants upon the ranch and these farm on shares, giving one quarter of the crop to the

In 1893 José Sansiñena planted extensive acreage in barley.[169] Wheat and barley were the initial crops grown on much of the former private sheep range.[170] By 1905 the citrus fruit boom began. Domingo Bastanchury had three thousand acres of oranges, making him the owner of the largest citrus grove in the world.[171] Later the oil exploration frenzy in southern California benefited some of those few Basque families with extensive landholdings. Substantial oil wells were developed on the Careaga ranches of San Luis Obispo County.[172] Even though Domingo Bastanchury was deceived into selling a part of his holdings to oil prospectors in 1905, his family later sued successfully and received a $1,200,000 settlement from the Murphy Oil Company.[173] According to one estimate the Bastanchury ranch was worth $15,000,000 by 1923 and included 5,000 acres of citrus groves.[174]

By the end of the nineteenth century the economic interests of the established Basque immigrants who had entered California prior to the new agricultural trends had evolved with the changing situation. Of the ninety-four men in our sample who were herders and/or independent sheep operators, forty-one purchased acreage, and a total of thirty-eight converted former sheep range into other forms of agriculture such as grain cropping, alfalfa, and, in southern California, citrus orchards. Many individuals shared a life pattern that began with wage employment as a sheepherder, followed by moderate economic success as an independent sheep operator, then the purchase or homesteading of acreage, a number of years devoted to cropping, and final retirement to an urban residence. In such families there appears to have been a continued involvement in agriculture among the first-generation American-born. Of a sample of twenty sons of immigrant Basque agriculturalists, seventeen continued in agriculture, although most were no longer in the sheep business.

Consequently, as California entered the twentieth century, there was a substantial and multifaceted involvement of Basques in the state's agriculture. Basques had practically displaced all other ethnic groups in the herding occupation. A large number of recently arrived, upward-mobile Basque immigrants dominated the ranks of the itinerant sheep operators. A combination of a few New World-born Basques and a larger number

---

company. These leases are made only from year to year and by this method the best farmers are permitted to remain as long as they desire and the unsuccessful ones are dropped."[168]

of Old World-born individuals were liberally represented in the ranks of the larger, more sedentary sheep operations of California.* Both New World- and Old World-born Basques were no longer in sheep, but remained in agriculture, participating in the new trends toward cropping. Gachiteguy found that in a sample of almost two thousand California Basques taken in the early 1950s, 71.4 percent were in rural surroundings and occupations and only 28.6 percent resided in cities. Of the total, 60.5 percent owned some land but more than half were no longer in livestock raising, prompting Gachiteguy to label them "cultivators."[175]

Although the Basques were the most firmly entrenched ethnic group at every level of the California sheep industry by the end of the nineteenth century, California itself had by that time been eclipsed as the major sheep producing state of the American West. The focus of the open range sheep industry had shifted inland to the Great Basin, the Columbia Plateau, and beyond. This new development was not to be without its Basque dimension as well.

CALIFORNIA EXODUS

The spread of the Basques throughout the American West was intertwined intimately with the movements of the Basque sheepmen.† Sketched in broad terms, Basque sheepmen first left their mark in southern California in the early 1850s. The Monterey and San Joaquin Valley areas show evidence of their presence in the following decade. Somewhat later they appear in the northern reaches of the Sacramento Valley. By about 1890 there are itinerant Basque sheepmen in the extreme northeastern corner of the state (Lassen and Modoc counties).[176]

---

*At present the largest single open-range sheep outfit in the American West, which controls huge properties in three states (California, Arizona, and Texas), is the Basque-owned Mendiburu Land and Livestock Company of Bakersfield, California. By employing an average of between fifty and sixty herders, Mendiburu is the largest single contractor of sheepherders in the United States. This is all the more impressive in light of the fact that cattle raising has become the major emphasis in the operation!

†We would reiterate that the denigration of the profession and the social isolation of the occupation insulated the sheepherder from public scrutiny and hence awareness. Our estimates of the period when Basques moved into a particular area are based on such primary sources as newspaper accounts and public records (e.g., vital statistics, tax rolls, deed lists, etc.) and published secondary sources (which are frequently less reliable). However, it is likely that in many cases the first Basques entered a particular area several years before any of them made local news or conducted business in a county courthouse.

By no later than 1870 Basques were present in western and northern Nevada. The greater Winnemucca region, bounded to the west by Reno, to the north by Jordan Valley (Oregon) and to the east by Elko, provided one major area for the activities of Basque sheepmen beginning in the early 1870s, an involvement that still exists.

From this base Basque sheepmen and sheepherders moved northward into southern Idaho. In 1889 two Vizcayans, Antonio Ascuenaga and José Navarro, left Winnemucca and narrowly averted dying of thirst in a difficult desert crossing before reaching Jordan Valley where they became established as sheepmen, attracting other Vizcayans to the area.[177] In 1891 another Vizcayan, José Uberuaga, set out from Reno to Boise with two companions, a journey that they made on foot in twelve or thirteen days.[178] Shortly before 1900 many of the Vizcayan sheepmen of Jordan Valley were extending their operations to the Boise Valley. During the first decade of the twentieth century, Boise was itself to serve as the support area from which Basque herders, itinerant sheepmen, and an occasional landowning rancher became established throughout southern Idaho to as far east as Pocatello.

The brunt of this expansion was borne by the Vizcayans, and the Basque colony of northern Nevada, eastern Oregon, and southern Idaho acquired an almost exclusively Vizcayan complexion. It might be argued that Vizcayan Basques, as relative latecomers to the American West, had more incentive in the waning years of the nineteenth century to strike out into previously underdeveloped areas than did their fellow ethnic French Basques and Navarrese, who were more likely to have established kinsmen in California who could be counted upon for protection and patronage.*

With the possible exception of the early days in southern California, Basques were not the founders of the open-range sheep industry of any particular area. But in many regions Basques were present shortly after sheep were in evidence and within a decade or two had largely supplanted others as the primary ethnic group in the business. It must be remembered that the open-range sheep industry of the American West was not restricted exclusively to the areas that we have discussed thus far. In 1910 Nevada (1,444,000 head) and Idaho

---

*Of course there were many exceptions, and not all newly arrived French Basques and Navarrese sought out the security of the established Basque colony.

(2,951,000 head) were major sheep producers, but Montana (5,220,000) and Wyoming (5,019,000) were even more so. Similarly, the states of New Mexico (3,113,000), Utah (2,010,000), Colorado (1,611,000), and Arizona (1,411,000) had substantial open-range sheep industries.[179]

Basques were participants in the development of the sheep industries of all of these states. However, their involvement was quite limited and tended to be highly localized.

There is indication of a few Basques in Arizona in the early years of the 1870s. According to one authority,

> A disastrous drought prevailed in southern California during 1870 and 1871 which led to driving into Arizona thousands of head of sheep and cattle. . . . More than likely some of these sheep remained in Arizona. A year or so later two Basques from California grazed their herds in the vicinity of Oracle, Pinal County. Later accounts of them, however, are lacking.[180]

In the 1890s there was still good range available in Arizona that brought in sheepmen from more crowded states.[181] A list of Arizona sheepmen compiled for the period 1891 to 1906 shows not a single Basque name among the established sheep ranchers, although the list does not appear to include itinerant operations. Among the herders, on the other hand, Basques occupied a prominent place. Haskett notes, "with few exceptions the herders and camptenders are Mexicans, Spaniards or Basques. . . ."[182] A series of published reports on the Arizona sheep industry in 1905−06 commented on individual outfits. While most employed Mexican herders, one report read,

> [Concerning Mr. Lockett's outfit] He for the most part employs on the range Basque Frenchmen, whose wages are $30 per month and found.[183] [Concerning the outfit of Mr. Scorce of Holbrook] Basque and Mexican herders are employed, usually two for each band.[184] [Concerning the outfit of Mr. Smith of Seligman, herders are] mainly Mexicans and French Basque, and both classes are about universally commended as exceedingly reliable and efficient.[185]

A pattern of transhumance developed in Arizona between the San Francisco Mountains in the north and the Gila and Salt river valleys in the south. During the twentieth century Basques have participated in this movement both as sheepmen and herders. As a consequence there is a small Basque population today in the greater Phoenix and Flagstaff areas.

While there are no present-day indications of its existence, there was a small Basque colony in the Tucson area during the 1890s, referred to occasionally in the newspaper *California'ko Eskual Herria*.[186]

At present there is a very sparse scattering of Basque sheepmen in New Mexico,[187] the legacy of three separate movements into the state. According to elderly informants, the arrival of Basque sheepmen in the extreme southeastern corner of New Mexico resulted from sheep drives out of California during a particularly severe drought year (1870). In the 1890s drought conditions again affected the California range, prompting some Basque sheepmen to remove their flocks to New Mexico.* Finally, about 1916 a plethora of homestead filings in southern Colorado reduced severely the sheep range on the public lands. There were a few Basques in the area who were displaced, most of whom resettled in and near Grants, New Mexico.

Extreme western Colorado and eastern Utah was one of the regions of the American West most beset with itinerant sheep bands. An 1894 article in *California'ko Eskual Herria* stated that crowded conditions on the California range had prompted four Kern County Basque sheepmen to leave for Colorado to examine the situation there. The article concluded with the prediction that, if conditions warranted, there would be a massive migration of California sheepmen to Colorado.[189] With respect to Carbon County, Utah, there is a specific reference to the first Basque sheepman into Clark's Valley:

> Sheepmen began to come into the valley to find grazing lands for their flocks. Gratien Etcheborne [*sic*] was the first to arrive. He came in 1910 and filed the first claim on the land in 1916.[190]

The largest concentration of Basques in the general area developed near the turn of the century in Grand Junction and Montrose, Colorado. Summer grazing was abundant in the high country of the western slopes of the Colorado Rockies, while the low desert lands between Grand Junction and Price, in Utah, provided adequate winter grazing.

---

*It seems that New Mexico Basques maintained ties with the California colony. In the December 19, 1896, issue of *California'ko Eskual Herria*, the editor welcomes Francisco Carricaburu *"gure herritar eta adichkide"* ("our compatriot and friend") to California. Carricaburu was a resident of Raton, New Mexico.[188]

It should be emphasized that the Basques were not the only sheepmen there. The area itself represented only a small percentage of the combined Colorado and Utah sheep production. Particularly in Utah, where sheepmen were Mormons whose sons were willing to herd their fathers' flocks, Basques have never gained much of a foothold at any level of the sheep industry.[191]

In Wyoming, Basque settlement was concentrated around the Rock Springs region and somewhat to the north. Johnson County, and particularly the town of Buffalo, has the largest single concentration of Basques to be found outside of the states of Idaho, Nevada, Oregon, and California. This colony was begun in 1902 when a French Basque was first employed by a large Anglo-owned Johnson County sheep outfit. Within twenty years, the Basques were well on their way toward controlling the area's sheep industry.*

The third issue (July 29, 1893) of *California'ko Eskual Herria* ran an article on the sheep industry of Montana.[192] Several Basque sheepmen got their start in the 1890s there by working for a large Béarnais-owned sheep outfit near Deer Lodge,† but no Basque names were on a list of over one thousand Montana sheepmen compiled about 1900.[194]

The ledger of operations in 1904–05 for a large ranching corporation, the Riverside Land and Livestock Corporation (located near Toston), lists two Basque sheepherders in a total herder labor force of about ten men.[195] By the early 1900s, a few Basques were becoming established as itinerant operators in one of the least inhabited areas of the state—the region between Glasgow and Plentywood.[195]

There was also a small Basque colony in the state of Texas, although present-day Basques of the American West have no awareness of its existence. In late 1893 and early 1894, *California'ko Eskual Herria* ran repeatedly the same favorable article on the sheep industry of Texas. Among the readership of the newspaper was at least one Basque resident of Corpus Christi and another of Van Horn.[197] The latter triggered a polemic when he refuted the notion current in the Basque colony of

---

*These developments are considered in greater detail in chapter 7.

†The June 27, 1896, issue of *California'ko Eskual Herria* reports the travel of the French Basque Jean Curutchet from Deer Lodge to the Basque country.[193]

California that Texas was an alien and dangerous land. The invitation he issued to California Basques to join their compatriots in Texas was worded in such a manner as to suggest that the Texas colony already consisted of more than a handful of Basques.[198]

We have also found evidence that, at the end of the nineteenth century, there was a Basque population thinly scattered throughout the ranching and logging districts of western Canada. Pierre Lhande lamented the fact that French Basques insisted on emigrating to the Anglo-dominated Canadian Far West when in fact there was ample opportunity for them in the Quebec area where they would have the added advantage of the familiar French culture. Lhande reports that the Quebec French community made efforts that proved unsuccessful to attract Basque immigrants.[199]

These brief comments complete our composite picture of the historical distribution and concentration of the Basque population of the American West. Appendix Seven lists by states the towns that have a notable Basque presence. We have indicated for each town its present-day or recent formal Basque ethnic manifestations, such as social clubs, folk dance groups, hotels, handball courts, festivals, picnics, dances, and radio programs. However, before considering in detail the history and nature of these ethnic institutions, we first turn to an analysis of the activities of the Basques in the Great Basin and the Columbia Plateau. Here the Vizcayans created a second major focus of Basque settlement in the American West.

CHAPTER SIX

Beyond California

Luck a la "Basquo"

(by C.C. Wright)

Some "Basquos" came from Spain last week
And all went out to herding sheep;
They passed some loafers on the way,
Who had some unkind things to say
About the country—how it's run—
To what dire end it's bound to come,
And how the poor man stands no show—
He might as well to Hazen go.
And so they sat and chewed the rag,
And went o'er and o'er that time-worn gag
About dividing up the wealth,
When each could travel for his health.
And as their cigarettes they smoked
They all about sheepherding joked,
And wished, meantime, some easy gink
Would come along and buy a drink.

Five years the Basque will follow sheep,
And every cent he gets he'll keep,
Except what little goes for clothes.
And then the first thing someone knows
He's jumped his job and bought a band
And taken up some vacant land;
And then the fellows who still prate
About hard luck and unkind fate,
And wail because they have no pull,
May help the "Basquo" clip his wool.[1]

CALIFORNIA SHEEP TRANSHUMANCE

California served as the first foothold for Basque immigration into the post-Hispanic American West. It was in California that Basque immigrants, many of whom had experience in South America, were able to establish livestock operations under what approached genuine frontier conditions. Just as in Argentina, some of these men who became entrenched in the industry during essentially lean and difficult years survived to witness developments that were to increase the value of their investments manyfold. But just as in Argentina, it required scarcely more than a generation of continued immigration of Basques, and the arrival of others interested in entering the sheep business, to convert the former sparsely inhabited sheep range into an arena of keen competition. As more and more itinerant sheepmen sought to earn a living on a land base that was dwindling due to the rapid expansion of other forms of agriculture, the crowded conditions on the California range became anything but a context of unlimited opportunity. Range-wise sheepmen, knowledgeable about the area's history of periodic lean years for stock growers, must have experienced considerable anxiety.

As pressure increased on the California range, the itinerant sheepmen began to incur the wrath of their more settled neighbors. Growing antitramp sentiment, coupled with dwindling economic opportunity, prompted many such sheepmen to look farther afield for better and less-crowded range conditions.

The vast interior regions of northern Arizona and the Great Basin proved attractive, and in these arid areas of harsh winters and scorching summers transhumance was, more than ever, a necessity. It was the successful transhumant California sheepman who was uniquely equipped to attempt year-round sheep raising in the interior. Furthermore, the "great circle" High Sierra pattern of transhumance initiated annually out of Kern County and southern California brought California sheepmen to the extreme western fringe of the Great Basin, the jumping-off point for penetration of the interior.

To what extent did Basques participate in these movements, and how were they viewed? There is confusing evidence on these points. In her book *The Flock*, written in 1906, Mary Austin describes sheep-raising conditions in southern Inyo County as if the movements of itinerant bands were a fairly late occurrence. She states:

> The best days of shepherding in California were before the Frenchmen began to appear on the mesas. Owners then had, by occupancy, the rights to certain range, rights respected by their neighbors. Then suddenly the land was overrun by little dark men who fed where feed was, kept to their own kind, turned money quickly, and went back to France to spend it.[2]

We might assume that the author was lumping French Basques with the ubiquitous Béarnais sheepmen under the general category of "Frenchmen," excepting that she herself states clearly that Basques are not to be confounded with French,[3] and that of the sheepherders trailing through the area, the majority "are French, then Basque, then Mexican and a few Portuguese. . . ."[4] In referring to the same movements, W. Storrs Lee, in *The Sierra*, agrees in spirit with Mary Austin's denunciations but probably errs in fact. He states with reference to the 1870s that herders were desperately needed, so the call went out to the Rhone Valley and the Pyrenees where the best herders in the world were to be found. "Suddenly the sheep lands were overrun with little dark silent men who cared not a whit about land rights, prerogatives, and American amenities."[5] Nor were the "foreigners" capable of forging a common front, since "Frenchmen despised the Portuguese and both united in common hatred of the Basques."[6]

An examination of the records for Inyo County establishes the fact that, by the 1890s, the seasonal movement of sheep bands through the area was considerable, and a large portion were Basque-owned. Table six lists the persons who paid sheep "licenses" or taxes to Inyo County in 1896–97.

TABLE 6
SHEEP LICENSES IN INYO COUNTY, 1896–97

Name of Operator	No. of Sheep	Name of Operator	No. of Sheep
*Juan Inda	11,300	†Escallier & Bress	5,500
*Juan Ospital	6,500	*Pedro Erro & Co.	4,200
*Antonio Erreca	3,550	*Esteban Zubiri	3,500
*Yldefonso Uxtasun	3,900	*Juan Arrembel	3,450
†Plantier Moynier	3,000	*Sandiago Ascarate	3,000
†Giradan Freres	3,100	†Espitallier	3,100
*José Irigoyen	2,800	*Domingo Saldumbehere	2,800
*Urretico & Saldumbehere	2,950	†Orcier Bros.	2,800
†Pourray Pellicier	2,600	*Juan Ardohain	2,550
*Juan Inchauspe	2,500	†Espitallier	2,500
†Girard Bros.	2,800	†Alphone Faure	2,000
†Léon Girandan	2,100	†Jean Scienturs	2,000
*Frank Bidart	2,300	*Arnaud Etchabendy	1,500
†Jean Blac	1,800	†Jean Reymond	1,900
Mark Matterson	1,600	†Guard Lombard	1,000
†Alfonso Rambaud	1,230	†Peirri Zonglard	5,000
A.L. Conklin	1,000	†P. Pon	800
Totals: 34 Operators		98,850 Sheep	

Source: Inyo County Sheep License Book.
*indicates clearly a Basque
†indicates *probable* non-Basque French
(Spellings are derived from county records and do not in all cases conform to usual Basque orthography.)

Several comments are in order. First, of the thirty-four operators, fifteen are clearly Basques and sixteen are probably French, but non-Basques. In terms of sheep numbers, the Basques definitely dominate, since of the 98,850 animals assessed, 56,800 were Basque-owned. The average holding of a Basque operator was 3,653 animals, whereas the average for the non-Basque French operator was 2,763 animals.

Second, practically all of the above sheep licenses were collected between April 30 and June 15, which suggests that the bands were passing through the area on their way to the High Sierra. By contrast, the two "Americans," A. L. Conklin and Mark Matterson, paid their assessments at the end of the calendar year, probably indicating that they were permanent residents of Inyo County.

Third, it is not to be assumed that these official records constitute an accurate picture of the numbers of bands moved through the area. We can be certain that no fewer operators and animals were involved since no one would pay taxes on imaginary sheep bands. Conversely, the itinerant operator became quite adept at dodging taxes. In part, this was a requisite for survival in the business, since a particular pattern of transhumance might take him across five or six counties, each of which tried to levy taxes against the band. The lore surrounding the movements of itinerant sheep bands is laced with stories of trailing sheep by county seats under the cover of darkness or trailing a part of one's animals through or near the county seat and paying taxes on them with considerable fanfare, while the remainder were being slipped by local vigilance.

Finally, the official practice of levying such taxes was a relatively late development. Inyo County instituted its sheep license ordinance on November 4, 1887, yet it is obvious that the movements of itinerant sheep bands through the area dated from considerably earlier. In the late 1860s and early 1870s the county allowed private individuals to build toll roads and exact fees. The usual charge per head for sheep was five cents. One suspects that this caused considerable resentment among the itinerant sheep operators, who did not require roads in order to move their outfits but who might find their passage blocked by an enterprising road "owner."

On balance, we believe that there is sufficient evidence to posit considerable annual movement of itinerant sheep bands out of southern California to the High Sierra by at least the early 1870s. It is also evident that the large majority of operators were either Béarnais or Basque in origin. We would also argue that this extensive involvement in southern California sheep transhumance presaged the movement of Basque itinerant sheep operators into the Great Basin regions of the American West. In the first place, the annual trailing along the eastern slopes of the Sierra gave the sheepmen a familiarity of range conditions along the western extremes of the Great Basin. Wentworth notes that in some years flocks would veer east into the higher ranges near the Nevada-California line. It was only natural that over time some of the itinerant sheepmen preferred the risks of stock raising in Nevada to the increasingly crowded winter range conditions of southern California and summer ranges of the High Sierra. Thus, while Argentina and Uruguay provided certain Basques with experience in large-scale, open-range,

sheep-raising practices, an experience which proved to be readily transferable to the conditions of southern California, the
latter area was itself to provide the lesson of transhumance,
without which sheepraising in most of the Great Basin region
would have been impossible.

GREAT BASIN SHEEPMEN

During the 1850s the vast area lying between the western
slopes of the Rockies and the eastern slopes of the Sierra Nevada
constituted, for a majority of the white population, a barrier to
be surmounted in the westward trek to California and Oregon.
The region, known as the Great Basin, is a harsh land of broken
topography and climatic extremes. The entire area is a huge
plateau tilted on a north-south tangent and laced with high
mountain ranges surpassing 10,000 feet above sea level in many
cases. The basic altitudes of the resulting valley floors vary
from approximately two thousand feet in extreme southeastern
California to six thousand feet in northern Nevada. Located to
the leeward side of the Sierra Nevada, the Great Basin has an
extremely arid continental climate in which a seasonal concentration of moisture in the winter months supposes locally heavy
snowfalls and extremely dry and hot summer conditions.

The population of the Great Basin in the 1850s consisted
largely of sparse numbers of nomadic Indians and the Mormon
settlers of Utah who, beginning in 1847, sought to create a
totally autonomous country out of one of the most neglected
corners of the American West. That such a venture could be
attempted at all is eloquent testimony to the lack of interest in
the region shared by the American government and most potential American settlers alike.

By the early 1860s the search for precious metals shifted
inland from the depleted mining districts of California.
Sporadic strikes were made throughout the Great Basin region,
e.g., the Comstock Lode in western Nevada (1859), the De
Lamar (1863) discovery in southwestern Idaho, and the Austin
(1862) and Tuscarora (1867) strikes in central and northeastern
Nevada. California miners swarmed over the mountains and
into the Great Basin region, following the rumors of new
bonanzas.

The inland mining boom was not without its significance
for livestockmen, Basques included. Each new mining camp
created its own demand for foodstuffs, and at considerably
inflated prices. Certain areas of the Great Basin, notably the

better-watered districts adjacent to the highest mountain ranges, began to be settled permanently by ranchers, most of whom emphasized cattle raising for the new local markets.

It might be argued that there was less initial attraction in sheep husbandry, since sheep could be trailed to local mining districts over greater distances and at less cost than could cattle. There is evidence as early as 1862 of sheep drives from Oregon and California to the Nevada mining towns of Austin and Eureka.[7] Also, the direction of the long overland sheep drives had been reversed by the 1860s, and California and Oregon sheepmen began to trail bands across the Great Basin to railheads east of the Rockies,[8] for marketing as well as for stocking new ranges. By the late 1870s it could be stated:

> Drives go out to Montana from the northern part of the state [California], generally above Lassen-Butte through south Oregon to Snake river; from middle California they go from Independence, thence up Owens river, and through Esmeralda County, Nevada, across Ralston desert to Humboldt Wells, from which, by Goose, Raft, and Snake rivers, they reach the divide of the Rocky Mountains between Idaho and Montana. From southern California to Arizona and New Mexico they go by the way of Mojave river and fort Mojave.[9]

Demand for mutton in mining camps along the sheep trails was filled easily out of passing drives.

There is little evidence that Basque sheep owners participated extensively in such sheep drives. According to a Bastanchury family tradition, however, Domingo trailed sheep to Idaho sometime in the 1860s, probably for sale in the mining camps. While the budding Basque sheep owners of California were little involved in the major sheep drives, it is probable that some Basque herders were employed as drovers and thereby became familiarized with Great Basin range conditions.

Yet there was early recognition of the potential of the Great Basin as sheep country in some California circles. In 1865 Flint wrote in the *Transactions of the California State Agricultural Society:*

> In the future this [the Great Basin] will be especially designated as the great pastoral region of the American nation, not because there may be a demand in distant markets for the wools which it may produce, but for the reason that the miners of the precious metals, sown thickly in every hill and mountain, will attract to this part of the continent a dense population for their development, which must find its chief supplies of food and

clothing from the produce of the herds grazed in its midst. Thus, in a great measure, will be settled the "difficult problem of transportation for these nearby inaccessible regions."[10]*

It is clear that a few small "farm" flocks of sheep were created on early Great Basin ranches, partly through the purchase of lame animals from the great sheep drive.[11] Consequently, by the late 1860s sheep were present in the Great Basin region under three distinct arrangements. Vast flocks crossed the area in the spring and summer months, moving eastward to railheads. A few farm flocks were maintained on the nascent ranches adjacent to the mining districts. And nomadic bands from southern and central California were summering along the basin's western fringes.

It is the movements of the nomads that are of greatest interest to the present study. In 1870 the *Elko Independent* reported, "Thousands of sheep have already been imported into Eastern Nevada, with results highly satisfactory. We may look for great activity in this branch of stock raising. . . ."[12] That the backbone of the movement consisted of the nomads is clear from an article that appeared the following year: "An immense drove of sheep . . . 80,000 head, says the *Silver State*, has reached Oreana from California, on its way to the eastern part of the State in search of mountain pasturage. . . ."[13] In a similar vein, an article in 1874 reports: "An immense amount of livestock is being gathered up in Kern and Tulare counties, Cal., preparatory for removal to other pastures, some for contiguous mountain valleys, but the larger portion to Nevada."[14]

From these modest beginnings there developed, within a few short decades, a major open-range sheep industry whose two prime characteristics were an almost total dependence upon use of public lands and transhumance between high country summer range and low-lying desert lands used for winter grazing. This was the dominant pattern both within the Great Basin and, near the end of the century, on the Columbia Plateau (the region of southern Idaho, eastern Oregon, and southern Washington, forming the headwaters of the Snake-Columbia river system). In 1880 there were no fewer than 7,493,864[15] sheep in the state of California; within a single decade, their

---

*Flint was correct in his prediction of the region's bright future as a livestock producer, but he was overly optimistic in his assessment of its mineral wealth and population potential. The livestock industry of the Great Basin was to thrive, although it solved its transportation problem with railroads rather than the expansion of internal markets.

numbers were halved to 3,712,310[16] animals. Meanwhile, Nevada and Idaho reported 504,710 and 501,978 sheep, respectively, in 1890.[17] California flocks continued to decline to 2,417,477 head in 1910, whereas in that year Nevada registered 1,154,795 sheep, and Idaho reported no fewer than 3,010,478 ovines.[18]

EARLY GREAT BASIN BASQUES

It is impossible to resolve with any degree of certitude the question of who was the first Basque to enter the Great Basin and Columbia Plateau regions. It is likely that he was one of the many California miners who followed the rumors of new strikes in the interior. There is a Humboldt County (Nevada) record from 1865 of a transfer of property deed involving the Zavala Mining Company.[19] While Zavala is a Basque surname, we cannot verify whether the founder, Pablo Zavala, was culturally Basque. It is just as likely that he was of remote Basque descent, but in a cultural sense the product of a Californio or Mexican background. Of unequivocal Basque origin, however, was the Viscaino Ledge Spanish Company, which transferred property in Unionville (Humboldt County, Nevada) as early as 1875.[20] The company was owned by three Basque partners, Florencio Crespo, José Manuel Apariz, and José Antonio Erquiaga. The latter filed a declaration of intent to become a United States citizen in Humboldt County on July 7, 1873.[21]

Julio Bilbao cites six individuals listed in the 1870 United States census of Idaho who *might* be Basque.[22] A possible candidate was the pack-train operator Jesús Urquides, known locally as the "Little Spaniard," who was reputed to have been in Boise Valley by 1862 or 1863.[23] Whether or not Urquides was aware of his possible Basque background is unclear. Militating against such an awareness was his birth in San Francisco* in 1833, the orthography of his last name (Urquid*es* is a hispanized version of the Basque last name Urquid*i*), and the fact that no Basques were pallbearers at his funeral.[25] On the other hand, at least one new Basque arrival to the American West in 1895, Francisco Odiaga, found his first employment with Urquides,[26] possibly indicating a mutual perception of Basque ethnic loyalties.

---

*However, one early newspaper account claims that Urquides was born in Spain.[24]

There is clear evidence of Basque personalities in the cattle industry of the Great Basin by 1871. It was in that year that two established Basque cattlemen of California—Pedro and Bernardo Altube—began ranching operations in Independence Valley (Elko County, Nevada), close to the mining town of Tuscarora.[27] By the time they were in their early forties, Pedro and Bernardo Altube occupied positions of wealth, prominence, and respect among California Basques. We have already considered some of their business dealings. According to one account, however, the Altubes felt the pressures of increased crowding on the California ranges and purchased 3,000 head of cattle in Mexico, trailing them to Independence Valley, where they established the huge "Spanish Ranch." When dissolved in 1907, the sale included 400,000 acres, 20,000 head of cattle, 20,000 head of sheep, and 2,000 horses.[28]

Jean Garat and his wife Grace were French Basques who, by 1871, had been successful cattle ranchers in the San Joaquin Valley for at least nineteen years. As with the Altubes, the attraction of uncrowded range conditions proved irresistible—probably all the more so given the fact that the Garat holdings in California bordered on Henry Miller's growing livestock empire, and Miller was prone to pressure his neighbors considerably when it came to use of the range.

In the summer of 1871 the Garat family crossed the High Sierra at Bridgeport with one thousand head of cattle and entered Nevada in search of a suitable ranch site. The first year, they wintered along the Humboldt River near Lovelock and the next summer ranged through the country north of Golconda. It was approximately three years after leaving California that the Garats purchased acreage on the Tuscarora Fork of the Owyhee River in Elko County and began what was to become known as the YP Ranch.[29] When the Garat family finally sold their holdings in 1939, the sale included 75,000 acres of deeded land, 7,500 cattle, and 500 horses.[30]

It may be surmised that both the Altube and Garat families viewed the mining boom in northeastern Nevada as a possible replay of the California opportunities of the 1850s. The silver discoveries in Tuscarora in 1869 were widely publicized and of such promising quality that the newspaper editor in the nearby town of Elko predicted that within a few years his community would surpass San Francisco in size.[31] In January 1869 city lots in Elko sold for $300 to $500 but by June of the same year had increased in value to between $1,500 and $2,000.[32] Yet, as late as the summer of 1870, it was estimated that the total cattle population of the rich Independence Valley was six hundred head.[33] For the range-wise Garats and Altubes, the opportunities for creating personal livestock empires* was clear.

By 1880 the Altubes alone were running five thousand head of cattle and were characterized as "one of the largest operators in this part of the state."[35] It is tempting to posit that these early Basque stockmen served as both the magnets and facilitators of the movement of their fellow Basques into the region. All the more so, since Pedro Altube is frequently cited as "The Father of the Basques in America."[36] There is an oral tradition extant among the Basques of extreme northern Nevada and parts of southern Idaho that he was the first Basque in the area and the patron of many subsequent Basque immigrants. In fact, it is evident that the man and myth of Pedro Altube are made to carry too great a burden in explaining the earliest entry of Basques into the Great Basin.

The Altubes were sympathetic to the needs of fellow Basques. We have already considered how both brothers, in their California dealings, entered into partnership with other Basques. Pedro made a large uncollateralized loan to another Basque on at least one occasion.[37] Both the Altubes and the Garats continued to maintain strong California ties after becoming established in Nevada. The November 16, 1895, issue of *California'ko Eskual Herria* reports the arrival of the Bernardo Altube family in San Francisco, where they planned to spend the winter.[38] Pedro constructed a mansion in San Francisco, and both brothers retired to the Bay area. Pedro died in San Francisco in 1905, while Bernardo passed away in Berkeley in 1916.[39]

The Garats likewise continued to maintain a California base. When Jean Garat moved to Elko County in 1871, at least one of his adolescent sons, John B. Garat, continued to reside in California until joining his father in 1877.[40] The Garat holdings became linked to Basque-owned California ranch interests in San Benito County through the marriage of John B. Garat and Matilda Indart in 1895.[41]

The ongoing California ties of both the Altubes and Garats might well have served as "channels" along which information

---

*The rapid growth of the Altube holdings was due to both a willingness to buy the ranch properties of others and their practice of encouraging their own employees to file homesteads, which the family then purchased.[34]

concerning conditions in the Great Basin reached the by then substantial Basque colony of California. Nor is it unlikely that a few Basques found employment on the YP and Spanish ranches during the 1870s.

On the other hand, there is considerable evidence that casts doubt upon the contention that the Altubes and Garats constituted the sole (or even major) factor in the subsequent migration of Basques to the Great Basin region. Both outfits were exclusively cattle-oriented for almost the first two decades of their existence; yet the majority of Basques entering the Great Basin were involved in the budding sheep industry. It was only after the severe winter of 1889−90 (in which both the Altubes and Garats suffered cattle losses of nearly 90 percent) that two adjustments were made in the Elko County livestock industry. First, summer haying was introduced for the winter feeding of cattle; second, the number of sheep bands (whose survival record during the harsh winter was considerably better) proliferated. The Garats opted for the first solution and remained a cattle operation exclusively. The Altubes, in addition to practicing haying, increased the number of sheep bands on their range (generally under the care of Basque herders). However, by at least one account, the Altubes were merely interested in parrying the thrusts of the Lovelock sheepman John G. Taylor onto Altube-claimed (but legally public) range in Elko County. In about 1900 the Altubes bought twelve thousand wethers that were purposely driven into Taylor flocks*—a tactic that will receive greater consideration at a later point.

While we know nothing about Garat employees, there is a partial published list of Altube ranch hands. The latter include several Mexicans and Californios, a Chinese cook, a few Anglos, and only a sprinkling of Basques.[43] As late as 1889, there was at least one Chinese sheepherder working for the Altubes.[44]

With the exception of the Nevada cattlemen Pedro and Bernardo Altube and Jean Garat, the entry of Basques into the Great Basin region was closely linked to the spread of open-range sheep raising. In no case do we have evidence that Basques were the *first* to introduce sheep into a particular area, but once sheep were introduced it took little more than a decade

---

*On one occasion, two of Taylor's herders beat an Altube herder and were subsequently arrested and fined, a decision hailed by Elko County cattlemen as a victory over sheep interests.[42]

for Basque herders and itinerant small-scale operators to become a ubiquitous sight. The earliest Great Basin sheep ranchers frequently employed Scottish, Mexican, Indian, Portuguese, Chinese, and American herders,[45] but, with few exceptions in all but the Mormon-dominated areas of the Great Basin, by 1900 the Basques were the preferred sheepherders in most outfits.

WINNEMUCCA BEGINNINGS

During the 1880s and 1890s the greater Winnemucca region was the major Great Basin destination of those Basque immigrants who were not bent upon reaching California. The area, despite being traversed in 1869 by the transcontinental railway, remained one of the least settled in the entire American West. With the exception of a few cattle and sheep ranches located in the extremely limited areas of watered river bottomlands, the small population was concentrated into railhead servicing centers like Winnemucca and Elko, or in the several mining districts. Vast amounts of range were in the legal status of public domain and hence, theoretically, open to anyone on a first-come basis. For the aspiring itinerant sheepman, there was the attraction (at least initially) that the settled livestock operations were too few and too widely scattered to exercise usufruct over all public lands. The stock industry of the greater Winnemucca area at this time was largely in its infancy. Yet the area, with its low desert winter range adjacent to high mountain summer pasturage, was ideal for transhumant sheep outfits.

There is evidence of Basque sheepmen in this area during the 1870s. At least four Basques—José Ugarriza,* Mateo Badiola, José Erquiaga, and Juan Aldamiz—were making local news by the 1880s as established and respected sheepmen. In the early accounts, the two men named José were both referred to by the Anglo editors as "Spanish Joe,"† and all were regarded locally as simply "Spaniards." The extent of their successes was noted in brief newspaper articles:

---

*Ugarriza is not a common Basque name, and it is very likely that this José was a kinsman (son? nephew?) of Segundo Ugariza ("Sendo") referred to in chapter 5 (p. 204).

†There is evidence that these two men did not get along well. *The Silver State* newspaper, in 1879, reports, "José Erquiga [*sic*], a Spaniard who is engaged in the sheep business in the Paradise mountains, entered complaint against another Spaniard named José M. Ugarriza, who, he alleges, compelled him, at the muzzle of a pistol, to sign a note for $206. . . ."[46]

Back from Spain

J. M. Ugarriza and Matio [*sic*] Badiola, who sold their sheep ranches in the Paradise range, a year ago, and went to the old country, returned here yesterday from Spain, and intend to remain in Humboldt. (1881)[47]

Industry Rewarded

In 1870 two Spaniards named Jose Erquiga [*sic*] and Juan Aldamiz came to this country direct from Spain. They could not speak a word of English, and could not do anything except herd sheep, having been raised in the mountains and followed the occupation of shepherds from childhood. They hired out to tend sheep at $30 per month and board, and in a few years invested their savings in flocks of their own. Last week they sold out their sheep and range for $18,000, and left for their native land, where they have a bank account of several thousand dollars, which they had sent home when they sold their wool last year and the year before that. They were sober and industrious men and accumulated a nice little stake under circumstances which would have discouraged less energetic men. They intend to return next Spring, if they succeed in getting mated this Winter. (1882)[48]

Sold out

The individual known as *"Spanish Joe"* [José Ugarriza] has sold his sheep and range in Pleasant Valley, south of John Guthrie's ranch, for $16,000, and is going home to Spain. He commenced in the sheep business a few years since with a capital of $3,000, and has industriously pursued his vocation. He has clipped a large yearly crop of wool, the value of which, added to his $16,000, will conduce to make his friends in his old home consider him a man of considerable wealth, on his arrival at his old home in Europe. (1885)[49]

On what was at least his second stint in Humboldt County, José Ugarriza had increased his capital fourfold in four years and once again went back to the Old World. In 1889 Ugarriza returned to Humboldt County, and during the early years of the 1890s, he again became established in the sheep business, near McDermitt.[50]* Nor did the other "Spanish Joe," José Erquiaga, leave Humboldt County permanently, since the July 3, 1888, issue of *The Silver State* reports his return from Spain.[52]

By the 1880s the greater Winnemucca region had its Basque sheepmen who were established as full-fledged

---

*The same José Ugarriza was to return to Winnemucca in 1913 after two decades' absence in Cuba where he established a sugar plantation.[51]

operators and were realizing fabulous returns on their investments. Significantly for the future immigration of Basques into
the area, these men (unlike the Altubes and Garats, for whom
we are unable to record trips to the Old World) were "birds-of-
passage," periodically changing their residence between
Europe and the American West. When José Ugarriza returned to
Winnemucca in 1889, *The Silver State* reported:

> José Ugarriza, better known as Spanish Joe, has returned from a
> visit to his native land with twenty able-bodied men and one or
> two boys. These immigrants are from the Basque province, and
> most of them have been engaged to herd sheep in the northern
> part of the county. . . . In a few years each and all of these men
> will doubtless have flocks or herds of their own and money at
> interest, if they are like those of their countrymen who preceded
> them here.[53]

In this article we see that, by 1889, there was a tradition of local
Basque successes in the sheep industry of Humboldt County and
new Basques were arriving in group strength to take advantage
of the opportunities in sheep.

By the late 1880s and the 1890s Basque ethnics were
recognized as such by their non-Basque neighbors and by the
newspapers, which regularly recorded their arrival:

> The population of Humboldt county has recently been increased
> by the arrival of twenty young men from the Basque province of
> Spain. They will engage in sheep-herding.[54]

> The Spanish Contingent
> A dozen or so hardy looking young men from the Basque
> province of Spain arrived here yesterday. These men are hardy
> and industrious and accustomed to life in the mountains, and,
> according to report, make first class sheep-herders.[55]

> More Basques
> The annual spring consignment of Basques (immigrants from
> the Basque provinces of Spain) arrived here this morning. They
> will go to work as sheepherders, and in a few years either own a
> band of sheep or have enough hard cash saved up to go back to
> Spain and live on easy street for the balance of their lives.[56]

The Silver State of March 10, 1894 announced that "A number
of Basques arrived here a few days ago. . . ." The same issue
maintained that:

> There is more inquiry for sheep by buyers who are in or con-
> template going into that business than there has been for the past
> several years. It is the only industry that the contraction of the

currency has not fatally crippled in this state. Although the price
of wool has been falling for years, the wool growers are about
the only ones engaged in our varied industries who have with-
stood the financial depression. A very industrious and intelligent gentleman, who has been in the business in this country
only three years, informs us that if he can get 10 or 12 cents a
pound for wool for the next four or five years he will be willing
to quit the business, go back to the old country and live like a
lord the balance of his days.[57]

By the turn of the century, the "Basque presence" in the
sheep industry of Nevada was ubiquitous. Agricultural officials
could state:

> The class of men which were in demand for herding the sheep
> were known as Basques or "Bascos." They come from the
> Pyrennees [sic] Mountains, and are designated French or
> Spanish Basques, according to the side of the mountains in
> which they lived. They naturally take to the life of solitude, as
> they and their ancestors have been employed in a similar occupa-
> tion in the Pyrennees [sic] Mountains for many years past. The
> wages paid them are from $30 to $40 a month, with board. Their
> savings are often spent in a trip to their homes in Europe, where
> they live a life of ease for one or two years, and then return to
> America to herd sheep again. Italians, Americans and other
> nationalities are sometimes employed, but they are rarely as
> contented and successful as the Basques. . . . Their [the herd-
> ers'] knowledge of English is usually very imperfect, so that
> even when they were willing to give out information they were
> unable to do so in a satisfactory manner. Some of them were
> very suspicious in regard to our motives, believing that we were
> government spies, or that we were trying to find out just what
> kinds of forage it was that made the mutton from Nevada sheep
> superior to others. By finding this out we could then introduce
> those particular forage plants into other States, which would
> then be able to produce equally as good mutton.[58]

The majority of Basques who entered were single males in
their middle and late teens, bent upon completing a pattern of
wage employment as herders to itinerant sheepmen before making an early and permanent return to the Basque country.* The
passage of time modified the plans of a small number of these

---

*Most of the elderly Basques interviewed by the present authors, includi
many who entered the United States prior to World War I, were in agreeme
on this point. There was, of course, the occasional exception. V., of Elko
Nevada, recounts that as he boarded his ship for the United States in 1914, he

young men. They became more oriented toward establishing themselves on a permanent basis in the American West. Others returned to Europe with the intention of remaining, only to be disillusioned by the changes in the Basque country and in themselves that had transpired during their absence. Some few returned to the United States, determined to remain there. These persons purchased lands or businesses and contracted marriages, generally with Old World-born Basque girls, and thereby laid the bases for the emergence of subsequent generations of United States-born Basque-Americans.

Between 1895 and 1915 some seventy-three marriages involving a Basque partner were recorded in the Winnemucca courthouse. In all but three cases, both partners were Basques.[59] Such marriages might result when a prospering sheepman sent to Europe for a boyhood sweetheart. In other cases, a couple might meet at one of the local Basque boarding houses or hotels where the woman was employed as a maid or waitress. Not infrequently, marriages were simply arranged as one friend put another in correspondence with his sister, cousin, or niece in the Basque country. Conversely, Basques were famed for returning to Europe on a visit for the main purpose of finding a spouse. The July 10, 1912, issue of *The Humboldt Star* stated:

> Joe Jaca, the McDermitt merchant, is in town today accompanied by four Basques who will leave for a visit to their old home in Spain. As they have all done well financially since they landed in Humboldt county it is presumed they will all return in a few months with wives.[60]

We find evidence that this process of forming an American orientation was emerging among at least a minority of the Basques of Nevada, eastern Oregon, and southern Idaho by the turn of the present century in the biographical sketches of Sol Silen's work, *Los Vascongados en el Oeste Americano*. Of the ninety-nine married men treated biographically, eight married prior to 1900, while fifty-five were wedded between 1901 and 1910. In the ninety-two Silen biographical sketches of married men in which both date of entry into the United States and date of marriage are provided, we find that eight men apparently

---

handed his beret to his brother. The brother said, "I'll save it for you," to which V. replied, "Keep it as I'll never need it again." V., unlike the majority of elderly Basque residents in the United States, has never paid so much as a short return visit to the Basque country in the last sixty years.

married in Europe prior to emigrating. Of the remaining eighty-four cases, only eight married within the first five years of their stay in the American West, whereas a total of thirty-five men required more than ten years to marry. Thus, the family-oriented permanent Basque settlers were in a decided minority, and the formation of their families was obviously a lengthy process.

The decision to purchase land was also indicative of a new sense of commitment to the New World. A purchase such as the sale reported in the February 13, 1911, issue of *The Humboldt Star* might unite the destinies of several fellow ethnics:

> The extensive agricultural holdings and other assets of the defunct Eureka Live stock company have been acquired by a coterie of wealthy Spaniards for a cash consideration of $119,163. Title to seventeen ranches in White Pine, Eureka and Nye counties has changed as a result of the transaction . . . to Pedro Urquiza, Fernando Petotequi [*sic*] Goni and Augusin Ga. . . . The new company also bought the Ruby Hill water works, 9,000 head of sheep, 550 head of catle [*sic*], 54 head of horses. . . .[61]

One means of acquiring capital to finance purchase of an outfit was to enter into partnership with a kinsman. The dissolution of such a partnership is noted in the March 16, 1914, issue of *The Humboldt Star*,

> Several days ago a deal was closed by which Mr. Aboitiz acquired his brother Eugene's half interest in their extensive sheep, cattle and ranching business. The ranch is located about fifteen miles north of McDermitt. Eugene Aboitiz will leave about March 25th for his old home in Spain to rejoin his family. He will not return to this country.[62]

However, not all budding Basque ranchers required or sought the partnership of fellow ethnics or kinsmen. On September 7, 1914, *The Humboldt Star* reported:

> Guy Saval of Elko is here [Ely] for the purpose of purchasing the Baker ranch in Snake valley. The Baker ranch, situated east of Jeff Davis peak in the richest portion of Snake valley, is undoubtedly one of the finest ranches in White Pine county.
> Mr. Saval is one of the largest cattle and sheep owners in Elko county and it is understood that he will go into the stock raising business in White Pine county on an extensive scale.
> Mr. Saval made an initial payment of $50,000. . . .[63]

The tone of such reporting is clear. The small minority of Basques who were willing to commit capital and self as permanent investment in the future of the American West were likely to elicit both praise and acceptance from their neighbors. The purchase of land was the most evident fashion of demonstrating such a commitment.*

Insofar as Basques were likely to be singled out for public praise, such behavior was underscored:

> A party composed of ten or fifteen people arrived here yesterday from the Basque provinces of Spain. Each year a number of these people arrive here until now the Basques form a large part of the county's [Humboldt] population. They are expert sheepmen and are an industrious people. Many of them own large flocks of sheep *and are land owners and have made this country their permanent home.*[64] (Emphasis supplied.)

But with respect to the total number of Basque immigrants in the early years, relatively few became land-owning, settled, family men. Most entered the American West with the intention of accumulating money as quickly as possible for an eventual life in the Basque country. Their ethnic reputation as sheepherders provided a first opportunity for employment, but few herders harbored the intention of living out their lives as employees. And for most Basques, economic mobility meant, at least at some stage in their stay in the American West, involvement in the ranks of the itinerant sheepmen. It was this group that rankled American sensitivities. As Major W. Shepherd, himself an alien (English), stated in 1885:

> The American does not like foreigners, but he tolerates their presence if they will follow his example and adopt his institutions; but to be a separatist, to live in small national colonies, to appear or behave differently to the accredited type, not to care for local topics or the politics of the saloon—these are all crimes which the American cannot allow.[65]

The life-style of the itinerant Basque sheepmen was the very antithesis of this preferred American way. From an American viewpoint, the "tramp" sheepman was a wanderer, a usurper, a potential trespasser, and aloof from local affairs to a greater degree than even the substantial social isolation inherent

---

*Of 129 biographies in the Silen book, 56 contain mention of land ownership. The figure is undoubtedly low, since Silen's interviews were uneven both in terms of quality of answers and questions asked.

in sheepherding would demand. It is in terms of such attitudes that anti-Basque sentiments were couched, and the simple announcement of the arrival of more immigrants might carry an appended ethnic slur. On April 10, 1896, *The Silver State* announced: "Seven more Basques arrived from Spain yesterday. *They are a better appearing lot than the average.*[66] (Emphasis supplied.)

In announcing departures on December 5, 1913, *The Humboldt Star* reported:

> So. Pacific train No. 10 today carried as passengers from this place five Basque sheepmen, en route to their old homes in Spain . . . some of them are going back for a few months' visit, while . . . two of them have sold their bands of sheep and will remain in the old country. *Incidentally, these latter took away with them several thousand dollars, which will also remain.*[67] (Emphasis supplied.)

Not so incidentally! This was a veritable charge leveled against the Basque sheepmen (obviously itinerants in this case, since no land sales are mentioned). In the vigorous but underdeveloped economy of the American West, the Basque who siphoned off local wealth to Europe was viewed as a distinct threat.

In areas settled by Basques with Spanish passports, the Spanish-American war colored relations between Basques and their neighbors. Some old-timers reported that during the war years they avoided the towns and thereby minimized their contacts with Americans. It is also said that in Jordan Valley the local Basque blacksmith awoke one morning to find his doorway festooned with a Spanish flag.[68] The *Carson Morning Appeal* published in its May 4, 1898, issue a somewhat tongue-in-cheek, yet double-edged article:

> A party of basque province sheepherders just passed through Ogden en route for Winnemucca . . . where they will herd sheep or enter some other line of work equally as severe upon their mental faculties. Following these there came through yesterday 23 more of these copper-colored bull fighters. . . . They were full of war talk and had many fairy stories about the prowess of their countrymen and their navy.
>
> "What will you do at Winnemucca?" was asked.
>
> "Ve vill be zere so zat ven ze var ees ofer ve can own efrysing."[69]

In the examples considered thus far, ethnic slurs remain implicit or couched in circumscribed language that appears to be designed to tone down insults while still making particular points. This was sane editorial policy in a community like Winnemucca, where, by the turn of the century, the Basque contingent was substantial.*

And so there was considerable ambiguity in the images held by their non-Basque neighbors of the early Basque settlers in the Great Basin. As a substantial and growing ethnic element within a generally sparse population, the Basques could not be overlooked. As a group in which a major sector was devoted to the socially denigrated and physically isolating task of sheepherding, Basques were neither particularly esteemed nor understood. Yet, as obvious practitioners of the American ideal of dedication to one's labors (whatever they may be) and the observance of thrift through moderation in one's life style, Basques earned respect. Finally, in the nascent society and economy of the Great Basin, the opportunities for upward mobility were many, and some Basques were quick to respond. The evident social and economic gulf between the more successful Basques and their sheepherding or itinerant-operator fellow ethnics was so evident as to make it difficult to apply a simplisitic and negative ethnic stereotype to the group as a whole. By the early 1900s there were Basque men like John Achabal of Boise who owned eighty thousand sheep and employed fifty-nine men;[71] José Bengoechea, who entered the country in 1897, worked initially as a sheepherder for Pedro Altube, but within twenty years was one of the largest sheepmen of southern Idaho, vice-president of the Mountain Home Bank, and owner of the town's finest hotel;[72] and Bertrand Duque, who parleyed an original investment of $50,000 in the Smoke Creek Ranch of Washoe County, Nevada, into a net worth of $860,000 and ownership of a large steam laundry in Reno.[73]

---

*Some Basques had become prominent citizens and advertisers in the local press. On May 24, 1912, *The Humboldt Star* ran the following article under the heading "Deals in Livestock; Is All-Around Hustler":

John Etchart, the well-known livestock dealer, was down from Golconda yesterday attending to business matters. He is one of Golconda's live wires and a consistent booster of his home town and the county in general. Mr. Etchart is a specialist in buying and selling livestock and is doing a large and constantly increasing business. Having been engaged in the sheep business for years, he knows when and where to buy to the best advantage and his customers receive the benefit of his knowledge and experience. He buys and sells on commission and gives the First National Bank of Winnemucca as his reference. . . . Attention is directed to Mr. Etchart's ad elsewhere in this paper.[70]

Such men commanded considerable respect in their communities.

This ambivalent view of the Basques, caused by their dual role as "solid citizens" on the one hand and "itinerant nomads" on the other, was reflected in a Nevada controversy surrounding the congressional testimony of the state's junior senator in 1913. In a speech assailing implementation of a wool tariff to protect the country's sheep industry, Senator Key Pittman argued that sheep raising in Nevada was controlled by a small number of men and institutions and that

> nearly all of the laborers employed in [the sheepherding] occupation are Basque sheep herders, who can hardly speak the English language, and get about $35 a month.
>
> The Basques come from the Pyrenees mountains in Spain. [The sheepmen] get that class of labor because they seem to be adapted for sheep herding, and they are lacking in intelligence, independence, or anything else. They are just about as near a slave as anybody could be under our present existing conditions.

In denouncing the Basques for failing to become naturalized citizens, Pittman stated:

> As a general thing they never associate with other people in the state; they live among themselves; they can only speak a few words of the English language; they live in the lowest possible way for a human being to live; and they are nothing but sheepherders.[74]

It is interesting to note that Pittman's statements struck an unresponsive chord back home. Newspapers like the *Reno Evening Gazette* and the *Carson City News* editorialized against Pittman's ethnic slurs, while private citizens wrote letters of protest. Mr. J. A. Langwith wrote to the editor of *The Silver State* newspaper:

> Why is it necessary to misrepresent a large number of Basques [*sic*] sheep men and sheep herders? It is untrue that the Basque sheep man is of a lower order than others engaged in the sheep business, or that they work for less. There are many Basques and descendants of Basques engaged in ranching, cattle and mercantile business as well as the sheep business. The Basque is usually a man of more than ordinary intelligence, with keen business ability, and is usually prosperous. They are, as a rule, law abiding, sober, and make good citizens. . . . Having for years been intimately acquainted with large numbers of these people I cannot understand Senator Pittman's attitude, or where he ac-

quired his information. Was it first hand, or was it from some person or persons jealous of the prosperity of the average Basque.[75]

In a June 27, 1913, editorial, *The National Miner* stated:

The fling and allusion to these descendants of Spain and France, hailing as they do from the Pyrenees mountains is cruel, unjust and indefensible. As a whole, *The Miner* has found these people good citizens, honest and straightforward in dealing with their fellows; always thrifty, enterprising and prudent. . . . *The Miner* regrets that the junior senator saw fit to attack an innocent people for the sake of supporting his position in Congress, for that position to win needs no brutal attack upon any individual citizen or class of foreigners who have become thrifty citizens and others, applying the test to become true Americans and who in time through the law of assimilation will become as advanced in the arts of civilized America as the foreigners did out of whose loins Senator Pittman sprung. The unjustness of this specious attack upon the Basque is glaring.[76]

If Senator Pittman was assailed in some quarters for his statements, the criticisms were not sufficient to dissuade him. On August 21, 1913, he again testified against the proposed duty on foreign wool, declaring that,

admitting for the sake of argument that these five or six hundred Basque sheep herders would receive some indirect benefit from the increased profits of the sheep owners by reason of the duty, I still maintain there is neither reason nor excuse for granting a bonus to these laborers who are imported from the Pyrenees Mountains between Spain and France, admitting allegiance to neither one nor the other of those great countries—men who do not know what a home is, and do not recognize the authority of government; men of the lowest type and the most inferior intelligence, who rarely seek to become citizens of the country to which they are imported. . . .[77]

Again,

As to the employment of foreigners in other branches of labor in my State, I wish to say that the other foreigners who are engaged in labor in the State are engaged principally in mining; not coal mining, for we have none, but hard-rock mining. There are no higher class laborers than miners. All of them are union miners. All of them stand for union wages. They are all capable, intelligent workers, and every one of them declares his intention to become a citizen of the United States just the minute the opportunity is offered to him. There is no comparison whatever between the ordinary foreigner and the Basque sheep herder from the Pyrenees Mountains.[78]

However, in the same testimony there is a clue to the real target of such rhetoric, for Senator Pittman states:

> in many instances the owners of the sheep are Basque sheep herders, who act as their own herders, their own foremen, and their own shearers. In other words, the Basque sheep herder, with 1,500 sheep, performs all the labor with regard to such sheep without any assistance.[79]

It was the small, independent, itinerant, or "tramp" operator who most frequently evoked anti-Basque sentiments. Where the itinerant sheepmen were concerned, polite language ceased and tempers flared. The extent of the animosity may be appreciated from the extreme language of an article that appeared in the *Caldwell Tribune* (Idaho) on July 17, 1909:

> ### Sheepmen and Biscayans
> The sheepmen of Owyhee countee [*sic*] are sorely beset by Biscayans, Bascos as they are commonly called, and trouble might result most any time. These Bascos are coming in great numbers and are driving the other sheepmen from the range. It's the same old story of the cupidity on the part of the sheepmen. They, themselves introduced the Biscayans into this country and instructed them in the sheep business, because they could get them for a smaller wage.
> The sheepmen are now thinking of trying to get their range taken into the forest reserve. This is the only method by which the Bascos can be kept out. Even then the sheepmen will have to wage a boycott in order to accomplish anything. The Bascos can buy sheep from men who have range allotments in the reserves and thus get on the range, reserve or no reserve. The scale of living and the methods of doing business of the Bascos are on a par with those of the Chinamen.
> However, they have some undesirable characteristics that the Chinese are free from. They are filthy, treacherous, and meddlesome.
> However, they work hard and save their money. They are clannish and undesirable but they have a foothold and unless something is done will make life impossible for the whiteman. One thing is certain, and that is that the sheepmen are not going to give up without a struggle. Trouble may be anticipated.[80]

ITINERANT SHEEPMEN AND THEIR FOES

Few, if any, Basques became sheepherders with the intention of remaining such. The previous chapter described the "hiving-off" of itinerant bands from existing flocks. This was the beginning of the general progression from sheepherder to itinerant operator to reemigrant to Europe, the pattern that characterized the initial aspiration of most early Basque immigrants and the realization of many. According to our description, the itinerant sheep bands were formed as a young man sought herder employment with an established kinsman or acquaintance, took his wages in ewes, ran both bands simultaneously for three or four years, and then struck out on his own. In point of fact, this was but one of a great number of arrangements which produced itinerant sheepmen. Many itinerant operations changed hands on a straight cash basis. An operator who had tired of life on the range was usually able to find a buyer among the ranks of the salaried herders. In many instances two herders pooled their savings in order to purchase an existing itinerant outfit. It was also common practice for some of the more successful Basque sheepmen to finance potential itinerant operators by providing them with a sheep band on a shares basis. For example, a biography of John Achabal of Boise, published in 1920, stated that, in addition to his own operations, "he has twelve men associated with him in the sheep raising industry as side partners. His plan . . . has been to provide these side partners with a certain number of sheep—from two to six thousand head, the men to care for them on shares."[81]

Generally speaking, the itinerant sheep outfit required a minimum of two partners. One had to stay with the animals constantly while the other laid in the supplies (frequently over considerable distances) and tended camp. Then, too, the problem with predatory animals was acute, requiring night herding that would ordinarily overtax the abilities of an unrelieved single herder. For the two partners to make a realistic start, they normally required about one thousand ewes, which could be handled in a single band. The numbers could be increased until they approximated two thousand, at which time a third person was hired to care for the new band. In this fashion, an itinerant operation might grow to several bands, each with herders who were themselves aspiring to repeat the successes of their employers.

In the initial formative stages of an itinerant outfit, it was common for one of the two partners to remain as a wage employee for an additional year or two while the other cared for their small flock alone and under the most trying of conditions. In this fashion the two partners managed to earn money while retaining their own lamb production to build up their band. But there was another reason for this arrangement. Except during the very earliest years of development of the sheep industry in a particular region, the itinerant operators were never welcome. As pressure on range resources increased, the existing sheepmen, Basque or otherwise, itinerant or settled, were not particularly interested in seeing new outfits (even under the ownership of close kinsmen) proliferate in their immediate area. Hence, there was considerable pressure upon the itinerant operators that constantly forced them to the most marginal districts of the existing open-range sheep industry areas. In this fashion, itinerant sheep bands spread to practically every suitable corner of the public lands of the American West between 1890 and 1910. For the itinerant operator, however, this frequently meant striking out into essentially unfamiliar country in search of feasible pasturage. He required summer range, high above the valley floors, and an area of low desert sufficiently protected from heavy winter snows, yet near snowline, to obtain water for the sheep. Even once such conditions were found, the itinerant operator was particularly vulnerable to inclement weather. A freak winter blizzard or a late spring storm that coincided with lambing invariably caught him out on the open range, without benefit of feed or protection for his animals.

Here is how the vicissitudes of the Nevada sheep industry were described in 1881:

> The limited plant necessary to engage in the sheep business, and the brief season which intervenes before an income from wool and increase may be derived, cause many to engage in it unprepared to sustain reverses. Although for several years the climate may prove favorable to the nomadic flock-owner, a season of unusual severity may come, finding him wholly unprepared to feed his sheep, and often annihilating the profits of previous years, as in the winter of 1879−80.[82]

On February 5, 1910, the *Goldfield Daily Tribune* reported:

> Frozen to death, with the pitiless snow drifting over them, two men lie on the desert near Donnelly mountain in northwestern Humboldt county, near the Washoe county line. Surrounding them are their faithful dogs, pack animals and three thousand sheep, all victims of the intense cold that has prevailed for the past six weeks in the northern country.
>
> News of the tragedy was brought to Reno today by a French sheep herder, who works for an outfit that is wintering its sheep in the vicinity.

O. W. Ward of the Washoe County bank, heard of the tragedy and sent for the herder. The latter was unable to speak English, but through an interpreter he said that the story, as outlined above is correct. He told Mr. Ward that the sheep belong to B. Lasaga, but he did not know the names of the herders.

The latter also stated that Mr. Lasaga, who lives at Eagleville in Surprise Valley, just over the line in California, has 3,000 more sheep in that country, which he offers for 25 cents a head, the buyer to take chances on getting them out alive.

It seems that there came a storm when the sheep were far from any hay and two feet of snow fell, which caused the sheep to huddle up and perish, while the herders and their trusty animals remained at their post of duty and perished during the blizzard that ensued.[83]

One week later the same newspaper reported on the general status of the sheep industry in northern Nevada under the trying severe winter conditions:

> while the reports of losses have been exaggerated, Nevada has lost in the neighborhood of 25,000 head, mostly lambs. . . . the cause of the great loss . . . has not been the result of any shortage of feed so much, *excepting among the bands owned by the Basque sheep men, who are the smaller handlers and unprepared for any emergency at any time.* . . . [84] (Emphasis supplied.)

The budding itinerant outfit had to operate under the pressure of existing livestock interests and at the caprice of a harsh natural environment. It is not surprising that in many of the partnerships one man continued in his secure employment while the other sought out that scarce commodity—the ideal sheep range.

A second point concerning the formation of Basque sheep interests is that the move from wage herder to itinerant operator was not necessarily irreversible. Operating on the narrowest of margins, the itinerants were easily ruined by minor fluctuations in the prices of wool and lambs; these markets fluctuated sharply at times. Wool sold for fifty cents a pound in 1919 and lambs for $13.05 a hundredweight; two years later wool prices were down to sixteen cents while lambs brought a scant $7.83.[85]* In

---

*A letter from a Basque herder in Sumner (California) to his mother and uncle in the Basque country states:

this is a year [1893] of very poor prospects; it scarcely rains, the feed is practically all gone, and the herders who have debts and who have no

boom years Basque herders were encouraged by local bankers*
to strike out on their own with financial assistance. While it was
widely held that "the word of a Basque is as good as a written
contract" prompting bankers to extend liberal credit to the
Basque sheepmen, these loans, frequently collateralized with
nothing but the sheep themselves, were highly vulnerable.
More than one banking fortune was made or lost in the American West due to sheep loans.[89]† There are many stories concerning the rising fortunes of individual Basque itinerant
sheepmen but there are even more accounts of herders whose
accumulated savings were wiped out. Significantly, the unqualified success story of the sheepherder who became an itinerant
operator and then a large sheep rancher is quite rare among the
Basques of the West. Even those who ultimately prospered
usually suffered several false starts occasioned by abnormal
sheep losses through inclement weather or financial disaster
resulting from thin capitalization of the sheep outfit in a highly
variable world market for sheep products.

Harshness of the natural environment and thin capitalization
were not the only dangers for the itinerant sheep outfit. An
elaborate game of wits developed between the settled livestockmen and the itinerants. On some occasions, the former
resorted to sheer intimidation or even violence. As one- or
two-man enterprises, itinerant outfits were no match for the
personnel of even the smaller ranches. Nor could the itinerant
operator expect much sympathy from either local authorities or

---

income are suffering a great deal. Wool prices have been very low until
now, although they are beginning to rise; also sheep prices have been
very low. A few months ago our boss Preyo sold four thousand wethers,
in which he lost 30,000 *pesetas*, at least with respect to last spring's
values. Our Yoanes and many others sold theirs last spring and they
were on target; had they sold now they wouldn't have received more
than half.[86]

*In many sheep-raising areas Basques sat on the boards of directors of local
banks. For example, José Bengoechea was vice-president of the Mountain
Home Bank (Idaho).[87] Vandor reports that John Bidegaray and Matias Erro
were cofounders and president and vice-president, respectively, of the Growers National Bank of Fresno (California).[88]

†Many bankers actually preferred making loans to the itinerants rather than
to settled livestock interests. Loans to the former were secured by the sheep
alone which were theoretically readily convertible to cash, whereas the latter
sought loans on the less liquid collateral of ranch properties. However, not
even the bankers were always able to anticipate the volatile price changes in
the sheep market.

public opinion. As the February 17, 1890, *Reno Evening Gazette* reported,

> John Torre, the "big Russian" was in Reno not long since and told Dan Wheeler that he wanted to buy 100 bucks.
> "What kind of bucks do you want?" inquired Dan.
> "I wanta scabby buck, litta wool with plenty long hair; I wanta s-- of b---- buck. You got em? I wanta cooka de sheep."
> It transpired that John wanted just what he called for, some scabby bucks to kill off straggling bands of sheep.[90]

More direct antitramp measures were reported in the August 8, 1902, issue of the *Nevada State Herald*:

> Cattlemen Slaughter Sheep
> Winnemucca, Nevada, Aug. 4—Armed men are visiting the sheep ranches near Disaster Peak, shooting the sheep and stealing horses. Eight invaders visited the camps in the mountains at the head of Kings river and Cottonwood creek a few nights ago and slaughtered all the sheep they came upon. Then they drove off many of the horses. Their object in taking the horses was to prevent pursuit. It is supposed the invaders were cattle men, who took this method of driving the sheepmen from the county.[91]

Less frequently, the herder himself might become the object of violence. On September 1, 1905, the *Nevada State Herald* reported that a man named Wallace shot a Basque herder, Simon Salas, in the shoulder:

> [Salas] was on a mountain with some sheep; Wallace was on a creek down the mountain. Wallace called to Salas to "come down." Salas refused and Wallace shot at him. . . . We understand that Wallace shot at another sheepherder about a year ago at Coon Creek. . . .[92]

Wallace was a homesteader, as was Thomas Brackney, who shot to death a Basque sheepherder in July 1924. Brackney was described as a "homesteader, said to possess an avowed dislike for sheepherders in general."[93] He was acquitted the following October.

In the early 1930s two young Basque itinerant sheepmen moved their bands close to a small Utah town and acquired leases to a hayfield that had formerly been rented to a local cattle rancher. The rancher was furious and went about the town threatening to shoot the "Greeks."* That night, the rancher, intoxicated, advanced on the sheep camp with a rifle. As he aimed at one of the Basques, the son of the farmer shot him in the back. The bullet passed through the rancher and struck the sheepman as well, killing both men instantly. Local feelings ran high, and while no charges were preferred, both local morticians, either from fear or hate, refused to bury the Basque's corpse. His partner took the body out into the desert, where he buried it himself. At the same time, he moved more sheep onto his leases, and for the remainder of the winter maintained a decoy camp. He laid out a bedroll next to the fire and then slept in the darkness at some distance from the camp as a precaution against an ambush (which never came).[94]

Many such instances of violence† directed against Basque sheepmen can be documented. In fact, however, the resort to serious violence was both rare and limited to the particularly hot-tempered. It is not that the enemies of the itinerant sheepmen were either cowed or adverse to using extralegal pressures. Violence was often threatened to make a sheepman move on, although such intimidation was merely a bluff. The few cases of actual bloodshed and death were widely publicized and served to underscore the seriousness of the matter for both parties to any confrontation.‡

The threat of legal charges of trespassing was another form of intimidation. Few itinerant operators were sufficiently versed in either local law or the English language to dispute a rancher's claim of private ownership to a particular area.

---

*Eastern Utah was one of the last areas of the extended Great Basin to receive Basque sheepmen. Greek sheep interests had entered the area somewhat earlier.

†By way of examples, other altercations involving Basque herders in an exchange of gunfire are reported in the April 30, 1913, issue of *The Humboldt Star* and the September 23, 1922, and June 26, 1926, issues of the *Battle Mountain Scout*. The May 30, 1896, and August 14, 1897, issues of *Califor-nia'ko Eskual Herria* reported the shooting of Basque herders in California and Arizona, respectively.[95]

‡It is interesting to note that, despite their vulnerability and their early entry into many remote corners of the American West, there are no nineteenth-century reports of trouble between Basque sheepmen and American Indians. In January 1911, in extreme northwestern Nevada, three Basques, John B. Laxague and Peter Erramouspe, and a man nicknamed "Indiano," in the company of a fourth sheepman, were slain by a small group of Shoshone Indians who had fled from a reservation. The Indians were later tracked by a posse and most of them killed. The incident is touted by popularizers as the "last Indian massacre in the history of the American West."[96]

Another favorite tactic of the large and settled operators, cattlemen, or sheepmen was to maintain a few bands of sheep for the express purpose of harassing the tramp outfits. The idea was to contest particular range by herding close to any invading outfits until the bands were "accidentally" mixed. This simple event, if repeated several times, could spell financial disaster for the smaller operator. It necessitated constructing a rough corral in the middle of the desert to separate the bands. This could take a couple of days, during which the animals became nervous and lost weight. The whole experience might put them off their feed for several days after the sorting. For the large operator, the loss of several pounds liveweight per lamb was easily absorbed, but for the itinerant herder, it might mean the difference between profit and loss.

Another tactic employed by settled interests was to claim and fence desert springs and waterholes. In an arid environment like the Great Basin region, this was particularly effective. The majority of trespass cases actually pressed in the courts involved violation of desert waterhole claims, rather than trespass on home ranch properties.

For their part, the itinerant operators showed remarkable adeptness at surviving, given the fact that the settled interests enjoyed a favorable balance of power in their mutual confrontation. The adage "there is safety in numbers" signals one of the real, if subtle, defenses of the itinerant operators. The October 1919 issue of the *Nevada Stockgrower* stated that a "large percentage" of sheep are owned by "Pirate Sheepmen":

These men, many of whom are not citizens, have no property or other interests in the State save their sheep, lack ownership of property used in connection with their stock, can not qualify for range privileges upon the National Forests. They roam with their bands at large, in a way outside the law, flocking to favored ranges disregarding the seasonal necessities of plant life and wiping out the ranges adjacent to the ranching communities which are necessary for the success of the settler and small rancher. . . . [They,] like the pirates of old, cruise upon the public domain setting aside without the slightest regard moral rights and customs which in the olden days made at least some provision for what was right and just.[97]

There is a keen sense of helplessness in this statement stemming from the fact that the problem of the itinerant outfits could not be disposed of in a single encounter that could be won or lost. The rancher's victory in driving off one tramp operator was made hollow by the presence of another itinerant band over the next hill.

Again, the nomadic habits of the itinerants gave them a certain edge in dealing with their settled adversaries. It was difficult to bring to bear the full weight of local law upon an individual whose delict (e.g., trespass) was not sufficiently grave to warrant imprisonment, yet whose wandering habits would place him outside local jurisdictions before the legal machinery of arrest, summons, and hearing could be employed.

One can only surmise that many itinerant operators realized that the extralegal pressures and intimidations of the ranchers were just that. While care had to be taken to avoid provoking the ranchers to out-and-out violence, the threats of the latter could be taken with a grain of salt. Thus, if one were ultimately to move on in the face of local threats, he could at least arrange to move as slowly as possible—grazing as he went. To this end, many itinerants employed a variety of tactics. One obvious means of delaying departure was, when ordered out, to feign even greater ignorance of the English language than was the case when dealing with, say, the wool buyer. Another tactic was for the camptender to hide when strangers approached. If ordered off, the herder would then reply politely that he would gladly leave but could not until his camptender returned in a couple of days with supplies from some distant town. Two days of good grazing was of great value to any sheepman.

These differences between settled livestock interests and the itinerant sheepmen were made irreconcilable by the land laws governing the use of the western ranges. The entire Great Basin region, except for a few squatters' holdings recognized by the government, was a part of the federally owned public domain. In 1862 the Homestead Act was passed. This law provided a quarter-section (160 acres) of free land to any settler, conferring upon him final ownership after five years' residence and evidence of cultivation.[98] These quarter-section homesteads might be viable farms under conditions east of the Rockies or in the particularly lush areas of the American West, but they were largely unviable under the arid conditions of the Great Basin. In this region, they were exercised to establish the home ranch of a livestock outfit. Great Basin homesteaders, however, remained dependent upon access to the public range for grazing.

If the Homestead Act did not lend itself to the formation of viable, self-contained agricultural enterprises under Great Basin conditions, it did provide the basis for establishing claims to that most valuable of all commodities—water. Ranchers filed a declaration of intent to homestead on most of the springs throughout the range they sought to control. According to Wentworth,

> emphasis on control of water grew from 1870 to 1890, for the unowned intervening land could not be grazed without it. Excessive values crept into homestead filings on water, stimulated by the grazing lands controlled. Land, worth much less than the minimum price, commanded sums several times greater because of the adjacent public grazing.[99]

While the homestead laws were eventually liberalized (as in 1877, when the Desert Land Act increased the homestead to 320 acres, and by the 1916 Stock Raising Homestead Act, which doubled the allowance to 640 acres for each settler), they were seldom effective in creating self-contained, self-sustaining agricultural units in the Great Basin. Ranchers continued (and continue today) to depend mightily upon the public ranges.

Throughout most of the nineteenth century there were no legislated restrictions upon the entry of herds and flocks onto the public lands. It is a part of the legend of the American West that there was considerable dispute over the use of the range among cattlemen, between cattlemen and sheepmen, and between livestockmen and farmers. While there were some instances of actual range wars, violence was absent in most areas; where it did occur, it tended to be short-lived. The laws of the marketplace tended to override the passionate commitments to particular ways of life that are at the core of many a confrontation in Hollywood depictions of the western scene. More mundane factors, such as the rainfall isomorphs, topography, and proximity to markets, were the real economic architects of the American West.

Use of the public range was usually arranged by way of a *modus vivendi* between the livestock interests of a particular area. While the federal government did not recognize such pacts, the settled livestock interests considered the public lands to be parcelized by a patchwork of division lines that defined individual claims of usufruct and demarcated cattle range from sheep range. In the last decade of the nineteenth century the itinerant sheepmen began their intrusion into this set of informal understandings. We have seen that the settled livestock interests sometimes reacted extralegally. However, they also launched a

legal campaign against the itinerants that covered the entire
political spectrum from town ordinances to federal legislation.

In 1885 the Nevada legislature passed a law prohibiting the
herding of swine, goats, or sheep within a mile of any city or
town. The act also declared that it was the duty of the sheriff and
the privilege of the citizen to impound sheep trespassing on
private land.[100]

The 1895 session of the legislature passed a Sheep License
Act, which required sheepmen to pay local county authorities
fees that varied according to the number of animals grazed on
the public lands. The itinerant sheepmen were the targets of this
legislation, since those owning one acre of Nevada land for each
two sheep grazed were to be exempted.[101] The constitutionality
of the law was tested and upheld in 1896. In hailing the decision, *The Silver State* declared, "The law will undoubtedly be
enforced, and roving sheep men will be compelled either to
purchase land, pay a license or remove from the state."[102]

In 1901 the Nevada legislature passed a law extending the
one-mile trespass limit to three miles from a town or village.[103]
Two years later the legislature prohibited the herding or grazing
of sheep within one mile of "a bona fide home or bona fide
ranch house."[104]

Within a single decade, Nevada—and other surrounding
states—established substantial fiscal and administrative measures to bring order to the otherwise chaotic and charged state of
affairs that existed between the itinerant sheepmen and their
enemies. Such legislation emanated from the settled livestock
interests, who, as respected land-owning taxpayers, were in a
better position to influence the lawmakers.

The new laws were invoked with some effect. The August 3,
1908, edition of *The Humboldt Star* reported:

> Sheriff Lamb and Deputy Assessor Nofsinger returned yester-
> day from the Pine Forest range, where they went a few days ago
> to intercept the migrating bands of sheep that are invading that
> section at the present time. They found conditions there as had
> been reported. P—— L——, a Basque from Oregon, has 6,000
> sheep roaming the hills of that choice range. Mr. Nofsinger
> brought in a check for $602.40 to secure the payment of taxes on
> the band and Sheriff Lamb collected $300 license.
>
> J—— L——, a brother of the other sheepman, is herding six
> bands of sheep, aggregating about 15,000 head, in the same
> vicinity, but he claims to have paid taxes for the year in Washoe
> County. If this be true, a pro rata of the tax will have to be paid to

Humboldt county by Washoe and an investigation will be made
by Assessor Leonard to ascertain whether the sheepman has told
the truth.

The Pine Forest mountains is one of the finest stock ranges in
northern Nevada and if these nomadic sheepmen continue to
pasture their bands there the range will be nothing but barren
waste in a few years.[105]

This article and others like it document successful tax and
license collections from the itinerant operators. However, it
also reflects problems that plagued local officials. It was a
lengthy and difficult procedure to verify claims of having paid
taxes elsewhere, particularly when their wanderings sometimes
took operators across state as well as county lines. Conversely,
while local ranchers sought legal harassments against the itinerants, local county officials might see taxes on the bands as a
desirable source of revenue. An article in the May 23, 1899,
edition of the *Tuscarora Times-Review* states:

> In several counties in the State sheep are being assessed at one
> dollar a head. The reason for the low assessment is that the sheep
> men entertain bids from the assessors and the county that offers
> the lowest rate gets the sheep to assess. The sheepman, if he
> does not get his figure, threatens to drive his sheep into another
> county, where he can get a lower rate.[106]

The second difficulty had to do with the enforcement of
controls in a vast, sparsely settled area in which it might require
a trip of several days for an outraged citizen to reach the seat of
authority in order to file his charges.

There was yet a third problem: violation of the laws was
deemed a misdemeanor, subject to fines of from $50 to $250 or
twenty-five to ninety days in jail. Since, in fact, a jail term was
rarely if ever imposed, the itinerant sheepman had little to lose
in chancing detection rather than paying voluntarily his sheep
license. At the same time, there was little incentive for a rancher
or other property owner to go to the trouble of filing formal
charges in trespass cases.* But if legislation at the local level
was ineffective the same could not be said of the federal laws.

---

*There were, of course, exceptions. The April 14, 1923, issue of the *Battle
Mountain Scout* reported that the Pacific Land and Livestock Company had
filed nineteen separate trespass cases against five Humboldt County sheepmen, four of whom were Basques.[107]

Federal Legislation and the Itinerant Sheepmen

Of greatest importance to the futures of the itinerant operators was the creation of the national forests. In 1891 the United States Congress passed the General Revision Act, of which Section 24 empowered the President to "set aside as public reservations any timbered section of the public domain."[108] Timber protection, rather than regulation of foraging, was the major purpose of the law. In 1891 the Yellowstone Timberland Reserve in Wyoming was established by presidential action, and in 1892 five more reserves were created in the American West; the largest was Oregon's Cascade Mountain Reserve. It was there that the first federal regulations prohibiting the "driving, feeding, grazing, pasturing, or herding of cattle, sheep, or other livestock"[109] within the reserves appeared. Officials explained that livestock grazing retarded reforestation, denuded water sheds, and polluted the water supply. In this manner access of stockmen to the higher mountain areas, critical as summer range in the more arid areas of the American West, was threatened.

By 1897 another fourteen reserves had been established. Unified regulation of all forest reserves was not authorized until passage of the Act of June 4, 1897. This legislation relegated power of administration to the secretary of the interior and his land office commissioner. Under the act, and in response to pressure from livestockmen, rules and regulations provided that: "The pasturing of livestock on the public lands in forest reservation will not be interfered with, so long as it appears that injury is not being done to the forest growth, and the rights of others are not thereby jeopardized."[110] Sheep grazing, however, was considered especially injurious. By 1900, sheep were excluded from all forest reservations except those in Oregon and Washington, where abundant rainfall aided rapid recovery of the forest's forage. This prohibitory order was issued by Land Office Commissioner Binger Herman, who used sheep and goats as the culprits for his forest conservation program.[111] It was also Herman who initiated the first grazing permits for federal lands in 1899. The 1897 act marks the first official legislation directed against sheep specifically. Under this same act the secretary of the interior was empowered to establish the Bureau of Forestry, which would oversee the forest reserves.

By 1901 most reserves were closed to sheep grazing. Sheepmen launched a series of attacks upon the constitutionality of the

Act of 1897 in federal district courts. (In 1911 the United States Supreme Court declared it unconstitutional.) Meanwhile, sheepmen continued, both intentionally and unintentionally, to trespass on forest lands. Gomez-Ibañez notes that approximately one hundred thousand sheep entered the Sierra forest reserve illegally in 1901. According to the Visalia (California) land office, of the twenty-three known violators all but one were "French, Basques, or Portuguese."[112] In 1903, the United States government was forced to institute a policy of using army troops to patrol the national parks to stop the illegal entry of sheep bands.[113]

By 1902 pressure from the ranchers forced modification of forest reserve policy. In those reserves where sufficient rainfall assured limited grazing, permits were issued for some 1.4 million sheep. Local and regional wool growers' associations were generally allowed to select the recipients of these limited permits.[114]*

All of these problems were compounded as more forest reserves were created. Through the efforts of Presidents Harrison, Cleveland, and McKinley, some forty-one reserves totalling 46,410,209 acres were created. These impressive statistics pale beside the achievements of conservation-minded Theodore Roosevelt. At the close of Roosevelt's term there were 158 reserves encompassing 194,505,325 acres.[116]

In 1905 the Department of the Interior transferred jurisdiction over its forest reserves to the Bureau of Forestry (renamed the Forest Service) of the Department of Agriculture, and in 1907 the forest reserves were renamed national forests.

Sheepmen who had been embittered by the required grazing permits were angered further in 1906 when the Forest Service imposed grazing fees—five to seven cents per sheep and from twenty to forty cents per steer and horse. Subsequent raises in

---

*The question of grazing privileges on the forest reserves was extremely complex, particularly where sheep were concerned. According to Wentworth,

The whole problem was far from simple. Provocative acts that incited attempts to bar sheep were common among the "hobo" sheep bands whose herders abused the ranges, and the prohibitive policies that caused legitimate sheepmen and cattlemen so much difficulty originated with amateur, but fanatical, conservationists influencing distant Washington officials. Furthermore, the divided authority that has always characterized federal administration of public lands created many issues for the sheep and cattle industries during early decades of this century.[115]

fees elicited more resentment against the newly created agency. Local support of Forest Service policy was curried through federal legislation in 1908 that allowed a 25 percent rebate on grazing fees to the states and territories.[117]

If their struggles with the Forest Service produced resentment among many sheepmen,* the itinerant operators were particularly embittered and disadvantaged. Insofar as sheepmen won concessions for sheep grazing on national forest land, they were allotted and administered through local woolgrower associations. Itinerant operators were not welcomed as members into such organizations.

The press generally heralded the new legislation and expressed pronounced anti-Basque sentiments. On March 26, 1909, *The Humboldt Star* reported:

Sheepmen Get Basques Excluded

An Ogden dispatch says that a ruling of vast importance to the sheep and cattle interests of Nevada was made in that city Wednesday by Gifford Pinchot, head of the forest service of the United States, who decided that the transient owners of sheep and cattle are not entitled to allotments within the national forests within this State. . . .

This ruling will exclude great herds, totaling several hundred thousand sheep, owned by Basques, who of late years have overrun the State with transient bands.

The decision has greatly pleased a delegation of Nevada sheepmen, headed by Senator Warren Williams, and representing extensive interests who were in Ogden to meet Mr. Pinchot.[119]

Similarly, on May 17, 1909, the same newspaper reported:

Basque Sheepmen are Excluded from Reserve

Nineteen sheep men and stock owners, who have grazed their flocks for the past few years in what is now known as the Mono National Forest, have been recently served with a notice, bearing on the point of citizenship which excludes aliens [sic] and non-property holders from grazing privileges in the forest. The

---

*While the initial reaction of the "legitimate" sheepmen to Forest Service control was negative, Wentworth believes that the establishment of the Forest Service accomplished much for the sheep industry, since it rid many of the summer ranges of itinerant bands, slowed the deterioration of the summer grazing, and provided for more orderly utilization of the summer range. "Reasonable routines," he wrote, "were gradually established in what had been a chaotic situation, and attempts were made to restore the natural pasture grasses, among which uncontrolled competition had caused havoc."[118]

ruling was made by the chief forester some weeks ago and after a personal investigation of conditions in the West. It was found that Basque sheep owners were fast gaining possession of the grazing rights and completely crowding the citizen and property holder from grazing their sheep in the forest. All persons who have grazed their sheep on these areas during the past two seasons will be allowed to use the range this season, but such persons must be citizens of the United States, or, if not citizens, must be bona fide residents of and owners of improved ranch property either within or adjacent to the national forest lands which they have formerly used. Anyone not in the above class will be treated as trespassers.[120]

The consequence of the spread throughout the American West of the national forest system—which ultimately included most of the high country summer sheep range—was the exclusion of Basque itinerant operators. Settled stock interests that initially opposed the creation of the reserves changed their attitudes once it was established that: (1) stock grazing would be permitted, (2) allotments would be assigned through local boards (made up of propertied ranchers), and (3) "foreign" itinerant sheepmen would be excluded. Although the settled livestock interests subsequently became disenchanted with Forest Service bureaucratic snarls, allotment reductions, and establishment of grazing fees, they initially supported the new program. In fact, in some cases local livestockmen proposed that areas that failed to meet the necessary criteria be incorporated into the national forests.[121] The overriding consideration in this support was the prospect of ridding the western ranges of the itinerants. A forest ranger writing about the establishment of the Ruby Mountain District (Elko County, Nevada) of the Humboldt National Forest described the extent of this preoccupation among the cattlemen:

Another incident which injected a bit of humor in the situation was after we had rejected so many applications of transients, who were almost all Basques. A merchant of Elko who had a number of them on his list of customers undertook to right their wrongs and persuaded [them] to subscribe to a fund to send him to Washington to get justice. They did and he took one of their number with him and went to see Senator Nixon. One of the larger stockmen who was a warm friend of the Senator's sent him the following telegram, "Jew Taylor and Basco sheepherders in route to Washington claiming to represent stockman; hog tie 'em, letter follows." This got in the eastern papers and created quite a fury.[122]

Forest Service officials were also concerned about the effect of the sheep. As one wrote in 1912:

> The livestock industry derives a benefit from the Forest Service administration, rather than an injury, for if it was not for the creation of this Forest, the sheep that grazed on the Diamond range, some twenty miles west of the Ruby range, would force their way through, and use up the feed, and there is in the neighborhood of sixty thousand head. These sheep, before the creation of the National Forest, or the largest per cent of them, used to graze on the Ruby Mountains, but as they [sic] were nearly all aliens, they were forced to move when the Ruby range was made a National Forest.[123]

Similarly, in 1919 another Forest Service official noted:

> Men engaged in the livestock industry realize that the National Forests are a great protection to them, this applies to parties who own improved ranch property as the public range is fast being destroyed by transient sheep owners who have no thought of preserving the range for future generations. These owners are for the most part Basques, who are not citizens of the United States, and are here simply to get what they can from the natural resources of this country with the least possible expense to themselves. There are some Basques who have taken out their naturalization papers and are good citizens, improving the ranch property and developing the country.[124]

There is considerable question as to the overall effect of the national forest system on the itinerant sheepmen. Undoubtedly, many were affected adversely. There is evidence of some displacement* in these latter two statements. Similarly, in reporting on the creation of the Santa Rosa Division of the Humboldt National Forest, the supervisor reported that sheep numbers had dropped from 70,000 to 17,000 in one year, "mostly through failure to make application."[125]

While the anti-alien aspects of Forest Service policy excluded many Basque sheepmen, some were able to avoid exclusion by forming dummy corporations with non-Basque partners who, for a consideration, lent their names to the operation.[126] It is also a part of the legacy of the open-range sheep

---

*In interviewing the descendants of one early Basque settler in the Glasgow, Montana, area we were told that he originally operated as an itinerant sheepman in Elko County, Nevada, but on being excluded from his summer ranges by creation of the Humboldt National Forest he struck out for Montana, where he had heard that sheep range leases on Indian lands were available.

industry that some tramp operators risked fines and trespassed on the Forest Service lands.

One measure of the impact of the new regulations was that many Basques filed for citizenship, probably in the hope of blunting what was clearly an anti-alien as well as an antitramp policy. In Winnemucca alone, where only 48 Basques had filed for United States citizenship between 1871 and 1906, an additional 108 Basques did so between 1906 and 1912.[127]*

It is clear that the creation of the national forests did not in itself suffice to eradicate itinerant sheep bands. The definition of national forest boundaries was determined, at least in principle, by patterns of forestation. In the Great Basin region forestation was sparse and limited to higher elevations. There were many mountain ranges sufficiently high to contain adequate summer pasturage yet too barren for inclusion within the network of national forests. Furthermore, the exclusion of itinerant bands from much of the former summer range had the effect of increasing their pressure upon the remaining areas. A 1920 issue of the *Nevada Stockgrower* stated:

> The tramp farmers, the old name for the Basques, are on the summer range the twentieth of March, this year, until an early snow ran them off. We are just run out with them. They run right to a man's fence. If something is not done we will have to quit running stock. It is hard to say a resident American has to quit business on account of aliens. . . .[128]

By the early 1900s, of course, Basque predominance as herders and owners within the open-range sheep industry was not restricted to itinerant operations. Yet even the "legitimate" Basque sheepmen clashed with Forest Service officials. In commenting upon the ethnic makeup of stockmen and their employees authorized to run sheep on the Santa Rosa National Forest in 1912, forest supervisor W.W. Blakeslee stated:

> There are three separate nationalities among the sheepmen on this Forest, namely the French, Italians, and Bascos. They depend almost entirely on Basco help, and as these people cling together it is very hard for the French and Italian owners to secure help should they have trouble with any one of the Basco herders. The Basco owners can secure all the help they need and

---

*Many of the requests were denied on the grounds that the individual was not a resident of the county, indicating that itinerant sheepmen from other areas tried to file in Winnemucca.

they are as a rule the least progressive of the three nationalities. The Italians and French owners are more liberal-minded and grasp the intent of the regulations and instructions more quickly than the Bascos, hence, in trying to make the herders obey their instructions they get into trouble often. The only remedy I know of is for the Service to deal directly with the herder and bar him from herding on the Forest for a time. . . .[129]

Forest Service records dealing with Elko County support the contention that Basques dominated the ranks of herders working for settled livestock owners who, by virtue of their ranch properties, were eligible for grazing privileges on the National Forests. In 1911 some forty-four livestock outfits qualified for grazing permits (of which only seven were clearly Basque-owned). These outfits employed a total of 192 sheepherders, of whom 97 were unquestionably Basques and another 65 were probably Basques.* There were only 14 Anglo herders, 8 Portuguese, 8 probable Mexicans, and 1 Chinese.[130]

The Forest Service records reiterate what we have already seen about the strain between officials and the Basque herders. The rangers were primarily concerned with such matters as watershed protection and sought to restrict the movements of sheep bands to a carefully regulated cycle of light grazing. Basques were notoriously "close" herders. That is, they favored intensive grazing by a tightly bunched, carefully controlled sheep band. Perhaps this was the heritage of their intensive competition on the open range, where each flockmaster had to "find" his forage and then utilize it to the utmost. In any event, the herding philosophies of the Basques and Forest Service rangers clashed from the outset. In reporting on the use of Basque herders in one outfit, a forest ranger stated in 1910,

They have Basque herders and I consider this fact a detriment to Forest interest as they do not handle the sheep in the manner to obtain the best possible result from the range. They do not seem to understand that they should take care of the range and try to keep it improving, they only figure on summering the sheep in a manner which would make it easy for them. They are not a working class and they always try to avoid all (to them) unnecessary labor. I believe in order to get the best possible results out of the range that it will be necessary for the Forest Service to adopt harsh methods with grazers who insist on hiring Basque herders.[131]

---

*The indecision derives from the fact that the last names of many herders were omitted, with the record simply identifying a man as "José," "Bautista," or even "Can't speak."

The exasperation the Forest Service officials felt concerning the Basque herders is elaborated further in the statements by L.L. Lindsay, written in 1913:

As the majority of the permittees on this district live at a considerable distance their sheep are sent here in charge of hired men. All of these men are foreigners, the majority of whom do not speak or understand enough English to do business with, so it is impossible for a Forest Officer to give them instructions in regard to handling the sheep or explain the Forest Service regulations to them. Many are without previous experience with sheep and unfamiliar with the range. All are provided with from one to three dogs and a burro, they use the dogs on every occasion and move their camps when and where they please, without consulting the camptender and with no regard for the best interest of the range. It is the universal practice among Basque herders to make the sheep stay in the shade of the timber along creek bottoms and close to their camps, during the greater part of the day in summer time when the weather is hot; in order to encourage the sheep to do this of their own accord, they are salted there, if this fails to hold them the dogs are used. The result of this practice is that each year the creek bottoms are over-grazed, the grass being completely fed off and tramped out. During the time the sheep are quiet the herders are usually off visiting neighboring camps, leaving their herds unprotected for hours at a time, giving coyotes and wildcats opportunity to kill without being molested, and if, as frequently happens during the summer, a storm comes up, cooling the atmosphere, the sheep start to graze, get beyond the control or completely away from the herder and trespass on adjoining allotments, often mixing with the sheep there. In the evening the sheep are allowed to graze until dark and are bedded where they are at that time, the herder moves his bed and sleeps near them, in the morning they are grazed till eight or nine o'clock, then if they do not seek the shade of their own accord they are dogged to it.[132]

The complaint that the Basques could not understand English was recurrent in Forest Service reports:

Sheep are herded in bands of about 1500 ewes with their lambs. They are herded by Basque herders most of them "No savy Mericano." They are a faithful hard working people for their employers, but it is almost impossible to get them to use the range to best advantage.[133]

The reports of the district supervisors regularly noted the problem of the Basque herder's failure to adhere to forest regulations, either through stubbornness or ignorance of such regulations. With respect to the latter, it was suggested that herding instructions and forest regulations ought to be published in Basque.* In 1920 they were published as a pamphlet in the Spanish language.[135]

Not all Basque herders were given bad marks by Forest Service officials. In commenting on an animal carrying capacity test conducted on a portion of the Humboldt National Forest in 1918, Forest Service official Mink noted,

> The employees are Spanish and Basque of the very highest type. They all seem to work conscientiously and to their employees [sic] interest and adhere strictly to the forest regulations.[136]

Yet as late as 1924, the assistant range examiner James O. Stewart wrote,

> The greatest evils to the Humboldt sheep ranges today, in my opinion, are the "Basque sheepherding practices." From questioning different rangers it was learned that it is the custom to drive the sheep to water daily and during the forenoon. In the afternoon they are driven onto the ridges to feed. The Basque herders are a company-loving class of people, and gather at some central sheep camp during the day to visit. While actually on the job they are close herders, which is not in the best interests of the range. Many of them can not understand English, or pretend that they can't, and the rangers often have their instructions disobeyed when they tell the herders to keep their sheep off certain deferred areas. . . . Every ranger that I came in contact with who has been on his district more than one year was able to show a pretty good deferred and rotation grazing plan. . . . The success of these plans in many instances was limited by the handling of sheep by Basque herders.[137]

What irked Basque sheepmen the most about Forest Service policy was the propensity of most rangers to create their own plans for range use. The sheepmen thought that the rangers were too frequently self-styled experts on the sheep industry who lacked sympathy for local problems, necessities, and aspirations. Moreover, the rangers were seen by some as extortionists, holding off use of "free" land until the ranchers had paid fees for grazing permits. Finally, there was the overriding fear of ranger arbitrariness in administering local arrangements.

---

*In 1918 the Agricultural Experimental Station of the University of Nevada published a Spanish-language translation of its bulletin, "Range Plants Poisonous to Sheep and Cattle in Nevada."[134]

Animal numbers on permits could be reduced or the permits themselves divided and redistributed.

American livestockmen as well as Basque herders viewed the concentration of this kind of power in the hands of the Forest Service and its field representatives as, at the very least, an enormous potential danger to their continued existence.

The Forest Service stabilized grazing on the traditional summer ranges of the American West, but the millions of lowland and foothill acres of the public domain remained uncontrolled and were subject to overgrazing through competitive use. On March 29, 1928, Congress passed an act that allowed the Secretary of Interior to withdraw certain public lands in Mizpah-Pumpkin Creek area of eastern Montana from homestead status. This move was part of a larger plan to create an experimentally controlled grazing district on semi-arid range lands. In all, the district comprised some 108,804 acres, which were to be grazed by both cattle and sheep.[138] The plan for the organization of the Mizpah-Pumpkin Grazing District was voted by Congress and legally administered by the Division of Grazing under the Department of Interior. However, the actual users, the local livestockmen, were the main managers. The plan called for a monthly fee of three cents an acre. Artificial dams were constructed to provide better water supplies, fences were built to help regulate range use, and the Forest Service advised district administrators on range loads and distribution. By 1932 the Mizpah-Pumpkin Creek Project had shown a 38 percent increase in forage cover, and more plans for grazing districts were in the offing.[139]

As a result of the apparent success of the Montana experiment, more districts were created in Montana and Utah. According to Gates, it was these successes, coupled with severe droughts in the West and the faltering livestock market of 1932—34, that brought about full-scale elaboration of the federal grazing district plan formalized in the Taylor Grazing Act of 1934.

In point of fact, pressure for the creation of grazing districts throughout the West came from at least three other sources as well: (1) a publicity campaign in the eastern United States that depicted the western ranges as deteriorating rapidly under anarchical competitive grazing practices, (2) demands from a segment of the western livestock industry for the addition of guaranteed grazing allotments on the public domain, in order to enhance the capital worth of ranch properties and hence forestall bank foreclosures that were becoming increasingly common in the depressed economy of the early 1930s, and (3) an exaggerated problem with itinerant sheep bands in eastern Utah and western Colorado.

The key piece of legislation, enacted in 1934, was introduced by Senator Edward Taylor of Colorado. It was almost identical to an unsuccessful bill proposed in 1932 by Congressman Colton of Utah. The Taylor Grazing Act proved to be enormously effective. That November, all remaining unreserved lands in the Dakotas and ten states from the Rockies to the Pacific coast, except for Washington, were closed to itinerant grazing. In February of the following year, public lands in twelve additional states were withdrawn, halting itinerant grazing except where there were preexisting rights.[140]

Thirty-two districts, comprising some 80 million acres, were created from these lands. By 1936, increases brought the total acreage to 142 million.[141] The immediate task of administering the new districts fell to the Department of the Interior's Division of Grazing (later rechristened the Bureau of Land Management). With the creation of arid lands grazing districts, the era of unrestricted use of forage on the public domain was closed.

The Taylor Grazing Act was passed over powerful opposition. Many western congressional representatives and state officials viewed the law as one more federal encroachment upon local life. Livestock growers did not unanimously welcome the creation of yet another federal bureaucracy governing their activities. Furthermore, there was some consideration of grazing fees at the outset. Proponents of the bill within the Department of Interior sought to gain the support of the settled livestock interests by minimizing fees and designating their revenues largely for local use; allocation was to be decided by advisory boards of local livestockmen, basing allotments upon ownership of private land and water rights, and by excluding aliens.[142]

The last two points held out the promise of abolishing the itinerant sheepmen once and for all. There were many anti-alien and antitramp sheepmen statements made in the hearings. The remarks of Associate Forester E. A. Sherman to the House's Committee on the Public Lands provide an example:

Let me say that in many places much of the range has gone to people who are not citizens of the United States. They have abused the territory. It was not their country. It did not make any difference to them what happened to our land, but within 2, 3, 4, or 10 years or even 15 years they can make a clean-up of from five to fifteen thousand dollars and then go back to the old country with their money. . . . [Questioned about where they came from, Mr. Sherman noted] Various and different places. A great many of them [are] Basques and Greeks.[143]

In defending his bill, Senator Taylor, of Colorado, dwelt upon the "evils" of the itinerant sheep bands:

I might mention that there were some 15,000 sheep from the State of Oregon in my congressional district for the past 2 or 3 years. There is no restraint on them whatsoever. They eat out both the summer and the winter range of the local people, and destroy the mountain roads and are a frightfully devastating nuisance.

But that is not the worst of it. There are thousands of small ranchers, local settlers, on all the little creeks, and those nomadic herds, paying little or no taxes [sic] and roaming around carrying on their grazing operations unrestrained, eating out the forage right up to the very gardens and doors of the local settlers.

. . . The actual residents and taxpayers help to maintain the country. As to these people I would say that from 90 to 95 percent of them are in favor of this policy of control but as to the very large sheep men who send out a Basque or Greek or some other nonresident with a band of sheep as a shepherd, those men go out with a large bunch of sheep and they roam all over the country, they are not especially concerned about the principle of conservation. They are instructed by the owner of the sheep to take care of their flock for that particular season, and therefore are not interested in preserving the range.[144]

With the exception of a few areas, however, the itinerant sheepman was no longer the burning issue among western livestockmen. By the 1930s the cumulative weight of all of the measures that we have considered, legal and extralegal, had crippled the itinerants and thinned their ranks considerably. The Depression itself had ruined many of these operators. The prospect of ridding the range of itinerants was no longer a sufficient goal to rally western stockmen to the ranks of the proponents of new federal controls.

Viewed from the perspective of the Basque ethnic group, however, the Taylor Grazing Act was a major milestone.

Basque sheepmen tend to reckon time in terms of before and after "Taylor Grazing," a kind of Old and New Testament in their group life in the American West. In 1934 the itinerant sheepmen, though severely reduced in numbers in terms of former years, were mostly Basques, and they constituted a significant portion of the overall Basque population of the American West. Passage of the Taylor Grazing Act spelled the demise of the itinerant outfits. As the grazing districts were established and allotments determined by government officials and the advisory boards of local, settled, ranch interests, the applications of itinerant operators for grazing allotments were uniformly denied.

In 1935, for example, fourteen Basque sheepmen applied for grazing permits in the Modoc-Lassen (California) Grazing District. Together they owned 32,972 sheep. The grazing district allotment committee, nevertheless, recommended that only 7,880 sheep, belonging to six of the operators, be licensed; three of these six were required to take cuts of half or more—one applied for 6,800 animals and was allotted grazing for 2,000. Of the eight remaining Basque sheepmen, three had their requests rejected, either as non-citizens or for having no private or leased ranchland, while the requests of the other five were suspended for further investigation of their questionable citizenship.[145]

In Harney County, Oregon, sheep numbers were slashed on Steen Mountain (formerly a major summer pasture for transient sheepmen). In 1932 some 145,780 sheep grazed the area. The sheep belonged to fifteen Harney County sheep outfits with ranch property, sixteen Harney County outfits with no ranch property, and no less than forty-six "transient sheepmen." According to the author of a grazing district report,

> The term "transient" is applied to sheepmen who come in from outside districts, own no land in Steen's Mountains [sic] and may, or may not, own land elsewhere. It may be taken as a fact that Basque sheepmen, generally, do not own land anywhere. Some of the Irish sheepmen also own no land.[146]

Of the Steens Mountain sheepmen, twelve Basques, with a total of 43,100 animals, were listed on the summer range. All but one were identified as owning no land, and he was described as a "small landowner."[147] By 1937 the Harney County tax assessor complained that sheep numbers on Steens Mountain had dropped to ninety-one thousand, damaging severely the local economy.[148] The transient sheepmen were the chief targets of the cuts.

The Jordan Valley (Oregon) Grazing District provides a particularly striking example of such cuts and highlights other problems posed by the creation of grazing districts for highly mobile sheepmen. In 1935, of fifty-five applicants for sheep permits for a total of 184,695 animals, thirty were Basques, representing 120,680 of the animal allotments requested. Only eight of the applicants, all but one* of whom were resident in the Jordan Valley area, were approved without cuts or conditions. Their total number of sheep was only 10,770.

Six applicants from major operations, whose sheep totaled 48,650 head, were rejected out of hand. Five lived outside the district and were rejected because they had no private or leased land within the district. In the case of the local sheepman, his application was rejected because he was not a citizen. The applications of four operators, owners of a total of 25,200 sheep, were suspended for further investigation of lands owned, stock numbers and, in one case, citizenship. Ten applications, representing 37,500 animals, were approved but on a one-year basis, since it was believed that the applicants possessed insufficient lands to warrant the sheep numbers requested.[149] By the 1940s the Jordan Valley area was well on its way to becoming what it is today—cattle country.

It is clear from the above accounts that the Taylor Grazing Act neatly speared the itinerant Basque sheepmen on the twin horns of his alien citizenship‡ and lack of commensurate private or leased property.

Another consequence of the Taylor Grazing Act is reflected in the Jordan Valley Grazing District Committee's rejections of the applications of five large outsider sheepmen. The traditional patterns of transhumance for a particular outfit might cross grazing district lines, yet each district's allotment was determined by its resident livestockmen. By simply claiming that outsiders had no *local* property, locals could eliminate powerful competitors from the area.

---

*From nearby McDermitt, Nevada.

‡A letter from Agent Foley to his supervisor concerning the citizenship of sheepmen in the Mojave Grazing District Number One suggests that the Taylor Grazing Act triggered a new spate of declaration of citizenship intent filings by alien sheepmen. "Thus," Foley states, "of 20 named in my summary . . . as not citizens and who had not filed declaration of intention to become such, eleven individual and one partnership applicants were reported upon favorably for the reason either that the individuals, or leading member of the partnership had made application to file such declaration. . . ."[150]

The Taylor Grazing Act abolished itinerant sheepmen, Basque and otherwise, from the western ranges. In the first few years of the act, there was a shaking out period in which trespass cases and other violations were frequent. We can catch a glimpse of a few desperate men, converted into renegades of the range, trying to carry on stubbornly as if the Taylor Grazing Act were nothing more than a bad dream. Such a man was the Basque, J—— O——, whose case, as reflected in the report of agent H. M. Galt of the Oregon District Number 3, tells a tale of particular frustration:

J—— O—— made an application for 1937 license to graze 900 ewes from March 15 to June 15 in the Skull Springs and Harper Basin Grazing Units. The Advisory Board at the meeting held January 25, 1937, recommended that the application be rejected on the grounds of "No dependent commensurate property." At the appeal meeting of the Board held February 22, 1937, Mr. O—— appeared and requested that his application be withdrawn, giving as the reason that he wished to wait for the decision on his case now pending in Federal Court.

On March 12, 1937, Mr. O—— presented two leases covering certain ranch property in the vicinity of Vale, Oregon. He requested that his application be reinstated and allowed on the bases of these properties. This property was classified as Class 2 [hence low priority] because of range priority. In order not to force liquidation of this livestock on short notice a license was recommended Mr. O—— for 1937. The terms of the notice was [sic] sent to Mr. O—— by registered mail. A receipt for same was signed April 29, 1937. In the terms of this license a particular allotment of public domain range was described upon which this licensee was permitted to graze.

Subsequent to this notice of the license a complaint came to the Division of Grazing that O—— was violating the terms of the license by refusing to go or stay on the allotment described. Because of this fact he was personally served with a notice on May 4, to appear before the Regional Grazier in Burns, Oregon, to give reason why his license should not be cancelled. He did not appear in the allotted time given in the notice, consequently the Regional Grazier notified him that his license was cancelled. This notice was also served upon Mr. O—— personally by Mr. C. Smith, Range Rider. On May 11, 1937, the Range Rider found Mr. O—— . . . approximately 18 miles distance from the allotment described in his license.

Another notice was served on O—— at this time giving him three days to get on the stock driveway, as he stated that he wished to go to his summer range out of the district. He crossed the Malheur River, at Riverside, Oregon, approximately May 14 and started out on the trail west and north through the Drewsey Grazing Unit. Another complaint was made that he was not respecting the trail regulations. The Division of Grazing, therefore, authorized Mr. Charles McConnell and Mr. Bud Anderson, who were then marking the stock driveway to keep a check upon Mr. O——'s movements.

From May 14 to approximately May 31 when he crossed the Forest Boundary, Mr. McConnell and Mr. Anderson served three trespass notices upon Mr. O—— for violations of the stock driveway regulations. These trespass notices were based upon the fact that Mr. O—— refused to stay on the stock driveway that was plainly marked for that purpose.[151]

In light of the restrictions on use of the range, some of the displaced Basque sheepmen purchased or leased small ranch properties and thereby qualified for allotments. Others sought employment as sheepherders, camptenders, or sheep foremen in larger outfits. Still others went into different lines of work in the American West. Some returned to Europe, disillusioned, and of course spread the word that the American West no longer offered much opportunity for immigrant sheepherders to become sheepmen in their own right.

THE INDISPENSABLE BASQUE SHEEPHERDER

Although the Basque itinerant sheepman and the Basque herder alike were capable of firing emotions and evoking extremely harsh criticisms, their labor was, by 1900, both highly appreciated and indispensable to the sheep industry of the American West. As the *Humboldt Star* commented in 1912, announcing the arrival of a new contingent of Basques in Winnemucca:

These men will all go to herding sheep. Flock owners say it is impossible to get Americans to herd sheep and stick to it, notwithstanding the pay is $40 or $45 a month and board and the work is the easiest in the country.[152]

Despite the wages, the sheepherding occupation was held in particularly low social esteem throughout the American West. In the words of one authority,

You could not fire a shotgun into the average crowd in the range country without hitting a man who had at some time herded sheep, but it would probably take the charge in the other barrel to make him admit it. About the only person who isn't ashamed to admit having herded is a sheepman, and he refers to it merely to show how far he has come.[153]

Social degradation was not the only consideration that thinned the ranks of the non-Basque herders. There was great risk to the herder's personal safety, and especially to his mental stability, under Great Basin conditions of open-range sheep transhumance.

The man who spent days and even weeks on end in total solitude had particular reason to fear death by illness or accident. Misfortunes such as a broken limb or an accidental gunshot wound, serious but manageable turns of events for town dwellers, could mean a horrible lingering death for the herder. The *Elko Free Press* reported the case of the twenty-two-year-old Basque herder who shot himself accidentally in the foot, and several hours later shot himself in the head.[154] Throughout the sheep-raising districts it was commonplace to report the accidental deaths of Basque sheepherders.[155]

The herder had also to fear illness, particularly "spotted fever." Transmitted by the ticks that infested the sage and underbrush, plaguing both the sheep and sheep dogs, the disease could be fatal.[156]

Fears for personal safety were well-founded; but of possibly even greater concern were fears for one's sanity. The open-range sheepherder even today lives in one of the most pristine contexts of social isolation occurring outside of the laboratory experiments of social psychologists.[157] Before the days of the transistor radio and the four-wheel drive vehicle, his isolation was much greater. In a somewhat tongue-in-cheek manner Gilfillan states,

> Some hold that no man can herd six months straight without going crazy, while others maintain that a man must have been mentally unbalanced for at least six months before he is in fit condition to entertain the thought of herding.[158]

Gilfillan's humor masks the profound pathos of one of the stereotypes in the sheep districts of the American West—that of the "crazy Basco sheepherder." *The Silver State* reported in its July 17, 1894, issue:

A Crazy Sheepherder

An insane Basque sheepherder was arrested yesterday morning and locked up. He was wandering around town carrying a shepherd dog on his back, and is supposed to have packed the animal all the way from the sheep camp where he was

employed, about 40 miles south of here. His insanity seems to
be of a religious turn, as since put in jail he spends most of the
time on his knees muttering prayers, interspersed with howls
almost hideous enough to scare a railroad "scab" into being a
gentleman. . . .[159]

Nor was this an isolated instance.[160]

The herders themselves are acutely aware of the occupational hazard of insanity. Included in their conversations is a
vocabulary of madness in which the unbalanced herder is described in Basque as being "sheeped" or "sage-brushed."
When the Boise Basques created a mutual aid society for health
care in 1908, special provisions were made for providing the
mentally ill with return passage to Europe.[161] Another expression of mental imbalance was the frequent occurrence of suicide
among the ranks of the Basque herders.[162]

Insanity and suicides reinforced the notion held by their
non-Basque neighbors that the Basque sheepmen were at least
slightly unbalanced by their years of solitude. To this was added
the notion that the sheepherder was sexually frustrated. On
January 3, 1913, *The Humboldt Star* reported,

> Young Man Returns After Four Years
> [J—— U——] returned to Winnemucca on New Year's day
> after four years absence, during which time he has working [*sic*]
> steadily for J—— J—— at McDermitt, never having been to
> town once during that time. Now J—— has money enough to
> buy diamonds for his girl, an automobile and a fine brick house.
> After four years of the quiet of the little northern settlement the
> excitement of the Humboldt county metropolis is telling on him
> and he is resting at the Busch. As soon as he gets out to buy some
> lavender socks he will call on his girl.[163]

This fairly polite editorial fun at the expense of the image of the
sheepherder had its less benign counterpart in popular joking
patterns and ethnic slurs, in which the Basque herder's girl
friend was selected from among his sheep.

RECRUITING THE HERDER

By the early twentieth century the Basque sheepherder was
the irreplaceable backbone of the open-range, transhumant
sheep outfits in the American West (itinerant and otherwise).
There was an established labor pool of Basque herders sustained
by continued immigration from the Basque country. Within the
pool there was a high turnover of personnel, as individuals
sought to get out of the herder profession as quickly as possible.

If kinship ties and contacts between fellow villagers served initially as the key factors in attracting Basque labor to the United States, by the early 1900s the labor pool of Basque herders was an independent entity. In fact there was a surplus of herders in many areas. Pierre Lhande published a letter, written in 1908, claiming that there were 150 unemployed Basques in the San Francisco hotels alone in October of that year.[164] One of our informants recounts that upon arriving in Elko in the winter of 1912 he found the Basque hotels filled to capacity with the unemployed, which he estimated at about seventy-five men.*

For the unemployed herder the many Basque hotels of the American West served as more than mere temporary havens; they also provided local employment information. As a part of a regional network of Basque hotels, each became a source of job information for the sheep industry of the entire American West.

There came to be less incentive for established sheepmen (Basque or otherwise) to send directly to the Old Country for young men. It might take several months for a potential herder to make the journey, and he would arrive unversed in the ways of the American sheep industry. He had to be taught how to herd under local conditions. Personal ties with the herders could themselves prove a source of embarrassment for the established sheepmen. The herder, as well as the rest of his family in Europe, frequently regarded the "American uncle" as obligated to give a young man special considerations and help him become established as a sheepman in his own right. For the sheepman to treat a young relative as equal to other herders in his employ was to risk criticism from family members in Europe that he was "exploiting" his kinsman.

Conversely, there were sufficient instances of sheepmen who sent to the Old Country for relatives whose naïveté in the ways of the American West might be exploited to build up the outfit. Typically, such relatives might be induced to continue working for their keep and a little spending money while their wages accumulated over the years on the books of their kinsman-employer. The wages of two or three herders, accumulated in this fashion, provided the operator with an added capital factor of several thousand dollars. Such arrangements could end

---

*On the next day an agent from a mining company in Eureka, Nevada, hired the entire bunch as day laborers. According to the informant, the agent had come from Eureka for the express purpose of finding Basque laborers, due to their reputation as hard workers.

in tragedy if the operation collapsed, destroying at a single stroke the herders' savings. Such instances, while infrequent, were nevertheless sufficiently common to create a cautious attitude in the Basque country. Needless to say, they also left in their wake torn and embittered family relations.

Consequently, during the first two decades of the twentieth century, the recruitment of sheepherders became increasingly dictated by the simple laws of supply and demand and less by networks of personal ties. In business terms it made considerably more sense for a sheepman in need of a herder to go to the local Basque hotel (where he would likely find one who was thoroughly experienced and possibly even familiar with the peculiarities of local grazing conditions) than to bear the expense of sending off to Europe for an untrained young man. But there was added incentive for the sheepmen to seek at least some of their employees within the impersonal labor pool. The transhumant sheep outfits of the Great Basin region developed a pattern of activities within which there was sharp seasonal fluctuation in the demand for sheepherders. During the late winter and early spring lambing season additional help was necessary for about a six-week period. (This problem has never been resolved satisfactorily, and lack of sufficient labor during lambing remains one of the most predictable annual anxieties of the sheepman.) Once lambing and shearing are completed, summer bands of between one thousand and fifteen hundred ewes and their lambs are formed, and the wethers likewise form separate bands, each under the care of a single herder. In the fall the lambs are shipped, and two summer bands are combined into one winter band. This means that in terms of actual herding the labor force of the sheep outfit may be halved during the winter months. Strict economics demand winter layoffs. Such layoffs were more difficult to implement if kinsmen were involved.

From the sheepherder's point of view, there were also certain advantages in a system of impersonal hiring of help. It was easier to demand top wages if one's employer was not also his brother. It was also considerably easier to quit a nonkinsman if one were unhappy with working conditions. To walk out on a kinsman would likely have family repercussions on both sides of the Atlantic. This freedom and flexibility to negotiate became increasingly important as the general campaign against itinerant sheep bands undermined their ability to function. By the 1920s there was considerable opportunity for sheepherders but a dwindling likelihood that the sheepherder could become a successful itinerant operator. Consequently, some Basques came to regard their stay in the American West as one devoted exclusively to wage employment as a sheepherder. If they were to return to Europe with much of a nest egg, it was imperative that the herders work for the highest possible wages.

Some herders preferred to parley the seasonal layoffs into personal advantage. The fluctuation in the labor demands of the Great Basin region were the mirror opposites of the situation in the California sheep industry. In California, lambing was scheduled for autumn, the largest bands were formed during the winter, lambs were shipped during the spring, and the major herder layoffs began in early summer. Enterprising sheepherders established a labor symbiosis between California and the other western states. Some* herders worked part of the year in California and the remainder in another state. By arriving in each area just prior to lambing, the herder was in a position to command the highest possible wage. Many regarded the opportunity to avoid the harsh Great Basin winters and searing California summers as a further attraction and compensation.

By the second decade of the twentieth century there was an independent and self-sustaining sheepherder labor pool within which sheepherders moved either permanently or seasonally to different employment and areas of the American West. On the other hand, there remained a broad correlation between the distribution of Basques in the American West and regional distinctions in the Basque country. French Basques and Navarrese continued to enter California, western Nevada, Arizona, and pockets of Wyoming and Montana, whereas Vizcayan immigrants regarded northern Nevada, eastern Oregon, and southern Idaho as their primary destination. Significantly, it was this latter region that experienced the greatest expansion of open-range, transhumant sheep outfits between 1890 and the First World War (see p. 242). The shift of the focus of the sheep industry inland proved to be a major stimulus to the immigration of Vizcayans, almost all of whom became herders. Although French Basques and Navarrese continued to provide herders, the Vizcayan influence began to be felt even within the California industry. Undoubtedly the seasonal movement of some Vizcayan herders to California accelerated this trend.

---

*The California demand was insufficient to absorb the entire contingent of seasonally unemployed sheepherders from the remainder of the American West.

Meanwhile, California Basques began to have an alternative to involvement in the sheep industry. By the turn of the present century the population growth of southern California created considerable demand for dairy products. Some former French Basque sheepmen converted their landholdings into dairy operations and began to employ kinsmen and fellow ethnics as field hands and milkers. The relatively low French Basque population—about one hundred twenty thousand in 1900[165]—and the continued French Basque emigration to Latin America meant that the competition of dairymen for the small supply of French Basque immigrants in California further facilitated the Vizcayan and Navarrese takeover of the sheepherder occupation.

The First World War accelerated this trend. French Basque emigration ceased almost entirely. Many French Basques living in the American West returned to Europe for the conflict as the October 2, 1914, issue of *The Nevada State Herald* points out:

> Eight Basko sheep herders, who had been employed by the O'Neil-Capell company, departed yesterday for Europe, where they will take sides with the French in the warfare now raging in that country.[166]

Spain remained neutral in the First World War, but the flow of Vizcayan immigrants to the American West did not remain unaffected. In the general climate of uncertainty, compounded by the partial disruption of shipping, few left for the United States during the war years. Departures of emigrants from the port of Bilbao* totaled 6,211 in 1912, but declined to only 1,273 in 1916.[167]

Sheepherder monthly wages, which were from forty dollars to forty-five dollars in 1912 climbed to $100 and more in the war years. Yet sheepherders became increasingly scarce. There were newspaper reports of women being employed to herd, and by 1917, large sheepmen were requesting that all sheepherders be given draft exemptions.[168] This 1919 letter to the editor of *The National Wool Grower*, expressed the sheepmen's concerns:

---

*In the early years of the twentieth century there were few direct shipping lines between Spanish and United States ports, since the two countries had just ceased fighting each other. Consequently, the two most frequent ultimate European ports of departure for Spanish Basque emigrants to the United States were Liverpool and Le Havre. Commercial shipping from these two ports was disrupted considerably during the First World War.

We are having hard times getting any sheep herders even though
we are raising wages all the seasons. I think the main factor is
that there were not any newcomers from France and Spain since
the war started in 1914. . . .[169]

When the United States was itself drawn into the conflict,
its economy suffered an acute labor shortage: defense industries
boomed, and men were drafted into the army. The sheep industry underwent its own boom, as meat and wool prices soared.
The impending war years' labor crisis in the sheep business was
in part averted by the fact that few Spanish Basques were willing
to enter United States military service, arguing that they were
citizens of a country that was neutral in the struggle.

The refusal of many Spanish nationals to be inducted into
the American army provided critics with further ammunition in
their campaign against the itinerant sheepman. As an article
from the 1919 issue of *The National Wool Grower* stated:

Throughout the Western states we have a large class of aliens
engaged in running sheep upon the public domain. These men
do not intend to become citizens of the United States, they do not
own land or improved ranches, nor do they respect the range
rights of established sheep- and cattlemen. When the draft was
calling men to the colors they claimed exemption on the ground
that they were residents of a country not engaged in the war.
This class of sheepman is a nuisance for which there is no longer
any room in the range country. No one ought to be allowed to
use the public domain unless he is a citizen of the United States
and every alien user of the public domain who asked exemption
from the draft on the grounds that he was not a citizen ought to be
deported.[170]

The refusal to serve in the army caused the rejection of
many Basque applications for United States citizenship filed in
the early 1920s. In extreme cases, some men who were drafted
in the war years and who avoided serving by renouncing formerly attained citizenship were denied future United States
citizenship forever (as well as their grazing privileges). The
March 20 and 22, 1919, issues of the *Elko Independent* report
no less than sixteen such decisions in Humboldt and Elko
counties alone.[171] Some Basque sheepmen so feared the
xenophobia that they offered considerable bribes to federal
officials for favorable action on their citizenship applications.[172]

In 1921 there was another development that had a profound
effect upon the sheepherder labor force: the United States Con-

gress passed legislation that limited immigration from western Europe by assigning a national origins quota of immigrants. The initial Spanish quota was set at 912 persons per year.[173] In 1924 a new Immigration Act reduced the Spanish quota to 131 persons.[174] Spanish Basques were included under this designation, which meant that the act all but ended their legal entry into the American West. While the quotas for French nationals remained considerably higher, the continued immigration of French Basques, for reasons already considered, was insufficient to replenish the sheepherder labor pool.

A shortage of sheepherders loomed. The August 4, 1923, issue of the *Nevada Stockgrower* reported that many Basque herders had returned to Europe and very few were coming over.[175] In the previous spring, the Nevada Woolgrowers Association had contracted 250 American-born Mexican herders. The February 1924 issue of the same publication stated that herders from northern New Mexico were available. The employer would advance travel, one-half of which was deducted from the man's first paycheck and then ten dollars a month thereafter. This deduction was returned to the herder if he remained for a minimum of six months with his employer.[176]

Some sheepmen resorted to extreme measures to circumvent the new restrictions on the entry of Basque herders, as evidenced by a 1925 newspaper article:

> G—— S——, a wealthy New Mexico and Nevada rancher and stockman, is made defendant in a civil suit for $5,000 filed by the United States Attorney at Carson City yesterday.
>
> S—— is alleged to have smuggled . . . five Basques through the "hole in the wall," the bridge across the Rio Grande at El Paso, Texas. The government is said to have information that the smuggling took place at midnight and S—— paid a taxicab driver $68 to take the men to Deming, N.M. . . .[177]

The new immigration policies were felt almost immediately in the Great Basin sheep industry, but the full adverse impact of the measures was postponed for a number of years. It required time for the ranks of the herders to become critically thinned through retirements, deaths, and departures to Europe. At the same time, as many itinerant sheep operations were closed down, their owners often went to work for others as herders.

After 1924 it was virtually impossible for all but those Spanish Basques with immediate (ie., parent, spouse, or child) family members in the American West to enter the United States legally. Many Basques signed on as merchant seamen, jumped ship in some United States port, and made their ways to distant relatives or friends in the Great Basin, and many were caught and deported. The budding labor crisis in the sheep industry, exacerbated by the involvement of the country in a new war, caused considerable concern and initiated a debate at the national level. This brief article from the February 20, 1941, *Elko Free Press* underscores that concern:

> Senators Discuss Bill to Deport Basque Aliens
> Fate of 64 Basque aliens in Nevada, Idaho and California facing deportation is still undecided, according to press reports from Washington.
> A bill authorizing dismissal of the deportation proceedings has been placed before the senate, but it is feared that an unfavorable report from the justice department may result in the loss of the bill.[178]

By the early 1940s the labor crisis in the sheep industry became so acute that an unusual series of bills appeared in Congress. Called the Sheepherder Laws, these were private bills legalizing the status of individual Basque aliens. The sponsors of such legislation were western senators, who were in turn pressured by the sheepmen of their respective states. Between 1942 and 1961, 383 men received permanent residency status under the Sheepherder Laws.[179]

With each passing year, the supply of Basque herders continued to dwindle, while the replenishment was minimal and required the most extraordinary of actions (illegal entry and/or special legislation). As the Second World War created a demand for sheep products and siphoned off more men from the ranks of the sheepherders, the labor shortage reached genuine crisis proportions. On December 29, 1942, desperate Western Nevada sheepmen met in Minden and formed the Nevada Range Sheep Owners Association. The sole purpose of the organization was to alleviate the sheepherder shortage by seeking ways to import Basques. J. B. Dangberg of Minden became the president and within a short time there were forty-two members.[180] Dangberg and the association sought the support of Patrick McCarran, a United States senator from Nevada and himself a former sheepman.

On May 4, 1942, McCarran wrote to Dangberg,

> I quite agree with you that Mexicans are not the best herders, but it may be we will have to resort to that. As you know, I am very familiar with the sheep herding question.

The Aguirre Hotel in San Francisco, sometime during the late nineteenth century. In its day this was the most important Basque hotel in the American West.

Basque *pelota* court in Stockton about the year 1900.

Ball court in Stockton, California, utilized for wedding celebration near the beginning of the twentieth century.

Jai alai player with his wicker *txistera* in Stockton, California.

Funeral held in Stockton about 1900. It was customary to commission such graveside photos to send to European relatives as proof that the deceased had received a decent Christian burial. Given the physical dangers of the herder's isolation and the commonly held image that the American West was a treacherous wilderness, the bereaved in Europe had to be assured that the deceased was not abandoned to fate.

Facsimile of business card issued by Valentín Aguirre to advertise his New York establishment. These cards were distributed to travel agents in the Basque country. Most Basque immigrants in the U.S. spent their first night in this hotel.

Basque sheepherders frequenting a bar in McDermitt, Nevada (circa 1910). (Courtesy of Nevada Historical Society)

Portrait of John Achabal, prosperous and influential Basque sheepman of Boise, Idaho.

Sheep wagons of the Jean Esponda outfit descending from summer camp in the Big Horn mountains near Buffalo, Wyoming (circa 1926).

The early Basque herders transported their supplies and equipment with burros. They rarely owned a home base and simply moved about the range according to the season.

Sheep camp near Jordan Valley, Oregon, in the early 1900s.

The burro or other beast of burden is still essential to the Basque sheepherder.

Loading wool sacks near Jordan Valley, Oregon.

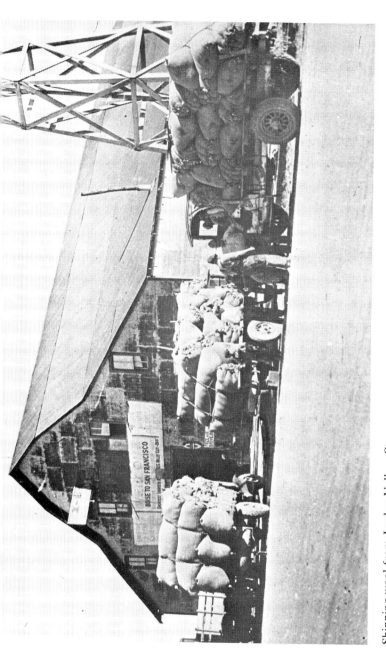

Shipping wool from Jordan Valley, Oregon.

Herder caring for sheep on the winter range in central Nevada. (Photo by Bill Belknap)

Bottle feeding a bummer lamb. Their willingness to give such care made the Basque herder particularly esteemed by sheep ranchers.

Herder in southern Idaho alongside his sheep wagon. The herders lived in such wagons while on the winter range. Coyotes were a major threat to the bands and the occasional sale of their pelts provided the herder with additional income.

There was a provision made in the Immigration Laws with regard to the importation of certain skilled labor. This was done with the vast sheepherder requirement definitely in mind.[181]

McCarran noted in the same letter that he had tried unsuccessfully to obtain Immigration Service approval to allow another Nevada sheep outfit to import herders. He promised to keep trying. On May 27, 1942, he wrote the rancher,

I am going to do everything in my power to assist with regard to the sheepherder question and in trying to secure Basque herders. However, let me warn you that the possibilities of getting this type of labor from the old country seem almost impossible.[182]

As the labor situation continued to worsen Senator McCarran stepped up his efforts. In a 1943 letter to the secretary of the Nevada Range Sheep Owners Association, he stated,

I have your letter of recent date, advising that your association has made a request for 100 herders from Mexico, and outlining why these men should be Spanish Basques.
I agree with you completely and have today taken the liberty of addressing a strong letter to the Secretary of Agriculture, urging that all herders brought in from Mexico be of Basque ancestry, rather than Mexican. I have also urged that the time has long since passed for consideration and consultation. What we need now is "Action" with a capital "A," and I intend to see that we get it.[183]

The plan apparently was to hire herders from among the Basque refugees of the Spanish Civil War resident in Mexico. However, the effort ran afoul of bureaucratic snarls. On July 8, 1943, McCarran sent a scathing letter to the Deputy Administrator of the War Food Administration denouncing the delays. He described the situation as "the now no longer threatened or impending shortage of experienced herders, but actual, present and existing disruption in the sheep industry in the Far West, directly due to the lack of competent herders. . . ." He further noted that "Basque herders are available not only in Mexico, but in many Latin American countries, and . . . sheep owners stand ready to advance all transportation costs, and do anything else that will get herders into this country."[184]

On July 15, 1943, McCarran received a reply to the effect that the War Food Administration office had already unsuccessfully negotiated the sheepherder issue with the Mexican government. The Mexican authorities were more interested in finding employment for their own nationals than for Europeans who happened to be resident in that country. Consequently, the War Food Administration suggested that the sheep ranchers ought to think in terms of alternatives, and specifically in the possibility of recruiting Spanish American herders in the state of New Mexico.[185]

The idea of employing New Mexican herders did not appeal to the sheep ranchers. On August 13, 1943, McCarran wrote to Dangberg,

> I have your . . . letter of July 30th in reply to mine of July 26th, concerning the use of Spanish-Americans in New Mexico as sheepherders.
>
> Your reaction to this proposal seems to be substantially the same as mine. I sent the communication along to you with my tongue in cheek, because I have never heard that these Mexicans are really experienced in herding. However, it seems that the powers that be in Washington, either refuse to face the serious situation, or continue to beg the question of the importation of Basque herders into the United States. . . .[186]

In October of 1943 J. B. Dangberg made application to the Immigration and Naturalization Service for permission to import seventy-five Basque herders from the Spanish Basque provinces. On November 4, 1943, he was informed,

> . . . permission has been granted for you to import 75 skilled Basque sheep herders for employment by members of your association for a period ending October 5, 1944, provided they are otherwise admissible than as contract laborers, upon condition that a blanket public charge and departure bond in the sum of $5000 is posted, guaranteeing departure of the workers, the sum of $500 to be forfeited for each person who fails to depart.[187]

While serving as a foot in the door this ruling did little to alleviate the situation. It was clearly impractical to recruit and import herders in Europe whose stay in the United States was to be limited to less than one year from the date that permission was granted. There were other problems as well. On December 29, 1943, the Spanish ambassador to the United States wrote McCarran,

> I am in receipt of your letter of December 28th, regarding the project of sending a Basque to Spain to recruit some other Basque herders . . .
>
> The Immigration Law in Spain reads as follows: "The recruiting of emigrants and propaganda to foster emigration, as well as

the existence of agencies directed to that purpose, are prohibited, under penalties established by law. (Articles 34 to 36 of the Emigration Law of December 21, 1907, as amended)."

Since this is the legal situation you may easily understand that neither the Consul in New Orleans nor I can help in this respect.

As I see it the only chance would be to take up the matter with your Embassy in Madrid through your Department of State here, and approach the Spanish Government explaining the case to see whether, in view of the situation created by the war, something could be done. . . .[188]

It was at this point that the United States government began to relent on the question of importing Basque herders. Two articles in the *Elko Free Press* refer to special war-related exceptions to the immigration policy that were allowed in 1944:

100 Basque Sheepherders Sought in Mexico
To alleviate the serious shortage of sheepherders in Nevada, D. A. Hughes, secretary-treasurer of the Eastern Nevada Sheep Growers' Association, and Pete Elia, Elko county sheepman, left by plane from Salt Lake City last week for Mexico to secure 100 Basque herders.

Permission was granted by the immigration service, and approved by various governmental departments to recruit 100 Basque refugees now in Mexico and Latin American countries, who had escaped from Spain during the revolution.

Under the plan 100 Basque herders will be brought to Nevada under $500 bond each to guarantee their departure one year after the close of the war, as they are being admitted for the duration of the war and one year thereafter, only.

Four Basque herders have previously been brought into White Pine county and arrangements have been completed under which 11 others will be admitted shortly into this country . . . The four, who arrived last November, have proven efficient and dependable, working out so well under the plan that it paved the way for the more extensive program.

Hughes has had requests from Idaho, Wyoming, Montana and Utah to cooperate with sheepmen's associations of those states in locating the same class of labor for them.

Special passports were secured for Hughes and Elia from the United States state department through the efforts of Senator Pat McCarran of Nevada, who has been working in close cooperation with the sheepmen for some time on this program.

In Mexico City it will be necessary for Hughes and Elia to work through the American embassy, as all Basque herders chosen to enter this country must first be approved by the American counsel [*sic*] officials.[189]

Forty-two Basques, who left their native province of Navarra in northern Spain a few weeks ago, arrived in Reno yesterday morning to become sheepherders on Nevada ranges. . . . When the train carrying these Spanish highlanders arrived here, there were 17 sheep growers gathered at the Southern Pacific station to greet the new herders and take them to various sections of the state. The Basque contingent arrived shortly after 9 a.m., and the men left the cars, many of them wearing the characteristic small black beret. Accompanying the group was Martin Goni, former Reno resident and at one time a business associate of Joe Elcano in Reno, but who returned to his native Spain 10 years ago. . . .

Dealing directly with agents in Spain the latter represented by Mr. Goni, and with the approval of both the United States and Spanish governments, the project to obtain sheepherders to relieve the acute Nevada labor shortage began about two years ago. . . . Through Sen. Patrick A. McCarran, who understood the Nevada livestock situation, negotiations sponsored by the Nevada Sheep Owners association were completed recently and passage from Spain was secured for 42 men.

Each member of the Nevada Sheep Owners Asociation [sic] who needed skilled herders posted a bond and paid one-way fare from Spain to Reno for the number of herders he wanted. Ranchers say that the Basques probably will save Nevada's sheep industry since 20,000 breeding ewes a year for the past two years have been sold for lack of herders to care for them. Estimates reached the 100,000 figure on the number of sheep sold in the past year for the same reason.

The Basque herders will be paid the prevailing wage for the area to which they will be sent. However, it was noted that they were hired only on a temporary basis, their permits to remain in this country expiring in a few months. It was the opinion of most interested ranchers that blanket permits for extension of their stay would be applied for thirty days before the expiration date.[190]

In the mid-1940s some Nevada sheepmen formed an organization for the purpose of securing herders. Between 1943 and 1949 the Eastern Nevada Sheep Growers Association imported more than one hundred herders, most of whom entered the United States under the temporary visitors provisions of the Immigration Act of 1924. It is clear, however, that such measures were inadequate and fraught with problems. Congressional testimony in 1949 noted that between 1942 and 1948 there was a 40 percent decline of breeding ewes in the western states.[191] Related testimony claimed a "Fifty percent decline in sheep flocks due to excessive operation costs against returns and factory jobs [that] have drained the sheepherders from isolated mountain ranges."[192]

Despite such conditions, Congress was wary of modifying the immigration laws and regulations. A report regarding importation of additional herders stated, "The committee emphasizes that the provisions of the bill would operate within the framework of our present quota law, and would merely provide a limited priority for a relatively short time in order to meet a serious situation."[193]

The private Sheepherder Laws and the special exemptions failed to alleviate the growing labor crisis in the open range sheep industry. Sheepmen continued to pressure their representatives for substantial legislation. In 1950 a bill sponsored by Senator McCarran passed the Senate. As Public Law 587, McCarran's bill permitted 250 herders to be allowed into the country. In 1952, Public Law 307 allowed an additional 500 herders into the United States. The law also authorized the sheepmen to recruit the new herders through collective action. Three years earlier a small number of California sheepmen had formed the California Range Association,* with headquarters in Fresno, for the purpose of recruiting herders for each member. The president and board of directors were all Basque sheepmen. This organization was authorized by the National Woolgrowers Association and eleven individual (western) state woolgrowers associations to conduct recruitment of sheepherders in foreign areas under Public Law 307.

While Public Law 307 represented a victory of sorts for sheepmen, it was not without its problems. Under the legislation, herders were to be imported according to an Immigration Law of 1917, which required that federal, state, and local employment services provide clearances declaring a need for imported foreign labor. A final certification for the importation of each herder had to be provided to the Secretary of State by the United States Attorney General. It was no easy matter to import men under Public Law 307. Furthermore, the law failed to provide for continuity in any sheepherder importation program that might be established.

With respect to the latter problem, the sheepmen were urging passage of the McCarran-Walter Omnibus Immigration

---

*The subsequent analysis of the history of the California Range Association and its outgrowth, the Western Range Association, was reconstructed from interviews in 1971 with officials of the latter and a study of its files.

Bill, which was designed to allow up to 50 percent of any country's annual quota of immigrants to be filled by skilled persons needed for jobs that could not be filled in the United States. This legislation also contained a proviso for the temporary importation of sheepherders on contracts, if a special labor crisis should arise. The McCarran-Walter Omnibus Immigration Bill became law on June 27, 1952, when it was passed over the president's veto.

Initially, sheepmen turned to the possibility of importing sheepherders from Mexico, Argentina, Canada, and France. But the Spanish Basque remained in the greatest demand. The California Range Association did not itself recruit herders but, rather, implemented the requests of sheepmen who, when making application for a herder, had to supply the name of a man willing to come to the United States. Many Basque sheepmen supplied the names of their Old World kinsmen, or through such relatives obtained the names of other Basques desirous of coming to the United States. Non-Basque sheepmen were able to acquire such names by working through the Old World ties of Basque herders who were already in their employ. Consequently, most of the applications received by the California Range Association listed Vizcayan and Navarrese candidates.* The extent to which activation of personal ties served as a channel for further recruitment of sheepherders is seen in the fact that of a sample of 556 alphabetically ordered herder applications on file with the Association (of more than five thousand such cards) there were fifty sets of two brothers, nine sets of three brothers, six sets of four brothers, and one instance of five brothers applying.

In the summer of 1952 the president and secretary of the association visited the Spanish Basque provinces where, working through the United States consulate in Bilbao, they processed the standing backlog of sheepherder applications. By the following November, 280 men had arrived in the United States, and new arrivals were anticipated.

A major difficulty plagued the program at a *sub-rosa* level on both sides of the Atlantic. The sheepmen of the American West wanted Basque herders. However, they were required to gain clearances from local employment services before pro-

---

*One of the difficulties for the recruiters was the tendency of many sheepmen to refine their requests even further, insisting upon a Vizcayan rather than a Navarrese, or vice versa. In extreme cases the sponsor might specify the herder's village of origin.

ceeding to import men from Europe. In some cases, the employment services insisted upon filling the posts with American citizens, particularly members of the Indian and Mexican-American minority groups. If these men were qualified, they had to be hired before application could be made for foreign herders. Furthermore, in its dealings with the Spanish government, the California Range Association had to employ considerable care to stress that the program was designed to import Spanish and *not* necessarily Basque herders. Theoretically, any Spanish national could apply. But when non-Basque Spanish nationals made application, the association was hard pressed to place them. The sheepman making application retained a right of refusal, which many exercised.

The demand for sheepherders continued to outstrip the supply, prompting the sheepmen and their associations to pressure Congress for additional sheepherder legislation. In 1953 the 50 percent skilled labor provision of the McCarran-Walter Act was applied to Spanish sheepherders, but Spain's low quota of immigrants limited severely the number of men who could be imported under such arrangement. Then, too, there was concern that the sheepherders who had entered under the special legislation might ultimately have to be deducted from Spain's quota.

During the first three months of 1954 only twenty-five herders arrived in the United States, and impatience among the sheepmen increased. Senator McCarran introduced new legislation, Senate bill 2862, which was to allow 385 herders to enter without quota restrictions, and which would permit the immediate entry of those men whose applications were on file with the California Range Association. At the same time, Senator Herman Welker of Idaho introduced Senate bill 2074, which was designed to legalize the status of a number of herders who were in the country illegally. Both bills were passed in amended form. McCarran's attempt to increase the Spanish quota or have sheepherders removed from quota calculations was rejected, while some forty-four illegal entrants were denied permanent residence status, but were simply allowed to stay in the United States on the grounds that they were needed. Deportation proceedings against them were terminated—for the time being.

New legislation, introduced during 1955 to increase the herder importation program, died in committee. In 1956 two groups of herders, numbering 174 and 193 men respectively, were imported under special State Department permission. These groups were not cleared through state employment services. An additional 350 men arrived in the same year with the authorization of the employment services in the states where they were to work.

By November 1, 1956, the California Range Association could report that, under the special sheepherder importation legislation, it had processed 1,593 applications for herders and succeeded in bringing 898 men* to the United States during the previous five years. Four hundred and twelve applications were pending, awaiting new legislation, while 283 men had been rejected for one or a combination of the following reasons: (1) denial by the United States consul as unqualified for sheepherding, (2) failure to pass a medical examination, (3) application cancelled by the sheepman sponsor, and (4) the candidate changed his mind about working in the United States. The membership of the California Range Association had increased to 391 sheepmen in ten different states of the American West.

The sheepherder importation program had obviously come of age, but internally it was plagued with two major problems that had appeared during the mid-1950s. Some sheepmen failed to join and instead resorted to pirating herders after an association member went to the expense and bother of importing and training them. This could be done by simply offering higher wages, since there were no legal restrictions requiring that the herder remain with his employer. The second problem had to do with the fact that many men who entered under sheepherder contracts were walking away from their jobs and finding better paying work as dishwashers, miners, janitors, and construction laborers. The members of the California Range Association felt particularly vulnerable on this point, since the Immigration Service launched an investigation that threatened all future sheepherder legislation. The association therefore went out of its way to obtain information on the whereabouts of ex-herders and to cooperate with government officials, who initiated deportation procedures. At the same time, the California Range Association sought to alter the agreement under which herders entered the United States. Notably, it sought successfully in 1957 to have the herders' legal status in the country changed from permanent resident to one of temporary entry permit holder. Under the conditions of the permit, the herder had to

---

*While the majority of herders entered under the auspices of the California Range Association, other state woolgrowers associations could also contract for men. The Wyoming Woolgrowers Association did so on a modest scale. Through 1960, it had imported fifty-five herders.

remain in sheepherding or face immediate deportation. What is more, he had to remain in the employ of a member of the association.

This arrangement still did not resolve the question of possible pirating of herders among association members. The herder remained free to change employers within the membership. There were cases of desperate sheepmen going after one another's herders. And there was the added problem of simple inequities that developed when herders changed employment for legitimate reasons, like incompatibility between the herder and his fellow employees, the desire of the herder to work in an outfit where he had friends or relatives, or the sheepman's decision to reduce his herds and, hence, the number of herders. There was the added consideration of the seasonal fluctuations in the demand for herders. As early as 1953, the California Range Association monitored the flow of herders between California and other western states in response to the peak demand for labor during their respective lambing seasons.

All of the above eventualities threatened to introduce inequities into the association membership, because one man incurred the total initial expenses of importing a herder, from whom others stood to benefit without outlay. To combat this problem, the association instituted a practice in 1958 of assessing members a fifteen-dollar monthly administration charge for each herder in their employment that they had not originally sponsored. Conversely, each member was given a credit of thirty-six months for each man brought in under his sponsorship. If he lost a herder to another, he retained these credits, less the number of months the herder worked for him, and could apply them to employ another contract herder already in the United States and desirous of changing employers.

Prior to 1957 the individual sponsor paid an annual fee of twenty-five dollars for membership in the California Range Association. He then placed on deposit $561.10 to cover the herder's fare from Europe (an advance to be deducted from wages) and an additional $150 to cover the expenses incurred by the California Range Association in recruiting and processing a herder. The association refunded the fare but retained the fee if a sponsor's herder failed (for whatever reason) to enter the United States and the sponsor did not request a substitute. The fees were used to cover such expenses as the processing of paper work, medical examination of the herder, transportation taxes, and meals and lodging for herders who incurred unexpected delays en route to the United States. Any excess would accrue in trust for the members.*

As of April 1, 1957, the United States Immigration Service required that the return fare for a herder be placed on deposit. This was calculated at a minimum of $295 per man and was added to the sponsor's initial outlay. The funds were to be used as a guarantee for the return fare. The sponsor was allowed to deduct this sum from the herder's wages over the first six months of his employment. Furthermore, the herders were to receive the local prevailing wage but never less than $180 monthly plus room and board. The herders were to register with a Spanish consulate. The employer was required to register his herders for local and state unemployment benefits.

As a condition for allowing 200 additional herders to enter, the United States Immigration Service required that herders no longer be asked to repay the fare from their port of entry to their final destination. Under this new arrangement, the herders were to repay a total of $543.30, calculated to be the round-trip fare between Madrid and New York. Sponsors were also to carry a pro rata share of Workmen's Compensation and Employer's Liability Insurance premiums. This was set at $60 annually as the herder's "off-the-job" policy, while the sponsor paid $108 yearly for Workmen's Compensation.†

By 1957 sheepherder importation had been established on a more or less regularized basis. The program had found its own level, nearly approximating a balance between supply and demand. The question of deducting herders from the Spanish immigration quota had become all but academic, as the number of herders entering annually outstripped the entire Spanish quota. Furthermore, the fact that herders were on temporary entry permit labor contracts (set at three years) and were not therefore qualified to file for citizenship (eligibility for which required five years of continuous residence), placed Basque sheepherders in a special class. After 1957 the numbers and status of contract Basque sheepherders in the American West was determined less by new laws and more by direct negotiations between the California Range Association (which became the Western Range Association in 1960), the United States Immigration Service and Department of Labor, state employ-

---

*In 1964 the Association returned more than $100,000 to its membership.

†There has been little increased cost in this area since herders were paying sixty-six dollars annually for insurance in 1970.

ment services, and the Spanish government. At another level, the flow of sheepherders was affected by the year-to-year labor demands of the sheepmen of the American West and the willingness of Old World Basques to contract out their services.

After 1958 herder wages began to rise in response to pressures on both sides of the Atlantic. The economic recovery of Franco's Spain lessened the gap between wages paid to a herder in the American West and salaries within the Spanish economy. To some degree, the wage earning opportunities in Common Market countries competed with United States sheepmen for the services of young Basques. In 1958 over the protests of sheepmen, the California State Employment Service dictated that herder wages in that state be set at $200 monthly (plus room and board). In 1964 this was raised to $225 monthly, and owners were ordered to pay wages at regular intervals.* In the other states, minimum official wage levels remained at $180 until 1966 when, through negotiations with the Spanish government, minimum wages in all states were set at $230 plus room and board. In 1967 the Western Range Association adopted a sliding schedule of paying $230 monthly for first-year men, $240 monthly for second-year men, and $250 monthly for the more experienced herders. This scale was increased ten dollars in each category as of June 1, 1969.

By the late 1950s the contracts of many herders were expiring. As it takes considerable time to train a good herder, sheepmen were loathe to lose their best men. For their part, many herders were desirous of staying on in the American West for an additional period of time. In 1959 the Immigration Service began to grant extensions, but these were limited in June 1963 to two per herder for a maximum of ninety days each. On the other hand, during the early 1960s, the Immigration Service allowed contract herders to return for a second three-year stint, if they left the United States after completing their first contract (to rule out their becoming eligible to apply for citizenship). In the mid-1960s herders were allowed to return for a third stay, but always with enforced departure between contracts. In 1965 there were 1,283 herders in the American West under contract to the Western Range Association and an

---

*Some owners were accused of withholding wages until the end of the three-year contract, enjoying the use of the money without paying interest on it.

additional 97 herders who had been imported under the Wyoming Woolgrowers Sheepherder Procurement Proram.[194]

Passing of an Era

The open-range sheep industry of the American West is clearly ailing. Sheepmen are beset on all sides by pressures that portend the ultimate demise of their operations. Pressures from conservationists and government agencies are applied relentlessly to lower grazing allotments on the public lands. Both the Forest Service and the Bureau of Land Management regard such allotments as a privilege rather than a right. Both pursue a policy of reducing allotments whenever an outfit changes hands or comes up for renewal. In 1915, 7,284,000 sheep and goats* grazed upon the National Forests; only 2,095,000 continued to do so in 1970.[195] Table 7 shows sheep numbers at thirty-year intervals, from 1910 to 1971 for the three key states in our account—California, Nevada, and Idaho.

TABLE 7
DECLINE OF SHEEP NUMBERS IN TWENTIETH CENTURY

State	1910	1940	1971
California	2,417,477	1,707,422	1,264,000
Nevada	1,154,795	513,541	206,000
Idaho	3,010,478	1,372,415	773,000

Source: *Census*, 1910, V, p. 402; *Census*, 1940, *Agriculture*, III, p. 646; *Statistical Abstract*, 1971, p. 605.

The trend toward decline is even more striking when we consider that the 1910 figures were undoubtedly low. Tax assessments were based on such counts, so itinerant operators and settled sheepmen alike commonly declared less than actual numbers. There were few controls that permitted officials to dispute the sheepman's claim. It is also likely that many itinerant bands escaped the account altogether. The 1940 and 1971 figures were highly accurate, since grazing allotments on the public domain were calculated by them. Forest Service and Bureau of Land Management controls are too stringent for the sheepman to risk declaring fewer animals than he actually introduces on the public domain.

But more telling than federal controls are the endemic labor shortages and the depressed market for sheep products. In

---

*Goat numbers are slight; figure excludes animals under six months of age.

1970 sheepmen were beneficiaries of a federal price support on wool sales, which was calculated at 102.8 percent of sales. The producer received more from the subsidy than from the sale of the product itself. Yet despite such aid, producers have not been able to compete with foreign suppliers, who still undercut domestic growers in the mutton market. As for wool, the combination of foreign sources and the trend toward synthetic fabrics in the textile industry has all but devalued the product. In 1970 some domestic sheepmen simply refused to sell their wool clip, since bids from woolbuyers scarcely covered shearing costs.

In 1973 there was an upsurge in lamb prices and a renewed interest in wool. While this has alleviated the sheepmen's crisis, it is too early to tell if the effects will be long term. Even with the more favorable market, scarcely a single sheepman in the American West views the future of his business with unqualified optimism. Sheepmen see their access to the public lands as jeopardized. They also fear a labor shortage. It is hardly an exaggeration to claim that the sheepherder importation program was the salvation of the industry during the 1950s and 1960s, since it provided sorely needed labor that was both devoted and relatively inexpensive. However, even though wages are rising, it is increasingly difficult to renew the pool of herders. The future participation of the Basque sheepherder in the open-range sheep industry of the American West is in considerable doubt at the present time.

Through the program of herder importation, 5,495 applications for sheepherder contracts were issued between 1957 and June 1970.* A random sample of 520 sheepherder applications from the files of the Western Range Association showed that 227 were Vizcayans and 177 were Navarrese; there were 4 French Basques,† 16 Guipuzcoans, 1 Alavese, 89 non-Basque

---

*Not to be confused with the number of individuals who have entered the United States under this program. Some men have signed as many as four different contracts and hence are counted more than once in this total. In any one year the Association issues between three hundred and four hundred contracts.

†We stated earlier that there has been a marked twentieth-century reduction in the numbers and percentage of French Basque immigrants in the American West who are engaged in sheepherding. However, the above figure should not be regarded as a ratio of French Basque to Spanish Basque herders. Most French Basque immigrants who do engage in herding do not enter the United States contracted to the Western Range Association.

Spanish nationals, 4 Peruvians, and 2 Greeks. Under this program, Basque representation in the ethnic makeup of the
sheepherders of the American West probably surpassed 95
percent by 1965. Only in the extreme Southwest (Arizona and
New Mexico) does the Mexican and Navaho Indian sheepherder
seriously challenge Basque control of the occupation. Only in
some Mormon outfits of Utah does the Anglo sheepherder
appear with any regularity. In the remaining open-range sheep-
raising areas of the American West, it is a rare outfit that has a
non-Basque herder, and in such cases he is likely to be a Spanish
national under Western Range Association contract. In the case
of such Spanish nationals, the man is likely to be a recent arrival
working on his first contract. Few non-Basque Spaniards were
recruited prior to 1965.

Of particular interest is the presence of the Peruvian herder, not because of the numbers he currently represents but
because of what his presence may portend for the future. In the
last few years the members of the Western Range Association,
now numbering in the neighborhood of four hundred sheepmen,
have become increasingly dissatisfied with the recruitment of
herders from Europe. In the initial years of the program
economic conditions in Spain were such that the $180 monthly
that a man could earn on a sheepherder contract represented as
much as four or five times his earning power in Europe. In the
early 1950s the Spanish nation was just emerging from a period
of extreme political and economic ostracism. As a country with
an avowedly fascist government, Spain was excluded from
normal political and economic relations with her neighbors.
This meant that the Spanish populace continued to lead a Spar-
tan existence of deprivation and sacrifice when much of western
Europe was undergoing rapid economic recovery under the
Marshall Plan. As a consequence, the early years of the
sheepherder importation program provided the herders, whose
isolated existence in the mountains and desert of the American
West was especially conducive to saving, with the opportunity
to acquire what in Spanish *pesetas* was substantial capital. The
earliest herders typically returned home to invest in business
enterprises, or to redeem a mortgaged family farm. For their
part, the sheepmen received the services of eager young men
accustomed to a life of postwar privation and grateful for the
opportunity presented to them.

With the passage of time the Spanish economy has recovered with incredible rapidity. Inflation has soared, making life

more dear in Spain, but also inflating wages far in excess of the American rate of increase. Furthermore, Spain entered into more normalized relations with her neighbors. This triggered a tourist boom and provided Spanish migrants with access to Common Market economies. The net result has been to narrow the gap between the sheepherder wage scale in the American West and wages obtainable in Europe. Furthermore, the former austerity of life in Spain is being transformed into one of affluence dominated by the two technological symbols of twentieth-century life—the television set and the automobile. French Basques have been even less willing than their Spanish counterparts to enter the United States as herders.

Consequently, the sheepherder importation program has suffered in two respects. There is growing concern among the employers over the quality and attitude of the herders. With increasing frequency, contract herders are proving to be unable or unwilling to acclimate to the simple and socially isolating existence of the transhumant sheepherder. This is so despite the fact that living conditions in most sheep outfits are considerably improved over what they were even twenty years ago, and today's contract is more attractive. Second, it is becoming increasingly difficult to recruit Spanish nationals under any circumstances. This is particularly true of the Basque provinces, which currently enjoy the highest per capita income of any region of Spain.[196]

In 1970 an ex-sheepman from Elko County (Nevada), returned to the Basque country for one of his frequent visits. Over the years this man had recruited dozens of herders in his natal area of northern Navarra, both for his own outfit and for other Nevada sheepmen. On this particular trip he promised to find a herder for a friend who gave him $100 to cover expenses. The man in turn offered the $100 as a commission to a taxi driver in his village who had recruited more than one hundred herders from the surrounding villages. He was regarded by all as the best local middleman in such dealings. By the end of the summer he failed to turn up a single candidate within the general area that has provided the Western Range Association with its greatest number of Navarrese herders. The recruitment efforts of the Western Range Association remain focused upon Vizcaya and Navarra.

By 1965 the young men of the Basque country were considerably less enthusiastic at the prospect of signing a sheepherder contract. No longer did barroom conversations turn to the fortunes to be made in the American West. Those few men who continued to leave for the United States did so almost furtively and apologetically. The most common explanation given by men about to leave was that the life-style of the sheepherder would force them to save their money. This, rather than an expectation of unusually high wages, still provided some incentive.

Of lesser, but nevertheless relevant, importance in the declining interest in the American West was the negative stereotype of the returnee sheepherder that had developed throughout the Basque country. In the world view of local villagers, those who went out to the American West suffered modifications in their personalities. They were characterized as withdrawn and unable to carry out normal human intercourse for a period of time after their return. A common joking explanation given by villagers for such shyness was that "All sheep speak the same language—b−a−a−a−."

Another aspect of the behavior of herders also evoked criticism. Many of the returnees underwent a period of emotional release once back in the Basque country. The herder who spent his hours of solitude dreaming of his return and planning it down to the minutest detail would frequently undergo a difficult readjustment. Having departed with fixed mental images of family, friends, and village, and having recalled them hundreds of times, the reality of inevitable change was not always taken easily in stride. His exaggerated mental state of excitement and exuberance at the prospect of his return might lead to disappointment when his arrival at home was indeed welcomed, but in a lower emotional key. Many of the young returnees, in part out of a sense of frustration, seek out the company of fellow ex-herders. The tendency for men who share the common experience of having lived in the American West to appear together in the bars, at handball matches, and at local festivals in turn fosters the notion that they are in some fashion to be distinguished from other villagers.

The growing disenchantment with sheepherding, noticeable in the Basque country at the grass roots level throughout the late 1960s and early 1970s, is reinforced by the press. In 1969 the newspaper *La Voz de España* (San Sebastián) published an article entitled, "Odyssey of Our Basque Sheepherders in America," with the subtitle "A Seductive Adventure Which Quickly Becomes the Reality of a Hard Life in Constant Solitude."[197] Similarly, *El Correo Español* (Bilbao) in 1971 featured articles documenting the declining interest in sheepherding. One of the articles is entitled, "Only One of Every Hundred Basque Herders in the United States Makes His Fortune."[198]

Meanwhile, during the summer of 1966 the sheepherder importation program encountered a new difficulty on this side of the Atlantic. Trouble had been brewing in the form of the attempts to organize a labor union among the contract herders. The movement was spearheaded by a Basque priest who was under the auspices of the bishop of Idaho and whose duties included serving as chaplain to the Basque sheepherders. The efforts of Father Santos Recalde and a small group of dissident herders were opposed stringently by the sheepmen and their associations, who viewed the specter of collective bargaining in an industry already declining at an alarming rate as simply inadmissible. For their part, the organizers sought to publicize what they regarded to be the sheepherder's intolerably low wages and primitive living conditions. They published a newsletter* and declared their willingness to serve as a kind of clearing house for information concerning abuses of either the spirit or the letter of the sheepherder contracts. Finally, they resolved to create a legal fund to initiate court cases against the more abusive employers. They requested that each herder join the group at a cost of $100 per man.

In this effort they were singularly unsuccessful, if herder participation is taken as the yardstick. Of the many hundreds of contract herders in the American West at the time, only a handful joined the movement. In part, this might be attributed to the difficulty of communicating with many herders, but there was more involved. On the one hand, the organizers miscalculated the measure of discontent among the majority of herders. On the other, even the unhappy herders were reticent to take on their employers, given the facts that they were contract foreign laborers in a strange land and that they were primarily interested in returning to Europe with their substantial savings upon completion of a contract. This rapid turnover in the ranks of the sheepherders was itself a major stumbling block to the potential labor organizers.

The effort to organize sheepherders in the American West proved abortive. But nevertheless it influenced the future direction of the sheepherder importation program. In the summer of

---

*Entitled *El Pastor*, or "The Herder," and distributed out of Boise, Idaho, the newsletter was short-lived, since only five or six issues were published.

1966, Father Recalde returned to the Basque country on a visit. He proceeded to give out a number of scathing interviews in which he denounced the existing situation as inhumane and exploitative. The articles were published in influential Spanish newspapers.[199]

In the face of a budding public scandal, the Spanish government threatened to terminate the program if the contract was not modified considerably. Under the new contract, three benefits accrued to the herder. He was guaranteed two weeks annual paid vacation. No part of the sponsor's initial $640 deposit for transportation to the United States could be deducted from his wages, and only $225 of the $295 return trip deposit fund could be so deducted. Finally, upon completion of his three-year contract, he was to become eligible to apply for permanent residency in the United States under the sixth-preference category of the revised Immigration and Naturalization Act. This last point required a change in Department of Labor policy, which had heretofore been one of refusing to qualify "farm labor" for consideration under the sixth-preference designation of permanent resident.*

The improved economic conditions and affluent life-style of Europe, in combination with a degree of low-key social ostracism of returnee herders and an unfavorable Spanish press, have served to hamper seriously the European recruitment efforts of the sheepherder importation program. The abortive attempt at collective bargaining by the herders and the liberalization of the conditions of the contract that resulted from it have increased the anxieties of the sheepmen. In 1969, in the hope of developing a new source of herders, the Western Range Association named a representative in Peru who actively recruits and processes herders from that nation. By early 1972, approximately fifty Peruvian herders had entered the United States on contract. At the present writing the jury is still out on the Peruvian herder.

---

*Initially, there was considerable concern among sheepmen that the new arrangement might cause mass defections of sheepherders once their status was adjusted. However, a Western Range Association survey in 1969 of 533 herders adjusted to permanent resident status showed that 232 continued to work in the sheep industry, 97 had returned to Spain, the circumstances of 28 were unknown, whereas only 176 men, or 33 percent of the total, were residing in the United States with employment outside of the sheep industry.

The role of the Basques in the development of the open-range sheep industry of the American West is both long-standing and many-faceted. From the days when Domingo Amestoy signed sheep range leases with Abel Stearns to the formation of the Western Range Association, Basques have been prominent among the ranks of the western sheepmen. They have occupied every rung of the ownership ladder, from the most meager of itinerant operations to the largest landed sheep ranches employing dozens of sheepherders. In the figure of the sheepherder, the Basques have provided the backbone and heroic figure of the sheep industry; in the person of the itinerant operator, its anti-hero. More than any other ethnic group, the Basques have affected the history and development of America's open-range sheep industry.

CHAPTER SEVEN

Ethnicity Maintenance
Among Basque-Americans

*Gizon batek bere herritik kanpora Indietara edo bertze lekhu urrun
batetara partitzen denean, eta oraiño bere herriko agerrian,
komarketan eta terminoetan denean, maiz behatzen du gibelat,
bere herriko mendietarat. Baiña aitzina iraganez gero, bere
herria eta herriko lurrak bistatik galduz gero, itzultzen da
bertze alderat, ioan behar duen eta dohan lekhu hartarat:
eta han aldiz, bere begiak, eta gogoa ere ibentzentu.*

*(When a man leaves his country for the Indies or some distant land,
while he is yet within sight of his town or still within its region, he looks
back frequently at the mountains of his homeland. But as
he goes forth, once he is beyond the view of his town and its
surroundings, he adjusts his thoughts to his country of
destination, fixing his gaze upon it and his will as well.)*

From the book Gero, *a devotional work published in 1643 by Pedro de
Axular and one of the earliest publications in the
Basque language.*[1]

Basques were among the first Europeans to emigrate to the Americas, and some five centuries later the process continues. We have seen that the emigrants' New World destinations were varied and subject to change. By now, the historical roots of the major New World Basque colonies are at least several generations deep. This raises the crucial question of the extent to which subsequent generations of Basque-Americans continue to express their ethnic identity. In chapter 3 we considered some of the ethnic institutions that developed in the several Basque colonies of Latin America. In the present chapter we shall consider Basque ethnicity maintenance in the American West.

Basques were present in California when the area was annexed by the United States in 1848; today Old World Basques and their descendants residing in the American West number at least fifty thousand persons.

This figure is nothing more than a rough estimate. It is both one of the ironies and the frustrations of the present study that it is impossible to determine the true magnitude of the population that constitutes our subject matter. Basques in the United States are simply never censused as such. There is also the problem of interpretation. After more than a century of immigration into the American West, and some intermarriage, the question of who is a Basque raises legitimate definitional problems. In the following discussion of ethnic institutions we examine aspects of the lives of those who consider themselves to be Basques and whose behavior is thereby affected in some fashion. However, not all of those with the requisite biological credentials continue to participate in the attendant ethnic heritage. If the definition of "Basque" requires that both of one's parents were biologically Basque and that one continues to self-identify with the ethnic heritage it is possible to reduce considerably the estimated numbers of Basque-Americans. Employing these criteria in the early 1950s, Gachiteguy, in his role as chaplain to the French Basque colony of the American West, set the combined Basque populations of Nevada and California at thirty-one hundred persons.[2] According to his calculation, there were several hundred additional Basques in Arizona, Wyoming, Colorado, New Mexico, Utah, and Montana. He failed to deal with the Pacific Northwest, but it seems clear that even if he had, this narrowest of definitions of Basques in the United States would have produced a total figure in the 1950s* of less than ten thousand persons.

Despite their relatively sparse numbers and their dispersion over a tremendous geographical area, Basque-Americans have demonstrated tenacity in maintaining their ethnic identity. Over the course of the past 120 years of western history, they have developed a number of practices or mechanisms that both express and reinforce their ethnic identity. Some, such as marital patterns and home life, are private and little noticed by their neighbors. Others, like the Basque hotels and festivals, are more public and contribute directly to the accepted stereotype of the Basques. Each Basque ethnic practice and institution† has a history and set of functions.

POPULATION

A considerable percentage of mid-nineteenth century Basque immigrants to the United States came from Latin America. By the latter third of the century, this was no longer the case. Only 3 of the 131 individuals whose biographies were published by Sol Silen in 1917 resided in Latin America prior to entering the United States.‡ There were not many instances of individuals who had resided personally in both Latin America and the American West; but it was increasingly common to find sets of siblings whose life experiences encompassed both worlds. Silen noted that Juan Archabal of Boise was one of six siblings, two of whom were South American businessmen, while the remainder lived in the Basque country.[4] Isidro

---

*It should be noted that Gachiteguy traveled the American West during the period when Basque immigration (particularly Spanish Basque) had been reduced severely for three decades by restrictive legislation. Since his stay, the sheepherder importation program, particularly in its early years and in the 1970s with the recent concessions of permanent residency, has provided renewed permanent settlement of Old World-born Basques.

†See Appendix Seven for a list of Basque ethnic institutions in communities of the American West.

‡A curious case of the American West providing a Basque immigrant *for* Latin America was reported in the April 23, 1913, issue of *The Humboldt Star:*

Joseph Ugarizza, who lived at McDermitt twenty years ago, when he was a large sheep owner, returned to Winnemucca a few days ago to visit his old home. . . . After leaving Humboldt county he went to Cuba and bought a sugar plantation. He has three sons living at McDermitt. . . .[3]

Madarieta, one of eight children, had five siblings in South America and two others in the Basque country;[5] Gervasio Mendiola had three siblings in South America and four others in the Basque area.[6]

Consequently, by the end of the nineteenth century the American West was established in its own right as a possible destination for the Old World Basque emigrant. Unlike the three families mentioned above, many families provided more than one emigrant to North America.[7] Silen reported that Miguel Gabica was one of six siblings residing in Idaho, while only a single sister remained in the Basque country. Of the four siblings of Bonifacio Bermensolo, two resided in Idaho and two in Europe.[8] Joaquín Solosabal had three siblings in Boise and two others in the Basque country.[9] Juan Madarieta of Elko had four siblings in Nevada and six in Europe.[10] Ignacio Arrascada of Winnemucca had four siblings in Nevada, one in California, one in South America, and one in the Basque country,[11] while Anacleto Achabal of McDermitt had seven siblings in Oregon and two in Europe.[12]

The immigration of several siblings to the same region of the American West is the most extreme expression of a strong tendency for Old World ties—family, village, and region—to be transferred overseas. In the Monterey-San Francisco area of California, there were kinship ties among the earliest Basque families—the Aguirres, the Arburuas, the Lugeas, the Yparraguirres, and many were from the one Navarrese village of Echalar. The July 15, 1893, issue of *California'ko Eskual Herria* identified many of the Basque settlers of Tehachapi as natives of the French Basque village of Banca.[13] To say that Vizcayans as such settled northern Nevada, eastern Oregon, and southern Idaho is not entirely accurate. In fact, the immigrants came primarily from a small area of that province—communities situated within a narrow belt of land running along the seacoast and bounded by Bermeo on the west and Ondárroa to the east (a straight-line distance of about thirty kilometers) and seldom penetrating inland for more than about twenty kilometers. Of the 215 Vizcayans* listed in Silen's work, there

---

*Silen's work deals with Vizcayans primarily, although he does list places of origin for some fourteen Guipuzcoans, eleven Navarrese, six French Basques, and one Alavese. It should be noted that Silen probably contacted many of his interviewees through personal referrals. There are several cases of two or more siblings appearing in his book. However, in other instances, the interviewee was the only one of several siblings residing in the American West to be included in the work.

is no indication of natal village for 11; 20 were from areas (generally near Bilbao) that fall outside of the above delineation, and 184, or fully 85 percent of the total, were from within the area. The map locates the villages in question, while table 8 lists numbers of emigrants from each village.

It may be noted that there is considerable further clustering within the delineated area. The five-village coastal cluster of Ea, Bedarona, Ispáster, Lequeitio, and Mendeja provided eighty-two emigrants, 44 percent of the sample. The drainage of the Artibay River, which includes Ondárroa, Berriatúa, Marquina, and Bolívar, provided twenty-seven men, 15 percent of the total. A third nucleus of twenty-eight emigrants, also approximately 15 percent of the total, emerged from the contiguous villages of Murélaga, Arbácegui, Navárniz, Guizaburuaga, and Amoroto. That they constituted a "natural" unit with shared interests is seen by the fact that their parish priests in the early 1960s jointly published a newspaper entitled *Zeutzat* (or "For You") that was designed to provide emigrants from the area with the intimate details of local life (e.g., births, deaths, marriages, sporting events, and local gossip). The paper was written primarily for the recently emigrated sheepherders. Of 227 Vizcayans in a sample of Western Range Association sheepherder applications, 208 (over 90 percent) were from the villages listed in table 8.

Just as it is necessary to avoid the overgeneralization that Vizcayans settled a wide swath in Nevada, Oregon, and Idaho, it would also be misleading to state that the colony in Buffalo, Wyoming, is French Basque. There is a great deal of evidence concerning the founding of this colony.* As early as 1910, the French Basque scholar Pierre Lhande stressed the importance of Jean Esponda, known as "Manech," in the colony's creation.[14] Esponda was born in St.-Etienne-de-Baigorry (Basse Navarre) in 1868. The common denominator of the Basque colony in Buffalo was Esponda himself, not an abstract category like "French Basque." Esponda's father had worked many years in the *saladeros* of South America and tried to convince young

---

*The sketch of the history of the Basques in Buffalo is derived (where not otherwise indicated) from personal interviews in the community and from unpublished biographical sketches of Jean B. Esponda, Martin Falxa, Peter Harriet, and John Camino, which were written for volume 4 of Bartlett's *History of Wyoming*. This volume was to appear in 1919, but its publication was cancelled after all typesetting was completed. A copy is available on microfilm at the Wyoming State Archives and Historical Department, Cheyenne.

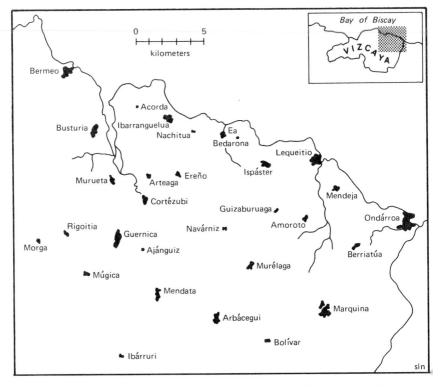

Communities of northeastern Vizcaya that provided the majority
of Vizcayan emigrants to the American West (see table 8).

TABLE 8

VILLAGE OF ORIGIN FOR 184 VIZCAYANS RESIDING IN
NEVADA, OREGON, AND IDAHO BY 1916

Name of Village	Number of Immigrants
Ispáster	29
Lequeitio	26
Ea	15
Marquina	14
Berriatúa	8
Guizaburuaga	8
Mendeja	6
Bedarona	6
Amoroto	6
Ereño	6
Arteaga	5
Mújica	5
Ibárruri	5
Navárniz	5
Nachitua	5
Murélaga	5
Arbácegui	4
Bolívar	4
Mendata	3
Rigoitia	3
Guernica	3
Ajánguiz	2
Morga	2
Cortézubi	2
Acorda	2
Busturia, Bermeo, Ibarrenguelua, Ondárroa, and Murueta	1 each

Source: Silen, 1917.

Jean that he should seek his fortune there. Instead, the young man struck out for California at the age of nineteen, and in 1888 he was herding sheep on the Mojave Desert for Juan Burubeltz of Bakersfield (Burubeltz was himself from the village of Urepel, which is near Esponda's home town).

Within a few years Esponda pooled his savings with those of three other men in order to purchase 5,000 sheep. Each became an itinerant operator in charge of a band of 1,250 animals. In 1896 Jean sold his sheep, then numbering 5,020. He entered the employ of their purchaser, the enormous Ardizzi and Olcese outfit of Bakersfield, and became sheep foreman of one of their ranches. He made at least one trip to New Mexico in order to sell sheep. He also owned milk cows for a time.

In 1902 he sold his private interests and left for the Basque country. After a six-month stay he returned to the United States. It was apparently while traveling westward on the train that he chanced to meet one of the owners of the Healy and Patterson Sheep Company of Buffalo, Wyoming (the largest existing sheep ranch in the northern part of that state). Jean was offered employment as a herder, which he accepted. As early as 1903 he was attracting other Basques to the employ of Healy and Patterson.[15] He went north to Montana for a year but returned in 1904 to Buffalo. That same year he was joined by a brother and two cousins, and the four men formed a partnership, purchasing lands as well as stock. Within three years the partnership was dissolved, and Jean began making a series of sheep and land purchases, which, by 1919, converted his outfit into one of the prominent sheep operations in Wyoming, totaling at times as many as twenty-five thousand head.

It is interesting to note that the Basques of Buffalo have been, from the outset, land-oriented, a fact that makes their early pattern of settlement unique when compared to that of Basques of other areas. Several factors help to explain this pattern. The movement of Basques into Buffalo was relatively late (1902) and postdates the first efforts at federal closure of the public domain to sheep interests. Jean Esponda, the first Basque in Buffalo, was thoroughly conversant with the tribulations of the itinerant operators in one of the most overcrowded open-range sheep areas—southeastern California. Finally, Esponda had considerable experience in the American West, some seventeen years, prior to making his first Wyoming land purchase in 1904. The fact that Esponda had returned recently from the Old Country suggests that he had experienced that critical shift in personal outlook wherein the New World comes to represent both "home" and "future," while the Old World becomes a cherished memory and possibly a sanctuary reserved for visiting only.

The arrival of new Basque immigrants in Buffalo between 1902 and 1920 can, in most cases, be linked directly or indirectly to the presence of Jean Esponda. Shortly after he began working for Healy and Patterson, another Basque, Peter Harriet, was employed by the firm. In 1907 Peter married Catherine Esponda (Jean's daughter). Martin Falxa was employed as a herder in this period by the same Healy and Patterson firm. Another early Basque arrival in Buffalo was John Camino, who first worked for Healy and Patterson and then entered partnership with Jean Esponda for a time. In 1914, Camino married Marie Harriet, Peter's sister. Bernard Marton came to Buffalo in 1914, where he was employed as a herder by Jean Esponda. In 1916 he entered partnership with Simon Harriet in their own sheep business.[16] All of these men became prominent northern Wyoming sheep ranchers and in turn helped other Basques to migrate to the Buffalo area. In this manner, the bases of the Buffalo Basque colony were established by an interlacing of kinship, marriage, and business ties between four or five prominent families. A recent study of the colony shows that of thirty-nine Basque families currently residing in Buffalo, thirty-four trace their Old World origin to villages that are located within eight miles of Jean Esponda's natal village of St.-Etienne-de-Baigorry.[17] The predominance of persons from the village of Arneguy, comprising over 30 percent of the Buffalo colony in the early 1950s and a considerably larger percentage prior to World War II, caused the observer Gachiteguy to state, "the Basque colony of Buffalo has been a colony of Arneguy."[18] In the same vein he finds that the majority of Basse Navarrese in the Fresno area are from the village of Esterençuby[19] and that at one time many Souletins resided in San Francisco where they were employed in the laundry business.[20]

The foregoing examples of the "chain migration" of Basques along kinship and Old World regional lines raises a key definitional problem for the present study. In a very real sense it is an artifice of the investigator to speak in terms of such a sweeping generalization as "Basques of the American West." For the Basques themselves, this is a vague secondary or tertiary feature in each man's concept of the ethnic self. Basque-Americans view the Basque population of the American West as clearly divided into two broad categories—French Basques and Navarrese of California, western Nevada, Arizona, New Mexico, Colorado, Wyoming, and Montana, and the Vizcayans of northern Nevada, eastern Oregon, and southern Idaho.

We have seen that the formation of the two colonies corresponds to distinct periods of Basque immigration into the American West. French Basques and Navarrese gained a foothold in southern California in the 1850s. By the 1860s and 1870s they were spreading throughout California and into western and northern Nevada. The California colony also provided the Basques who formed small colonies in Arizona, New

Mexico, Colorado, Wyoming, and Montana. Conversely, the entry of Vizcayans was a later movement, becoming noticeable in the 1880s. It was concentrated in northern Nevada (where Vizcayans quickly eclipsed French Basques and Navarrese as the most representative element in the local Basque populace), eastern Oregon, and southern Idaho.

Gachiteguy found that by the 1950s, 52.4 percent of California Basques were from Basse Navarre and 36.6 percent from Navarra, while only 5.5 percent were from Vizcaya, 2.6 percent from Labourd, 1.7 percent from Guipúzcoa, 1 percent from Soule and 0.2 percent from Alava.[21] The transitional nature of the Nevada colony was evident in the fact that 48.8 percent of the Nevada Basques in the Gachiteguy sample were from Vizcaya, 36.1 percent were from Basse Navarre, 12 percent from Navarra, 2.5 percent from Labourd and 0.6 percent from Soule.[22] While published figures are unavailable, it is clear that the Vizcayans in the Basque populations of Idaho and Oregon represent all but 1 or 2 percent of the total.

There is ample evidence to indicate that well before the Vizcayan colony emerged in the Great Basin there was a substantial French Basque and Navarrese colony in California. By the mid-1880s it was sufficiently developed to encourage Martin Biscailuz, an American-born attorney of Los Angeles, to found the Basque-language newspaper *Escualdun Gazeta*. By his estimate, there were at that time two thousand Basques residing in the Los Angeles area alone.[23]* However, the effort proved premature, and it was not until the following decade that a new Basque newspaper, *California'ko Eskual Herria*, became successful.

---

*Martin Biscailuz was a key figure in both the southern California Basque colony and wider Los Angeles society. Born in California, educated in Europe and fluent in the Basque language, he had a virtual monopoly on the legal business of the Basques.[24] He reportedly amassed a personal fortune of $100,000 while still a young man.[25] His son, Eugene Warren Biscailuz, who later became sheriff of Los Angeles County, was a personality in his own right. His life was even made the subject of a book-length biography.[26]

The career of Martin Biscailuz had its tragic side as well. When the millionaire Simon Oxarart died in 1886, it was rumored in the Basque colony that Biscailuz, as lawyer of the estate, had mishandled some seventy-five thousand dollars. The accuracy of the rumor notwithstanding, it cost him his Basque trade. By the mid-1890s, he was in desperate straits and prone to excessive drinking.[27] In the space of a few months, he was tried twice for defrauding clients and served a short prison sentence.[28] Goytino, as editor of *California'ko Eskual Herria*, berated Biscailuz mercilessly for being a scandalous representative of the Basque community.[29]

The pages of *California'ko Eskual Herria* reflect the maturity of the California Basque colony in a variety of ways. Several issues of the paper carried a debate concerning the feasibility of importing a Basque chaplain to minister to the state's Basque population, estimated at five thousand persons.[30]

José Goytino, the newspaper's editor, was concerned that the Basque language might die out in the California colony. He editorialized on the importance of retaining it as the chief means of expressing Basque ethnic loyalties.[31] To this end Goytino frequently ran Basque verses, famous ones from the folk traditions of the Basque country and others that were composed by his readers and, occasionally, by himself.

In many other respects the newspaper reflected the aging of the California colony. The October 7, 1893, issue reports the banquet held by the San Francisco Basques to honor the six forty-niners in their midst (including both José Aguirre and his wife).[32] There were two Basque-American attorneys in the state. Martin Biscailuz practiced in Los Angeles.[33] Orel M. Goldarecena, reputed to know French, Spanish, Portuguese, Italian, and Basque in addition to English, had his offices in San Francisco.[34] Advertisements listed a Basque beverage distributor in Los Angeles,[35] as well as a pharmacist[36] and doctor[37] in that city. A private Catholic school, St. Vincent's College of Los Angeles, advertised for Basque students.[38] In 1895, the paper announced a tour back to the Basque country, organized by Goytino.[39]

At the same time *California'ko Eskual Herria* almost totally ignored the growing Vizcayan colony to the north. There were advertisements for steamship departures from Montevideo,[40] suggesting that the paper circulated in the Río de la Plata area, and news from Mexico was a regular feature. However, news from northern Nevada and southern Idaho was notably lacking, except when it involved persons of French Basque origin[41] or with California ties.[42]

For the Basques themselves the distinction between "California Basques" and "Idaho Basques" is conceptually important. Historically, however, there have been at least three factors that promoted mingling of the French Basque-Navarrese and the Vizcayans.

First is the movement of some herders back and forth annually between California and the inland states, responding to the fact that the demand for herders in the two areas peaks at different times of the year (relating to differences in the lambing cycle). This movement of herders has partially modified the fairly rigid subethnic distinctions by area in the original settlement pattern of Basques in the American West.

Second, since the turn of the present century, but particularly in the last twenty years, the majority of Basque herders have been Spanish nationals. In the 1950s when herders were plentiful, most of the Navarrese contracted went to California and the traditional areas of French Basque-Navarrese settlement, and the majority of Vizcayans worked in northern Nevada and Idaho. However, as the supply of young men willing to come to the American West dwindled, ranchers became more willing to accept the first available man. In this fashion, a number of Vizcayans went directly to California under contract to the Western Range Association.

Finally, in recent years there has been a trend for herders desirous of leaving the sheep industry to move to large cities. In the greater Los Angeles area, Basques have become involved in the dairy industry, and there is considerable demand for young Basque workers as milkers. In the San Francisco Bay area Basques have become established as one of the major ethnic groups in gardening. While French Basques and Navarrese traditionally controlled both the dairying and gardening, Vizcayans with herding experience in the interior states have increasingly made their way to the California cities.

Consequently, the two substantial Basque colonies have become intermingled to some extent. There is a light sprinkling of Vizcayans in California, and one finds an occasional French Basque or Navarrese in northern Nevada. There are also transitional areas like the Reno colony, where there is substantial representation of the several Old World regions in the local Basque population. Recently, there has been a conscious attempt to increase rapport between the two greater colonies. In 1972 a meeting was held in Reno at which representatives of several Basque clubs agreed to initiate a federation called the "North American Basque Organizations, Incorporated." The first elected president was from the Boise colony, and the vice-president represented the San Francisco club. Nevertheless, the indicated geographical division remain basic features of the world view of the Basques of the United States.

Many incidents demonstrate the extent to which the two Basque colonies of the American West are ignorant of each other's activities. For instance, an effort was begun to renovate or construct one or more Basque handball courts in the Boise area. All of the former ones had fallen into disuse. Enthusiasm increased when the organizers learned that there might be the possibility of inter-sectional competition, since the French Basques of California had their own federation of handball players. The Boise Basques had been unaware of the existence of organized Basque handball competition in California.

Furthermore, there is transfer to the New World context of the perceived regional characterological distinctions among Old World Basques (see chapter 1). To a degree this has introduced an axis of animosity into group life that is manifested in a certain mutual aloofness and frequent double-edged joking between French Basques and Vizcayans. In the transitional communities with sizeable contingents of both colonies, this axis poses a low-key, yet discernible, threat of schism in local Basque clubs or dance groups. By way of illustration, one social club dominated by Vizcayans debated at length the question of the colors to be employed in the costumes of its dance group. The small French Basque contingent, although finally outvoted, resisted the red and white folk costume characteristic of Vizcaya in favor of the green and black common in the French Basque area. A social club dominated by French Basques overruled its Vizcayan minority and refused to sponsor a local performance of a Vizcayan Basque ballet on its American tour.

In most features of their social life the activities of the two greater Basque colonies remain mutually exclusive. Each has a history of founding its own hotel, organizing its own network of sporting events and festivals, importing its own Basque chaplains, organizing its own clubs and dance groups, and arranging its own charter flights to the Basque country. It is significant that there are two book-length studies of American Basques, each of which purports in its title to be a general work (Silen, *La Historia de los Vascongados en el Oeste Americano* and Gachiteguy, *Les Basques dans l'ouest Americain*). Yet each is narrowly sectarian. Few French Basques and Navarrese are represented in the Silen work, and Gachiteguy ignores almost entirely the Vizcayans of Oregon and Idaho.

A definition of the Basque population of the American West must also take account of what has become its quasi membership. There has been a long-standing relationship between Basques, the Béarnais French, and the *montañés* Spaniards (both from regions that border on the Basque country). In our treatment of Latin America we indicated that

Basques, Béarnais French, and *montañeses* at times traveled in the same circles, an arrangement that carried over into the American West.

We have already noted the simultaneous presence of Basque and Béarnais sheepmen in the sheep transhumance of southern California. The biographies of Béarnais sheepmen like Peter Arbios of Stockton,[43] Prosper Bergon of Fresno,[44] Pierre Sartiat of Kern County,[45] or John Cassou of Orange County[46] underscore the similarity in the life experiences of the Béarnais French and the Basques. An 1893 issue of *California'ko Eskual Herria* stated that the Basques and Béarnais French of Tehachapi planned to hold a joint festival, complete with handball competition.[47] In tracing the subsequent movement of Basques into other areas of the American West, one is likely to encounter Béarnais.

Gachiteguy also notes that in the older French Basque colonies of the American West, Dauphinois French are frequently found in association with the Basques. Like the Béarnais, the Dauphinois were prone to engage in the livestock business and found hotels patronized by the Basques.[48]

Similarly, a few *montañés* Spaniards entered California and became involved with Basques. The most outstanding figure is that of Faustino Noriega of Santander, who became the sheep foreman of Miller and Lux in 1882 and employed many Basque herders. He later erected the Hotel Pyrenees in Bakersfield as the partner of the Basque Fernando Etcheverry.

There were also occasional marriages between Basques and Béarnais, Dauphinois, or *montañeses*. The Basque Matias Erro, a widower, married a Béarnais widow, Marie Camy, in 1913.[49] In 1893 Faustino Noriega married Louise Inda, a French Basque.[50] At present one occasionally encounters persons of Béarnais, Dauphinois, or *montañés* descent in the American West who regard themselves as Basques and whose claim, for most purposes, is not challenged by those with stronger Basque genealogical credentials.

Finally, we should mention the Basque colonies of the New York City and Miami areas. Throughout the last three decades of the nineteenth century, after the transcontinental railway began service, New York City became the first New World destination of Basque immigrants and the prime way-station on their journey to the American West. By at least as early as the 1890s Basque-owned boarding houses, succeeded by regular hotels and a travel agency, were established in New

York City to service the traffic. By the first decade of the twentieth century this colony had acquired a life of its own, as some immigrants who arrived with the intention of continuing on westward were offered employment in New York and remained. In turn, they provided security, advice, and sometimes advance employment to Old World kinsmen or fellow villagers.

Elderly informants estimate that by 1920 there might have been as many as eight to ten thousand Basques residing in New York City, with most concentrated in a thirty-square-block area around Cherry Street. The occupations of members of the colony ranged from manual laborers to well-to-do manufacturers. At different periods groups of Basques based initially in the New York City area have found employment in the Pennsylvania mines and on the New Jersey docks.

In 1913 the New York City Basque colony formed an organization called the Vasco-American Benevolent Association, Inc. Each year the club sponsored two or three open air picnics in Olmen Park, where it fielded a soccer squad that played against the team of the Gallegan center. Informants note that as many as five or six thousand persons attended these picnics. In New York City today, both the *Centro Vasco* and the *Centro Gallego* have a number of New York-born members of Basque-Gallegan descent.

In 1925 the Basque organization purchased its own building, renting out the ground floor to a tailoring firm and installing a bar and ball court on the second floor. The latter also served as a dance hall. At that time the New York *Centro Vasco* had approximately seven hundred members. In later years United States governmental restrictions on immigration blocked further entries of legal immigrants (although the illegal entries of Basque seamen jumping ship in the New York port continued), and the membership of the New York City colony eroded. In 1926 a splinter group of political activists, unsuccessful in their attempts to convince the club to engage in pro-Basque nationalist political action, formed their own club in Brooklyn, called *Aberria*. The club closed in 1938.

In 1941 the *Centro Vasco* incorporated as a mutual aid society. Originally each member paid fifty cents monthly, then one dollar, and at present three dollars. In return he receives assistance when ill (today, a maximum of twenty-three dollars weekly). But above all the society pays funeral expenses up to $500, provides the announcements, and buys a wreath of flowers. Each year, the New York City colony organizes an *Aberri*

Eguna ("Day of the Fatherland") celebration to commemorate the declaration of the political autonomy of the Basques.

An urban renewal project demolished the building of the *Centro Vasco*, and the organization was forced to seek new quarters. Because of the thinning of its membership, it rented rather than purchased a new locale. At present the *Centro Vasco* is located in the heart of New York City's Chinatown. Its quarters are modest, consisting of a small bar and banquet room. Its membership has been reduced to 237 families. Each afternoon the bar opens to the few elderly men who come to play cards, and once monthly there is a no-host banquet for the membership. The young people have a Basque folk dance group.

The second eastern United States focus of Basque settlement is in Florida. For the past several decades professional *jai alai* players have been contracted in the Basque country for the Florida courts. Occasionally a player has married and settled in the area, thereby providing the initial base for a growing Florida colony. The numbers of Basques in the state increased manyfold with Fidel Castro's rise to power in Cuba. Basques were well represented in the ranks of the entrepreneurs and professionals who abandoned the island.

ENDOGAMY AND KINSHIP

The most characteristic Basque immigrant into the American West was the young single male. Of the 104 Old World-born males in the California biographies for whom we have information concerning their age on entry, 4 entered prior to their fifteenth birthday, 49, or almost half, entered between the ages of fifteen and twenty, 39 were between twenty-one and twenty-five, only 10 were over twenty-five upon their arrival, and none was over thirty-five. Most were single upon entering, yet of the 110 males in the California sample, 104 subsequently married.*

A similar analysis of the biographies in the Silen account shows that, of 116 males for whom age at United States entry is provided, 17 were under fifteen, 62 were between the ages of

---

*This should not be taken as an accurate indicator of the rate of bachelorhood among Basques, which was considerable. We again remind the reader that in order to be included in the history books a person had to be a "substantial citizen" in many ways, one of which was being the father of a family.

fifteen and twenty, 29 were twenty-one to twenty-five, 8 were over twenty-five, and only one was over thirty. Silen provides evidence that all but 28 eventually married.*

A consideration of the marriage choices of both Old World-born Basques and the subsequent generations of Basque-Americans is illuminating on three counts: 1) the extent to which Basques were endogamous is one indicator of their relations with the wider non-Basque populace, 2) in marriages in which both partners were Basque, the extent to which choices were made within one's subethnic category provides an additional demonstration or denial of the validity of our subdividing of the total Basque population of the American West, and 3) the patterning of the marriage choices of subsequent generations of American-born Basques is one indicator of the extent of Basque assimilation into the wider American populace.

In the California sample 9 of the 10 *Vascongado* (Vizcaya and Guipúzcoa) male immigrants married, and only 2 married non-Basques. In the remaining 7 marriages all of the spouses were *Vascongadas*! Of the 40 male Navarrese immigrants, 37 were married. Of this total, only 1 married a non-Basque, 2 married *Vascongadas*, 7 married French Basque girls, while 27 of the 37 married Navarrese. In the case of the 58 married French Basque males, 8 had married non-Basques, 2 had married *Vascongadas*, 10 were married to Navarrese, and 38 were married to French Basque girls. Clearly, marital patterns reinforced Basque exclusivity in the immigrant generation, since there were 91 Basque-to-Basque marriages out of a total of 104; moreover, these marriages reinforced the persistence of Old World regional distinctions.

Silen's sketches from southeastern Oregon, northern Nevada, and southern Idaho provide evidence of the same strong tendency for immigrant Basques to marry not only within their group, but also within their subethnic category. Of the 96 married Vizcayan males for whom Silen provides data on the ethnic background of the spouses, 94 married Vizcayan or Guipuzcoan girls, 1 married a Navarrese, and 1 married a

---

*It is likely that the figure of twenty-eight bachelors should be reduced considerably since: 1) Silen was not always careful to mention marital status and 2) he collected his biographies in 1917, when the Idaho Basque colony was barely out of its formative stage. Consequently, in contrast to our sample of California biographies, Silen interviewed young persons who were relative newcomers, many of whom subsequently married.

non-Basque. In the remaining 5 cases there are 2 Navarrese-to-Navarrese marriages, 2 Navarrese-to-French Basque marriages, and 1 French Basque-to-French Basque marriage.

But what of the second generation? In a sample of 39 marriages involving California-born Basques, 14 married Old World-born persons of Basque descent, 2 married New World-born persons of Basque descent, and 23 married non-Basques. These statistics may be interpreted as simultaneously reflecting *both* reinforcement and disintegration of Basque endogamy. On the one hand, 14 New World-born persons (including 5 girls) married Old World persons. This would indicate that Basques were maintaining mutual ties insofar as they were in a position to make the acquaintances of new arrivals from the Old World that might ultimately culminate in marriage. Sather notes that in every such case in Shoshone (Idaho) the girl was the daughter of a Basque hotel owner and hence raised in a highly ethnic home environment.[51] On the other hand, the fact that considerably more than half of those persons sampled married non-Basques reflects the progressive Americanization and growing involvement over time of (at least some) Basques in their local community.

Gachiteguy provides more recent figures (the early 1950s) and a much larger sample of marital choices of the Basques of California and Nevada. Of a total of 500 California Basque marriages, in 70.2 percent both partners were Old World-born Basques (region of origin unspecified), 16.4 percent involved an Old World-born and New World-born Basque, and in 13.4 percent of the cases a Basque married a non-Basque.[52] Of 324 Nevada Basque marriages, 77.7 percent were between Old World-born Basques, 4 percent between an Old World-born and New World-born Basque, and 18.3 percent involved a non-Basque partner.[53] He regards the lower proportion of mixed marriages in Nevada than California (4 percent versus 16.4 percent) as symptomatic of the more recent founding of a Basque colony in the former state.[54]

It should be noted that neither in the case of the 39 older California biographies cited above nor in Gachiteguy's samples should the statistic on Basque-to-non-Basque unions be construed as a ratio of intermarriage. In the former instance we are dealing with children of the successful immigrant (prominent enough to make the vanity section of a county history book). It may well be that such marriages (23 of 39) were a function of social class considerations overriding ethnic group loyalties.

Gachiteguy's results are affected considerably by the circumstances of his profession as chaplain of the French Basque colony in the American West. This limited his experience to persons who in some sense self-identified with their Basque ethnic heritage. This identification was frequently diminished by intermarriage. Even with these reservations it is clear that there remains to this day a tendency for Basques to marry within their ethnic group.

However, other recent studies have also tended to confirm the impression that the first generation of American-born Basques intermarries readily with non-Basques. Pagliarulo found that of forty-four Old World-born Basque males in Stockton in the 1940s, only one had married a non-Basque. However, of the American-born offspring of these unions, in forty-two cases, thirty-six married non-Basques.[55] Sather found that in Shoshone, Idaho, in the 1960s over half the marriages of American-born Basques are with non-Basques.[56]

While there is a Basque propensity for preferential endogamy, particularly in the immigrant generation, our interpretation of the statistics of Basque-to-non-Basque marriages must be qualified on other grounds. The young immigrant who becomes a sheepherder is both physically isolated from frequent contact with the non-Basque population and excluded from many of its social circles. A sheepherder in town for a few days' relaxation for the first time after many months of solitude and speaking little or no English is not in a position to enter the regular patterns of dating and courtship. Rather, his few contacts with non-Basque girls are likely to be made in bars and, in some parts of the West, houses of prostitution. The herders keep alive a tradition of accounts of Basques who have been bilked out of years of savings by American girls they have met in a bar. In some cases, the man is said to have married the girl only to have her divorce or simply abandon him as soon as his savings ran out. While it is difficult to assess accurately the extent to which Basque ambivalence concerning American women reinforces Basque endogamy, it is certainly a factor. Similarly, Basque herders feel that the rising frequency of divorce and the breakdown of parental authority have brought about a disintegration of the American family. For these reasons, Basques were reluctant to marry even "respectable" non-Basque girls.

Conversely, the Basque identification with the socially stigmatized role of sheepherder undermined their desirability as marriage partners in many areas of the American West. This was particularly true during the years of range conflict. Presently, however, the Basque ethnic group is held in high esteem by its neighbors, an attitude that is also reflected in a willingness to marry a Basque. A recent survey conducted in Reno, Nevada, designed to measure acceptance of ethnic groups and attitudes toward intermarriage, found 92 percent of all respondents favorably inclined toward Basques.[57]

The simple presentation of marital statistics, while heavily weighted in the direction of preferential Basque endogamy, fails to reflect the extent to which marriage was actually a socially integrative mechanism among the Basques. Brother-sister exchanges were not uncommon. To cite a few of the many examples: in Bakersfield two Echenique brothers married Etcheverry sisters;[58] three Erreca brothers married three Laxague sisters in Merced County;[59] and Vandor reports that two cousins from the same Navarrese village, Miguel Villanueva and Florencio Serrano, married two sisters in Fresno. The cousins were in the sheep business together.[60]

Furthermore, from the beginning there was chain migration of Basques into California whereby each immigrant was a potential attractor of kinsmen, fellow-villagers, or friends. Thus, the 1910 marriage of two Old World-born Basques in Fresno County united "Martin Irigaray who was one of six brothers residing in California and Marie Yraceburu who was one of nine brothers and sisters residing in the United States."[61] In 1905 Jean Arrabit came to the West as a tourist because "of his six children five were residing in California. The four boys were all sheepmen while his daughter was also married to a Basque sheepman."[62]

In sum, preferential Basque endogamy was in many cases superposed on an existing kinship network of siblings and cousins to such an extent that early maintenance of Basque ethnicity may have been as much a matter of playing out the intimate associations of family life as a conscious, impersonal, collective enterprise.

This network of marriage and kinship ties held together the early California Basque colony and served an important business function. Of the seventy sheepherders in our sample, thirty-one had one or more employers* who were explicitly identified as fellow Basques. Frequently, it is a question of a

---

*In many cases, information on the employer's identity is lacking. Were it available in every case, the incidence would undoubtedly be higher.

nephew working for an uncle or a younger brother coming over to herd sheep for an elder one. The same pattern is apparent at the level of partnerships. Of the seventy-one independent operators, twenty-four were in business at some time with a fellow Basque and, more often than not, a kinsman. The experiences of Miguel Erreca are a good illustration:

> Miguel Erreca came to California with his brother Juan in 1873. They made their way to San Juan Capistrano where they had a cousin, Bernardo Erreca, in the sheep business. After working for a Mr. Landell for two months he entered the employ of his cousin Bernardo where he remained for seven and one-half years. Bernardo had four partners among whom were the two Orroqui [sic] brothers. Miguel then entered into a partnership with his brother Juan and they jointly purchased a half interest in Bernardo's operation. Two years later they bought more sheep from Bernardo's old partners, leased a large ranch, and increased their flocks to a total of 20,000 head. In two years the brothers bought out Bernardo's interest and a short time later Miguel bought out Juan's share and the latter returned to the Basque country.[63]

A particularly complicated example of a combination of Basque kinship and ethnic ties being activated over two generations for business purposes is found in this account:

> In 1851, Jean Etchemendy, a French Basque, founded one of the first bakeries in Los Angeles. In 1865 he married Juana Equirala [sic] from Vizcaya. In 1872 he died and she married Pierre Larronde, a local French Basque sheepman.[64] One of Larronde's herders was named Martin Lifur. Lifur later quit Larronde to form an independent sheep operation with Augustine Echeverria whose sister he later married.[65] In the next generation Larronde's first-born, Pierre Domingo, and Martin Lifur's first-born John, completed the cycle by entering into partnership in the Franco-American bakery of Los Angeles.[66]

Similarly, the Silen sample provides many examples of the interweaving of marriage and kinship ties which stimulated chain migration, provided persons with their first employment in the New World, and served as the subsequent basis for the formation of business partnerships.

In Old World Basque society kinsmen are reckoned cognatically. Just as in the American kinship system, relatives are traced through both one's paternal and maternal side. We have noted that kinship ties were frequently invoked to assist an Old World youth to join a relative who was established in the

American West. In some cases the Old World relatives initiated the matter; in others the New World sheepman activated kinship ties to get a much-needed herder. Continued contacts with Old World kinsmen through correspondence and occasional trips by former emigrants back to Europe were the prime channels along which information about the American West permeated the Basque country. At the same time kinship ties for the emigrant generally proved to be his most durable links with the Old World over time. Nostalgia for Europe was expressed more frequently by the desire to see one's relatives than to return to his natal village.* This sense of continued orientation to Old World relatives persists over more than one generation in many Basque families. It is not uncommon for New World-born Basques to write family news to Old World relatives whom they have never met. Similarly, they may exchange news with family members residing in Latin America.

In the Basque system of reckoning kinsmen there is a principle that may be stated, "the spouse of a relative is a relative, but the relative of a spouse of a relative is not a relative."[67] Two consequences follow from the application of this principle in the social life of the Basques in the American West. One is how far the kinship networks are extended and the other is the matter of the inclusion of non-Basques into the system.

The most extensive kinship networks are those that have at their core a sheepman and his wife. Over time, this couple will likely have assisted numerous relatives, reckoned bilaterally through both partners. Many of these kinsmen, in turn, will have established themselves in the sheep business, frequently moving farther afield to less-crowded areas of the western range. In the next generation the couple's descendants are likely to have a large number of cousins, themselves descended from sheepmen, who are residing at considerable distances. The kinship networks of such people may encompass four or five states and include dozens of persons. Among those remaining in sheep, these ties have been frequently activated for the purpose of forming business partnerships or acquiring a herder in an emergency situation. To some extent, there is a pattern of

---

*This is the reverse of the situation in some areas like southern Italy, where emigrants are more prone to verbalize nostalgia in terms of desire to return to a particular community.

visiting among such kinsmen, which is frequently a factor in choosing a vacation destination.

The extensive kinship networks generated by reckoning the ties of a key or core couple that once actively imported kinsmen-herders may be contrasted with the kinship reckoning of the assisted herder himself. The subsequent reckoning of New World kinship ties for his first-generation descendants will be restricted to the side of that partner in the sponsoring couple who was a blood relative (since the spouse of a relative, while a relative, is not a conduit for further extension of kinship reckoning). Thus, by definition, the descendants of the herder are likely to have a less-extensive network of *New World-resident* relatives than the descendants of his sponsor.

Finally, not all Basque immigrants entered the American West along kinship lines. Those who did not were likely to have a highly fractured network of kinsmen in the United States, and the importance of kinship in their personal lives pales accordingly. Thus, such a man residing in California might be aware that a cousin whom he has not seen since leaving home has himself emigrated and is working in Montana. But for him this remains little more than a vague point of information.

There is a second consequence of the application of the kinship principle. While we have noted a tendency toward preferential endogamy among Basque ethnics, we have also found intermarriage, the rate of which has increased substantially over time. Under the kinship principle, when a non-Basque marries a Basque, he or she is defined as a relative by spouse's relatives, but the new extension of kinship stops at that point. The non-Basque married to a Basque, and hence the kinsman of other Basques, acquires status within the Basque ethnic group by virtue of marriage. Such individuals are accorded full membership in the Basque social clubs (some have held office, including the presidency). The children of the ethnically mixed marriages are regarded as holding full Basque credentials. There is very little notion among the Basques that so and so is a "half-Basque" or a "quarter-Basque." The claim to the identity of a person with one Basque grandparent will not be disputed, nor will he be denied membership in the local Basque club. Therefore, the continued application of a principle of the Old World Basque kinship system provides New World Basques with a means of coping rather smoothly with the thorny question of how an ethnic group maintains an identity in a pluralistic society that promotes interethnic marriages.

EDUCATION AND OCCUPATION

In a generational or long-term perspective, key barometers of any immigrant group's success within its host society are its educational level and occupational mobility. Among Basque immigrants, attitudes towards schooling were heavily influenced by Old World experiences, where instruction—obtained in rural schools—was frequently dogmatic, of poor quality, and of short duration. The curriculum was in French or Spanish, whereas most children arrived at school age as monolingual Basque speakers, thus guaranteeing them a large measure of personal frustration in their early years. Moreover, rural Basque society has a generally negative attitude toward formal education of any kind, with the one exception of preparation for a religious vocation.

To this anti-intellectual background in the attitudes of the immigrant parental generation may be added certain handicaps in educational opportunity for the first generation of Basque-Americans. Their parents' involvement in the sheep business meant that many Basque-Americans were raised on isolated ranches or in tiny towns in remote corners of the western range where the quality of the local school system was questionable. The poor Old World educational background of the parental generation and its continued involvement in an occupation that guaranteed them a large measure of social isolation meant that the immigrants were slowed in their own efforts to acquire English skills. The first generation of Basque-Americans was exposed to a strong Basque ethnic flavor at home, which slowed its initial progress in the Anglo school system. Finally, the preoccupation of the immigrant generation with financial success gained through hard physical labor made them less prone to encourage the young to postpone their entry into the labor force in favor of devoting several years to acquiring a college education.

All of the above factors have contributed to a certain amount of indifference toward formal education among many Basques of the American West. This is not to say that education is not esteemed, but rather it is not regarded by them as the *prime* means of succeeding in life.[68]* While some Basque-

---

*It is interesting to note that, while they are in school, many Basque children tend to excel.[69] However, the same Basque-American student who leads his high school class is less likely to go on to college than some of his

Americans have used formal education to gain access to the professions, there are to this day relatively few Basque doctors, lawyers, teachers, and statesmen in the American West, particularly when compared with the many successful ranchers and businessmen of Basque descent.[70]

The specialization of the Basques in the sheep industry has been so extensive that, for the Basque and non-Basque alike, sheep-industry occupations (and particularly herding) are regarded as an ethnic marker of the group. From the turn of the century to the present, Basques have dominated the sheepherding occupation. They have enjoyed considerable socioeconomic mobility within the sheep industry, and today many of the largest open-range sheep outfits of the American West are Basque-owned. Basques have also made their marks as wool and lamb buyers and as livestock transporters.

In specific localities, Basques are identified as an ethnic group with other occupations. In southern California they are regarded as the best milkers in the large commerical dairies. In San Francisco they now constitute the greatest challenge to Japanese control of the gardening business. Throughout central and southern California there are several Basque-owned bakeries famed for their sourdough bread. In the Oregon towns of Burns and Eugene there is a growing Basque colony dependent upon work in lumber processing. Throughout the American West many Basques are employed as construction workers. Generally, the persons in question in all of these occupations are Old World-born and are undergoing horizontal job mobility, moving from one type of menial job, herding, to another.

There is also the question of occupational mobility in the subsequent generations of New World-born BasqueAmericans. If relatively few have entered the professions, it is also true that the majority fail to follow in their parents' footsteps by remaining in agriculture.* Some remain in essentially rural or small-

---

classmates. The school system became one more arena in which the highly competitive Basques underscored their ethnic pride. Today's middle-aged Basque-Americans frequently recount negative feelings about their experiences in school—fights on the playground triggered by an ethnic slur or exclusion from the high school prom. Until recently, the Basque student tended to view excelling in class and in school sports as immediate goals unrelated to long-range career aspirations. The reticence to attend college, however, is diminishing.

*Most Basque-Americans who do inherit ranches convert them from sheep to cattle operations. In some cases this is dictated by economics and governmental restrictions on sheep range. However, the younger generation also views cattle raising as both easier and more prestigious.

town settings, while others migrate to the cities. Their occupations become so varied as to defy generalization, except to note that there is some clustering in both the areas of manual labor and ownership of small-scale business enterprises.

Gaiser's study of the Basques of southeastern Oregon and Boise, Idaho, during the 1940s noted considerable differential mobility among Basque-Americans of the same family. Frequently only one or two children would be given educational opportunities while the remainder stayed in the parental home and in an ethnic environment. Over time, the more educated and Americanized members became, in Gaiser's view, "strangers" to their less privileged siblings.[71]

While few Basque-Americans remain in sheep, or in agriculture for that matter, there is a sense in which even the urban Basque recognizes the group's identification with the sheep industry. This is reflected in his knowledge of the sheep business, his attendance at rural festivals, his visits to the ranches owned by relatives and childhood friends, and his joking patterns. An urban Basque may humorously excuse his behavior with the statement, "What do you expect from a sheepherder?" Similarly, he may couch self-praise in the statement, "Pretty good for a sheepherder." Such statements may be made by persons two generations removed from the sheep business.

Today, in many communities of the American West, both Old World- and New World-born Basques benefit from the group's reputation for honesty and hard work. Although this reputation was originally earned in the sheep industry, it has been transferred to other sectors of the economy. There are supermarket companies in California and construction companies in Nevada that are willing, even anxious, to hire Basques solely on the basis of the group reputation. Again, the prospective Basque entrepreneur who is seeking to establish a small business may sometimes receive easier credit because of his ethnic credentials. Basques are quite aware of this situation and are protective of it. Within the group the harshest criticism is reserved for the shirker or untrustworthy individual who, by his undependability, threatens to undermine that group asset, "the word of a Basque."*

---

*By way of example we have noted the unsympathetic treatment accorded to Martin Biscailuz in the pages of *California'ko Eskual Herria* after he was convicted of defrauding clients in his law practice.[72] Similarly, Laurent Etchepare, financial advisor to the widow of Miguel Leonis, was upbraided in the newspaper after he was arrested for embezzlement in managing her funds.[73]

A further means of evaluating the educational level and occupational patterns of the Basques of the American West lies in a comparison of their overall socioeconomic mobility with that of the Basques of the Río de la Plata nations. Within the society of the American West, Basques are little understood and often unknown as an ethnic group. Few of their successes have been outside of the livestock industry. In the Río de la Plata region the Basques are today regarded as one of the most successful and dynamic ethnic groups and are disproportionately entrenched in the circles of high finance, the professions, and the military, religious, and national leaderships. Consequently, there is general knowledge about the Basque ethnic group in the wider society of southern South America. Furthermore, there is little tendency to confuse Basque ethnics with other Spanish or French nationals, as happens frequently in the American West.

There are several factors that would seem to explain the differing histories of Basque immigrants in the two areas. It might be argued that, with respect to language skills, Basques who entered South America were advantaged over their counterparts in the American West. The former entered a society where their proficiency in Spanish (albeit differing from individual to individual) was of immediate use. The latter entered a nation having both alien language and culture. The majority of Basque immigrants required several years to acquire even rudimentary English skills, and some never did. This handicap served to brake their involvement in the wider society, and in many cases that of the first-generation BasqueAmerican as well.

The differing language situations on the two continents further conditioned Basque immigration by influencing the choice of destination of certain potential Old World emigrants. Both areas received emigrants from the rural districts of the Basque country, but the majority of urban emigrants with professional skills opted for South America. There they could hope to use their Old World training, usually by settling in cities like Buenos Aires or Montevideo. In doing so they established an educated urban dimension to the Río de la Plata Basque colony that was essentially lacking among the Basques of the American West.

Other factors may be cited as well. A frequent theme in the analyses of the economic development of the United States is the importance ascribed to the American work ethic and puritanical life-style. Conversely, historians frequently describe the economic life of Latin American society as turning upon the concern with appearances and the quest for leisure. While it is a dangerous oversimplification to depict whole economies and national characters in such terms, there is some element of truth in the contrast. Evaluated in terms of the present study, it might be argued that the Basques' work ethic, and particularly their willingness to engage in hard physical tasks, gave them a particular economic advantage in the South American context whereas in the American West it gave them less of a competitive edge *vis-à-vis* others.

The initial economic successes of Basques in both areas were achieved mainly in the livestock industry. On both continents Basque livestockmen acquired considerable fortunes, but economic successes in ranching had differing social and political implications in the two societies. Until recently Argentina and Uruguay were agrarian nations. The rural large-scale landowners were enormously influential in national affairs, and a number of the leading families of Buenos Aires and Montevideo were absentee landlords. Thus, in the Río de la Plata region there was an extension of the rural class structure into the urban centers. Successful landowners, Basques included, educated their sons in the capitals, using both their influence and wealth to establish them in urban professions and enterprises.

The situation in the United States differed considerably. In the American West success in the livestock industry was not readily transferred to other areas of American life. Livestock fortunes were not the linchpins of upper class social status and the major source of capitalization of urban enterprises. There was not a pattern of absentee landlordism, since even to this day the successful ranchers tend to spend all of their active lives residing on their ranches or in nearby small communities. Thus, the successes of Basque livestockmen have not necessarily meant entry of their sons into urban professions.

Finally, the Basque colony of the Río de la Plata region may be on the order of ten times larger than that of the American West. Employing the most conservative of estimates, the present-day population of Old World- and New World-born persons of Basque descent in Argentina alone may approach one million people, whereas the total Basque population of the United States likely falls somewhere between fifty and one hundred thousand individuals. The difference is even more pronounced when we consider that the present-day population of the United States is roughly ten times larger than that of Argentina. The sheer magnitude of the Basque colony within the society of the Río de la Plata region made it considerably likelier that individuals within the group would achieve notable socioeconomic mobility.

It is interesting to note that, in both societies, the Basques have attained an ethnic group reputation for honesty and hard work that has increased their social esteem and economic success. In both areas ethnic group loyalty prompts Basques to assist and trust one another. Today, however, this trust remains a more viable factor in the formation of business partnerships, the extension of credit, and other economic affairs in the American West. In the Río de la Plata region Basque ethnic credentials serve more as a basis for social presumption, but are insufficient in themselves for forming lasting social and business ties. What best expresses the difference in use of ethnic heritage between the South American and North American Basques is that the former display their family escutcheons in the home, whereas the latter hang their regional Basque escutcheons.

RELIGION

The fact that Old World Basques are almost all baptized Roman Catholics, as are their New World-born descendants, provides an additional difference between the Basque ethnic group and some of its neighbors. There is also a further distinction between Basques and other non-Basque Roman Catholics.

Old World Basque Catholicism is characterized to this day by almost universal church attendance. The laymen place great emphasis upon strict adherence to religious duty and ritual, leaving theological concerns to authoritarian clergy. The asceticism of Old World Basque Catholicism* and the practice of universal involvement of the congregation stand in marked contrast to the more pragmatic approach of southern European Catholicism in which the participation of adult males is notably absent.

The occupational specialization of Basques in the sheep industry has affected their religious life considerably. In some areas such as Jordan Valley, Oregon,[75] Volta[76] and Fullerton,[77] California, and Elko[78] and Gardnerville,[79] Nevada, there is evidence that Basques were instrumental in erecting the first

---

*Basque Catholicism was heavily influenced by the Jansenist movement of the early seventeenth century.[74]

local Catholic church. In Boise, Idaho, they are reported to have constructed their own ethnic church.[80] In most instances, though, their dispersed settlement pattern ruled out the creation of Basque-dominated church congregations. For similar reasons there has developed a differential participation of Basque men and women in church activities. The men, who spend much of the year on the range, far from established churches, become unaccustomed to attending church services. According to one Basque priest, many limit their attendance to major feast days, such as Christmas, Easter, and the Assumption, while others enter a church only when attending a wedding or funeral.[81] A higher proportion of the women maintained permanent residence in towns or close to them, and their involvement in the local church activities was considerably greater. To a certain degree, however, Basques of both sexes are somewhat reticent to become active in the "American" Catholic congregations. This is seen clearly in the persistence and appeal of the practice of importing Old World Basque clergymen to minister to the Basques of the American West.

In two 1894 issues of *California'ko Eskual Herria* there are extensive articles on a group of Basque priests who had founded a mission in Oklahoma territory.[82] In the May 18, 1895, issue a priest from the Basque country chastised the California colony for not having taken steps to secure a Basque chaplain.[83] Although this triggered a polemic in future issues, it failed to produce immediate results. Meanwhile, the Benedictine priests of the Sacred Heart mission in Oklahoma territory maintained correspondence with the newspaper. In the February 1, 1896, issue it was announced that Reverend Hippolyte Topet had arrived at the Oklahoma mission from the Basque country,[84] and the May 23, 1896, issue welcomed to California two visitors from the mission—a Father Leo Gariador and companion.[85] Apparently, the Benedictines were favorably impressed by their visit.* Pierre Lhande reports that they founded a church in Montebello at the request of Bishop Conaty of Los Angeles. The California bishop had solicited priests from the bishop of Bayonne so that his Basque parishioners could confess in their maternal language.[86]

From Montebello the Basque priests travelled widely. A 1912 article in the *Humboldt Star* states:

---

*Beginning in 1897, a Benedictine priest published a regular column in *California'ko Eskual Herria* that dealt with the lives of the saints.

Basque Priest will Visit Northern Section
Father Enright of Lovelock, accompanied by Father Hippolite
Topet of Los Angeles, left yesterday morning by automobile for
Paradise. Father Topet is of Basque nationality and comes to do
spiritual work among his countrymen. . . .[87]

In 1918, when the Basques of Buffalo, Wyoming, organized a
festival, they asked Father Gariador, resident near Los Angeles,
to provide religious services.[88] Northern Nevada, which still
had a considerable French Basque and Navarrese population at
the time, is the farthest afield (from Los Angeles) that we can
document Father Topet's travels. However, to the north, in
Boise, there was another organized effort to provide the Vizcayan community with a chaplain. In 1910 the Bishop of Idaho
wrote directly to the Bishop of Vitoria (whose jurisdiction
included Vizcaya and Guipúzcoa), requesting a Basque priest
for Boise. The Bishop of Vitoria published the request in the
monthly diocesan bulletin, and Father Bernardo Arregui of
Tolosa volunteered. Father Arregui had the added advantage of
knowing English, since he had studied in England for six
months. He arrived in Idaho in 1911 where, according to Silen,
"his zeal and activity . . . made him a focal point not only for
the Basque colony of Idaho but also from adjacent states."[89]

As in other areas of the social life of the Basques of the
West, we can detect an early and almost absolute distinction
between the two greater Basque colonies in religious matters.
To the present, there has been an effort to maintain a Basque
priest in California. For the last twenty years the Bishop of
Bayonne and the Premonstratensian friars of the monastery of
Belloc (in the French Basque area) have provided a chaplain to
the California colony. From his home base in Fresno he travels
widely throughout the French Basque-Navarrese areas of the
American West. From San Francisco and western Nevada
through southern California, Arizona, Utah, Colorado, Wyoming, and extreme northeastern Montana, the French Basque
chaplain logs thousands of miles annually, celebrating Mass at
Basque festivals and picnics, in private homes, and in sheep
camps, hearing confessions, sermonizing, and conducting religious retreats in the Basque language. Significantly, he never
visits northern Nevada, eastern Oregon, or southern Idaho.*

*In the transitional areas between the two greater Basque colonies, the
question of which priest to invite to say the Mass at the annual festival
sometimes leads to debate between the local French Basques and Vizcayans.

Similarly, in both southern Idaho and northern Nevada, a number of Old World-born Basque priests minister to the Basque colony, particularly to the sheepherders.

Within the framework of the Basque Catholic religious experience, the ritual that receives the greatest elaboration is the funeral. In Old World Basque society a death triggers a series of events lasting for several years that involves all levels of local social organization. Members of the deceased's domestic group, kindred, neighborhood, and village all enter into a complex series of religious rituals, funerary banquets, and offerings for the salvation of his soul.[90]

When a Basque emigrant dies in a foreign land there may be a funeral in his natal village, complete with a block of wood serving as a substitute coffin. The decision as to whether or not to hold the funeral turns on the marital status of the deceased. To have married is to relinquish all claims upon one's natal household and, by extension, to its church floor *sepulturie.** If the emigrant remains unmarried, he retains his right to return to his natal household and resume residence at any time. When news of his death reaches his natal domestic group it has the obligation of initiating and sponsoring the entire gamut of funerary practices, as if the deceased had never left home.

The "death theme"[91] of Old World Basque society is reflected as well in the activities of the associations founded by Basque emigrants. Burial crypts and cemeteries were established by the *Cofradía de la Nación Vascongada* of Sevilla (sixteenth century), the *Hermandad de Nuestra Señora de Aránzazu* of Mexico City (seventeenth century), the *Asociación Vasco-Navarra de Beneficencia* of Havana (nineteenth century), the *Euskal Echea* of Argentina, and the *Asociación Vasca de Socorros Mutuos* of Caracas (twentieth century). The *Real Compañía Guipúzcoana de Caracas* reserved shares in the enterprise to meet the expenses of providing memorial services for deceased employees (eighteenth century). Both the *Centro Vasco* of New York City and the *Sociedad de Socorros Mutuos* of Boise provide burial insurance for their members.

---

*Each household has a rectangular space on the church floor called the *sepulturie*. The women of the household arrange their chairs on this site whenever attending a church service. If there is a death in the household, the *sepulturie* is draped in black cloth, adorned with candles, and becomes the focal point for much of the funerary ritual. Today the *sepulturie* is a symbolic burial site; until the seventeenth century, it was the actual burial plot, as the dead were interred beneath the church floor.

The discharge of these funerary obligations constitutes an ethnic marker of the Basques of the American West. The pages of *California'ko Eskual Herria* contained frequent obituaries as well as announcements of anniversary masses for the souls of the deceased. To this day the Basques in America retain a strong sense of obligation to attend the funerals of business associates, kinsmen, friends, or employees. It is not at all unusual for persons to travel as much as one thousand miles for the occasion, so that one finds residents from four or five states of the American West attending a Basque funeral. Nor is participation limited to Old World-born persons. In an era when most Americans tend to deemphasize funerary ritual, Basque funerals* attract the attention of their non-Basque neighbors. The funerals also serve the Basques themselves as a prime social context for meeting and mingling, exchanging news, and renewing old ties.

POLITICS

Ethnic politics among the Basques of the American West can be divided into the separate concerns of their continued orientation to Old World politics on the one hand and their involvement in American politics on the other.

For the most part, Basque-Americans have been either indifferent to or disaffected from Spanish and French politics. Many of the Spanish Basque emigrants to the New World left Europe in the nineteenth century either directly or indirectly as a result of Basque defeats in the Carlist wars. Similarly, the French Basques were disenchanted with nineteenth-century centralized political control exerted from Paris. Their alienation was exacerbated further by the disruptions of the Revolution of 1848. The most eloquent testimony of Basque political disaffection from French and Spanish national purposes was their rate of evasion of military service. Throughout the late nineteenth and early twentieth centuries the Basque provinces had by far the highest percentage of military evaders in the respective nations,

---

*Except in those cases where a Basque priest is available to conduct a Basque-language Mass and sing Basque religious music, the format of the actual funeral does not differ from the funerals of non-Basque Catholics. However, until about thirty years ago, it was common to hold a *gauela*, or wake, either in the home of the deceased or, if he was unmarried, in one of the Basque hotels. Also, there is strong persistence of the Old World custom of *artu-emon* (literally to "take and give"), which refers to donations of a Mass for the soul of the deceased, the recording of the donation, and the future reciprocity in kind by the family of the deceased. At one recent Basque funeral in Nevada 159 families from four different states gave such Masses.

in some years approaching fifty percent of all men conscripted.

Although Basques in the New World remain indifferent or hostile to French and Spanish national politics, the question of Basque regional politics—Basque nationalism—has always been of interest. In chapter 3, we noted that segments of the Latin American Basque colonies have actively supported Basque nationalism since the end of the nineteenth century. In part, this is due to the fact that leaders of the movement who have been exiled at various times were professionals or well-educated middle-class persons, rather than men drawn from the urban lower classes or rural areas. When forced to emigrate they have opted for Latin American countries where their knowledge of the language and their general understanding of Hispanic society allowed them to put their profession to immediate use.

Thus, insofar as Basque intellectuals have migrated at all, their destinations have been Latin America. Since the defeat of the Basque forces in 1937, all of the various Basque underground organizations such as the *Partido Nacionalista Vasco*, the *Euzkadi ta Azkatasuna* and the *Eusko-Gaztedi* groups have organized chapters in Mexico, Venezuela, Argentina, and Chile. The Basque government-in-exile, headquartered in Paris, maintains representatives in all of the major Basque colonies of Latin America. In the late 1930s and early 1940s the government-in-exile sponsored the emigration to Latin America of literally thousands of refugees. Many were provided with the capital to establish themselves in business. Today several are millionaire industrialists who retain strong loyalties to the Basque cause. Consequently, Latin America, and notably Mexico City, Caracas, Buenos Aires and Santiago, is presently the prime staging area for funding the various phases of the Basque resistance in Europe. Much of the literature of the Basque nationalist groups originates in Latin America.

By way of contrast, the American West has never proven to be fertile ground for Basque nationalism. The language difficulty and the main occupational opportunity of sheepherding discouraged politicized Basque intellectuals from emigrating to the area. As we have seen, the Basque colony of the American West was constituted largely of emigrants from the rural sectors of Old World Basque society. Furthermore, the characteristic emigrant was the single male, twenty years old or younger. His poor educational background, derived through sporadic attendance at country schools, made him semiliterate and hence not easily influenced by the published propaganda of Basque nationalism.

In the American West he had to cope simultaneously with the hardships and isolation on the range and the alien culture of the wider society. Furthermore, he was acutely aware of his own alien status and, therefore, avoided collective manifestations of his ethnic identity. It may be surmised that an effort to organize a conspicuous pro-Basque nationalist movement oriented toward Old World politics would have been a risky enterprise for the Basques of the American West. Even assuming that there was sufficient interest in the Basque community for such a movement (a point of speculation), it might have served as an irritant in its relations with the wider society.*

The only evidence of organized Basque nationalist sentiment in the United States is to be found in the New York City colony. In 1926 a small group of New York City Basques seceded from the *Centro Vasco* and founded their own club in Brooklyn and began to subscribe funds for the *Partido Nacionalista Vasco* (Basque Nationalist Party). They published a newspaper entitled *Aberri* (or "The Nation"), which was an official organ of the party. The effort involved only a minority of the colony, and from the beginning, it foundered in economic difficulty. The last issue of *Aberri* appeared in 1928.

During the Spanish Civil War the Basques of the American West, and particularly the Vizcayan colony, were placed in an agonizing position. Vizcaya and Guipúzcoa established an autonomous government, loosely affiliated to the Spanish Republic, and fielded an army to oppose Franco. Within nine months they were overrun and thousands of persons went into exile in southern France while thousands more were put in prison. At the same time, the Spanish Republic was depicted as communistic in a segment of the American press. The American Catholic clergy praised Franco from the pulpit as the savior of religion in traditionally Catholic Spain. Basques were torn between a fear of being identified as procommunist and a concern for their relatives in Europe. Consequently, little or no aid for the Basque military cause was forthcoming from the American West, although war relief was provided. For example, the proceeds from the Sheepherders' Ball in Boise were used to purchase one thousand blankets for Basque women prisoners in Spain. At the same time leaders of the Basque community were at pains to

---

*Note that in Senator Pittman's 1913 anti-Basque speeches before the United States Senate, Basque ethnic politics and an unwillingness to become citizens were singled out as evidence of their undesirability as a people (cf. pp. 268–270).

denounce communism. An article in the *Boise Statesman* reflects this concern:

> Basque Leader Defends People. Boisean Vigorously
> Denies Hints that Group Communistic
>
> . . . Denouncing what he termed allegations that his people in Idaho and neighboring states espoused communism, a Basque leader Sunday declared the claims "contemptible and malicious accusations made by contemptible and malicious persons."
>
> . . . "The Basque people throughout the entire United States clearly and fully realize the Third International Communist Party, headed by Stalin, methodically fomented the recent Spanish civil war which kept our people in a blood bath for three long years. . . ."[92]

When France was invaded by Germany, the Basque government-in-exile was again forced to flee. The president, José Antonio Aguirre, settled in New York and traveled extensively in Latin America, seeking support for his cause. As the United States was drawn into the Second World War, Franco's identification with Hitler and Mussolini prompted United States government support for exiled Spanish opposition groups like the Basque government. Aguirre believed that the shape of postwar Europe after an allied victory would be heavily influenced by the United States. He felt that his presence in this country was imperative if the Basques were to obtain autonomy through negotiation.

Aguirre's expectations that Franco would be removed by the victorious allies were not realized. But the creation of the United Nations headquarters in New York City justified maintenance of a Basque delegation there in order to plead the Basque case in an international forum. The presence of the delegation in New York City further politicized the local colony, but efforts to influence the Basques of the American West were a total failure. The delegation sent out emissaries to places like Boise and Elko, where they were received with politeness, but nothing resulted from the visit.

To this day the Basques of the American West have little understanding of the intricacies of the Basque nationalist movement. Furthermore, there is little sympathy among them for its political aspirations. Occasionally, they mobilize on humanitarian grounds to protest a particular excess of the Franco regime. For example, the trial at Burgos in 1970, when sixteen separatists were tried for assassination, caused a storm of international protest. There was sufficient outrage in the

Basque colony to cause the governors of Oregon, Idaho, and Nevada to send official protests to Madrid. But on a day-to-day basis, Basque nationalism is scarcely a subject of conversation among the Basques of the American West. A few persons, generally Old World-born and politicized before emigrating, subscribe to one or more publications of the resistance groups. One can find an occasional Basque nationalist zealot, embittered to the point of silence by the generally unsympathetic hearing that his views receive among his companions. In sum, Basque nationalism is simply not a viable issue with the Basque-Americans.

The other aspect of Basque ethnic politics is their involvement in the American political scene. Again, the nature of the Basque experience in the American West was not conducive to their participation in politics.

With the exception of Jordan Valley, Oregon,[93] and Buffalo, Wyoming,[94] communities where Basques represent a considerable portion of the overall population, few Basques have entered politics at even the community level.

The tendency for most Basques to harbor a desire to return to Europe meant that some of those who ultimately never returned resided in the United States for decades before taking out citizenship. The physical and social isolation of sheep-industry occupations slowed their acculturation and crippled their understanding of local issues. It is only with the establishment of generations of United States-born Basque-Americans that there has been a growing involvement of Basques in the political scene of the American West. Small-town politics in the region are conservative, and the Basque voters are no exception. In the past twenty years a few political leaders of Basque descent have emerged. The three most notable, Paul Laxalt (former governor of Nevada and currently United States senator from that state), Peter Cenarruza (secretary of state of Idaho), and Anthony Yturri (speaker of the Oregon Senate), are all Republicans; Peter Echeverria (a former member of the Nevada State Legislature and presently head of the Nevada Gaming Commission) is a Democrat.

The campaigns of Basque politicians tend to reflect considerable ethnic flavor. The aspiring Basque politician was identified with an ethnic group whose relations with the wider society were, until quite recently, tinged with controversy. At the same time, the Basque population is scattered so widely and sparsely throughout the American West that it scarcely constitutes a significant voting bloc in any one electoral district. Thus, the first Basque candidates incurred the liabilities of an ethnic label with few of its benefits. For the Basques themselves the early candidacies constituted a source of anxiety as a public measure of the success or failure of their attempt to enter the American mainstream.* The victories of Basque candidates likewise became a source of ethnic pride, and today no Basque festival is really complete without the presence of at least one Basque officeholder.

LANGUAGE

The most striking ethnic marker of the Basques is their language. Basque, unlike most other European languages with representative speakers in the American West, is rarely learned by others. As a non-Indo-European tongue with few Old and New World speakers, the language is almost never taught in the school system or in any other formal context.† We have already noted the paucity of literature about the Basques in any language, and printed Basque-language materials are particularly rare. The upshot is that Basque, for its speakers, is tantamount to a secret code, a medium that can be used with absolute impunity and without fear of penetration in the presence of non-Basques.

Here are several generalizations about language retention, particularly from generation to generation, among the Basques of the American West:

1) Most first-generation Basque-Americans have at least some knowledge of the Basque language, which erodes rapidly in the course of their own lifetimes. Thus the New World-born first-generation Basque may reach school age as a monolingual Basque speaker; by the time he graduates from high school or college, he may be able to understand very little of what is said to him in Basque and may be unable to speak it at all.

2) While Old World-born persons are bilingual Basque/Spanish or Basque/French speakers, the first generation Basque-American, insofar as he is bilingual at all, tends to be a

---

*With improvement in the image of the Basques held in the wider society, Basque candidates have become less private about their ethnic origins. In a recent municipal election held in Reno one aspirant used the slogan, "Let this Basque do the task."

†Recent exceptions are a Basque-language course sequence at the University of Nevada, Reno, and Basque language courses in Boise, Idaho, sponsored by the Idaho System of Higher Education.

Basque/English speaker, thus underscoring the fact that Basque is the preferred language of the home in the immigrant generation.

3) Language retention in New World-born children of Old World parents may be correlated with the parents' occupation, on the one hand, and sibling age order, on the other. If the parents remain in the sheep business, the children are exposed regularly to Old World-born herders and have their language skills reinforced. If the parents are proprietors of a Basque hotel, the child is raised in a strong ethnic context, again reinforcing his Basque-language ability. The eldest children of immigrant parents are considerably more likely to learn Basque than are the younger siblings. As the parents themselves learn English, they are more prone to use it in the home. And, of course, as the eldest children learn colloquial English in the schools, they influence their younger siblings.

4) Second-generation Basque-Americans rarely retain any Basque-language competence or comprehension.

In any social situation among the Basques of the American West, four different languages—Basque, Spanish, French, and English—are potentially at play. Language use has clear significance as a marker of each individual's ethnic credentials. The selection of language is not neutral; rather, there is a "grammar of grammars," a kind of "language of languages," operative among Basques of the American West, the careful manipulation of which can affect profoundly the outcome of any social situation. One's selection of language can convey intimacy, as when two Vizcayans take pleasure in conversing in their dialect; sternness, as when a parent switches in mid-sentence from English to Basque in order to admonish a child; or distance, as when two Basque speakers revert into Basque in the presence of a Basque-American whom they know to be ignorant of the language.*

At the same time, the simultaneous presence of four languages provides an almost mercurial quality to the flow of conversation. At the boarders' table of the Basque hotel, the picnic tables of the Basque festival, or the meetings of the social club, the language of individual conversations may shift frequently, as new participants arrive and others depart, or merely at the speaker's whim. The recounting of a single short episode

---

*For example, an American-born Basque recently resigned from the board of directors of one of the Basque clubs because whenever the other directors wanted to discuss his controversial stands, they did so in Basque.

may begin in Basque, shift to English, and terminate in Spanish or French, thus adding to the bewilderment of the monolingual or strictly bilingual listener.

The question of language skills can affect seriously the dealings between Basques and others. Ignorance of English has historically been a great handicap; however, feigned ignorance could be an effective means of frustrating a cowboy who tried to order an itinerant sheepman off a particular stretch of rangeland. In courtroom circumstances, as either defendants or plaintiffs, Old World Basques sometimes feigned ignorance of Spanish as well as English, as the following tale illustrates. In 1873, thirteen years after his arrival in southern California, Domingo Bastanchury was tried for killing another man's dog. One Basque signed an affidavit that Bastanchury knew no English.[95] Bastanchury signed an affidavit that he knew little Spanish,[96] while a third Basque testifying for the defense swore that he had informed Bastanchury in Spanish of the charges against him.[97] For his part, the plaintiff produced a Basque witness who testified that he was:

> a Basco, or native of the Basque provinces, of which the defendant is also a native; That the vast majority of the natives of such provinces understand and familiarly speak and use the Spanish tongue, though they also have a local native tongue of their own; That the defendant, in all the conversations aforesaid, spoke the Spanish language with ease and facility.
>
> That he, the said defendant, uses the said Spanish language in all his business transactions, and has no difficulty whatever in making himself understood in said language, or in understanding it when spoken by others.[98]

In such cases it was common for the court to appoint a Basque translator.

In the broadest sense, the Basque versus English distinction is the most fundamental language differentiator within the Basque ethnic group. Using one language rather than the other means much more than simply choosing an alternate means of expression. Each language encapsulates an experience, a world that is not totally translatable into the terminology of the other.

It is in this respect that even the most bilingual of speakers compartmentalizes experience in the privacy of his thoughts. There are public expressions of this compartmentalization. For instance, one Basque social club currently publishes a bilingual newsletter. While some points of information are presented in both languages, the Basque and English sections also discuss different issues, as well as the same issues from differing perspectives.

Finally, there is a sense in which a generalized dialect of spoken Basque is emerging in the context of the American West. In part, there is the influence of English loan words derived largely from the sheep camp experience, e.g., *kornfliek* (cornflakes) and *trelie* (trailer). In part, there is a mingling in the American West of speakers of the several Old World dialects.* It is in the American West where a French Basque might work in a Spanish Basque-dominated sheep outfit and find that Basque is the only language that he shares in common with his fellows. In such circumstances dialectal difficulties are quickly overcome. At the same time Basque speakers in the American West participate less directly in the Old World evolution of the language. Certain expressions are retained in the New World context after falling into disuse in the Basque country. Conversely, many new words and phrases that become popular in the Old World never enter the speech of New World Basques. As a consequence, when New World-born Basque speakers travel to Europe as visitors, Old World Basques recognize them immediately because of the "quaintness" of their speech.

LITERATURE AND COMMUNICATIONS

Literature concerning the Basques of the American West is extremely sparse. The occupational specialization of the Basques isolated them physically from their neighbors and identified them with one of the least prestigious activities in the region's economy. Consequently, the Basques remained a "phantom-like" element within the society of the American West, largely ignored by the literati.† Insofar as Basques were mentioned in the local newspapers, they were often presented in a controversial light.

It is clear that the majority of Basque immigrants had limited educational backgrounds and a relative disdain for formal education. Consequently, they were not prone to produce their own literary spokesmen. To this day, the only exception is Robert Laxalt, whose book *Sweet Promised Land* describes his father's life as a sheepman in Nevada and California.[101] More

---

*Francisco Grandmontagne reports a similar process at work among the Basques of Argentina.[99]

†See Wilbur Shepperson's book, *Restless Strangers*, for an analysis of the few short stories and novels in which Basques are protagonists.[100]

recently Laxalt has written *In a Hundred Graves: A Basque Portrait*,[102] which deals with life in the Basque country as seen through the eyes of a Basque-American.*

Similarly, the limited educational background and reading habits of the Basque immigrants crippled efforts to create a Basque-language press. There were only two nineteenth-century attempts to do so. The American-born lawyer Martin Biscailuz founded a newspaper entitled *Escualdun Gazeta* (Basque Gazette) in Los Angeles in 1885. In his first editorial he made the immodest, yet correct, claim that he was launching the first exclusively Basque-language newspaper ever published.[104] The newspaper provided some international and national news, emphasized success stories of both Basques and non-Basques, railed against the rising divorce rate, and provided the reader with such information as train schedules and the results of the New Orleans lottery. By the third issue, the newspaper was in financial trouble and Biscailuz was asking the readership "should we continue?"[105] Apparently, the answer was negative.

In 1893 José Goytino, a journalist by trade, founded the newspaper *California'ko Eskual Herria* (California Basque Land). It proved to be considerably more successful than the *Escualdun Gazeta*, since it was published until 1898. It had distributors in San Francisco, San Diego, and Mexico City.†

We have already referred to *Aberri*, the journal published between 1925 and 1928 by the Basque nationalist splinter group in the New York colony. Like the *Escualdun Gazeta*, it had financial problems from the outset, and it soon folded. In 1938 and 1939 the newspaper, *The Boise Capital News*, published a weekly "Basque Section" with news of the local colony in English, Spanish, and Basque. In 1943–44 an English-language Basque nationalist periodical entitled *Basques* was published in New York City by the delegation of the Basque government-in-exile. And, finally, in 1946–48 a Basque-language cultural review (literature, art, and music) called *Argia* (Light) was published in New York City. In 1975 a newspaper

---

*Two Old World-born persons have published English works about the Basque country.[103]

†This is further evidence that, by the end of the nineteenth century, there were still ties between Basques in the American West and in Latin America. Goytino's efforts were praised in the journal *La Vasconia* of Buenos Aires as well.[106]

with national distribution, *The Voice of the Basques*, began publication in Boise.

With these few exceptions there has been no ethnic literature generated by the Basques of the United States. There is, however, a growing popular literature on the Basques written by non-Basques. After the passage of the Taylor Grazing Act in 1934 had removed the itinerant sheepman as a source of irritation between Basques and others, the image of the Basque sheepherders underwent transformation in the popular literature of the region. Articles in periodicals, as well as feature stories in western newspapers, began to extol the Basques as hardworking, productive citizens. Perhaps inevitably, the Basque sheepherder became the frequent subject of the journalistic backlash against the rampant and too-rapid ubranization of American society. The new depiction of the herder as a romantic figure set amidst idyllic scenes, free from urban ills, engaged in a simple, wholesome task as he contemplated western sunsets, did much to distort the reality of the sheepherder's circumstances,[107] but it contributed to the emerging positive image of the Basque ethnic group. Since the 1940s there has been a growing scholarly literature on the American Basques.

Finally, there is a modest literature in Europe that deals with the experiences of the Basques in the American West. Two of the priests who have served as chaplains among the Basque-Americans have written about them.[108] There are a few novels about the life of the herder, but they usually offer a highly romanticized and distorted account.[109]* In other novels[110] and plays,[111] the returnee emigrant is included as one of the protagonists. There is also a published account of the life of the sheepherder.[112] Of considerable interest are the few literary efforts in the Basque language produced by individuals with personal experience as herders in the American West.

In rural Basque society verses set to music, composed spontaneously by individuals known as *bertsolariak*, or versifiers, are extremely popular. The *bertsolari* is himself likely to be of rural origin, and a few persons with *bertsolari* skills have worked as herders in America. In some cases, verses describing their tribulations and aspirations while herding have been conserved and published. Possibly the best examples are found in the work *Paulo Yanzi ta Bere Lagunen Bertsoak* ("The Verses

---

*Much of the distortion derives from the popularity in Europe of Hollywood films and fanciful novels about the American West.

of Paulo Yanzi and his Friends").[113] In this compendium of the verses of the well-known *bertsolari*, there is a section of correspondence in verse between Paulo (who had himself herded sheep in the United States) and his nephew José (who at the time of their composition was working as a sheepherder in Nevada). José's verses include *Artzaien bizimodua* ("Herder's life"), *Negu gogorra* ("Hard winter"), and *Kaskabel sugeari* ("To the rattlesnake").

This literature emphasizes the harsher realities of sheepherding. *California'ko Eskual Herria* regularly published verses on the difficulties of life on the range. For example, in the July 7, 1894, issue there was a poem entitled *California'ko Miseriak* ("California Miseries").[114] In the sobered view of the experienced herder, America is described as a land where one can no longer acquire great wealth with little effort.

There are other forms of communication used by Basques of the American West. Several of the Basque clubs have their own newsletters that circulate among the membership. Also, there are weekly Basque-language radio broadcasts in the communities of Elko and Winnemucca, Nevada; Boise, Idaho; and Buffalo, Wyoming. The programs emphasize Basque music and news of the local colony, and are particularly aimed at the Old World herders in the nearby hills.

THE BASQUE HOTEL

The boarding house, or hotel, is undoubtedly both the oldest and the most important ethnic institution found among the Basques of the American West. Historically, the Basque hotels constituted a network of ethnic establishments along which Basque immigrants could enter and move about the United States with a maximum of protection and a minimum of culture shock. They provided the key employment agencies and recreational centers for local Basques as well as a source of information concerning the wider Basque colony of the American West. Subsequently, the Basque hotels have acquired additional functions. They came to provide the American-born Basque population with a context in which both to renew and to express their ethnic selves. They also attracted tourists whose presence in turn provided Old World-born boarders with exposure to non-Basques in a controlled ethnic context.

The Plaza Hotel in San Juan Bautista is the oldest Basque hotel establishment in the American West of which we have evidence. Founded sometime during the 1850s, it served as a

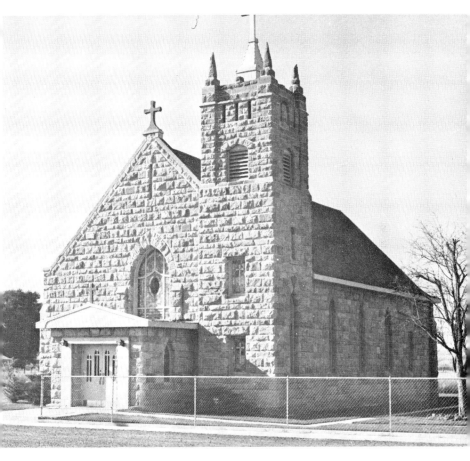

Catholic church of Jordan Valley, Oregon, which was constructed by a congregation that was primarily Basque.

Ranch house near Jordan Valley, Oregon, that is one of the rare examples in the American West of Old World Basque architecture.

Nevada and Star hotels of Elko, Nevada. Throughout the American West Basque hotels were usually located within sight of the train station so that new arrivals who knew no English could locate them with ease. (Photo by Bill Belknap)

Dinner in the Basque hotels is frequently served family style to boarders and guests alike. The unique atmosphere and hearty fare have made these establishments popular throughout the American West. (Photo by Bill Belknap)

Informal, yet large, picnics such as this one held near Buffalo, Wyoming, about 1924 were the precursors to today's Basque festivals. This particular event was held annually in Buffalo on August 15, the feast day of Our Lady of the Assumption, an important holy day in the French Basque area.

Scene from the annual Sheepherders' Ball at Boise sometime during the 1930s. Admission was restricted to Basques and their guests.

In the 1930s Dan Bilbao successfully bid $1,270 for this lamb auctioned at the annual Sheepherders' Ball in Boise.

Basque children of Boise, Idaho, present an ethnic heritage production entitled "Song of the Basque." This was possibly the first major public display of Basque ethnic pride in the American West.

The Basque center of Boise, Idaho, founded in 1951.

Novelist Robert Laxalt (left) and attorney Peter Echeverria, coorganizers of the First National Basque Festival held in 1959 in Sparks, Nevada. This event set the format for future Basque festivals.

Benedicto Goitiandia, for many years the champion Basque weight lifter in the American West, performs at a Basque festival. The steel cylinder weighing 225 pounds is lifted to the shoulder as many as fifty times in a six-minute period. (Photo by Don Normark)

Woodchopping is a popular traditional Old World Basque sport. Scene from a competition held in the Basque country.

The woodchopping competition is now a regular feature of the New World Basque festival. Photo is from the first North American Basque Festival held in Sparks, Nevada, in 1959.

Weight carrying is another popular event at a Basque festival. Victory goes to the person who carries the two 110-pound weights the greatest distance. (Photo by Don Normark)

Emphasis upon *indarra*, or strength, in Old World Basque culture is displayed by men engaged in stone-dragging competition.

Basque-American folk dancers perform traditional flag dance substituting the American flag for the Basque *ikurriña*. (Photo by Bill Belknap)

Dancer displays the athletic prowess and physical strength inherent in Basque folk dances.

The Oinkari dance group of Boise, Idaho, is the epitome of Viscayan dancing to be found in the American West. (Photo by Don Normark)

French Basque handball champions performing in downtown San Francisco.

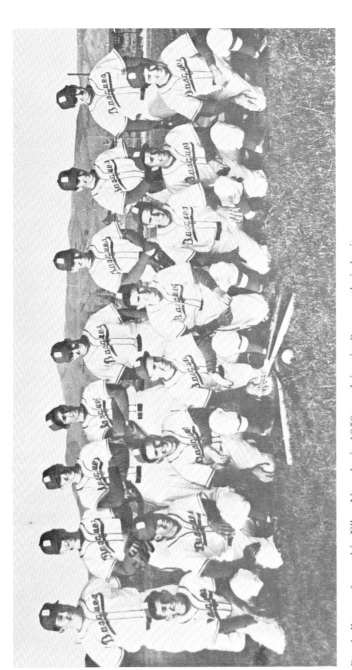

Baseball team formed in Elko, Nevada, in 1950 proclaims its Basque ethnic heritage.

Ethnic pride is now a strong feature of Basque-American life, as displayed by young woman attending a Basque festival. (Photo by Don Normark)

center for the business transactions of the sheepmen and cattle-men of a large region.[115] However, it was San Francisco that was destined to have an early and important Basque hotel district. José Aguirre founded a Basque hotel in the city as early as 1866. San Francisco was the main port of entry for those arriving in California by sea. After the transcontinental railway was completed in 1869 the city continued to be the main initial destination of Basque immigrants, even though they sub-sequently settled in other parts of the American West. The notion that "California" and the "American West" were synonymous persisted in the Basque country well into the twen-tieth century. The young man leaving Europe to join a relative in Nevada might announce *"Kalifornia'ra banoa"* ("I am going to California"), while letters arrived from Europe with addresses like "Boise, Idaho, California."

San Francisco remained California's major wool-exporting center and mutton market; consequently, the business activities of the Basque sheepmen were frequently oriented toward the city. A powerful Basque-owned wool brokerage, the George Alferitz Company, was based there. It would send out buyers all over the state. It also provided financing for many California Basque sheep outfits. On occasion, Basques from as far away as the southern California range drove their own animals (and others on commission) to the San Francisco mar-ket.[116]

For Basques in the central valleys, San Francisco was an important social center. In many instances, Basques traveled to the city to be married, and they honeymooned in the Aguirre hotel or one of the several others that appeared there by the late nineteenth century.* The French hospital in San Francisco became the key medical center for California Basques. Throughout its years of publication, *California'ko Eskual Her-ria* ran a regular column entitled *San Francisco'ko Berriak* ("San Francisco News"), which consisted largely of lists of persons from all over California and from adjacent states who were visiting the city. Most of them stayed in the Basque hotels.

In our sample of California biographies of the 110 Old World-born Basque males, 14, including 9 French Basques, 4

---

*It is extremely difficult to get specific information on San Francisco Basque hotels established prior to 1906, since they, and their records, were destroyed in the earthquake. However, after the calamity, an entire district of Basque hotels emerged on Broadway Street. Today there are six Basque hotels in the North Beach district within a three-block area.

Navarrese, and 1 Vizcayan, were hotel owners at some time in their careers.* Wherever the Basque sheepmen became established in susbstantial numbers, one or more Basque hotels were quickly established. In the words of one informant, "California towns had a French [usually Béarnais], French Basque, and Spanish Basque hotel." In the areas of extensive Basque settlement, several hotelkeepers competed for the ethnic trade. The third issue of *Escualdun Gazeta* carried ads for eight local hotels. Of this total, three were clearly Basque-owned (proprietors: A. Dalgalarrando, M. Hirigoyen, and J. Arroqui), four were likely Béarnais French (proprietors: V. Dol, J. Sartiat, P. Ballade, and S. Celestin) and one was owned by a Jerry Illich. The individual ads reflect keen competition among the hotelkeepers as each sought to provide a unique service unavailable from the others. One ad emphasized good wines and fresh fruit. Another advertised the convenience of its location next to the railway station. A third touted its handball court, a fourth its bar, a fifth its fine stable. One hotelkeeper advertised his willingness to lend money, while another appealed to Old World regional sentiments announcing that his hotel was "home" for people from the French Basque village of Aldudes ("Aldudaren Etchea").[129]

Advertisements in *California'ko Eskual Herria* reveal the existence of additional Basque hotels in the state. The December 30, 1893, issue lists as Basque establishments in Los Angeles the Hotel des Pyrénées, the Hotel d'Europe, the Buena

---

*After the Plaza and Aguirre hotels, the earliest reference is to Esteban and Domingo Oyharzabal who, in 1878, founded the French Hotel in the southern California town of San Juan Capistrano.[117] Another southern California hotel operator was Paul Bengochea, who came to California from Cuba and built and operated the Royal Hotel in Los Angeles, beginning in 1923.[118] In the San Joaquin Valley area we find that Fernando Etcheverry owned the Pyrenees Hotel in Bakersfield in 1894.[119] In 1895 Jean-Pierre Martinto constructed the Basses Pyrenees Hotel in Tehachapi,[120] while Jean Burubeltz, after having hotel interests in Los Angeles during the 1890s, built the Hotel d'Europe in East Bakersfield in 1901.[121] Further to the north, in Fresno, John Bidegaray owned a hotel in 1899.[122] Dominique Bordagaray operated the Pyrenees Hotel from 1900 to 1902.[123] George Bazterra became proprietor of the Hotel Bascongado shortly after 1900.[124] José Michael Lugea, one of the United States-born Basques in our sample, was the owner of the Hotel Spanio in Fresno between 1909 and 1917.[125] In the Stockton area, Raymond Narbaitz and José Oyarbide were partners in the Royal Hotel from about 1920 on,[126] and Nick Ylarraz became the owner of the Hotel Central in 1919.[127] Joseph Yriberri was a hotel manager in Reno, Nevada, shortly after 1896, and later established his own hotel in San Francisco sometime prior to 1919.[128]

Vista House, the Eskualdun Ostatua, and the Hotel de Bayonne. In San Diego there was the Hotel d'Europe. In Kern City, there was the Iberia Hotel, and the Piute Hotel (although operated by F. Young) advertised in the paper. To the north there was the Yparraguirre Hotel in San Francisco and the New Lake House in San Jose.[130] By 1895 Mr. H. Fletcher of Bishop Creek, Inyo County, was advertising his Ostatua Frantsesa ("French Hotel"), and by 1897 there were ads for the Maritonia Hotel of Los Angeles.[131]

The Vizcayan Basques showed this same propensity to found hotels in the regions they dominated in northern Nevada, southeastern Oregon, and southern Idaho. Silen lists twenty-eight individuals who established hotels at some time in their careers (see Appendix Eight). As in the case of our California data, the Silen account is not complete, but we have been able to fix approximate dates for the hotelkeeping activity of those persons cited by him.

The two hotels in Ogden, Utah, are of particular historical interest. The town emerged in the 1890s as a key community for understanding the distribution and movement of Basques throughout the American West. By the late nineteenth century most Basque immigrants traveled westward on the transcontinental railway as far as Ogden. There many Vizcayans changed to the spur line that curved northward into southern Idaho.* Others continued on to northern and western Nevada and San Francisco. While the greater Ogden area was not particularly characterized by heavy Basque settlement, the town itself developed a small Basque hotel district with both French Basque and Vizcayan establishments. Just as the Basque hotels of San Francisco were a focus for the social life of California Basques, many of the Basque sheepmen of the Great Basin who sent to Europe for wives met them in Ogden, were married there, and honeymooned in the hotels. Ogden also became a major stopover for Basques traveling between Montana or Wyoming and the large Basque colony of southern California. By the early years of the twentieth century it was common for the more successful Basque sheepmen of the rigorous northern climes to spend the harshest winter months in the southern California area, frequenting its Basque hotels.

_____

*On April 11, 1896, *The Silver State* of Winnemucca reported, "Nine more Basques, including a woman and young child, arrived yesterday. Four of them are bound for Boise City and will have to return to Ogden and go to their destination over the Ogden short line."[132]

Paralleling the San Francisco and Ogden hotels in the West, there was a crucial eastern seaboard dimension to the network of Basque hotels. By the late nineteenth century, the majority of Basques disembarked in New York. In the 1890s, there were two Basque boarding houses in New York City, outgrowths of private homes.

By 1910 one of the boarding house operators, Valentín Aguirre (no relation to the San Francisco hotel keeper José Aguirre) established a hotel called the *Casa Vizcaina* and a travel agency. His hotel and travel agency are today legendary among the Basques of the American West. Until the advent of regular transatlantic air travel, it was a rare Basque immigrant who did not spend his first night in the United States sleeping in Aguirre's hotel. The traveler left the Old World without a specific New World destination or with only the address of a California or Idaho relative to calm his anxieties as he contemplated crossing a continent with an alien culture and language. Aguirre's efficient aid and direction was a welcome solace.

Elderly Basques residing in the American West today still retain vivid memories, spanning more than half a century in some cases, of getting off the boat in New York City filled with trepidation, only to hear the welcome words, *"Euskaldunak emen badira?"* ("Are there Basques here"). Aguirre's agents were sent to meet every vessel arriving from Europe. Within a short time, the new arrivee was esconced in a Basque establishment, regaled with familiar food, immersed in conversation in the maternal language, and given the opportunity to work out the tensions of the voyage on a nearby handball court. No longer need he fear for the future. In the hotel he was given specific information about conditions in the American West. Aguirre frequently had standing requests for new herders and could place the man whose major concern was his lack of guaranteed employment. Nor need the newcomers entertain the persistent fear of being unable to cope with the train schedules, fares, and the other unknowns of a strange land. Aguirre determined each man's itinerary, purchased his tickets, provided him with detailed instructions concerning transfers and layovers, and gave him the address of a Basque hotel establishment in the town of his destination. In many cases, Aguirre wrote this on a card and pinned it to the traveler's lapel, so that the railway conductor would be certain to put him off. Whenever possible, Aguirre sent out groups of persons with the same destination.

Certain hotels were particularly important in funneling Basque immigrants into the American West, but the total network of hotels was considerably more extensive. In key towns throughout the open-range sheep districts, Basque boarding houses or hotels appeared shortly after the arrival of the sheepherders. As a rule, it would take about five years for the first establishment to appear, and usually within a decade of the first "Basque presence" within a particular area, there would be two or more Basque hotels established in its major community. Normally, such centers were stopoffs on a railroad line, and the hotels were established within sight of the station. In most cases the newly arrived immigrant needed only to cross the street in order to enter an ethnic haven.

The founders of the hotels tended to be individuals with extensive experience in the sheep business who, after many years in the American West, resolved to marry and "settle down." The life of a herder or itinerant sheepman was not conducive to marriage. The majority of married sheepmen simply maintained their families in the Basque country while enduring total separation from them during their years in the sheep business. There were a few cases in the American West in which Basque women stayed with their sheepmen husbands in a tent on the open range, however most lived either on a home ranch or in a town residence. Many itinerant sheepmen established the latter, and in such cases it was not uncommon for the wife to take in boarders. The seasonal fluctuation in the demand for herders meant that many men experienced long layoffs. They would gather in the nearest town and seek to minimize their spending until new employment was available. The cheapest and most agreeable solution was to find room and board in a Basque home.

In this fashion some private homes became boarding houses, and from this experience the proprietor family either purchased or constructed a regular hotel in the railroad station district of the town.* Typically, the hotel was a two-story structure with plain but clean lodgings on the top floor (usually a combination of private rooms and small dormitories sleeping several men) while the ground floor consisted of a bar (with ample space for card playing and occasional dancing) and a large dining room, where the boarders ate together at long tables.

---

*Some hotel proprietors went directly from the sheep business into ownership of a commercial hotel without passing through the boarding house phase.

The Basque hotel operation was dependent upon the sheep industry, and the most effective hotel proprietor was a man with personal experience in sheep. Of the fourteen California hotel proprietors listed above, thirteen had sheep industry experience; eleven of the fourteen had been independent sheep operators. Only José Aguirre did not have personal experience in the sheep business. Nor was involvement in the hotel business necessarily a move out of the sheep industry for these men. Domingo Oyharzabal, Fernando Etcheverry, George Bazterra, and Raymond Narbaitz all owned sheep bands while they were hotel keepers, whereas John Bidegaray, Dominique Bordagaray and José Michael Lugea all were hotel keepers after working as herders but prior to later forming their own sheep outfits. Of the twenty-eight hotel proprietors in the Silen account, sixteen were described as having had involvement in the sheep industry in some capacity.

Competition in the hotel business was keen. As a general rule, before there was sufficient trade in a particular area to support its one Basque hotel in style, another would surely be established. Consequently, hotel owners did their utmost to attract business by creating a festive atmosphere. One might construct a handball court onto the side of the building, another would hire a local accordionist to provide music for frequent dances. Most hotels came to serve Old World Basque festive cuisine as ordinary fare. In rural Basque society, banquets held on special occasions would most certainly include garbanzo beans, a stew dish, and chicken. In the hotels, these items, as well as an additional meat dish,* became the basis of everyday four- and five-course meals. But, of course, once initiated by one hotelkeeper, such fare was copied by the others. In this fashion, the competitive edge of offering superior cuisine was neutralized, while at the same time a Basque cuisine was established throughout the American West.

For its Old World-born clientele, the Basque hotel was both a first way station for the newly arrived immigrant and a haven for the unemployed. However, the hotels also became a base of operations for the Basque sheepman in town on business

---

*This was a concession to the eating habits of the American West as well as a reflection of the difficulty of acquiring seafood in the Great Basin areas at the turn of the century. Old World Basque cuisine is given to a wide array of seafood dishes.

or in search of a few days' pleasure. The drinking* and card-playing atmosphere of the hotels proved particularly attractive to the single males. The hotels occasionally sponsored dances that were sure to be attended by the few unattached Basque girls in the area. The hotels themselves were the greatest source of single Basque girls. Each generally employed two or three, brought out directly from the Basque country by the hotelkeepers, as domestics. Needless to say, there was a high rate of turnover among these female employees, the majority of whom married within a few months after reaching the American West. Most hotelkeepers had more or less standing arrangements to sponsor such girls. Thus, employment in the hotels, with the related possibility of employment as domestics within private homes, was the major channel along which young Basque women arrived in the United States.

The hotels were involved in the business of helping clients to earn a living. Each was a focus of local employment information. Sheepmen in need of herders usually began the search in the local Basque hotels. Each hotel served as a node in a network of employment information that spread throughout the American West. As Basques traveled from one area to another, they almost invariably stayed in the hotels. The steady turnover of travelers provided the hotelkeeper with fairly detailed and up-to-date information on employment opportunities in other areas. Finally, it was through the intervention of the hotelkeepers that Basques found occasional employment in lines of work other than sheep, notably as ranch hands on cattle outfits and in the mines.

The hotel served the nomadic Basque sheepherder and itinerant operator as the closest thing that he had to a "home." It was his mailing address, and the hotelkeeper would save his letters for many months, if need be. It was the place where he left his good town clothing when out on the range, and his bedroll and rifle when in town. Each hotel had a special storeroom reserved for such items. In one hotel, the present authors encountered one hundred and fifty bedrolls, stored

---

*A favorite drink in Europe near the turn of the century, made of picon liqueur, grenadine, brandy, and soda, was extremely popular among the Basques of the West. Today the "picon punch" is regarded as a Basque ethnic drink in the American West, although it is presently all but impossible to buy a picon punch in the Basque country.

carefully, despite the fact that some of their owners had not been
heard from in over twenty years.

For the man who was either injured or ill, the hotel served
as a clinic where he could recuperate. San Francisco and Salt
Lake City emerged as major regional medical centers, and the
hotelkeepers in those cities acquired a special clientele of sick
and injured Basque herders and sheepmen. In the early years it
was common for Basque women living on isolated ranches to
board in a Basque hotel during the latter stages of pregnancy.
The baby was born in the hotel, and the hotelkeeper's wife
frequently served as midwife. As a Basque child living on an
isolated ranch entered his school years, he might be boarded
during the school term at one of the Basque hotels. Over time
the hotels functioned as old-age homes, acquiring a population
of retired bachelor herders who, whether shamed by their lack
of financial success or grown too accustomed to life in the
American West, preferred not to return to the Basque country in
their waning years. And in some instances, the hotel functioned
as a funeral parlor where a corpse might spend its last night
before interment.

But the real secret to success for the hotelkeeper was his
ability to become each client's confidant in the delicate areas of
financial affairs, legal matters, and general dealings with the
Anglo world. The Basque sheepherder tended to be a person of
limited educational background. Furthermore, the isolation inherent in his occupation prevented him from learning the English needed to understand American society. Thus, he was a
man who was sorely unprepared to deal with the local banker,
lawyer, or doctor. He was equally hard pressed to handle such
simple matters as making purchases. In all of these areas, the
hotelkeeper could be counted upon to serve the herder as both
interpreter and protector of his interests. It was not uncommon
for a hotelkeeper to be entrusted with thousands of dollars, a
man's accumulated savings from years of privation; or if a man
needed a loan, he would likely get it from his favorite hotelkeeper. If he was entering into a complicated business matter
requiring the signing of contracts (e.g., a land purchase), he
might place blind faith in the opinion of the hotelkeeper who,
sitting by his side in a lawyer's office, urged him to sign the
unintelligible English-language document. One of the most
frequent demands placed upon the hotelkeeper was to serve as
interpreter in the doctor's office.*

_____

*The impersonality of American medical practices, in contrast to the

Initially, the Basque hotel emerged in response to the needs of an Old World Basque population of single males. As we have seen, these needs went far beyond the simple provisioning of room and board, and the hotel became the single most important social institution for the immigrant Basque population of the American West. From the perspective of the client, the ideal hotelkeeper was the man with whom he shared the same Old World regional background, thereby ruling out possible conflicts between French Basques and Vizcayans. Secondly, the ideal hotelkeeper should himself be Old World-born and fluent in Basque, the clientele's language of intimacy. Only the man with a similar background and language skills was capable of appreciating fully his clients' outlooks. Even first-generation American-born Basques were likely to view life differently as a result of their exposure to the American school system and their deeper involvement in the wider society, and few Basque-Americans retained total fluency in the Basque language. For an Old World-born sheepherder, whose intention it was to return to Europe permanently, the New World-born generation was somewhat inscrutable, if not downright suspect. Thus, few American-born Basques have ever been successful hotelkeepers.

On the other hand, the hotelkeeper had to be somewhat conversant in the ways of the wider American society. He had to possess sufficient English skills to serve as interpreter as well as sufficient *savoir faire* to act as the herder's protector in a totally alien world. Not every Basque who had resided in the United States for ten years was capable of being a hotelkeeper. The position was multifaceted and exceptionally demanding. It is not by chance that many failed as hotelkeepers and that the successful ones tended to be leaders in the local Basque colony. While it seems obvious to argue that the nature of the Basque hotel thrust upon its owner the role of leader, one suspects that the opposite was equally true: it required a talented man with leadership qualities to be a success in the Basque hotel business.

The hotelkeeper's choice of spouse could be equally critical to the success of the enterprise. The business was inevitably understaffed and demanded the full participation of husband and wife. The latter, if Old World-born, likely devoted herself to organizing the kitchen and/or the maid service. However, in many cases hotelkeepers married New World-born Basque

---

emphasis upon at-home, family-circle medical care in the Basque country, has proven to be most difficult for the Old World Basque.

girls, or, in a few instances, non-Basques. Such a person could be particularly useful in helping her husband discharge his role as interpreter and protector for the clientele. She, even more than her husband, possessed English fluency and a working familiarity with local ways.

Basque hotels have a history of a high rate of turnover in their ownership. There are several reasons for this. From the viewpoint of the individual owner, the hotel business might, if successful, provide him with the wherewithal either to return permanently to Europe or to invest in other endeavors. Many hotel owners continued in the sheep industry with hired labor during the years that they were in the hotel business. Others used their hotel profits to purchase substantial sheep ranches. Other hotel men invested their funds in urban enterprises. But whatever the future direction of their investments, most proprietors sold out after a few years to escape the tensions and drudgery of operating a hotel. The hotel owners and their wives generally worked in the business together and full time. He might be at the bar while she was in the kitchen. Even if two families were in partnership (a frequent arrangement), there were excessive demands on all concerned. The hotel operated with its single shift from the crack of dawn until far into the night. While other employees might be given time off, the owner and his wife usually worked a seven-day week. Accounts of working five years without a vacation were not uncommon.

There is yet another reason for frequent changes of hotel ownership. The Basque hotel proved to be a particularly fragile business with respect to the possibility of transferring ownership between the generations in the same family. When an American-born Basque who did not happen to marry an Old World Basque attempted to continue the family's hotel business, there would likely occur one of two developments. Either the business would lose most of its clientele and simply fail, or the owner would become obligated to convert the establishment into a luxury restaurant with a specialized ethnic cuisine, patronized largely by non-Basques. The latter possibility occurred with increasing frequency as Basque cooking acquired an excellent reputation among non-Basques of the American West.

The Basque hotels also provided a range of services for the growing population of American-born Basques, who demanded a substantial Old World atmosphere and ownership of the establishment. The hotel, more than any context other than his family circle, served the Basque-American with the opportunity of articulating and expressing his ethnic identity.

Until the recent emergence of Basque social clubs and festivals, the Basque-American lived in a thoroughly Anglo world. A combination of factors created in Basque-Americans a sense of confusion concerning their ethnic identity. In part there was the general erosive effect of the American melting pot philosophy. Then, too, Basques are racially Caucasian and were therefore not readily subjected to the exclusion characteristic of the historical treatment of nonwhite minorities in American society, an exclusion that might have reinforced their sense of sharing a collective ethnic group destiny. On the other hand, the negative image of the Basque sheepman held in some circles has discouraged Basques from a public display of their ethnic identity. Parents who imparted a keen sense of ethnic pride to their offspring discouraged them from expressing it outside of intimate Basque circles. This ethnic pride operated more at the level of a mental image than as outward behavior.

The fact that Old World Basque culture lacked a substantial intellectual or literary tradition further isolated New World-born Basque-Americans from information about their ethnic heritage and ruled out Basque militancy or even interest in creating an ethnic literature or ethnic schools (as was the case with many groups). Curious Basque-Americans, to a greater degree than the members of any other ethnic group, were without reading matter dealing with either their Old World or New World history and traditions. The question with which we began this work, namely, "What is a Basque?" was perplexing for many Basque-Americans as well. While the average Basque-American possessed a notion of ethnic identity as an aspect of self, he had little substantive knowledge concerning its heritage.

The hotels gave the Basque-American some semblance of ethnic tradition. Entering a hotel he found an ethnic context in which he was regarded as holding at least some credentials. Here he could practice his incorrect Basque, and converse with herders,* thereby becoming somewhat familiar with Old World conditions and concerns. In a very real sense the Basque hotel

---

*Since contract sheepherders may now apply for permanent residency in the United States and seek other forms of employment, the hotels are also acquiring young and single male boarders who work at town jobs.

provided Basque-Americans with a means of recharging their ethnic batteries. Over the years both local and out-of-town Basque-Americans have come to constitute an important segment of the clientele of the Basque hotels. While most successful Basque-Americans, when traveling, balk at actually staying overnight in the simple lodgings of the hotels, they are likely to be found there at the dinner hour.

The Basque hotel has come to serve Americanized New World-born Basques with an opportunity to become at least partially versed in Old World Basque traditions. However, this is not the only instance of acculturation discernible in the Basque hotel. The hotel also promotes considerable mingling of Old World Basques from diverse regions of the Basque country. As we have noted, there are usually both French and Spanish Basque hotels in communities with a large and heterogeneous Basque population. But this exclusiveness is never absolute, and there are many communities with only one hotel. It is in the American West that a French Basque bartender frequently interacts with Vizcayan clients, or vice versa. Out of this interaction there has developed a greater understanding of Old World regional differences than one encounters in the Basque country itself. The hotel context lends itself to a greater tolerance of dialectical differences in spoken Basque. The hotelkeeper from Soule who, prior to coming to the United States, regarded Vizcayan Basque as totally incomprehensible, quickly acquires fluency in Vizcayan as a New World resident and may even lace his speech with Vizcayan expressions when dealing with his fellow Souletins. Ironically, it is in the context of the American West that Old World Basques broaden their Basque perspectives. Similarly, it is in the American West that Basque is the *lingua franca* for a heterogeneous population of French national, Spanish national, and New World-born Basques. Some young herders remark that they actually improved their Basque in the sheep camps and hotels of the American West, especially since the language is falling into disuse in many parts of the Basque country.

During the last thirty years the Basque hotels have acquired a considerable non-Basque tourist trade. Although the hotels advertise but little, there are many devotees of the Basque hotel cuisine and atmosphere who make a point of discovering and frequenting the obscure Basque establishments. Part of the attraction lies in the hearty, ample, and inexpensive fare, part in the camaraderie of eating meals "family style" at a long table (the heritage of the boarding house tradition) in the company of strangers.* Of particular delight to the tourists is the Old World atmosphere of the bar, where questions concerning the "mystery" of the Basques may be directed at the bartender.

In this situation the hotelkeeper becomes an adept popularizer of his ethnic heritage. He is likely to emphasize or "stage" those aspects that are most conducive to an aura of ethnic uniqueness, and hence most marketable to the casual tourist. The discussion turns to the unsolved riddle of Basque origins, the reputed impossibility for a non-Basque to learn the Basque language, the art of drinking wine from a bota bag, or romantic anecdotes and tales of hardship in the life of the Basque sheepherder. It is in this manner that much of the image held of Basques by their non-Basque neighbors is derived from casual conversation and observation during occasional evenings spent in the hotels.

Just as tourists can learn about Basques in the hotels, the Basques are exposed to additional sources of information about the wider American society.† It is in the hotels that the boarders peruse the local newspaper, play American music on the juke box and, most importantly, watch American television on the inevitable barroom set. In this fashion, they are exposed to local issues that transcend the narrower interests of the boarding house.

The presence of the tourists provides the Old World-born boarders with a daily opportunity to interact with non-Basques in a context in which the Basque is both relaxed and at an advantage. Upon entering the Basque hotel, the tourist is anxious to enjoy an "ethnic evening" and is at great pain not to give offense. To a greater degree than when patronizing an American eating establishment, the tourist in the Basque hotel is likely to

---

*Basque hotel dining rooms vary in their eating arrangements. In some, Old World-born herders and tourists eat at the same table. In others, the boarders have their own table while tourists are served a different menu at individual tables. In still others there are separate dining rooms for the boarders and the tourists.

†At the same time, through residence in the hotels, the boarders maintain close contact with their Old World heritage. The hotel is likely to receive a steady flow of Old World periodicals, which circulate among the residents. Through conversations with hotel guests recently arrived from Europe, the boarders learn the latest developments in the Basque country. Similarly, persons departing for Europe frequently spend their last few days in the United States in a Basque hotel. They may be asked by the boarders to deliver messages and presents to relatives in the Basque country.

comport himself as a "guest." In this respect his behavior is controlled, his demeanor friendly, his conversation open, and his interest genuine. Consequently, his presence does not threaten the "home-like" atmosphere of the establishment or disturb the boarders, who indeed do regard the hotel as home. In his relaxed dealings with the tourist, the herder can practice his faltering English without fear of ridicule. He can deal with a non-Basque at a level that has none of the added overtones of an employer-employee relationship or the charged negative aspects that can sometimes color relations between "Americans" and "foreigners." The tourist is the most innocuous of the non-Basques, a person whose intentions are patently benign and who in any event may never be encountered again.

As an ethnic haven for the Old World herder and a "safe" context for his acculturation into the wider society, a context for versing Basque-Americans in their Old World heritage, and a common meeting ground for the Basques and their non-Basque neighbors, the hotel is a prime architect of the ethnic image of the Basques of the American West as well as a key mechanism in its maintenance. Unlike other institutions, such as Basque social clubs and festivals, the hotel functions every day of the year.

Social Clubs

Social clubs appear relatively late in the development of Basque settlements. In most cases it is an emerging generation of American-born Basques who work in concert with the immigrant generation to form the organization.

The earliest mention of an abortive attempt to form a club is in Stockton in 1907.[133] In 1924 the Zazpiak Bat Club was formed in San Francisco. It managed to survive for a little more than a decade, disbanding due to internal tensions between French and Spanish Basques. The Basques of Kern County were more successful. They founded a club in 1938 that still exists. Two years later, the Basque colony of La Puente, in the Los Angeles area, mustered the cooperation of several Basque groups and created the La Puente Handball Club. The club had its own court and clubhouse, which still serve as a social center for the members. In 1946 nine southern California Basques founded the Southern California Eskualdun Club, which continues to function with a highly limited membership.

The earliest effort of the Vizcayan colony to organize was the founding in Boise of the *Sociedad de Socorros Mutuos*

(Mutual Aid Society) in 1908. The society was organized strictly for the purpose of providing health and burial insurance; it paid medical bills, gave the member a daily stipend while he was incapacitated, paid funeral expenses, and, in the case of those permanently physically disabled or mentally deranged, paid their passage to the Basque country. The health insurance aspect of this plan is still in effect.

In 1949 Euzkaldunak, Inc., was organized in Boise. By 1951 the group had constructed its own building, complete with bar and banquet facilities. The Boise Basque Center, as it is known, still operates. More recently there has been considerable organizational activity among the Basques of Boise. In 1972 a group of Boiseans formed the *Idaho'ko Euzko Zaleak* nonprofit corporation in order to foment Basque studies in the area by raising matching funds for a Basque cultural appreciation grant of the National Endowment for the Humanities awarded to the Idaho Office of Higher Education. The group sponsored a successful Basque festival. At about the same time a women's auxiliary called *Aiztan Artean* was founded by several ex-members of Boise's *Oinkari* dance group (see below). Finally, in 1973 several interested persons formed the *Anaiok Danok* organization. Its purpose is to disseminate information about conditions in the Basque country, provide assistance to political refugees, and support the *ikastolak* or Basque language schools in Europe. The organization has also formed a Basque choir.

The remainder of the Basque social clubs in the American West are considerably more modern than the Boise Basque center. The Chino, San Francisco, Los Banos (California), Reno, Elko, Ely (Nevada), and Grand Junction (Colorado) clubs all postdate the celebration of the First National Basque Festival (see below) and were in some measure influenced by it.

In 1973 representatives of several of the Basque clubs met in Reno and formed the North American Basque Organizations, Inc. It was a conscious attempt to overcome the regional divisions between the two Basque communities of the American West. The geographical representation of the new organization is propitious, since the president and secretary are from Boise, the vice-president is from San Francisco, and the treasurer is from Elko. It is premature to evaluate the success of the organization. However, there appears to be considerable potential, since the combined memberships of the Basque clubs of the American West surpass 3,000 persons (including Boise, 800 members; Kern County, 538 members; Reno, 325 members; and San Francisco, 300 members).

Membership in the clubs is reserved to "all persons of Basque extraction or part Basque extraction and their spouses whether of Basque extraction or not."* This statement is congruous with the Basque kinship principle that views the spouses of relatives as relatives.

Historically, leadership in the social clubs, as in the total Basque community, tends to devolve upon men of native intelligence rather than of polished education—the hotelkeeper, the successful rancher—persons of Old World origins, who thereby enjoy the confidence of other immigrants but who also acquire sufficient language skills and familiarity with Anglo ways and institutions to command respect in the wider community. Such men as John Achabal of Boise, José Bengoechea of Mountain Home, Jean Esponda of Buffalo, and Guy Saval of northeastern Nevada were so instrumental in orchestrating the affairs of their fellow Basques that they were sometimes referred to and perceived by the wider populace as the local "king" or "father" of the Basques. To this day, the mantle of leadership within the ethnic community has not been transferred entirely to the subsequent generations of Basque-Americans. In the organization of the social clubs and the Basque festivals, Basque-Americans play important roles, but in the final analysis the Old World contingent weighs in more heavily, and decisions are made against the backdrop of the latter's opinions. Consequently, the emphasis in organized activities is placed almost exclusively upon association and recreation rather than upon education. The Basque organizations of the American West have not, with very few exceptions, emulated other ethnic groups in creating language classes, library facilities, or lecture and publications series. They do, however, engage in charitable activities, such as providing scholarships and making donations to needy families and institutions.

The clubs sponsor a local festival as their major undertaking. There is also likely to be an annual winter dance (possibly as a Christmas or New Year's Eve party, and in Idaho a "Sheepherders' Ball") that is less public than the festival. The clubs may also organize one or two "members only" picnics or dinners during the year, and they frequently sponsor a folk dance group for the junior members. In recent years the Boise and San Francisco Basque clubs have sponsored charter flights to the Basque country for their members.

---

*This is an identical quote in the first article of the bylaws of both the Elko and Ely clubs, and is generally characteristic of all club bylaws.

PICNICS AND FESTIVALS

The social life of each Basque colony during the earliest years of its formation focused upon the local Basque hotels. With the passage of time, it became customary in many areas to hold picnics or other kinds of get-togethers, frequently under the sponsorship of one of the more prominent Basque ranchers. Cramer, reporting on Basque social life in rural southern California of the late nineteenth century, notes:

> Basque traditions were part of the life on the Sansiñena-Eseverri sheep ranch. Many of the close friends were other Basque people—the Bastanchurys, Hualdes, Oxararts, Yriartes, and others—and many of the customs from the "old country" were carried on here by these families. They gathered for huge barbecues and traveled to the Bastanchury Ranch frequently to watch the Basque handball games played on the special courts there. . . .[134]

By the 1880s the Basques in western Merced County gathered weekly at the Arburua ranch for a day of relaxation.

> Since the adjacent lower country was almost exclusively inhabited by Basques what could better entertain these people than a good game of pelota (Basque handball)? Miguel converted the front wall of his very large and solidly built barn into a court. Lines were painted on the wall, and the ground in front was smoothed out, rolled and sprinkled. Practically the entire neighborhood living within a distance of five or six miles gathered every Sunday (weather permitting) to play and watch the game. Frequently, as many as 25 or more, including women and children attended.[135]

In Buffalo, Wyoming, the "founder" of the local colony, Jean Esponda, built a handball court on his property. By 1918 the Basques of Buffalo were holding an annual picnic in their summer ranges of the nearby Bighorn Mountains. The festival was held on August 15, the feast day of Our Lady of the Assumption, patron of many French Basque villages. Gachiteguy reports that for the first of these occasions, Jean Esponda sent for Father Gariador, a Basque Benedictine monk residing in Montebello (near Los Angeles).[136]

In 1929 John Achabal initiated the annual Sheepherders' Ball in Boise. The affair is still held each winter, and the proceeds go to charity. On the day of St. Ignatius, the patron saint of Vizcaya, in 1933, the Basques held a picnic at the Boise municipal park. This may have been the first such affair in the area.[137]

These Basque get-togethers all shared the characteristic of being closed ethnic affairs. With the exception of the Boise Sheepherders' Ball, they were unheralded, inconspicuous events on the local social calendar. They were often held at some distance from the local population centers. None of this is surprising when we consider that the dates coincide with the periods of tension between the Basques and their neighbors. Anglo ambivalence regarding the Basque ethnic group fed upon the latter's identification with the sheep industry, and particularly with the Basque role as itinerant sheepmen. In a period of competition over the range, sometimes leading to violence, the Basque was frequently the target of insults, barbed ethnic jokes, and epithets such as "black Bascos."

In such a climate the Basques were not prone to display their ethnic identity publicly. If the Basque hotel and the private picnic or dance served as an ethnic refuge, where the immigrant could enjoy Basque cuisine, conversation, and company, he attempted in his dealings with the wider society to remain as inconspicuous as possible. Elderly informants relate that for this reason Basque herders around the beginning of the century consciously cultivated cowboy ways in both dress and the habit of drinking American whiskey.

We have noted that American attitudes toward the Basque ethnic group, even during the years of tension, were not unanimously negative. That the Basques were hard-working, dedicated in the face of adversity, and prone to well-earned economic success was recognized even by their detractors. It was also generally acknowledged that the Basques, with few exceptions, were trustworthy in their business dealings. However, the very successes of the Basques underscored the threat that they posed in the competition for an ever more crowded range.

The restrictive immigration laws of the 1920s and the cumulative legislation restricting access to the public lands, culminating in the Taylor Grazing Act of 1934, hamstrung Basque immigration into the American West, but it also created the bases for a new relationship between the Basques and their neighbors. Once range use was stabilized and regulated, the itinerant sheepman became extinct. By the 1940s sheepherders were in such short supply in the American West that the highest level of American politics was set in motion; within a decade, the pro-Basque forces had succeeded in singling out Basques as especially desirable immigrants who were to be accorded special treatment by immigration policy. The public image of the Basque changed during this period, as popular writers began to depict the Basque herder as a romantic and a heroic figure.

It was against this backdrop of a new ethnic group image that the First National Basque Festival, held in Sparks, Nevada, just outside of Reno, took place in 1959. The sponsor of the festival was a casino operator who, while not a Basque himself, was married to an Idaho-born Vizcayan. The local Basques who organized the festival spared no expense in their attempt to make the event as authentic as possible, although many retained only vague notions of their Old World ethnic heritage. They were confident of a financial success, but their objectives went far beyond the commercialization of ethnicity. They encouraged participants to wear folk costumes, they assembled folk music groups from distant areas, and they invited the French and Spanish ambassadors, who attended. Basque athletic contests, including wood chopping and stone lifting, were held. A sheep dog trial was organized, and a banquet with Basque-American food highlighted the festivities. Significantly, the event was open to the public. The festival received considerable attention in the news media.

During the two days, between five and six thousand Basques and almost as many non-Basques attended. The choice of the Reno area was fortuitous in terms of attracting the widest possible participation of Basques of the American West. Reno is centrally located with respect to the Vizcayan colony of northern Nevada and southern Idaho and the California French Basque colony. The Reno colony itself is transitional, representing all Old World Basque regional origins in its makeup. The two prime organizers were Basque-Americans, one of Vizcayan descent, the other of French-Basque parentage.

The first national Basque festival stands as the largest single gathering of Basques in the American West. Even more significantly, the festival served as both a stimulus and model for future Basque festivals, which began to proliferate throughout the American West during the 1960s. It sparked the creation of many of the Basque clubs mentioned in the previous section of this chapter. All sponsor annual picnics that are in some measure open to the public.* The festivities usually include a

---

*This can vary from the relatively closed picnic of the Ely club, in which the only non-Basques attending come at the invitation of a club member, to the conscious attempts of the Elko organizers to sell tickets to tourists. In 1964, Elko christened its first festival as the Second National Basque Festival. Each

Basque-language Mass celebrated by one of the Basque chaplains in the American West, Basque athletics, in which herders vie for prizes in wood chopping and stone lifting, folk dance performances, an open-air barbecue with Basque cuisine, and a public dance in the evening. The festivals are scheduled on different weekends throughout the late spring and summer months. Attendance at each varies between one and three thousand persons.

These local festivals have acquired regional importance. Even national magazines and other news outlets[138] have given the festivals exposure and made them somewhat of a tourist attraction. Our concern here, however, is the role of the festivals as a regional social institution for the Basques themselves. Individual Basques travel great distances to attend them. Furthermore, local Basque colonies invite the participation of folk dance groups and athletic contestants from other colonies. The festival becomes the vehicle for persons residing at great distances from one another to renew old friendships or make new ones. For the Basques themselves, visiting is as important a part of the proceedings as any of the official events. Festival attendance is an important integrative mechanism. In some measure it provides the cohesiveness required to convert a population into an ethnic group.

On the other hand, the patterns of Basque attendance at the various festivals also serve to reinforce some of the divisions within the Basque community that we have already discussed. Few, if any, Boise Basques attend the California festivals. French Basques are notably absent at Boise Basque affairs. It is not simply a question of distances, since a sizeable contingent of Basques from Buffalo, Wyoming, attend the picnic in Chino, California. In festival attendance, as in other contexts, there are clearly two major spheres of Basque activities in the American West.

The festivals serve to introduce strong local competition among the Basque colonies. Each local club tries to outdo others in staging a successful festival. In the folk-dancing performance at a particular festival the children's dance groups from two or three outside communities may perform along with the sponsoring club's group, and all are subjected to critical eyes and tongues.

---

year it continues the "national festival" billing. In 1972 the Basques of Boise organized a large and successful festival. However, no provisions have been made to continue it on a regular basis.

Finally, the festival permits the Basque community to project its self-image to non-Basque society. The Basques simultaneously reassert ethnic pride and take cognizance of their "differences" as they acknowledge their membership in the broader American society. A delicate balancing of cultural symbols during the festival is necessary to achieve both these aims. In the parade, on the bandstand, and at the athletic events, the American and Basque flags are flown together. The festival program might contain an essay on the merits of the Basque cultural heritage as well as contributions emphasizing the Basques' adherence to the American dream and their specific contributions to the society of the American West. The non-Basque Catholic bishop and state politicians receive prominent exposure throughout the proceedings. Basque children dressed in traditional costume might sing "God Bless America" before performing their own national anthem, *"Gernika'ko Arbola."* The Basque festival is the major event in which non-Basques are invited to view the Basque ethnic group, and the entire event is highly structured by its organizers to present "on stage" those aspects of the heritage and Basque character that the Basques themselves wish to publicize.

PELOTA

A clear manifestation of the Basque ethnic heritage is the game of pelota, or handball, and the variant *jai alai*. There is not a village in the Basque country where some form of handball is not played, and with a passion. In most communities the village plaza is flanked by both the church and the ball court. Pelota is to Basque youngsters what sandlot baseball is to their American counterparts. Like baseball, pelota is the sport of grown men as well—amateurs, semiprofessional, and professional players. No event in a Basque village creates as much interest as a match that pits a local player or team against players from a neighboring community. In the major towns and cities of the Basque country, professional matches are held regularly. Each year there are both amateur and professional tournaments, in which champions of the entire Basque country are determined. Of particular interest are the games that acquire an international flavor when the best Spanish Basque *pelotaris* are matched against the French Basque champions. One form of the many variations of the Basque ball game has thrilled audiences in such widely disparate places as Shanghai and Manila, South America, Cuba, Mexico City, Tijuana, and Miami: the game of *jai alai* (which means, "happy festival" in Basque).

While *jai alai* was never organized on a commercial scale among the Basques of the American West, the handball form was popular sport among the Basque sheepherders. Handball courts were a part of many of the early Basque hotel establishments; as we have also noted, some private individuals even built their own courts. The pelota matches were a social event in the Basque community. Until well into the twentieth century, whenever there was a substantial Basque population there was almost certain to be a pelota court.

There is also evidence that matches of regional interest were sometimes organized in the American West. The November 15, 1907, issue of the *Elko Independent* reported that a new Basque hotel planned to inaugurate its business by sponsoring a handball match between the champions of Nevada and California. The paper stated that the wagering was heavy and that each side had placed $1,000 on the line.[139]

As time passed, and particularly in the years between 1921 and 1950, when Spanish Basques were largely prohibited from entering the United States, most of the courts fell into disuse. Few American-born Basques showed an interest in the game. Today, there are few active pelota courts in the Spanish Basque areas of the American West. The Oregon Historical Society is currently attempting to restore the court in Jordan Valley. The Boise Basques have recently restored a court and now sponsor local tournaments. In the summer of 1975 a new court was inaugurated in Elko, Nevada; it was erected with the financial support of the Spanish government.

The French Basque colony of California was not affected as adversely by the United States Immigration Service quota system as was its Spanish counterpart. Consequently, today there are active handball courts in San Francisco, Stockton, Los Banos, Fresno, Bakersfield, Chino, and La Puente. Matches are organized with some regularity, particularly in conjunction with picnics and festivals. Intersectional pelota matches serve as an axis of competition within the California Basque colony: a player is regarded a *Chino'tar* or a *San Francisco'tar*, a representative of a local colony, and feelings run high concerning the outcome of the matches. The enthusiasm of the California Basques for pelota was underscored in the autumn of 1971, when they sponsored a tour of California by ten French Basque national champions and officials of the French federation. The group toured the California colonies and gave several exhibition matches.

DANCE GROUPS

The earliest descriptions of life in the Basque hotels of both the Río de la Plata region and the American West emphasize the popularity of dancing. There is frequent reference to the *jota*, a folk dance that originated in northeastern Spain, but which is enormously popular in the Basque country as well. The *jota*, while more "folk" than "social," was and continues to be danced by the Basques of the American West as a regular part of any social dance. On occasion, festivals and dances may have a *jota* competition to select the best couple.

While the *jota* may be danced by a single couple or even a single individual, there are many Basque folk dances that require group performance and that are most effective when the dancers wear folk costumes. Most of the Basque clubs of the American West presently sponsor dance groups or have sponsored them in the past. Some clubs have two dance groups—one for very small children and one for adolescents. In the case of the French Basque clubs of San Francisco and a southern California dance group that straddles the Chino and La Puente clubs, the dancers are young adults.

All of the dance groups develop a repertoire of folk dances that again reflect and reinforce the Old World regional origins of the local Basque community. In Boise the dances performed and costumes worn are Vizcayan and Guipuzcoan, whereas in San Francisco they are French Basque. The dancers perform at functions of the local club, such as the Christmas party and its festival. They are also likely to perform on invitation at other Basque festivals. They may perform at a local school affair or for a service club, but in the main, the dance groups do not perform publicly except in the context of Basque public events.

There is an exception to the above generalization. In 1960 a group of young Basque-Americans from Boise traveled to the Basque country. While attending a local festival, they observed the performance of a folk dance group from San Sebastián called the *Oinkari*. The Idaho group was invited to attend several Oinkari rehearsals and traveled with it on a dance tour in the French Basque area. On their return to Idaho, these young people formed their own organization which they, too, called the Oinkari Basque Dancers.

During the early 1960s the Boise Oinkari group gave many public performances in Idaho. In 1962 they performed at the Seattle World's Fair, and in 1964 they represented Idaho at the New York World's Fair. On that same tour they performed in the Capitol in Washington, D.C. They performed at the national folk festival in Milwaukee in 1966, at Expo '70 in Montreal, and at the Spokane World's Fair in 1974.

There has been additional exposure of the American public to Basque dancing through the American tours of Old World Basque dance groups. Since 1967 the Olaeta Basque ballet of Bilbao has toured the United States on three occasions, playing concert engagements before non-Basque audiences in places like Carnegie Hall in New York and performing before predominantly Basque audiences in the American West. These dance groups furnish another medium in which an aspect of the Basque character and ethnic heritage is displayed.

The Basque ethnic manifestations that we have described may be analyzed in two fashions. On the one hand, they reflect and contribute to the continued maintenance of the Basque ethnic heritage in the American West. Taken as a whole, they provide a fascinating example of an ethnic group elaborating a series of institutions that reinforce a sense of ethnic cohesiveness among a population that is small and lightly sprinkled over an enormous territory. Through its regional festivals, the network of Basque hotels, preferential endogamy, the kinship system, sense of funerary obligations, social clubs, dance groups, the travels of Basque chaplains, and Basque-language radio broadcasts, the Basque community has been able to create and to project one of the most viable ethnic heritages in the American West. A close look at the organizational details of any one ethnic manifestation reveals tendencies within the Basque community, ranging from Old World regionalism and New World regionalism to generational differences between the Old World- and the New World-born. Considerable social diversity is masked under the single label of "Basque."

On the other hand Basque ethnic manifestations may be viewed from the perspective of the outsider. Our account has documented the transformation of the Basque stereotype from that of the despised itinerant herder of the days when men fought for use of the open range to that of the romantic hero, the humble worker, or the established hotelkeeper. Basques are now one of the most highly respected ethnic groups in the American West. Non-Basques frequent Basque hotels and attend Basque festivals; newspaper editorials and feature stories praise the virtues of the group. But there is a sense in which a new misconception now colors the Basque stereotype. The person who frequents the hotel and the festival observes the Basques in the context of relaxation and recreation. He comes away with the impression that Basques are addicted to good food, wine, dancing, and sport. This is only one aspect of Basque group life, the reverse side of a personality that can be dour to an extreme and pragmatic to the point of obsession. American society is most tolerant of ethnic differences in the areas of cuisine and innocuous folk arts. To contribute a new dish to America's "cafeteria culture" or to titillate audiences with unique dances, sports, and costumes is the surest way to gain approval. In their public displays of their ethnic heritage, Basques, like other groups, are prone to emphasize these features. The result is that "a good time is had by all," but, in many respects, the Basques remain as inscrutable as ever.

CHAPTER EIGHT

Conclusion

It is in viewing Basque emigration against the backdrop of almost five centuries of history in Europe and both continents of the New World that the problem of interpreting the Basques is fully apparent. For those who stereotype the Basque emigrant as a simple sheepherder, there is a lesson in Spanish colonial history. For those who stereotype him as an elitist administrator, clergyman, mariner, or financial magnate of the Spanish Empire, there is the sobering reality of the Basque sheepmen of the *pampas* and the American West. Some Basque emigrants have risen to the dizzying heights of imperial political and financial circles, while others have served as the lonely guardians of the flocks under the most primitive of living conditions.

Nevertheless, we have emphasized certain aspects of Basque emigration, and in doing so, we have identified several of its most salient themes. From the time in the early sixteenth century, when the king of Spain was at particular pains to recruit rural Basques for Hispaniola, to the most recent signings of Western Range Association shepherder contracts, the majority of Basque emigrants have come from the rural sector of Basque society. The impartible inheritance system of the rural farmsteads (in combination with the tendency of rural Basques to produce large families) provided the structural basis for extensive emigration in each generation. But if the typical

Basque emigrant was of peasant origin, this background itself requires further consideration.

Students of peasant society are prone to consider that it is rooted in a traditional, and frequently anachronistic, way of life. This rootedness, according to this view, is a major impediment to the individual peasant's attempts to exploit new opportunities and life styles. Peasants leave their communities as a reaction against the restraints (economic and otherwise) of tradition. By implication, the narrowness of the traditionalist peasant background means that the individual emigrant likely makes his adaptation to the outside world *after* leaving the confines of his community.

In our opinion, the view we have described ignores the fact that life on the farmstead provided the individual with a generalized background. He was a jack-of-many-trades, without becoming overly specialized in any one of them. He was a carpenter, furniture maker, stone mason, grain cropper, animal raiser, mule skinner, charcoal maker, logger, and contraband runner. The successful operation of the Basque farmstead required a certain amount of business acumen and the ability to weigh many factors. The Basque farmstead is in miniature a complicated enterprise.

Basque children were initially socialized into agricultural roles, although it was expected that not all members of the family would pursue a career in agriculture. Those who left were normally provided with dowries or other financial assistance so they had at least some initial capital as they sought a new start in life. To the degree that Basque emigrants were able to exploit an Old World experience or, conversely, were trapped by it, such experience was more generalized and more widely adaptable to a variety of situations than might be assumed, and the act of emigration was itself subsidized. Although the Basque emigrant did not possess polished intellectual skills, he left the Old World with a variety of practical trades and, in many cases, with some money in his pocket. He was in a position to consider a wide range of New World opportunities.

Thus, there are *several* admissible stereotypes of the Basque emigrant, each of which may be understood only in historical context. Such a context would include the interplay between events and conditions in Europe, the immigrant's host country, *and* the other areas of the world that clearly served him as viable alternatives when making the selection of his overseas destination. It has been one of our tasks to interpret in depth one major stereotype of the Basque emigrant—that of the sheepman. In order to do so, it was necessary to describe the history and life of the Basques in two widely separated regions of the New World—southern South America and the American West. The emergence of Basque sheepmen in the latter can be understood only if interpreted in light of Basque experiences in the former.

The parallels between the economic development of the *pampas* and the American West are striking. In both cases the pioneers who developed the ranches had a frontiersman mentality. The risks were great, the living conditions primitive, but the adventurous individual could dream of acquiring great wealth with a minimal investment of capital. We have seen that Basque emigrants were particularly prone to risk-taking in the more marginal areas of the newly opened ranges. If most enjoyed only modest economic success or even tasted outright failure, others forged personal empires in the vast hinterlands of the New World. Success stories from both South America and the American West flowed back to the Basque country to fire the imagination of its youth.

As an example of New World opportunity, there was much to recommend the South American sheepman's experience. The Basque presence in Río de la Plata was older and hence both more extensive and better organized. By the time that the first few Basques had arrived in California in the early 1850s, cities like Buenos Aires and Montevideo already had their Basque districts and businesses designed to service Basque immigration. The sheer size of the South American colony multiplied the number of kinsmen and acquaintances that the emigrant might call upon for assistance. As a group, Basques were esteemed in South American society. All of this was in sharp contrast to the "foreigner" or "greaser" treatment that awaited the southern European immigrant in Anglo California.

Furthermore, outside of his ethnic districts and circles the Basque immigrant in South America encountered a society with which he had some working familiarity. Even for French Basques the acquisition of Spanish posed little difficulty, and many arrived in the New World with some knowledge of it.*

---

*In 1850 François Jaureguy published a method for learning Spanish in Buenos Aires. His book was written in a French Basque dialect.[1]

Most Spanish Basques were practically bilingual.* Life in California (even the Hispanic south) meant struggling with the difficulties of the English language and the less-familiar Anglo culture.

The first Basques to arrive in California, after the annexation of the area by the United States, were clearly drawn by the attraction of the gold discoveries. There is no reason to suspect that they would have gravitated to the area had they simply been in search of new rangeland. The distances between California and either Europe or South America were too great, and the favored Argentine *pampas* were only relatively crowded by the early 1850s. But for the Basques who joined the ranks of the argonauts and then became disillusioned with the mining camps, the California range must have looked like a replay of the Argentine scene of the 1830s—but with the added advantage of a highly inflated local demand for animal products. They were quick to respond.

Nevertheless, there remains the question as to why this initial entry into California of several hundred South American and Old World Basques was converted into a wave of Basque immigration encompassing the entire American West. There are at least two explanations. The first has to do with the relative maturity of the two modern thrusts of Basque emigration—the one to South America and the other to the American West.† The very fact that by the 1860s and 1870s massive Basque emigration to South America was an established tradition meant that the volume of feedback of information to Europe was substantial and included the negative aspects as well. Despite his 1852 pamphlet that eulogized agricultural opportunities in Argentina, Dr. Brougnes's own attempts at founding a colony in the *pampas* ended in failure. By 1852 the bishop of Pamplona had

---

*Grandmontagne argues that most Basques who arrived in the Río de la Plata region were monolingual Basque speakers. He believes that this difficulty with the language is what prompted many Basques to leave the cities and strike out into the solitude of the *pampas*.[2] We regard this view as exaggerated. One need only note that both the *Laurak Bat* of Montevideo and the *Laurac Bat* of Buenos Aires published their newspapers in Spanish to appreciate that the majority of Spanish Basques in the area were bilingual.

†In neither case does there appear to have been continuity of Basque migration from the days when the two areas formed part of the Spanish Empire to that of American independence. The xenophobia of both newly independent Argentina and Mexican California largely ruptured the colonial patterns of Basque New World emigration. We can date the modern period of Basque emigration to Argentina from the 1830s and to California from the 1850s.

mobilized opinion against emigration to South America. The book by José Cola y Goiri, published in 1883, which denounced in vivid terms every aspect of life in Uruguay, received wide circulation and official support in the Basque country. Descriptions of life in the *saladeros* could not have proven too attractive to the potential emigrant. Meanwhile, word from the American West was at best sketchy and, in part, gilded with California gold and plated with Nevada silver.

By the 1880s and 1890s sounder and more detailed information about the American West began to reach the Basque country, largely in the form of first-person accounts as some members of the first generation of Basque sheepmen retired to their homeland. It became apparent that the development of agriculture in the Río de la Plata area was at least several decades ahead of farming in the interior of the western United States. By 1880 much of the Argentine countryside was settled and in the midst of a plow agriculture boom that inflated land prices and restricted the movements of sheepmen to the most marginal areas. In the American West the majority of land was still in the public domain, and vast areas of potentially good sheep range were practically devoid of stockmen.

Nevertheless, during the last two decades of the nineteenth century more Basques undoubtedly left Europe for South America than for the United States.* In 1895 *California'ko Eskual Herria* estimated that the Basque population of the state was five thousand persons;[4] it is unlikely that there were more than ten thousand Basques in the entire American West. At that time the Vizcayan colony of northern Nevada, southern Idaho, and southeastern Oregon was still in its infancy. The official

---

*This generalization, however, is not applicable to the emigration from every area of the Basque country. We have noted that the majority of the earliest Basque emigrants to California were French nationals and that the French Basque presence in the American West had matured considerably before Spanish Basques, and notably Vizcayans, entered in great numbers. Gachiteguy finds that, of all eighteen-year-old males born during the years 1862–65 in the village of Aldudes, 78 percent emigrated to the American West while 9 percent left for South America. Of those eighteen-year-olds born during the period 1870–73 in nearby Esterençuby, 60 percent of the young men left for the United States while only 4 percent selected a Latin American destination. During the same period, however, only 31.8 percent of the young men of the village of Arneguy opted for the American West while 36.4 percent went to South America. Of those eighteen-year-olds born during 1876–79, in all three villages, the majority elected to emigrate to the American West. Even in Arneguy 39.3 percent opted for this destination while only 26 percent left for South America.[3]

AMERIKANUAK

United States census figures of 1900 list 12,256 French nationals and 896 Spanish nationals resident in the state of California. Nevada had 303 French nationals and 178 Spanish nationals, while Idaho had only 194 French citizens and 77 Spanish ones.[5]*

Immigration to Argentina boomed during the 1880s, due in part to governmental subsidies to immigrants. Many Basques were among the newcomers. In that decade the Argentine nation had a net gain of 846,000 persons in its population.[6] During this period, the *Laurac Bat* periodical of Buenos Aires noted that it was the goal of most of the Basque immigrants to obtain the wherewithal to return to the Basque country, purchase a farmstead, and become an *echekojaun*. The paper remarked that "only a true Basque can understand the powerful influence that the elevated and plausible idea of becoming a proprietor exerts among Basque laborers." The paper also notes that it was likely to take at least ten years to realize this dream, and that many failed altogether.[7]

By 1890 the Argentine rural economy showed genuine signs of crisis. In 1891 thirty thousand more persons actually left than entered as immigrants. By 1895 real wages in the nation were down 50 percent from the levels of the previous decade.[8] At about the same time a period of rampant lawlessness broke out in the rural districts, and crimes of violence were an everyday occurrence. The authorities treated the matter lightly, and Argentina acquired a black reputation among potential European emigrants.[9] In the words of one social historian:

> Letters from established relatives and newspaper reports turned many a prospective immigrant in Italy, Spain, and England away from the Río de la Plata area and helped to account for twelve times as much immigration to the United States as to Argentina.[10]

---

*Several comments are in order. First the statistics are of unnaturalized residents only and do not include Old World-born naturalized citizens. Second, the statistic for French nationals may not be construed as a figure of French Basque residents. Probably at least one-half of the total were from other regions of France. However, the Spanish statistic, in our opinion, is largely constituted by Spanish Basques (and a few *montañeses*), since no other area of the Spanish nation provided more than a handful of emigrants to the American West. Third, we doubt that the United States census reflects accurately the number of French and Spanish nationals employed in the sheep industry. Both the wage herder and itinerant sheepman were elusive quarry for the census taker. Newspaper accounts suggest that, by 1900, there were probably several hundred Basques in Humboldt County, Nevada, alone.

These developments, in combination with the chain migration of European relatives, friends, and fellow villagers to the California Basque colony, had a cumulative effect. By the 1870s the California colony had grown to such an extent that some of its members were striking out into the lesser-developed regions of the American Southwest.

Consequently, there was a discernible shift in the aspiring Basque sheepman's choice of New World destination by the beginning of the twentieth century. As if word that the *pampas* were becoming crowded, that sheep range was scarce and expensive, that the Argentine economy was foundering, and that there was widespread public disorder were not enough to dissuade the Basque emigrant, disastrous floods of 1900 in Argentina coincided with a sharp drop in wool prices offered by the French and Belgian textile manufacturers.[11] The crisis in Argentina was reflected most noticeably in its sheep industry.

Massive emigration of Europeans to Argentina resumed in the decade 1900 to 1910. No fewer than 652,658 Spanish nationals entered the South American nation during the period. However, the majority were short-term labor migrants *(golondrinas)* or persons seeking small farm holdings. The proportion of Basques in the ranks of the Spanish immigrants had diminished considerably.

During the first two decades of the twentieth century, xenophobia swept Argentina, culminating in a highly restrictive immigration policy. While there were similar developments in the United States, there was greater awareness in the Basque country of such developments in the Río de la Plata nations. By the end of the last century there was a Basque intelligentsia in Argentina and Uruguay that produced its own newspapers, journals, and books. These works were in Spanish and were circulated in the Basque country. In the American West, by way of contrast, there were just two short-lived newspapers, *Escualdun Gazeta* and *California'ko Eskual Herria*, which were of more limited scope and circulation. Letters from relatives and first-person accounts of a few returnees remained the major sources of information concerning the United States. Consequently, as Argentina's problems were compounded and information about them permeated the Basque homeland, emigration to the American West increased dramatically.* Its high point was concentrated between 1900 and 1920.

---

*Gachiteguy finds that in the three French Basque villages of Aldudes, Esterençuby, and Arneguy emigration for eighteen-year-olds born between

During this period 263,183 French nationals and 178,947[13] Spanish citizens entered the United States, an annual average of 13,159 and 8,949 persons, respectively. Even if departures are subtracted from arrivals, the increase is substantial. Between 1908 and 1920, 205,180[14] French nationals entered the United States while only 53,342[15] departed, an annual net gain of 11,645 French residents for the thirteen-year period. During the same years, 147,316[16] Spanish nationals entered the United States and 44,994[17] departed, an annual average gain in the American Spanish nationals population of 7,870 persons. Between 1900 and 1920, as table 9 shows, the population of Spanish- and French-born unnaturalized residents of California, Nevada, and Idaho increased considerably.

TABLE 9
FRENCH AND SPANISH ALIEN POPULATIONS IN
CALIFORNIA, NEVADA, AND IDAHO, 1900–1920

Year	Nationality	California	Nevada	Idaho
1900	French nationals	12,256	303	194
	Spanish nationals	896	178	77
1910	French nationals	17,407	653	333
	Spanish nationals	4,229	778	1,047
1920	French nationals	18,523	566	398
	Spanish nationals	11,123	1,180	1,416

Source: *Abstract of the Twelfth Census* . . . (1902:60, 63); *Statistical Abstract* . . . (1913:63); *Statistical Abstract* . . . (1923:60, 62).

A published study of Spanish emigration between the years 1911 and 1915 provides some general information regarding the departures of Spanish Basque nationals. During the period 6,211 persons embarked from the port of Bilbao and it was estimated that an equal number of Spanish Basques sailed from Bordeaux in defiance of Spanish emigration regulations.[18] The number of legal departures from all Spanish ports of persons with residence in one of the four Basque provinces was 18,367 persons.[19] Unfortunately, there is no breakdown according to destination, although it seems that more than half selected a South American country.

1903 and 1910 was down considerably from former periods. However, *none* of those who left (i.e., during the 1920s) selected a South American destination.[12]

THE BASQUE SHEEPMEN

By the middle of the nineteenth century Basques were the sheepmen of the *pampas*. In the late nineteenth and early twentieth centuries Basques as a group became the dominant ethnic element in the open-range sheep industry of the American West. Why did Basques make such a success of the sheep business? For many the answer is simple. An article in the May 3, 1920, issue of the *Nevada Stockgrower* states it clearly:

> The herders are largely Basques, commonly called "Baskos."
> These Basques hail from the north of Spain, the early home of
> the merino, so they take naturally to the "call of the woolies."
> They are not unused to the lonesome life, nor the hardships of
> rough mountainous country.[20]

Grandmontagne voices similar sentiments in accounting for the Basque success in the livestock industry of the *pampas*.[21]

Considerable ink has been spilled concerning the supposed Old World background of the Basques in sheep raising, as well as their supposed psychological conditioning for the isolation inherent in the sheepherding profession. As the argument runs, Old World Basques spend their lives on scattered farmsteads isolated at considerable distance from village centers and cities. Hence the Basque, by both experience and character, is accustomed to minimal contact with his fellows and able to endure social privation that might unbalance others.*

When examined in more critical light, it is evident that the Old World background argument is made to carry too heavy an explanatory load. While it is true that sheep are raised in the Basque country, the conditions and scale in most of the area bear so little resemblance to sheep raising in either South America or the American West as to provide the potential emigrant herder with little practical experience for his future (beyond a general working familiarity with animals that is the heritage of every rural Basque). In the sheep industry of the Basque country flock size rarely surpasses one hundred animals. Furthermore, in most cases the sheep are not herded, but simply pastured without constant surveillance in nearby mountain tracts, within easy walking distance of the farmstead. During much of the year flock care consists of an occasional visit (weekly or biweekly) of the owner to see how the animals

---

*Cf. Bieter's article "Reluctant Shepherds" for a rare refutation of this view.[22]

are doing. This relative neglect is feasible, since there are no longer large predators in the Basque country. During the spring of the year the ewes and lambs are kept near the dwelling and milked twice daily for cheese making.

All of this is in marked contrast to New World sheep-raising practices, where a minimal band is one thousand animals, the use of sheep dogs is critical, protection from predators is a constant problem, and (in many areas) seasonal transhumance of the herds—sometimes involving treks of several hundred miles—is the rule. In the Basque country itself, there is some pooling of farm flocks for transhumance between the main ridges of the Pyrenees and the coastal foothills of the north or the arid plains of southern Navarra. Professional herders accustomed to handling large numbers of animals under constant supervision are employed. Yet very few of these professional herders entered the ranks of the nineteenth- and twentieth-century Basque emigrants to the New World. For example, in 1915 only one person of the 33,199 male emigrants departing from Spanish ports listed his occupation as "sheepherder." The destination of this herder was not one of the New World livestock districts but rather the island of Cuba![23] In six years of fieldwork among Basque herders of the American West, the present authors have encountered only one man who had actually worked professionally in the sheep transhumance of the Basque country.

Nor may it be argued that Basques somehow do not suffer from the social isolation inherent in the herder's life. There is a certain aloofness in the Basque character that conveys an impression to others of extreme reserve and a kind of emotionless self-sufficiency. Once beyond the mask, however, we find admissions of men weeping openly in the solitude of desert and mountains. Accounts of insanity and suicide among herders are common, and among the men there is a vocabulary of madness in which the individual who has spent too much time alone in the hills is characterized as "sheeped" or "sagebrushed." So the arguments that Basques possess an Old World background in sheep raising and that they are psychologically conditioned for the solitude of the herding profession cannot account fully for their success in the open-range sheep industry of the American West. We must turn to a contributing factor of an historical nature.

While we have argued that Basques did not simply transfer an Old World experience to the United States, it is likely that they did bring South American sheep industry techniques to the western ranges. It was sufficient for a few men to apply the South American example, tailoring it to local conditions when need be, to establish, by the late 1850s, a Basque (and Béarnais) sheep-raising complex in California. In the 1860s the continued arrival in the state of Basque immigrants corresponded almost exclusively to the labor demands and entrepreneurial opportunities in stock raising. However, this near total commitment of immigrant Basques to sheep raising was not necessarily a reflection of an Old World or even a South American fixation with ovines. Rather, California provided opportunities in stock raising that were easily recognized by the Basque who had previously resided in the Río de la Plata region. Financing a sheep outfit required considerably less capital than financing a cattle operation; close herding also gave the sheep outfit great mobility, making it possible to graze exclusively on the public domain and thereby ruling out the necessity of investing in a home ranch; sheep remained more adaptable than cattle to the climatic extremes of southern California (drought) and the Great Basin (hard winters); and during the decade of the 1860s sheep values remained high while cattle prices sagged. It is in this combination of factors—the South American model, the California opportunity, and the specific economics and conditions of sheep husbandry—that we find much of the explanation of the role of the Basque immigrants as partial founders of the sheep industry of the American West.

Yet, to say that Basques applied a South American example in California climes is to beg the question of why, by the early 1830s, they became a significant ethnic element in the livestock industry of the *pampas*, and most notably as sheepmen. Can it be that we have simply distorted the image of a crucial and explanatory Pyrenean sheep-raising background by passing it through a South American prism? We do not believe so. However, in order to appreciate a major factor in the success of the Basque sheepmen of both North and South America, it is necessary to consider an aspect of the ethos of Old World Basque society. There are highly esteemed values in Old World Basque culture that are expressed by the terms *indarra* and *sendotasuna*. *Indarra* may be translated as "force" or "strength." *Sendotasuna* includes "physical prowess" and "strength of character."*

---

*The suffix *-tasuna* in Basque means "quality of." While it is not employed commonly with *indarra* it is used with *sendoa*, which, like *indarra*, is also sometimes translated as "force."

Rural forms of sport and recreation are one clear context in which the *indarra* and *sendoa* of both animals and men are put to the test. Thus popular events include ram-butting contests, which continue until one ram retires, and stone-dragging contests, in which teams of oxen drag enormous blocks of marble or granite until one outdistances the other. Human endurance is tested in contests that determine who can scythe the most grass, chop through the greatest number of tree trunks, or lift a stone weight the greatest number of times. In all cases, the time allotted is sufficiently generous to guarantee eliminating the player who, while possibly more skillful, lacks stamina. Similarly, foot races and rowing regattas are popular in the Basque country, but in neither case is innate quickness rewarded. The hundred-yard dash, for instance, is foreign to the Basque mentality. Rather, the runner, or *korrikalari*, must prove himself over a distance of several kilometers. The rowing teams are likely to compete over a course that takes them from one port to another.

Given the emphasis upon the test of *indarra* and *sendoa* rather than polished skill, it is common for Basque sporting events to pit a woodchopper against a weight lifter or a runner against both: the runner must cover a certain distance before the axeman cuts through so many trunks and the weight lifter accomplishes a specified number of lifts. This is not seen as a "mixing of apples and oranges" in a world where stamina and personal mettle are being tested.

The appreciation of these qualities is readily evident in the reactions of Basque audiences at sporting events. The sport of *jai alai* has international appeal and remains popular in the Basque country as well. Basque players have been in demand in such widely separated sports centers as Miami and Manila, Havana and Hong Kong. The popularity of *jai alai* is derived in part because it lends itself to betting, but also because of the game's speed and the almost ballet-like grace of the players. When witnessing a *jai alai* match in the Basque country, one is struck by the different standards of appreciation that are applied by the non-Basque and Basque fans. For the former the attraction lies in the coordination and quickness of the professional player that allow him to take two steps up a vertical wall to make a seemingly impossible return. For the latter it is the crushing shot, driving one's opponent to the farthest reaches of the back court, that causes a low murmer of admiration and elicits the spontaneous remark, *"Au da indarra!"* ("That's *indarra*!").

The player who manifests great stamina throughout the match is rated a *gizon sendoa* ("strong man").

Sports provide a public staging of *indarra*, but the value permeates many other areas of rural Basque life. *Sendotasuna* is the quality shown by the woman who is able to work in the fields alongside the men. The woman also manifests *sendoa* when she sustains the emotional burden of the sudden loss of her child. Males manifest *indarra* through feats requiring extraordinary strength and *sendoa* through unswerving dedication to the hard work that is characteristic of labor-intensive peasant agriculture. Old World Basque society has a work ethic that deems physical labor prestigious, in contrast to the attitude held in neighboring Latin cultures. Devotion to daily tasks, tasks of a hard physical nature, becomes a point of honor and criterion of self-estimation for Basque men and women alike.

In a sense, economic success is an obsession in the rural Basque society, not so much for the present comforts or future security it provides, but as a validation of one's past performance. This is a crucial point that escapes those who suggest that the Basque emigrant undergoes great personal privation in order to return to his homeland with savings that will permit him a work-free existence for the rest of his days. In point of fact, *sendotasuna*, and the sense of personal worth that it confers, require constant reaffirmation in Old World Basque society. The returnee uses his savings to gain a foothold in a new economic arena. He may purchase a farm or small business, but he is then likely to drive himself as he strives to make it the *best* farm in the valley or *best* business on the block.* By the same token, the fact that Basques are so obsessed with a validation of personal worth within Basque circles partially explains why the emigrant generation remains so strongly fixated upon its Old World homeland.

In sum, as a product of the *indarra/sendoa* value complex of Old World Basque society, the Basque emigrant combines an obsession with success as validation of personal worth and a predisposition to engage in hard physical and/or psychologically trying tasks. These qualities proved to be advantageous to

---

*As a corollary to the *indarra/sendoa* complex, with its emphasis upon prowess and stamina, there is an obsession in Basque society with physical health. In fact, ill health is regarded as the only "legitimate" excuse for failure. Thus, it is not admissible to stay home from work because one is tired or seeking relaxation. If one is suffering from pain or illness it is a different matter.

the Basque colonial entrepreneurs who willingly engaged in the mundane (and frequently disparaged) world of business affairs with a zeal that was rarely equalled by others. Similarly, while the claim to collective *hidalguía* provided many Basques with easy entry into the administrative circles of the Spanish Empire, their devotion to task made them formidable competitors for promotions. The demise of the empire in the early nineteenth century ended three centuries of elitist opportunity for the Basque emigrants. However, the world view based upon *indarra/sendoa* proved equally adaptable in the tenuous enterprise of gaining an immigrant's foothold in the alien economies of sometimes hostile societies.

This argument must not, however, be overdrawn as there are other hard realities and contradictory trends at play as well. For instance, Gachiteguy estimates that only about 3 percent of the Basques who emigrated to the American West made great fortunes and that these men were prone to remain in America. He further estimates that about another 15 percent were successful, but on a scale that required their ongoing involvement in the enterprise. He is here referring to the sheepman that has four to six thousand animals, the cattleman that has two to five hundred head, or the hotel proprietor.[24] The remainder presumably never achieved entrepreneurial status and either failed in their own terms or achieved a success based more upon favorable currency exchange and salary schedules than personal business acumen.

It may be argued that the more recent immigrants were under even greater pressure than their forebears to succeed in the New World. The several centuries of successful Basque participation in Spain's colonial venture left an exaggerated local view in the Basque country of the intrinsic wealth of the Americas. To fail to make one's fortune reflected more on one's own worth than upon shortcomings in New World opportunity.

The validation of *sendoa* disposed the Basque emigrant to a life of hard physical labor, but the high expectations of family and friends prompted him to seek out opportunities that promised at least a long-range prospect of substantial economic success. In this respect it might be argued that Basques, possibly to a greater degree than most emigrant groups, are prone to subordinate short-range comforts and a modicum of security to long-range aspirations. In the same vein Basques are particularly given to risk taking. Thus, the Basque emigrant might enter the *saladeros* of Argentina or work with livestock for wages, but only as a temporary measure prior to launching his own enterprise. It is hard to conceive of a riskier business than wandering about the range of the American West with one's savings tied up in an itinerant sheep band that is beset on all sides by settled ranchers, predators, the elements, and fluctuating market values.

Given this drive for personal success, the Basque emigrant has been quick to seize upon those opportunities in the host countries that are either unrecognized or disparaged. It so happened that Basque immigrants began to enter both Argentina (1830s) and the American West (1850s) at the precise moment when their respective sheep industries were in infancy. In both regions livestock raising was dominated by cattle interests, and cattle operations required greater capitalization than sheep outfits. Basques became established sheepmen just prior to a set of economic developments that were to favor greatly the sheep industry. The successful Basque sheepmen served as magnets for fellow Old World Basques desirous of emigrating, *but only insofar* as there was the prospect that they, too, could aspire to similar success.*

If Basques became the sheepmen of both North and South America, it was due primarily to the availability of an economic opportunity that was ignored or disparaged by others in the host country. It was the Basque emigrants' willingness, even impatience, to pay a higher price in terms of personal privations (both physical and psychological) for quick success, rather than an Old World preoccupation with sheep raising, that made them the most prominent ethnic group in New World open-range sheep-raising circles.

The experience of a more recent current of Basque emigration supports this view. In the 1930s Basques, particularly Vizcayans, began to emigrate to Australia. There, almost to the man, they became involved in the sugar industry as cane-cutters. The job is well paid but requires considerable immigrant labor, since it is so extremely dirty and tedious that few Australians are willing to do it. Over the years the Basques of northeastern Australia established an ethnic group reputation as

---

*In this vein it should be noted that the majority of contract herders who have entered the American West in recent years have sought the surrogate reward of savings, which allow them to launch a business enterprise back in the Basque country. The point is that even today, with the possibility of obtaining permanent residence in the United States, most contract herders believe that their future is in Europe.

the best cane-cutters, and several rose through the ranks to acquire their own sugar holdings. On the other hand, despite Australia's role as a leading sheep-producing nation, to our knowledge not a single Basque is involved in the Australian sheep industry!

Document of Departure of Pedro Altube Prepared in Oñate, Guipúzcoa 6 May 1845

. . . José Miguel de Altube, resident of this town, presented himself and declared that his brother Pedro de Altube, profession farmer, bachelor, native, and resident of this town, with the blessings and approval of the declarant, lacking parents now deceased, has decided to embark and travel to the city of Buenos Aires in America, to join Don Santiago de Altube and two other brothers who reside in that locality. [The declarant] desiring to guarantee the payment of the board and passage to Buenos Aires of the above stated young man, and noting that the ship *Irurac Bat* is readied to sail shortly from the port of Bilbao, said ship belonging to Espalza and Sons of the firm of that name, agrees to guarantee with his belongings and to transfer in payment to the stated firm Espalza and Sons, or their representatives, in cash, the amount or expenses of the board and passage of said young man Pedro de Altube. The payment or payments in the form agreed upon mutually will be made without delay or excuse, under pain of legal action and collecting costs in the event of default. . . . [As an article of faith the declarant herewith] mortgages specifically and expressly among his other family holdings, a portion of chestnut forest, with its land and trees, belonging to the declarant, and with a sale's value of three thousand *reales vellon*, situated in the district called Escorta erreca, barrio Zubillaga, in this municipality, and bordered on one side by the chestnut forest of the farmsteads Urteaga-garaicoa and Antuena, and on the other by that of the farmstead Azpicoa. . . .

Source: Archivo de la Universidad de Oñate, Legajo 3610, folio 159.

Persons with Basque Names, or Associated with Basques, Who Applied for Passports in Buenos Aires Listing California as Their Destination

Abadia, Bernardo   December 31, 1850
[Abadie] Avadie, Juan   February 14, 1851
Abeledo, Bernardo   February 14, 1851
Aicaguerre, Salvador   February 18, 1851
[Altube] Alduve, Bernardo   February 14, 1851
Amestoi, Domingo   February 14, 1851
Arambidi, Juan   February 20, 1851
Arrecha, Francisco   February 22, 1851
Arrosbide, Arnot   February 14, 1851
Asalegui, María   February 22, 1851
Asme, Juan   December 7, 1850
Bardenave, Victor   February 14, 1851
Bayart, Eugenio   February 20, 1851
Bordarampe, Pedro   February 19, 1850
Burnague, Juan   February 14, 1851
Cahuare, Juan   February 22, 1851
Cedarry, Juan   February 20, 1851
Darrico, Pedro   February 14, 1851
Echemendi, Lorenzo   October 23, 1849
Erreca, Bernardo   February 20, 1851
Galdo, Pedro   February 14, 1851
Garaus, Bernardo   February 14, 1851
Garciarena, Lorenzo   February 22, 1851
Garciarena, Martín   February 22, 1851
Gastigne [Gortigue?], Francisco   December 31, 1850
Gustale, Carlos   February 14, 1851
Haeguy, Catalina   February 21, 1851

Haspura, Antonio   February 20, 1851
Hauscarriaga, Graciano   February 14, 1851
Hauscarriaga, Santiago   February 14, 1851
Heguy, Juan   February 18, 1851
Hoyan, Juan   March 7, 1850
Inubia, Martín José   February 21, 1851
Iturralde, Juan   February 20, 1851
Jaureguiberry, Pedro   February 22, 1851
Larrondo, Pedro   February 14, 1851
Lasarte, Juan   February 22, 1851
Latape, José   September 25, 1850
Lazboren, Pedro   February 14, 1851
Lestrade, Juan   February 21, 1850
Lisarrebe, José   February 14, 1851
Lopetegui, Bernardo   February 22, 1851
Luceruz, Juan   September 26, 1850
Luzaire, Ramón   December 8, 1850
Mandagaran, José   September 25, 1850
Mane, Juan Bautista   February 19, 1850
Massa, José   February 18, 1851
Maza, Juan   February 23, 1851
Ohet, Domingo   February 20, 1851
Orosco, Antonio   December 6, 1850
Oxarat, Gaston   February 18, 1851
[Oyhenard] Doyhenard, Pedro   February 22, 1851
Sartu, Bautista   February 14, 1851
Tavas, Juan   February 14, 1851
Vidarte, Pedro   February 23, 1851
Ypar, Bernardo   February 14, 1851
Zavaleta, Juan   February 18, 1851

Source: List compiled by C. Vilgre La Madrid employing the *Diario de la Tarde* and
Diario de Avisos of Buenos Aires. (Spellings from originals.)

I. Passports with Basque Names, Issued by the *Intendencia de Valparaíso*, to Persons Listing California as Their Destination, 1849

JANUARY

30   Vicente Alvarez Araya; Santos Araos; Ramón Arellano; Felipe A. Basaure; Juan Figueroa

FEBRUARY

1   Pedro Arancibia (worker); Salvador de Arevalo with his manservant

2   Gacinto Garate (worker); Manuel Madreaga (worker); José Navarrete; Enrique Tapia (worker)

3   Francisco Landa (worker); Pedro A. Muga (worker)

14   Ramon Abasolo; Manuel Arancibia (worker); Rafael Arancibia (worker); José Elías Arauz (worker); Agustin Araya (worker); Eugenio Araya (worker); José Niceto Araya; Concepción Baranao with maid; Ignacio Díaz Bilbao; Santiago Madriaga; Pedro León Zuluaga

MARCH

2   Juan de Dios Arancibia (worker); José María Aros (worker); Tomás Gamboa (worker); Juan Urmazabal; Juan José Urmazabal (worker); Francisco Urtado (worker); José María Zarrigueta

3   José del Carmen Arancibia (worker); Juan Eyzaguirre (worker); Juan de Dios Ivaceta (worker); Justo Olabarria (worker); Feliciano Oyaneder; Santiago Oyaneder; Pascual Sambuesa (worker); José Antonio Ugalde (worker); Dionisio Luis Urtabey with wife and daughter

20   Francisco Pascual de Achurra; José Serein; Pedro Juan Tapia (worker)

27   Domingo Carricondo; Juan Francisco Mugica with his manservant Manuel Ubilla; Rufino Odriosola

APRIL

9   Eugenio A. Arnais
10   Remigio Lacube
25   Miguel Aguirre; José de Fano; Cirilo Guevara; Blas Larrain and servant Ramon Atela; S. Zulueta
28   Nicolás Esquivel (worker); María Lacarse
29   Francisco Garay; Blas Larrain and a manservant; José Antonio Luco y Huici

MAY

11   Graciella Hiriart with son
16   Francisco Duo; Ignacio Olarte; María Orbes; Fabián Oyarzun; Joaquín Vera
18   José Francisco Aldunate and six workers
19   Antonio Aliaga; Serapio Gana; Juan de Dios Manterola; Agustín Vidaurre
21   José Segundo Marambio
24   Ignacio Guicolea
25   José de Aguinaga and his servant; Francisco Prado Aldunate
26   Manuel Garate

JUNE

1   Juan de Dios Aeta; José T. Alegria; José Aravena; Cipriano Ezquer; Cayetano Gundian; Manuel Marcoleta; Joaquín Mardones and son; Diego Mondica; Luis Mondica; Santiago Ortuzar y Gandarillas; Candelario Oyarzun; Fermín Ureta; Celestino Urquieta
2   Juan Ayala; Pedro Ayala; Luciano Ayala; Paulino Duarte; Feliciano Galea; José Santos Galea; Gregorio Irigoyen
4   Casimiro Aliaga; Anselmo Arabena; Andrés Layseca and servant; Ildefonso Luco; Ramón Luco; José Antonio Orrego; Javier Requena
13   Juan Antonio Aranguez (worker); Pedro Ureta y Carrera; Ramón J. Ureta
15   Victoriano Echanes; Laureano Ituza; Aranzasus Latorre
19   Marcos Vildosola; Vicente Vildosola
21   Francisco Esquivel; Antonio Larrain; Pedro Larrain; Tomás Larrain; Pascual Loyola; Cupertino Sumaeta; Domingo Sumaeta; José Antonio Ureta; Benero Uriarte; Domingo Veas; Estanislao Zabala

JULY

7   Antonio Arancibia; Miguel Colart; Félix Gatica; Domingo
    Hara and wife; Miguel Sanhueza
10 Narciso Amaya (worker); Manuel Rios Egaña
11 Reperto Allendes; Calisto Basualto; Toribio Larrain;
    Francisco Leroy; Miguel Moya; Julián Navarrete
13 Rosario Arancibia with son
14 José Araviola with wife; Pedro Barraza; Juan de Dios Goñi
18 José del C. Narvaez
27 Mariano Araya; Luis Larrain; Manuel Urbano Larrain

AUGUST

3   Juan de Dios Arlegui; Germán Lasserre

II.   Passengers with Basque Last Names Who Embarked in Valparaíso for California, 1849

JANUARY

13 Brigantine *Félix Araucano*: José Arriasola, wife and two
    sons; José Chopitea; Santiago Dazarola; Juan Laborde;
    Pedro T. Larranaga

MARCH

5   The *Oberón*: Gregorio Urizar
10 The Chilean ship *Europa*: Toribio Araos
    The Chilean Brigantine *Ovalle*: José Santos Abarca; Blas
    Arredondo; Dionisio L. Urtuber, wife and daughter
19 American Frigate *Huntress*: José del C. Arancibia; Félix
    Araos; Ramón Araos Juan de Dios Ibaceta; Agustín
    Lecanda; Justo Olavarria; Antonio Oyaneder; Feliciano
    Oyaneder; Pedro Sanhuesa; Vicente Sanhuesa; José An-
    tonio Ugarte; José María Vera

APRIL

27 Ship unlisted: Eduardo Beeche and the workers Buenven-
    tura Uvilla; Lorenzo Duarte; Blas Arteaga and José Acuna

MAY

5   The *Almirante Blanco*: Miguel Aguirre; Evaristo Ache-
    rreca and four workers; Juan B. Elissegaray and worker,

Santiago Ogada; Antonio Olea; Manuel Orrian; Vicente Orrian

16 The Chilean Brigantine *Huemul*: F. Prado Aldunate; José Francisco Aldunate and six workers; José Arancibia; Lorenzo Basaure (miner); Francisco Duo; Estanislao Gacitua; Francisco Gacitua; Serapio Gana and five workers; José Segundo Marambio; José Manuel Olano; Rufino Odriosola; F. Oyarzun and two workers; Joaquín Vera

16 United States Brigantine *Walcott*: José Aguinaga; Manuel Garate; Mariano Inostroza

JUNE

7 The *Juana Josefa Font*: Juan de Dios Aeta; José Aravena; Ulises Calbeti; Antonio Elgueta; Vicente Elgueta; Cayetano Gundian; Leandro Lopategui; Manuel Marcoleta; Fernando Ureta; Celestino Urqueta

13 The English Corvette *Flash*: Joaquín Mardones and son; Bruno Parragui

13 United States Frigate *Florence*: José M. Adaro; Ramón Arrieta; Andrés Layseca and worker; Saturnino de Oro; José Antonio Orrego

JULY

5 The Chilean Frigate *Catharines*: Pedro Larrain, two sons and five workers; Juan de Dios Mujica

12 Chilean vessel *Ballena*: José Besoain; José María Manterola and son; José Mondaca

12 Chilean Brigantine *Delfín*: Agustín Aguirre; Gumersindo Gaviola

16 Unidentified Chilean Vessel: Mariano Lechee(?) and family; Francisco Leroy(?)

16 Belgian Vessel *Schelde*: E. Garin and family; Antonio Jatzo and five workers; Marcos Vildosola, son and three workers

20 French Frigate *Martinique*: Diego Araya; José Manuel Larrain; Ventura Luco; Crisóstomo Mardones; Laureano Mardones; José Saldames (Galdames?)

DECEMBER

26 The *Staouli*: Domingo Aldunate de Lastra; Ramón Aldunate de Lastra; Juan Fagalde; José Antonio Hurtado; José M. Olavarria; Juan Urbina with two workers; José María Urrejola

Year 1850

JANUARY

22   United States ship *Rosa*: Lorenzo Araos; Antonio Araya;
      José María Araya; Félix Araya

25   French vessel *Cardenal de Cheverus*: Bartolomé Arriola;
      Lorenzo Echemendi; David Silauter; Domingo Zabaret

FEBRUARY

3   United States vessel *Caribe*: Joaquín Mayorga and brother
      Manuel Mayorga; José Orrego

MARCH

12   United States Frigate *Orpheus*: Eusebio Araos; José del
      Carmen Araos; Lorenzo Araya and two children

Year 1852

FEBRUARY

8   English Frigate *Princess Royal*: José Abalos; Francisco
      Aracena; Diego Arancibia; José Vicente Belche;
      Leonardo Corta; Manuel José Garay and wife; Fabricio
      Garratea; Guillermo Lecaroz; Juan Lodi; José D. Oro;
      Eusebio Tapia; Rosario Tapia

Source: Zarrantz, Santiago de, "Pasajeros Salidos de Valparaíso para California,
años 1849–1852 (febrero), ms, Basque Collection, University of Nevada, Reno.
(Spellings from originals.)

Basque Biographies in
California County Histories

1. Armor, Samuel (ed.). *History of Orange County, California*. Los Angeles: Historic Record Company, 1911: Domingo Oyharzabel.

2. Armor, Samuel. *History of Orange County, California*. Los Angeles: Historic Record Company, 1921: Bernard Arroues, Domingo Bastanchury, Marie Eugenia and Jean-Pierre Daguerre, Bautista Duhart, Domingo and John Erramouspe, Miguel Erreca, Francisco Errecarte, Dolores Eseverri, Juan Ordoqui, Martin and Salvador Labat, Esteban Oyharzabal, Peter Oyharzabal, Jose Sansinena, Felix Yriarte, Patricio Yriarte.

3. Brown, Robert R. *History of Kings County*. Hanford, California: A. H. Cawston, 1940: Peter Irigaray.

4. Elliott, Wallace W. and Co. (ed.). *History of San Diego County*. San Francisco: Wallace W. Elliott and Co., 1883: Bernardo Etcheverry.

5. Gabbett, John Raymond. *History of Riverside City and County*. Phoenix and Riverside: Record Publishing Company, 1935: Joseph A. Aguirre.

6. Gidney, et al. *History of Santa Barbara, San Luis Obispo and Ventura Counties, California*. Vol. II. Chicago: The Lewis Publishing Company, 1917: Alfonso and Mariano Erburu.

7. Guinn, J. M. *Historical and Biographical Record of Southern California*. Chicago: Chapman Publishing Company, 1902: A. J. Amestoy.

8. Guinn, J. M. *History of the State of California and Biographical Record of Santa Cruz, San Benito, Monterey and San Luis Obispo Counties*. Chicago: Chapman Publishing Company, 1903: Pedro Zabala.

9. Guinn, J. M. *A History of California*. Vol. II. Los Angeles: Historic Record Company, 1907: Miguel Antonio Aguirre, James LaBorde, Domingo, under John Olhasso, Cadet Yribarne.

10. Holes, Elmer W. *History of Riverside County, California*. Los Angeles: Historical Record Company, 1912: Antonio Aguirre.

11. Jurmey, Honoris. *History of Sonoma County, California*. Vol II. Chicago: The S. J. Clarke Publishing Co., 1926: E. Aguirre, Raymond Legaretta, Joseph Yriberri.

12. Ludwig, Ella A. *History of the Harbor District of Los Angeles*. Los Angeles: Historic Record Company, 1927: Paul Bengoechea, Frank Bilbao.

13. McGowan, Joseph A. *History of the Sacramento Valley*. Vol. I. New York: Lewis Historical Publishing Company, 196?: Joaquin, under Albert J. Arostegui.

14. McGroarty, John Steven. *Los Angeles from the Mountains to the Sea*. Chicago: The American Historical Society, 1921: Martin C. Aguirre, Domingo Amestoy, John B. Amestoy, Michael F. Amestoy, Jean Etchemendy, Pierre Larronde.

15. McGroarty, J. S. *History of Los Angeles County*. Chicago: The American Historical Society. 1923: Baptiste and Jose D. Batz, Martin Lifur, Jose A. Magonacelaya.

16. McGroarty, John Steven. *California of the South: A History*. Vol. V. Chicago: S .J. Clarke Publishing Co., Inc., 1935: Domingo Amestoy, Martin and Eugene Biscailuz, Jean Etchemendy, Pierre Larronde, Peter Oyharzabal.

17. Millard, Frank Bailey. *History of the San Francisco Bay Region*. Vol. II. Chicago: The American Historical Society, Inc., 1924: Santiago Arrillaga.

18. Miller, Thelma B. *History of Kern County, California*. Chicago: The S. J. Clarke Publishing Co., 1929: John Burubeltz, Thomas Echenique.

19. Morgan, Wallace M. *History of Kern County, California*. Los Angeles: Historic Record Company, 1914: Gratian Ansolabehere, Michel Ansolabehere, Michael Ansolabehere [different persons], John Bidart, Domingo Borda, Jean Burubeltz, Pierre Duhart, Miguel and Thomas Echenique, Fernando Etcheverry, Michel Etcheverry, Peter Etcheverry, Jean B. Estribou, Jean Pierre Martinto, Agustin Sanzberro, Peter Tuculet.

20. Morrison, Annie L. and John H. Haydon. *History of San Luis Obispo County and Environs*. Los Angeles: Historic Rec-

ord Company, 1917: Bernardo F. Careaga, Charles M. Careaga, James F. Careaga, Ramon A. Careaga, Ramon F. Careaga.

21. O'Neill, Owen H. (ed.). *History of Santa Barbara County.* Santa Barbara: The Union Printing Company, 1939: Bruno and Mercedes Orella Careaga.

22. Outcalt, John. *History of Merced County, California.* Los Angeles: Historic Record Company, 1925: J. Miguel Arburua.

23. Phillips, Michael James. *History of Santa Barbara County, California.* Vol. II. Chicago: The S. J. Clarke Publishing Co., 1927: Miguel Erro.

24. Pleasants, Mr. J. E. *History of Orange County, California.* Los Angeles: J. R. Finnell and Sons Publishing Co., 1931: Ysidoro Eseverri, Martin and Joseph Etchandy, Esteban and Peter Oyharzabal, Jose Sansinena.

25. Radcliffe, Corwin. *History of Merced County.* Merced, California: A. H. Cawston, 1940: Frank J. and J. Miguel Arburua, Jean B. Erreca, Martin Erreca, Peter Erreca.

26. Thompson and West. *History of Santa Barbara and Ventura Counties, California.* Berkeley: Howell-North, 1961: J. M. Andonaegui, U. Yndart.

27. Tinkham, George H. *History of Stanislaus County, California.* Los Angeles: Historic Record Co., 1921: John B. Arrabit, John L. Bernadicon, Saturnino Celayeta, Domingo Changala, Rufino Echandi, Joseph Etcheto, Martin Etcheto, Etienne Lacost, Joseph Larranaga, Raymond Narbaitz, Jean Ospital, Jose Oyarbide, Nick Ylarray, Gregorio Yrigoyes, Domingo Yroz.

28. Vandor, Paul E. *History of Fresno County.* Los Angeles: Historic Record Company, 1919: Martin Ardohain, Jean Arosteguy, Angel Arriet, Pedro Arriet, George Bazterra, Domingo Bidegaray, John Bidegaray, Dominique Bordagaray, Juan Camino, Mariano Eticheche, Matias Erro, Andres Errotabere, Martin Ingaray, Lucas Juanche, Jose and John Michael Lugea, Dominique Martinto, Jean Sahargun, Bernard Sallaberry, Natalio Semper, Florencio Serrano, Matias Serrano, Juan Miguel Urrutia, Miguel Villanueva, Joe Yraceburu, Jose M. Yraceburu, Firmin Yzurdiaga, Jose Zandueta.

29. Warner, J. *An Illustrated History of Los Angeles County, California.* Chicago: The Lewis Publishing Co., 1889: Martin C. Aguirre.

30. Warren, Charles S. *History of Santa Monica Bay Re-*

gion. Santa Monica, California: A. H. Cawston, 1934: Martin and Eugene Biscailuz.

31. [Author unknown]. *Memorial and Biographical History of the Counties of Fresno, Tulare, and Kern, California.* Chicago: The Lewis Publishing Co., 1892: S. Arrillago, Bernard Iribarne, John Iribarne, Pedro Yribarne.

32. [Author unknown]. *History of the Greater San Francisco Bay Region.* Vol. III. New York and West Palm Beach: Lewis Historical Publishing Co. [n.d.]: John Felix Etcheverry (under Nellie E.), Domie Indart, Juan Indart.

(Spellings from originals)

Synopses of Biographical Sketches of Fourteen Basques who Entered California Between 1845 and 1860

1. Jean-Baptiste Batz—was residing in Buenos Aires until 1850 when he came to California to seek his fortune in the mines. He became disillusioned and in 1852 bought a quarter section of land near Los Angeles that served him as home base for a sheep operation (McGroarty 1923:353).

2. Jean Etchemendy—born in 1830; by 1847 he was residing in South America. In that year he came to California and entered the mines. By 1851 he was in Los Angeles after enjoying some success in the mining camps. He established a bakery, but shortly thereafter bought into the sheep business in the Los Angeles area (McGroarty 1935:473).

3. Pierre Larronde—a carpenter by trade; before he was twenty he sailed for Buenos Aires [in the early 1840s]. In 1847 he moved to California. He spent the next four years in the mines and found considerable gold. In 1851 he moved to Los Angeles and established a sheep outfit (McGroarty 1935:479).

4. Domingo Amestoy—at age fourteen, in 1838, he went to Buenos Aires where he learned the trade of shoemaker. In 1851 he moved to California. He entered the mines but without success. He went to Santa Barbara County and found employment on the Noriega ranch. He saved his money, purchased a small band of sheep, and moved them to Los Angeles. In later years he acquired considerable acreage in Los Angeles County and at one time ran 50,000 sheep (McGroarty 1935:397).

5. Domingo Bastanchury—entered California in 1860, seeking work in Los Angeles as a sheepherder. He later acquired his own band, becoming the biggest sheepman in Orange County (Armor 1921:264).

6. Juan Ordoqui—a carpenter by trade, came directly from Europe to the goldfields of California in 1849. He left for Spain after several successful years but decided to return to the American West with his family. In 1872, he settled in Los Angeles County where he became a sheepman (Armor 1921:599).

7. Ulpiano Yndart—in 1844, at age sixteen, and educated in commerce, he accepted a position in a business in Mexico. Attracted by the gold rush, he came to California in 1849. Rather than going to the mines, he engaged in commerce in Los Angeles for five years. In 1854 he bought a large cattle ranch in Santa Barbara. He was ruined by the drought of 1864 and at that time entered politics, holding many posts in local government (Thompson and West 1961:232-233).

8. José María Andonaegui—in 1842 at age seventeen, he traveled to Buenos Aires and worked as a tailor for seven years. In 1849 he entered the ranks of the California argonauts. He spent but one year in the mines, returning to San Francisco, where he worked as a tailor until 1854. In that year he transferred his residence to Santa Barbara, and he developed a successful tailoring and mercantile firm (Thompson and West 1961:241-242).

9. Bernardo Etcheverry—in 1856, at age twenty, he came directly from Europe to the California gold fields. He mined with success for three years and later settled in Santa Barbara for ten years (no occupation given). In 1869 he returned to the Basque country, where he remained for three years. In 1872 he returned to California. In 1879 he purchased an extensive ranch in San Diego County and he raised 12,000 sheep (Elliot 1883:110d).

10. Juan Indart—came directly to the mines from Europe in the mid-1850s. Later he established a cattle ranch in the San Joaquin Valley near Tres Pinos (Lewis 1892:III:376).

11. Pedro Zabala—in 1846, at twenty-one years of age, he emigrated to South America, where he was a merchant. In 1849 he joined the California gold rush. Instead of entering the mines, he established a mercantile business in Monterey. After eight years, he acquired a large cattle ranch near Salinas (Guinn 1903:303).

12. Bernard Iribarne—a stonemason by trade, he came to California prior to 1851 and settled for fifteen years in Murphy's camp. After much financial success he moved to Los Banos, Merced County, where he established a cattle and sheep operation (Lewis 1892:326).

13. José Lugea—at age seventeen went to Buenos Aires where he was a livestockman in partnership with his brothers. In the 1850s, he came to California, and his brothers later joined him. He became a sheepman in the Los Banos and later the Tres Pinos areas in partnership with his brothers and another Basque, Miguel Arburua (Vandor 1919:2558).

14. Juan Miguel Aguirre—after serving on the losing side in the First Carlist War, he emigrated to Montevideo in 1845, where he engaged in the hide and tallow business. He came to San Francisco in May 1849. Rather than going to the mines, he stayed in the city and peddled water from door to door. He later purchased property in the downtown area [where he constructed San Francisco's first Basque hotel] (Hunt 1932:III:121-122).

"Conbenio" or Contract Between Don Abel Stearns and Don Domingo Amestoy

THIS CONTRACT concluded today, the 26th of June, 1854, in the city of Los Angeles, between the Messers Don Abel Stearns first party and Don Domingo Amestoy second party, both parties residents of the County of Los Angeles, states:

1. That the first party agrees to give and turn over immediately to the second party a band of sheep in the Rancho de los Alamitos, the numbers and classes of which are as follows: eight hundred (800) ewes, three hundred and eighty five wethers, one hundred and eighteen rams, and four hundred and twelve lambs of the present year, along with one hundred and fourteen goats, comprising both large and small, with the intention that the second party herd them for a period of two years and six months; reckoned from the 15th of last May of the present year. The first party will provide the ranch for this herding.

2. That the second party obligates himself to care for and herd this band for all of the specified time, and toward this end will devote his personal attention to the work along with the necessary employees. All the work in this care, and the expenses, will be paid by the second party, and remain his obligation. Further, the second party obligates himself to reimburse the first party for any loss that results from his neglect or bad management during the indicated period. At the end of the period the second party promises to turn over to the first party the number of eight hundred ewes and half of all the increase in the referred to band during the period of this contract; the other half remaining with the second party as compensation for his labor and expenses incurred in the care of said band. The wethers and rams of this arrangement that remain shall always belong to the first party and revert at the end of the referred period.

3. The first party reserves the right to reclaim, from time to time during the expressed period, any sheep from among the wethers and rams, which belong to him [presently] or after lambings will belong to him with the exception that the first party will not retire the rams necessary to the increase of the band. Moreover [the first party] will have the right to sell the goats when he wishes.

4. The second party obligates himself to pay immediately in cash the sum of one *peso* and *cuatro reales* [$1.50] for each of the lambs born this year in order to have half ownership in this year's lambing; the number of these lambs is mentioned in the first clause of this contract.

5. The second party agrees to shear the stated band at the proper time and turn over on demand to the first party all of the wool. And this task will be done at the expense of the second party.

6. Both parties agree that during the period of this contract there will be no sale in any form of the ewes, either [those of the initial] capital or [those of] the lambings of the said band. If either party fails to comply with this contract it is immediately and irrevocably voided from the time of the infraction.

Signed on the above date

7. Before signing the present document both parties agree that the second party must castrate the lambs of the band at the proper time, and mark all lambs with the brand of the first party. At the end of this contract, when the aforementioned increase, ewes, wethers, and rams are returned to the first party, the stated increase will be divided equally between the two parties, with both parties observing that the division is equal.

Signed on the above date,

> Abel Stearns
> Domingo Amestoy

Witness: Ulpiano Yndart

Source: Abel Stearns papers, Henry E. Huntington Library, San Marino, California (our translation).

Communities of the American West that have at present, or have had in the past, Basque ethnic group organizations and manifestations

KEY OF SYMBOLS

H = Basque Hotel or Boarding House
SC = Basque Social Club
HC = Handball Court
RB = Basque Language Radio Broadcast
D = Dance Group
F = Festival
P = Picnic
N = Newspaper or Newsletter
PP = Physical Plant for
      Social Club
BC = Basque Chaplain

1. ARIZONA
a. Flagstaff   H

2. CALIFORNIA
a. Bakersfield   H, HC, SC, F, D, N
b. Bishop   H
c. Chino   H, HC, SC, F, D (with La Puente)
d. Fresno   H, HC, P, D, BC
e. La Puente   H, HC, SC, F, D (with Chino), PP
f. Los Angeles   H, N, BC
g. Los Banos   H, SC, HC, F
h. Redwood City   SC
i. Sacramento   H
j. San Diego   H
k. San Francisco   H, SC, HC, D, F, N

Communities of the American West with Basque ethnic institutions. Diagonal hatchings identify areas of predominantly French Basque and Navarrese population; vertical hatchings cover areas of predominantly Vizcayan population; horizontal hatchings show the area of Basque settlement where all three groups are present.

l. San Juan Bautista   H
m. Stockton   H, HC, P, SC
n. Susanville   H

3. COLORADO

a. Grand Junction   H, SC
b. Montrose   H

4. IDAHO

a. Boise   H, SC, P, F, D, HC, RB, N, PP, BC
b. Caldwell   SC, H
c. Cascade   H
d. Emmett   SC
e. Hailey   H
f. Mountain Home   SC, H, HC, D, P
g. Parma   BC
h. Pocatello   H
i. Rupert   BC
j. Shoshone   H

5. MONTANA

a. Miles City   H

6. NEVADA

a. Austin   H
b. Carson City   H
c. Elko   H, SC, D, F, RB, N, HC, BC
d. Ely   H, SC, D, F
e. Eureka   H
f. Gardnerville   H
g. Golconda   H
h. Lovelock   H
i. Reno   H, SC, D, F, N, HC
j. Winnemucca   H, SC, D, RB

7. NEW MEXICO

a. Grants   H

8. OREGON

a. Burns   H, SC, P
b. Jordan Valley   H, HC, D
c. Ontario   H, SC, P, N
d. Vale   SC

9. UTAH
a. Ogden   H, HC
b. Price   H
c. Salt Lake City   H

10. WASHINGTON
a. Yakima   H

11. WYOMING
a. Buffalo   H, SC, RB, P
b. Rock Springs   H

It should be noted that the New York City Basque colony has several ethnic manifestations including: H, HC, D, N, F, PP, BC.

Basque Hotelkeepers in Idaho, Oregon, Nevada, and Utah, according to Sol Silen, *La historia de los vascongados en el Oeste de los Estados Unidos*

(Where two dates are given, the actual founding of the hotel is somewhere in between)

(Place: name of hotelkeeper; date hotel was founded)
Boise, Idaho: José Mendiota; 1900 ?
    Francisco Aguirre; 1905 ?
    Antonio Letamendi; before 1916
    José Uberuaga;† before 1916
    Anastasio Jayo; 1916
    Ventura Beristain; 1916
Nampa, Idaho: Luis Bermensolo; before 1916
Mountain Home, Idaho: José Bengoechea; before 1916
Shoshone, Idaho: Manuel Beitia; 1910
    Julián Pagoaga; 1914
    Francisco Onaindia; 1915
Jordan Valley, Oregon: Domingo Yturri; 1902–1916
    Eulogio Mandariaga; 1906–1916
    Sotero Maguna; 1911–1916
Elko, Nevada: Domingo Calzacorta; 1904–1916
    Ignacio Arrascada;* 1905
    Domingo Sabala; 1906 ?
    Pedro Jauregui; 1906
    Celso Madarieta; 1913
    Andrés Inchausti; 1916
Jack Creek, Nevada: Félix Plaza; 1902–1916
Gold Creek, Nevada: Ignacio Arrascada;* 1900 ?

Paradise Valley, Nevada: José Gastanaga; 1900 ?
  Hermenegildo Aramburu; 1898—1916
Winnemucca, Nevada: Ignacio Arrascada;* 1908 ?
Golconda, Nevada: Jean Etchebarren;** 1899 ?
Reno, Nevada: Jean Etchebarren;** 1899—1916
  J. P. Aldaz; 1905—1916
Ogden, Utah: José Laucirica; 1906
  Damián Telleria; 1914—1916

---

†José Uberuaga also founded the *Restaurante Vasco* in Boise, probably as early as the 1890s, according to Silen, *La historia*, p. 183.

?=approximate date

*=same individual

**=same individual

Notes

CHAPTER 1

1. Goti (1972:176)
2. Boyd (1963:1063)
3. Moya (1971:553−61)
4. Barandiarán (1953:40, 41, 60); Bosch y Gimpera (1966:3)
5. Maluquer de Motes (1966:118)
6. Gallop (1930:283)
7. *Anuario Estadístico* (1971:52)
8. Sollube (1969:201−5)
9. *Recensement* (1968:791−802)
10. Yrizar (1973:74−76)
11. Caro Baroja (1941)
12. Douglass and DaSilva (1971)
13. For greater detail, see Douglass (1975)
14. Lacarra (1957:51)
15. Mezquíriz (1969:3, map)
16. Lacarra (1957:52−53)
17. Ibid:59
18. Tacitus: *Historia* book IV, chapter 33 (Tacitus 1942:615)
19. García Bellido (1954)
20. Mohrmann (1951:II:146)
21. Caro Baroja (1945)
22. Mezquíriz (1958:31)
23. Thompson, E. A. (1952:16−17); Vigil and Barbero (1965:293)
24. Vigil and Barbero (1965:296)
25. Nieto Gallo (1958:132)
26. Ausonius: *Epist. XXIX:*57, 59 (Ausonius 1919:II:116)
27. Mezquíriz (1956:471)
28. Dubarat (1901:vii−xi); Vigil and Barbero (1965:275)
29. Vigil and Barbero (1965:274−78)
30. Zosimus (1967:252)
31. Lacarra (1957:54)
32. Vigil and Barbero (1965:300) gives the text of Idatius; see also Isidorus (1970:40)
33. Ibid. (citing Idatius 171)
34. Ibid.
35. Ibid.
36. Ibid.
37. Isidorus (1970:20)
38. Torres López (1963:101); Vigil and Barbero (1965:302−4) and González Echegaray (1966:232−33) for documentation and commentaries.
39. Biclara: anno VIII Iustini, qui est Leovigildi VI annus, 2 (cited by Vigil and Barbero 1965:302)
40. Ibid.: anno V Tiberii, qui est Leovigildi XIII annus, 3 (cited by Vigil and Barbero 1965:303)

41. Gregorius (1927, book VI:12)
42. Fortunatus *Carmina* X, 19 ad Galactorum comitem 10-12 (cited by Vigil and Barbero 1965:305)
43. Gregorius (1927, book IX:7)
44. Isidorus (1970:26, 27, 29)
45. Van Bath (1963:33)
46. Ibid.
47. Fredegarius (1960:14). For documentation of this period see Jaurgain (1898)
48. Cuzacq (1948:11)
49. Caro Baroja (1945:178-79)
50. Ausonius (1919:I:129)
51. Pérez de Urbel (1969:I:12)
52. Ubieto Arteta (1953:map 1)
53. Fredegarius (1960:67)
54. Caro Baroja (1943:181-82)
55. Urkina (1935)
56. Navascues (1947)
57. Fredegarius (1960:48)
58. Ibid.:66
59. Wallace-Hadrill (1967:77)
60. Taio XXXI, 172 (cited by Vigil and Barbero 1965:311)
61. Isidorus (1970:29); Latin text in Vigil and Barbero (1965:308)
62. Vigil and Barbero (1965:322-23)
63. Jaurgain (1898:I:44); Caro Baroja (1943:183)
64. Jaurgain (1898:I:44-45)
65. Ibid.:44
66. Ibid.:45
67. Jullian (Bishop) VI, 549 (cited by Vigil and Barbero 1965:312-13)
68. Ubieto (1969:24)
69. Ibid.
70. Codera (1903:102)
71. Ibn al-Qutiyyah (1926:116)
72. Levi-Provençal (1938:70)

73. Pérez de Urbel (1969:I:89-92)
74. Whitehead (1962)
75. Ferrarotti (1973:278-80)
76. Campión (1929:92)
77. Menéndez Pidal (1960)
78. Gurruchaga (1958)
79. Jaurgain (1898:I:144)
80. Lacarra (1971:41)
81. Ibid.:42
82. Ubieto (1969:56)
83. Ibid.
84. Arbeloa (1969:I:174-75)
85. Lacarra (1957:57)
86. Caro Baroja (1971:26)
87. Mañaricua (1971:275)
88. Ibid.:281-86
89. Ibid.:279
90. Ibid.:289
91. Lacarra (1957:67)
92. Ibid.:68
93. See Arteche (1941, 1951) for biographies of the two saints.
94. Ubieto (1969:57)
95. Ibid.:60
96. Ubieto (1960)
97. Ubieto (1953:30-32)
98. Arocena (1964:76)
99. Mañaricua (1972:19)
100. Barandiarán (1972:220)
101. Ubieto (1969:63)
102. Pliny (1952:IX:234-35)
103. Vie (1938); Gascue (1908)
104. Laborde (1956:226, 228)
105. Caro Baroja (1958:241)
106. Laborde (1956:225)
107. Arteche (1963:173)
108. Churruca (1951:13)
109. Labayru III:414, 433
110. García de Cortázar (1966:124)
111. Churruca (1951:8)
112. Ciriquiain (1951)
113. Mezquíriz (1964:26)

114. Aguirre-Andrés (1955:190)
115. Ausonius: Moselle verses 144−45 (Ausonius 1919:II:235)
116. Ciriquiain (1952:75−82)
117. Ciriquiain (1961:159); Jenkins (1971:69)
118. Arne (1943:194)
119. Herubel (1934:60−61)
120. Lefebvre (1933:259)
121. Ciriquiain (1952:162)
122. Sauer (1968:64−65)
123. Caro Baroja (1958:102)
124. Berraondo (1932:137)
125. Ducéré (1893:246−74)
126. Sauer (1968:73)
127. Fernández de Navarrete (1955:II:116)
128. Fernández Duro (1882)
129. Ibid. (1886:325)
130. Ispizua (1914:I:17−22)
131. Idoate (1969:251−52, 263)
132. Bélanger (1971:33−58 *passim*)
133. Howley (1908)
134. Lancre (1937:147)
135. Isasti (cited by Ciriquiain 1961:217)
136. Biard (1959a:163)
137. "Journal 1646" (1959:219); Vimont (1959:147)
138. Le Jeune (1959a:297); Bélanger (1971:65−67)
139. Le Jeune (1959b:VIII:29)
140. Biard (1959b:III:69)
141. Biard (1959a:173)
142. Laure (1959:101)
143. Deen (1937)
144. Michelena (1961:333)
145. Purchas (1625:III:709−10)
146. Jenkins (1971:83)
147. Ibid.:83−84
148. Dégros (1940:173)
149. Ibid.
150. Markham (1881−82)
151. Dégros (1940:175)
152. Le Jeune (1959c:IX:169)
153. Palacio Atard (1971:416)
154. Lhande (1910:56)
155. Chaunu (1969:263−64); Sauer (1968:67)
156. Harris (1920)
157. Chaunu (1969:258, 264)
158. Ballesteros-Beretta (1968:41−76)
159. Sauer (1968:73)
160. Fernández Duro (1881:232), cited in Sauer (1968:67−68)
161. Procacci (1970:70−114)
162. Vicens Vives (1969:270)
163. Ibid.:362
164. Chayette (1970:41)
165. Suárez Fernández (1969:87)
166. Ferrer I Mallol (1964:604)
167. Colas (1927)
168. Wright (1916:234)
169. Nogaret (1925:174)
170. Thierry (1932:9, 61)

CHAPTER 2

1. Cervantes Saavedra (1950:73)
2. Elías de Tejada (1963:47)
3. Ibid.:54
4. Celaya Ibarra (1970b:613)
5. Elías de Tejada (1963:142); *Nueva recopilación* (1919:478−79)
6. Zurita (1580:I, fol. 208v)

7. Valera, Diego (as cited by Labayru III, 269)
8. Uranzu (1955:142)
9. Labayru (1895-1903:III:280)
10. Sarasola (1950:97)
11. Suárez Fernández and Fernández Alvarez (1969:56-57)
12. Ibid.:57-58
13. Ibid.:58
14. Bilbao (1958:89-90)
15. Lynch (1964:29)
16. Ibid.
17. Vicens Vives (1969:326)
18. Martyr (1826)
19. Vicens Vives (1969:366)
20. Bilbao (1958:89-90)
21. Areitio (1959a:69-70)
22. Garibay (1628:I:190); Lojendio (1969:345)
23. Areitio (1959b:15-16)
24. Garmendia (Papers)
25. Chaunu (1955-59:VIII(1):255)
26. Ibid.:251
27. Ibid.:284
28. Lynch (1964:154)
29. Chaunu (1955-59:VIII (1):257)
30. Lynch (1964:155)
31. Bilbao (1958:192-209)
32. Chaunu (1955-59:VII(1):288
33. Ibid.:I:126
34. Pike (1972:127)
35. Ibid.
36. Chaunu (1955-59:VIII(1):254)
37. "Descripción del Convento de San Francisco de Sevilla" 1690 (MS.)
38. "Estatutos de Gobierno de la Cofradía de la Nación Vascongada, 1561," cited by Garmendia (1972)
39. Lynch (1964:159)
40. Ibid.:165
41. Nadal (1966:72)
42. Ibid.:75-76
43. Ibid.:73
44. Ibid.:20
45. Ibid.:79
46. Boyd-Bowman (1967:208)
47. "Documento Histórico Curioso" (1887:394)
48. Ibid.:399
49. Ibid.
50. Nadal (1966:79)
51. Goyheneche (1967)
52. Caro Baroja (1958:124)
53. "Liste des maisons" (1963)
54. Manzano (1970:450-54)
55. Las Casas (1951:I:357-58)
56. Herrera (1944-47:I:277); Bilbao (1958:92-97)
57. Fernández de Oviedo (1944-45:VII:31-32)
58. Ispizua (1914:I:145-46)
59. Ispizua (1917:III:39)
60. Ibid.
61. Lascurain (1956:110)
62. Ibid.:104
63. West (1949:6)
64. Ibid.
65. Ibid.
66. Estornés Lasa, M. (1970:620)
67. Lascurain (1956:229-30)
68. Ibid.:111
69. Estornés Lasa, M. (1970:611)
70. Thayer y Ojeda (1904:13-14)
71. Sáenz de Santa María (1969:482)
72. Thayer y Ojeda (1904:32-35)
73. Ibid.:23
74. Madariaga (1950:463-64)
75. Ibid.:465
76. Ibid.:469
77. Ibid.:629
78. Ibid.

79. Cited in Ibid.:629
80. Crespo R. (1969:83-141 *passim*)
81. Madariaga (1950:633-34)
82. Idoate (1954:407)
83. Ibid.:408
84. Ibid.:409
85. Ibid.
86. Ibid.:410
87. Ibid.
88. Zaragoza (1876:498-99, 502)
89. Zuñiga (1865:229)
90. Caro Baroja (1968)
91. Madariaga (1950:623)
92. Hussey (1934:8-32)
93. Morales Padrón (1955:26)
94. Ibid.:20
95. Crouse (1966:4)
96. Hussey (1934:87)
97. Ibid.:57
98. Ibid.:54
99. Estornés Lasa, J. (1948:16)
100. Hussey (1934:61); Estornés Lasa, J. (1948:17)
101. Hussey (1934:62)
102. Arocena (1933:43)
103. Hussey (1934:74)
104. Estornés Lasa, J. (1948:22)
105. Hussey (1934:65)
106. Ibid.:72
107. Ibid.:74
108. Mendizabal (1947:260)
109. Díaz Bravo (1754)
110. For genealogical evidence of the founding of several important Basque lineages in Venezuelan society of the 18th century, see Amezaga Aresti (1966), Mendizabal (1947:260-61), and Sangróniz (1943).
111. Estornés Lasa, J. (1948:67)
112. Ibid.:72
113. Hussey (1934:77)
114. Ibid.:79
115. Morales Padrón (1955:26)

116. Hussey (1934:82-83)
117. Cited in Morales Padrón (1955:27)
118. Ibid.:46
119. Ibid.:52
120. Ibid.:7
121. Ibid.:9
122. Ibid.
123. Ibid.:50
124. Hussey (1934:122-55)
125. Morales Padrón (1955:91)
126. Ibid.:92-93
127. Hussey (1934:110)
128. Cited in Morales Padrón (1955:103)
129. Ibid.:139
130. Hussey (1934:169-70)
131. Ibid.:171
132. Ibid.:241
133. Ibid.:266
134. Ibid.:166
135. Mendizabal (1947:264)
136. Hussey (1934:297)
137. Obregón (1949:15)
138. Sierra (1969:118)
139. Echabe (1971:84)
140. Obregón (1949:17)
141. Ibid.:24-25
142. Ibid.:21
143. Olavarría y Ferrari (1889:11)
144. Obregón (1949:159-62)
145. Obregón (1949:25)
146. Ibid.
147. Olavarría y Ferrari (1889:Appendix, 3)
148. Ibid.:8
149. Ibid.:55-92
150. Ibid.:91-92
151. Dorcasberro de Baragorri (1929:517)
152. Obregón (1949:55-56)
153. Olavarría y Ferrari (1889:56)
154. Ibid.:26; Obregón (1949:60)
155. Letter from Aldaco to

Meabe, June 14, 1752, cited in Olavarría y Ferrari (1889:30); Obregón (1949:61).

156. Olavarría (1889:33); Obregón (1949:63)
157. Olavarría y Ferrari (1889:36)
158. Ibid.:63
159. Ibid.
160. Obregón (1949:70)
161. Olavarría y Ferrari (1889:68−69)
162. Ibid.
163. Ibid.:81−83
164. Caro Baroja (1969)
165. Ibid.:24
166. Ibid.:81−170
167. Ibid.:225−56
168. Ibid.:254
169. Ibid.:267
170. Ibid.:34, 318
171. Ibid.:78−79
172. Ibid.:309−16
173. Ibid.:125
174. Ibid.:289−300
175. Ibid.:419−29
176. Davies (1970:273)
177. Ibid.:18
178. *Noticia* (1896:11−12)
179. Ibid.:49−60
180. "Documento Histórico Curioso" (1877)
181. Caro Baroja (1969)
182. Urquijo (1925:11−12)
183. Aralar (1942:14)
184. Shafer (1958:28−29)
185. *Estatutos* (1766)

186. *Código de Ynstitución*, titles 2 and 4
187. Urquijo (1945:253−269 *passim*)
188. *Código de Ynstitución*, title 1, article 22
189. Shafer (1958:24−27 *passim*)
190. Elorza (1971:354)
191. Ibid.
192. "Tratado de Basilea, 1795 (July 22)"
193. Aralar (1942:92−96)
194. Ibid.:160−80
195. *Extractos* (1777:v)
196. Ibid.:lxviii−lxix
197. "Proyecto" (1775:175)
198. *Extractos* (1777:lv)
199. Noticia (1896:18)
200. *Extractos* (1777:xxxviii)
201. Ibid.:lxvii
202. Shafer (1958:45)
203. Martínez Ruiz (1972)
204. "Catálogo" (1793)
205. Caro Baroja (1969:180)
206. Ibid.:294
207. Ruiz González (1972:434); Vicens Vives (1968:117)
208. Shafer (1958:44−45)
209. Ibid.
210. Ibid.:45−70, 140, 148, 158, 161, 259
211. Ibid.:119
212. Ibid.:166
213. Ibid.:236
214. Ibid.:246
215. Luque Alcaide (1962:60)
216. Shafer (1958:73)
217. Ibid.:43

CHAPTER 3

1. Grandmontagne (1933:29)
2. Irujo (1964:104−6)
3. Nadal (1966:112−13)
4. Panettieri (1970:16−17)

5. Deffontaines (1952:6)
6. Etcheverry (1886:493)
7. Deffontaines (1952:6)
8. Brie (1841:24)
9. Ibid.:18

10. Barrère (1842)
11. Deffontaines (1952:6)
12. Lamarque (1951:17)
13. Brougnes (1851)
14. Deffontaines (1952:6)
15. Michel (1857:193)
16. Ibid.:193–94
17. Oñate (Guipúzcoa): Archivo de la Villa. Legajo 3607, folios 24, 25, 39, 45, 47, 49, 53, 57, 62, 66, 71, 73, 81, 83, 98, 287, 328.
18. Zumalde (1972)
19. L'International (1855)
20. Andriani (1852)
21. Cuccorese and Panettieri (1971:395)
22. Deffontaines (1952:6)
23. Nadal (1966:153)
24. Ibid.
25. Conseil General (1855 [Sept. 3], p. 42)
26. Ibid.:41
27. Ibid. 1862 (Aug. 27), p. 78
28. Etcheverry (1886:494-95)
29. Ibid.:497
30. Lhande (1910:12, note 1)
31. Etcheverry (1903:806)
32. Gachiteguy (1955:187)
33. Etcheverry (1886:494)
34. Cola (1882:19)
35. Conseil General (1842 [Sept. 13], p. 36)
36. Michel (1857:197)
37. Lhande (1910:xix)
38. Consejo Superior de Emigración (1916:460)
39. Etcheverry (1886:494)
40. Lhande (1910:xxi)
41. Ibid.:xx
42. Ibid.:xxii
43. Altadill (1918:13)
44. Urabayen (1959:362)
45. Múgica (1918:233)
46. Ibid.:234
47. Instituto Nacional de Estadística (1960:53)
48. Jiménez (1970:304–5)
49. Ibid.:800
50. Douglass (1975:124)
51. Instituto Nacional de Estadística (1960:54-55)
52. Vicens Vives (1961:V:246)
53. Ibid.:251
54. Ibid.:276
56. Ibid.
57. Ibid.:295
58. Ibid.:298
59. Ibid.:25
60. Ibid.:19
61. Lhande (1910:12)
62. Lefebvre (1933:700)
63. Douglass (1975:133–35)
64. Ibid.: passim
65. Consejo Superior de Emigración (1916:75)
66. Ibid.:452
67. Goyheneche (1961:62–64)
68. For adversities experienced by two Spanish Basque villages (Echalar, Navarra, and Murélaga, Vizcaya), see Douglass (1975:74–83).
69. For a particularly poignant account of the emigration of a family from Guipúzcoa to Buenos Aires in order to flee the First Carlist War, see Garaico Echea (1965).
70. Etcheverry (1886:500)
71. Ibid.:501
72. Douglass (1975:46–48)
73. Caro Baroja (1958:265)
74. Douglass (1971:1100–1114)
75. Ibid.
76. Lhande (1910:19, note 1)
77. Michel (1857:7)
78. Lhande (1910:3–34)
79. O'Shea (1886:165)
80. Etcheverry (1903:806)
81. Dirección General de Inmigración (1925:9)
82. Ibid.:10

83. Ibid.:4
84. Ibid.:29
85. Ibid.:31
86. Alsina (1898:45)
87. Lhande (1910:xxii)
88. Scobie (1964a:78)
89. Ferns (1969:74)
90. Scobie (1964a:84)
91. Clemens (1886:130−31)
92. Scobie (1964a:97−99)
93. Denis (1922:183)
94. Scobie (1964a:83)
95. Latham (1866:19−20)
96. Cuccorese and Panettieri (1971:422)
97. Latham (1866:15)
98. Ibid.:19
99. Ibid.
100. Ibid.:20−21
101. Ibid. 185−90
102. Ibid.:194−96
103. Ross (1916:7−8)
104. Scobie (1964a:99)
105. Latham (1866:17); Denis (1922:186−87)
106. Latham (1866:17)
107. Ibid.:16
108. Cuccorese and Panettieri (1971:425)
109. Denis (1922:184)
110. Scobie (1964a:83)
111. Daireaux (1901:115−20)
112. Latham (1886:25)
113. Jefferson (1926:46−49)
114. Lauriente (1953:52)
115. Department of Agriculture (1904:24−31)
116. Denis (1922:186)
117. Scobie (1964a:119)
118. Alsina (1898:275−83)
119. Cuccorese and Panettieri (1971:527−33)
120. Alsina (1898:58−59)
121. Ibid.:179, 181
122. Uriarte (1919:401)

123. Ibid.:403
124. Ibid.:406
125. Ibid.:104−5
126. Martinez and Lewandowski (1911:176−77)
127. Larden (1911:304)
128. Denis (1922:185)
129. Daireaux (1901:273−78) gives a description of one Basque livestock agent.
130. Grandmontagne (1933:146−66)
131. Garriga (1958:75)
132. Garciarena (1955:33)
133. Sagastume (1912:78−79)
134. Ibid.:93
135. Ibid.:99
136. Morales Padrón (1948:114)
137. Lhande (1910:185)
138. Zoleta (1902:263)
139. Lesca (1907:36−37)
140. Ibid.:35
141. Garriga (1958:75)
142. Macchi (1971:154−58)
143. Lesca (1907:42)
144. Ibid.
145. Martin (1906:71)
146. Hammerton (1915:309)
147. Uriarte (1919:424−25)
148. Ibid.:422−28
149. Ibid.:427
150. Department of Agriculture (1904:87)
151. Lesca (1907:37)
152. Grandmontagne (1933:32)
153. Hammerton (1915:309−13)
154. Lesca (1907:41)
155. See Grandmontagne (1933:31) and Otaegui (1943:160)
156. Lesca (1907:42)
157. Grandmontagne (1933)
158. Ibid.:380
159. Ibid.

160. Ibid.:251
161. Garaico Echea
    (1965:164–76)
162. Grandmontagne
    (1933:28–40)
163. Ibid.:146–66
164. Imaz (1964:107)
165. Gori (1958:119)
166. Ibid.
167. Imaz (1964:121)
168. Ibid.:59–61 *passim*
169. Ibid.:174
170. Guaresti (1950:15)
171. Imaz (1962:13)
172. Lesca (1907:39)
173. Lhande (1910:185–86)
174. Cola y Goiti (1882)
175. Lhande (1910:236)
176. Ibid.:245–46
177. Grandmontagne
    (1933:143)
178. "Los Vascos en el
    Uruguay" (1881:65)
179. R.C. (1880:177–79)
180. Otaegui (1943:160)
181. Daireaux (1901:88–89)
182. Pellegrini (1968:128–29)
183. Hammerton (1915:299)
184. Sagastume (1912:31)
185. Ortiz y San Pelayo
    (1915:19, 25)
186. Garciarena (1956:135)
187. Cola y Goiti (1882:50)
188. Irujo (1964:104)
189. Sagastume (1912:104–10)
190. Lesca (1907:37)
191. Etcheverry (1886:495)
192. Ibid.:496
193. Consejo Superior de
    Emigración (1916:56–57)
194. Moch (1909:12–13)
195. Sarthou (1947:88–93)
196. Mieya and Azpiazu
    (1950:314)
197. Lamarque (1951:17)

198. Lhande (1910:231)
199. Cola y Goiti (1882:51–60)
200. "Fiestas éuskaras en
    Montevideo" (1881:39–40)
201. "Miscelánea" (1881:142)
202. Ortiz y San Pelayo
    (1915:34)
203. Ibid.:75
204. *Laurac Bat* (1878:I:no 1
    and no 4)
205. Ibid.:no 5
206. Ibid.
207. Ibid.:no 9
208. Ibid.:no 3
209. Ibid.:no 6 and 7
210. Ibid. 1879:II:no 23
211. Ibid.
212. Ibid.:1881:IV:no 77
213. Ibid.:no 80
214. Lhande (1910:159–60)
215. Iriart (1950:114–15)
216. Ibid.:115
217. Beramendi (1958)
218. Ortiz y San Pelayo
    (1915:39–45)
219. Ibid.:51, 56
220. Lhande (1910:162)
221. Baylac (1955:24)
222. Ibid.:103
223. Lhande (1910:164–78)
224. Lefebvre (1933:705)
225. Espil (1950:71)
226. Lefebvre (1933:705)
227. Solberg (1970:38)
228. Ridal (1883:571)
229. Thayer y Ojeda (1919:61)
230. Ibid.:164
231. Ibid.
232. Ibid.:162
233. Ridal (1883:571)
234. *Laurac Bat* (1882:V:no 86)
235. Ibid.:1883:VI:no 89
236. Lefebvre (1933:705)
237. Espil (1950:71)
238. Lefebvre (1933:705)

239. Thayer y Ojeda (1919:141)
240. Ibid.:142
241. Ibid.:143
242. Hagen (1962:353–384 *passim*)
243. Lefebvre (1933:706)
244. López Alen (1895:478)
245. "Los Bascongados en América" (1887:447–48)
246. "Los Bascongados en La Habana" (1884:403–9)
247. Gurat (1885:504)
248. Rojas (1874:21)
249. Ibid.:22
250. Ibid.
251. Ibid.:23
252. Binayan (1970:185–86)
253. Etcheverry (1892:1102)
254. Gachiteguy (1955:66)
255. Ibid.:98
256. Uriarte (1919:398–422)
257. Ibid.:393
258. Garciarena (1955:136)
259. Iriart (1950:136)
260. Garciarena (1955:136)
261. Uriarte (1919:395)
262. Lamarque (1930:491)
263. Amorrortu (1970:122–27)
264. "Cincuentenario del Retoño" (1969:88)
265. Scobie (1964a:120)
266. Solberg (1970)
267. Ibid.:170–72
268. Arciniegas (1957:16)
269. Ibarbia (1970:133–34)
270. Lamarque (1930:490–91)
271. Bilbao (1947)
272. Garriga (1958:77)
273. Centro Laurak Bat (1971)
274. Centro Vasco Francés (1970)
275. Espil (1950:73)

CHAPTER 4

1. Alegre (1956:II:100–101)
2. Ibid.
3. "Relación" (1622:678)
4. Ibid.:704
5. Dunne (1968:29)
6. Ibid.:30
7. Ibid.:36
8. Burrus (1971:18)
9. Dunne (1968:138)
10. Ibid.:178
11. Ibid.:432
12. Ibid.:436
13. Bancroft (1884c:468)
14. Dunne (1968:417–18)
15. Thurman (1967:95–98, 233)
16. Florez (1788:91)
17. Thurman (1967:26)
18. Cook (1973:70, 71n)
19. Thurman (1967:144)
20. Ibid.:149
21. Ibid.:159
22. Bancroft (1884b:246; 1885a:689)
23. Thurman (1967:24)
24. Ibid.:313
25. Bancroft (1884a:248–49)
26. Thurman (1967:315–17)
27. Ibid.:351–59)
28. Ibid.:51
29. Priestley (1916:143)
30. Ibid.
31. Ibid.:142–46
32. Ibid.:154
33. Ibid.:151–52
34. Olavarría (1889:87–90)
35. Ibid.:Appendix:19
36. Thurman (1967:114)
37. Ibid.:114–15
38. Bancroft (1884b:140)
39. Ibid.:131
40. Ibid.:732–44
41. Ibid.:181–82
42. Ibid.:170–71

43. Ibid.:195–96
44. Bancroft (1885a:9)
45. Lamadrid (1963:II:93)
46. Ibid.:338
47. Guest (1966:200)
48. Ibid.:208
49. Lamadrid (1963:I:165)
50. Ibid.:197
51. Ibid.:174
52. Ibid.:298–301
53. Ibid.:362
54. Ibid.:II:452
55. Luzuriaga (1686)
56. Engelhardt (1897:493–94)
57. Bowman (1958:138–39)
58. Ibid. (1959:58–64)
59. Bancroft (1884b:446)
60. Ibid.:448
61. Moorhead (1968:68)
62. Adams and Algier (1968:49–50)
63. "Catálogo" (1793)
64. Bancroft (1884b:732–44)
65. Lamadrid (1963:II:416)
66. Ibid.:450
67. Ibid.:200
68. Ibid.:203
69. Landaeta (1949:31–32)
70. Bancroft (1884b:503)
71. Bancroft (1885a:703)
72. Ibid.:207
73. Valdes (1874)
74. Lamadrid (1963:II:258)
75. Bancroft (1885a:724)
76. Suárez (undated)
77. Bancroft (1885a:724)
78. Guest (1962:37)
79. Bancroft (1885a:47)
80. Ibid.:158
81. Ibid.
82. Ibid.:195
83. Ibid.:197
84. Madinabeitia (1898:575)
85. Bancroft (1885a:195)
86. Ibid.:220
87. Ibid.:426–27
88. Montoya (1971)

89. Bancroft (1885b:47)
90. Ibid.:15
91. Reynolds (1945:291–94)
92. Bancroft (1885b:23)
93. Ibid.:90 (note 6); Duhaut Cilly (1929:151)
94. Bancroft (1885b:100)
95. "Reglamento" (1834)
96. Bancroft (1885b:100)
97. Ibid.:361
98. Ibid.:284
99. Ibid.:282–83 (note 17)
100. Ibid.:1886a:286
101. Galindo (1877:47)
102. Bancroft (1886a:287)
103. Bancroft (1884b:484)
104. Ibid.:607
105. Guest (1967:309)
106. Ibid.:310
107. Ibid.:327
108. Landaeta (1949:355ff)
109. Bancroft (1884b:440)
110. Ibid.:438–43
111. Ibid.:1885b:132
112. Duhaut Cilly (1929:143)
113. Arnaz (1878:2–4)
114. Guide (1940:206)
115. *La Gaceta Mercantil de Lima* (Sept. 1, 1834)
116. Bancroft (1885a:688)
117. Romer (1961:126)
118. Davis (1967:192)
119. Guinn (1907:III:1740)
120. Davis (1967:3)
121. Bancroft (1885a:710)
122. Nasatir (1945:279)
123. Bancroft (1885a:688)
124. Olavarría (1889:120)
125. Bancroft (1886a:12, 104)
126. Ibid.:2–15
127. Estudillo (1878:1)
128. Koch (1936:61)
129. Davis (1967:192)
130. Ibid.:239
131. Ibid.:193
132. Estudillo (1878:1)
133. Bancroft (1885b:282)

134. Davis (1967:13)
135. Pedrorena (1840)
136. Bancroft (1885b:752)
137. *Comercio del Plata* 1848 (Aug. 4) (Pasaportes)
138. Arnaz (1878:46−47)
139. Bancroft (1886a:620−21; 1886b:619)
140. Hayes (B.) (n.d.:41v)
141. Pitt (1970:43)
142. Arnaz (1878:8); Guinn (1902:259)

143. Santa Barbara Mission. Marriages 1
144. Hammond (1955:V:159)
145. Saint Amand (1854)
146. Oreña C-B:584:4, Schedule 3
147. Thompson (1883:233)
148. Ibid.:232
149. Santa Barbara Mission. Marriages 1868 (Oct. 31)
150. Santa Barbara County. Death Records 1902 (Nov. 7)

CHAPTER 5

1. Shepherd (1885:123)
2. Account collected by Jon Bilbao in Boise (Idaho) in 1939. Possibly the captain was Leon Aguirre, captain of the *Orion*, a brigantine that left Valparaíso for California on January 20, 1849, according to *El Comercio de Valparaíso*, of that date (Zarrantz 1972:II:1)
3. Handwritten note by deceased Boise resident, Bonifacio Garmendia, in *Garmendia Papers*.
4. Mason (1849−50:533)
5. Kenny (1955:30)
6. Almanach (1850:116)
7. Vallejo (1850:289)
8. Morenhout to Minister, in Nasatir (1945:286)
9. Perkins (1964:86)
10. López Urrutia (1967:17; 1969:191−92)
11. Perkins (1964: Introduction, 29−30)
12. King (1850:28)
13. Pitt (1970:60)
14. Paul (1965:108−9), citing Borthwick

15. Perkins (1964: Introduction, 27)
16. Chinard (1944:4)
17. Dillon (1850), in Nasatir (1945:555)
18. Nasatir (1945:36)
19. Ibid.:555
20. Almanach (1850:86, 90)
21. Meany (1953:22)
22. Almanach (1850:111)
23. Census (1852:XI:102)
24. Massey (1926:240)
25. Gachiteguy (1955:8)
26. Vilgre manuscript notes
27. Derbec (1964:217)
28. Gerstaecker (1856:160−61)
29. Ibid.
30. Ibid.:165
31. Perkins (1964:300−301)
32. Arnaz (1878:8)
33. Tuolumne County. *Deeds.* Book 1, p. 492; Book 2, p. 618.
34. Ibid.: Book 1, p. 345; Book 2, p. 590
35. Beaudreau (1932:45); Elliot (1883:110d)
36. Calaveras County. *Deeds.* Book E, pp. 252, 313.
37. Cureton (1953:101)
38. Caughey (1953:261)
39. Cleland (1941:137)

40. Ibid.:142
41. Pitt (1966:83−103)
42. Cleland (1941:137−42);
    Guinn (1915:I:285)
43. Cleland (1941:144)
44. Ibid.:145
45. Georgetta (1972:36)
46. Ibid.:39−56
47. Guinn (1915:286)
48. Ibid.
49. Cleland (1941:180)
50. Ibid.:148
51. Carrillo (1861)
52. Pitt (1966:247)
53. Kindall (1959:34)
54. Raup (1937:11)
55. Guinn (1915:285); Cleland
    (1941:149)
56. Cleland (1941:146−47)
57. Ibid.:151, 156
58. Ibid.:180
59. Milliken (n.d.:412−13)
60. Calaveras County. *Deeds*.
    Book B, p. 288 (April 22,
    1856)
61. Ibid.: Book B, p. 533 (Dec.
    26, 1856)
62. Pitt (1966:174−75)
63. Calaveras County. *Deeds*.
    Book F, p. 230 (March 6,
    1860)
64. Santa Barbara County.
    Miscellaneous Records, pp.
    250−54
65. Patterson, *et al*. (1969:387)
66. Gachiteguy (1955:9)
67. Patterson, *et al*. (1969:387)
68. Ibid.
69. Bilbao (1970)
70. Bell (1930:183)
71. Ibid.:181
72. Russell (1959:28)
73. Pitt (1966:250)
74. Bell (1930:183)
75. Gaye (1965:25)
76. Fortnight (1956:XIX[5]:
    54−55)
77. Russell (1959:29−30)
78. *California'ko Eskual Herria*
    (Ostailaren [May] 9, 1895
    Lib. 3, no 24, p. 2)
79. Ibid.: (Urriaren [Oct.] 26,
    1895, Lib. 4, no 9, p. 2)
80. Ibid.: (Urthailaren [Jan.] 11,
    1896, Lib. 4, no 20, p. 2)
81. Gaye (1965:25)
82. Bell (1930:188, 190)
83. *Escualdun Gazeta* (1885:no
    1, p. 3, col. 1)
84. Shochat (1950:275)
85. Borica (1796−97)
86. Cleland (1941:186)
87. Ibid.
88. Wentworth (1948:128−29)
89. Cleland (1941:187)
90. Wentworth (1948:130)
91. McGowan (n.d.:I:159)
92. Cleland (1941:144)
93. *Sacramento Union* (Sept.
    22, 1852, p. 3, col. 1)
94. Wentworth (1948:168−69)
95. Carman, Heath, and Minto
    (1892:448)
96. Cleland (1941:187)
97. Hayes, J. (1872:490)
98. Wentworth (1948:169)
99. Cramer (1969:57)
100. Wentworth (1948:174)
101. Hayes, J. (1872:492)
102. Ibid.
103. McElrath (1967:34)
104. Raup (1937:11)
105. Wentworth (1948:174)
106. Hayes, J. (1872:490)
107. *San Francisco Bulletin*
     (April 5, 1864: p. 5, col. 4)
108. Newmark (1970:328−29)
109. Census (1870:25)
110. Hayes, J. (1872:490)
111. Cleland (1941:191)
112. Armor (1911:347)
113. Case (1927:63)
114. Friis (1965:78)
115. Newmark (1970:422)

116. Powers (1870:141)
117. *San Andreas Independent*
     (March 23, 1860: p. 2, col. 3)
118. Gomez Ibañez (1967:1−6,
     46)
119. McGroarty (1921:II:112)
120. McGroarty (1923:II:393)
121. Beaudreau (1932:29)
122. Amestoy (1857)
123. Beaudreau (1932:58)
124. Ibid.:29
125. Stearns (SG Box)
126. Cramer (1969:56−57)
127. Newmark (1970:310)
128. *California'ko Eskual
     Herria* [Abendoaren (Dec.)
     18, 1897; Lib. 5, no 18, p. 3]
129. Bixby−Smith (1926:126)
130. Carr (1935:195)
131. Census (1883:1030)
132. Batz (1876)
133. *Escualdun Gazeta* (1885
     [Dec. 24], p. 1, col. 2)
134. Gordon (1883:87)
135. Ibid.:144
136. Ibid.:1896:239
137. Ibid.:1864:10
138. Gates (1967:211−12, 215)
139. Talbott (n.d.)
140. Arburua (n.d.)
141. Ibid.
142. Fisher (1945:208−11)
143. Ibid.:211−12
144. Ibid.:208
145. Indart (1933:III:515)
146. Merced County. *Deeds*.
     Book B, p. 122 (Aug. 9, 1862)
147. Census (1883:144)
148. Morgan (1814:50)
149. Wentworth (1948:196)
150. Ibid.
151. Ibid.:197
152. Winchel (n.d.:8); Burcham
     (1957:154−55)
153. Winchel (n.d.:8)
154. Wentworth
     (1948:192−95)
155. *California'ko Eskual
     Herria* (Uztailaren (July) 15,
     1893, p. 4)
156. Flint (1865:284−85)
157. Muir (1911:4)
158. Le Conte (1960:79)
159. McGowan (n.d.:I:271)
160. Merced County Records.
     Homstead Book.
161. Morgan (1914:50)
162. Hellinger (1966:2)
163. Morgan (1914); Vandor
     (1919); Tinkham (1921, 1923)
164. Census (1883:1036)
165. McGroarty (1923:202);
     Guinn (1901:128)
166. Crouch (1915:18)
167. Cleland (1941:224−27)
168. Armor (1911:342)
169. Cramer (1969:24)
170. Lewis, *et al.* (1924:65)
171. Armor (1921:264);
     Pleasants (1931:I:424)
172. Morrison and Haydon
     (1917:217)
173. Cramer (1969:180)
174. Rouget de Lisle (1928:115)
175. Gachiteguy (1955:66)
176. Tierney (1946:Chap. 8, p.
     1)
177. Silen (1917:51−52)
178. Ibid.:183
179. Census (1913)
180. Haskett (1936:20)
181. Ibid.:32
182. Ibid.
183. Reeve (1964:52)
184. Ibid.:153
185. Ibid.:1963:332
186. *California'ko Eskual
     Herria* [Abostuaren (Aug.)
     24, 1895, p. 2]
187. Gachiteguy (1955:129)

188. *California'ko Eskual Herria* (Dec. 19, 1896, Lib. 5, no 16, p. 2)
189. Ibid. (Aphirilaren [April] 7, 1894, Lib. 2, no 23, p. 2)
190. O'Driscoll (1948:171)
191. Parker (1951:154–55)
192. *California'ko Eskual Herria* [Uztailaren (July) 29, 1893, Lib. 1, no 3, p. 2]
193. Ibid. (Ereraroaren [June] 27, 1896, Lib. 4, no 43, p. 2)
194. Montana Historical Society Archives. manuscript case, item 636.3;M76
195. Ibid.:SC2, p. 112
196. Dionne (1970:331–32); see also Sallaberry (1956:3)
197. *California'ko Eskual Herria* (Hazilaren (Nov.) 10, 1894, Lib. 3, no 11, and Otsailaren (Feb.) 6, 1897, Lib. 5 no 23, p. 2)
198. Ibid. (Hazilaren [Nov.] 10, 1894, Lib. 3, no 11, p. 1 and (Hazilaren [Nov.] 24, 1894, Lib. 3, no 13, p. 2)
199. Lhande (1910:206–17)

CHAPTER 6

1. *The Humboldt Star* (March 29, 1912, p. 4, col. 4)
2. Austin (1906:9)
3. Ibid.:60
4. Ibid.:62
5. Lee (1962:206)
6. Ibid.:208
7. Georgetta (1972:39)
8. Ibid.:39–56
9. Census (1883:1036)
10. Flint (1864–65:285)
11. Georgetta (1965:20)
12. *The Elko Independent* (Dec. 14, 1870, p. 2, col. 3)
13. Ibid. (Sept. 9, 1871, p. 4, c. 1)
14. Ibid. (June 27, 1874, p. 2, c. 2)
15. *Report* (1881:201)
16. Ibid.:1892:313
17. Ibid.
18. Census (1913:402)
19. Humboldt County (Nevada) *Book of Deeds*, no 13, p. 155
20. Ibid. *Notices*, Book C, p. 209
21. Ibid. *Declaration of Intention Record Book*, no 1, p. 27
22. Bilbao, Julio (1971:29)
23. Ibid.:28
24. *Oregon Journal* (July 27, 1929, p. 4)
25. *Boise Statesman* (April 29, 1928)
26. Silen (1917:320)
27. Patterson *et al.* (1969:387–88)
28. Ibid.:391
29. Ibid.:419
30. Ibid.:421
31. See *The Elko Independent* (July 24, 1869, p. 1)
32. Ibid. (June 19, 1869, no 1)
33. Ibid. (Nov. 25, 1870)
34. Patterson *et al.* (1969:388)
35. *Elko Weekly Post* (April 10, 1880)
36. Silen (1917:321)
37. Arburua, "Rancho Panocha"
38. *California'ko Eskual Herria* (Hazilaren (Nov.) 16, 1895, Lib. 4, no 12, p. 2)

39. Patterson *et al.* (1969:390–91)
40. Scrugham (1935:II:422)
41. San Benito County (California) *Index to Marriages* (1874–1900). John B. Garat and Matilda Indart were married on April 29, 1895, in Tres Pinos.
42. Patterson *et al.* (1969:389)
43. Ibid.:388–390
44. *Tuscarora Times-Review* (April 27, 1889, p. 3, c. 2) reports the man as missing.
45. See Sawyer (1971:165)
46. *The Silver State* (Aug. 15, 1879, p. 3, c. 3)
47. Ibid. (Oct. 25, 1881, p. 3, c. 1)
48. Ibid. (Jan. 21, 1885, p. 3, c. 1)
50. *The Humboldt Star* (April 23, 1913, p. 1, c. 1)
51. Ibid.
52. *The Silver State* (July 3, 1888, p. 3, c. 1)
53. Ibid. (April 16, 1889, p. 3, c. 1)
54. *Tuscarora Times-Review* (March 17, 1888, p. 3, c. 2)
55. *The Silver State* (March 13, 1888, p. 3, c. 1)
56. Ibid. (April 5, 1892, p. 3, c. 1)
57. Ibid. (March 10, 1894, p. 3, c. 1 and p. 2, c. 1)
58. Kennedy and Doten (1901:19–20)
59. Humboldt County (Nevada) *Marriages*, Books C and D
60. *The Humboldt Star* (July 31, 1912, p. 1, c. 6)
61. Ibid. (Feb. 13, 1911, p. 1, c. 7)
62. Ibid. (March 16, 1914, p. 1, c. 3)
63. Ibid. (Sept. 7, 1914, p. 1, c. 4)
64. Ibid. (March 27, 1911, p. 1, c. 1)
65. Shepherd (1885:123)
66. *The Silver State* (April 10, 1896, p. 3, c. 1)
67. *The Humboldt Star* (Dec. 5, 1913, p. 1, c. 4)
68. Hanley (1973:278)
69. *Carson Morning Appeal* (May 4, 1898, p. 3, c. 1)
70. *The Humboldt Star* (Dec. 5, 1913, p. 1, c. 1)
71. Silen (1917:69)
72. Ibid.:261
73. Ibid.:397
74. Quoted in *The Reno Evening Gazette* (June 18, 1913, p. 4, c. 3 and 4)
75. Reprinted in *The Carson City News* (July 26, 1913, p. 1, c. 5)
76. *The National Miner* (June 27, 1913, p. 1, c. 5 and 6)
77. *United States Congressional Record*. 63rd Congress. 1st Session (1913), vol. 50, pt. 4, p. 3581
78. Ibid.:3582
79. Ibid.:3580
80. *Caldwell Tribune* (July 17, 1909, p. 4)
81. Hawley (1920:Deluxe Supplement, p. 102)
82. Census (1883:1066)
83. *Goldfield Daily Tribune* (Feb. 5, 1910, p. 2, c. 3 and 4)
84. Ibid. (Feb. 13, 1910, p. 3, c. 4)
85. Fleming and Brennen (1940:27)
86. Satrústegui (1971:297–98)
87. Silen (1917:261)
88. Vandor (1919:1585, 916)
89. Georgetta (1972:383–426)

90. *The Reno Evening Gazette* (Feb. 17, 1890, p. 3, c. 2)

91. *Nevada State Herald* (Aug. 8, 1902, p. 5, c. 3)

92. Ibid. (Sept. 1, 1905, p. 5, c. 4)

93. *Elko Free Press* (July 11, 1924)

94. From an interview with the partner of the deceased in Grand Junction (Colorado) in July 1971.

95. *California'ko Eskual Herria* (Maiatzaren [May] 30, 1896, Lib. 4, no 39, p. 2; Aboztuaren [Aug.] 14, 1897, Lib. 5, no 50, p. 3)

96. See Bartley (1968)

97. *The Nevada Stockgrower* (Oct. 1, 1919, p. 12) (Statement by Vernon Metcalf)

98. Robbins (1962:206–07)

99. Wentworth (1948:495)

100. *Statutes* (1885:Chap. LXVI, pp. 67–68)

101. Ibid.:53–54

102. *The Silver State* (April 6, 1896, p. 3, c. 2)

103. *Statutes* (1901:Chap. XXVI, p. 37)

104. Ibid. 1903:Chap. XXVIII, pp. 47–48

105. *The Humboldt Star* (Aug. 3, 1908, p. 1, c. 1)

106. *Tuscarora Times-Review* (May 23, 1899, p. 3, c. 3)

107. *Battle Mountain Scout* (April 14, 1923, p. 3, c. 3)

108. Robbins (1962:306)

109. Coville, as cited in Wentworth (1948:502)

110. Clawson (1950:252)

111. Gates (1968:583)

112. Cited in Gomez-Ibañez (1967:59, 62)

113. *Annual Reports* (1903:152–53); Austin (1906:193–95)

114. Gates (1968:583)

115. Wentworth (1948:503)

116. Gates (1968:580)

117. Ibid.:582

118. Wentworth (1948:506)

119. *The Humboldt Star* (March 26, 1909, p. 1, c. 3)

120. Ibid. (May 17, 1909, p. 1, c. 5)

121. Lane (1973; chapter V)

122. Tremewan n.d.

123. "Annual Grazing Report" (1912)

124. Templeton (1919)

125. Martineau (1922:17)

126. See testimony in Buckman (1935:40)

127. Humboldt County. *Declaration of Intent*, Books 1–3

128. *Nevada Stockgrower* (April 1920, p. 8)

129. Blakeslee (1913)

130. From *The Humboldt National Forest* list of sheep permittees (1911)

131. Keas (1910)

132. Lindsey (1913)

133. Keas (1911)

134. Fleming (1918)

135. United States Forest Service (1920)

136. Mink (1918)

137. Stewart (1924)

138. Gates (1968:608–609)

139. Ibid.:610

140. Ibid.:612–13

141. Ibid.:613–14

142. Taylor Grazing Act (1934)

143. Sherman (1933:43–44)

144. "Taylor Testimony" (1934:25, 28)

145. Federal Records Center,

San Francisco (California) (1935a)

146. Walker (1933:15)
147. Ibid.:16–18
148. Loggan (1937)
149. Federal Records Center (1935b)
150. Foley (1935)
151. Galt Statement
152. *The Humboldt Star* (March 22, 1912, p. 1, c. 1)
153. Gilfillan (1930:5)
154. *The Elko Free Press* (July 25, 1923, p. 1, c. 7)
155. For example, see *The Humboldt Star* (Aug. 5, 1914, p. 1, c. 1) (death by gunshot self-inflicted and accidental); (March 4, 1910, p. 1, c. 1) (frozen in a blizzard); (Sept. 16, 1910, p. 1, c. 5) (crushed by haying derrick); Jan. 19, 1910, p. 1, c. 5) (frozen); *The Elko Independent* (June 2, 1911, p. 2, c. 4 and 5) (frozen body found in snowbank); *The Humboldt Star* (June 25, 1913, p. 1, c. 1) (found dead, bucked from horse).
156. For examples of Basque herders either dying from spotted fever or arriving in town suffering from the disease, see *The Humboldt Star* (April 17, 1911, p. 1, c. 6, April 28, 1911, p. 1, c. 2; April 8, 1910, p. 1, c. 1.)
157. Douglass (1973c)
158. Gilfillan (1930:1)
159. *The Silver State* (July 17, 1894, p. 3, c. 1)
160. For examples of other insane herders, see *The Humboldt Star* (June 6, 1910; Jan. 29, 1913, p. 1, c. 3; March 25, 1914, p. 1, c. 1); *The Elko Free Press* (Oct. 8,

1920; Aug. 29, 1927, p. 1, c. 3)
161. *Estatutos* (1908:11)
162. For examples, see *The Elko Free Press* (Nov. 22, 1920, p. 1, c. 6 and April 14, 1933, p. 1, c. 4)
163. *The Humboldt Star* (Jan. 3, 1913, p. 1, c. 5)
164. Lhande (1910:213)
165. Ibid.:xvii
166. *The Nevada State Herald* (Oct. 2, 1914, p. 5, c. 1)
167. Consejo Superior de Emigración (1916:235)
168. *The Elko Independent* (Sept. 28, 1917, p. 4, c. 3)
169. Etchart (1919:18)
170. *The National Wool Grower* (July 1919:39)
171. *The Elko Independent* (March. 20, 1919, p. 1, c. 2 and March 22, 1919, p. 1, c. 3)
172. *The Elko Free Press* (Sept. 28, 1923, p. 1, c. 5)
173. United States Department of Labor (1922:5)
174. Ibid. 1925:6
175. *The Nevada Stockgrower* (Aug. 4, 1923)
176. Ibid. (Feb. 1924)
177. *The Nevada State Journal* (April 8, 1925, p. 3, c. 2)
178. *The Elko Free Press* (Feb. 20, 1941, p. 1, c. 3)
179. Ruiz (1964:58–67)
180. Georgetta (1972:291)
181. McCarran to Dangberg, May 4, 1942
182. McCarran to Dangberg, May 27, 1942
183. McCarran to D. W. Park (undated, but 1943)
184. McCarran to Lt. Col. Jay L. Taylor, July 8, 1943
185. Bruton, Philip S., to

McCarran, July 15, 1943
186. McCarran to Dangberg,
August 13, 1943
187. Shoemaker, T. B., to
Dangberg, November 4, 1943
188. de Cardenas, Juan F., to
McCarran, December 29,
1943
189. *The Elko Free Press* (May
1, 1944, p. 1, c. 4)
190. Ibid. (June 23, 1944, p. 1,
c. 2, p. 4, c. 5)
191. House Report (1949a:2)
192. House Report (1949b:2)

193. House Report (1949a:2)
194. Gomez–Ibañez (1967:23)
195. Statistical Abstract
(1973:627)
196. Linz and De Miguel
(1966:282)
197. *La Voz de España*. San
Sebastián (Sept. 16, 1969, p.
14)
198. *El Correo Español*. Bilbao
(Jan. 2, 1971, p. 4 and Jan. 7,
p. 4)
199. Ibid. (May 5, 1966, p. 5)

CHAPTER 7

1. Axular (1964:161–62)
2. Gachiteguy (1955:66, 98)
3. *The Humboldt Star* (April 23,
1913, p. 1, col. 3)
4. Silen (1917:69)
5. Ibid.:82
6. Ibid.:183
7. Ibid.:69
8. Ibid.:72
9. Ibid.
10. Ibid.:319
11. Ibid.:395
12. Ibid.
13. *California'ko Eskual Herria*
(Uztailaren [July] 15, 1893, p.
2)
14. Lhande (1910:197)
15. Gachiteguy (1955:118)
16. Chamblin (1954:882)
17. Castelli (1970:100–101)
18. Gachiteguy (1955:121)
19. Ibid.:186
20. Ibid.:60
21. Ibid.:66
22. Ibid.:98
23. *Escualdun Gazeta* (Jan.
1886, p. 1)
24. McGroarty (1935:543)

25. *California'ko Eskual Herria*
(Aphirilaren [April] 18, 1896,
Lib. 4, no 33, p. 2)
26. Bynam and Jones (1950)
27. *California'ko Eskual Herria*
(Hazilaren [Nov.] 23, 1895,
Lib. 4, no 13, p. 2; Hazilaren
[Nov.] 30, 1895, Lib. 4, no
14, p. 2.)
28. Ibid. (Hazilaren [Nov.] 16,
1895, Lib. 4, no 12, p. 2;
Urtharrilaren [Jan.] 18, 1896,
Lib. 4, no 21, p. 2;
Aphirilaren [April] 4, 1896,
Lib. 4, no 31, p. 2)
29. Ibid. (Hazilaren [Nov.] 30,
1895, Lib. 4, no 14, p. 2;
Aphirilaren [April] 18, 1896,
Lib. 4, no 33, p. 2;
Aphirilaren [April] 25, 1896,
Lib. 4, no 34, p. 2)
30. Ibid. (Maihatzaren [May]
18, 1895, Lib. 3, no 38, p. 1)
31. Ibid. (Uztailaren [July] 29,
1893, Lib. 1, no 3, p. 1)
32. Ibid. (Urriaren [Oct.] 7,
1893, Lib. 1, no 13, p. 3)
33. Ibid. (Abendoaren [Dec.]
30, 1893, Lib. 2, no 9, p. 4)

34. Ibid. (Urtharrilaren [Jan.] 18, 1896, Lib. 4, no 21, p. 2)
35. Ibid. (Abendoaren [Dec.] 30, 1893, Lib. 2, no 9, p. 4)
36. Ibid.
37. Ibid.
38. Ibid. (Otsailaren [Feb.] 20, 1897, Lib. 5, no 25, p. 3)
39. Ibid. (Urtharrilaren [Jan.] 12, 1895, Lib. 3, no 20, p. 2)
40. Ibid. (Urtharrilaren [Jan.] 26, 1895, Lib. 3, no 22, p. 3)
41. See Ibid. (Madama Mathilda Garat news) (Otsailaren [Feb.] 29, 1896, Lib. 4, no 27, p. 2)
42. See Ibid. (Bernardo Altube news item) (Hazilaren [Nov.] 16, 1895, Lib. 4, no 12, p. 2)
43. Tinkham (1923:1368)
44. Vandor (1919:2532)
45. Morgan (1914:651)
46. Armor (1921:571)
47. *California'ko Eskual Herria* (Uztailaren [July] 15, 1893, Lib. 1, no 1, p. 2)
48. Gachiteguy (1955:174)
49. Vandor (1919:651)
50. Morgan (1914:128)
51. Sather (1961:51)
52. Gachiteguy (1955:66)
53. Ibid.:98
54. Ibid.:103
55. Pagliarulo (1948:34)
56. Sather (1961:48)
57. Price (1972:27)
58. Morgan (1914)
59. Outcalt (1925)
60. Vandor (1919)
61. Ibid.:2581
62. Tinkham (1923:1410)
63. Armor (1921:1291–92)
64. McGroarty (1935:473)
65. Ibid.:1923:II:290
66. Ibid.:291; Ibid. 1935:474
67. Douglass (1969:Chap. 5)
68. *E.g.*, Pagliarulo (1948:36)
69. Gaiser (1944:101–3)
70. Ibid.:89; Pagliarulo (1948:36–37)
71. Gaiser (1944:175–78)
72. *California'ko Eskual Herria* (Hazilaren [Nov.] 30, 1895, Lib. 4, no 14, p. 2; Aphirilaren [April] 18, 1896, Lib. 4, no 33, p. 2; Aphirilaren [April] 25, 1896, Lib. 4, no 34, p. 2)
73. Ibid. (Urriaren [Oct.] 26, 1895, Lib. 4, no 9, p. 7)
74. See Arteche (1958)
75. Gaiser (1944)
76. Arburua (n.d.)
77. Cramer (1969)
78. Gachiteguy (1955:140)
79. Ibid.
80. Cornell (1959:38); Bradley and Kelly (1953:I:340–41)
81. Gachiteguy (1955:135–46 *passim*)
82. *California'ko Eskual Herria* (Aboztuaren [Aug.] 18, 25, 1894)
83. Ibid. (Maihatzaren [May] 18, 1895, Lib. 3, no 38, p. 1)
84. Ibid. (Otsailaren [Feb.] 1, 1896, Lib. 4, no 23, p. 2)
85. Ibid. (Maihatzaren [May] 23, 1896, Lib. 4, no 38, p. 2)
86. Lhande (1910:197)
87. *The Humboldt Star* (Nov. 27, 1912, p. 1, col. 5)
88. Gachiteguy (1955:120)
89. Silen (1917:40)
90. See Douglass (1969:Chap. 2)
91. Ibid.
92. *Boise Statesman* (Nov. 25, 1940)
93. Gaiser (1944:146)
94. Castelli (1970:110–11)
95. California Supreme Court (1873:17)
96. Ibid.:16
97. Ibid.:17–18

98. Ibid.:19
99. Grandmontagne
     (1933:226–234)
100. Shepperson
     (1970:167–72, 210–13,
     219–20, 222, 242)
101. Laxalt (1957)
102. Ibid.: 1972
103. Cornu (1970); Isasi and
     Kenny (1942); Isasi (1940)
104. *Escualdun Gazeta* (Dec.
     24, 1885, no 1, p. 1)
105. Ibid.: (Jan. 16, 1886, no 3,
     p. 1)
106. *La Vasconia* (Dec. 10,
     1898, IV [no 187], p. 78)
107. Bieter (1955); Douglass
     (1973)
108. Gachiteguy (1955);
     Recalde (1973)
109. Castillo Puche (1963)
110. *E.g.*, Arrizabalaga (1967)
111. *E.g.*, Labayen (1969)
112. Ossa Echaburu (1963)
113. Zavala (1968)
114. *California'ko Eskual
     Herria* (Uztailaren [July] 7,
     1894, Lib. 2, no 45, p. 1)
115. Talbott Papers
116. Arburua (n.d.)
117. Armor (1921:1644)

118. Ludwig (1927:893–94)
119. Morgan (1914:1191)
120. Ibid.:1351
121. Ibid.:1335
122. Vandor (1919:1585)
123. Ibid.:1901
124. Ibid.:2515
125. Ibid.:2559
126. Tinkham (1923:1622)
127. Ibid.:1452
128. Juvmey (1926:382)
129. *Escualdun Gazeta* (Dec.
     24, 1885, no 1, p. 4)
130. *California'ko Eskual
     Herria* (Abendoaren [Dec.]
     30, 1893, Lib. 2, no 9, pp.
     3–4)
131. Ibid. (Abendoaren [Dec.]
     15, 1895, Lib. 4, no 16, p. 3
132. *The Silver State* (April 14,
     1896, p. 3, col. 1)
133. Pagilarulo (1948:54)
134. Cramer (1969:66)
135. Arburua (n.d.)
136. Gachiteguy (1955:20)
137. Baker (1972)
138. Laxalt (1966); Toll (1968)
139. *Elko Independent*
     (November 15, 1907, p. 1,
     col. 4)

CHAPTER 8

1. Jaureguy (1850)
2. Grandmontagne (1933:30)
3. Gachiteguy (1955:187)
4. *California'ko Eskual Herria*
   (Mainhatzaren [May] 18,
   1895, Lib. 3, no 38, p. 1)
5. Scobie (1964b:124)
6. *Laurac Bat* (1880:III:no 3)
7. Scobie (1964b:124)
8. Ibid.:158–59

9. Ibid.:124
10. Ibid.:120
11. Lhande (1910:196)
12. Gachiteguy (1955:187)
13. *Statistical Abstract . . .*
    [hereafter referred to as SA]
    (1911:82); SA (1916:83); SA
    (1921:93)
14. SA (1921:93)
15. SA (1911:85); SA
    (1912:90); SA (1913:106); SA
    (1914:90); SA (1915:88); SA

(1916:86); SA (1917:101); SA (1918:101); SA (1919:99); SA (1920:93); SA (1921:96)

16. SA (1911:82); SA (1916:83); SA (1921:93)

17. SA (1911:85); SA (1912:90); SA (1913:106); SA (1914:90); SA (1915:88); SA (1916:86); SA (1917:101); SA (1918:101); SA (1919:99); SA (1920:93); SA (1921:96)

18. *Consejo Superior* (1916:245−46)

19. Ibid.:75

20. *Nevada Stockgrower* (May, 1920:3)

21. Grandmontagne (1933:30−31)

22. Bieter (1957)

23. *Consejo Superior* (1916:49)

24. Gachiteguy (1955:186−87)

Bibliography

Aasheim, Magnus
  1970 *Sheridan's Daybreak: A Story of Sheridan County and its Pioneers.* Great Falls (Montana).

Abstract of the Twelfth Census of the United States
  1902 U.S. Department of Commerce, Bureau of the Census. *Abstract of the Twelfth Census of the United States, 1900.* Washington.

Adams, Eleanor B., and Keith W. Algier
  1968 "A Frontier Book List—1800." *New Mexico Historical Review.* Albuquerque. XLIII:49–59.

Adams, John
  1850 "On modern democratic republics: Biscay." In *The Works of John Adams.* Boston. Vol. I, pp. 310–13.

Aguirre-Andrés, Antonio
  1955 *Materiales arqueológicos de Vizcaya.* Bilbao.

Alegre, Francisco Javier
  1956– *Historia de la Provincia de la Compañía de Jesús de Nueva*
  1960 *España. Nueva edición por Ernest J. Burrus, S.J. y Félix Zubillaga, S.J.* 4 volumes Rome.

Almanach
  1850 *Almanach Californien pour 1851. Guide de l'émigrant.* Paris.

Alsina, Juan A.
  1898 *La inmigración europea en la República Argentina.* 3rd ed. Buenos Aires.

Altadill, Julio
  1918 *Provincia de Navarra.* In Carreras y Candi, Francisco (ed.): *Geografía general del País Vasco-Navarro.* Barcelona.

Amestoy, Domingo
  1857 "Domingo Amestoy receipt, June 2, 1857," Abel Stearn Collection. Huntington Library, San Marino (California), Box 75.

Amezaga Aresti, Vicente de
  1966 *El elemento vasco en el siglo XVIII venezolano.* Caracas.

Amorrotu, Pedro María de
  1970 "Centenario del Dr. Tomás de Otaegui (1870–1932)." *Boletín del Instituto Americano de Estudios Vascos.* Buenos Aires. XXI:122–27.

Andriani Escofet, Severo Leonardo
  1852 *Circular en que reprueba como immoral el sistema de "enganchar" jóvenes de ambos sexos para conducirlos al Continente*

Americano bajo las seductoras promesas de una estable fortuna y de un feliz porvenir. Pamplona.

"Annual grazing G report for Ruby Mountain District, 1912." National Forest Service, Humboldt National Forest, Elko, 1912.

Annual Reports
    1903   Department of the Interior. Washington.

Anuario Estadístico de España. Presidencia del Gobierno, Instituto Nacional de Estadística. Vol. XLVI, 1971. Madrid: Imprenta Nacional del Boletín Oficial del Estado.

Aralar, José de
    1942   *El Conde de Peñaflorida y los Caballeritos de Azcoitia.* Buenos Aires.

Arbeloa, Joaquín
    1969   *Los Orígenes del reino de Navarra (710−925).* 3 vols. San Sebastián.

Arburua, Joseph
    n.d.   "Rancho Panocha de San Juan y los Carrizalitos." Manuscript in the Basque Collection, University of Nevada, Reno

Arciniegas, Germán
    1957   "Los vascos en Caracas." In Centro Vasco de Caracas: *Los Vascos en Venezuela.* Caracas. p. 16.

Areitio, Darío de
    1959a   "El Colegio de Pilotos Vizcaínos en Cádiz, existía antes del siglo XV." In Areitio, *Los vascos en la historia de España.* Bilbao. Pp. 69−70.
    1959b   "Sevilla y los vizcaínos." In Areitio, *Los vascos en la historia de España.* Bilbao. Pp. 15−16.

Armor, Samuel (ed.)
    1911   *History of Orange County, California.* Los Angeles.
    1921   *History of Orange County, California.* Los Angeles.

Arnaz, José
    1878   "Recuerdos de José Arnaz, residente en San Buenaventura, español de nacimiento y comerciante en el tiempo pasado. Los dictó a Thomas Savage para la Bancroft Library." Manuscript in Bancroft Library, Berkeley (California).

Arne, Paul
    1942−   "La baleine des Basques." *Bulletin du Musée Basque.* Bayonne.
    1943   XVIII−XIX:189−96.

Arocena, Fausto
    1933   "La Compañía Guipuzcoana de Caracas. Notas para su historia." *Yakintza.* San Sebastián. I:42−44.
    1964   *Guipúzcoa en la Historia.* Madrid.

Arrizabalaga, Bernardo de
    1967   *Los Barroeta.* Bilbao.

Arteche, José de
    1941   *San Ignacio de Loyola.* Barcelona.
    1951   *San Francisco Javier.* Zaragoza.
    1958   *Saint-Cyran. De caracteriología vasca.* Zarauz.
    1963   "Ferrones vascos del siglo XV en el Alto Garona." *Boletín de la Real Sociedad Vascongada de Amigos del País.* San Sebastián. XIX:173.

Ausonius, Decimus Magnus
1919 *Ausonius, with an English translation by Hugh G. Evelyn White.* 2 vols. London.

Austin, Mary
1906 *The Flock.* Boston.

Axular, Pedro de
1964 *Gero (Después). Introducción, edición y traducción de Luis Villasante.* Barcelona.

Baker, Sarah
1972 "Basque American Folklore in eastern Oregon." M.A. Thesis. University of California, Berkeley.

Ballesteros Beretta, Antonio
1968 *La marina cántabra. I. De sus orígines al siglo XVI.* Santander.

Bancroft, Hubert Howe
1884a *History of the Northwest Coast. Vol. I. 1543–1800.* San Francisco. *(Works* XXVII)
1884b *History of California. Vol. I. 1542–1800.* San Francisco. *(Works* XVIII)
1884c *History of the North Mexican States and Texas.* Vol. 1, 1531–1800 *(Works* XV).
1885a *History of California. Vol. II. 1801–1824.* San Francisco. *(Works* XIX).
1885b *History of California. Vol. III. 1825–1840.* San Francisco. *(Works* XX).
1886a *History of California. Vol. IV. 1840–1845.* San Francisco. *(Works* XXI).
1886b *History of California. Vol. V. 1846–1848.* San Francisco *(Works* XXII).

Barandiarán, José Miguel de
1953 *El hombre prehistórico en el País Vasco.* Buenos Aires.
1972 *Diccionario Ilustrado de Mitología Vasca.* Bilbao.

Barrère, B.
1842 *Emigration à Montevideo et à Buenos Aires.* Pau.

Bartley, Lee
1968 "The last massacre." *True Frontier* I (6):25–27, 55–56.

"Los bascongados en América." *Euskal Erria.* San Sebastián, 1887:XVI:447–48.

"Los bascongados en la Habana." *Euskal Erria.* San Sebastián, 1884, X, 403–9.

Battle Mountain Scout. Battle Mountain (Nevada), 1923.

Batz, Catalina
1876 "Catalina Batz lease application letter." Los Angeles County Museum, Manuscripts (no. DE851).

Baylac, Natividad E.
1955 *Euskal Echea. Su obra a través de cincuenta años, 1904–1954.* Buenos Aires.

Beaudreau, Charles
1932 "A record of the activities of people of French origin in southern California." In Loyer, F., and Charles Beaudreau.

Bélanger, René
1971 *Les Basques dans l'Estuaire du Saint-Laurent, 1535–1635.* Montreal.

Bell, Major Horace
    1930   *On the West Coast. Being Further Reminiscences of a Ranger.*
          Edited by Lanier Bartlett. New York.

Beramendi, E. F.
    1958   "Centro Navarro, extracto de su historia social." In *Centro
          Navarro, LXIII aniversario de su fundación.* Buenos Aires.

Berraondo, Ramón
    1932   "Sellos medievales de tipo naval." *Revista Internacional de Es-
          tudios Vascos.* San Sebastián. XXIII:130−38.

Biard, Pierre
    1959a   "Letter from Father Biard to Reverend Father Christopher Bal-
          tazar, Provincial of France, at Paris, June 10, 1611. In Thwaites
          1959:I, 139−83.

    1959b   "Relation of New France, of its lands, nature of the country, and
          of its inhabitants, also, of the voyage of the Jesuit Fathers to said
          country, and of their work there up to the time of their capture by
          the English. Written by Father Pierre Biard of Grenoble, of the
          Society of Jesus, 1616." In Thwaites 1959:III, 23−283; IV,
          1−165.

Bieter, Pat
    1957   "Reluctant shepherds: The Basques of Idaho." *Idaho Yesterdays,*
          I:no. 2:10−15.

Bilbao, Jon
    1947   "Publicaciones periódicas vascas aparecidas en América entre
          1936−1946." *Ikuska.* Sare (B.P.) I (nos. 4−5), 164.

    1958   *Vascos en Cuba (1492−1511).* Buenos Aires.

    1970   *Eusko Bibliographia. Dictionary of Basque Bibliography. A
          Cataloguing of books, pamphlets, leaflets and journal articles
          referring to the Basque Country, classified by author, subject
          matter, and place names.* San Sebastián.

    1972   "Pedro Altube." Manuscript.

Bilbao, Julio
    1971   "Basque names in early Idaho." *Idaho Yesterdays* XV(2):26−29.

Binayan, Narciso
    1970   "La población vasca de la Argentina." *Boletín del Instituto
          Americano de Estudios Vascos.* Buenos Aires. XXI:185−87.

Bixby Smith, Sarah
    1926   *Adobe Days.* Cedar Rapids (Iowa).

Blakeslee, W. W.
    1913   "Supervisors annual work plan for 1913." Santa Rosa National
          Forest, filed under Humboldt National Forest.

Boise Statesman, 1928, 1940.

Borica, Diego de
          Governor Borica to the Com. of Santa Barbara, 1796−97. Man-
          uscript in the Bancroft Library, Berkeley (California).

Bosch y Gimpera, Pedro
    1966   "Sobre el planteamiento del problema vasco." *IV Symposium de
          prehistoria peninsular.* Pamplona, pp. 3−6.

Bowman, J. N.
    1958   "The Resident Neophytes (Existentes) of the California missions
          (1769−1834)." *The Historical Society of Southern California
          Quarterly.* XL:138−48.

1959 "The Comenzada dates of the California missions." *The Histori-cal Society of Southern California Quarterly*. XLI:58−64.

Boyd, William C.
1969 "Genetics and the human race." *Science*. Washington. CXL:1057−64.

Boyd-Bowman, Peter
1964 *Indice Geobiográfico de Cuarenta Mil Pobladores Españoles de América en el Siglo XVI. Tomo I. 1493−1519.* Bogotá.
1967 "Regional origins of the early colonists." In Lewis Hanke (ed.), *History of Latin American Civilization: Sources and Interpreta-tions.* Vol. I, pp. 206−10. Boston.
1968 *Indice Geobiográfico de Cuarenta Mil Pobladores Españoles de América en el Siglo XVI.* Mexico, D.F.

Bradley, Rt. Rev. Cyprian, and Most Rev. Edward J. Kelly
1953 *History of the Diocese of Boise 1863−1952.* 2 vols. Boise, Idaho.

Brandes, Stanley H.
1973 "On Basque migration." *American Anthropologist* 75(1):299−300.

Brie, F.
1841 *Considérations sur l'émigration basque à Montevideo.* Bayonne.

Brougnes, M. A.
1851 *Extinction du pauperisme agricole par la colonisation dans les provinces de la Plata, etc.* Bagnères-de-Bigorre.

Bruton, Philip S., Colonel, Corps of Engineers, Deputy Administrator to Patrick McCarran, July 15, 1943. In McCarran Collection, Itemized Files, The College of the Holy Names, Oakland, California, Item nos. A641−642.

Buckman, Thomas E.
1936 "The Taylor Grazing Act in Nevada." *University of Nevada, Agricultural Extension Service, Bulletin.* no. 76, p. 40.

Burcham, Levi Turner
1957 *California Range Land, an Historico-ecological Study of the Range Resource of California.* Sacramento.

Burrus, Ernest J.
1971 *Juan María de Salvatierra, S.J. Selected papers about Lower California.* Los Angeles.

Bynum, Lindley, and Idwal Jones
1950 *Biscailuz, Sheriff of the New West.* New York: Morrow.

Calaveras County (San Andreas, California) *Deeds.*

Caldwell Tribune. Caldwell (Idaho), 1909.

California Supreme Court
1873 *California Reports,* Sacramento.

California'ko Eskual Herria. Berriketari eskualduna aguertzen dena Larum-bate guziez. Los Angeles (California), 1893−96.

Campión, Arturo
1929 *Euskariana. Novena serie. Nabarra en su vida histórica. Segunda edición (corregida y aumentada).* Pamplona.

Cardenas, Juan F. de, Spanish Ambassador, to Patrick McCarran, December 29, 1943. In McCarran Collection, Itemized Files, The College of the Holy Names, Oakland, California. Item nos. A645-A646.

Carman, Ezra A., H. A. Heath, and John Minto
1892 U.S. Department of Agriculture. *Bureau of Animal Industry Re-*

port 18. *Special Report on the History and Present Condition of the Sheep Industry of the United States.*

Caro Baroja, Julio
    1941   "Retroceso del vascuence." *Atlantis* XVI:35−62.
    1943   *Los pueblos del Norte de la Península Ibérica.* Madrid.
    1945   *Materiales para un estudio de la lengua vasca en su relación con la latina.* Salamanca.
    1958   *Los vascos.* Segunda edición. Madrid.
    1968   *El señor inquisidor y otras vidas por oficio.* Madrid.
    1969   *La hora navarra del siglo XVIII. Personas, familias, negocios e ideas.* Pamplona.
    1971   "San Amando y los vascones." *Príncipe de Viana* XXXII:7−26.

Carr, Henry
    1935   *Los Angeles, City of Dreams.* New York.

Carrillo, Pedro C.
    1861   Pedro C. Carrillo to Abel Stearns, June 1861. In Gaffey manuscript. Huntington Library. Cited in Cleland (1941:168).

The Carson City News. Carson City (Nevada) 1913.

Carson Morning Appeal, 1898

Case, Walter H.
    1927   *History of Long Beach and Vicinity.* Vol. I. Chicago.

Castelli, J. R.
    1970   "Basques in the Western United States: a functional approach to determination of cultural presence in the geographic landscape." Ph.D. Dissertation, University of Colorado, Department of Geography.

Castillo Puche, José Luis
    1963   *Oro blanco.* Madrid.

"Catálogo General alfabético de los individuos de la Real Sociedad Bascongada de los Amigos del País." 1793 In *Extractos,* 1793.

Caughey, John Walton
    1953   *California.* Second Edition. New Jersey.

Celaya Ibarra, Adrián
    1970a   "Las declaraciones de derechos y el Fuero de Vizcaya. (En el año de los derechos humanos.)" *La Gran Enciclopedia Vasca.* Bilbao. IV, 569−87.
    1970b   "El derecho foral de Vizcaya en la actualidad." *La Gran Enciclopedia Vasca.* Bilbao. IV, 589−673.

Census
    1935   *Census of 1852. California. County of Tuolumne.* Copied under the direction of the Genealogical Records Committee, Daughters of the American Revolution of California. (Typed copy at State Library, Sacramento, California).
    1864   *Census 1860. Agriculture in the United States in 1860,* compiled from the original returns of the Eighth Census. Washington.
    1883   *Report on the Productions of Agriculture as Returned at the Tenth Census (June 1, 1880).* Washington.
    1896   The miscellaneous documents of the House of Representatives for the first session of the Fifty-second Congress, 1891−92. Vol. 50, pt. 10. *Reports on the Statistics of Agriculture in the United States . . . at the Eleventh Census: 1890.* Washington.

1913   *Thirteenth Census of the United States Taken in the Year 1910.*
        Vol. V. *Agriculture 1909 and 1910.* General report and analysis.
        Washington.
1943   *Sixteenth Census of the United States, 1940. Agriculture.* Vol. III.
        General Report. Statistics by subjects. Washington.
Centro Laurak Bat. *El Hogar de los Vascos. Memoria y balance correspon-
        diente al ejercicio 1970, sometidos a la consideración de la Asamblea
        General Ordinaria del día 27 de marzo de 1971.* 1971 Buenos Aires.
Centro Vasco Francés. *Memoria y balance correspondiente al 75 ejercicio. 1
        de agosto de 1969 - 31 de julio de 1970.* 1970 Buenos Aires.
Cervantes Saavedra, Miguel de
        1950   *The Adventures of Don Quixote.* J. M. Cohen (translator). Bun-
                gay, Suffolk.
Chamblin, Thomas (ed.)
        1954   *The Historical Encyclopedia of Wyoming.* Wyoming Historical
                Institute.
Chaunu, Pierre
        1955–   *Séville et l'Atlantique (1504–1650).* 8 vols. Paris.
        1959
        1969   *Conquête et exploitation des nouveaux mondes (XVIe siècle).*
                Paris.
Chayette, Fredric L.
        1970   "The Sovereign and the Pirates, 1332." *Speculum. Journal of
                Mediaeval Studies.* Vol. XLV, pp. 40–68.
Chinard, Gilbert
        1944   *When the French came to California.* San Francisco.
Churruca, Alfonso de
        1951   *Minería, industria y comercio del País Vasco.* San Sebastián.
"Cincuentenario del retoño del Arbol de Guernica de Buenos Aires." *Boletín
        del Instituto Americano de Estudios Vascos.* 1969 Buenos Aires,
        XX:88–90.
Ciriquiain Gaiztarro, Mariano
        1951   *Los puertos marítimos vascongados.* San Sebastián.
        1952   *La pesca en el mar vasco.* Madrid.
        1961   *Los vascos en la pesca de la ballena.* San Sebastián.
Clawson, Marion
        1950   *The Western Range Livestock Industry.* New York.
Cleland, Robert Glass
        1941   *The Cattle on a Thousand Hills. Southern California 1850–1870.*
                San Marino (California).
Clemens, E. J. M.
        1886   *La Plata Countries of South America.* Philadelphia.
Codera, Francisco
        1903   *Estudios críticos de historia árabe española.* Zaragoza.
"Código de Ynstitución. Seccion 1a. Ordenanzas relativas a la dirección y
        gobierno del Ynstituto Patriótico Bascongado." Manuscript in the Archives
        of the Convento de Aránzazu, document no. XVI–43.
Colas, Louis
        1927   *Marins basques du temps passé: baleiniers, filibustiers et Cor-
                saires.* Biarritz.
Cola y Goiti, José
        1882   *La emigración vasco-navarra.* Vitoria.

Comercio del Plata. Montevideo, Chap. IV, note. 134. 1846.

Conseil General des Basses-Pyrenees
1808– *Rapport du prefet et proces-verbaux des seances.* Pau.
1891

Consejo Superior de Emigración
1916 *La emigración española transoceánica 1911–1915.* Madrid.

Cook, Warren L.
1973 *Flood Tide of Empire, Spain and the Pacific Northwest, 1543–1819.* New Haven & London.

Cornell, Joseph R.
1959 "The acculturation of the Basque ethnic community in southwestern Idaho." Senior Essay. University of Notre Dame, Department of Sociology, Indiana.

Cornu, Jean
1970 *The Innocent Ones.* Philadelphia.

El Correo Español. El Pueblo Vasco. Bilbao. 1966, 1971.

Cosgrave, George
        see Gerstaecker

Coville, Frederick V.
1898 "Forest growth and sheep grazing in the Cascade mountains of Oregon." Division of Forestry, United States Department of Agriculture, *Bulletin* 15:10 as cited in Wentworth 1948:502.

Cramer, Esther R.
1969 *La Habra, the Pass Through the Hills.* Fullerton (California).

Crespo R., Alberto
1969 *La guerra entre Vicuñas y Vascongados. Potosí 1622–25.* La Paz (Bolivia), 2d ed.

Crouch, Herbert
n.d. *Reminiscences of Herbert Crouch, 1915.* Manuscript in the San Diego Historical Society, The Serra Museum Research Library. San Diego, California.

Crouse, Nellis M.
1966 *The French Struggle for the West Indies (1665–1713).* New York.

Cuccorese, Horacio Juan, and José Panettieri
1971 *Argentina, manual de historia económica y social.* Vol. I. *Argentina criolla.* Buenos Aires.

Cureton, Gilbert
1953 "The cattle trail to California 1840–1860." *The Historical Society of Southern California Quarterly* XXXV:99–109.

Cuzacq, Rene
1948 *Géographie historique des Landes.* Mont-de-Marsan.

Daily Alta California. San Francisco. 1851.

Daireaux, Godofredo
1901 *Tipos y paisajes criollos.* Buenos Aires.

Davies, R. Trevor
1970 *The Golden Century of Spain, 1501–1621.* London.

Davis, William Heath
1967 *Seventy-five Years in California. Recollections and Remarks by One Who Visited These Shores in 1831, and Again in 1833, and Except When Absent in Business was a Resident from 1838 Until*

the End of a Long Life in 1909. Edited by Harold A. Small. San Francisco.

Deen, N. G. H. (ed.)
1937   *Glossaria duo Vasco-Islandica.* Amsterdam.

Deffontaines, Pierre
1952   "Participation des Pyrénées au peuplement des Pays de la Plata." In *Primer Congreso Internacional de Estudios Pirenaícos.* Zaragoza. pp. 269−97.

Dégros, Maxime
1940   "La grande pêche basque, des origines à la fin du XVIII siècle." *Bulletin de la société des Sciences, Lettres et Arts de Bayonne.* Bayonne. Pp. 148−79, 204−10.
1941   Ibid., pp. 27−33, 89−92, 156−63.
1942   Ibid., pp. 23−26, 75−78, 137−45.
1943   Ibid., pp. 39−53, 95−101, 165−83, 221−26.
1944   Ibid., pp. 17−28, 75−81, 127−31.
1945   Ibid., pp. 34−44.

Denis, Pierre
1922   *The Argentine Republic. Its Development and Progress.* Translated by Joseph McCabe. London.

Department of Agriculture (Argentina)
1904   *Sketch of the Argentine Republic as a country for immigration.* 2d ed. Buenos Aires.

Derbec, Etienne
1964   *A French Journalist in the California Gold Rush. The Letters of Etienne Derbec.* Edited by A. P. Nasatir. Georgetown (California).

"Descripción del Convento de San Francisco de Sevilla, 1680." Manuscript in the Archivo de la Provincia. Seville (in Garmendia, 1972).

Díaz Bravo, José Vicente (Bishop of Durango, Mexico)
1754   *El ayuno reformado, según práctica de la primitiva Iglesia, por los cinco Breves de nuestro Santíssimo Padre Benedicto XIV. Obra histórica, canónico-médica, necessaria à los señores obispos, curas, confessores, médicos, sanos y enfermos. Con noticia particular de los privilegios, que aun después de los Breves, gozan en España los soldados. Y una disertación histórica, médico-chymica, physico-moral de el Chocolate, y su uso, después de los nuevos preceptos.* Pamplona.

Díaz Trechuelo, María Lourdes
1965   *Navegantes y Conquistadores Vascos.* Madrid.

Dillon, Patrice
1850   "La Californie dans les dernières mois de 1849." *Revue des Deux Mondes.* Paris. Pp. 193−219. Cited by Nasatir 1945:555.

Dionne, Harvey
1970   "John Etcharen." In Aasheim 1970:331−32.

Dirección General de Inmigración.
1925   *Movimiento migratorio en la República Argentina. Años 1857−1924.*

"Documento Histórico Curioso"
1887   "Proposiciones que hace el M.N. y M.L. Señorío a sus hijos residentes en las Indias, Flandes, Italia y otras provincias, en

consideración a las necesidades que padece Vizcaya." (written in 1639) *Euskal Erria*, vol. VIII, no. 16, May 10, 1887, pp. 394–400.

Dorcasberro de Garagorri, Carlos
1929 "Le Collège de las Viscainas à Mexico." *Revista Internacional de Estudios Vascos*. San Sebastián, XX, 516–28.

Douglass, William A.
1969 *Death in Murélaga*. Seattle.
1971 "Rural exodus in two Spanish Basque villages: a cultural explanation." *American Anthropologist* LXXIII:1110–14.
1973a "Reply to Brandes." *American Anthropologist* LXXV:300–2.
1973b "Reply to Kasdan and Brandes." *American Anthropologist* 75(1):304–6.
1973c "Lonely lives under the big sky." *Natural History* LXXXII(3):28–39.
1975 *Echalar and Murelaga: Opportunity and Rural Depopulation in Two Spanish Basque Villages*. London and New York.

Douglass, William A., and Milton da Silva
1971 "Basque nationalism." In Oriol Pi-Sunyer (ed.), *The Limits of Integration: Ethnicity and Nationalism in Modern Europe*. Research Reports no. 9, Department of Anthropology, University of Massachusetts, Amherst. Pp. 147–86.

Dubarat, V.
1901 *Le Missel de Bayonne de 1543*. Bayonne.

Ducéré, Edouard
1893 "Les Pêcheurs Basques a Terre-Neuve," *Bulletin de la Société des Sciences, Lettres et Arts de Pau*. Pau. XXII:221–351.

Duhaut Cilly, A.
1834 *Voyage autour du monde, principalement à la California et aux Iles Sandwich pendant les annees 1826, 1827, 1828 et 1829*. Paris.
1929 "Duhat-Cilly's account of California in the years 1827–28. Translated from the French by Charles Franklin Carter." *California Historical Society Quarterly* VIII:130–66.

Dunne, Peter M.
1968 *Black Robes in Lower California*. Berkeley. (1st ed. 1952)

Echave, Balthasar de
1971 *Discursos de la Antigüedad de la Lengua Cantabra Bascongada*. Bilbao. (Facsimile of original edition published in 1607, Mexico City)

Echegaray, Carmelo
1918 *Provincia de Vizcaya*. In Carreras y Candi, Francisco (ed.): *Geografía general del País Vasco-Navarro*. Barcelona.

Elías de Tejada, Francisco
1963 *El Señorío de Vizcaya (hasta 1812)*. Madrid.

Elko Free Press. Elko (Nevada), 1920, 1923, 1924, 1927, 1941, 1944

The Elko Independent. Elko (Nevada), 1869, 1870, 1907, 1911, 1917, 1919.

Elko Weekly Post. Elko (Nevada), 1880.

Elliot, Wallace W. (ed.)
1883 *History of San Diego County*. San Francisco.

Elorza, Antonio
1971 "Las *Conferencias* inéditas de Larramendi." *Revista de Oc-cidente.* Madrid. Pp. 350—55.
Enciclopedia general ilustrada del País Vasco. Cuerpo A. Diccionario enci-clopédico vasco. San Sebastián, 1968.
Engelhardt, Zephyrin
1897 *The Franciscans in California.* Harbor Springs (Michigan).
Escualdun Gazeta, 1885—86, Los Angeles.
Espil, Pierre
1950 "Les basques au Chili." *Gure Herria.* Bayonne. II:71—79.
"Estatutos de gobierno de la Cofradía de la nación vascongada," 1561. Manuscript (cited by Garmendia, J.: "Los vascos en Sevilla").
Estatutos de la Sociedad Bascongada de los Amigos del País según el acuerdo de sus juntas de Vitoria por abril de 1766. San Sebastián, 1766 (facsimile in *La Gran Enciclopedia Vasca.* Bilbao, 1967, II:463—78).
Estatutos de la Sociedad de Socorros Mutuos. Boise (Idaho), 1908.
Estornés Lasa, José
1948 *La Real Compañía Guipuzcoana de Navegación de Caracas.* Buenos Aires.
Estornés Lasa, Mariano
1970 "América." In *Enciclopedia general ilustrada del País Vasco. Cuerpo A.: Diccionario,* pp. 603—22.
Estudillo, José María
1878 "Datos históricos sobre la Alta California por don José María Estudillo, vecino de San Diego." Manuscript in the Bancroft Library, Berkeley, California.
Etchart, P.
1919 "Letter to the Editor." *The National Wool Grower.* Salt Lake City (Utah), p. 18.
Etcheverry, Louis
1886 "Les Basques et leur émigration en Amérique." *La Réforme Sociale.* Paris. XI:491—515.
1892 "L'émigration dans les Basses-Pyrénées pendant soixante ans," *Association Française pour l'Avancement des Sciences.* II:1092—1104.
1903 "De l'expansion familiale considérée comme source de l'expan-sion coloniale: l'exemple des Basques." *La Réforme Sociale.* Paris. XLVI. pp. 798—808.
Extractos de las Juntas Generales celebradas por la Real Sociedad Bascon-gada de los Amigos del País. Madrid, Vitoria, 1772—93.
Federal Records Center, San Francisco (Box 38928)
1935a "Summary of grazing applications, 1935, sheep list no. 1, Modoc-Lassen District."
1935b "Taylor Grazing Committee Report, Jordan Valley District, 1935."
Fernández Duro, Cesareo
1886 "El descubrimiento de Terranova." *Euskal Erria.* San Sebastián XV:325—27.
1882 "Expediciones precolombinas de los vizcaínos a Terranova y a los paises del litoral inmediato." *Congreso Internacional de Americanistas. Actas de la IV reunión.* Madrid. I:216—18.

Fernández de Navarrete, Martín
1955   *Colección de los viajes y descubrimientos que hicieron por mar los españoles desde fines del siglo XV.* 3 vols. Madrid. *(Biblioteca de Autores Españoles,* vol. 75 − 77).
Fernández de Oviedo, Gonzalo
1944−   *Historia general y natural de las Indias, islas y tierrafirme del*
1945   *Mar Océano.* Asunción del Paraguay.
Ferns, H.S.
1969   *Argentina.* London.
Ferrarotti, Franco
1973   *Per conoscere Pareto.* Milano.
Ferrer I Mallol, María Teresa
1964   "Documents Sobre el Consolat de Castellans a Catalunya: Balears." In *Anuario de Estudios Medievales.* Barcelona. No. 1, pp. 599 − 605.
"Fiestas éuskaras en Montevideo." *Euskal Erria.* San Sebastián, 1881, II:39 − 40.
Fisher, Anne B.
1945   *The Salinas: Upside-down River.* New York.
Fleming, C. E.
1918   *Range plants poisonous to sheep and cattle in Nevada.* University of Nevada, Reno, Agricultural Experiment Station, Bulletin no. 95.
Fleming, C. E., and C. A. Brennen
1940   *Range sheep production in northeastern Nevada.* University of Nevada, Reno, Agricultural Experiment Station, Bulletin no. 151, p. 27.
Flint, Wilson
1864−   *Textile fibres of the Pacific states.* Transactions of the
1865   California State Agricultural Society, 1864 and 1865. pp. 271 − 89.
Florez
1788   "Letter from Viceroy Florez to Minister of the Indies, Valeds, dated April 26, 1788." In Kuykendall 1922:91.
Foley
1935   "Letter from Agent Foley to Special Agent J. H. Favorite, Feb. 19, 1935." Federal Records Center, San Francisco, California, Box 38927.
Fortnight
1956   XIX(5):54 − 55.
Fredegarius
1960   *The Fourth Book of the Chronicle of Fredegar with its Continuations.* Translated from the Latin with introduction and notes by J. M. Wallace-Hadrill. London.
Friis, Leo
1965   *Orange County Through Four Centuries.* Santa Ana (California).
La Gaceta Mercantil de Lima. Lima (Peru), 1834.
Gachiteguy, Adrien
1955   *Les Basques dans l'Ouest Américain.* Bordeaux.

Gaiser, Joseph H.
1944 "The Basques of the Jordan Valley area, a study in social process and social change." Ph.D. Dissertation, University of Southern California.
Galindo, José Eusebio
1877 "Apuntes para la historia de California." Manuscript in the Bancroft Library, Berkeley, California (C-D-87).
Gallop, Rodney
1930 *A Book of the Basques.* London. Reprint ed., Reno, 1970.
Galt, H. M.
Statement regarding J. O. case. Exhibit, S.F. 21. Federal Records Center, San Francisco (California), Box 38931.
Garaico Echea, Abraham Ignacio
1965 *De Vasconia a Buenos Aires o la venida de mi madre al Plata.* Buenos Aires.
García Bellido, A.
1954 "Los *vardulli* en el ejército romano." *Boletín de la Real Sociedad Vascongada de Amigos del País.* San Sebastián X:131−39.
García de Cortázar, José Angel
1966 *Vizcaya en el siglo XV. Aspectos económicos y sociales.* Bilbao.
Garciarena, José María
1955 "Los campesinos vascos en América y sus descendientes argentinos." *Boletín del Instituto Americano de Estudios Vascos.* Buenos Aires. VI:128−38.
Garibay, Esteban
1628 *Los Quarenta libros del compendio historial.* Barcelona. (Cited by Lojendio 1969)
Garmendia, Bonifacio
n.d. "Papers." (Manuscript in the Basque Collection. University of Nevada, Reno)
Garmendia, J.
1972 "Los vascos en Sevilla." (Manuscript in possession of the author, Zaldibia, Guipúzcoa).
Garriga, Gabino
1958 "El euskera en América." *Boletín del Instituto Americano de Estudios Vascos* IX:67−79. Buenos Aires.
Gascue, F.
1908 "Los trabajos romanos de Arditurri (Oyarzun)." *Revista Internacional de Estudios Vascos* II:465−73. San Sebastián.
Gates, Paul W. (ed.)
1967 *California Ranchos and Farms 1846−1862.* The State Historical Society of Wisconsin.
1968 *History of the Public Land Law Development.* Washington, D.C.
Gaye, Laura B.
1965 *The Last of the Old West. A Book of Sketches about the Calabasas Area.* Woodland Hills (California).
Gerstaecker, Friedrich
1856 *Californische Skizzen.* Leipzig. The chapter "Die franzoesische Revolution," pp. 159−95, was translated by George Cosgrave from the French version *(Scenes de la vie californienne traduites*

de l'allemand, par Gustave Revilliod. Génève, 1859) and published under the title "The French Revolution" in *California Historical Society Quarterly,* 1938, XVII, 3−17. Our quotations are literal translations from the German.

Georgetta, Clel
1965   "Sheep in Nevada." *Nevada Historical Society Quarterly* VIII(2):15−39. Reno (Nevada).
1972   *Golden Fleece in Nevada.* Reno (Nevada).

Gilfillan, Archer B.
1930   *Sheep.* Boston.

Goldfield Daily Tribune, Goldfield (Nevada), 1910.

Gomez Ibañez, Daniel
1967   "The rise and decline of transhumance in the United States." M.A. Thesis, University of Wisconsin.

González Echegaray, Joaquín
1966   *Los cántabros.* Madrid.

Gordon, Clarence
1883   "Report on cattle, sheep, and swine." *Tenth Census of the United States, 1880.* Vol. 3. Washington.

Gori, Gastón
1958   *El pan nuestro. Panorama social de las regiones cerealistas argentinas.* Buenos Aires.

Goti Iturriaga, José Luis
1972   "Aportación a la antropología de la población vascófona." *Estudios de Deusto* XX:173−79. Bilbao.

Goyheneche, Eugène
1961   *Notre terre basque.* Bayonne.
1967   "L'introduction du maîs en Euskal Herria et en Europe (1523)." In *Homenaje a don José Miguel de Barandiarán.* Bilbao, II:109−20.

Goytino, J. P.
1898   "J. P. Goytino." *La Vasconia* IV(187):78. Buenos Aires.

Grandmontagne, Francisco
1933   *Los inmigrantes prósperos.* Madrid.
1967   "Interviu con Angela Querejeta Iparraguirre en América." In Antonio Arrillaga (ed.), *Lo que se ha dicho de Iparraguirre.* Bilbao.

Gregorius
1927   *The History of the Franks,* by Gregory of Tours. Translated with an introduction by O. M. Dalion. Oxford.

Guaresti, Juan José
1950   "Notas para un apunte sobre la influencia vasca en la Argentina." *Boletín del Instituto Americano de Estudios Vascos.* I:13−17. Buenos Aires.

Guest, Florian
1962   "The establishment of the Villa Branciforte." *California Historical Society Quarterly* XLI:29−50. San Francisco.
1966   "The Indian policy under Fermin Francisco de Lasuen, California's second president." *California Historical Society Quarterly* XLV:195−224. San Francisco.

Guest, Francis F.
  1967   "Municipal government in Spanish California." *California His-
          torical Society Quarterly* XLVI:307—35. San Francisco.
Guide, Erving Gustav (ed.)
  1940   "Edward Vischer's first visit to California." Translated and edited
          by E. G. Guide. *California Historical Society Quarterly*
          XIX:193—216. San Francisco.
Guinn, James Miller
  1901   *Historical and Biographical Record of Los Angeles and Vicinity.*
          Chicago.
  1902   *Historical and Biographical Record of Southern California.*
          Chicago.
  1903   *History of the State of California and Biographical Record of
          Santa Cruz, San Benito, Monterey and San Luis Obispo Counties.*
          Chicago.
  1907   *A History of California.* 3 vols. Los Angeles.
  1915   *A History of California and Extended History of Los Angeles and
          Environs.* 3 vols. Los Angeles.
Gurat, G.
  1885   "Eskualdunak-Orok-Bat." *Euskal Erria* XII:504—5. San Sebas-
          tián.
Gurruchaga, Ildefonso
  1958   "La expedición de Abd-al-Rahman I a tierra de Vascones y del
          Pirineo aragonés en el año 781." *Boletín del Instituto Americano
          de Estudios Vascos* IX:102—24, 161—75. Buenos Aires.
Hagen, Everett E.
  1962   "The transition in Colombia." In Hagen, *On the Theory of Social
          Change.* Homewood (Ill.).
Hammerton, J. A.
  1915   *The Real Argentine. Notes and Impressions of a Year in the
          Argentine and Uruguay.* New York.
Hammond, George Peter (ed.)
  1951—   *The Larkin papers, Personal, Business, and Official Correspon-
  1962   dence of Thomas Oliver Larkin, Merchant and United States
          Consul in California.* 8 vols. Berkeley.
Hanke, Lewis (ed.)
  1967   *History of Latin American Civilization: Sources and Interpreta-
          tions.* Vol. I. Boston.
Hanley, Mike (with Ellis Lucia)
  1973   *Owyhee Trails: The West's Forgotten Corner.* Caldwell, Idaho.
Harris, J. R.
  1920   *The Last of the Mayflower.* Manchester.
Haskett, Bert
  1936   "History of the sheep industry in Arizona." *Arizona Historical
          Review* VII (3):20—32.
Hawley, James H.
  1920   *History of Idaho.* Chicago.
Hayes, Benjamin
          Benjamin Hayes Papers. Bancroft Library, Berkeley, California.
Hayes, John
  1872   "Sheep farming in California." *Overland Monthly* VIII:489—97.

Hellinger, Charles
 1966   "The long sheep trail through California." *San Francisco Sunday Chronicle and Examiner. Punch Section* (July 3), p. 2.
Herrera, Antonio de
 1944–   *Historia general de los hechos de los castellanos en las islas y*
 1947   *tierras firmes de el Mar Océano.* 10 vols. Asunción del Paraguay.
Herubel, M. A.
 1934   *Les origines des ports de la Gironde et de la Gascogne maritime.* Paris.
House Report 2268 (11381)
 1949a   *House Miscellaneous Reports.* 81st Congress, 2nd Session. Vol. IV.
House Report 3066 (11384)
 1949b   *House Miscellaneous Reports.* 81st Congress, 2nd Session. Vol. VII.
Howley, Michael Francis
 1908   "Les anciennes tombes basques à Placentia." *Revista Internacional de Estudios Vascos.* San Sebastián. II:734–48.
Humboldt County, Nevada
         Book of Deeds. Notices. Declaration of Intention Record Book. Marriages.
Humboldt National Forest, Elko
 1911   List of Sheep Permittees.
The Humboldt Star, Winnemucca (Nevada). 1908–14.
Hunt, Rockwell D.
 1932   *California and Californians.* Chicago.
Hussey, Roland Dennis
 1934   *The Caracas Company 1728–1784. A study in the history of Spanish monopolistic trade.* Cambridge (Massachusetts).
Ibarbia, Diego Joaquín
 1970   "Homenaje al presidente Dr. Roberto M. Ortiz y al Comité Pro-Inmigración Vasca." *Boletín del Instituto Americano de Estudios Vascos* XXI:133–34. Buenos Aires.
Ibn al-Qutiyyah
 1926   *Historia de la conquista de España de Abenalcotía el Cordobés, seguida de fragmentos históricos de Abenalcotía, etc. Traducción de don Julián Ribera.* Madrid.
Idoate, Florencio
 1954   "Una matanza de vascos y navarros en el Perú." In Idoate, *Rincones de la historia de Navarra.* Pamplona, pp. 408–10.
 1969   *Catálogo de la sección de Comptos, Documentos, Diputación Foral de Navarra.* XLIX, Años 1500–1780. Pamplona.
Imaz, José Luis de
 1962   *La clase alta de Buenos Aires.* Buenos Aires.
 1964   *Los que mandan.* Buenos Aires.
Indart, Marie
 1933   Interview, 1933. Milligan Museum, Los Banos (California). Milligan papers, vol. III:515.
Instituto Nacional de Estadística
 1960   *Reseña estadística de la provincia de Vizcaya.* Madrid.
L'International; Politique, commerce, législation, littérature
 1855   (April 1–June 23). Buenos Aires.

Inyo County Sheep License Book. Independence (California). 1896−97.

Iriart, Michel
  1950   "El Centro Vasco-Francés de Buenos Aires. *Boletín del Instituto Americano de Estudios Vascos* I:114−18. Buenos Aires.

Irujo, Andrés M. de
  1964   "Los vascos y el euskera en la Argentina." *Boletín del Instituto Americano de Estudios Vascos* XV:104−6. Buenos Aires.

Isasi, Mirim, and Melcena Burns Denny
  1942   *White Stars of Freedom.* Chicago: Albert Whitman and Co.

Isidorus of Seville
  1970   *History of the Goths, Vandals and Suevi.* Translated from the Latin with an introduction by Guido Donini and Gordon B. Ford. Second revised edition. Leiden.

Ispizua, Segundo de
  1914−   *Historia de los vascos en el descubrimiento, conquista y civiliza-*
  1919   *ción de America.* 6 volumes, Bilbao.

Jackson, J. A.
  1969   "Migration. Editorial introduction." In J. A. Jackson (ed.), *Migration, Sociological Studies 2.* Cambridge (Mass.). Pp. 1−10.

Jaurgain, Jean
  1898−   *La Vasconie. Etude historique et critique.* 2 volumes. Pau.
  1902

Jefferson, Mark
  1926   *Peopling the Argentine Pampa.* New York.

Jenkins, J. T.
  1971   *A History of the Whale Fisheries from the Basque Fisheries of the Tenth Century to the Hunting of the Finner Whale at the Present time.* 2nd ed. London.

Jiménez, Joaquín
  1970   "Alava. Población." In *Enciclopedia general ilustrada del País Vasco. Cuerpo A. Diccionario enciclopédico vasco.* San Sebastián. I:300−307.

Journal 1646
  1959   "Journal of the Jesuit Fathers, in the year 1646." In Thwaites XXVIII:143−251.

Juvmey, Honoria
  1926   *History of Sonoma County, California.* Los Angeles.

Kasdan, Leonard
  1965   "Family structure, migration, and the entrepreneur." *Comparative Studies in Society and History* 7:345−57.

Kasdan, Leonard, and Stanley H. Brandes
  1973   "Basque migration again." *American Anthropologist* 75(1):302−4.

Keas, Charles
  1910   "Quarterly grazing G report, District 6, Oct. 31, 1910." Humboldt National Forest. Elko.
  1911   "Grazing G report, District 6, 1911." Humboldt National Forest.

Kennedy, P. Beveridge, and Samuel B. Doten
  1901   *A preliminary report of the summer ranges of western Nevada sheep.* University of Nevada, Reno, Agricultural Experimental Station, Bulletin no. 51, pp. 19−20.

Kenny, William Robert
1955   "History of the Sonoma Mining Region of California,
        1848 – 1860." Ph.D. Dissertation, University of California,
        Berkeley.
Kindall, Cleve E.
1959   "Southern vineyards. The economic significance of the wine
        industry in the development of Los Angeles, 1831 – 1870." *The
        Historical Society of Southern California Quarterly* XLI:26 – 37.
King, Th. B.
1850   *California, the Wonder of the Age.* New York.
Koch, Carlota
1936   "La Guipuzcoana." Manuscript in Bancroft Library, Berkeley,
        Calif.
Kuykendall, Ralph S.
1922   "An American ship-builder for Spanish California." *Hispanic
        American Historical Review* V:90 – 92.
Labayen, Antonio M.
1969   *Kalifornia kuku.* Zarautz (Guipúzcoa).
Labayru. Estanislao J.
1895 – *Historia general del señorío de Vizcaya.* (6 vol.) Bilbao.
1903
Laborde, Manuel
1956   "Datos sobre los orígines de la minería e industria del hierro en
        Guipúzcoa." *Homenaje a D. Joaquín Mendizábal Gortazar.* San
        Sebastián. Pp. 225 – 36.
Lacarra, José María
1957   *Vasconia medieval. Historia y filología.* San Sebastián.
1971   *Estudios de historia navarra.* Pamplona.
Lafarga Lozano, Adolfo
1973   *Los Vascos en el Descubrimiento y Colonización de América.*
        Bilbao.
Lamadrid Jiménez, Lázaro
1963   *El alavés fray Fermín Francisco de Lasuén O.F.M.
        (1736 – 1803), fundador de las misiones de California.* 2 volumes.
        Vitoria.
Lamarque, Jean
1930   "Français et basques d'Argentine." *Gure Herria* X:481 – 92.
        Bayonne.
1951   "Soldats et missionnaires français en Uruguay et Argentine."
        Gure Herria XXIII:14 – 17. Bayonne.
Lancre, Pierre de
1937   "Tableau de l'inconstance des mauvais anges et demons ou il est
        amplement traicte des sorciers et de la sorcellerie. Paris, 1622."
        Bulletin du Musée Basque. Bayonne, pp. 129 – 231.
Landaeta, Martín de
1949   *Noticias acerca del puerto de San Francisco.* Mexico.
Lane, Richard H.
1973   "The cultural ecology of sheep nomadism: northeastern Nevada,
        1870 – 72." Manuscript.
Larden, Walter
1911   *Argentine plains and Andine Glaciers.* London.

Las Casas, Bartolomé de
1951 *Historia de las Indias.* 3 vols. Mexico.
Lascurain, Vicente
1956 "Los grandes caudillos en la conquista de Mexico." *Boletín del Instituto Americano de Estudios Vascos* VII:101–11, 219–38. Buenos Aires.
Latham, Wilfred
1866 *The States of the River Plate: Their Industries and Commerce.* London.
Laurac Bat. Buenos Aires, 1878–1882.
Laure, Pierre
1959 "Relation of the Saguenay, 1720 to 1730, by Reverend Father Pierre Laure." In Thwaites LXVIII:23–117.
Lauriente, Camille
1953 *The Chronicles of Camille.* New York.
Laxalt, Robert
1966 "Lonely sentinels of the American West. Basque sheepherders." *National Geographic Magazine* CXXIX:870–88. Washington.
1957 *Sweet Promised Land.* New York.
1972 *In a Hundred Graves: A Basque Portrait.* Reno (Nevada).
Le Conte, Joseph
1960 *A Journal of Ramblings Through the High Sierra of California by the University Excursion Party.* San Francisco. (Originally published in 1875 by Francis Valentine, San Francisco).
Lee, W. Storrs
1962 *The Sierras.* New York.
Lefebvre, Theodore
1933 *Les modes de vie dans les Pyrénées Atlantiques Orientales.* Paris.
Le Jeune, Paul
1959a "Relation of what occurred in New France in the year 1634." Sent to the Reverend Father Provincial of the Society of Jesus in the Province of France, by Father Paul le Jeune, of the same Society, Superior of the Residence of Kebec. In Thwaites 1959: VI:90–317.
1959b "Relation of what occurred in New France in the year 1635." Sent to the Reverend Father Provincial of the Society of Jesus in the Province of France, by Father Paul le Jeune of the same society, Superior of the Residence of Quebec. In Thwaites 1959: VII:250–303; VIII:7–281.
1959c "Relation of what occurred in New France in the year 1635." Sent to the Reverend Father Provincial of the Society of Jesus in the Province of France, by Father Paul le Jeune of the same Society, Superior of the Residence of Kebec. In Thwaites 1959: VIII:199–281; IX:5–303; X:6–317.
Lesca, F. H.
1907 *Les Basques et le Béarnais dans l'Argentine et l'Uruguay.* Bordeaux.
Lévi-Provençal, E.
1938 *La péninsule ibérique du Moyen Age d'après le Kitab Ar-Rawd Al-Mi'tar . . . Texte arabe des notices relatives à l'Espagne, au*

Portugal et au Sud-Ouest de la France, publié avec une introduction, un répertoire analytique, une traduction annotée, un glossaire et une carte, par E. Lévi-Provençal. Leiden.

Lewis, Alice Bradbury, *et al.*
1924   *The Valley of San Fernando.* The San Fernando Chapter of the Daughters of the American Revolution.

Lewis Publishing Co.
1892   *History of the Greater San Francisco Bay Region.* New York.

Lhande, Pierre
1910   *L'émigration basque.* Paris.

Lindsey, L. L.
1913   "Quarterly grazing G report, District 4, Sept. 30, 1913." Humboldt National Forest. Elko.

Linz, Juan J., and Amando De Miguel
1966   "Within-nation differences and comparisons: the eight Spains." In Merritt and Rokkan 1966:267−319.

"Liste des maisons de Baigorry en 1670. Document se trouvant à la Bibliothéque Nationale de Paris." *Gure Herria* XXXV:225−29. Bayonne, 1963.

Loggan, C. W.
1937   "Interview, May 7, 1937." Federal Records Center. San Francisco (California), Box 38929.

Lojendio, Luis María de
1969   "Referencias a la historia vasca (temas, sucesos y personas) que se contienen en *Los quarenta libros del Compendio historial* de Esteban de Garibay." *Principe de Viana* XXX:121−146, 329−400. Pamplona.

López Alen, Francisco
1895   "Recuerdos de Cuba, llegada de los Tercios Bascongados en 1869." *Euskal Erria* XXXIII:477−79. San Sebastián.

López Urrutia, Carlos
1967   "1849: El asalto a Chilecito." *La Gaceta Chilena.* San Francisco (California), pp. 17−19.
1969   *Historia de la marina de Chile.* Santiago de Chile.

Loyer, F., and Charles Beaudreau
1932   *Le guide français de Los Angeles et du Sud de la Californie.* Los Angeles.

Ludwig, Ella A.
1927   *History of the Harbor District of Los Angeles Dating from its Earliest History.* Los Angeles.

Luque Alcaide, Elisa
1962   *La Sociedad Ecónomica de los Amigos del País de Guatemala.* Sevilla.

Luzuriaga, Juan de
1686   *Paraninfo celeste, historia de la mystica Zarza, milagrosa imagen y prodigioso santuario de Aránzazu.* Mexico.

Lynch, John
1964   *Spain Under the Hapsburgs. Vol. I: Empire and Absolutism (1516−1598).* New York.

McCall, Grant
1968   *Bibliography of Basque Materials.* Reno (Nevada).

McCarran, Patrick, U.S. Senator, to J. B. Dangberg, May 4, 1942. In McCarran Collection, Itemized Files, The College of the Holy Names, Oakland, California, Item no. A546.

McCarran, Patrick, U.S. Senator, to J. B. Dangberg, May 27, 1942. In McCarran Collection, Itemized Files, The College of the Holy Names, Oakland, California, Item no. A543.

McCarran, Patrick, U.S. Senator, to J. B. Dangberg, August 13, 1943. In McCarran Collection, Itemized Files, The College of the Holy Names, Oakland, California, Item no. A635.

McCarran, Patrick, U.S. Senator, to D. W. Park, Secretary, Nevada Range Sheep Owners Association, Minden, Nevada (undated but 1943). In McCarran Collection, Itemized Files, The College of the Holy Names, Oakland, California, Item no. A633.

McCarran, Patrick, U.S. Senator, to Lt. Col. Jay L. Taylor, Deputy Administrator, War Food Administration, Washington, D.C., July 8, 1943. In McCarran Collection, Itemized Files, The College of the Holy Names, Oakland, California, Item nos. A636-39.

McElrath, Clifford
    1967   *On Santa Cruz Island. The Ranching Recollections of Clifford McElrath.* Los Angeles.

McGowan, Joseph A.
    n.d.   *History of the Sacramento Valley.* Vol. I. New York.

McGroarty, John Steven
    1921   *Los Angeles from the Mountains to the Sea.* 3 vols. Chicago.
    1923   *History of Los Angeles County.* 3 vols. Chicago.
    1933   *California of the South. A history.* 4 vols. Chicago.
    1935   *California of the South. A history.* Vol. V. Chicago.

Macchi, Manuel
    1971   *Urquiza el saladerista.* Buenos Aires.

Madariaga, Salvador de
    1950   *Cuadro histórico de las Indias. Introducción a Bolívar.* 2nd ed. Buenos Aires.

Madinabeitia, Miguel de
    1898   "Marinos ilustres guipuzcoanos." *Euskal Erria* XXIX:575-76. San Sebastián.

Maluquer de Motes, J.
    1966   "Consideraciones sobre el problema de la formación de los vascos." *IV Symposium de prehistoria peninsular.* Pamplona, pp. 115-28.

Mañaricua, Andrés E. de
    1971   "Los vascos vistos en dos momentos de su historia." In *Primera Semana Internacional de Antropología Vasca.* Bilbao: Editorial La Gran Enciclopedia Vasca.
    1972   "Orígenes del Señorío de Vizcaya." In Excma. Diputación Provincial de Vizcaya, *Edad Media y Señoríos: El Señorío de Vizcaya.* Bilbao.

Manzano, Juan
    1970   "El motín de los Vizcaínos del 6 de octubre [de 1492]." In "Los motines en el primer viaje colombino." *Revista de Indias* XXX:450-54. Madrid.

Markham, C. R.
1881– "On the whale fisheries of the Basque provinces of Spain."
1882 *Nature* XXV:365–68.
Martin, Percy F.
1906 *Through Five Republics (of South America).* London.
Martineau, Bryant S.
1922 "Report on range classification, Santa Rosa Division." *Humboldt National Forest Report,* Winnemucca, no. 2210.
Martinez, Albert B., and Maurice Lewandowski
1911 *The Argentine in the Twentieth Century.* London.
Martínez Ruiz, Juan
1972 *Filiación de los seminaristas del Real Seminario Patriótico Bascongado y Noble de Vergara.* San Sebastián.
Martyr (bishop of Arzendjan)
1826 "Relation d'une voyage fait en Europe et dans l'Ocean Atlantique, à la fin du XVe siecle, sous le regne de Charles VIII, par Martyr, évéque d'Arzendjan, dans la grande Armenie, écrite par lui-même en armènien, et traduite en français par M. Saint-Martin." *Journal Asiatique* IX:321–46.
Mason, R. B.
1849– "Gov. Col. R. B. Mason's report to the Adjutant General." In
1850 *31st Congress. 1st Session. House,* Ex.Do.no. 17, p. 533.
Massey, Ernest de
1926 "A Frenchman in the Gold Rush. The journal of Ernest de Massey, argonaut of 1849." *The California Historical Society Quarterly* 5:3–43, 139–77, 219–54, 342–77; 6:37–57. San Francisco.
Meany, Andrée
1953 *La Californie. Une merveilleuse aventure.* San Francisco.
Mendizabel, Javier de
1957 "Real Compañía Vascongada de Caracas." *Revista General de Marina* CXXIII:255–65. Madrid.
Menéndez Pidal, Ramón
1960 *La Chanson de Roland et la tradition épique des Francs.* Paris.
Merced County, Merced (California). *Deeds.*
Merced County Recorder. *Homesteads Book.*
Merritt, Richard L. and Stein Rokkan
1966 *Comparing Nations: the Use of Quantitative Data in Cross-Sectional Research.* New Haven.
Mezquíriz, M. A.
1956 "Excavación estratigráfica en el área urbana de Pompaelo." *Príncipe de Viana* XVII:467–71. Pamplona.
1958 *La excavación estratigráfica de Pompaelo. I: Campaña de 1956.* Pamplona.
1964 "Notas sobre la arqueología submarina en el Cantábrico." *Munibe* XVI:24–41. San Sebastián.
1969 *Romanización.* Pamplona.
Michel, Francisque
1857 *Le pays Basque, sa population, sa langue, ses moeurs, sa littérature et sa musique.* Paris.

Michelena, Luis
  1961   "Ballenas y grasa de ballena." *Boletín de la Real Sociedad Vas-congada de Amigos del País* XVII:332−34. San Sebastián.
Mieya, P., and I. Azpiazu
  1950   "L'oeuvre de Saint-Michel de Garicoïts en Argentine." *Gure Herria* XXII:313−15. Bayonne.
Milliken, Ralph Leroy
  n.d.   "San Juan book," Vol. I. Manuscript in Ralph Leroy Milliken Museum, Los Banos, California.
Mink, Oscar
  1918   "Carrying capacity test, District 4, 1918 (Jan.)." Humboldt National Forest.
"Miscelánea"
  1881   *Euskal Erria* II:142. San Sebastián.
Moch, Andrea
  1909   *Del Cantábrico al Plata.* Buenos Aires.
Mohrmann, Christine
  1951   "Etudes sur le latin des Chrétiens." *I Congrès Internationale des Etudes Clasiques. Actes.* II. Paris.
Montana Historical Society Archives, Missoula (Montana).
Montoya, Pío de
  1971   *La intervención del clero vasco en las contiendas civiles (1820−23).* San Sebastián.
Moorhead, Max L.
  1968   *The Apache Frontier. Jacobo Ugarte and Spanish-Indian Relations in Northern New Spain (1769−1791).* Norman (Oklahoma).
Morales, Ernesto
  1948   *Fray Mocho.* Buenos Aires.
Morales Padrón, Francisco
  1955   *Rebelión contra la compañía de Caracas.* Sevilla.
Morgan, Wallace M.
  1914   *History of Kern County, California.* Los Angeles.
Morrison, Annie L., and John H. Haydon
  1917   *History of San Luis Obispo and Environs (California).* Los Angeles.
Moya, J.
  1971   "Los grupos sanguíneos de los sistemas Kelly Duffy en los vascos." In *Primera Semana Internactional de Antropología Vasca.* Bilbao: Editorial La Gran Enciclopedia Vasca.
Múgica, Serapio
  1918   *Provincia de Guipúzcoa.* In Carreras y Candi, Francisco (ed.): *Geografía general del País Vasco-Navarro.* Barcelona.
Muir, John
  1911   *My First Summer in the Sierra.* Boston.
Nadal, Jorge
  1961   In Vicens Vives 1961, vol. V.
  1966   *La población española (Siglos XVI a XX).* Barcelona.
Nasatir, Abraham P.
  1945   *French Activities in California. An Archival Calendar Guide.* Stanford.

The National Miner, 1913.

The National Wool Grower. 1919.

Navascues, L. J.

1947 "John Adams y su viaje a Vizcaya en 1779." *Eusko Jakintza* I:395–419, 583–91. Sare (B. P.)

Nevada State Herald, Wells (Nevada) 1902, 1905, 1914.

The Nevada State Journal, Reno (Nevada), 1925.

The Nevada Stockgrower, 1919–20.

Newmark, Harris

1970 *Sixty Years in Southern California (1853–1913). Containing the Reminiscenses of Harris Newmark.* Fourth edition. Los Angeles.

Nieto Gallo, Gratiniano

1958 *El Oppidum de Iruña. Memoria de las excavaciones.* Vitoria.

Nogaret, Joseph

1925 *Saint Jean de Luz des origines a nos jours.* Bayonne.

Noticia del origen, fundación, objeto y constituciones de la Real Congregación de Naturales y Originarios de las tres Provincias Vascongadas, establecida bajo la advocación del glorioso San Ignacio de Loyola. Madrid, 1896.

Nueva recopilación de los Fueros, Privilegios, Buenos Usos y Costumbres, Leyes y Ordenes de la M.N. y M.L. Provincia de Guipúzcoa. Reimpresa por acuerdo de la Excma. Diputación de 28 de noviembre de 1918. San Sebastián, 1919.

Obregón, Gonzalo

1949 *El Real Colegio de San Ignacio de México (Las Vizcaínas).* Mexico.

O'Driscoll, Irene

1948 "Kiz." In Reynolds 1948:171.

Olavarría y Ferrari, Enrique de

1889 *El Real Colegio de San Ignacio de Loyola, vulgarmente Colegio de las Vizcaínas, en la actualidad Colegio de la Paz. Reseña histórica.* Mexico.

Oñate (Guipúzcoa)

Archivo de la Villa de Oñate (Guipúzcoa). Legajo 3607.

Oregon Journal, 1929.

Oreña, Gaspar

"Documentos." Manuscript in the Bancroft Library, Berkeley, California.

Ortiz y San Pelayo, Félix

1915 *Los Vascos en América.* Buenos Aires.

O'Shea, Henri

1886 "La maison basque." *Revue des Basses-Pyrénées et des Landes.* Paris. IV:179–244.

Ossa Echaburu, Rafael

1963 *Pastores y pelotaris vascos.* Bilbao.

Otaegui, Tomás

1943 *Los vascos en el Uruguay.* Buenos Aires.

Otazu y Llana, Alfonso de

1970 *Hacendistas Navarros en Indias.* Bilbao.

Outcalt, John

1925 *History of Merced County, California.* Los Angeles.

Pagliarulo, Carol Maria
1948   "Basques in Stockton; a study in assimilation." M.A. Thesis, College of the Pacific, Stockton (California).
Palacio Atard, V.
1971   "Pescadores Vascos en Terranova en el siglo XVIII." In *Primera Semana Internacional de Antropología Vasca.* Bilbao. pp. 409 – 17.
Panettieri, José
1970   *Inmigración en la Argentina.* Buenos Aires.
Parker, L. Mayland
1951   "Economic geography of Utah's sheep industry." M.S. Thesis, University of Utah, Salt Lake City.
Patterson, Edna B., Louise A. Ulph, and Victor Goodwin
1969   *Nevada's Northeast Frontier.* Sparks (Nevada).
Paul, Rodman W.
1965   *California Gold, the Beginning of Mining in the Far West.* Lincoln (Nebraska).
"Pedrorena to Stearns, October 1840." Letter in the Huntington Library.
Pellegrini, Carlos
1968   "Los vascos y la Argentina." *Boletín del Instituto Americano de Estudios Vascos* XIX:126 – 29. Buenos Aires.
Pérez de Urbel, Justo
1969 –   *El Condado de Castilla.* 3 vols. Madrid.
1970
Perkins, William
1964   *Three Years in California. William Perkins' Journal of Life at Sonora (1849 – 1852).* With an introduction and annotations by Dale L. Morgan and James R. Scobie. Berkeley.
Pike, Ruth
1972   *Aristocrats and Traders in Sevillian Society in the Sixteenth Century.* Ithaca and London.
Pitt, Leonard
1966   *The Decline of the Californios. A Social History of the Spanish-speaking Californians (1846 – 1890).* Berkeley.
Pleasants, J. E.
1931   *History of Orange County, California.* 3 vols. Los Angeles.
Pliny
1952   *Pliny Natural History, with an English translation.* London 1952, vol. IX (Book XXXIV, Chap. XLIII).
Powers, S.
1870   "A flock of wool; on sheep raising in California." *Overland Monthly* IV:141 – 46.
Price, John A.
1972   "Reno, Nevada: The city as a unit of study." *Urban Anthropology* I:14 – 28.
Priestley, Herbert Ingram
1916   *José de Galvez, visitador-general of the New Spain (1765 – 1771).* Berkeley (University of California Publications in History, vol. V).
Procacci, Giuliano
1970   *History of the Italian People.* London.

"Proyecto de una Escuela Patriótica presentado a la Junta General de la Real Sociedad de los Amigos del País por su Junta de Institución a 17 de septiembre de 1775." In *Extractos.* Vitoria, 1775.

Purchas, Samuel
1625   *Hakluytus Posthumus or Purchas his pilgrimes.* 5 vols. London.

R. C.
1880   "La inmigración vasca en el Uruguay." *Euska Erria* I:177−79. San Sebastián.

Raup, Hallock F.
1937   "Rancho Los Palos Verdes." *Historical Society of Southern California Quarterly* XIX:7−21.

Recensement de 1968; Population de la France; Départements; Arrondissements; Cantons et Communes. Paris: Direction des Journaux Officiels, 1968.

Reeve, Frank D. (ed.)
1963   "The old observer. The sheep industry in Arizona, 1905−6." *New Mexico Historical Review* XXXVII:244−52, 323−42.
1964   Ibid., XXXIX:40−79, 111−56.

"Reglamento provisional para la secularización de las misiones de Alta California, 9 de agosto de 1834." In Bancroft, 1885b: 342−344 (note 4).

Rekalde, Santos T.
1973   *Deunor. Idaho'n artzain ta euskaldun.* Zarautz.

"Relación de las fiestas que se hicieron en esta ciudad de Mexico en la canonización del glorioso S. Ignacio y San Francisco Javier, en 26 de noviembre de 1622 y por todo su octavario." (Published by Jorge Schurhammer) *Missionalia Hispánica* IX:677−717, Madrid, 1952.

The Reno Evening Gazette, Reno (Nevada), 1890, 1913.
Report of the Commissioner of Agriculture, 1880. Washington, 1881.
Report of the Commissioner of Agriculture, 1891. Washington, 1892.

Reynolds, Keld J.
1945   "Principal actions of the California Junta de Fomento, 1825−27." Translated with introduction and notes by Keld J. Reynolds. *The California Historical Society Quarterly* XXIV:289−320.
1946   Ibid., XXV:57−78, 149−68, 267−77, 347−66.

Reynolds, Thursey J. (compiler)
1948   *Centennial Echos from Carbon County (Utah).* Price (Utah).

Ridal, Francesco
1883   "L'émigration dans l'Amérique du Sud." *La Réforme Sociale.* Paris.

Robbins, Roy M.
1962   *Our Landed Heritage. The Public Domain, 1776−1936.* Lincoln (Nebraska).

Rojas, Aristides
1874   *El elemento vasco en la historia de Venezuela.* Caracas.

Romer, Margaret
1961   "The story of Martin Aguirre, famed Los Angeles County sheriff." *Southern California Historical Quarterly* XLIII:125−36.

Ross, Gordon
1916   *Argentina and Uruguay.* New York.

Rouget de Lisle, Madame Agnès
1928 "Les Basques en Amérique." *Gure Herria* VIII:113—20. Bayonne.
Ruiz, Allura Nason
1964 "The Basques, sheepmen of the West." M.A. Thesis, University of Nevada, Reno.
Ruiz Gonzalez de Linares, Ernesto
1972 "Las Sociedades Económicas de los Amigos del País." In *Las Reales Sociedades Económicas de Amigos del País y su Obra.* San Sebastián.
Russell, J. H.
1957 *Cattle on the Conejo.* Los Angeles.
Sacramento Union, 1852.
Sáenz de Santa María, Carmelo
1969 "Don Juan Martínez de Landecho, primer presidente-gobernador de la Audiencia de Guatemala." *Estudios de Deusto* XVII:405—27. Bilbao.
Sagastume, José Pío
1912 *Los vascos en la Argentina.* Buenos Aires.
Saint-Amand, M. de
1854 *Voyage en Californie et dans l'Oregon.* Paris.
Sallaberry, John
1956 "John Sallaberry sketch. Culbertson Historical Society, Old Timers Roundup." *The Poplar Standard.* Poplar (Montana) (Oct. 26), p. 3.
San Andreas Independent, 1860.
San Benito County, California. *Index to Marriages.*
San Francisco Bulletin, 1864.
Sangróniz, José Antonio de
1943 *Familias coloniales de Venezuela.* Caracas.
Santa Barbara County. Court House, *Record of Deeds.* 1852—75.
Santa Barbara County. Court House, *Miscellaneous Records.* 1857—90.
Santa Barbara Mission. *Book of marriages.* 1786—1885.
Sarasola, Modesto
1950 *Vizcaya y los Reyes Católicos.* Madrid.
Sarthou, B.
1947 *Vida popular de San Miguel de Garicoïts.* Buenos Aires.
Sather, Clifford A.
1961 "Marriage patterns among the Basques of Shoshone, Idaho." Senior Thesis, Reed College, Division of History and Social Sciences, Portland (Oregon).
Satrústegui, J. M.
1971 "Correspondencia familiar vasca del siglo XIX." *Fontes Linguae Vasconum* III:291—306. Pamplona.
Sauer, Carol O.
1968 *Northern Mists.* Berkeley and Los Angeles.
Sawyer, Byrd Wall
1971 *Nevada Nomads.* San Jose (California).
Shochat, George
1950 "The Casa-Adobe de San Rafael (The Sanchez Adobe) in Glendale, California." *Historical Society of Southern California Quarterly* XXX:269—308.

Scobie, James R.
  1964a *Argentina, a City and a Nation.* New York.
  1964b *Revolution on the Pampas, a Social History of Argentine Wheat, 1860 1910.* Austin.
Scrugham, James G.
  1935 *Nevada, a Narrative of the Conquest of a Frontier Land.* Chicago.
Shafer, Robert Jones
  1958 *The Economic Societies in the Spanish World (1763 – 1821).* Syracuse.
Shepherd, Major W.
  1885 *Prairie Experiences in the Handling of Cattle and Sheep.* New York.
Shepperson, Wilbur S.
  1970 *Restless Strangers.* Reno (Nevada).
Sherman, E. A.
  1933 "Sherman testimony. Hearing before the Committee on Public Lands on HR 2835." *House of Representatives, 73rd Congress, 1st Session.* Washington, Pp. 43 – 44.
Shoemaker, T. B., Assistant Commissioner, Immigration and Naturalization Service, to J. B. Dangberg, November 4, 1943. In McCarran Collection, Itemized Files, The College of the Holy Names, Oakland, California, Item no. 643.
Sierra, Justo
  1969 *The Political Evolution of the New Mexican People.* With notes and a new introduction by Edmundo O'Gorman. Prologue by Alfonso Reyes. Translated by Charles Ramsdell. Austin (Texas).
Silen, Sol
  1917 *La historia de los vascongados en el Oeste de los Estados Unidos.* New York.
The Silver State, Winnemucca (Nevada), 1879, 1881, 1882, 1885, 1888, 1894, 1896.
Solberg, Carl
  1970 *Immigration and Nationalism: Argentina and Chile, 1890 – 1914.* Austin.
Sollube, I. de
  1969 *Geografía del País Vasco.* Vol. 1. San Sebastián.
Statistical Abstract
  1911 U.S. Department of Commerce, Bureau of the Census. *Statistical Abstract of the United States, 1910.* Washington.
  1912 U.S. Department of Commerce, Bureau of the Census. *Statistical Abstract of the United States, 1911.* Washington.
  1913 U.S. Department of Commerce, Bureau of the Census. *Statistical Abstract of the United States, 1912.* Washington.
  1914 U.S. Department of Commerce, Bureau of the Census. *Statistical Abstract of the United States, 1913.* Washington.
  1915 U.S. Department of Commerce, Bureau of the Census. *Statistical Abstract of the United States, 1914.* Washington.
  1916 U.S. Department of Commerce, Bureau of the Census. *Statistical Abstract of the United States, 1915.* Washington.

1917   U.S. Department of Commerce, Bureau of the Census. *Statistical Abstract of the United States, 1916.* Washington.

1918   U.S. Department of Commerce, Bureau of the Census. *Statistical Abstract of the United States, 1917.* Washington.

1919   U.S. Department of Commerce, Bureau of the Census. *Statistical Abstract of the United States, 1918.* Washington.

1920   U.S. Department of Commerce, Bureau of the Census. *Statistical Abstract of the United States, 1919.* Washington.

1921   U.S. Department of Commerce, Bureau of the Census. *Statistical Abstract of the United States, 1920.* Washington.

1923   U.S. Department of Commerce, Bureau of the Census. *Statistical Abstract of the United States, 1922.* Washington.

1971   U.S. Department of Commerce, Bureau of the Census. *Statistical Abstract of the United States, 1971.* Washington.

1973   U.S. Department of Commerce, Bureau of the Census. *Statistical Abstract of the United States, 1973.* Washington.

Statutes of the State of Nevada. 1885, 1895, 1901, 1903.

Stearns, Abel
            Papers. Huntington Library.

Stewart, James O.
1924   "Inspection, Nov. 6, 1924." Humboldt National Forest.

Súarez, Jacinto
            "Diccionario biográfico vasco-mexicano." Manuscript in the Basque Collection, University of Nevada, Reno.

Suárez Fernández, Luis, and Manuel Fernández Alvarez
1969   *La España de los Reyes Católicos (1474 – 1513).* Madrid. (Tomo XVII, vol. II of Menéndez Pidal, R., *Historia de España*).

Tacitus
1942   *The Complete Works of Tacitus.* Translated from the Latin by Alfred John Church and William Jackson Brodribb. New York.

Talbott, Elena. "Papers." Manuscript in the Basque Collection, University of Nevada, Reno, Nevada.

The Taylor Grazing Act
n.d.   Reprint by the Bureau of Land Management. Information Bulletin No. 5. Washington.

"Taylor testimony. Hearings before the Committee on Public Lands and surveys on HR 6462." *U.S. Senate, 73rd Congress, 2nd Session, April 20 to May 2, 1934.* Washington, pp. 25, 28.

Templeton, Earl
1919   "Annual grazing G report, District 6." Humboldt National Forest. Winnemucca.

Thayer y Ojeda, Luis
1904   *Navarros y vascongados en Chile.* Santiago de Chile.
1919   *Elementos étnicos que han intervenido en la población de Chile.* Santiago.

Thierry, Sandre
1932   *Le corsaire Pellot qui courut pour le Roi, pour la République et pour l'Empereur, et qui etait Basque.* Paris.

Thompson, E. A.
1952   "Peasant revolts in late Roman Gaul and Spain." *Past and Present* (no. 2), pp. 11 – 23.

Thompson, Thomas H.
1883   *History of Santa Barbara and Ventura Counties, California.*
Thompson, Thomas H., and Albert A. West
1961   *History of Santa Barbara and Ventura Counties, California.*
        Berkeley.
Thurman, Michael E.
1967   *The Naval Department of San Blas, New Spain's Bastion for Alta
        California and Nootka, 1767 to 1798.* Glendale (California).
Thwaites, Reuben Gold (ed.)
1959   *The Jesuit Relations and Allied Documents. Travels and Explora-
        tions of the Jesuit Missionaries in New France 1610 – 1791.* New
        York.
Tierney, Hollie
1946   *The History of Modoc County.* Alturas (California).
Tinkham, George H.
1921   *History of Stanislaus County, California.* Los Angeles.
1923   *History of San Joaquin County, California.* Los Angeles.
Toll, D. W.
1968   "Westerners in blue berets." *Westways* LX(7):38 – 40. Los
        Angeles (California).
Torres López, Manuel
1963   "Las invasiones y los reinos germánicos de España (años
        409 – 711)." In R. Menéndez Pidal (ed.), *Historia de España.
        Tomo III. España visigoda.* Madrid, pp. 3 – 140.
"Tratado de Basilea, 1795 (Julio 22)." *Enciclopedia Universal Ilustrada
        Europeo-Americana.* Bilbao, Madrid VIII:1048.
Tremewan, C. S.
n.d.   "A brief history of the Forest Service in Nevada." Humboldt
        National Forest. Archives. Elko.
Tuolumne County, *Deeds.* 1850 – 1957.
Tuscarora Times Review. Tuscarora (Nevada), 1888, 1889.
Ubieto Arteta, Antonio
1953   *Las fronteras de Navarra.* Pamplona.
1960   *Estudios en torno a la división del Reino por Sancho el Mayor de
        Navarra.* Pamplona.
1969   *Ciclos económicos en la Edad Media española.* Valencia.
United States Census for Cattle, 1910.
United States Congressional Record, 63rd Congress, 1st Session, 1913.
        Washington.
United States Department of Agriculture
1964   *Report of the Chief of the Forest Service, 1964.* Washington.
United States Department of Labor, Bureau of Immigration
1922   *Annual Report of the Commissioner General of Immigration to
        the Secretary of Labor. Fiscal Year Ended June 30, 1922.*
        Washington.
1925   *Annual Report of the Commissioner General of Immigration to
        the Secretary of Labor. Fiscal Year Ended June 30, 1925.*
        Washington.
United States Forest Service
1920   *The Handling of Sheep on the National Forests. La manipulación
        de las ovejas en los bosques nacionales.* Washington.

Urabayen, Leoncio
1959 *Una geografía de Navarra.* Pamplona.
Uranzu, Luis
1955 *Lo que el río vió. Biografía del río Bidasoa.* San Sebastián.
Uriarte, José R. de
1919 *Los Baskos en la Nación Argentina.* Buenos Aires.
Urkina, J. de
1935 *La democracia en Euzkadi. Ensayo histórico-jurídico.* San Sebastián.
Urquijo, Julio de
1925 *Menéndez Pelayo y los Caballeritos de Azcoitia.* San Sebastián.
1945 " Vergara en el último tercio del siglo XVIII según un minerólogo sueco. El primer platino enviado a Suecia." *Boletín de la Real Sociedad Vascongada de los Amigos del País* I. San Sebastián.
Valdes, Dorotea
1874 "Dictation, June 1874." Manuscript in Bancroft Library, Berkeley (California).
Vallejo
1850 *Noticias estadísticas.* Mexico.
Van Bath
1963 *The Agrarian History of Western Europe.* London.
Vandor, Paul E.
1919 *History of Fresno County, California.* 2 vols. Los Angeles.
La Vasconia. Buenos Aires.
"Los Vascos en el Uruguay." *Euskal Erria* II:65. San Sebastián, 1881.
Vicens Vives, Jaime
1969 *An Economic History of Spain.* With the collaboration of Jorge Nadal Oller. Princeton.
1970 *Approaches to the History of Spain.* Berkeley, Los Angeles, and London.
Vicens Vives, Luis (ed.)
1961 *Historia de España y América.* Barcelona.
Vie, Georges
1938 "Les anciennes mines du Pays Basque et du Béarn." *Bulletin de la Société des Sciences, Lettres et Arts de Bayonne.* Bayonne, pp. 59−62.
Vigil, M., and A. Barbero
1965 "Sobre los Orígenes sociales de la Reconquista: Cántabros y Vascones desde fines del Imperio Romano hasta la invasión musulmana." *Boletín de la Real Academia de la Historia* CLVI:271−339. Madrid.
Vilgre Lamadrid, César
Manuscript notes. In Basque Collection, University of Nevada, Reno.
Vimont, Barthelemy
1959 "Relation of what occurred in New France in the years 1644 and 1645." Sent to the Rev. Father Provincial of the Society of Jesus in the Province of France. By Father Barthelemy Vimont of the same Society, Superior of the Residence of Kebec. In Thwaites 1959:XXVII:123−305.
La Voz de España. San Sebastián (Guipúzcoa), 1969.

Walker, C. B.
1933   "Report on stock-raising in the Steen's Mountains, Oregon."
          Federal Records Center, San Francisco (California), Box 38928.
Wallace-Hadrill, J. M.
1967   *The Barbarian West, 400 – 1000.* London.
Wentworth, Edward Norris
1948   *America's Sheep Trails.* Ames (Iowa).
West, Robert C.
1949   *The Mining Community in Northern New Spain: The Parral
          Mining District. Ibero-Americana 30.* Berkeley and Los Angeles.
Whitehead, F.
1962   "Menéndez Pidal and the Chanson de Roland." *Bulletin of His-
          panic Studies* XXXIX:31 – 33. Liverpool.
Winchell, Lilbourne Alsip
n.d.   *History of Fresno County.* Fresno (California).
Wright, Irene A.
1916   *The Early History of Cuba (1492 – 1586).* New York.
Yrizar, Pedro de
1973   "Los dialectos y variedades de la Lengua Vasca: Estudio
          Lingüistico-Demografico," Separata del *Boletín de la Real
          Sociedad de los Amigos del País.* Año XXIX, cuadernos 1, 2, 3.
          San Sebastián.
Zaragoza, Justo
1876   *Castellanos y vascongados.* Madrid.
Zarrantz, Santiago de
1972   "Pasajeros salidos de Valparaíso para California, años
          1849 – 1852 (febrero)." Manuscript in the Basque Collection,
          University of Nevada, Reno.
Zavala, Antonio
1968   *Paulo Yanzi ta bere lagunen bertsoak.* San Sebastián.
Zoleta, Ignacio
1902   "La industria lechera y los vascos en la Argentina." *Euskal Erria.*
          San Sebastián XLVII:262 – 63.
Zosimus
1967   *Historia Nova. The Decline of Rome.* Translated by James J.
          Buchanan and Harold T. Davis. San Antonio (Texas).
Zumalde, Ignacio
1972   "Los pastores vascos en los Estados Unidos y Pedro de Altube."
          Manuscript. In author's possession. Oñate, Guipúzcoa.
Zuñiga, Gonzalo de
1865   "Relación muy verdadera de todo lo sucedido en el Río del
          Marañon, en la provincia del Dorado, Hecha por el Gobernador
          Pedro de Orsua, Dende que fue enviado de la ciudad de Lima, por
          el Marqués de Cañete, Visorey de los Reinos del Pirú, y de la
          muerte del dicho Pedro de Orsua y el comienzo de los tiranos D.
          Fernando de Guzman y Lope de Aguirre su subcesor, y de lo que
          hicieron Fasta llegar á la Margarita y Salir della." In *Colección de
          documentos inéditos, relativos al descubrimiento, conquista y
          organización de las antiguas posesiones españolas de América y
          Oceania.* 42 vols., 1864 – 84. Madrid. 1865 IV:215 – 82.
Zurita y Castro, Gerónimo
1580   *Historia del rey don Hernando el Cathólico.* 2 vols. Zaragoza.

Index